TRANSNATIONAL COMMERCIAL DISPUTES IN AN AGE OF ANTI-GLOBALISM AND PANDEMIC

In this book, senior judges and academics at the forefront of transnational commercial law in Asia, Australia, Europe, the US, and elsewhere, reflect on the implications of anti-globalism and the COVID-19 pandemic on international commercial dispute resolution (ICDR).

The chapters consider: (1) What types of cross-border commercial disputes will arise in the future and what resources will be needed to respond to them in a cost-effective, time-efficient, and equitable manner? (2) Is there still merit in a multilateral approach to transnational commercial law and ICDR, despite the closing of borders, the rise of protectionism, and the disruption of global supply chains? (3) What reforms and innovations should courts, arbitrators, and mediators contemplate when navigating the post-pandemic landscape? (4) Can the accelerated use of remote technology in ICDR (as prompted by the pandemic) be leveraged to enhance access to justice for all?

With a focus on the current crisis in globalism, as well as the associated problems of ensuring justice and fairness in the resolution of cross-border commercial and investment-state disputes along the Belt-and-Road and elsewhere, the book will be an invaluable resource for academics, judges and practitioners alike.

Transnational Commercial Disputes in an Age of Anti-Globalism and Pandemic

Edited by
Sundaresh Menon
and
Anselmo Reyes

•HART•
OXFORD • LONDON • NEW YORK • NEW DELHI • SYDNEY

HART PUBLISHING

Bloomsbury Publishing Plc

Kemp House, Chawley Park, Cumnor Hill, Oxford, OX2 9PH, UK

1385 Broadway, New York, NY 10018, USA

29 Earlsfort Terrace, Dublin 2, Ireland

HART PUBLISHING, the Hart/Stag logo, BLOOMSBURY and the Diana logo are trademarks of Bloomsbury Publishing Plc

First published in Great Britain 2022

A catalogue record for this book is available from the British Library.

A catalogue record for this book is available from the Library of Congress.

ISBN: HB: 978-1-50995-497-1
ePDF: 978-1-50995-499-5
ePub: 978-1-50995-498-8

Typeset by Compuscript Ltd, Shannon

FOREWORD

This book flows out of papers prepared for a 2021 meeting of judges and legal academics to discuss the imperatives for dispute resolution of transnational commercial disputes. That gathering occurred amid a global pandemic, the response to which was dependent in part on the transnational movement of goods (vaccines in particular) and ideas. And it occurred at a time when in most nations people were actively challenging, through word and through action, the accepted order of things, including the desirability and even the inevitability of globalised trade.

It is perhaps no surprise, then, that the discussion that ensued was wide-ranging, placing issues arising from the resolution of transnational commercial disputes in the context of some of the larger themes of our time – the role the globalisation of business and trade has played in climate change and in the increasing wealth disparity between and within nations, and the implications of international trade agreements and dispute resolution mechanisms and bodies, for the sovereignty of nations and the rule of law.

This book is, as a consequence, relevant, helpful and engaging. The assembled papers analyse the different types of transnational commercial disputes in order to assess the best methods of dispute resolution. They examine the international instruments, laws and tribunals that are brought to bear on those disputes – an examination which will be of great assistance to lawyers, arbitrators and judges. The strengths and weaknesses of the status quo are explored, and pragmatic reforms that could be implemented to build efficiency and reduce cost are identified. But the authors also examine how the law and procedure that is applied in these disputes feeds into the broader themes I have mentioned and, in doing so, reflect upon the changes that may be needed to strengthen the legitimacy of institutions and of globalisation itself.

This approach to the topic by a group comprised predominantly of judges is bold and refreshing. The papers it has produced are evidence of the cogency of the frame of reference, and remind us how important it is for judges, charged with the development of the common law as they are, to understand the broader context, and reflect upon what that context tells us about the substance of the law and the processes we use.

There is also a nice symmetry to the book. In the opening paper Chief Justice Menon lays down a challenge for those whose work is the law – he suggests that if the law is truly to serve as the currency of trust in a globalised world, then we need to fundamentally rethink and re-engineer our justice systems in a manner that will better serve that purpose. The book closes with a further challenge – from the academics who attended the 2021 gathering – suggesting that if the goal is indeed to address some of the challenges facing the world through the development of international commercial law, judges many need to understand their roles not just as dispute resolvers, but also as law developers and as global citizens.

I congratulate the group that gathered in 2021 for both the ambition of their project, and the quality of the book that it has produced.

Helen Winkelmann
Chief Justice of New Zealand
May 2022

PREFACE

A Word about this Book and its Organisation

This book considers how judges, arbitrators, lawyers, policy-makers, and other stakeholders can and should respond to the current wave of discontent over the way in which international commercial dispute resolution is carried out.

Since the early nineteenth century, globalisation has been a significant transformative force, bringing about an interconnected world defined by massively increased trade and cultural exchange.[1] By allowing countries to capitalise on their competitive advantages and businesses to reap greater economies of scale across borders, globalisation has brought about substantial economic benefits in terms of efficiency, competitiveness and prosperity overall. Since the 1990s, more than one billion people have been lifted out of extreme poverty and the proportion of under-nourished persons in developing regions has fallen by close to half. Other human development indicators, such as literacy and child mortality rates, have also improved significantly.[2] However, especially in recent years, a growing anti-globalisation sentiment has begun to gain momentum across the world, even among those who had hitherto benefitted from and favoured globalism. Chief among the criticisms is unhappiness over how the wealth generated by globalisation has been distributed among the world's populations. It was noted in The World Inequality Report 2018 that, despite nearly four decades of unprecedented economic growth since 1980, income inequality has increased sharply in nearly all world regions. The global top one per cent of earners have accumulated twice as much of the growth in global income as the 50 per cent poorest individuals, even as the bottom 50 per cent enjoyed some income growth. Globalisation has also been criticised for contributing to job displacement and a loss of national sovereignty and identity. These and other criticisms have led to claims that globalisation is now rightly in retreat, so much so that between 2008 and 2017, the global trade openness index (defined as the sum of world exports and imports divided by world GDP) fell for the first time since World War II.[3]

[1] See outline of a history of globalisation: Peter Vanham, 'A brief history of globalization' World Economic Forum, Chairman's Office (17 January 2019).

[2] M Kituyic, Secretary-General of UNCTAD, Foreword in the 'Developmental and Globalisation: Facts and Figures 2016 Report' ii.

[3] S Donnan, 'Globalisation in retreat: capital flows decline since crisis' *Financial Times* (22 August 2017); DA Irwin, 'Globalisation is in retreat for the first time since the Second World War' Peterson Institute for International Economics (23 April 2020).

The COVID-19 pandemic has exacerbated discontent with globalisation in two ways. First, the pandemic has entrenched the global wealth divide since the greatest economic devastation has been visited on the poorest and most vulnerable. This is despite the epicentres of severe outbreaks having largely been in relatively wealthy and industrialised countries.[4] According to the World Bank, after years of steady progress in reducing the number of persons living below the poverty line (less than US$1.90 per day), 2020 ushered in the first reversal in a generation by pushing an additional 88 million people into extreme poverty.[5] This effect has been asymmetrically distributed in geography and industry, with the impact being felt most strongly in South Asia and Sub-Saharan Africa, and being evidenced by the loss of jobs related to informal services, construction and manufacturing. Second, the pandemic has brought the pros and cons of globalisation into sharp contrast and propelled the debate on the virtues and risks of globalisation to the fore of public and political consciousness. Some have argued that globalisation has increased our vulnerability to pandemics and created the perfect conditions for the spread of disease by promoting concentrations of human and economic activity in a few 'global cities' and facilitating frequent travel between them. The breakdown of global supply chains due to travel and quarantine restrictions imposed to combat the pandemic has been attributed to the high degree of inter-dependency inherent in a globalised economy. Critics of globalisation have observed that governmental responses to the pandemic have often involved reversing or at least suspending the key features of globalisation, for example through the closing of national borders or the repatriation of extraterritorial manufacturing facilities.[6] Others have countered that the groundwork of infrastructure rolled out by globalisation over the years has in fact preserved and improved public health and facilitated vaccine research and the development of efficacious vaccines at a speed and scale that would otherwise have been impossible if undertaken exclusively at a national level.[7] While the net effect of globalisation as a contributor or solution to the pandemic can be debated, there is little doubt that the pandemic has fuelled scepticism, in at least some quarters, that global peace, prosperity and justice are best achieved through the pursuit of greater interconnectivity and interdependence among nations.

In a recent speech, the Senior Minister of Singapore, Mr Tharman Shanmugaratnam,[8] described the present global situation as the coming of a 'perfect long storm' – *perfect*, because it represents an unprecedented confluence of several adverse conjunctural factors; and *long*, because these factors are not random or even cyclical; they represent

[4] M Fujita and N Hamaguchi, 'Globalisation and the COVID-19 pandemic: a spatial economics perspective' Centre for Economic Policy Research (CEPR), VOX-EU (16 August 2020).

[5] P Blake and D Wadhwa, '2020 year in Review: The impact of COVID-19 in 12 charts' The World Bank Group (14 December 2020).

[6] Fujita and Hamaguchi, 'Globalisation and the COVID-19 pandemic' (2020).

[7] See transcript of interview with Charles Kenny, senior fellow at the Center for Global Development, at the National Public Radio programme 'Disease in a Globalised World'. See also S Lincicome, 'COVID-19 Vaccines Depend on Globalisation (And, Therefore, So Does the Trump Administration)' Cato Institute (12 October 2020).

[8] Senior Minister Tharman Shanmugaratnam, 'Responding to a Perfect Long Storm', speech at IMAS-Bloomberg Investment Conference on 9 March 2022, available at www.mas.gov.sg/news/speeches/2022/responding-to-a-perfect-long-storm.

structural shifts in the world order that will be with us for a long time. Minister Tharman raised five factors that contribute to this storm: first, geopolitical instability; second, stagflation and the slowing of global economic growth; third, the climate crisis; fourth, global health security; and fifth, the problem of less inclusive growth, which will only fuel and exacerbate each of the previous four factors. To this list there may be added a sixth factor – the problem of truth decay, and the general erosion of fact and truth in public discourse, which could seriously undermine efforts by governments to rally the public behind painful but necessary initiatives to address the aforementioned challenges. Together, these factors present a daunting challenge to the legitimacy of the existing international order.

It is in this regard that Sundaresh Menon, in the Introduction to this book, argues that globalism and the spirit of interconnectedness it entails remain our best shot at addressing the global challenges facing the world today, and that our response to the present backlash against globalism should not be to abandon it, but rather, to mould a more economically and socially *sustainable* vision for globalisation – an endeavour in which the law can play a significant part. The chapter begins by highlighting the important part that international commercial dispute resolution has played in supporting the development of a truly *global* economy. As cross-border trade has flourished, so, inevitably, has the propensity for disputes to arise. By providing mechanisms for the resolution of cross-border commercial disputes quickly and fairly at a proportionate cost, the law served to create the conditions necessary for engaging in cross-border commercial activity. In this way, globalism and international commercial dispute resolution have developed hand in hand, the latter supporting and facilitating the former.

Yet, over the decades, it would appear that cracks have begun to form in the façade. Just as the law has been instrumental in the rise of globalisation, there is a sense that it has, at least partially, also been complicit in its fall. This has manifested in what seems a growing wave of discontent with various aspects of international commercial dispute resolution; from investor-state dispute settlement to international commercial arbitration, there are now mounting concerns both within and without the legal fraternity as to whether the legal processes by which justice is delivered remain fit for their purpose in terms of being accessible, efficient and contextualised to the dispute. These concerns go directly to the legitimacy of the global institutions which depend upon these legal processes and indeed of globalism as a whole. These challenges to the legitimacy of international commercial dispute resolution and its role in supporting globalism must be addressed. But how precisely should judges, arbitrators and other stakeholders engaged in cross-border dispute resolution respond? That is the subject of this book. It approaches the question by breaking down 'international commercial dispute resolution' into its components and examining three aspects: (A) how each element has so far supported and complemented globalism; (B) what problems have arisen as a result; and (C) how those problems might be addressed by way of a response to the anti-globalist critique and the upheaval wrought by COVID-19.

The core of this book is found in the six parts which follow the Introduction and build on the themes highlighted there. Part one argues that, in formulating an appropriate response to anti-globalism and the pandemic, it would be helpful to regard the idea of the 'international commercial dispute' as pertaining to a complex ever-evolving system of many parts. Part one thus begins by considering what it means for a dispute to be 'international' and 'commercial' in nature. It then asks why, given this, international commercial disputes should be treated as a unique category of disputes, the resolution of which merits special treatment. It concludes by highlighting different parts of the system and how they contribute to international commercial dispute resolution as a whole.

Succeeding parts then examine how the individual parts of the system identified in part one can respond to the contemporary challenges confronting them. Part two compares the resolution of an international commercial dispute by arbitration and through litigation. International commercial courts have begun to proliferate over the last decade. Why is this and are such courts an answer to the pervasive complaint that international commercial arbitration has become prohibitively expensive, excessively technical, and far too lengthy as a means of cross-border dispute resolution?

Part three delves into a specialised area of dispute resolution – investment treaty arbitration (also known as investor-state arbitration). In addition to the complaints about cost- and time-efficiency that have beset international commercial arbitration, the complaint here is over a lack of transparency, with arbitral tribunals comprising arbitrators (who, even if they did know a lot about public international law, might have little or no first-hand experience of the economic and development problems facing a state party) issuing substantial awards against developing state parties with little means and few resources to fulfil those awards. Part three explores how the problems that currently beset investment treaty arbitration might be better handled.

Parts four and five move from considering modes of dispute resolution to looking at how procedural and substantive questions are dealt with by international commercial dispute resolution service providers. Part four focuses on the need for certainty and finality in the determination of commercial disputes. It asks whether there are limits to the attainment of certainty and finality in the resolution of transnational commercial disputes. If so, then what should those limits be and how are they imposed across borders?

Part five considers the substantive law which is applied to determine international commercial disputes. It analyses the extent to which there is a harmonised or convergent body of principles (known as the *lex mercatoria* or the law merchant) which govern commercial disputes across borders. If there is such a substantive body of law, then how is it developed, and is it robust enough to offer a credible response to the anti-globalist challenge?

Part six considers the system of international commercial dispute resolution during and after the COVID-19 pandemic. How has the system changed, for better or worse, due to the pandemic and where should it now be heading? Is going back to the way things used to be still an option?

The Conclusion to the book pulls together the themes discussed in the Introduction and six parts of the book and charts a way forward for international commercial dispute resolution as a system.

Since preparation for this book began, the world has been shaken by yet another unexpected crisis – the eruption of war in Ukraine. The implications are not just political or economic; the war has also exerted significant pressure on the existing global legal order and its institutions. We deal with this topic and its implications, albeit briefly, in the Postscript.

This book originated as a series of background and discussion papers that were presented and discussed at the 3rd Judicial Roundtable on Commercial Law which took place using a remote conferencing platform on 29 and 30 September and 1 October 2021. The Judicial Roundtable was jointly organised by Shanghai University of Political Science & Law (SHUPL) and the Law Faculty of the University of Hong Kong and was attended by judges, arbitrators, academics, and legal practitioners from civil and common law jurisdictions around the world.[9] The Judicial Roundtable comprised six sessions corresponding to the six parts of this book. The background and discussion papers have been reworked as the constituent chapters of this book and have been edited and revised to incorporate observations made and address queries raised by participants during the Judicial Roundtable.[10] The edited chapters consequently represent the fruits of the discussions that took place during the Judicial Roundtable. Although written by individual contributors, the edited chapters can (and are meant to) be read straight through as an integrated view of how judges, arbitrators and other stakeholders dealing with international commercial dispute resolution might respond to the anti-globalist critique and the 'new normal' ushered in by pandemic.

This book is, first and foremost, directed at judges and arbitrators. That does not, however, mean that it is exclusively written for them. It has also been designed to cater for an audience of policy-makers, lawyers, lay persons and academics who may have varying degrees of knowledge of and experience in international commercial dispute resolution, but who are nonetheless interested in obtaining perspectives on what it is like today and what it could become in the future. Indeed, because transnational business currently has so many dimensions, it is unlikely that even judges and lawyers who deal with cross-border commercial disputes day-to-day will be familiar with all areas covered by this book. They may have deep expertise in the highly specialised areas of commercial dispute resolution in which they practise, but may not have as clear a view of the far bigger picture that lies beyond.

Within the six parts of the book, odd-numbered chapters (that is, chapters one, three, five, seven, nine and eleven) provide readers with little or no knowledge of the subject matter of a part with an overview of the same. These chapters, which started out as the background papers prepared for the Judicial Roundtable, are designed to bring readers up to speed on the current state of debate on controversial issues within the topic covered by a part. They deal with Aspect A mentioned above. Even-numbered chapters (that is, chapters two, four, six, eight, ten and twelve) consider how the major problems flagged in the odd-numbered chapters might be handled in the future in response to the headwinds that globalism presently faces and the upheavals wrought by the pandemic. The even-numbered chapters began life as the discussion papers prepared for the corresponding section of the Judicial Roundtable. They deal with Aspects B and C referred to above. Readers who feel that they are sufficiently knowledgeable about the state of play within the subject matter of a part may wish to

[9] The full list of participants in the Judicial Roundtable appears at the end of the book.

[10] To encourage a frank exchange of views, all discussions at the Judicial Roundtable were subject to the Chatham House Rule.

skip the odd-numbered chapters and go directly to the even-numbered chapter within that part. But it is hoped that even knowledgeable readers will benefit from skimming through the odd-numbered chapters.

One might find, reading through the rest of this book, that the discussion that follows raises more questions than it answers. That is entirely to be expected. The themes discussed in this book are all drawn from the interface between the law and the broader macro and global trends that shape the world. The issues that arise at their junction are complex, and they are dynamic. When we were developing the themes of the Judicial Roundtable some three years ago, we did so with the modest aim of furthering the development of a transnational system of dispute resolution fit for purpose in an increasingly globalised and interconnected age. But the events of recent years – from the COVID-19 pandemic to the Russian invasion of Ukraine – have thrust deep-rooted discontents with globalisation into the spotlight, discontents which call the future of globalism into serious question. The solutions to the issues that these challenges raise will almost certainly lie beyond the realm of the law. The problems are multifaceted and addressing them will require the cooperation of multiple stakeholders, not just across jurisdictions, but across disciplines, especially those from related fields like economics, politics, security, climate change and technology. As we quickly realised following the discussions at the Judicial Roundtable, we cannot and do not purport to offer conclusive or comprehensive solutions to the issues highlighted. Instead, our more modest goal has been to lay the groundwork for further discussion by outlining the contours of the debate and then offering a perspective on possible ways forward bearing in mind that more remains to be done within a rapidly changing environment. In short, this book serves not to cap the discussion we had at the Judicial Roundtable, but to *further* it.

ACKNOWLEDGEMENTS

As explained more fully in the Preface, this book is based on the discussions that took place during the 3rd Judicial Roundtable which, due to COVID-19, took place online on 29 September to 1 October 2021. The editors would like to thank the Shanghai University of Political Science and Law (SHUPL) and the Law Faculty of the University of Hong Kong (HKU) for their sponsorship, organisation and support of the Judicial Roundtable. The participants in the Judicial Roundtable are listed at the end of the book. We thank them all for their individual contributions and insights.

Many individuals were involved in logistics of the Judicial Roundtable and in the subsequent compiling of this book. We hope that we do not offend them if we do not name them all individually, but simply express our gratitude. We should, however, mention the critical assistance that we received from the following: Xiaohong Liu, Guojian Xu, Lihua Wang, and Zhengyi Zhang of SHUPL; Hualing Fu and Alan Tsang of HKU; and Jiahui Huang, Reuben Ong, Ee Kuan Tan, Elton Tan, and Kenneth Wang of the Supreme Court of Singapore. Finally, we express our gratitude to the Hong Kong artist Brian Kwan Lok Chan for creating a bespoke artwork *Causal Circle* for the cover of this book.

The Editors
1 May 2022

CONTENTS

Foreword ... v
Preface: A Word about this Book and its Organisation ... vii
Acknowledgements ... xiii
List of Contributors ... xxiii

Introduction: Justice in a Globalised Age ... 1
Sundaresh Menon

I. Overview ... 1
II. Globalisation and the Law: A Brief History ... 3
A. The Twin Triumphs of Globalisation and Law ... 3
B. Globalisation on the Rocks ... 6
III. Evaluating Globalisation: A Faith Misplaced? ... 8
A. The Fall of an Ideology ... 8
B. The Case for Hope ... 11
IV. Keeping a Light on for Globalisation ... 14
A. A More Sustainable Footing ... 15
B. A Robust, Truth-Based Space for Discussion ... 17
C. Building Legitimacy ... 18
V. Conclusion ... 25

PART I
WHAT IS AN INTERNATIONAL COMMERCIAL DISPUTE?

1. *A Bird's Eye View of International Commercial Dispute Resolution* ... 29
Pak Hei Li

I. About this Chapter ... 29
II. Special Features of International Commercial Disputes ... 29
III. Party Autonomy and its Limits ... 33
IV. Means for Achieving Convergence ... 35
A. Instruments ... 36
B. Institutions ... 37

2. *International Commercial Dispute Resolution as a System* *43*
James Allsop and Samuel Walpole

I. The Nature of an International Commercial Dispute 43
A. Introduction 43
B. Describing an International Commercial Dispute 45
II. The Distinctiveness of International Commercial Dispute Resolution 49
III. Understanding International Commercial Dispute Resolution as a System 55
A. Foundations 56
B. Institutions 58
C. Rules and Principles 61
D. The Human Element 62
IV. Balancing Competing Interests 62
A. Arbitrability 64
B. Mandatory Rules 66
C. Public Policy 68
V. Continued Convergence in International Commercial Dispute Resolution 71
A. The *Lex Mercatoria* Today 72
B. International Commercial Courts 75
C. A Facilitative Dispute Resolution Culture 79
VI. COVID-19, the International Order and the System of International Commercial Dispute Resolution 81
VII. Conclusion 87

PART II
THE SWINGING PENDULUM: INTERNATIONAL COMMERCIAL ARBITRATION AND THE RISE OF SPECIALIST COMMERCIAL COURTS

3. *The Landscape of International Commercial Courts* *91*
Jianping Shi

I. Introduction 91
II. ICCs in Different Countries 91
A. The Commercial Court in London 91
B. The International Chamber of the Paris Commercial Court 93
C. The Singapore International Commercial Court 95
D. The Dubai International Financial Centre Courts 97
E. The Netherlands Commercial Court 98
F. The China International Commercial Court 99
III. Reasons for the Establishment of ICCs 100
A. International Trade and Dispute 100
B. Providing an Alternative to Arbitration 103

IV. The Benefits of ICCs ... 103
A. Making Up for the Shortcomings of Arbitration ... 103
B. Greater Professionalism, Expertise, and Flexibility ... 105
C. Diversity ... 106
D. Breaking through the Limits of National Boundaries ... 107
E. Simplification of Proceedings ... 108
F. Unification of Litigation Language ... 108
V. The Problems of ICCs ... 109
A. Recognition and Enforcement of Judgments ... 109
B. Imperfection and Ambiguity of Regulations ... 110
C. Disadvantages of Litigation in Some ICCs ... 111
D. Lack of Foreign Lawyers in Some ICCs ... 112
VI. Conclusion ... 112

4. *The Driving Forces behind the Swinging Pendulum* ... *115*
Bernard Eder

I. Introduction ... 115
II. Historical Perspective: What are the Reasons for the Swinging Pendulum? ... 116
III. Pros and Cons of the Swing ... 121
IV. The Rise of ICCs ... 127
V. Supposed Shortcomings of ICCs ... 130
VI. Conclusion ... 133

PART III
DAVID AND GOLIATH: INVESTOR–STATE DISPUTE SETTLEMENT

5. *An Introduction to Investor–State Dispute Settlement* ... *137*
Jianjian Ye

I. The System of Investor–State Dispute Settlement ... 137
A. Jurisdiction under the ICSID Convention and UNCITRAL Rules ... 137
B. What is a Minimum International Standard? ... 139
C. Favourable Treatment and MFN Clauses ... 140
D. Expropriation, FET and FPS Clauses ... 141
E. Dealing with Corruption ... 142
F. Umbrella Clauses ... 143
G. The Mauritius Convention ... 144
H. Set-Offs and Counterclaims ... 145
I. Multi-Party Arbitration and Consolidation ... 146
J. A Word on Awards ... 146
II. Problems with ISDS ... 147
A. Transparency ... 147
B. Certainty ... 148
C. Accountability ... 150

D. Expense 150
E. Enforcement 151
F. Diversity of Arbitrators 152
III. Proposals for Reform and Possible Future Trajectories 153
A. Appeal Mechanism 154
B. Appointment of Arbitrators 155
C. Reducing Costs and Duration 155
D. The Future 156
IV. A Radical Proposal: Formation of an Investment Court and Use of International Commercial Courts 156
A. Two Levels of Adjudication 157
B. Adjudicators 157
C. Enforcement 157
D. Financing 158
E. Application to Existing Treaties 158

6. *The Way Forward in Investor–State Dispute Settlement: How Do We Balance the Needs of States with the Demands of Investors?* *159*
Anselmo Reyes

I. Introduction 159
II. Four Propositions 160
A. Proposition 1 160
B. Proposition 2 173
C. Proposition 3 173
D. Proposition 4 174
III. A Glimpse into a Possible Future 177

PART IV
THE PERFECT AS THE ENEMY OF THE GOOD – THE IMPORTANCE OF FINALITY AND CERTAINTY

7. *The Need for Finality and Certainty in International Commercial Dispute Resolution* *183*
Wilson Lui

I. Introduction 183
A. The Virtues of Finality and Certainty 183
B. The Limits of Finality and Certainty 185
II. Concurrent Proceedings 187
A. *Forum Non Conveniens* and *Lis Alibi Pendens* 187
B. Anti-Suit Injunctions 188
C. Applications for the Stay of Arbitral Proceedings 190

D. Applications for the Stay of Court Proceedings on Case Management Grounds.......191
E. *Res Judicata* and Issue Estoppel.......192
III. Recognition and Enforcement of Judgments and Awards.......194
A. Indirect Jurisdiction.......194
B. Reciprocity.......196
C. Due Process.......197
D. Public Policy.......198
E. Enforcing Awards Set Aside by a Supervising Court.......200
F. The 2005 and 2019 Hague Conventions.......202
IV. Post-Pandemic Considerations.......204

8. *Towards the Just Resolution of Disputes: How Do We Balance Commercial Certainty and Achieving the Right Result?*.......*209*
Nallini Pathmanathan and Joanne Tan Xin Ying

I. Introduction.......209
A. Finality.......209
B. Certainty.......211
II. Defining and Evaluating the Policies of Finality and Certainty in International Commercial Dispute Resolution.......212
A. Finality.......212
B. Certainty.......212
C. Comity, Sovereignty and Party Autonomy.......213
III. Managing Concurrent Proceedings.......215
A. *Lis Alibi Pendens*.......215
B. *Forum Non Conveniens*.......216
C. Anti-Suit Injunctions.......217
D. Applications for Stay of Proceedings.......219
E. *Res Judicata* and Issue Estoppel.......220
IV. Recognising and Enforcing Judgments and Awards.......223
A. Jurisdictional Considerations.......224
B. Grounds for Refusing to Recognise or Enforce Judgments and Awards.......226
C. Enforcing Awards Set Aside by a Supervising Court.......232
D. Requirement of Reciprocity.......235
V. Impact of 2005 and 2019 HCCH Conventions on the Recognition and Enforcement of Foreign Judgments.......236
A. 2005 HCCH Convention.......236
B. 2019 HCCH Convention.......239
VI. Issues Arising from the COVID-19 Pandemic.......240

PART V
THE *LEX MERCATORIA* AND THE CONVERGENCE OF INTERNATIONAL COMMERCIAL LAW

9. *An Anatomy of the* Lex Mercatoria *245*
Jason Lin

I. The Concept of *Lex Mercatoria* 245
A. Is the Concept too Nebulous? 246
B. What Principles Make up the *Lex Mercatoria*? 248
C. Is it Fit for the Purpose of International Commercial Dispute Resolution? 251
D. Do Parties Actually Choose the *Lex Mercatoria* as Governing Law? 253
II. Convergence of the *Lex Mercatoria* 257
A. Efforts at Identifying the Principles of the *Lex Mercatoria* 257
B. Evaluating Efforts at Convergence 259
C. Will International Commercial Mediation Detract from the *Lex Mercatoria*? 264
D. Will International Commercial Arbitration Detract from the *Lex Mercatoria*? 265

10. *Developing the* Lex Mercatoria *269*
Tiong Min Yeo

I. Focusing the Inquiry 269
II. Finding Common Ground 273
A. National and Municipal Interests 274
B. Diversity and Competition 275
C. Scope and Modality of Convergence 276
III. Towards a System of Transnational Civil Justice 282

PART VI
THE IMPACT OF COVID-19

11. *How the Pandemic has Changed the Landscape of International Dispute Resolution* *285*
Cedric Yeung

I. Introduction 285
II. The Past 286
III. The Present 286
IV. The Future 288

12. *Shaping the Future of International Dispute Resolution* ... *293*
Douglas Jones AO and Jonathan Mance

I. The Lessons of the Pandemic ... 293
II. COVID-19, Technology and Cross-Border Dispute Resolution Procedure ... 294
A. Innovations in Dispute Resolution Procedure ... 294
B. Positive Impact of Technology ... 297
C. Limitations of Technology ... 299
D. Conclusion ... 301
III. Fully Asynchronous Dispute Resolution Proceedings ... 302
A. The Concept of Asynchronicity ... 302
B. Asynchronous Dispute Resolution ... 303
IV. Overall Conclusion ... 311

Conclusion: Transnational Dispute Resolution, International Commercial Courts, and the Future of International Commercial Law ... *313*
Pamela Bookman and Alyssa King

I. New and Old Challenges in International Dispute Resolution ... 313
A. Chief Justice Menon's Introduction ... 314
B. International Commercial Law in an Age of Uncertainty ... 315
II. Commercial Courts: Old Private Wine, New Public Bottles ... 322
A. Familiar Themes from Arbitration ... 323
B. The Role of International Commercial Courts ... 326
III. Charting a Course for the Future of International Commercial Courts ... 329
A. Why International Commercial Courts? A Bridge from the Past to the Future ... 330
B. How Convergence Might Happen ... 331
C. International Commercial Law and Global Problems: Cause and Solution? ... 334
D. What Can a Court Do? ... 336
IV. Conclusion ... 339

Postscript ... *341*
List of Participants in the 3rd Judicial Roundtable: 29 September to 1 October 2021 ... *351*
Index ... *353*

LIST OF CONTRIBUTORS

James Allsop is Chief Justice of the Federal Court of Australia.

Pamela Bookman is an Associate Professor at Fordham University School of Law in New York.

Bernard Eder is an International Judge of the Singapore International Commercial Court and an independent arbitrator. He was formerly a judge of the High Court of England and Wales.

Douglas Jones AO is an International Judge of the Singapore International Commercial Court and an independent arbitrator.

Alyssa King is an Assistant Professor at Queen's University Law School in Ontario.

Pak Hei Li is a Hong Kong barrister.

Jason Lin is a trainee solicitor in London.

Wilson Lui is a Pre-Doctoral Fellow and Lecturer at the Faculty of Law of the University of Hong Kong.

Jonathan Mance is Chief Justice of the Astana International Financial Centre Court and an International Judge of the Singapore International Commercial Court. He was formerly Deputy President of the UK Supreme Court.

Sundaresh Menon is Chief Justice of Singapore.

Nallini Pathmanathan is a Justice of the Federal Court of Malaysia.

Anselmo Reyes is an International Judge of the Singapore International Commercial Court and a Visiting Professor at the Law Faculty of Doshisha University in Kyoto.

Jianping Shi is a Professor of Law at the Shanghai University of Political Science and Law, where she is Deputy Dean of the International School of Law.

Joanne Tan Xin Ying is a Senior Assistant Registrar at the Federal Court of Malaysia.

Samuel Walpole is a barrister in Queensland and an Adjunct Fellow at the University of Queensland.

Jianjian Ye is an Associate at Quinn Emanuel Urquhart & Sullivan LLP in New York.

Tiong Min Yeo is Yong Pung How Chair Professor of Law at the Singapore Management University (SMU), where he was formerly Dean of the School of Law.

Cedric Yeung is a Hong Kong barrister.

Introduction: Justice in a Globalised Age

SUNDARESH MENON*

I. Overview

The chapters in this book resulted from discussions that took place when a group of judges and academics gathered virtually at the Third Judicial Roundtable on Commercial Law. The themes for the Roundtable were initially developed and shaped by the evident need to fashion a *transnational system of justice* that could better serve a highly interconnected world that has seen explosive growth in transnational trade and commerce. While this growth had undoubtedly led to important, albeit piecemeal, changes in the supporting justice infrastructure, these had generally emerged in a reactive way rather than as a thoughtful review of key aspects of that infrastructure, in order to come to a better understanding of how the *system* as a whole could be improved. While this remains a worthwhile and necessary exercise, the passage of time and the emergence of new challenges and developments have raised doubts as to the continued viability of the fundamental assumption that underlies any discussion of this sort – namely, that the connectedness and linkages that bind us in a globalised world are necessary elements for our common good. And so, this introductory chapter focuses on that anterior point and proposes a framework for thinking about 'Justice in a Globalised Age'.

The term 'globalisation' means many different things to different people, but most definitions converge on the central idea that it refers to a growing interconnectedness and interdependence across the world in various spheres – whether economic, social, or cultural – and at an inter-nation level as well as between individuals, businesses and communities.[1] The late Professor David Held, an eminent scholar of globalisation and global governance, perhaps put it best when he suggested that globalisation

* Chief Justice, Supreme Court of Singapore. This article is adapted from the keynote speech delivered at the 3rd Judicial Roundtable on Commercial Law on 29 September 2021. I am deeply grateful to my law clerk, Joshua Foo, my colleagues, Assistant Registrars Kenneth Wang, Huang Jiahui and Reuben Ong, as well as my former law clerk and colleague, Elton Tan for all their assistance in the research for and preparation of the address and this chapter.

[1] NRF Al-Rodhan and Gerard Stoudmann, 'Definitions of Globalization: A Comprehensive Overview and a Proposed Definition' (19 June 2006), available at citeseerx.ist.psu.edu/viewdoc/download?doi=10.1.1.472.4772&rep=rep1&type=pdf.

means that we now live in a world of 'overlapping communities of fate'.[2] Indeed, we are today interconnected to a degree never before seen in human history. As the ongoing pandemic reminds us, the choices we make and the actions we take within our own nations can have significant consequences for others half a world away.

In this chapter, the focus is on the relationship between globalisation and the law, and the mutually transformative effect that each has had, and will continue to have, on the other. There are perhaps two uncontroversial observations about this relationship that can be stated at the outset and which might help explain why it is helpful first to direct attention to the anterior question. The first observation is that the law has been a force that has helped to *sustain* globalisation. In an increasingly interconnected world, the law has served the essential function of bringing structure and order to an ever-expanding scope of relationships and connections that individuals, communities and nations have with one another. This has certainly been the case in the context of transnational trade and commerce. The second observation, which follows from the first, is that globalisation on its part has correspondingly also *shaped* the law. For if the object of the law is to bring order to societal relationships, and if globalisation has radically and fundamentally altered the nature, pattern and intensity of those relationships, then the law and its institutions will inevitably have to change in order to meet the changing needs of those they serve and be shaped and influenced by the new realities of a globalised world.

Taken together, these observations suggest that before one considers the future of the law, and especially transnational commercial law, one should first consider the future of globalisation itself. Indeed, this is particularly apposite given the *normative* uncertainty that has come to plague globalisation in recent years. Rising socio-economic inequality, growing distrust of public institutions, and the breakdown of traditional media and informational sources – all of which are trends stemming from or exacerbated by globalisation – together threaten to halt and even reverse the heretofore seemingly inexorable trend towards greater interconnectedness.

In light of all this, what does the future hold for the globalised world? This question is approached in the three main sections of this chapter. Section II sets out a brief history of globalisation including its rise and decline since the World Wars. The role that the law has played in this journey is then considered, and it is suggested that, for better or for worse, globalisation and the law are symbiotically and inextricably linked. In section III, the possible reasons for the decline of globalisation, and the role that the law and legal systems might have played in exacerbating that decline are identified and evaluated. This sets the stage for weighing the strengths of globalisation and proposing the reasons why it might yet remain our best hope in securing humanity's shared future. Finally, in section IV, it is suggested that despite the present headwinds, our best course to the future is not to jettison the idea of globalisation, but rather to take a concerted effort to develop a more *sustainable* vision of it – one that is grounded in the idea of legitimacy so that we might achieve a degree of consensus about the purposes and limits of globalisation, and the trade-offs that we should be willing to accept in exchange for its benefits.

[2] D Held, 'Democracy and Globalization: MPIfG Working paper, No 97/5' (May 1997) Max Planck Institute for the Study of Societies, available at www.mpifg.de/pu/workpap/wp97-5/wp97-5.html.

II. Globalisation and the Law: A Brief History

A. The Twin Triumphs of Globalisation and Law

The modern wave of globalisation was born out of the ashes of the Second World War, as the US-sponsored Marshall Plan kickstarted a worldwide economic recovery by rebooting cross-border trade and investment after years of global warfare and nationalism. This process of economic and cultural integration continued apace until the 1990s, at which time it was supercharged as the European single market began to take shape, and then even more so in the succeeding years as China and India became key players in the world economy.

It is undeniable that globalisation has played a significant role in advancing global economic prosperity, and this has been marked by a broad trend of economic liberalisation that has facilitated the flow of capital and resources to where they can be most profitably applied, as well as the emergence of new technologies which have fostered global interconnectedness on an unprecedented scale.[3] Since 1990, transnational trade has seen tremendous growth. As a share of global output, it rose from under 40 per cent in 1990 to almost 60 per cent in 2018.[4] In the same period, global gross domestic product (GDP) more than tripled.[5] Globalisation has also been instrumental in alleviating the plight of the poorest and most economically vulnerable in the global community. Between 1990 and 2010, the number of persons living in poverty as a share of the total population of developing countries *fell by half*. And about a *billion* people were freed of the scourge of poverty in just those two decades.[6] China alone accounted for three-quarters of that stunning achievement.[7] Other human development indicators too, such as literacy and child mortality rates, have improved significantly.[8]

Whatever one's view on globalisation and its continued viability, it cannot be denied that globalisation has done a tremendous amount of good over the past decades. What is perhaps less known, but no less important, is the indispensable role that the law has played in bringing order to the tangle of invisible threads that has increasingly bound and connected the world. There are at least three aspects to this.

First, the law has served as the globalised *currency of trust*. The days are long gone when the sphere of one's interactions was largely limited to members of the same, close-knit

[3] 'The global list: Globalisation has faltered' (24 January 2019) *The Economist*, January 2019, available at www.economist.com/briefing/2019/01/24/globalisation-has-faltered.

[4] See ibid: world trade as a share of global GDP in 1990 was 39%, and had by 2018 increased to 58%.

[5] See the World Bank, 'GDP (current US$)' (updated as of 20 August 2021) World Bank Data2019, available at data.worldbank.org/indicator/ny.gdp.mktp.cd?end=2018&start=1990: in 1990, global GDP in current US dollars was $22.762 trillion, whereas this had increased to $86.344 trillion by 2018, and increase of approximately 3.8 times.

[6] 'The world's next great leap forward: Towards the end of poverty' (1 June 2013) *The Economist*, June 2013, available at www.economist.com/leaders/2013/06/01/towards the end of poverty.

[7] In 1990, more than 750m Chinese lived below the international poverty line, and this was a staggering two-thirds of the national population. By 2012, however, that number had fallen to fewer than 90m and, by 2016, it had further fallen to just over 7m, or 0.5% of China's population. See J Goodman, 'Has China lifted 100m people out of poverty?' (28 February 2021) BBC News, February 2021, available at www.bbc.com/news/56213271.

[8] M Kituyic, Secretary-General of UNCTAD, Foreword in the 'Developmental and Globalisation: Facts and Figures 2016 Report' ii.

community. Instead, globalisation has created a new *transnational* marketplace, and this has witnessed a proliferation of commercial relationships with counterparties one might not really know, fully understand, or even trust. Thus, while transactions of the past could stand on nothing more than one's word and a firm handshake, dealing in the modern global marketplace calls for a more 'arm's-length' regulatory framework – or a rules-based system – requiring the law to play a crucial role. We can see this at all levels of the economy. In businesses, legal contracts have supplanted the exchange of memos as the primary means of economic command and control.[9] Between nations, the international law of obligations has also lent structure and given order to international trade. The UN Convention on Contracts for the International Sale of Goods, and the World Trade Organization's (WTO) General Agreement on Tariffs and Trade (GATT), are but two well-known examples.

If legal rights can now be considered the new *currency* of trust, then it follows that our legal frameworks have become the notional 'bank' in which we can safeguard and realise those rights. Among the clearest illustrations of this are the methods for transnational commercial dispute resolution that have evolved dramatically in recent decades. Leveraging on the advantages of international enforceability, neutrality and procedural flexibility, arbitration has emerged as the pre-eminent means of resolving transnational commercial disputes. The New York Convention on the Recognition and Enforcement of Foreign Arbitral Awards, widely regarded as one of the most successful international treaties,[10] boasts an impressive 168 state parties and has reshaped the manner in which transnational commercial justice is pursued and enforced. In like manner, instruments like the UNCITRAL Model Law on International Commercial Arbitration and the ICSID Convention for Investor-State Arbitration have gained significant currency and acceptance.[11] More recently, we have seen the rise of international commercial courts, which complement – and, some might say, *compete* with – international arbitration. These developments are but a part of the growing assembly of specialised institutions and procedures that pertain to the resolution of *international* commercial disputes, and this raises interesting and important questions as to whether, and if so, to what extent, the internationality of such disputes justifies treating them differently than we would domestic commercial disputes. In any case, developments like these underscore how, in these and other ways, the law has played a crucial role in oiling the wheels of transnational commerce which have, in turn, been powered by the engine of globalisation.

Second, driven by the desire to overcome the risks and costs of regulatory fragmentation and arbitrage, global commercial laws have gradually been converging towards a

[9] M Shapiro, 'The Globalization of Law' (1993) 1 *Indiana Journal of Global Legal Studies* 37, 40.

[10] Arbitration Academy, 'Benefits of the New York Convention', available at arbitrationacademy.org/wp-content/uploads/2018/07/7.pdf.

[11] The UNCITRAL Model Law has been adopted in 85 states, and the ICSID has 164 signatory and contracting states: see United Nations, 'Status: UNCITRAL Model Law on International Commercial Arbitration (1985) with amendments as adopted in 2006' (updated as of January 2021) United Nations Commission On International Trade Law, available at uncitral.un.org/en/texts/arbitration/modellaw/commercial_arbitration/status; International Centre for Settlement of Investment Disputes, 'Database of ICSID Member States' (updated as of June 2021) ICSID, available at icsid.worldbank.org/about/member-states/database-of-member-states.

set of shared principles that provide a measure of legal consistency regardless of locality. This has seen the blending of trade usages, model contracts and standard clauses into a body of supra-national norms and principles.[12] The success and proliferation of various standard form contracts – such as the Institution of Civil Engineers (ICE) Conditions of Contract[13] – testify to the appetite for the law's standardising function. This is also reflected in the emergence of institutions such as the UNCITRAL, the European Law Institute, and the Asian Business Law Institute (ABLI), among others, which are all engaged in the bid to minimise unnecessary obstacles to free and seamless trade.[14] And even in judicial contexts, the ability to refer to the decisions of other jurisdictions – enabled by the proliferation of technologically enabled research tools – has facilitated a gradual convergence in the attitudes and approaches taken by national courts to commercial issues, with clear examples in the field of cross-border insolvency and international commercial arbitration.[15] Taken together, this trend towards the standardisation of commercial practices fostered by the law has provided something approaching a common framework within which any person from any jurisdiction could, with a reasonable degree of stability, engage and participate in the global economy.

Third, the law has furnished the underlying infrastructure of rules and rights needed to encourage commercial entrepreneurship and innovation while limiting the potentially ruinous consequences of business failure. This includes legal developments in the recognition of a wider range of property rights from intellectual property to crypto assets, the trend towards a universalist approach in international insolvency and restructuring, the development of antitrust and competition law principles to guard against monopolistic excesses, and perhaps most foundationally, the principle of separate legal personality that limits the personal liability of businesspersons. In this sense, the law has undoubtedly, in the words of Lord Bingham, played a vital role as the handmaid of commerce.[16]

Thus, it might be said that the triumphs of globalisation have in some ways also been the triumphs of the Rule of Law. Their intertwined histories showcase a relationship that has proven both profoundly symbiotic and immensely successful. If globalisation may be said to have built a system of superhighways for the more efficient movement and utilisation of money, materials and labour, then the law has dutifully served as its system of traffic rules, road markers and crash barriers – organising and regulating its flows, illuminating the cracks and curbing its more brutish tendencies.

[12] M Vacarelu, 'Globalization, Modernity and Law' (2017) *Academic Journal of Law and Governance* 58, 62.

[13] See B Eggleston, *The ICE Conditions of Contract*, 7th edn (Blackwell Science Publishing, 2001).

[14] See, for example, the work of the Asian Business Law Institute and its reports on regulatory and legal approaches in Asia concerning personal data, corporate restructuring, and the recognition and enforcement of foreign judgments. See abli.asia/Publications. See also S Menon, 'Transnational Commercial Law: Challenges and A Call for Meaningful Convergence' 2 *Singapore Journal of Legal Studies* 231.

[15] See, for instance, the converging jurisprudence concerning the interpretation of the UNCITRAL Model Law on International Commercial Arbitration. See also C Molineaux, 'Applicable Law in Arbitration: The Coming Convergence of Civil and Anglo-Saxon Law via Unidroit and Lex Mercatoria' (2000) 1 *The Journal of World Investment* 127.

[16] Lord Bingham of Cornhill, 'The Law as the Handmaid of Commerce' (5 September 2001), speech at the Sixteenth Sultan Azlan Shah Law Lecture 2001.

B. Globalisation on the Rocks

Yet, for all of globalisation's past achievements, a new page seems to have been turned in its history. One might trace this back to just before the turn of the millennium, when a number of events with regional or global repercussions tore national economies apart. In 1997, Asia suffered a serious financial crisis after an economic bubble inflated by a rapid inflow of short-term funds into Thailand rapidly collapsed. A decade later, a collapse in the US subprime mortgage market swiftly developed into a full-blown international banking crisis and global economic downturn,[17] plunging several nations into serious debt.[18] Out of the questions that were raised as to how the risks that had pooled in what were then relative backwaters of the global financial system had so rapidly and devastatingly impacted all corners of the world economy,[19] it emerged that at least part of the answer lay in the fact that the very connections that had propelled the world's markets to unprecedented heights of prosperity had also served as conduits for the ensuing financial contagion. Furthermore, as we entered the first decade of the new millennium, a series of threats to our common peace and security also emerged in relatively quick succession which were perceived, whether justifiably or otherwise, as being a result of globalisation and the interconnectedness it necessarily entails.

First, in 2001, the US was rocked by major attacks masterminded by a global terrorist organisation and executed by an international cell of attackers, one of whom had been born in Egypt, radicalised in Hamburg and trained as a pilot in Florida.[20] The attacks sparked a global war on terror, the implications of which continue to reverberate throughout the world. Although often perceived as a preoccupation of the US, this is a war against an enemy that is insidious and invisible; is not uniformed; operates without resources even remotely comparable to those of conventional forces; does not regard itself as being bound by any rules of war or engagement; and has a sphere of operations that is neither confined in geography nor affected by the military or civilian status of its targets. This, in fact, is a war that concerns and involves all of us.

Second, climate change has come to the fore as one of the gravest existential threats to humanity. In 2009, alarms were raised that the decade about to end had been the

[17] Academics have warned of signs of a similar impending collapse in late-2020 and early-2021. See E Harrell, 'Are we on the verge of another financial crisis? An interview with John Macomber, Senior Lecturer at Harvard Business School' *Harvard Business Review* (18 December 2020), available at hbr.org/2020/12/are-we-on-the-verge-of-another-financial-crisis.

[18] R McCauley, 'The 2008 crisis: transpacific or transatlantic?' (16 December 2018) *BIS Quarterly Review*, December 2018, available at www.bis.org/publ/qtrpdf/r_qt1812f.pdf.

[19] M Carson and J Clark, 'Asian Financial Crisis' Federal Reserve History (22 November 2013), available at www.federalreservehistory.org/essays/asian-financial-crisis, noting that the crisis that had started in Thailand in July 1997 had by 1998 spread across East Asia and led to spillover effects as far away as in Latin America and Eastern Europe. I Goldin, 'Globalisation has created substantial benefits, but global governance must evolve to meet the challenges posed by new systemic risks' (1 September 2014) London School of Economics Blogs, September 2014, available at blogs.lse.ac.uk/europpblog/2014/09/01/globalisation-has-created-substantial-benefits-but-global-governance-must-evolve-to-meet-the-challenges-posed-by-new-systemic-risks.

[20] L Keay, '9/11 anniversary: Who were the September 11th attackers and what are the links with the new Taliban regime?' Sky News (11 September 2021), available at news.sky.com/story/9-11-anniversary-who-were-the-september-11th-attackers-and-what-are-the-links-with-the-new-taliban-regime-12402917.

warmest since modern record-keeping started in the 1880s.[21] Two decades on, the situation has only deteriorated further.[22] In its recent 2021 Report, the Intergovernmental Panel on Climate Change found that the world was warming faster than previously expected, and warned that unless immediate, rapid and large-scale reductions in emissions are achieved, humanity's ability to limit the warming of our planet will soon slip out of our collective reach.[23]

Third, the ongoing COVID-19 pandemic has highlighted global public health as another pressing issue of worldwide concern. Within months, COVID-19 had spread throughout the world, paralysing economies and healthcare systems and illustrating in the starkest terms possible just how interconnected – and therefore vulnerable – we all are.

This succession of existential crises has laid bare the costs of global interconnectedness. Each of these threats has powerfully demonstrated the extent of our interlocking fragility, and strengthened the case of those who view global interconnectedness not as a means of advancing collective progress but as a slippery slope towards excessive interdependence, shared vulnerabilities and a loss of self-determination. This has led to calls for states to 'take back control';[24] some going as far as to declare that 'globalisation is dead' and that the future of the world ahead lies instead in 'deglobalisation'.[25] Unfortunately, anti-globalisation rhetoric today is no longer the preserve of a vocal minority, but has manifested in ways that are much more concerning. Between 2008 and 2017, in the wake of the global financial crisis, measures of global trade openness indicated a decline for the first time since World War II.[26] In 2016, the EU, once the poster child of transnational integration, suffered a major setback when the UK voted to leave the EU. Then in 2017, a change of administration in the White House brought with it a sharp pivot away from multilateralism and global free trade. In the ensuing years, the

[21] A Voiland, '2009: Second warmest year on record; end of warmest decade' 22 January 2009, NASA Global Climate Change, available at climate.nasa.gov/news/249/2009-second-warmest-year-on-record-end-of-warmest-decade.

[22] In its 2021 Report, the Intergovernmental Panel on Climate Change found that the world was warming faster than previously expected, and it warned that unless immediate, and large-scale reductions in emissions were achieved, humanity's ability to limit the warming of our planet will soon slip out of our reach: see Intergovernmental Panel on Climate Change, 'AR6 Climate Change 2021: The Physical Science Basis' (updated as of 7 August 2021) IPCC Sixth Assessment Report, August 2021, available at www.ipcc.ch/report/ar6/wg1/#FullReport. Despite the potentially devastating scenario we face collectively, the political will and incentive to take action against climate change appears wanting.

[23] ibid.

[24] R Horner, et al, 'How anti-globalisation switched from a left to a right-wing issue – and where it will go next' The Conversation (26 January 2018), available at theconversation.com/how-anti-globalisation-switched-from-a-left-to-a-right-wing-issue-and-where-it-will-go-next-90587, noting the rallying call for supporters of Brexit who seek to 'Take Back Control' from Brussels. In a speech at the 2017 World Economic Forum at Davos, British Prime Minister Theresa May acknowledged that 'talk of greater globalization can make people fearful. For many, it means their jobs being outsourced and wages undercut. It means having to sit back as they watch their communities change around them'.

[25] M O'Sullivan, *The Levelling: What's Next After Globalization* (PublicAffairs Publishing, 2019); see also 'Globalisation is dead and we need to invent a new world order' *The Economist* (28 June 2019), available at www.economist.com/open-future/2019/06/28/globalisation-is-dead-and-we-need-to-invent-a-new-world-order.

[26] S Donnan, 'Globalisation in retreat: capital flows decline since crisis' *Financial Times* (22 August 2017), available at www.ft.com/content/ade8ada8-83f6-11e7-94e2-c5b903247afd; DA Irwin, 'Globalisation is in retreat for the first time since the Second World War', Peterson Institute for International Economics (23 April 2020), available at www.piie.com/research/piie-charts/globalization-retreat-first-time-second-world-war.

Trans-Pacific Partnership[27] was abandoned by the US, appointments to the Appellate Body of the WTO[28] were blocked, and the US withdrew from the Paris Climate Accord on the stated basis that the agreement was prejudicial to American jobs.[29] The continuing trade tensions between the US and China are yet another example of the shift in attitude towards globalisation that has had implications not only for the US and Chinese markets,[30] but also for every other national economy.[31] It is too early to tell how this will be affected by the change of administration in Washington in 2021.[32]

Given all this, it may consequently be said that we are today, more than ever in the past 50 years, living in a world that is both intensely and intractably interconnected and yet also deeply divided; one that, in many respects, increasingly resembles a scatter of anxious states preoccupied by threats that they know to be common, but yet, somehow choose to face these challenges within national, or, at best, regional silos, rather than as part of a dynamic, unified whole.

III. Evaluating Globalisation: A Faith Misplaced?

A. The Fall of an Ideology

The foregoing portends a worrying future for globalisation and the globalised world. In the search for answers as to why the tide has turned, and what lessons we might glean from this, three points may be made.

[27] M Solis, 'Trump withdrawing from the Trans-Pacific Partnership' (24 March 2017) Brookings Institute, March 2017, available at www.brookings.edu/blog/unpacked/2017/03/24/trump-withdrawing-from-the-trans-pacific-partnership.

[28] P Baker, 'Trump Abandons Trans-Pacific Partnership, Obama's Signature Trade Deal' *New York Times* (23 January 2017), available at www.nytimes.com/2017/01/23/us/politics/tpp-trump-trade-nafta.html. See also an author's suggestion that the 2019 WTO crisis possibly presented '*déjà vu*', ie a pattern that has recurred in WTO over the years, albeit the author's view is that the actions by the Trump Administration as regards the Appellate Body were arguably more severe: R Ricupero, 'Chapter 2 – WTO in crisis: déjà vu all over again or terminal agony?' in *The WTO Dispute Settlement Mechanism* (Springer, 2019) 17–23.

[29] J Jacobo, 'The US is leaving the Paris Agreement: How that will affect the global mission to affect climate change' ABC News (2 November 2020), available at abcnews.go.com/US/us-leaving-paris-agreement-affect-global-mission-affect/story?id=73861889: US President Trump had announced his intention to withdraw from the agreement, saying that it would 'undermine [the US] economy, hamstring [US] workers, weaken [US] sovereignty [and] impose unacceptable legal risk'.

[30] 'Trump's Tariffs Led to Billions of Losses, Fed Research Shows' (updated as of 23 June 2021) Bloomberg Economics, available at www.bloomberg.com/news/articles/2021-06-22/u-s-china-tariffs-distorted-trade-billions-lost-fed-says.

[31] K Itakura, 'Evaluating the Impact of the US-China Trade War' (2019) 15 *Asian Economic Policy Review* 77, available at doi.org/10.1111/aepr.12286; S Goulard, 'The Impact of the US-China Trade War on the European Union' (2020) 12 *Global Journal of Emerging Market Economies* 56, available at doi.org/10.1177/0974910119896642.

[32] See O Wang, 'US-China relations: American efforts to reshore supply chains blasted as 'empty talk' by former minister' *South China Morning Post* (28 June 2021), available at www.scmp.com/economy/global-economy/article/3139057/us-china-relations-american-efforts-reshore-supply-chains. Perhaps as a harbinger of what is to come, one *New York Times* headline from March this year proclaimed that 'In Washington, 'Free Trade' Is No Longer Gospel'. See A Swanson, 'In Washington, 'Free Trade' Is No Longer Gospel' *New York Times* (17 March 2021), available at www.nytimes.com/2021/03/17/business/economy/free-trade-biden-tai.html.

First, much of the discontent with globalisation may be attributed to a fundamental failure to achieve consensus on its primary objectives and purposes, and therefore, also on its *limits*. The precursor to contemporary globalisation was the age of colonialism. The colonial powers saw the globe and its resources as theirs for the taking, and the 'global interconnectedness' of that age was largely founded on starkly asymmetrical relationships between the colonisers and the colonised,[33] with few if any normative limits on the ability of a colonial power to exploit those relationships for economic gain. Over time, these attitudes have given way to a somewhat more inclusive and enlightened approach to globalisation that is more conscious of the need to ensure that all are allowed to *share* in the benefits of the global economic growth.[34] But what has not changed is humanity's seemingly single-minded desire to maximally exploit global resources without restraint – relying on the trade and legal infrastructure provided by globalisation – in a bid to sustain what are, in truth, *unsustainable* levels consumption and affluence, even though those levels will only be attained by very few and at inordinate cost. And today, even in the face of overwhelming evidence that current practices are unsustainable,[35] we continue to resist the idea that there are costs associated with the untrammelled exploitation of our natural resources,[36] and that *sustainable* development requires us to take these costs into account even as we continue to pursue economic prosperity.[37]

Second and relatedly, lulled perhaps into a false sense of security by the past successes of globalisation, we have failed to trim the sails of globalisation to better navigate the changing winds of threats to our collective humanity. Our inability to develop a cohesive response to the dangers posed by climate change is a prime example of this. So too is our inability to develop any meaningful or concerted effort to address the problem of global economic inequality. Despite the unprecedented prosperity brought about by globalisation, the World Inequality Report states that between 1980 and 2016, income inequality had increased sharply in nearly *all* world regions, and that even as there was general economic growth across all income groups, the global top one per cent of earners had captured twice as much of the growth in global income

[33] As evidenced by, for example, what has been called the 'Scramble for Africa', which took place in the late 19th century. The colonisers – 13 European countries and the US – met in Berlin to agree the rules of African colonisation, and promptly proceeded to divide up the continent amongst themselves: see St John's College, University of Cambridge, 'The Scramble for Africa', available at www.joh.cam.ac.uk/library/library_exhibitions/schoolresources/exploration/scramble_for_africa.

[34] See JA Du Pisani, 'Sustainable development – historical roots of the concept' (2006) 3 *Environmental Sciences* 83, 88. This latest iteration of globalisation has a central concern the widening gap between the developed and developing countries, and there seems acknowledgment that high international economic growth rates could only be maintained if wealth could be distributed more evenly on a global scale.

[35] See, among others, the United Nations Intergovernmental Panel on Climate Change (IPCC) Special Reports on Global Warming dated 8 October 2018 and 9 August 2021.

[36] Pisani, 'Sustainable development' (2006) 87–88, 90.

[37] UN Conference on the Human Environment (Stockholm, 1972): 'A point has been reached in history when we must shape our actions throughout the world with a more prudent care for their environmental consequences. Through ignorance or indifference we can do massive and irreversible harm to the earthly environment on which our life and well being depend. Conversely, through fuller knowledge and wiser action, we can achieve for ourselves and our posterity a better life in an environment more in keeping with human needs and hopes … To defend and improve the human environment for present and future generations has become an imperative goal for mankind', cited in Pisani (n 34) 92.

as the poorest 50 per cent. While globalisation may not at its core be a *distributive* concept, these numbers highlight that we have yet to come to terms with the distributive *consequences* of globalisation or to develop a consensus on the distributive *norms* that could and perhaps should have underpinned globalisation as the defining trend of the twentieth century.

The third and final point relates to the role of the law in the decline of globalisation. Just as the law has played a complementary role to the rise of globalisation, it seems also at least partly responsible for its decline. If legal rights are the *currency* of trust in a globalised world, they seem to suffer the very same problems that the fiat currencies now suffer from – that of unequal distribution and a growing sense that they may no longer be fit for purpose. Across the developed and developing worlds, the issue of access to justice has been an enduring problem that manifests in various ways – long waiting times for hearings, delayed judgments and the prohibitive costs of legal services and court fees, among others.[38] The issue of *inadequate* access comes hand in hand with the problem of *unequal* access,[39] since it tends to be the poorest and most marginalised who lack the resources necessary to surmount these barriers to justice. In its 2016 report on inclusive growth, the Organisation for Economic Co-operation and Development (OECD) stated that the 'inability to resolve legal problems diminish access to economic opportunity, reinforces the poverty trap, and undermines human potential and inclusive growth'.[40]

To this end, target 16.3 of the UN Sustainable Development Goals expressly commits Member States to 'promote the rule of law at the national and international levels, and ensure equal access to justice for all'. Yet, on a global scale, there remains a disquieting justice gap despite the economic gains of the past decades. According to one UN estimate, 85 per cent of the populations of 179 developing nations live in areas that are beyond the reach of the law, meaning that over *four billion people* lack effective recourse to justice through the law.[41] Even in countries as developed as the US, it has been reported that four-fifths of low-income Americans have no effective access to legal help.[42] It should be a matter of deep concern that instead of serving as a bulwark against evolving threats and growing inequality in a globalised world, the law and legal systems might in fact have perpetuated and exacerbated the failings of globalisation.[43]

[38] See, for example, E Hadrian, 'Optimizing the implementation of mediation to overcome civil case backlog in Indonesia' (2019) 20 *South East Asia Journal of Contemporary Business, Economics and Law* 151–57, available at www.endanghadrian.co.id/images/Journal per cent20internasional.pdf; S Kalantry, 'Litigation as a Measure of Well-Being: The Threat of India's Case Backlog' (2013) 62 DePaul Law Review 247, available at osf.io/preprints/lawarxiv/dr92f; L Dearden, 'Crown court backlog hits record high of 60,000 cases as victims wait years for justice' *The Independent* (24 June 2021), available at www.independent.co.uk/news/uk/home-news/crown-court-backlog-coronavirus-cuts-b1872051.html; P Stinson and JE Cutler, 'Texas Court backlog could last five years without more funding' Bloomberg Law (24 May 2021), available at news.bloomberglaw.com/us-law-week/Texas-court-backlog-could-last-five-years-without-more-funding.

[39] S Menon CJ, 'Technology and the Changing Face of Justice' (14 November 2019), speech at the Negotiation and Conflict Management Group ADR Conference 2019 delivered in Lagos, Nigeria ('NCMG Speech') at para 9.

[40] OECD, 'Towards Inclusive Growth – Access to Justice: Supporting people-focused justice services' (2016).

[41] UN Report of the Commission on Legal Empowerment of the Poor, 'Making the Law Work for Everyone' vol 1 (2008) 19 and 90, available at un.org/ruleoflaw/files/Making_the_Law_Work_for_Everyone.pdf.

[42] 'Addressing the Justice Gap' *New York Times* (23 August 2011), available at nytimes.com/2011/08/24/opinion/addressing-the-justice-gap.html.

[43] NCMG Speech at para 9.

B. The Case for Hope

The common thread underlying these three contributory factors to the decline of globalisation is that they are complex, multifaceted and near-intractable problems that cannot easily be resolved or mitigated. But before one concludes that globalisation ought therefore to be abandoned, there is another perspective that must be considered – namely, the strengths of globalisation and the reasons why it might remain our best hope for securing humanity's shared future. From that perspective springs a simple but compelling argument for doubling down on our commitment towards a certain vision of globalisation; and that is that the most urgent, important and existential issues that plague humanity today *require* multilateral solutions, and our best chances of achieving them lie in an interconnected and open global society with a realistic appreciation of both our inter-dependency and our shared vulnerabilities. As the saying goes, 'global problems require global solutions'.[44] Three such issues have already been discussed – the threat of terrorism, climate change and the ongoing pandemic. And there are of course others; in a speech at the 76th Session of the UN General Assembly, Singapore's Foreign Minister stressed the importance of *multilateral* action to tackle a range of global issues including data regulation and the governance of the world's oceans and ocean resources.[45] The underlying commonality that these problems share is that they cannot be solved by any one state alone; they require collective action and multilateral solutions.

Take the fight against climate change, for example. Limiting global warming requires that we keep greenhouse gas emissions to a certain level. Individually, each country lacks both the capacity and the incentive to achieve this; and since no single country *can* do it alone, no country standing alone *will* do it. Issues like these, which implicate the global commons, require that we stand together. Uneven participation, even if involving a relatively small band of abstainers, creates a free-rider problem that undermines the incentives for those onside to stay onside. Take, for instance, the commitments made by the signatories to the Kyoto Protocol and the Paris Agreement to reduce greenhouse gas emissions, for which the fruits of participation – the slowing of global warming – accrue to the benefit of *all*, even the abstainers who share none of the costs of participation.[46]

The COVID-19 pandemic is another contemporary example of the need for multilateralism. It cannot be denied that hyperconnectivity, whether in terms of cross-border economic relations or air travel, contributed to the speed and reach of the pandemic's impact. Within half a year of COVID-19 being declared a global pandemic

[44] United Nations News Centre, 'Global problems need global solutions, UN officials tell ministers at development forum' (17 July 2017), available at www.un.org/development/desa/en/news/intergovernmental-coordination/high-level-segment.html.

[45] Ministry of Foreign Affairs Singapore, 'Minister for Foreign Affairs Dr Vivian Balakrishnan's National Statement at the General Debate of the 76th Session of the United Nations General Assembly in New York, 25 September 2021' (26 September 2021), available at www.mfa.gov.sg/Newsroom/Press-Statements-Transcripts-and-Photos/2021/09/j20210926-76th-UNGA-national-statement.

[46] See E Ostrom, *Governing the Commons* (CUP, 1990) (online republication in October 2015).

in March 2020, every economy had plunged into recession.[47] By November 2021, COVID-19 had spread to at least 220 countries and territories, infected well over 250 million people, and killed over five million.[48]

Across the world, the initial response of almost every state was to shut its borders and turn inward. By May 2020, *every* country in the world had imposed travel and entry restrictions. Singapore, for instance, took the unprecedented step of closing its land border with Malaysia, one of the busiest land crossings in the world that used to see over 300,000 people and 145,000 vehicles crossing each day.[49] By April 2020, more than half of humanity – or just under four billion people – had their travel restricted and had been asked or ordered to stay at home to prevent the spread of the virus.[50] Globally, air travel came to a standstill and plummeted to levels not seen since the 1970s.[51] Fears over the scarcity of medical resources also prompted some countries to introduce legislation to ban the export of face masks and other medical supplies.[52]

The pandemic has shown us that in the face of an existential threat, the state's priority is to offer protection and support to its own people, and it is to the state, rather than the global community, that people tend to turn in times of crisis. This autarkic reflex is neither new nor surprising, and reflects, in some senses, the influence of the Westphalian construct of nationhood and sovereignty. But imagine an ideal world. In the face of a serious global pandemic, the optimal course of action to stop its spread at minimal collective cost might have been a simultaneous, globally coordinated lockdown across the world. Such a lockdown would likely have been more effective than the patchwork of national lockdowns that we saw, because like a forest fire that cannot be put out without a coordinated plan, there will be flareups, reinfections, and cross-infections if our responses are siloed and indifferent to the plight and situation of others.

Of course, this is an *ideal* world scenario, and we do not live in a utopia. But thankfully, the concepts of collective action and shared consequence are not unknown even in our *reality*. The COVAX initiative is one example. It aims to bring countries, businesses and civil society together with the goal of providing equitable access to COVID-19 vaccines.[53] The initiative has seen considerable success – the US announced

[47] G Yip, 'Does COVID-19 Mean The End For Globalization?' Forbes (8 January 2021), available at www.forbes.com/sites/imperialinsights/2021/01/08/does-covid-19-mean-the-end-for-globalization?sh=4d538881671e.

[48] Statista, 'Number of coronavirus cases worldwide as of November 11, 2021 by country', available at www.statista.com/statistics/1043366/novel-coronavirus-2019ncov-cases-worldwide-by-country.

[49] ChannelNewsAsia, 'Clearing the Causeway', available at infographics.channelnewsasia.com/interactive/causewayjam/index.html.

[50] A Sanford, 'Coronavirus: Half of humanity now on lockdown as 90 countries call for confinement' Euro News (3 April 2020), available at www.euronews.com/2020/04/02/coronavirus-in-europe-spain-s-death-toll-hits-10-000-after-record-950-new-deaths-in-24-hou.

[51] Washington Post, 'The virus that shut down the world', available at www.washingtonpost.com/graphics/2020/world/coronavirus-pandemic-globalization.

[52] R Fontaine, 'Globalization Will Look Very Different After the Coronavirus Pandemic' Foreign Policy (17 April 2020), available at foreignpolicy.com/2020/04/17/globalization-trade-war-after-coronavirus-pandemic.

[53] S Berkley, Gavi Vaccine Alliance, 'COVAX explained' (3 September 2020), available at www.gavi.org/vaccineswork/covax-explained.

in September 2021 that it would donate 500 million doses, while the UK announced a donation of a further 100 million doses.[54] The EU has pledged €500 million, and Chinese manufacturers have agreed to provide up to 550 million vaccines.[55] Whether this is borne out of altruism or enlightened self-interest, responses to the pandemic like COVAX demonstrate that when faced with a global problem, we know, in our rational minds, that a global response is optimal and indeed necessary. Our nativist instincts may lead us to turn inward when threatened, but we eventually seek multilateralism and tap on our global infrastructure and relationships because that is the *only* way to truly resolve the threats that confront us. And this is so not only for the pandemic but for most of the major challenges that plague humanity.

There is a final reason why hope remains for the future of globalisation – and that is that we are perhaps already past the point where globalisation *can* be reversed or disavowed. The reality is that we live in a world today that will not easily be untied. Importantly, this growing sense of global interconnectedness exists not just between states or national governments, but indeed at a grassroots, *inter-personal* level.[56] Technology – and, in particular, the Internet – has enabled millions of small companies and individuals to directly participate in globalisation by tapping into global markets and networks. According to one 2016 estimate, some 900m people have international connections on social media networks like Facebook and LinkedIn, and over 360m have taken part in cross-border e-commerce.[57] Tens of millions of small businesses worldwide have become 'micro-multinationals' by tapping on digital marketplaces like Amazon, eBay and Alibaba to directly reach customers and suppliers.[58] It should not come as a surprise, then, that there seems an increasing consciousness of and sense of attachment to our membership in these global communities. In a 2016 BBC survey of over 20,000 people from 18 countries, more than half said that they see themselves more as 'global citizens' than citizens of their home country.[59] While the

[54] 'COVAX: How many Covid vaccines have the US and the other G7 countries pledged' BBC (11 June 2021), available at www.bbc.com/news/world-55795297.

[55] E Farge, 'Chinese drugmakers agree to supply more than half a billion vaccines to COVAX' Reuters (12 July 2021), available at www.reuters.com/world/gavi-signs-covid-19-vaccine-supply-deals-with-sinovac-sinopharm-covax-2021-07-12.

[56] Putting the temporary disruptions wrought by the pandemic aside, the volume of international flows of tourists, university students and migrants extended their long-term rising trends in 2019: DHL, 'DHL Global Connectedness Index 2020' (2020) 41, available at www.dhl.com/content/dam/dhl/global/dhl-spotlight/documents/pdf/spotlight-g04-global-connectedness-index-2020.pdf. The proportion of persons living outside their birth countries, for instance, was 23% above its 1990 level in 2019: see 19; cross-border Internet bandwidth has grown by 45 times since 2005: McKinsey Global Institute, 'Digital Globalization: The New Era of Global Flows' (March 2016) vii, available at www.mckinsey.com/~/media/McKinsey/Business Functions/McKinsey Digital/Our Insights/Digital globalization The new era of global flows/MGI-Digital-globalization-Full-report.ashx; and the proportion of voice calls made internationally has seen a marked threefold increase in the past two decades from about 2% in 2001 to nearly 7% in 2015: DHL Global Connectedness Index 2020, 36.

[57] McKinsey Global Institute, 'Digital Globalization' vii.

[58] ibid vi–vii.

[59] Interestingly, this was particularly true for respondents from emerging economies; in China, for instance, this view was held by 71% of respondents, and, in Nigeria, by 73% of respondents: see N Grimley, 'Identity 2016: 'Global citizenship' rising, poll suggests' BBC (28 April 2016), available at www.bbc.com/news/world-36139904; F Garza, 'Survey: People are increasingly identifying more as 'global citizens' than national citizens' Quartz (29 April 2016), available at qz.com/672396/people-are-now-more-likely-to-identify-as-global-citizens-than-national-citizens.

likelihood of the concept of 'global citizenship' being realised in any true, political sense in the foreseeable future is remote, what these results nonetheless show is the extent to which people already *identify* with the global networks and communities of which they are a part.

In sum, not only is the world more connected than ever before, but more importantly, the depth and nature of those connections has changed in a fundamental way. The global flows of trade, information and people which are the lifeblood of globalisation flow not just through major inter-state arteries but also through the network of millions of capillaries formed between individuals. As a result, the keys to globalisation are no longer exclusively held by governments or indeed by any one stakeholder. In short, through our shared history, the evolution of technology, and the need to collectively confront global issues and threats, we are *already* inextricably interconnected and integrated. In the words of the great eighteenth-century philosopher Immanuel Kant, we are all '*unavoidably side by side*'.[60] On this view, a 'de-globalised world' is simply unimaginable. And even if multilateral cooperation were renounced and its institutions deserted, all that would accomplish is to abandon the governance and regulation of the vast, interconnected economy of people, goods and services to nothing more than the whims of fate. By stepping away from engagement and integration, we would not, in fact, be taking back power for ourselves; rather we would be *giving up control* over our futures – futures that are and will remain inextricably tied to one other.

IV. Keeping a Light on for Globalisation

Before turning to consider what the future holds for globalisation, it might be helpful to take stock of the foregoing discussion and to revisit two propositions that have been advanced. First, that globalisation has serious conceptual and distributive issues almost all of which will not be easy to correct, and some of which are in fact contributed to by the failings of the law and legal systems. Second, that despite the difficulties that bedevil it, globalisation nonetheless remains the best, if not the only, solution to meet the major challenges that confront the world, and that it offers the best hope for securing humanity's shared future. There is clearly some tension between the two propositions, but the unescapable reality is that we *must* live in and with a globalised world. If we accept that we are better off together than apart, then we have no choice but to confront and overcome the failings of globalisation, to revisit its assumptions, and to remodel it in a manner that will better serve the demands of the times.[61] This will not be an easy task.

[60] See D Held and P Hirst, 'Globalisation: the argument of our time' (22 January 2002) Open Democracy, available at www.opendemocracy.net/en/article_637jsp/.

[61] M Wolf, 'Globalisation and Interdependence', speech to the UN General Assembly (October 2004), available at www.un.org/esa/documents/un.oct.2004.globalisation.and.interdependence.pdf: 'What we must do is build upon what has been achieved, not, as so many critics wish, throw it all away. In the era after 11 September 2001, that co-operative task has certainly become far more difficult. For people to sustain openness to one another is far harder at a time of fear than at a time of confidence. But the task has also become more urgent. A collapse of economic integration would be a calamity'.

There are at least three aspects we should consider: (1) to place globalisation on a more sustainable footing; (2) to build a more robust and constructive space for discourse about globalisation; and (3) to ground globalisation, like the law, in a notion of legitimacy. In all of these, the law can and should have an important role to play.

A. A More Sustainable Footing

We must place globalisation on a more sustainable footing. There are several dimensions to the notion of sustainability, some of which have already been discussed. One such dimension is the idea that there are normative limits on the extent to which globalisation should permit and facilitate the exploitation of our natural and human resources. The heady optimism and unbridled expectations of unlimited economic growth sparked by the post-war economic boom of the 1950s must, especially with our current understanding of the sciences and the world we inhabit, give way to a realisation that there are limits to our resources and that exceeding those limits carries serious human and environmental consequences for us and for our future generations.[62] This is not new, and steps have already begun to be taken to introduce the concept of sustainability into the global economic agenda. The previously mentioned UN Sustainable Development Goals (SDGs) are a good example of this. Adopted in 2015 and intended to be achieved by the year 2030, the SDGs are a collection of 17 interlinked global goals designed to serve as a 'blueprint to achieve a better and more sustainable future for all'.[63] And, since a little over a decade ago, sustainability clauses have started to feature in free trade agreements.[64]

Similar observations may also be made regarding distributive inequality arising from the uneven distribution of the impacts of, and opportunities from, globalisation. Ed Miliband, a UK politician, once remarked: 'They used to say a rising tide lifts all the boats. Now the rising tide just seems to lift the yachts'.[65] One may or may not agree with the politics, but it is undeniable that there is now an emerging sense that a more sustainable approach to globalisation is needed, and that ensuring the social sustainability of globalisation requires that inequality be kept in check.[66] As Larry Summers, a former US Treasury Secretary and Chief Economist of the World Bank puts it, 'there is little hope for maintaining integration and cooperation if [globalisation] continues to be seen as leading to local disintegration while benefiting only a mobile, global elite'.[67]

[62] Pisani (n 34) 87–88, 90.

[63] See UN Department of Economic and Social Affairs, Sustainable Development Unit, available at sdgs.un.org.

[64] See, for an overview, M Bronckers and G Gruni, 'Retooling the Sustainability Standards in EU Free Trade Agreements' (2021) 24 *Journal of International Economic Law* 25.

[65] P Wintour, 'Ed Miliband stakes the house on huge new-build programme and tax cut' *The Guardian* (24 September 2013), available at www.theguardian.com/politics/2013/sep/23/labour-ed-miliband-housebuilding-pledge.

[66] E Aisbett, 'Why are the Critics So Convinced that Globalization is Bad for the Poor?' in A Harrison (ed), *Globalization and Poverty* (University of Chicago Press, 2007) 41.

[67] LH Summers, 'Global Trade Should be Remade from the Bottom Up' (18 April 2016) Social Europe, available at socialeurope.eu/global-trade-remade-bottom.

Indeed, inequality that is sustained and extreme is the *very antithesis* of sustainability. While there remains room for debate on the adequacy of the initiatives taken to address these sustainability dimensions,[68] it is nonetheless true that these are promising developments reflecting a growing recognition and awareness that economic growth is not the unitary policy objective, and that there needs to be a weighing of costs and policies to arrive at a balance we are prepared to live with.

The problem is that different states may well have different interests, and different views as to exactly where and how that balance ought to be struck, whereas the solutions to global problems will undoubtedly require that we *cooperate* and act *collectively* instead of pulling in different directions. While two neighbours may conceivably be able to work out a mutually acceptable compromise, the same might not be the case where dozens of states are involved; large-scale cooperation would not be possible without a rules-based framework for mutual forbearance, the balancing of conflicting interests, and the mediation of disputes where they do arise. The law can play an integral role in supplying that rules-based framework and serve at least two key functions in this context.

To begin with, the law facilitates *promise-keeping*, and therefore creates the regularity that is necessary for actors to orient themselves to others and plan for the future.[69] The law holds states to agreements, and provides disincentives for breach through, for example, the imposition of sanctions that raise the cost of non-compliance, or, even where no express sanctions are stipulated, through such mechanisms as reputation, reciprocity and the threat of retaliation.[70] Apart from upholding an agreed consensus, the law can also play an important role in *shaping* it. This *coordinating* function of the law is particularly useful in situations which call for universal adherence to a single rule or standard. Take, for instance, the treaty which created the 1865 International Telegraph Union (ITU), in which states standardised, amongst other things, the equipment and language used to transmit telegraphic messages internationally.[71] By setting certain rules as equilibrium points, the law can facilitate the coalescence of consensus; the more that states join the treaty, the more it becomes the dominant equilibrium.[72] Even *non-binding* legal instruments can generate this coordinating effect if they gain sufficient initial traction and buy-in; the UNCITRAL Model Laws relating to international commercial arbitration and cross-border insolvency are good examples of this. In this way, though consensus may, at least initially, prove elusive in certain more controversial areas of global concern, the *process* of transnational law-making can itself provide a useful framework for balancing conflicting interests, allowing the contestation of different approaches or views, and, ultimately, enshrining the emergent pre-eminent norm.[73]

[68] See for instance, Bronckers and Gruni Gruni, 'Retooling the Sustainability Standards' (2021) on the adequacy of the EU-championed sustainability standards in FTAs.

[69] CE Pavel, 'Hume's Dynamic Coordination and International Law' (2021) 49 *Political Theory* 215, 226.

[70] ibid 230–31.

[71] International Telecommunications Union, 'International Telegraph Conference (Paris, 1865)', available at www.itu.int/en/history/Pages/PlenipotentiaryConferences.aspx?conf=4.1.

[72] Pavel, 'Hume' (2021) 230.

[73] ibid 231: The development of norms in the highly controversial area of international human rights has been cited as an example of how the law can shape norms, even where black letter legal rules are more honoured in the breach rather than in the observance. It has in this context been argued that 'norms of individual accountability for large scale human rights abuses have been changing in the past thirty years, from

B. A Robust, Truth-Based Space for Discussion

The second idea is that we should encourage and facilitate a more robust global discourse about the purposes and limits of globalisation, and the trade-offs that we are willing to accept in exchange for its benefits. This might seem obvious and uncontroversial today, but the truth is that discussions about globalisation have not always been as critical or robust as they should have been. In its heyday, few dared to question the wisdom of globalisation. An American journalist, George Packer, recalled that at the turn of the millennium, the prevailing attitude was that 'Rejecting globalisation was like rejecting the sunrise. Only the short-sighted, the stupid, the coddled, and the unprepared would turn against it'.[74] It is now obvious that such attitudes have not aged well; but the fact that propositions like these were seemingly unassailable just two decades ago speaks to the importance of breaking free of echo chambers and building a safe and truth-based space for the discussion of the issues that matter. Equally, as a global community of communities, we must recognise that the path of globalisation will not be singular. As with our own communities, we must come together to discuss, debate and build consensus on our choices and the trade-offs that we are willing to accept.

The construction of a healthy and constructive space for discourse on globalisation will not be easy. One challenge is the politicisation of the issues. Another challenge is what has been referred to as 'truth decay',[75] which is the worrying erosion of truth in the modern society as traditional, trusted sources of information – ranging from government authorities to the mainstream media – are increasingly supplanted by a jungle of unverified facts and opinions, enabled by the rise of social and alternative media which have afforded just about anyone a platform to reach a global audience and project any message. The worry is that this will, in time, lead to the emergence of 'alternative facts', echo chambers, the blurring of the line between opinion and fact, and, ultimately, the decline of the role of facts and reason in public discourse. This will not be conducive to *any* rational, constructive, fact-based debate, including one about globalisation. As the world continues to grapple with this problem, the law will assume an increasingly significant role in regulating the veracity and flow of information in the emergent post-truth era.

In Singapore, the Government introduced legislation in 2019 that empowers a minister to issue a take-down or correction order against falsehoods published on the Internet, provided that the statutory requirements are satisfied, and subject to appeals to the court and other processes.[76] The law has been used in response to online circulation of an allegation that a new Singapore-variant of COVID-19 had spread from Singapore to a foreign state.[77] Other jurisdictions may choose to adopt different responses, but

a norm of sovereign immunity which precluded prosecutions of heads of states and other officials, to one in which accountability becomes more common and the norms of sovereign immunity ceases to be absolute'.

[74] G Packer, 'Hillary Clinton and the Populist Revolt' *The New Yorker* (31 October 2016), available at www.newyorker.com/magazine/2016/10/31/hillary-clinton-and-the-populist-revolt.

[75] J Kavanagh and MD Rich, 'Countering Truth Decay' RAND, available at www.rand.org/research/projects/truth-decay/about-truth-decay.html.

[76] POFMA Office, 'Protection from Online Falsehoods and Manipulation Act (POFMA)', available at www.pofmaoffice.gov.sg/regulations/protection-from-online-falsehoods-and-manipulation-act/.

[77] M Yong, 'POFMA directive issued to Facebook, Twitter, SPH Magazines over "Singapore variant" of COVID-19 falsehood' ChannelNewsAsia (20 May 2021).

ultimately, because information and fake news do not respect geographical borders or national identity, this is yet another example of a global problem that calls for a multilateral response.

C. Building Legitimacy

Legitimacy must be the bedrock upon which all aspects of globalisation are grounded. The concept of 'legitimacy' will not be unfamiliar to judges and lawyers. In this context, it connotes the willingness of people to respect the institutions, principles and practices associated with globalisation, and the decisions and outcomes that are derived by those actors and from those norms, even if individually, they may not agree with any particular instantiation of the globalist philosophy.[78] It is suggested that the future of globalisation will depend to a very large extent on its ability to build and regain legitimacy in the eyes of the global polity. There are a few reasons for this. First, imbuing globalism and its institutions with a true sense of legitimacy is the best long-term response to the present climate of growing anti-globalisation sentiment. Like national governments, global governance institutions[79] claim the authority to issue rules, and demand compliance with those rules on pain of real and significant consequences for breaching them.[80] Take, for instance, the WTO, membership of which entails the acceptance of a whole range of rules and obligations authoritatively applied by an internal dispute settlement system. To the extent that global institutions claim the authority to limit the exercise of state sovereignty, constrain policy choices, and thereby affect matters of public interest and policy, they must be grounded in legitimacy. Otherwise, their claims to authority will prove baseless and unworthy of support.[81] Second, the issues that globalisation gives rise to operate on an international plane, where there is no supranational mechanism of compulsion and enforcement. It is therefore moral suasion, deriving from legitimacy, that will enable us to agree on the norms and standards of conduct and nudge us towards adherence.[82] Third, legitimacy bears a self-compounding effect. An institution considered to be legitimate will benefit from greater influence and compliance; this begets stability and efficacy, which will, in turn, allow it to command greater respect.[83] The converse also holds true, and therefore on this premise, it is simply impossible to conceive of any effective or sustainable model of globalisation without legitimacy.

[78] S Menon CJ, 'A Tale of Two Systems: The Public and Private Faces of Investor-State Dispute Settlement' (27 May 2021) Lalive Lecture 2021 ('Lalive Lecture') at para 5.

[79] The concept of 'legitimacy' is usually applied to evaluate whether institutions of governance at a domestic level are worthy of support. But globalisation has created entirely new supranational or transnational spheres of activity directed and regulated by institutions of global governance.

[80] A Buchanan and RO Keohane, 'The Legitimacy of Global Governance Institutions' (2006) 20 *Ethics & International Affairs* 405, 407.

[81] ibid 407.

[82] D Bodansky, 'Legitimacy in International Law and International Relations' in J Dunoff and M Pollack (eds), *Interdisciplinary Perspectives on International Law and International Relations: The State of the Art* (Cambridge, Cambridge University Press, 2013) 327, citing A Hurrell, 'Legitimacy and the Use of Force: Can the Circle Be Squared?' (2005) 31 Review of International Studies 15, 32.

[83] ibid 327.

Admittedly, many of the challenges associated with securing the legitimacy of globalisation lie in the realm of extra-legal factors such as politics, geopolitics and economics.[84] But the law also has a vital role to play. For one, if the law is truly to serve as the currency of trust in a globalised world, then we need to fundamentally rethink and re-engineer our justice systems in a manner that will better serve that purpose. Three overarching themes emerged in the course of the discussions at the Judicial Roundtable which serve as excellent guideposts for how the process of reform might be taken forward.

The first guidepost theme concerns the importance of *procedure* and procedural design in the pursuit of justice and in securing *access* to justice. Developments in the *substantive* law often attract the most attention, whether in the legislative chambers, the courtroom or the lecture hall. But the *means* of delivering justice are just as important as the *ends*, for even the best rules and rights are worthless without an accessible and effective procedure through which they may be actualised and delivered.[85] Seen in this light, *access to justice* is at least as important as, and is in fact an integral part of, *doing* justice; for justice cannot be done if the process by which it is dispensed is, for practical purposes, out of reach of those who seek to invoke it. And because a justice system which is ineffectual or inaccessible cannot claim to be credible or legitimate, establishing legitimacy requires a multifaceted effort to enhance access to justice by ensuring that the procedures by which justice is done are (1) accessible, and (2) fit for their intended purpose.

Beginning with the latter point, to be fit for purpose, the legal process must *cohere* with and be *contextualised* to the specific dispute, such as the nature of the parties and legal interests involved. This can be illustrated with an example from the field of investor-state dispute settlement (ISDS),[86] which is one of the core aspects of the transnational legal infrastructure developed to support globalisation. Unlike *private* commercial dispute resolution, which is concerned primarily with the vindication of the private rights of private parties, the ISDS process involves sovereign states and state interests, and ISDS decisions can, and often do, affect the interests of polities *beyond* the disputing parties and engage issues of significant *public* interest.[87] These *public* dimensions to the ISDS process arguably call for a greater focus on such values as transparency, accountability and consistency of outcomes – values which the *private* arbitral process, which has incorporated features such as confidentiality, party-appointment and the lack of an appellate mechanism, subordinates to party autonomy and choice.[88]

[84] See Bruegel, 'Should we give up on global governance?' (24 October 2018), available at bruegel.org/reader/global_governance#, citing problems of: (i) the over-representation of certain countries (Europe, the US and Japan) in key institutions and the need to redistribute power and influence in favour of emerging and developing countries; (ii) difficulties arising from governance through sectorial institutions, each of which dealing with a specific field, but none dealing with cross-sectoral issues.

[85] Sundaresh Menon CJ, 'Gateway to Justice: The Centrality of Procedure in the Pursuit of Justice', delivered as the 36th Annual Lecture of the School of International Arbitration in Dispute Resolution (30 November 2021) ('SOIA Lecture') at para 9.

[86] See further ch 6 of this book.

[87] Lalive Lecture at para 14. ISDS adjudication can implicate public interests in at least two ways: (i) by influencing and constraining States' exercise of their power to make domestic policy; and (ii) by contributing to the development of international investment law.

[88] Lalive Lecture at paras 24, 34, 38 and 47.

While these features may have been appropriate in the context of private arbitration, which originated as means of resolving *private* disputes and is therefore focused on disputing parties and how *they* wish their dispute to be resolved,[89] the *public* nature of investor-state disputes entails a very different approach to the dispute resolution process – one which must account for the far broader scope of interests that the ISDS process engages. And there is a growing sense that much of the criticism levied at the ISDS process stem from the dissonance between its public nature and goals and the private procedure by which they are to be achieved.[90]

The field of family justice offers yet another example of the value of contextuality. In the family and matrimonial context, beyond the fair resolution of the dispute, doing justice entails helping the parties emerge from the legal process with a sense of reconciliation, the tools to make lasting peace, and a true sense of closure and catharsis. Family justice, unlike *civil* justice, is not about vindicating rights and redressing wrongs; it is fundamentally about problem-solving and helping the parties work through the difficult issues that arise when a family breaks down, and therefore places a far greater premium than general commercial law would on such interests as the preservation of relationships and the management of emotions.[91] Transplanting the procedural framework for *civil* justice, which has at its core an *adversarial* approach to dispute resolution, would be incompatible with the effective pursuit of the unique interests and goals of family and matrimonial law if, for instance, it ends up increasing the acrimony between the disputing spouses.[92] Instead, what is needed is a bespoke, *therapeutic* approach to family procedure which is: *holistic*, because the legal issues visible at the surface often belie more deep-rooted underlying non-legal causes; *restorative*, because the most broken relationships are also often those most in need of urgent repair; and *forward-looking*, because the parties must be able to move on from past hurts and focus on their shared futures which will most often revolve around the lives of their children.[93] This vision might be brought to life through, for instance, the incorporation of non-adversarial methods within the dispute resolution process.[94] Mediation, which offers the parties a means of resolving the dispute amicably, is already a fixture of family procedure in many jurisdictions. The introduction of simplified processes for uncontested divorces can also help to blunt the sharp, adversarial edge of litigation; instead of subjecting the parties to the litigation process, with the risk that dormant tensions might thereby be reignited, simplified divorce procedures[95] offer the parties a quicker, cheaper and less traumatic

[89] Lalive Lecture at para 31. Arbitration, having been developed within a purely private commercial paradigm, was primarily concerned with the interests of the disputing parties and giving effect to their choices in terms of the process by which their dispute would be resolved. In this way, arbitration might be said to have, by design, chosen to prioritise certain values favoured by disputing parties over other core Rule of Law values; eg, parties' desire for confidentiality over the values of transparency and open justice; the party-appointment of arbitrators over concerns to assure the fact and appearance of impartiality of the adjudicators; and the general preference for speed and finality over consistency and accuracy.

[90] Lalive Lecture at para 8.

[91] Sundaresh Menon CJ, 'Through the Eyes of a Child', delivered at the 8th Family Law & Children Rights Conference: World Congress 2021 (12 July 2021) ('Family World Congress') at para 6.

[92] SOIA Lecture at para 23.

[93] Family World Congress at para 6.

[94] ibid at para 11.

[95] In Singapore, six out of 10 divorcing couples file for divorce on a 'simplified track', which is available where the parties are able to reach agreement on the ground for divorce and all ancillary matters (eg, on

way to deal with what is itself already a traumatic event. The point is that there can be no 'one-size-fits-all' approach taken to procedure; if our legal procedures are to serve as gateways to justice they must be contextualised to the particular dispute and what the ends of justice are within that particular context.[96]

Besides contextuality, the *accessibility* of the process is essential to its practical utility in ensuring that justice is actualised and delivered into the hands of those who seek it, and therefore, to its legitimacy. The challenge of enhancing access to justice might be seen as an extension of the scarcity problem; we live in a world of limitless wants but finite means, and there are, therefore, limits to the quantity of resources that can be expended on the administration of justice.[97] But, we cannot simply do *less*, for *unequal* access to justice is anathema to the notion that all are equal before the law. Instead, we must find ways to *do more with less*, and part of this might entail a re-examination of certain long-held beliefs as to what justice is and what it requires.

Consider, for instance, the belief that justice *necessarily* requires and entails an exhaustive search for the truth. While accuracy and rectitude are undoubtedly important objectives of the legal process, it is now widely accepted that these imperatives must be balanced against other values, such as efficiency and proportionality.[98] The need to rebalance these priorities will become even more urgent as our disputes become ever more complex. Advances in information technology and the proliferation of electronically stored information have led to an explosion in the quantities of data (and therefore, potential evidence) that both counsel and the courts might be called on to consider.[99] Hyper-complex cases present access to justice challenges at two levels: first, at the level of the individual case, which can sometimes be so large and factually rich that it becomes virtually impossible for the adjudicator to properly understand, much less decide;[100] and second, at a *systemic* level, because complex cases are a severe drain on judicial time and resources and can therefore have serious consequences on access to justice for the countless others left waiting in line.[101] And since complexity is driven by forces which cannot be stopped, we must expect that the problem will only get worse.[102]

Complex cases can, to a point, be managed by keeping a firm hand on the timelines and evidence, but there will inevitably come a point where the complexity of the case exceeds the bounds of that which even robust case management can manage. The answer might instead lie in reconsidering the notion that justice invariably requires an *exhaustive* search for the truth, and in embracing solutions which, whilst not as

any child issues, maintenance and the division of matrimonial assets): see Ministry of Social and Family Development, Family Assist, 'Types of Divorce Proceedings', available at familyassist.msf.gov.sg/content/proceeding-with-divorce/divorce-proceedings/types-of-divorce-proceedings.

[96] SOIA Lecture at para 19.

[97] NCMG Speech at para 36.

[98] Sundaresh Menon CJ, 'The Complexification of Disputes in the Digital Age', delivered as the Goff Lecture 2021 (9 November 2021) ('Goff Lecture') at para 49. Many jurisdictions expressly recognise this in their civil procedure rules; rule 1.1 of the UK Civil Procedure Rules, for instance, states that the 'overriding objective' of procedure is to enable the court to deal with cases 'justly and at proportionate cost'.

[99] Goff Lecture at paras 18–20.

[100] ibid at paras 34.

[101] ibid at para 37.

[102] ibid at para 40.

thorough as a full-blown trial, are nonetheless capable of producing a fair and satisfactory resolution to the parties' dispute.[103] This might, for example, include the use of representative sampling,[104] or the use of simplified adjudication procedures for certain lower-value claims.[105] Procedures like these might detract somewhat from the view that justice requires the fullest possible determination of all the facts, but if we accept that adjudication is ultimately about resolving the dispute fairly, then we should remain open to them.

Another set of beliefs that we may need to re-examine relate to the integration of technology in the delivery of justice.[106] Technology has been, and will continue to be, a powerful enabler in our efforts to bridge the various aspects of the justice gap and thereby enhance access to justice for all. Indeed, one need look no further than the pandemic for an example of the vital and integral role that technology can play in bridging the *physical* gap[107] between our institutions of justice and the constituencies who seek justice, by keeping *remote* avenues of access open even as courts worldwide were forced to shutter their physical premises. Technology also holds tremendous potential in closing the *resource* gap[108] by increasing efficiency and reducing costs. Online dispute resolution platforms, for instance, integrate technology-assisted negotiation or mediation with simplified adjudicatory processes to resolve millions of low-value consumer disputes quickly and at low cost.[109]

Finally, technology is perhaps best suited for bridging what has been referred to as the *literacy* gap,[110] which affects those who lack the legal literacy to even realise that their problem has a legal dimension and might be capable of being addressed by legal means. Here, even the most basic of technological tools can significantly improve the user experience, and therefore, the *accessibility* of legal procedures. Take, for instance, the introduction in England and Wales of an online system for divorce filings. Users report that the online forms take only half the time to complete as compared to the old paper forms, and because technology automatically and interactively guides the user through the process, less than one per cent of online applications have to be rejected because of user error, compared to 40 per cent under the old system. The project has

[103] ibid at para 52.

[104] ibid at paras 58–59. Under this approach, the result obtained in relation to a smaller, representative sample is then extrapolated to a wider set; see *Amey LG Limited v Cumbria County Council* [2016] EWHC 2856 (TCC).

[105] ibid at para 60. See, for example, the Singapore International Commercial Court's Technology, Infrastructure and Construction List's simplified adjudication process protocol, under which parties may agree to carve out a set of lower-value claims in respect of which recovery is then pegged to the percentage eventually recovered in respect of the main 'non-excluded' claims, available at www.sicc.gov.sg/guide-to-the-sicc/the-technology-infrastructure-and-construction-list.

[106] There remain doubts both within and beyond legal circles is that technology-assisted means of delivering justice would lead to the emergence of two distinct 'classes' of service within the justice system: a superior 'business class' service dispensed by judges in courts assisted by lawyers, and an inferior 'economy class' service for the less well-off who must rely on automated chatbots instead of lawyers, and algorithms rather than judges: see NCMG Speech at para 35.

[107] NCMG Speech at paras 15–17.

[108] ibid at paras 18–24.

[109] Goff Lecture at footnote 67: see J Barnett and P Treleaven, 'Algorithmic Dispute Resolution – The Automation of Professional Dispute Resolution Using AI and Blockchain Technologies' (2018) 61 *The Computer Journal* 399, 406.

[110] NCMG Speech at paras 25–27.

achieved a remarkable 87 per cent user satisfaction rate, and seven out of 10 divorces are now filed online.[111]

In these and other ways, technology can serve as the *interface* between the law and its subjects. This is critical to the legitimacy of our justice systems, for if the law and its institutions seem distant and unfamiliar, that could foster distrust and anxiety which might deter those with legitimate justice needs from seeking recourse. Technology could therefore serve to enhance the legitimacy our legal institutions if it is harnessed to facilitate the delivery of justice in a manner in which the public is already familiar with (for example, through mobile app interfaces), and thereby increase the *psychological* accessibility of our justice systems.[112]

In short, establishing the legitimacy of our justice systems demands a concerted, multifaceted effort at enhancing access to justice. This will entail ensuring that our legal procedures are *contextualised* to the dispute at hand, and also widening our conception of the Rule of Law to encompass the provision of *accessible* and *proportionate* justice:[113] accessible, because justice that is out of reach to some in our society is not justice, and will instead erode trust and build resentment against the system; and proportionate, because in a world of limited judicial resources, we should dispense with the fallacy that justice requires an unlimited outpouring of resources towards an exhaustive search for the truth, and instead recognise that what parties truly require is a fair and acceptable resolution to their dispute. We must ensure that our legal procedures are designed with these values of the Rule of Law in mind so that they are accessible and fit for purpose. If we accept that globalisation must be grounded upon the Rule of Law and therefore commit to the realisation of this vision of justice on a global level, we would have taken an important step towards shoring up the normative and distributive weaknesses of globalisation and addressing at least some of the cracks that have appeared in its façade.

The second guidepost theme is that, in thinking about procedural reform, we ought not to lose sight of the fact that each forum or dispute resolution mechanism is ultimately part of a larger *system* of transnational justice.[114] From international commercial arbitration to international commercial courts, and even investor-state dispute settlement – each of these are but parts of the wider *system*, and therefore should not be understood in isolation, but rather in relation to each other and the different and often complementary roles they play in advancing the administration of transnational justice. We see this, for instance, in the coexistence of international commercial courts and international commercial arbitration, each of which offers litigants a *different* blend of processes and procedures, and therefore unique value propositions.[115] Viewing each in isolation might lead one to conclude that both are locked in a Darwinian race to develop the 'best' or 'perfect' means of resolving commercial disputes. But this view misses the

[111] HM Courts & Tribunals Service, 'Case Study: Divorce online: guided by service users' (22 September 2020), available at www.gov.uk/government/case-studies/divorce-online-guided-by-service-users.

[112] NCMG Speech at para 27.

[113] ibid at para 56; see also S Menon CJ, 'Mediation and the Rule of Law', speech delivered at the Law Society Mediation Forum (10 March 2017).

[114] See further ch 2 of this book.

[115] See further ch 4 of this book.

valuable point that arbitration and litigation might in fact be viewed as *complementary* mechanisms which, together, offer a more varied and therefore holistic menu of options from which litigants may select the mechanism most suited to their dispute.

Viewing transnational dispute resolution as a *system* might also shed light on how other potential tensions between diversity and uniformity might be managed. Take, for instance, the call for greater harmonisation of substantive and procedural laws. This is undoubtedly valuable, especially where differences in procedure lead to inefficiencies and problems of coordination. But where procedural diversity is part of a system of intentionally different processes catering to different needs and interests, one might conclude that there ought to be *some* room for divergence, and, relatedly, that what harmonisation requires is not necessarily uniformity, but interoperability.[116] In a similar vein, taking a systems-oriented lens to the issue of jurisdictional conflicts might provide a framework for understanding why and when courts ought to yield to one another when jurisdictional conflicts arise, as well as the centrality of party autonomy in coordinating and avoiding such conflicts, if, for example, courts view themselves not as competing jurisdictions but as parts of a system which has as its goal the fair and effective resolution of the parties' disputes.[117]

The third guidepost theme is that, apart from structural legal reforms, we should also not underestimate the role that individual lawyers, judges, and legal professionals can play in contributing to the legitimacy of globalisation. One way we can do this is by norm-building, through the articulation and, where appropriate, the institutionalisation of Rule of Law values whenever we discuss and debate transnational legal systems and issues. This extends also to taking a strong and unified stance against the known ills of globalisation, such as cross border corruption, money laundering, and tax evasion, all of which may seem like disparate wrongs but in fact insidiously contribute to our current climate of distrust. Another way is by fostering legal convergence in areas of shared interest. Even if full convergence is not possible or ideal, there may be benefit in maintaining open lines of communication in fields that require coordinated solutions. The Hague International Network of Judges is an example of an institution that addresses the problem of international child abduction in such a way;[118] and the Judicial Insolvency Network (JIN) is yet another example that seeks to improve the management of cross-border restructuring matters.[119] One of the realities of our multipolar, globalised world is the dispersal of power into the hands of different actors who must commit to coming together and acting collectively in the many areas where it is sensible, and indeed *necessary* to do so. Within that context, legal professionals can play a significant part as honest brokers, whose role as interlocutors is to bring the relevant actors together, facilitate communication, and assist them

[116] See further ch 10 of this book.

[117] See further ch 8 of this book.

[118] HCCH, 'The International Hague Network of Judges', available at www.hcch.net/en/instruments/conventions/specialised-sections/child-abduction/ihnj.

[119] Judicial Insolvency Network: 'Judicial Insolvency Network: A network of insolvency judges from across the world', available at jin-global.org.

with solving their problems, all in adherence to the framework of a more sustainable version of globalisation.[120]

V. Conclusion

Globalisation and the law have had and will continue to have a mutually transformative effect on each other. But, as we stand here buffeted by headwinds that seem to push us away from a unified world, it is clear that we cannot abandon the project of globalisation. The real challenge is to muster the will and the ability to formulate a better vision of globalisation. This is a necessary undertaking because the most pressing problems that the world faces require more, not less, multilateral cooperation. The significant scale, proliferation, and consequences of our contemporary problems mean that no state alone, however powerful, can effectively serve as a bulwark. And so, if we accept that globalisation remains the best, and perhaps only, solution to these major challenges of our times, then we must directly confront the reasons for its decline and acknowledge that we cannot continue to enjoy its benefits without also sharing in its costs and addressing its failings. The real question is how those downsides can best be managed. This task will fall ultimately on the global polity, as well as all of us within the law and justice systems worldwide, to steer globalisation onto a more sustainable footing, grounded in a restored sense of legitimacy.

[120] FJ Garcia, 'Introduction: Globalization, Power, States, and the Role of Law' (2013) 54 *Boston College Law Review* 903, 910–11, citing Prof Anne-Marie Slaughter: 'Globalization, however, has brought to the fore another kind of power more suited to the new, flatter, and multi-polar environment: horizontal power … One consequence of globalization is that on an international level, nation-states must increasingly operate through the mode of horizontal power. This mode also brings law and lawyers to the fore, as law creates spaces for horizontal power and structures for interconnection and cooperation. Moreover, to be able to achieve desirable outcomes through horizontal power, someone must bring together actors to solve problems and mediate disputes. As lawyers are trained to think in terms of rights and obligations from all sides of an issue, they are ideally placed to exercise power in a globalized world'.

PART I

What is an International Commercial Dispute?

1

A Bird's Eye View of International Commercial Dispute Resolution

PAK HEI LI

I. About this Chapter

This chapter introduces key elements of the system of international commercial dispute resolution. It does so by looking into three questions. First, what features justify giving international commercial disputes special treatment as far as their resolution is concerned? Second, to what extent is international commercial dispute resolution about party autonomy and holding parties to their agreement? Third, on the basis (as suggested in chapter two) that there is a need for convergence in the management and resolution of commercial disputes across borders, what are the means through which such convergence might be attained?

II. Special Features of International Commercial Disputes

The UNCITRAL Model Law on International Commercial Arbitration[1] ('the Model Law') is a useful starting point for a definition of the phrase 'international commercial disputes'. There is no difficulty in understanding the word 'disputes'. The question is how 'international' and 'commercial' should be understood.

[1] The Model Law was adopted by the United Nations Commission on International Trade Law (UNCITRAL) in 1985 and amended in 2006. UNCITRAL's membership is drawn from the Member States of the United Nations (UN). Currently, the representatives of 60 countries sit on UNCITRAL. Those 60 countries are selected by the UN to reflect the geographical regions and the economic and legal systems of the world. The Model Law is a soft law instrument, which means that, in distinction to a bilateral treaty or a multilateral convention which is legally binding on countries that ratify or accede to it, the Model Law is not binding. A soft law instrument, such as the Model Law, is indicative of international best practice in the particular subject matter covered by the instrument. A soft law instrument can be adopted by a country in whole or part. Its provisions function as guidelines and may be modified or varied to suit the conditions of a country. Thus, a country wishing to enact a state-of-the-art international commercial arbitration law may enact all or some of the Model Law as best suits its circumstances. In practice, a country wishing to reform its arbitration law along the lines of the Model Law will seek advice and technical assistance from UNCITRAL on how best to integrate the Model Law into its laws.

Consider first the adjective 'international'. According to Article 1(3) of the Model Law, an arbitration is 'international' if:

(a) the parties to an arbitration agreement have, at the time of the conclusion of that agreement, their places of business in different States; or
(b) one of the following places is situated outside the State in which the parties have their places of business:
    (i) the place of arbitration if determined in, or pursuant to, the arbitration agreement;
    (ii) any place where a substantial part of the obligations of the commercial relationship is to be performed or the place with which the subject-matter of the dispute is most closely connected; or
(c) the parties have expressly agreed that the subject matter of the arbitration agreement relates to more than one country.

The definition in Article 1(3) can be generalised to cover any commercial transaction. Accordingly, a transaction will be 'international' if one or more of the following conditions are met:

(1) The parties to the transaction have their places of business in different countries.
(2) If the parties have stipulated a forum (such as a court or arbitral tribunal) in which disputes arising in connection with their transaction are to be resolved, that forum will be outside the country or countries of the parties' relevant business.
(3) A substantial part of the performance of the parties' transaction is to be undertaken outside of the country or countries of the parties' relevant business.
(4) The envisaged performance is most closely connected with a place which is outside the country or countries of the parties' relevant business.
(5) The transaction relates to more than one country.

The Model Law having been adopted in some 85 countries, it makes sense to adopt the foregoing generalised definition of 'international' for the purposes of this book.

The Model Law does not have an exhaustive definition of the adjective 'commercial'. Instead, a footnote to Article 1(1) of the Model Law states:

> The term 'commercial' should be given a wide interpretation so as to cover matters arising from all relationships of a commercial nature, whether contractual or not. Relationships of a commercial nature include, but are not limited to, the following transactions: any trade transaction for the supply or exchange of goods or services; distribution agreement; commercial representation or agency; factoring; leasing; construction of works; consulting; engineering; licensing; investment; financing; banking; insurance; exploitation agreement or concession; joint venture and other forms of industrial or business cooperation; carriage of goods or passengers by air, sea, rail or road.

Again, given the adoption of the Model Law by many countries, it makes sense to adopt this non-exhaustive definition for the purposes of this book. The point to note is that the definition is a wide one, covering just about all forms of business transaction and excluding only consumer, labour, family and other relationships of status where the parties do not deal with each other as equals.

Reference to other instruments, by way of a cross-check, confirms that our definitions of 'international' and 'commercial' are widely accepted. A contract is regarded as 'international' under Article 1(2) of the Hague Principles on Choice of Law in

International Commercial Contracts[2] 'unless each party has its establishment in the same State and the relationship of the parties and all other relevant elements, regardless of the chosen law, are connected only with that State'. With the launch of international commercial courts (such as the Singapore International Commercial Court (SICC)), the definition of what constitutes an 'international commercial dispute' has gained significance for the purposes of determining jurisdiction (that is, an international commercial court's ability to hear a case). According to Order 2, Rule 1(3)(a) of the SICC Rules 2021,[3] an action is 'international' if:

(i) any of the following places is situated in a state other than Singapore:
 (A) the place of business of at least one party to the action;
 (B) the place where a substantial part of the obligations of the commercial relationship between the parties is to be performed;
 (C) the place with which the subject matter of the action is most closely connected; or

(ii) all parties named in the case when it was first filed have expressly agreed that the subject matter of the action relates to more than one State;

Order 2, Rule 1(3)(b) of the same Rules further provides that an action is 'commercial' in nature if:

(i) the subject matter of the action arises from a relationship of a commercial nature, whether contractual or not;
(ii) the action relates to an *in personam* intellectual property dispute; or
(iii) all parties named in the case when it was first filed have expressly agreed that the subject matter of the action is commercial in nature.

Given our definitions of 'international' and 'commercial', why then single out 'international commercial' disputes for special treatment?

A compelling reason is that unique issues arise from the 'international' and 'commercial' nature of the disputes. These issues must be addressed in a manner that achieves a fair and just resolution of the differences between commercial parties who are likely to come from different economic and legal systems with possibly different expectations as to the process and effects of dispute resolution. Such differences, if not addressed, will impede the growth of cross-border transactions. Hence, to foster international trade, different states will want to work towards a harmonised or convergent legal framework in resolving international commercial disputes. The consequence will be that entrepreneurs from different countries doing business with each other will have a degree of certainty and comfort that their commercial disputes will be dealt with in a

[2] The Hague Conference on Private International Law (usually abbreviated HCCH) is an intra-governmental organisation based in The Hague. Its purpose is 'to work for the progressive unification of the rules of private international law' (Art 1 of the Statute of the Hague Conference on Private International Law (1955)). HCCH presently has 89 countries and one Regional Economic Integration Organisation (REIO) (the European Union (EU)) as members. HCCH has traditionally worked towards achieving its purpose by promulgating conventions. The Hague Choice of Law Principles on Choice of Law in International Commercial Contracts, which was approved in 2015, was the first soft law instrument promulgated by HCCH. Rule H of the HCCH's Rules of Procedure require that 'To the furthest extent possible, all decisions shall be taken by consensus'.

[3] Singapore International Commercial Court Rules 2021, S 924/2021.

fair, cost-effective and time-efficient manner, regardless of the forum or state in which such disputes are considered. By 'fair' it is meant that the commercial principles applied in one jurisdiction will not be radically different from those applied in another – like cases should essentially be treated in a like manner regardless of the country or forum in which a dispute is being resolved. By 'cost-effective' it is meant that the costs of resolving a dispute will be proportionate and not exorbitant, regardless of the forum chosen for determination of the dispute. By 'time-efficient' it is meant that the time taken to resolve parties' commercial disputes will be short or at any rate not inordinately long, so the parties can go on with their normal business with a minimum of disruption. In the absence of such basic expectations, it is doubtful that commercial persons will take the risk of doing business in a foreign state in any great numbers.

This rationale for the separate treatment of international commercial disputes is underscored by a report published by the Singapore International Commercial Court Committee[4] when weighing the need for a specialised court (the future SICC) to deal with international commercial disputes:

> 12. In the context of investment arbitration, inconsistent arbitral decisions undermine the legitimacy of the investment arbitration regime, while in the broader commercial context, the existence of different legal systems within Asia itself leads to uncertainties and increases transaction costs. This may impact the growth of trade and investment in the region.
> 13. The need for a freestanding body of international commercial law in tandem with Asia's continued growth as a trade and investment hub serve as compelling impetus for Singapore to improve upon our existing legal infrastructure to leverage upon these opportunities.
> 14. There is therefore scope for the SICC to provide an internationally accepted dispute resolution procedural framework for the resolution of international commercial disputes in accordance with substantive principles of international commercial law.

The rationale is further supported by reference to the '2018 International Arbitration Survey',[5] which observed that 97 per cent of its respondents preferred international arbitration as a method of dispute resolution, either on a standalone basis or in conjunction with other forms of alternative dispute resolution.[6] For the respondents, the three most valuable characteristics of arbitration were: (1) the enforceability of awards across borders; (2) the avoidance of specific legal systems or national courts; and (3) flexibility. The first two characteristics suggest that, in an international commercial dispute, parties prefer uniformity and convergence across borders. Certainty and foreseeability can thereby be achieved in two senses. The parties will have a better understanding of their respective rights and obligations in connection with a transaction. Additionally,

[4] The Singapore International Commercial Court Committee, 'Report of the Singapore International Commercial Court Committee' (November 2013), available at www.sicc.gov.sg/docs/default-source/modules-document/news-and-article/-report-of-the-singapore-international-commercial-court-committee-_90a41701-a5fc-4a2e-82db-cc33db8b6603-1.pdf.

[5] White & Case, '2018 International Arbitration Survey: The Evolution of International Arbitration', available at www.whitecase.com/sites/whitecase/files/files/download/publications/qmul-international-arbitration-survey-2018-19.pdf.

[6] The expression 'alternative dispute resolution' (ADR) is typically used to describe means of dispute resolution which are 'alternative' to court proceedings. Thus, arbitration is a form of ADR. Other commonly used forms of ADR are mediation, adjudication, neutral evaluation and expert determination.

the outcome of dispute resolution will be readily recognised and enforced in any other jurisdiction where enforcement is sought.

III. Party Autonomy and its Limits

From a realist viewpoint, when determining disputes, judges, arbitrators and other adjudicators are called upon to apply legal principles in a way that balances among competing individual, commercial and social interests. Typically, the issue is whether to hold commercial parties to the terms of their contract, however harsh the consequences may be to one of the parties or possibly society in general. A court, tribunal or other forum essentially has to decide whether: (1) to uphold party autonomy (that is, the principle that, having freely agreed to undertake certain obligations, the parties should be held to their contract); or (2) to conclude instead that a party need not perform part or all of its obligations for some reason (such as misrepresentation (including fraud), mistake, undue influence, duress (including economic duress), unconscionability, incapacity, illegality, force majeure or frustration, mandatory law, or public policy). Where there is a straightforward clash between the interests of the parties to the contract, the decision-maker's task is to determine on the evidence and applicable law: (1) what as a matter of fact the parties actually agreed to do by their contract; (2) whether some factor (such as misrepresentation, mistake, undue influence, duress, unconscionability, incapacity, illegality, *force majeure*, frustration or unconscionability) excuses a party from performance; (3) whether, in the absence of any vitiating factor, the parties fully performed their respective obligations; and (4) whether, where a party has failed to perform, such party must compensate the other. The foregoing might be characterised as the paradigm issues in a commercial dispute, whether domestic or international.

But there are additional dimensions where a 'commercial' dispute is 'international' in the sense just defined. Parties to an international commercial contract are normally entitled to choose the law that will govern their agreement.[7] They can also designate the forum (such as litigation before the court of a specified state, or arbitration whether ad hoc or under the rules of some administering institution[8]) in which disputes arising

[7] In *Robinson v Bland* (1760) 1 W Bl 234, 96 ER 129 Lord Mansfield famously observed: 'The general rule established *ex comitate et jure gentium* [by comity and the law of nations], is that the place where the contract is made and not where the action is brought, is to be considered in expounding and enforcing the contract. But this rule admits of an exception where the parties (at the time of making the contract) had a view to a different kingdom'.

[8] International commercial contracts will often (but not invariably) include a dispute resolution clause. The clause may be in the form of a choice of court agreement requiring disputes to be litigated before the court of a specified country. The clause may alternatively take the form of an arbitration agreement, requiring the parties to settle their differences arising out of the contract by arbitration. Such arbitrations may be administered or ad hoc. An administered arbitration is carried out under the arbitration rules of an administering body (such as the International Chamber of Commerce (ICC), the Singapore International Arbitration Centre (SIAC), the Hong Kong International Arbitration Centre (HKIAC), the Chins International and Economic Trade Arbitration Commission (CIETAC), etc). An ad hoc arbitration, in contrast, is simply carried out pursuant to a set of arbitration rules (often the UNCITRAL Arbitration Rules (not to be confused with the UNCITRAL Model Law on International Commercial Arbitration (Model Law) discussed above) without there being any administering body overseeing the conduct of proceedings.

out of their contract are to be determined. The agreed chosen law can be (and often is) different from the laws of the countries in which the parties have their business. Because of the role played over the centuries by the English courts in the development of mercantile law, parties frequently chose English law to govern their contracts, although neither party may have a connection with England and the parties' contractual obligations are to be performed somewhere else. The parties' chosen forum for the determination of their disputes may likewise have no link with the parties or their contract. Parties commonly stipulate that differences arising from their commercial contract are to be determined: (1) by a court in a state having no link to either party or their contract; or (2) by an arbitration seated[9] in a neutral state having those characteristics.

There are, however, numerous situations where parties' choices of law or forum are overridden or disregarded. A few examples will suffice for present purposes. Where the parties have chosen a court in a neutral jurisdiction for the adjudication of their dispute, that court may nonetheless decline to hear their case on account of *forum non conveniens*.[10] But suppose that the designated court hears the parties' dispute and delivers a judgment in favour of a party. Despite having obtained a judgment from the agreed forum, the latter may not be able to enforce the judgment against the assets of the losing party in that party's country of business (the enforcing state) because the court of the latter state (the enforcing court) takes the view that enforcement would be contrary to the enforcing state's mandatory law or public policy.[11] A typical scenario is where the enforcing court finds that the parties' choice of a foreign court breached domestic law conferring exclusive jurisdiction in specified disputes on the enforcing state's courts. Another common scenario is where the enforcing court finds that the parties' choice of law and thus the law applied in the judgment sought to be enforced was contrary to mandatory or overriding provisions in the enforcing state's law.[12] In international commercial arbitration, a losing party may apply to the court of the seat of arbitration to set aside the relevant award due to the award being contrary to the public policy of the seat of arbitration.[13] Where it is sought to enforce an arbitral award, an enforcing court may refuse to recognise and enforce the award because the

[9] The 'seat' of an arbitration is the state whose courts have supervision over the conduct of any arbitration proceedings between the parties. For example, when an arbitration is seated in Singapore, the Singapore court will have supervisory jurisdiction over the arbitration. Conventional wisdom holds that every international commercial arbitration must have a seat. However, it is clearly possible to have a delocalised arbitration (that is, an arbitration without a seat). An instance of this would be investment treaty arbitrations conducted pursuant to the ICSID Convention. See Pt 3 of this book for a fuller discussion of ICSID arbitrations.

[10] *Forum non conveniens* is the legal doctrine that the court of another state is more appropriate and convenient for the fair, timely and cost-effective disposal of the parties' dispute.

[11] See, eg, Art 9(e) of the 2005 HCCH Convention on Choice of Court Agreements, which entitles an enforcing court in a Contracting State to refuse recognition and enforcement of a judgment by the parties designated court if 'recognition or enforcement would be manifestly incompatible with the public policy of the requested State, including situations where the specific proceedings leading to the judgment were incompatible with fundamental principles of procedural fairness of that State'.

[12] In these cases, the enforcing court will typically find that the parties' choice of law was an attempt to evade the application of the enforcing state's domestic law (for example, foreign exchange legislation).

[13] See Art 34(2)(b) of the Model Law giving the court of the state in which an arbitration is seated the discretion to set aside an award 'if the court finds that: (i) the subject-matter of the dispute is not capable of settlement by arbitration under the law of this State; or (ii) the award is in conflict with the public policy of this State'.

award concerns a dispute that is incapable of settlement by arbitration under law of the enforcing state or because enforcement of the award would be contrary to the public policy of the enforcing state.[14]

In short, party autonomy is not absolute. The parties' agreements as to forum and choice of law may be disregarded. Party autonomy has limits which may vary from country to country depending on the country's fundamental legal, social, cultural, religious, etc norms. Different countries may carry out the requisite balancing exercise between upholding the sanctity of contract and upholding the state's values in different ways with potentially different outcomes.

IV. Means for Achieving Convergence

Chapter two will put the case for a degree of uniformity and convergence in the way that international commercial disputes are resolved throughout the world. But, given the possibility of divergent outcomes highlighted in the previous parts of this chapter, one might ask how in practical terms convergence can be attained. Does harmonisation simply happen as by an invisible hand? That is unlikely. Left purely to chance, there can be no certainty that harmonisation will materialise, at least within any reasonable timeframe. Instead, if harmonisation is to transpire, judges, arbitrators and other dispute resolution service providers will need to proactively strive to bring about a convergence of principles. If so, what means do they have at their disposal? Part A of this section will comment on instruments that, used in conjunction, can lead to a requisite degree of uniformity. Part B will conclude with remarks on three institutions (the courts, arbitral tribunals, and mediators) for bringing about convergence.

However, before discussing the means for achieving convergence, three points should be made. First, convergence involves the harmonisation not just of substantive commercial law principles, but also of the way that dispute resolution is carried out. Thus, for example, standards of due process in arbitration or litigation should not vary widely from country to country. Second, convergence (whether as to procedure or substance) is not merely a task for judges, arbitrators and dispute resolution service providers. Governments, legislators – indeed, the public at large – also need to work together to bring about a desirable degree of harmonisation. Governments and legislatures interested in attracting trade and investment into their countries will wish to implement commercial laws that facilitate the carrying out of these activities within their territories by traders and enterprises from abroad. That will include putting in place procedural mechanisms for ensuring access to justice, the fair, cost-effective

[14] See Art 36(2)(b) of the Model Law giving the court of an enforcing state the discretion to refuse recognition and enforcement of an award 'if the court finds that: (i) the subject-matter of the dispute is not capable of settlement by arbitration under the law of this State; or (ii) the recognition or enforcement of the award would be contrary to the public policy of this State'. In this respect, Art 36(2)(b) simply reflects Art V(2) of UNCITRAL's 1958 New York Convention on the Recognition and Enforcement of Foreign Arbitral Awards (popularly known as 'the New York Convention'). The New York Convention, which is a treaty or hard law instrument (in contrast to the Model Law), is binding on its Contracting States. The New York Convention is probably one of the most successful treaties ever promulgated. As at February 2022, it had 168 signatories. This is 86% of the 195 countries in the world. See further section IV.B of this chapter.

and timely resolution of cross-border commercial disputes, and the prompt recognition and enforcement of foreign judgments and arbitral awards. Third, convergence and harmonisation does not mean that all jurisdictions must approach cross-border disputes in precisely the same manner. For instance, Judge Renaud Sorieul, formerly Secretary-General of UNCITRAL, was fond of observing that the Model Law was not intended to set up monolithic regimes of international commercial arbitration everywhere. There will be a high degree of convergence, insofar as international commercial arbitration practice is concerned, as more and more jurisdictions adopt the Model Law. But the Model Law itself allows significant scope for diversity and variation in the way that it is applied – for example, as to what is contrary to the public policy of a state or what matters are deemed to be incapable of settlement by arbitration under national law. Consequently, even with harmonisation, there will be room to take account of a state's fundamental social, economic, cultural, religious and other norms. There will likewise be space for jurisdictions to compete with one other in attracting trade and investment by highlighting features of their laws which, although fully compatible with accepted transnational commercial norms, are not present elsewhere.

A. Instruments

Harmonisation may be attained through the implementation of non-state (transnational) norms as found in different instruments. There are four broad categories of such instruments: (1) multilateral treaties or conventions promulgated by UNCITRAL, Hague Conference on Private International Law (HCCH) and other intragovernmental organisations which countries may ratify; (2) soft law instruments (such as model laws or codes of principles, eg UNIDROIT Principles of International Commercial Contracts and the HCCH Choice of Law Principles) that states may adopt in whole or part into their law; (3) trade usages; and (4) non-codified norms (that is, the *lex mercatoria* or the common law of merchants) aimed at creating a transnational legal order. These categories are not mutually exclusive. There is no reason, for instance, why a state cannot treat as a convention (such as the 2005 HCCH Convention on Choice of Court Agreements) as a Model Law and, instead of acceding to the same, simply incorporate some or all of its provisions into its national law. Nor are the categories exhaustive. Instruments may straddle categories. For example, several courts have recently concluded memorandums of guidance (MOGs) with each other. These set out the procedures to be followed when a party wishes to have the commercial judgment of one court party to the memorandum in the territory of the other court party. MOGs are not treaties since they are not binding. Neither are they soft law instruments in the sense just described, as they are only statements of the procedural law in effect within the territories of the court parties to the MOGs. But a preponderance of MOGs setting out similar procedures for the recognition and enforcement of foreign judgments can evidence a general practice in relation to the treatment of judgments in commercial matters. MOGs taken can therefore function as evidence of an international commercial usage. Similarly, in connection with trade usages, widely used international standard form commercial contracts are important to the achievement of harmonisation. Examples of such standard form contracts are:

(1) in shipping transactions: The Baltic and International Maritime Council's (commonly known as BIMCO) charterparties and bills of lading;
(2) in financial transactions: the International Swaps and Derivatives Association (ISDA) Master Agreement;
(3) in construction matters: the International Federation of Consulting Engineers (FIDIC) Contracts;
(4) in commodity trades: the Grain and Feed Trade Association (GAFTA) Contracts.

The terms of standard form contracts and the obligations to which they give rise, as clarified by the pronouncements of judges in different jurisdictions, will have an impact on how business in relevant commercial fields will and should be carried out. Such contracts are accordingly capable of generating transnational commercial norms.

B. Institutions

It has already been suggested that in effect everyone – governments, legislators, judges, arbitrators, businesses, trade associations, chambers of commerce – has a role to play in the development of a harmonised system of international commercial dispute resolution. Of these stakeholders, undoubtedly much of the heavy lifting when it comes to bringing about convergence will fall upon courts and arbitral tribunals, which will have to discern and apply the procedures and substantive law relating to international commercial disputes on a nearly daily basis.

As between litigation before the courts and arbitration, for a long time the preferred mode of international commercial dispute resolution has been international commercial arbitration.[15] There may be various reasons for this. But a principal one must be the existence of the New York Convention. That instrument performs two important functions. First, by its Article II(3), the Convention requires the court of a Contracting State to stay or dismiss a case which is brought before that court in breach of an international commercial arbitration agreement. The court must instead refer the parties to arbitration in accordance with their agreement, unless the agreement is 'null and void, inoperative or incapable of being performed'. Second, by its Article V, the Convention requires a court in a Contracting State generally to recognise or enforce an international commercial award. The court may only refuse recognition or enforcement in the limited circumstances set out in sub-paragraphs (1) and (2) of Article V. Among those circumstances is the situation where a foreign award deals with a matter which is 'not capable of settlement by arbitration' under the law of the enforcing state or where recognition or enforcement would be contrary to the 'public policy' of the state.

Thus, for a commercial party, the attraction of being able to enforce an arbitral award against the assets of a contractual counterpart in the 167 other Contracting States (that is, excluding the Contracting State in which the arbitration leading to

[15] See 2018 International Arbitration Survey (n 5) 5.

the award was seated) will be near irresistible, especially where there is no equivalent convention for the enforcement of judgments handed down in commercial matters by a court designated in a choice of court agreement.[16] The nearest direct equivalent to the New York Convention in cross-border litigation would be the 2005 HCCH Convention on Choice of Court Agreements, and although the HCCH Convention is in effect, only 32 states are bound by it at present.

But there is a dark side to arbitration. The perennial complaint has been that over the years international commercial arbitration has become too expensive, too technical and too protracted in terms of the proceedings required.[17] Arbitration is effectively a one-shot proceeding. A losing party will normally not be able to appeal against an award. It may apply to the court of the seat of arbitration for the award to be set aside. However, the grounds for recourse against an award are typically limited. In Model Law jurisdictions, the grounds are similar (but not wholly identical) to the grounds for refusing recognition or enforcement of an award under the New York Convention. Of these limited grounds, reliance is nowadays usually placed on the alleged failure of an arbitral tribunal to give the losing party a reasonable or full opportunity to present its case – that is, a lack of due process in the way that an arbitration was conducted. This has led arbitrators to become acutely conscious – some have suggested overly conscious – about the way in which proceedings are conducted. Because of a fear of having their awards set aside or refused recognition and enforcement as a result of the failure to follow due process, many arbitrators bend over backwards to allow a party to amend pleadings, advance new evidence or arguments, prepare voluminous closing submissions, and apply for extensions of time almost without limit. This phenomenon, often disparagingly referred to as 'due process paranoia' on the part of arbitrators, has led to the costs of an arbitration building up, proceedings taking too long,[18] and arguments being overly technical and legalistic. So much so, that arbitration may now be even more legalistic and technical in nature than litigation before the courts. Nonetheless, as judgments are generally perceived to be less portable across borders in comparison to arbitration, businesses may feel that they have little option but to stipulate for arbitration, rather than litigation, in their international commercial contracts.

Dissatisfaction with what international commercial arbitration has become has led some stakeholders in international commercial arbitration to take a closer look at litigation. Is it really the case that a judgment in a commercial case is more difficult to enforce across borders than an arbitral award? Does the absence in litigation of an equivalent to the New York Convention with its 168 jurisdictions really make so much difference in the recognition and enforcement of an award?

[16] ibid: '"Enforceability of awards" continues to be perceived as arbitration's most valuable characteristic, followed by "avoiding specific legal systems/national courts", "flexibility" and "ability of parties to select arbitrators"'.

[17] ibid: '"Cost" continues to be seen as arbitration's worst feature, followed by "lack of effective sanctions during the arbitral process", "lack of power in relation to third parties" and "lack of speed"'.

[18] Interestingly, the 2018 International Arbitration Survey (n 5) 27 observes: 'A number of respondents and interviewees referred to what the 2015 survey called the "due process paranoia" of arbitrators as a probable reason for this continued lack of proactiveness [that is, the failure to hold parties to procedural orders and deadlines]. This phenomenon continues to be a source of concern to many. On a related note, both the 2015 survey and the current survey … found that the "lack of effective sanctions during the arbitral process" is seen

Recent studies suggest that is not actually the case.[19] The studies point out that commercial judgments for the payment of monetary amounts can be readily recognised and enforced in most modern common and civil law jurisdictions. Most common law jurisdictions (including the individual US states) have a proceeding whereby summary judgment can be obtained on a judgment debt. 'Summary judgment' means that there is no trial on the merits. Having obtained a judgment from the court of an originating state which holds the respondent liable to the claimant for a sum under a commercial contract, the claimant can then start an action in the court of a common law enforcing state based on the debt established by the judgment. Provided several conditions[20] are satisfied, the common law enforcing court will not reopen the merits of the claim underlying the originating state's judgment. In such a situation there will usually be no arguable defence to the judgment debt meriting a trial. Accordingly, the judgment debt having been established, the common law will simply deliver judgment summarily in the claimant's favour. The claimant can then enforce the summary judgment in the enforcing state in the same way as any other domestic judgment of that state.

In the same vein, the codes of civil procedure of many civil law jurisdictions have been modernised to allow for the recognition and enforcement of foreign judgments even where the originating and enforcing states are not party to a treaty or convention for the mutual recognition and enforcement of commercial judgments. Again, provided that certain conditions are met, many civil law jurisdictions will recognise and enforce a debt due pursuant to the judgment of another state.[21] The foregoing analysis is hardly surprising. An arbitral award is at best merely a piece of paper to which the parties

as the second worst characteristic of arbitration. Interviews for both studies nuanced this finding by revealing that many users are of the opinion that the bigger problem is that arbitrators do not make sufficient use of the sanctioning powers they already possess [to control the parties]'. Nonetheless, the 2018 International Arbitration Survey (n 5) 27 found that the position was not so clear-cut: 'This year, however, the legitimacy of this "due process paranoia" phenomenon was vigorously contested by a number of counsel and arbitrators. It was argued that explaining arbitrators' conduct by referring to this "paranoia" is misleading because arbitrators should be confident enough that the courts at the seat would support arbitration. Some went on to explain that the popularity of "arbitration-friendly" jurisdictions stems partly from the fact that local courts have no trouble deferring to arbitrators as far as the approach to conducting the arbitral proceedings is concerned. If this is indeed the case, then perhaps the phenomenon might arise more where arbitrators are conscious that their awards may need to be enforced in jurisdictions where the support of the local judiciary for arbitration may not be so assured'.

[19] See, for example, A Chong (ed), *Recognition and Enforcement of Foreign Judgments in Asia* (Asian Business Law Institute, 2017); A Chong (ed), *Asian Principles for the Recognition and Enforcement of Foreign Judgments* (Asian Business Law Institute, 2020); A Reyes (ed), *Recognition and Enforcement of Judgments in Civil and Commercial Matters* (Hart, 2019).

[20] Where commercial judgments are concerned, the conditions are normally that: (1) the originating court had jurisdiction over the claimant's action under a recognised ground of indirect jurisdiction (sometimes also called 'international jurisdiction'); (2) the originating court's judgment is final and conclusive; (3) the originating court's judgment was obtained through due process; (4) recognition of the originating court's judgment would not be contrary to the public policy of the enforcing state; and (5) the originating court's judgment is not contrary to a prior judgment of the court of the enforcing state. The designation of the originating court in a choice of court agreement as the forum for the resolution of the parties' disputes will ordinarily satisfy the requirement of indirect jurisdiction.

[21] The conditions are similar to those enumerated in n 20 for common law jurisdictions, save that a number of civil law countries add the requirement of reciprocity. By 'reciprocity' is meant that it must be established that the originating state will recognise like judgments of the enforcing state. The trend today, however, is for reciprocity to be presumed. That is, in the absence of proof to the contrary, it will be presumed that an originating state will recognise and enforce like judgments of the enforcing state. See B Elbalti, 'Reciprocity and

by their arbitration agreement have contracted to give binding force as between themselves. In contrast, a judgment is an official act of a sovereign state. Considerations of international comity among nations mean that, in the absence of good reason (such as public policy concerns), states should respect and honour each other's judgments.

Given the situation just described, it does not follow from the absence of a New York Convention equivalent in litigation that judgments determining international commercial disputes are less likely to be enforced across borders than arbitral awards. The reality is that the opposite may be the case, precisely because judgments are official acts of sovereign states. The implication of this is that recourse to litigation should not be excluded from consideration as at least part of the answer to the costs, protracted nature and over-technicality of international commercial arbitration. Instead of arbitration agreements, commercial parties have been considering incorporating choice of court agreements into their international commercial contracts. Considerations such as these have led over the last decade to a rise in the number of international commercial courts. The SICC is one such example. The nature of these international commercial courts and the effect that they might have on the development of international commercial dispute resolution is the subject of part two of this book. For present purposes, it will be sufficient to note that, moving forward, international commercial courts will undoubtedly play a significant role in achieving convergence and harmonisation in the conduct of international commercial dispute resolution.

There is one other institution that is likely to play a significant part in international commercial dispute resolution in the future: international commercial mediation. Mediation is a form of alternative dispute resolution (ADR) whereby a neutral third party (the mediator) assists the parties to a dispute to reach a settlement.[22] The mediator meets with the parties jointly or in caucus (that is, without the other party being present). In the latter instance, unless a party authorises otherwise, everything that a party communicates to a mediator during mediation will not be disclosed to the other party to the dispute. The settlement will not necessarily be confined to a party agreeing to accept all, some or none of the legal remedies that it is claiming in a contractual dispute.

The power of mediation lies in the mediator's ability to facilitate settlement on a range of terms going beyond what a court or an arbitral tribunal can order in proceedings before them. Thus, the mediator can broker a settlement where a party accepts an apology or the prospect of further commercial contracts from the other side in return for giving up all or some of a claim. A rule of thumb is that mediation is typically successful in 70 per cent of cases. Mediations can be undertaken at any time, including at the start of a dispute. Settlement is often reached after a couple of days, in contrast to the months, possibly years, taken by arbitration proceedings. Mediation is consequently

the Recognition and Enforcement of Foreign Judgments: A Lot of Bark But Not Much Bite' (2017) 13 *Journal of Private International Law* 184.

[22] Article 1(3) of the 2018 UNCITRAL Model Law (n 1) defines 'mediation' as 'a process, whether referred to by the expression mediation, conciliation or an expression of similar import, whereby parties request a third person or persons ('the mediator') to assist them in their attempt to reach an amicable settlement of their dispute arising out of or relating to a contractual or other legal relationship'. Article 1(3) stresses: 'The mediator does not have the authority to impose upon the parties a solution to the dispute'.

a way of substantially lowering the costs and time taken up by an international commercial dispute. The mediator can fashion the mediation proceedings so that they are more or less formal depending on the circumstances of the parties and the dispute.

With the coming into force of the Singapore Convention on Mediation on 12 September 2020, international commercial mediation has come into its own as a means of resolving international commercial disputes. The Singapore Convention enables international mediated settlement agreements to be enforced in Contracting States. The latter may only refuse enforcement on limited grounds, including where enforcement would be contrary to the public policy of the enforcing state or where under the law of the enforcing state the party's dispute is not one capable of resolution through mediation. As more states adopt the Singapore Convention,[23] it will become a game-changer as parties will have the confidence and comfort that, much as with judgments and awards, their settlement agreements will be enforceable abroad.

A major difference between the three institutions is that commercial litigation is premised on open and public justice. That means outsiders can attend proceedings and read a court's judgment resolving a dispute. In contrast, arbitration and mediation are wholly private. Members of the public may not sit in on arbitrations or mediations. Everything that takes place in those proceedings is confidential, including the text of an arbitral award or any mediated settlement agreement. There have been efforts by arbitral institutions to publish redacted versions of their arbitral awards. This practice has had some success in relation to the publication of final (as opposed to interlocutory) awards in investment treaty arbitrations. But the practice has yet to become common and matter of course in respect of awards in international commercial arbitrations. A consequence of this is that as institutions for achieving convergence, arbitration and mediation are limited to the introduction and development of procedural innovations. They can accomplish this through the rules and soft law guidelines on aspects of procedure regularly issued by bodies associated with the conduct of arbitrations and mediations. Courts can do the same through the publication of their procedural rules and practice directions. But courts can do more: through their judgments, they can shape the substantive development of commercial law (specifically, the *lex mercatoria*).

[23] As of January 2022, there are 55 signatories to the Singapore Convention and nine ratifications. In 2018 UNCITRAL also put out a Model Law on International Commercial Mediation and International Settlement Agreements Resulting from Mediation 2018 (amending the UNCITRAL Model Law on International Commercial Conciliation 2002).

2

International Commercial Dispute Resolution as a System

JAMES ALLSOP AND SAMUEL WALPOLE

I. The Nature of an International Commercial Dispute

A. Introduction

The title of part one of this book is 'What is an international commercial dispute?'. This may appear to be a simple enough question to answer. However, it belies a number of complex, multifaceted issues that attend international dispute resolution: Why do we accord international commercial disputes special status? How do we accommodate the differing interests that are involved in international commercial disputes? How does party autonomy and the private nature of commercial dispute resolution interact with national sovereignty and the other public interests involved? Furthermore, to what extent should we seek convergence and uniformity in international dispute resolution? How should we do so? Above all, these are questions about what the aims of an international commercial dispute resolution system should be.

In suggesting possible answers to these questions, it is important to first recognise what has been achieved in international commercial dispute resolution in recent decades. The inheritance of the latter part of the twentieth century and early part of the twenty-first can be seen in what has developed: a decentralised (but interlinked), complex and dynamic system of international commercial dispute resolution. It assists in the upholding of the international rule of law, and contributes to the stability of the global order by securing the fair and just resolution of cross-border commercial disputes. The recognition that there is a dynamic and diffuse system of international dispute resolution has implications for the questions canvassed above. We must be cognisant of the fact that we are dealing with a system – this should also shape our attitudes to harmonisation, uniformity and convergence. Different tools may be more useful for different components of the system.

The aim must be to continue to develop the system – together with promoting the continued use of international commercial dispute resolution as a means of vindicating the international rule of law in relation to commercial matters. The continued prosperity and security of the international economic order demands no less. Within the Asia-Pacific region alone, there have been further developments in international trade in recent years, such as the Comprehensive and Progressive Agreement for Trans-Pacific Partnership, which was concluded in 2018.[1] However, these developments have taken place at a time of greater geopolitical tension, division and insular thinking. If it is to continue to operate as a part of the international order, the international commercial dispute resolution system will need to continue to develop as commerce in the Asia-Pacific region itself grows.

This chapter will reflect on some ways in which we might shape our approach to a selection of the continuing issues in international commercial dispute resolution to achieve this aim. In doing so, it will canvass the following matters:

- the identification and description of an international commercial dispute;
- the distinctiveness of international commercial disputes;
- the components of the international commercial dispute resolution system;
- the interests involved in international commercial disputes, which are themselves intimately linked to questions of what really is an 'international commercial dispute'; and
- the achievement of continued convergence in international dispute resolution.

It is not possible to address all aspects of the international commercial dispute resolution system or of the associated issues and debates in a single volume, let alone a chapter. This chapter will instead focus on some of the key issues, assessed from a systemic perspective.

In thinking about international commercial dispute resolution as a decentralised – but globalised – system, it is beneficial to step back and consider what its broader function may be, beyond the settling of commercial disputes and the facilitation of international trade. On a higher level, the system is a part of the rules-based international order that developed following the end of World War II. It represents part of that commitment to law, not *war*;[2] to the promotion of the peaceful resolution of commercial disputes, not militaristic ones; to the furtherance of justice, fairness, and good faith in international relations, rather than arbitrariness, caprice and injustice; and, to the advancement of rules-based, mutually respectful interactions between nations rather than the enhancement of the power of the strong man.

The international commercial dispute resolution system is as crucial a part of this order as the WTO, IMO, World Bank and other institutions. Investment arbitration developed to lessen the temptation to resort to 'gun boat diplomacy'.[3] In addition, we have developed a sophisticated, diverse and rules-based system for the resolution of a broad range of international commercial disputes between private parties. That this could be achieved in an effective way should not be forgotten. Indeed, it should strengthen our willingness to ensure that the system endures.

The role of international commercial dispute resolution as a component of the rules-based international order is particularly apposite at present. This chapter was

[1] See Australian Department of Foreign Affairs and Trade, 'Comprehensive and Progressive Agreement for Trans-Pacific Partnership (CPTPP)', available at dfat.gov.au/trade/agreements/in-force/cptpp/Pages/comprehensive-and-progressive-agreement-for-trans-pacific-partnership.aspx.

[2] A phrase used by Benjamin Ferencz, one of the prosecutors at the Nuremberg Trials.

[3] SM Schwebel, 'Keynote Address: In Defence of Bilateral Investment Treaties' in International Arbitration – Legitimacy: Myths, Realities and Challenges' (2012) 18 *ICCA Congress Series* 5.

originally to be presented at the Judicial Roundtable on Commercial Law to be held in Shanghai in May 2020. A draft of this chapter was prepared. Then, suddenly, COVID-19 intervened. The pandemic has gripped the globe for the past two years. Its effects have been profound, and unprecedented in our lifetimes. Hundreds of millions have been infected and millions have died from a pathogen to which humanity had no prior immunity. The broader consequences have also been catastrophic. Economies have been battered. Millions have lost their employment as governments have been forced to take drastic actions to protect lives and livelihoods. The prospect of seamless international travel disappeared. The pandemic has also disrupted – and transformed – the work of courts and tribunals around the world.

Despite the promise of vaccination, it remains impossible to predict what the world, both politically and economically, will look like as COVID-19 transitions from a pandemic to something endemic within our daily lives. With the aftermath of COVID-19 will come the potential for more of the insular thinking that has grown in prevalence in recent years. We cannot allow such thinking to lead us away from a rules-based international order, of which the international commercial dispute resolution system is a signal example. Rather, we should consider what lessons can be learnt from the pandemic, and how these can be used to strengthen, and further develop, our international system.

B. Describing an International Commercial Dispute

It is appropriate to give some consideration to what an 'international commercial dispute' is and why such a dispute should be treated as distinct from commercial disputes generally. The key feature to note is the need for a wide definition to facilitate international commerce and not restrict the availability of international commercial dispute resolution mechanisms through artificially rigid or constrained definitions or categories.

Although by no means dispositive of the two questions just posed, the definition of 'international commercial arbitration' in Article 1 of the UNCITRAL Model Law on International Commercial Arbitration[4] ('the Model Law') provides some guidance as to the meaning of an 'international commercial dispute'. An arbitration is 'international' within the meaning of the Model Law if:

(a) the parties to an arbitration agreement have, at the time of the conclusion of that agreement, their places of business in different States; or
(b) one of the following places is situated outside the State in which the parties have their places of business:
    (i) the place of arbitration if determined in, or pursuant to, the arbitration agreement;
    (ii) any place where a substantial part of the obligations of the commercial relationship is to be performed or the place with which the subject-matter of the dispute is most closely connected; or

[4] UNCITRAL Model Law on International Commercial Arbitration (as adopted by the United Nations Commission on International Trade Law on 21 June 1985, and as amended by the United Nations Commission on International Trade Law on 7 July 2006) Art 1.

(c) the parties have expressly agreed that the subject-matter of the arbitration agreement relates to more than one country.[5]

There must be some element of the dispute, or its resolution, that involves more than one country – it must be properly international. Traditionally, in order to be considered 'international', an arbitration had to involve parties of different nationalities or the dispute had to be of an 'international character'.[6] As the authors of *Redfern and Hunter* identify, the definition of 'international' in the Model Law builds on this and incorporates the internationality of the parties and the internationality of the dispute, and also gives the parties the liberty to state that the subject matter is international.[7] This approach is sensible – it involves asking, with due regard to the autonomy of the parties, whether the dispute could conceivably be seen as relating to more than one state.

What of the breadth of the word 'commercial'? A note to Article 1(1) of the Model Law offers the following guidance on the term 'commercial':

> The term 'commercial' should be given a wide interpretation so as to cover matters arising from all relationships of a commercial nature, whether contractual or not. Relationships of a commercial nature include, but are not limited to, the following transactions: any trade transaction for the supply or exchange of goods or services; distribution agreement; commercial representation or agency; factoring; leasing; construction of works; consulting; engineering; licensing; investment; financing; banking; insurance; exploitation agreement or concession; joint venture and other forms of industrial or business cooperation; carriage of goods or passengers by air, sea, rail or road.[8]

The Model Law merely offers interpretive guidance on the word 'commercial'. It does not define it. Definitions exist in other instruments that are similar. In many respects, and rightly so, these are descriptions rather than rigid definitions.

The English Commercial Court is 'the original specialised court for international commercial matters',[9] though it hears both 'national and international business disputes'.[10] Its subject matter jurisdiction concerns 'commercial claims', which are widely and practically defined as:

> [A]ny claim arising out of the transaction of trade and commerce and includes any claim relating to (a) a business document or contract; (b) the export or import of goods; (c) the carriage of goods by land, sea, air or pipeline; (d) the exploitation of oil and gas reserves or other natural resources; (e) insurance and re-insurance; (f) banking and financial services; (g) the operation of markets and exchanges; (h) the purchase and sale of commodities; (i) the construction of ships; (j) business agency; and (k) arbitration.[11]

The breadth of international commerce dictates description, rather than rigid definition. The language used by the English Civil Procedure Rules in relation to the jurisdiction

[5] ibid Art 1(3).

[6] As is required under the ICC Rules of Arbitration: see N Blackaby et al, *Redfern and Hunter on International Arbitration*, 6th edn (OUP, 2018) [1.27]–[1.29].

[7] ibid [1.29].

[8] UNCITRAL Model Law on International Commercial Arbitration Art 1(1).

[9] J Walker, 'Specialised International Courts: Keeping Arbitration on Top of Its Game' (2019) 85 *Arbitration* 1, 3.

[10] UK Government, 'Commercial Court', available at www.gov.uk/courts-tribunals/commercial-court.

[11] Civil Procedure Rules 1998 (UK) r 58.1(2).

of the Commercial Court – 'any claim arising out of the transaction of trade and commerce' – is helpful as it directs attention to the commercial relationship in which most international commercial disputes will arise.

The Singapore International Commercial Court (SICC) takes a similar approach. For the purpose of its jurisdiction, a claim is commercial if it 'arises from a relationship of a commercial nature, whether contractual or not, including (but not limited to)' the transactions listed in the Model Law.[12] The Rules also expressly include an 'in personam intellectual property dispute' as within jurisdiction, along with a claim where 'the parties to the claim have expressly agreed that the subject matter of the claim is commercial in nature'.[13]

Such definitions cannot be dispositive of the question of what is an 'international commercial dispute' because, given the nature of international commerce, it is not possible rigidly to define the adjective 'commercial' in this context. To do so would be to seek to set the limits of international commerce. Indeed, it has been said that 'the draftsmen of the Model Law considered defining the word "commercial" but gave up the attempt',[14] instead settling on the interpretive guidance set out above.

The limits of any attempt to define the term 'commercial' arise not only from the broad range of legal issues and subject matters that may be involved in an international dispute, but also from the fact that a dispute that appears to be non-commercial in some respects may properly be considered to a commercial one. Or it may shade into a dispute that is commercial, depending on the particular factual matrix. There is no binary choice between two competing categories. There are questions of degree involved. Ultimately, the decision is one of characterisation.

An illustration of this is *Hancock Prospecting Pty Ltd v Rinehart*,[15] which involved an agreement for domestic arbitration, albeit under an arbitration regime based upon the Model Law. The underlying dispute was complex. In its simplest form, it related to a dispute between family members over the control of significant commercial assets that had resulted in a proceeding filed in the Federal Court of Australia. It included challenges to the validity of various deeds entered into by the parties in relation to the substantive matters in dispute. One group of interests brought an interlocutory application under section 8(1) of the Commercial Arbitration Act 2010 (NSW) seeking an order that the parties be referred to arbitration in respect of the matters in dispute that were the subject of the various arbitration agreements contained in the deeds, by staying the proceedings in the Federal Court.

One of the issues on the application, both before the primary judge and on appeal to the Full Court of the Federal Court, was whether the dispute was a 'commercial' one that was capable of resolution by 'commercial arbitration'. The Full Court rejected an argument that to be the subject of a 'commercial arbitration' within the terms of the Model Law there needed to be a pre-existing 'commercial relationship' between the parties to the arbitration.[16] Furthermore, it was not a matter of determining whether

[12] Rules of Court (Singapore) O 110, r 1(2).
[13] ibid.
[14] Blackaby et al, *Redfern and Hunter* (2018) [1.38].
[15] *Hancock Prospecting Pty Ltd v Rinehart* [2017] FCAFC 170, 257 FCR 442.
[16] ibid [119]–[124].

the dispute was 'commercial' or whether it was a 'family' or 'trust' dispute. The Court emphasised 'the point that the enquiry is not binary. That the dispute may be seen as a family dispute does not mean that it and the arbitration to resolve it are not to be characterised as commercial'.[17] It explained that 'the disputes the subject of the proceedings [were] "quintessentially" commercial. The word commercial is intended to be given a wide interpretation, as the note from the Model Law makes clear'.[18] Applied to the facts of the case, the Court said the following about the process of characterisation that was involved:[19]

> It is, of course, also true to say that in one sense the dispute is capable of being described as one between a mother and her children, about the destruction of a family relationship under the crushing weight of wealth, about the alleged maladministration of family trusts, and about the asserted loss of a large part of an inheritance that the childrens' grandfather … had intended them to have. *But, in our opinion, the choice between a dispute being 'commercial' on the one hand, or 'family' on the other, is not, as the applicants' submissions imply, a binary one. Such questions of characterisation rarely involve the existence of mutually exclusive categories. Questions of characterisation are not questions of definition ….*
>
> … *The applicants' characterisation of the dispute is not necessarily inconsistent with its characterisation as a 'commercial dispute'. In our view, to characterise this dispute only as a family dispute or a family trust dispute, which is the view propounded by the applicants, is to ignore the overwhelming commercial nature and circumstances of the dispute*

There are other types of dispute which should be considered as international commercial disputes. For example, cross-border insolvency, which is now the subject of the UNCITRAL Model Law on Cross-Border Insolvency that has been adopted by several jurisdictions within the Asia-Pacific. At the same time, such matters are distinct: they do not solely concern private rights and interests; they also involve the supervisory jurisdiction of a national court over an insolvent entity and they involve questions about the response and cooperation of states to an insolvency with impact in multiple nations. This does not mean, however, that such disputes should be considered outside the family of 'international commercial disputes'.

Conversely, there are other matters that should be treated as distinct. For example, investor-state dispute settlement under investment treaties. In one sense, these disputes are international commercial disputes – investment arbitration was developed to protect private commercial investments in foreign countries. However, the fact that such an arbitral claim by an investor is against a sovereign state in its capacity as a state raises issues of democratic legitimacy and sovereignty that are absent in typical international commercial disputes. Both raise issues about the public interest – but the interests are not the same. Investment arbitration and international commercial arbitration should not be treated as one and the same.[20] Importantly, however, if we think about international commercial disputes as being dealt with by an international dispute resolution system that exists for the purpose of enhancing the international rule of law in relation

[17] ibid [126].
[18] ibid [132].
[19] ibid [134]–[135] (emphasis added).
[20] See J Allsop, 'Commercial and Investor-State Arbitration: The Importance of Recognising Their Differences' (ICCA Congress 2018, Sydney, 16 April 2018).

to commercial law then we can accommodate a broad variety of claims – and the differences among them – within the adjudicative mechanisms of that system.

II. The Distinctiveness of International Commercial Dispute Resolution

Although its current scale, pace and pervasiveness are unique to the modern era, the interconnected nature of global trade is not a modern phenomenon, nor one confined to a particular part of the world. In his books *The Silk Road* and *The New Silk Roads*,[21] the historian Peter Frankopan explains the connections and exchanges that have occurred between Asia, the Middle East and Europe since antiquity. In Frankopan's words, concepts used to describe those relationships, such as that of 'the Silk Roads', permit us 'to see the rhythms of history in which the world has been connected for millennia as being part of a bigger, inclusive global past'.[22]

Another Oxford historian, the great Richard Southern, wrote of 'the growth in Mediterranean trade' in the High Middle Ages, and the well-established trading routes in that period including between Eastern Germany and Muslim Spain, 'Italian ports and the mouth of the Nile', and between Constantinople and the West.[23] This route must have, in turn, connected with those routes into Central and East Asia. Southern identifies one of the contributing factors to the impressive growth in international trade over this period as the 'conditions of relative peace [which] brought stability and confidence'.[24] Such a statement could also be made about recent decades.

The recognition of the need for a specialised body of law, and specialised system of dispute resolution, for commercial matters with an international character is also not unique to our period of history. Nor is the idea that such a body of law should be harmonised amongst trading nations. Such bodies of law as they have developed throughout history arose to meet the requirements of trade.

The medieval law merchant that developed out of the activities of European merchants trading during the Middle Ages is an important example. Sir William Blackstone acknowledged the law merchant as a particular body of law applicable in England, and referred to it as:

> a particular system of customs used only among one set of the King's subjects, called the custom of merchants or lex mercatoria; which, however, different from the common law, is allowed for the benefit of trade, to be of the utmost validity in all commercial transactions.[25]

[21] P Frankopan, *The Silk Roads: A New History of the World* (Bloomsbury, 2015); P Frankopan, *The New Silk Roads: The Present and Future of the World* (Bloomsbury, 2018).

[22] Frankopan, *The New Silk Roads* (ibid) 3.

[23] RW Southern, *The Making of the Middle Ages* (Yale University Press, 1953) 41–43.

[24] ibid 44–45.

[25] W Blackstone, *Commentaries on the Laws of England*, Book I (Clarendon Press, 1769) 75. The needs of merchants during the medieval period also influenced legislative changes to the common law of England: see S Walpole, 'The Medieval Law of Debt and the Interests Served by the Statutes Merchant' (2020) 49 *Australian Bar Review* 167.

In his treatise of 1686 entitled *The Ancient Law-Merchant*, Gerard Malynes described the law merchant as follows:

> Every man knoweth, that for Manners and Prescriptions, there is great diversity amongst all Nations; but for the customs observed in the course of traffic and commerce, there is that sympathy, concordance, and agreement, which may be said to be of like condition to all People, diffused and spread by right reason, and instinct of nature consisting perpetually. And these customs are properly those observations which Merchants maintain between themselves, and if these be separated from the Law of Nations, the remainder of the said Law will consist of but few points.[26]

Disputes arising under the law merchant were determined using a unique system of courts. These included merchants' courts and maritime courts that came to be established in ports. One early example of these merchants' courts was England's Piepowder Court, which dealt with mercantile disputes in relation to a fair or market. These courts were described as 'the lowest and at the same time the most expeditious court of justice known to the law of England'.[27] These were the courts 'in which the disputes of wayfaring merchants, the dusty-footed men, were settled'.[28] The relationship between the Piepowder Courts and the development of the law merchant is described by Charles Gross in his 1906 study of these institutions:

> It is evident that the procedure of the court of piepowder resembles the procedure of the international law merchant as it was administered in all European tribunals. The 'lex mercatoria' was a customary law that grew up gradually through the intercourse of merchants; and special rules relating to litigation in mercantile transactions existed already in the eleventh century. Outside of Italy little is known, however, concerning the law merchant before the thirteenth or fourteenth century, when it is administered in the cities of Italy and Spain and in the great fairs of Champagne. In England such a separate body of law was in operation in the piepowder courts long before the creation of special commercial tribunals, like those of the staple, which were adapted mainly to the needs of alien merchants. Already in the twelfth century there seems to have been a 'lex de pede pulveroso' in Scotland and England,' and in the thirteenth century there is a body of rules in English boroughs, markets, and fairs known as the 'lex mercatoria,' which must have originated largely in the piepowder courts. We may, indeed, safely assume from the evidence afforded by royal grants of fairs and markets with toll and jurisdictional rights that such courts were active throughout Western Europe during the eleventh and twelfth centuries, and through the decisions of the merchant doomsmen were establishing legal precedents which must have exerted a powerful moulding influence upon the law merchant.[29]

The intimate connection between the law merchant and the customs of merchants, together with its symbiotic relationship with the common law, has been succinctly summarised by Chief Justice Kiefel as follows:

> [T]he law merchant existed for some time in parallel with the legal systems of the continent and of England. It developed by reference to customs and best practices in medieval times

[26] G Malynes, *The Ancient Law-Merchant*, 3rd edn (1686) 2.
[27] C Gross, 'The Court of Piepowder' (1906) 20 *Quarterly Journal of Economics* 231, 231.
[28] ibid.
[29] ibid 245–46.

> and was used by merchants throughout England and Europe, at least until these countries developed their own commercial laws. There can be little doubt about its influence on the English common law as much as on civilian law.[30]

The role of commercial parties themselves in the settlement of international commercial disputes can be seen also in the origins of arbitration, which is now a mainstay of international dispute resolution. From the time of its origin in antiquity, arbitration has had an intimate relationship with commercial expectations:

> In its early days, arbitration would have been a simple and relatively informal process. Two merchants, in dispute over the price or quality of goods delivered, would turn to a third whom they knew and trusted, and they would agree to abide by his decision – and they would do this not because of any legal sanction, but because this was what was expected of them in the community within which they carried on their business.[31]

Perhaps the greatest historic – but also contemporary – example of a system of international commercial law can be seen in the development of the general maritime law. While the story of the law merchant is primarily European in focus, the development of maritime law owes much to the great cultures of Asia and the Middle East, with their affinity for free navigation and free trade.[32] The trading world was interconnected, even in antiquity.

In the West, the mariners of the island of Rhodes developed a body of maritime law referred to as the 'Rhodian Code' that was in operation around the eighth or ninth century BC.[33] Though its exact character is unclear, it appears that this was a form of customary maritime law, based upon the practice and customs of merchants, seafarers and other traders.[34] It may have had its origins in oral tradition,[35] with aspects of it later formed into the 'Rhodian Code' and then incorporated into the Digest of Justinian.[36] Later, in the Byzantine period, a sophisticated written codification of maritime law was promulgated, called the 'Rhodian Sea Law'.[37]

Further codifications of the maritime law of the West occurred in the Middle Ages. Prominent among these was the *Roles of Oleron*, which came to influence other maritime codes in Europe such as the *Judgments of Damme*, the *Laws of West Capelle* and the *Laws of Wisby*.[38] Another was the *Consolato del Mare*, which derived from local custom in ports around Barcelona.[39] Italian city states also developed codes based on local customs, and the customs of the merchants of Lübeck were also codified and used

[30] S Kiefel AC, 'Legal Influences – across centuries and borders' (Hellenic Australian Lawyers Association Alexander Christy Freeleagus Oration, Brisbane, 26 August 2016).

[31] Blackaby et al (n 6) [1.13].

[32] W Tetley, *International Maritime and Admiralty Law* (Editions Yvon Blais, 2002) 5.

[33] ibid 9; W Tetley, 'The General Maritime Law – The Lex Maritima' (1994) 20 *Syracuse Journal of International Law and Commerce* 105, 109.

[34] Tetley, *International Maritime and Admiralty Law* (2002) 9; Tetley, 'The General Maritime Law' (1994) 109. See also RD Benedict, 'The Historical Position of the Rhodian Law' (1909) 18 *Yale Law Journal* 223.

[35] Tetley (n 33) 109; Tetley (n 32) 9; Benedict (n 34).

[36] ibid.

[37] ibid 10–11. For the text, see W Ashburner, 'The Rhodian Sea-Law' (Clarendon, 1909).

[38] ibid 12.

[39] ibid 13.

to govern maritime trading relationships in the Baltic Sea.[40] The progressive development and codification of maritime law in Europe continued into the Renaissance, in the form, for example, of the Guidon de la Mer and the Ordonnance de la Marine in France, and the Codice Ferdinando in Sicily.[41]

These great maritime codes were by no means restricted to the waters of the West.[42] Far from it. In the waters of Asia and the Middle East, maritime trading networks founded upon principles of 'free navigation' had been in existence since antiquity.[43] As Professor Tetley has described, these trade routes linked up with those in the West, but also went further afield:

> The Phoenicians, Rhodians, Greeks and Romans, in the ancient world, engaged in extensive seaborne trade with Arabia and India. India and Ceylon, in turn, sent merchant ships to the East Indies and China. China itself developed a sophisticated system of ports, and even port customs services, as early as the eighth century AD, while foreign merchants were permitted to establish themselves in Canton and other Chinese ports as early as the seventh century.[44]

By the time of the Han Dynasty,[45] and certainly by that of the Tang Dynasty,[46] maritime trading routes connecting the regions of South-East Asia, Indo-China, North Sumatra, Myanmar and South India were well established, whilst land trade had expanded with the development of the Silk Roads which eventually connected China, the Indian subcontinent, Persia, Europe, the Horn of Africa and Arabia.[47] Land-based trade during the reign of the Tang Dynasty occurred along the Silk Roads,[48] with trade occurring in a wide array of goods: horses, silk, tea, furs, carpets and precious stones, to name but a few.[49]

Later, through the medieval period, maritime trade in the Asian and Middle Eastern regions continued to develop, with the voyages of Arab mariners extending 'from the Red Sea ports to Canton and the marts of China'.[50] Major trading ports, attended by mariners and merchants from all over Asia and the Middle East, arose in places such as Calicut in India, Zayton (Quanzhou) in China, and Malacca and Macassar in South-East Asia.[51]

A distinctive *lex maritima* developed in Asia during this period. In Malacca, a 'written maritime code', based upon custom, was drafted in the late fifteenth century.[52]

[40] ibid.

[41] ibid 14.

[42] The discussion that follows in this section draws upon that in J Allsop, 'Comity and Commerce' (Address to the 16th Conference of Chief Justices of Asia and the Pacific, 8 November 2015) [16]–[17].

[43] RP Anand, 'Maritime Practice in South-East Asia until 1600AD and the Modern Law of the Sea' (1981) 30 *International and Comparative Law Quarterly* 440, 443–45.

[44] Tetley (n 32) 5.

[45] See A Schottenhammer, 'The "China Seas" in world history: A general outline of the role of Chinese and East Asian maritime space from its origins to c. 1800' (2012) 1 *Journal of Marine and Island Cultures* 63.

[46] P Beaujard, *The Worlds of the Indian Ocean: A Global History* vol 1 (CUP, 2019) 26–30.

[47] See Schottenhammer, 'The "China Seas" in world history' (2012).

[48] Beaujard, *The Worlds of the Indian Ocean* (2019) 25.

[49] ibid.

[50] Anand, 'Maritime Practice in South-East Asia' (1981) 445.

[51] JL Abu-Lughod, *Before European Hegemony: The World System AD 1250–1350* (OUP, 1989); JL Abu-Lughod, *The World System in the Thirteenth Century: Dead-End or Precursor?* (American Historical Association, 1993); Anand (n 44) 445.

[52] Anand (n 44) 445.

It addressed many matters familiar to maritime lawyers today: the authority of the master; the role of pilots; wreck; ships in distress; and the jurisdiction of harbour masters.[53] Another regional code, that of Macassar, also set out legal principles relating to charterparties.[54]

Professor Anand explains that 'Codified or not, similar rules were applied by other maritime States in south, south-east and east Asia.'[55] In 1822, Sir Alexander Johnson, the third Chief Justice of Ceylon, described the 'maritime laws and usages as prevail respectively amongst all the different maritime people of Asia, consisting of Arabs, Maldivians, Malays, [Hindu] and Chinese, who from time immemorial have had separate maritime laws and usages of their own.'[56] He noted that this body of law was comprised

> partly of [Hindu], partly of Malay, partly of Maldivian, partly of Persian, partly of Arabian, partly of [Sinhalese], and partly of Chinese origin; that a few of them are derived from the laws of Rhodes, Oleron, Itisbury, and the *Consolato del Mare*; some of which were introduced by the Arabs, from the Mediterranean, into the Indian seas, during the fifteenth and sixteenth centuries.[57]

As in the West, one can see the origins of maritime law in the customs and practices of mariners and merchants.

The international and mercantile heritage of maritime law was recognised by the great British (more accurately, Scottish) jurist Lord Mansfield, who in 1759 in *Luke v Lyde*, made reference to the laws of ancient Rhodes, the *Consolato del Mere*, the laws of Oleron, the *Roccius de Navibus et Naulo* and the Ordinance of Lewis in order to discern the appropriate legal principles applying to a dispute as to freight.[58] His Lordship opined that 'the maritime law is not the law of a particular country, but the general law of nations.'[59]

This acknowledgement that international maritime law has an international character founded in mercantile custom was also adopted, in 1953, in the opinion of Robert Jackson J of the United States Supreme Court[60] in *Lauitzen v Larsen*.[61] His Honour said the following about the existence of a general maritime law, derived from the custom of mariners and merchants:

> [C]ourts of this and other commercial nations have generally deferred to a non-national or international maritime law of impressive maturity and universality. It has the force of law, not from extraterritorial reach of national laws, nor from abdication of its sovereign powers by any nation, but from acceptance by common consent of civilized communities of rules designed to foster amicable and workable commercial relations.[62]

[53] ibid 446.
[54] ibid.
[55] ibid.
[56] A Johnston, 'Administration of Justice in India – Sir Alexander Johnston's Plan of Reform' (1830) 3 *Law Magazine and Review: A Quarterly Journal of Jurisprudence* 581, 590.
[57] ibid 592.
[58] *Luke v Lyde* (1759) 2 Burr 382; 97 ER 614, 619–20.
[59] ibid 617.
[60] Having been one of the prosecutors at the Nuremberg Trials, Jackson J was a jurist uniquely acquainted with the norms of the law of nations.
[61] *Lauritzen v Larsen* 345 US 571 (1953).
[62] ibid 581–82.

Thus, the foundation of international commercial law upon the principles of international traders – and the continuing recognition of the need for an appropriately tailored, harmonised but decentralised, body of law for international commercial disputes – can be seen throughout history and into the modern era.

Why tell this historical story? First, to dispel any notion that the current approach to international commercial disputes is some untested new product of twentieth-century globalisation. Rather, the contemporary architecture for international commercial dispute resolution that has developed is a continuation of this approach, taken throughout history, to the law governing international trade. Secondly, to shed light on why international commercial disputes may require unique treatment. If not, why else would societies, in different parts of the world and over millennia, have considered a distinctive approach to cross-border mercantile law necessary? These historical approaches to the distinctive treatment of international commercial dispute resolution show that a key feature of these developments was the unifying role they played, both in the substance of the law and in the means of dispute resolution.

What they also show is that the content of that unification paid careful regard to the customs and needs of international commerce, and the merchants involved in that activity. Debate (in the Anglo-American world at least) has attended the extent to which the ancient law merchant or the beginnings of the general maritime law represented a body of law that was separate to the common law, the extent to which it was really separate from national jurisdiction, and the extent to which its organs of dispute resolution were really separate from national courts.[63] Whether treated distinctly or not, one would expect different national laws to influence – but not control – any transnational body of commercial law. We would also expect to see a relationship in the opposite direction, as we do today. Furthermore, we would not expect a dispute resolution system operating in a state, even if applying mercantile law, to be wholly independent of that sovereign state's legal system. It is all a question of degree, and a question of the extent to which the national system supports the broader cross-border system of dispute resolution. This does not militate against treating international commercial disputes as distinctive or striving for consistency in approach in the treatment of such disputes amongst different nations.

The more interesting question is why there is a continued need for the unique treatment of international commercial disputes. Part of an answer can be derived from the remarks of the then Lord Chief Justice of England and Wales, Lord Thomas of Cwmgiedd, in 2016 about the benefits that strong national commercial courts provide to commercial parties:

> Fundamental to the rule of law is an effective justice system in each nation state. It is constituted of accessible courts, presided over by an independent and highly qualified judiciary, which delivers quality justice and commands public confidence. It is fundamental for a number of reasons. It underpins the operation of the markets and commerce. It enables contracts to be enforced and debts paid through a just and fair process. It provides a sound

[63] See, eg, L Trakman, 'The Twenty-First Century Law Merchant' (2011) 48 *American Business Law Journal* 775.

> framework for just dispute resolution: enabling businesses to resolve their disputes, if necessary, on their substantive merits. It is, in short, essential to economic prosperity.
>
> Effective courts thus give life – and where necessary give teeth – to the framework of law within which markets and businesses operate, and their lawyers advise. Such a framework enables entrepreneurs to be confident that they can develop their businesses, promote and market their products, and develop new products secure in the knowledge that their rights will be respected, vindicated and enforced.[64]

Expanding upon these themes, his Lordship noted that the 'strategic objective' of commercial courts adapting to respond to a globalised world must be based upon the aim of 'strengthening the rule of law in our global village'.[65] These comments can be generalised further. The reason for treating international commercial disputes uniquely, and for ensuring an appropriate *system* of international commercial dispute resolution, is best expressed as a reflection of the need for the application of an international rule of law to global commerce in order to secure and facilitate globalised trade. The lesson throughout history, and particularly through the achievements of the past few decades, has been that the best way to do this is through constructing a legal order that provides an appropriate foundation of legal security to commercial relationships, but which is also sufficiently adapted to the requirements of those relationships.

III. Understanding International Commercial Dispute Resolution as a System

The system of international commercial dispute resolution that has developed in recent decades has a level of complexity, reach and dynamism that has not been seen before. It differs from those of centuries past in that it relies, to a greater extent, on instruments and institutions that are the products of the individual or collective acts of sovereign state actors. It also has more moving parts than those simpler, merchant-focused and administered bodies of law. However, it is none the worse for that. It reflects the greater complexity of modern international trade. While these features provide the foundations and tools to be used in international commercial dispute resolution, the system remains intimately connected to the actions of commercial parties and the people who work within it.

Indeed, perhaps the key task for the enduring success of international commercial dispute resolution as a system into the future is the embedding within it, as a shared norm of the persons engaged in the system, of an appropriate litigation culture. For the system to function effectively and efficiently – and so retain legitimacy – this must be a culture of problem solving, rather than process. There must be a commitment, by the parties, to working together to use the components of the international commercial dispute resolution to resolve their mutual problem within the bounds of the system. Such a norm cannot be established by the black letter of rules or codes of conduct alone.

[64] Lord Thomas of Cwmgiedd, 'Commercial Justice in the Global Village: The Role of Commercial Courts' (DIFC Academy of Law Lecture, 1 February 2016) [7]–[8].

[65] ibid [52].

That would allow a culture of process to dominate. Instead, such a norm must develop as part of the system through the conduct and attitudes of the persons that comprise its constituent parts.

This norm can be developed through the actions of national courts. Commercial courts have the capacity to develop a problem-solving culture through the approach they take to commercial disputes within their jurisdiction. In turn, such an approach can influence the arbitration culture of that particular jurisdiction, through those courts' approach to the supervision of arbitration and through the impact that national courts have on the attitudes, behaviour and values of the practitioners that practice before them. As such a culture develops in national courts around the world, it will come to be infused in the broader international commercial dispute resolution system.

Other norms of international dispute resolution that deserve highlighting are those surrounding judicial support for arbitration.[66] What is required is full support for arbitration. However, this must be done properly. National courts must be sympathetic to arbitration. This does not mean that they should be reluctant to intervene in the exercise of their supervisory jurisdiction where appropriate. Appropriate judicial supervision is not to be equated with a light touch in all circumstances. Rather, judicial supervision should entail acting to protect the institution of arbitration through *interfering properly*. Through doing so, commercial courts can steward the development of a litigation culture that promotes the continued vitality of international commercial dispute resolution through arbitration. What is required is the development of an appropriate culture – again, not rigid rules – in commercial courts supervising arbitration. Arbitrators, and commercial parties, should be able to rely upon a sympathetic, competent and interested commercial court that will act with a light touch generally whilst also intervening with proper despatch when the circumstances of the case and the protection of the system as a whole demand it.

Keeping those matters in mind, it is appropriate to consider the structure of international commercial dispute resolution. The system can be seen to have a particular architecture, though it is more like Gaudi's Sagrada Familia than any classical structure – heterogeneous and constantly evolving. Certain key aspects can be discerned. These different interlocking components might be grouped into its foundations, institutions, rules and principles, and the human element. These are discussed in turn below.

A. Foundations

The foundations of international commercial dispute resolution comprise several important legal instruments developed over the past 60 years. These permit a truly international system of commercial dispute resolution to operate. The most important of these is arguably the New York Convention, concluded in 1958.[67] Chief Justice Bathurst

[66] See the discussion in J Allsop, 'The Authority of the Arbitrator' (2014) 30 *Arbitration International* 639.

[67] Convention on the Recognition and Enforcement of Foreign Arbitral Awards, opened for Signature 10 June 1948, 330 UNTS 3 (entered into force 7 June 1959) ('New York Coventention').

has described 'the enforcement aspect of the New York Convention' as the 'pillar' on which the 'international system for the peaceful and civilized resolution disputes, under international rule of law principles' rests.[68] Without widely available enforcement, an international arbitral award could be close to worthless. From 24 signatories, the New York Convention has come to have, at last count, 169 state parties.[69] The success of the New York Convention is underpinned by the requirement in Article III to:

> [R]ecognize arbitral awards as binding and enforce them in accordance with the rules of procedure of the territory where the award is relied upon, under the conditions laid down in the following articles. There shall not be imposed substantially more onerous conditions or higher fees or charges on the recognition or enforcement of arbitral awards to which this Convention applies than are imposed on the recognition or enforcement of domestic arbitral awards.

The regime is completed by the fact that enforcement may only be refused in the limited circumstances set out in Article V.

The second key foundational instrument also relates to arbitration. It is the Model Law. It was promulgated in 1985 and amended in 2006. Although not a treaty like the New York Convention, it has been embraced widely internationally, and should be interpreted as an international instrument. It was designed for implementation into national legislation. UNCITRAL reports that 'Legislation based on the Model Law has been adopted in 80 States in a total of 111 jurisdictions'.[70] The adoption of the Model Law into national legislation has helped to establish a coherent and harmonised approach to international commercial arbitration. With the New York Convention, it has created a framework for international arbitration that is an integral component of the international commercial dispute resolution system. Like the New York Convention, the Model Law secures the strength of the arbitral order. It limits the opportunities for intervention of a supervising court of the seat of the arbitration. The policy of the Model Law is to respect the authority of the arbitrator. This can be seen particularly in Article 16 of the Model Law which deals with the arbitral tribunal's competence to rule on its own jurisdiction. The Model Law also significantly limits the grounds upon which an arbitral award can be set aside (Article 34) or upon which recognition and enforcement can be refused (Article 36).

Another UNCITRAL Model Law that is critical to international commerce is the UNCITRAL Model Law on Cross-Border Insolvency. Its foundational role is reflected in its preamble:

> The purpose of this Law is to provide effective mechanisms for dealing with cases of cross-border insolvency so as to promote the objectives of:
>
> (a) cooperation between the courts and other competent authorities of this State and foreign States involved in cases of cross-border insolvency;
>
> (b) greater legal certainty for trade and investment;

[68] TF Bathurst, 'The Role of the Courts' (ACICA New York Convention Symposium, Sydney, 4 July 2018) [7].

[69] New York Convention Guide, 'New State Party to the New York Convention', available at newyorkconvention1958.org/index.php?lvl=cmspage&pageid=7&id_news=1021&opac_view=-1.

[70] UNCITRAL, 'Status: UNCITRAL Model Law on International Commercial Arbitration (1985), with Amendments as Adopted in 2006', available at uncitral.un.org/en/texts/arbitration/modellaw/commercial_arbitration/status.

(c) fair and efficient administration of cross-border insolvencies that protects the interests of all creditors and other interested persons, including the debtor;
(d) protection and maximization of the value of the debtor's assets; and
(e) facilitation of the rescue of financially troubled businesses, thereby protecting investment and preserving employment.

Instruments such as the Hague Choice of Court Agreements Convention of 2005 may also come to serve a facilitative role in regard to enforcement of court judgments, much as the New York Convention has for arbitral awards. It applies to exclusive choice of court agreements in 'civil or commercial matters'[71] and provides in Article 8 that:

> A judgment given by a court of a Contracting State designated in an exclusive choice of court agreement shall be recognised and enforced in other Contracting States in accordance with this Chapter. Recognition or enforcement may be refused only on the grounds specified in this Convention.

Uptake of this Convention has been slow, however,[72] and it may be that the Hague Convention on Recognition and Enforcement in Civil or Commercial Matters of 2019 (the 2019 Hague Convention),[73] which is not limited to exclusive jurisdiction agreements, will become the foundational instrument that underpins enforcement of commercial court judgments. That more recent convention is designed to be 'complementary' of the Hague Convention on Choice of Court Agreements,[74] according to its Preamble. It is broader, applying generally 'to the recognition and enforcement of judgments in civil or commercial matters'.[75] This is reflected in the key operative provision in Article 4 of the 2019 Hague Convention:

> A judgment given by a court of a Contracting State (State of origin) shall be recognised and enforced in another Contracting State (requested State) in accordance with the provisions of this Chapter. Recognition or enforcement may be refused only on the grounds specified in this Convention.

If it receives international acceptance, the 2019 Convention would be a significant development in the assured enforcement of commercial court judgments internationally. It would do a lot to strengthen the role of national commercial courts in the international commercial dispute resolution system.

B. Institutions

The institutions of the international commercial dispute resolution system are critical. These institutions rely on the foundational instruments for their effectiveness. Similarly, these instruments would not be effective without these institutions. The institutions

[71] Convention on Choice of Court Agreements 44 ILM 1294 (Opened for Signature 30 June 2005) Art 1.
[72] AS Bell, 'An Australian International Commercial Court – Not a Bad Idea or What a Bad Idea?' (2019 ABA Biennial International Conference, Singapore, 12 July 2019) [56]–[57].
[73] Hague Convention on Recognition and Enforcement in Civil or Commercial Matters of 2019 (Opened for signature 2 July 2019) (not in force).
[74] Hague Convention on Choice of Court Agreements 44 ILM 1294 (Opened for signature 30 June 2005, entered into force 1 October 2015).
[75] Hague Convention on Recognition and Enforcement in Civil or Commercial Matters (n 73) Art 1.

of the system are heterogeneous. To a certain extent, they compete with each other. Competition between different parts of the system is not necessarily a bad thing.[76] Just because they are somewhat competitive with one another, does not mean they do not also support one another.[77] For example, arbitral tribunals are dependent upon national commercial courts for enforcement of their awards. Considered as part of an interlocking system, this duality can be supportive of effective dispute resolution.

The most prominent contemporary 'institution' of international commercial dispute resolution is international commercial arbitration. Its connection to the international rule of law has been described by other commentators.[78] Arbitration's popularity has continued to grow worldwide over the past decade, particularly in the Asia-Pacific.[79] The Model Law has done much to embed international arbitration into national legal systems. Ad hoc arbitrations continue. There are also a range of arbitral institutions, which have only continued to grow. Within the Asia-Pacific, these include the Singapore International Arbitration Centre (SIAC), the Singapore Chamber of Maritime Arbitration (SCMA), the Hong Kong International Arbitration Centre (HKIAC), the Asian International Arbitration Centre (AIAC), and the Australian Centre for International Commercial Arbitration (ACICA). In China, the institutions include the Beijing International Arbitration Centre (BAC) and the Chinese International Economic and Trade Arbitration Commission (CIETAC). Globally, they include the London Court of International Arbitration (LCIA), the London Maritime Arbitrators' Association (LMAA), the International Chamber of Commerce (ICC) in Paris, and the Permanent Court of Arbitration (PCA) in The Hague, along with the arbitral bodies of the US, such as the New York International Arbitration Centre and New York's Society of Maritime Arbitrators.

While recognising the role of arbitration, one must be careful not to downplay the role of skilled commercial courts. Lord Thomas has devoted much energy to promoting the role of national commercial courts in the international commercial dispute resolution system.[80] His Lordship has criticised the growing use of arbitration as a 'serious impediment to the development of the common law', and suggested that greater emphasis needs to be placed on the utility of skilled commercial courts in resolving international commercial disputes, as the Commercial Court in London has done with great renown since the nineteenth century.[81] Such a view, however, is premised on the idea that only courts legitimately make law, which is not the approach that the international system has adopted. Arbitrators can, and do, make law.[82]

[76] See J Allsop, 'National Courts and Arbitration: Collaboration or Competition' (CIArb Centenary Conference, July 2015); Allsop (n 20).

[77] ibid.

[78] See Lord Neuberger, 'Arbitration and the Rule of Law' (CIArb Centenary Celebration, Hong Kong, 20 March 2015).

[79] S Jhangiani and I Hopkinson, "The Changing Face of International Arbitration in Asia: Innovating to Stay Afloat" Clyde & Co, available at www.clydeco.com/uploads/Blogs/employment/CC008357_ArbitrationThirdly_Edition5_WEB_23_09_15.pdf.

[80] See, eg, Lord Thomas, 'Commercial Dispute Resolution: Courts and Arbitration' (National Judges College, Beijing, 6 April 2017).

[81] Lord Thomas, 'Developing commercial law through the courts: rebalancing the relationship between the courts arbitration' (BAILII Lecture, 9 March 2016) [6], [22]–[23].

[82] See J Allsop, 'The role of law in international commercial arbitration' (CIArb Inaugural Annual Lecture, Melbourne, 15 October 2018).

The better view, we respectfully suggest, is that commercial courts and arbitration both compete with, and also complement, each other. Commercial parties will select the appropriate forum for their dispute. Commercial courts also play an important role in supervising arbitration. This is where the complementarity can perhaps best be observed. This requires commercial courts to be commercially aware and sympathetic to the role of arbitration in the international legal order. Lord Thomas has himself emphasised the symbiotic relationship between arbitration and commercial courts in a more recent paper, stating that:

> [T]he role of a Commercial Court cannot simply be seen as a forum for court based litigation. It has an essential role in relation to arbitration, provided that a Commercial Court and arbitrators and arbitral institutions work together and respect the complementary nature of their respective roles.
>
> … A successful arbitral centre therefore needs a Commercial Court that can provide what is required, but it must do so on the basis that the parties right to opt for arbitration is a right that must be respected and upheld by a Commercial Court. It is not always appreciated that arbitral centres need strong Commercial Courts to ensure that arbitration can function effectively.[83]

A more recent institutional development has been the increasing number of international commercial courts.[84] These now include the Singapore International Commercial Court (SICC), the Dubai International Financial Centre (DIFC) Courts, the Abu Dhabi Global Markets (ADGM) Courts, the Qatar International Court and Dispute Resolution Centre of the Qatar Financial Centre (QFC), the Astana International Financial Centre (AIFC) Court and the new Chinese International Commercial Court (CICC). They also include the international chambers that have recently been established, or are in the process of being established, in Amsterdam, Paris, Frankfurt and Brussels.[85] The precise scope of each court's jurisdiction varies. The courts of the Gulf were formerly limited to matters arising in the DIFC, ADGM or QFC, but have since expanded the cope of their jurisdiction.[86] The SICC from the outset allowed parties to consent to its jurisdiction.[87] The CICC sits in Shenzhen and Xi'an. As Professor Walker has explained, it has a broad jurisdiction:

> The CICC provides options for mediation, arbitration and litigation in a range of matters including: matters in excess of RMB 300 million where the parties consent; matters within the jurisdiction of the Higher People's Court that it seeks to have the CICC decide; international commercial matters that have a nationwide impact; and other matters that the SPC considers appropriate for determination by the CICC. The CICC also has jurisdiction over applications for interim measures in support of arbitrations and the enforcement of arbitral awards. The CICC does not hear investor-state disputes or state-state trade disputes …
>
> … [T]he CICC seeks to provide within mainland China an alternative to the local PRC courts or arbitration commissions for international matters involving foreign and PRC parties that is acceptable to both.[88]

[83] Thomas, 'Developing commercial law through the courts' (2016) [18]–[19].
[84] As to which see Walker, 'Specialised International Courts' (2019).
[85] See further ch 3 of this book.
[86] Walker (n 9) 5–7.
[87] ibid 7.
[88] ibid 8–9.

Two aspects of the institutional components of the system should be noted. The first is the range of different institutions that have now developed. This means they can, and do, compete with each other. Usually, the institution will be selected by the parties. The procedural rules of the institution, or the identity and skill of its arbitrators or judges may prove critical. Second, one has to appreciate how the different institutions complement each other.

C. Rules and Principles

The next part of the system that should be briefly surveyed is the substantive law – the rules and principles to be applied to resolve an international commercial dispute. The sources and content of these is also heterogenous and substantially subject to the desires of the parties. The substantive rules may include international conventions or treaties, such as the United Nations Convention on Contracts for the International Sale of Goods (CISG), which has been enacted in municipal legislation in many countries.[89] To this hard law may be added the various model laws and soft law instruments that form the corpus of international commercial law. Within this mixture of documents, the standard form contracts that facilitate global trade should also be included. The names of many of these are instantly recognised amongst international commercial lawyers: INCOTERMS, GENCON, BIMCO, ASBATANKVOY and so on.

One cannot, however, underestimate the continuing role of national law in the resolution of international commercial disputes. A specific national law will commonly be adopted in choice of law clauses relating to particular international transactions. In the interpretation of standard form maritime contracts, English law will regularly be of particular assistance. In the interaction between international or industry instruments and national law, one can again see a symbiotic relationship in operation among different parts of the international system: national law gains its force from its promulgation by national entities, including the decisions of national commercial courts. These decisions interpret and develop principles contained in relevant international instruments. At the same time, the text, context and purpose of those instruments influence the shaping of national law relating to international commerce. Through these interactions, international instruments influence municipal commercial law.

In an arbitral context, parties have the right to choose the substantive law to be applied. Article 28(1) of the Model Law makes this clear: 'The arbitral tribunal shall decide the dispute in accordance with such rules of law as are chosen by the parties as applicable to the substance of the dispute'. The interaction of international bodies of law with a national law may lead parties to select a law that is particularly attuned to the rules of international commercial practice. However, the internationalised and decentralised nature of the system is now such that the parties may also select a non-national law. Parties may select soft law instruments or generally recognised principles of international commercial law to govern the dispute. Alternatively, they may select a

[89] See, eg, Sale of Goods (Vienna Convention) Act 1986 (NSW); Sale of Goods (United Nations Convention) Act (Sing).

combination of different national laws, with international commercial law to be used where there is conflict, as occurred in the *Channel Tunnel* case.[90] Article 28(3) of the Model Law even permits parties to require the arbitrators to decide the dispute *ex aequo et bono*, without reference to a defined body of law.[91]

All of these options are available even without turning to the arguments for and against the existence of a modern *lex mercatoria*, which will briefly be considered later in this chapter and in more detail in part five of this book. The discussion here is simply intended to highlight the broad scope of different sources of law that are part of the international commercial dispute resolution system, and how they might interact to resolve a particular dispute, depending on the choices of the parties and the forum involved.

D. The Human Element

The final aspect of the system which it is important to highlight is that of the persons involved in international commercial disputes. At its core, all commercial activity, whether international or domestic, concerns human relations. Within international commercial dispute resolution, the skill, attitudes and culture of the different actors is important. It will affect the choices of the parties, as to the forum and the law to be applied. It will affect the response of judges and arbitrators to particular arguments, and the responses of national commercial judges to arbitration generally. Ensuring a legal culture exists that is sympathetic to international commercial dispute resolution is critical and, as noted above, ensuring that this is a culture that promotes problem-solving, rather than process for the sake of process, is essential.

What does this short survey reveal? The interlocking, though different, nature of national and international approaches, and the preferences of commercial parties. Having outlined the system, it is appropriate to examine some of the interests at play in debates about international commercial disputes, and how the system might continue to evolve in order to respond to international commerce and the demands on the system insofar as upholding the international rule of law is concerned.

IV. Balancing Competing Interests

The subject matter of international commercial disputes principally focuses on private parties, the determination of private disputes, and questions of private law. The centrality of the concept of party autonomy to the international commercial dispute resolution system reflects this. It has been a key driver of the growth in the popularity of international mechanisms for resolving commercial disputes. Party autonomy is embraced in

[90] *Channel Tunnel Group Ltd v Balfour Beatty Constructions Ltd* [1993] AC 334.

[91] See discussion in N Teramura, '*Ex Aequo et Bono*: An Overlooked and Undervalued Opportunity for International Commercial Arbitration' (18 November 2018) Kluwer Arbitration Blog, available at arbitrationblog.kluwerarbitration.com/2018/11/18/ex-aequo-et-bono-an-overlooked-and-undervalued-opportunity-for-international-commercial-arbitration/.

the default position under Article 28(1) of the Model Law as to the substantive law to be applied to a dispute. Article 28(1) was partially quoted above, but it is worth setting it out more fully:

> The arbitral tribunal shall decide the dispute in accordance with such rules of law as are chosen by the parties as applicable to the substance of the dispute. Any designation of the law or legal system of a given State shall be construed, unless otherwise expressed, as directly referring to the substantive law of that State and not to its conflict of laws rules.

We also see this in the selection of the procedural rules to be applied. Article 19(1) of the Model Law provides: 'Subject to the provisions of this Law, the parties are free to agree on the procedure to be followed by the arbitral tribunal in conducting the proceedings'. Further, the limitations placed upon the intervention of the supervising courts of the seat in an arbitration that are imposed by Article 5 of the Model Law reflect the importance placed on party autonomy, together with the authority of the arbitrator: 'In matters governed by this Law, no court shall intervene except where so provided in this Law'. The limited grounds for setting aside an award or denying enforcement under the New York Convention and the Model Law can also be seen as reflections of party autonomy, in the sense that they respect the parties' decision to resolve their dispute through arbitration.

However, when one reflects upon international commercial dispute resolution as a system, it becomes clear that the resolution of international commercial disputes is not only about private interests and party autonomy. Private interests cannot explain all aspects of the system. All components of the system form part of a true international legal order. The globalised system of international commercial dispute resolution – as part of a rules-based international order – also involves public interests, both domestic and international. Continued international support for the system from nations, legislatures and judiciaries is derived from two key aspects: (a) a respect for the autonomy of the individual private party; and (b) the role of the system as a fair way of vindicating the international rule of law. Maintenance of these two integral aspects of the system requires a recognition and balancing of both private and public interests. In achieving that balance, it is important also to recognise that there is a public interest – rather than solely a private interest – in ensuring the continued vitality of an international commercial dispute resolution system that gives power to the parties to determine how disputes about their commercial affairs should best be resolved. Nonetheless, just as there is a need to promote party autonomy, there is a need to promote the national and transnational public interests that attend such disputes, so that the system retains the support of the international community of nations upon which it depends.

The ways in which the international commercial dispute resolution system accommodates these competing public and private interests include concepts such as arbitrability, mandatory rules and the power to set aside or refuse recognition and enforcement of an arbitral award on the ground of public policy. These concepts are also inter-related, and often act upon similar subject matter. For example, a dispute may be arbitrable, but the tribunal may be required to apply the mandatory rules of a particular state. The failure to apply such mandatory rules may lead to the award being set aside on the ground of public policy. Through these concepts, the system places limits on the autonomy of the parties that it otherwise strives to promote, so as to uphold national and transnational interests recognised by the international community which has itself created the system. In recent decades, these issues have often arisen in relation to matters of competition law and matters relating to bribery, corruption and corporate crime. This reflects increasing focus by the international community on such matters, and the greater reliance by states on laws that have extraterritorial effect to address these issues. Accordingly, the potential for such matters of public policy to come into contact with international commercial dispute resolution has increased.

A. Arbitrability

It is useful to discuss the concept of 'arbitrability' first. Arbitrability relates to the 'question whether the dispute is of the type that comes properly within the domain of arbitration'.[92] It is central to the New York Convention and the Model Law, which both require a dispute to be 'capable of being settled by arbitration'[93] if an award is ultimately to be enforced.[94] As was observed in *Comandate Marine Corp v Pan Australia Shipping Pty Ltd*:

> [T]he common element to the notion of non-arbitrability was that there was a sufficient element of legitimate public interest in these subject matters making the enforceable private resolution of disputes concerning them outside the national court system inappropriate. Secondly, the identification and control of these subjects was the legitimate domain of national legislatures and courts. Thirdly, in none of the *travaux préparatoires* [for the *New York Convention* or Model Law] was there discussion that the notion of a matter not being capable of settlement by arbitration was to be understood by reference to whether an otherwise arbitrable type of dispute or claim will be ventilated fully in the arbitral forum applying the laws chosen by the parties to govern the dispute in the same way and to the same extent as it would be ventilated in a national court applying national laws.[95]

The inquiry into whether a dispute is 'arbitrable' relates to whether the public interest favours the matter being determined by a national court, rather than by part of the delocalised international commercial dispute resolution system. The authors of *Redfern and Hunter* note that 'it is precisely because arbitration is a private proceeding with public consequences [for instance, in the recognition and enforcement of the award] that some types of disputes are reserved for national courts, the proceedings of which are generally in the public domain'.[96]

The consensus over what is arbitrable has changed over time. Arguably, this is because of states' increased acceptance of, and respect for, the international commercial dispute resolution system. For instance, under the national law of many states,

[92] [2006] FCAFC 192, 157 FCR 45 [200].
[93] ibid [200].
[94] New York Convention Art V(2)(a); UNCITRAL Model Law on International Commercial Arbitration Arts 34(2)(b)(i), 36(1)(b)(i).
[95] [2006] FCAFC 92, 157 FCR 45 [200].
[96] Blackaby et al (n 6) [2.126].

competition law issues are now arbitrable.[97] This was not always the case. In the US, for example, antitrust claims were originally not as arbitrable,[98] until the Supreme Court held in *Mitsubishi Motors Corp v Soler Chrysler Plymouth Inc* that, despite the public interests involved, an antitrust dispute could be the subject of resolution by arbitration.[99] The Court said that:

> [W]e conclude that concerns of international comity, respect for the capacities of foreign and transnational tribunals and sensitivity to the needs of the international commercial system for predictability in the resolution of disputes require that we enforce the parties' agreement, even assuming that a contrary result would be forthcoming in a domestic context.[100]

For systemic reasons, the Court permitted competition law issues to be the subject of arbitration. Similarly, in England it has been held that there was 'no realistic doubt' that competition law claims are arbitrable, if they come within the scope of an arbitration clause.[101] It has also been argued that competition law disputes would be arbitrable in Australia,[102] though others have noted that this issue remains unresolved.[103]

The arbitrability of other subject matters continue to attract debate, along with differing answers in different states. Securities transactions, insolvency and corporate law disputes are examples.[104] Matters of corporate law attract diverging national views: Dutch and Russian law do not allow such matters to be the subject of arbitration,[105] while in England shareholder disputes may be the subject of arbitration, provided that the dispute does not affect third parties and the arbitration does not represent 'an attempt to delegate to the arbitrators what is a matter of public interest which cannot be determined within the limitations of a private contractual process'.[106] Again, it has been argued that under Australian law, oppression and winding-up actions could be the subject of arbitration, although the types of award that an arbitrator could make are argued to be limited.[107]

What of the arbitrability of claims of bribery and corruption? With the increasing focus both nationally and transnationally on combating white collar crime, this is an important question. Arbitral tribunals routinely deal with claims of bribery, corruption and fraud. The most significant English case on arbitration law in recent decades, *Fiona Trust & Holding Corporation v Privalov*,[108] illustrates this. In *Fiona Trust*, the House of Lords held that an allegation that a charterparty had been obtained by bribery came within the arbitration clause and so the arbitrator had jurisdiction to

[97] ibid [2.134].
[98] *American Safety Equipment Corporation v JP Maquire Co* 391 F 2d 821 (2nd Cir, 1968).
[99] *Mitsubishi Motors Corporation v Soler Chrysler Plymouth Inc* 473 US 614 (1985).
[100] ibid 629.
[101] *ET Plus SA v Jean Paul Welter & The Channel Tunnel Group* [2005] EWHC 2115 (Comm).
[102] See, eg, M Bonnell, 'Arbitrability of competition disputes in Australian law' (2005) 79 *Australian Law Journal* 585.
[103] J Sher, 'Arbitrability and the impact of fraud or corruption on international arbitration'(2010) 84 *Australian Law Journal* 702, 708.
[104] Blackaby et al (n 6) [2.139]–[2.160].
[105] ibid [2.157]–[2.158].
[106] *Fulham Football Club (1987) Ltd v Sir David Richards* [2011] EWCA Civ 855.
[107] A Marchesi and K Dharmananda, 'The arbitrability of oppression and winding-up actions' (2013) 87 *Australian Law Journal* 258.
[108] *Fiona Trust & Holding Corporation v Privalov* [2007] UKHL 40, [2008] 1 Lloyd's Rep 254.

determine the bribery allegation. The arbitration would only be affected if the allegations involved an attack on the arbitration agreement.[109] This contrasts with earlier decisions internationally which considered that such allegations could not be resolved in arbitration.[110]

Another current area of debate is the arbitrability of intellectual property and technology disputes. The willingness of parties to resolve international intellectual property disputes through arbitration has increased in recent years.[111] An arbitration framework has even been established under the auspices of the World Intellectual Property Organization.[112] As Professor Vincente explains, there is controversy about such disputes because intellectual property disputes relate to 'monopolies granted by states' and, accordingly, states have been reticent to allow such matters to be litigated outside of national courts, 'at least when matters of validity and registration are at stake'.[113] Indeed, some intellectual property disputes, such as those relating to invalidity, have continued to be seen as solely within the domain of national courts.[114] On the other hand, matters that do not involve invalidity, such as contractual disputes in relation to intellectual property rights, are more clearly arbitrable.[115]

It remains to be seen whether international tensions about technology and intellectual property rights will cause a move away from the arbitrability of intellectual property disputes in their entirety. It is submitted that it should not. While it may make sense for invalidity disputes to not be arbitrable, due to the national public interests involved, it would be incongruous with the scope of the concept of arbitrability in contemporary international commercial jurisprudence to declare matters relating to intellectual property non-arbitrable in their entirety.

From this discussion one can observe a trend in favour of greater arbitrability – and so greater promotion of party autonomy. At the same time, there remains a recognition that certain disputes should remain firmly within the domain of national legal systems.

B. Mandatory Rules

While a dispute may be arbitrable, and while parties may select the law applicable to the resolution of the dispute, mandatory rules may constrain this choice by applying national laws to a dispute. Often, mandatory rules involve, but are not limited to, laws relating to taxation, trade practices or other regulatory regimes. Barraclough and Waincymer have explained mandatory rules as follows:

> Mandatory rules are laws that purport to apply irrespective of a contract's proper law or the procedural regime selected by the parties. In this sense, whether they are 'mandatory' does

[109] ibid [17]–[19] (Lord Hoffmann).

[110] See, eg, ICC Case No 1110, Award of 1963, discussed in Blackaby et al (n 7) [2.148]–[2.150].

[111] See DM Vicente, 'Arbitrability of intellectual property disputes: a comparative survey' (2015) 31 *Arbitration International* 151, 161–62. M Woller and M Pohl, 'IP Arbitration on the Rise' Kluwer Arbitration Blog (16 July 2019), available at arbitrationblog.kluwerarbitration.com/2019/07/16/ip-arbitration-on-the-rise.

[112] Woller and Pohl (ibid).

[113] Vincente, 'Arbitrability of intellectual property disputes' (2015) 152.

[114] ibid (n 111) 162.

[115] Woller and Pohl, 'IP Arbitration' (2019).

> not depend on whether they will ultimately end up applying via the relevant conflict of laws analysis, but only on how the law itself defines its sphere of application. Mandatory rules can reflect states' internal or international public policy, and generally protect economic, social or political interests. They can be either procedural, for example requiring due process, or substantive, such as certain tax, competition and import/export laws. Unsurprisingly, it is the application of substantive mandatory rules that creates the most controversy.[116]

They suggest that there are several groups of circumstances in which the application of mandatory rules has become so established as to be 'uncontroversial'.[117] First, mandatory rules can apply to render contractual obligations impossible and so constitute a *force majeure* event.[118] Second, mandatory rules that reflect aspects of transnational public policy, including human rights, *bonos mores*, fair hearing and due process. Prohibitions on bribery and corruption may also be considered to be norms of transnational public policy.[119] It has been asserted that mandatory rules applicable to the parties' choice of law should not be applied if they conflict with transnational public policy.[120] Third, mandatory rules of the law governing the contract under which the dispute arises should be applied.[121] Finally, although this is more controversial, the mandatory procedural and substantive rules of the seat should be applied.[122]

Other applications of mandatory rules may be somewhat more controversial. The examples provided in *Redfern and Hunter* illustrate this well.[123] For example, US anti-bribery laws are applied to US companies even if they conclude an agreement in another country that is subject to the laws of that country. Similarly, Russian corporate law will apply to a Russian-domiciled company even in a dispute governed by another nation's national law. In the context of competition law, determining whether antitrust laws are to be applied as mandatory rules may be complex given that 'antitrust law has its own rules of application, commonly determined by the object or effect of the allegedly anticompetitive agreements or practices on trade or competition in the markets'.[124] As Korzun has noted, the fact that antitrust laws may have extraterritorial application further complicates this. Both US antitrust and EU competition laws have such application. It follows that:

> These rules may have to be considered by arbitral tribunals where the contract at the center of a dispute has direct effects on the US and EU markets, even if the contract was concluded and

[116] A Barraclough and J Waincymer, 'Mandatory Rules of Law in International Commercial Arbitration' (2005) 6 *Melbourne Journal of International Law* 205, 206.

[117] ibid 217.

[118] ibid 218.

[119] CF Concepcion, 'Combating Corruption and Fraud from an International Arbitration Perspective' (2017) 11 *Dispute Resolution International* 23, 27–36; ibid 218. The law of the contract may also incorporate express prohibitions on bribery and corruptions that would be applicable: W Fox, 'Adjudicating Bribery and Corruption Issues in International Commercial Arbitration' (2009) 27 *Journal of Energy and Natural Resources Law* 487, 500–01.

[120] Barraclough and Waincymer (n 116) 218–19.

[121] ibid 219–23.

[122] ibid 223–24.

[123] Blackaby et al (n 6) [3.129].

[124] V Korzun, 'Arbitrating Antitrust Claims: From Suspicion to Trust' (2016) 48 *NYU Journal of International Law and Policy* 867, 893.

> performed outside of these jurisdictions. Thus, irrespective of the will of the parties, which may choose to arbitrate abroad and apply the substantive law of a third country, the applicability of antitrust law in international arbitration may ultimately be determined by its own criteria of application established in such law. This has been referred to by Radicati Di Brozolo as the 'self-connection' principle of antitrust law.[125]

Similarly, anti-bribery statutes such as the Foreign Corrupt Practices Act of 1977 (US) and the Bribery Act 2010 (UK) have extra-territorial effect.

Ultimately, whether mandatory rules should apply depends on the proper construction of those rules, as well as how one conceives of international commercial dispute resolution. If one sees it as a purely private arrangement between the parties, the application of mandatory rules beyond those which form part of the governing law selected by the parties will seem inappropriate. However, if one takes the system-focused view of international commercial dispute resolution that has been advocated in this chapter, it becomes clear that a balancing process is appropriate, and that there is scope for the application of a broader range of mandatory rules. The difficulty is in determining where to strike that balance between party autonomy, the mandatory rules of states, and the public policies that underlie those rules: when is the application of mandatory rules to a private, decentralised dispute appropriate, and when is it not?

C. Public Policy

Finally, there is the concept of 'public policy' as a basis for declining to recognise and enforce arbitral awards under the New York Convention, or as a basis for setting aside an award and refusing recognition or enforcement under the Model Law. Article V(2)(b) of the New York Convention provides that recognition and enforcement of an award may be refused where 'the competent authority in the country where recognition and enforcement is sought finds that … The recognition or enforcement of the award would be contrary to the public policy of that country'. Similarly, under Article 34(2)(b)(ii) of the Model Law, an award may be set aside where it 'is in conflict with the public policy of this State'. Article 36(1)(b)(ii) of the Model Law also permits recognition and enforcement of an award to be refused where it 'would be contrary to the public policy of this State'.

The focus here is upon the 'public policy' of the country in which the setting aside, or recognition and enforcement, of the award is sought. What does this mean, however?

In *TCL Airconditioner (Zhongshan) Co Ltd v Castel Electronics Pty Ltd*,[126] the Full Court of the Federal Court of Australia was required to interrogate the meaning of this term, as used in this part of the New York Convention and Model Law. The appellant sought to argue that an award should be set aside, or refused recognition and enforcement, on the basis that there had been a breach of natural justice in connection with the making of the award, such that the award was contrary to the public policy of Australia. It submitted that three central findings of fact were made in the absence of

[125] ibid 893.
[126] [2014] FCAFC 83, 232 FCR 361.

evidence and that the appellant had been denied the opportunity to make submissions and provide evidence on these matters. In relation to the concept of 'public policy' in the New York Convention, the Court said:

> [T]hree things of relevance may be presently noted. First, the common law term 'public policy' was recognised as broadly equivalent to the civilian notion of 'ordre public', though the latter could perhaps be seen to have had or have a wider application, sufficiently wide to include principles of procedural justice. ... Secondly, the legislative history of Art V(2)(b) of the New York Convention reveals that the phrase was understood to be directed to fundamental principles and was not to be given a broad interpretation that might pick up particular national domestic policy manifestations ... Thirdly, care needs to be exercised in the use of the expressions of 'international' public policy and 'domestic' public policy. van den Berg states that the legislative history of Art V(2)(b) points to 'international public policy' being referred to. Yet, of course, the text of Art V(2)(b) is 'the public policy of that country'. The point being made by van den Berg was that those words do not mandate particular domestic national public policy, rather they denote a concept recognising the international place of the Convention and the need for public policy to be restricted to the state's most basic, fundamental principles of morality and justice in order that there be the fullest commonality of international approach to the question. This usage of 'international' public policy is to be distinguished from some truly international or transnational public policy comprising fundamental shared values or rules of natural law of universal application that is discussed by some authors ...[127]

Articles 34 and 36 of the Model Law reflect aspects of these features of the New York Convention. A review of the international jurisprudence leads to the conclusion that the interpretation of public policy in Article V of the New York Convention and Articles 34 and 36 of the Model Law is as it was understood at the time of the completion of the preparatory work: 'It is limited to the fundamental principles of justice and morality of the state, recognising the international dimension of the context'.[128] The Full Court endorsed the remarks of Bokhary PJ and Sir Anthony Mason NPJ in *Hebei Import & Export Corporation v Polytek Engineering Company Ltd*.[129] In that decision, Bokhary PJ summarised the position as follows, in relation to the New York Convention:

> Before a Convention jurisdiction can, in keeping with its being a party to the Convention, refuse enforcement of a Convention award on public policy grounds, the award must be so fundamentally offensive to that jurisdiction's notions of justice that, despite its being a party to the Convention, it cannot reasonably be expected to overlook the objection.[130]

Sir Anthony Mason NPJ added the following: 'It has been generally accepted that the expression "contrary to the public policy of that country" in Article V(2)(b) means "contrary to the fundamental conceptions of morality and justice" of the forum'.[131] In *TCL Airconditioner*, the Full Court held that the principles of natural justice were part of Australian public policy.[132] However, in an arbitration context, conduct such as that

[127] ibid [64] (citations omitted).
[128] ibid [65] (citations omitted).
[129] *Hebei Import & Export Corporation v Polytek Engineering Company Ltd* [1999] 2 HKC 205.
[130] ibid 215–16.
[131] ibid 232–33.
[132] *TCL Airconditioner (Zhongshan) Co Ltd v Castel Electronics Pty Ltd* [2014] FCAFC 83, 232 FCR 361 [111].

alleged in the case would only breach the rules of natural justice if it resulted in 'real unfairness or real practical injustice'.[133] That had not been established by the appellant in *TCL Airconditioner* and so the award was not able to be impugned on the basis of public policy.

What are some examples of where parties have sought to invoke the enforcing state's public policy? In *Soleimany v Soleimany*,[134] the Court of Appeal of England and Wales refused to enforce in England an award based upon an arbitration agreement relating to carpet smuggling that was contrary to English law. Waller LJ explained that:

> When considering illegality of the underlying contract, we do not confine ourselves to English law. An English court will not enforce a contract governed by English law, or to be performed in England, which is illegal by English domestic law. Nor will it enforce a contract governed by the law of a foreign and friendly state, or which requires performance in such a country, if performance is illegal by the law of that country. That is well established as appears from the citations earlier in this judgment. This rule applies as much to the enforcement of an arbitration award as to the direct enforcement of a contract in legal proceedings.[135]

Conversely, in *Westacre Investments Inc v Jugoimport-SPDR Holding Co Ltd*,[136] the Court of Appeal of England and Wales permitted enforcement of an award where allegations of bribery had been made in the arbitration, on the basis that the arbitrator had considered the matter, as had the courts in Switzerland. Mantell LJ explained that in those circumstances, and without fresh evidence, refusing to enforce the award could not be justified.[137] Another of the judges, Sir David Hirst, opined that even if corruption had been established, the public policy in favour of finality would have led him to enforce the award.[138] In dissent, Waller LJ formed the view that the Court should have refused enforcement, given that 'the principle against enforcing a corrupt bargain … is … based on public policy of the greatest importance and almost certainly recognised in most jurisdictions around the world' and that it was 'important that the English Court is not seen to be turning a blind eye to corruption on this scale'.[139] It has been suggested that it would have been difficult to argue that enforcement would not be contrary to public policy if bribery had been established in the arbitration.[140] Furthermore, Michael Hwang SC and Kevin Lim have argued that, since enactment of the Bribery Act 2010 (UK), an English court is likely to take a more interventionist approach in relation to allegations of corruption.[141]

In summary, what these concepts and principles demonstrate is how the system of international commercial dispute resolution seeks to balance competing private and public interests in its operation, in different ways. In the main, the system does so

[133] ibid [112].
[134] *Soleimany v Soleimany* [1999] QB 785.
[135] ibid 803–04.
[136] *Westacre Investments Inc v Jugoimport-SPDR Holding Co Ltd* [1999] 2 Lloyd's Rep 65.
[137] ibid 81.
[138] ibid 82. See also *R v V* [2008] EWHC 1531 (Comm).
[139] ibid 80.
[140] W Fox, 'Adjudicating Bribery and Corruption Issues in International Commercial Arbitration' (2009) 27 *Journal of Energy and Natural Resources Law* 487, 500.
[141] M Hwang and K Lim, 'Corruption in Arbitration – Law and Reality' (Herbert Smith-SMU Asian Arbitration Lecture, Singapore, April 2011) 71–72.

effectively. Nonetheless, there remain unresolved matters of principle in certain areas. This is particularly so in relation to the application of mandatory rules in statutes of extraterritorial application.

V. Continued Convergence in International Commercial Dispute Resolution

Convergence, unification, and harmonisation have been objectives of contemporary international commercial law since its earliest instruments. The Hague Rules are an early example of a successful attempt. The full title of the Hague Rules (International Convention for the Unification of Certain Rules of Law relating to Bills of Lading) demonstrates its aim. This objective is also evidenced in the preamble, which refers to the decision to 'conclude a convention', 'having recognised the utility of fixing by agreement certain uniform rules of law relating to bills of lading'. Economic arguments for greater convergence in international commercial law have only grown since. The globalising economic forces of the last decades of the twentieth century have been identified as the drivers of greater convergence over that period:

> The motive force for the recent changes is easy to identify. Local economic markets during the past two generations have been enlarged to national and international markets. Trade among nations has multiplied more than tenfold. Barriers to trade, while significant, are small in comparison to the historic past. The new ease of communication and transportation has supported the creation of world markets for many kinds of goods and services. These commercial changes have created a competitive climate for legal rules and have fed the convergence of legal practices in trade transactions.[142]

Professor Rosett argued that:

> The primary function of commercial law is to provide tools for economic and social enterprise. Viewed functionally in an international context, harmonization of results, that is, general consistency in substantive outcomes, will allow those who engage in transactions a higher level of confidence in a worldwide market.[143]

Similarly, the Hon James Spigelman AC, when he was Chief Justice of New South Wales, considered that a lack of convergence in commercial law leads to transaction costs for commercial parties:

One of the barriers to trade and investment, as significant as many of the tariff and non-tariff barriers that have been modified over recent decades, arises from the way the legal system impedes transnational trade and investment by imposing additional and distinctive burdens including:

- uncertainty about the ability to enforce legal rights;
- additional layers of complexity;

[142] A Rosett, 'Unification, Harmonization, Restatement, Codification, and Reform in International Commercial Law' (1992) 40 *American Journal of Comparative Law* 683, 685.

[143] ibid 683.

- additional costs of enforcement;
- risks arising from unfamiliarity with foreign legal process;
- risks arising from unknown and unpredicatable legal exposure;[144]

The economic case for greater steps toward unification and convergence in how different jurisdictions deal with international commercial disputes is a powerful one. However, the matter can also be put in another way, one which potentially hints of the approach that should be taken in future efforts toward convergence: greater convergence should be seen as a means of strengthening the international rule of law as it applies to transnational commercial disputes. This has economic benefits, but not through the mere reduction of 'transaction costs'. Rather, the benefit is in the shaping of commercial expectations and the providing of certainty as to one's legal position in international commerce. Greater convergence should be directed toward enhancing the *system* of international commercial dispute resolution identified in this paper.

This way of thinking about further efforts towards convergence, unification and harmonisation has several implications. First, that this is not something that will happen on its own. The system developed through the efforts of multitudes of different actors – states, supranational organisations, trade bodies, and commercial parties. Its further development will require careful thought and negotiation within and between these different groups of actors. However, as a second consideration, the heterogeneity of the system means that there is no single means of achieving convergence that should alone be pursued. It would be wrong, for example, to think that all future attempts at convergence should be through an international convention incorporated into national law. The system is more complex than that.

There are three key mechanisms of uniformity and convergence that may be especially beneficial for the future development of the international commercial dispute resolution system at this stage of its existence: (a) the continued development, in a variety of ways, of a modern *lex mercatoria*, influencing and being influenced by both national and international commercial law; (b) the establishment and strengthening of international commercial courts as institutions that compete with and complement both arbitration and national commercial courts; and (c) the elaboration of a culture within international commercial dispute resolution that is committed to efficient dispute resolution with an understanding of how international commercial dispute resolution operates as a heterogeneous but interlocking system.

A. The *Lex Mercatoria* Today[145]

Much has been written (positively and negatively) over the past several decades about the emergence of a modern *lex mercatoria* constituted by the principles of international commercial law adopted globally over the course of the twentieth century. References to a modern *lex mercatoria* began to appear in the 1960s through the work of Clive

[144] JJ Spigelman AC, 'Cross-Border Issues for Commercial Courts: An Overview' (Second Judicial Seminar on Commercial Litigation, Hong Kong, 2010).

[145] See for further detail Pt 5 of this book.

Schmitthoff and others.[146] These early scholars noted that international commercial transactions were 'based on uniform, industry-specific contractual arrangements through model contracts and standard clauses that were detached from a specific national legal system' and were resolved using arbitration procedures that deployed rules that were not tied to a particular national legal system.[147] Different views arose as to whether the *lex mercatoria* was an 'autonomous legal order' that arose solely from party autonomy, or whether its recognition depended upon national law.[148]

As the latter half of the twentieth century progressed, understandings as to what comprises the *lex mercatoria* also diverged.[149] This was understandable, given that over this period there was a great explosion in the promulgation of different international instruments on commercial law. These ranged from traditional, 'hard law' treaties such as the United Nations Convention on Contracts for the International Sale of Goods of 1980, to 'soft law' instruments such as the UNIDROIT Principles of International Commercial Contracts and Principles of International Civil Procedure, through to standard form agreements used throughout international commerce, such as charterparties like GENCON and ASBATANKBOY, and sale of goods contracts like INCOTERMS. Theorists like Schmitthoff considered all of these instruments to comprise the *lex mercatoria*, while others suggested it was only those completely independent from the acts of nation states or supranational organisations that were truly part of a modern law merchant.[150] Beyond the proponents of the existence of a modern *lex mercatoria*, there are critics who argue, essentially, that no body of commercial law can exist without implementation in municipal law.[151]

Why raise this debate here? The question of whether there is a *lex mercatoria* and its scope has implications for what approach should be taken toward greater convergence in principles of international commercial law into the future. The better view of the *lex mercatoria* for these purposes, we respectfully suggest, involves rejection of the two extreme positions. The better view is to consider the *lex mercatoria* to encompass the entire corpus of international commercial law rules and principles – treaties, soft law and instruments created by commercial parties. National law, to the extent that it has embraced principles of international commercial law, or has been harmonised with the law of other trading nations, may also have a case for being considered to be a constituent part. One should also add the foundational instruments of the international commercial dispute resolution system such as the New York Convention and the UNCITRAL Model Laws on International Commercial Arbitration and Cross-Border Insolvency.

This raises another extreme position that should be rejected: the idea that national law is the only real law of international commercial dispute resolution. Parties in an international commercial arbitration are entitled to select generally recognised principles of international commercial law or request that the arbitrator decide the matter

[146] SW Schill, '*Lex mercatoria*' in *Max Planck Encyclopaedias of International Law* (OUP, 2014) [9].
[147] ibid [10].
[148] ibid [16].
[149] ibid [17].
[150] ibid [18].
[151] ibid [28]–[29].

ex aequo et bono.[152] At the same time, one also should reject the idea that national and international commercial law principles are somehow wholly independent. In a great many cases, the law applied by international arbitrators will typically be national law. Even then, it may be national law that interprets an internationally recognised standard form. The English Commercial Court developed its reputation to a large degree on its interpretation of standard form bills of lading and charterparties, technically under English law. Due to the proliferation of these forms in industry and the respect accorded to English commercial maritime law, English commercial judges came to shape shipping law around the world. Conversely, international arbitrators will rely on national law, incorporating principles of international commercial law, for enforcement of their award, regardless of the law governing the dispute. In addition, the supervising court of the seat of an arbitration will apply its national law in supervising the arbitration, although that law is likely based on the Model Law. In another dispute, an arbitrator may be required to apply, and a court may be required to rule on, the validity of such a choice of law – a combination of different national laws, with recourse to principles of international commercial law where there is conflict.[153]

These examples show how the substantive and procedural laws of international commercial dispute resolution operate in a complex and interlocking manner, incorporating, in many disputes, a mixture of international principle, domestic law and industry standards. What is the lesson for convergence? The lesson is that there cannot be a single mode of convergence in the substantive and procedural rules that apply to international commercial law. We cannot, and should not try to, enact everything in a treaty. We should not try to require all parties to apply the UNIDROIT Principles to every international commercial dispute. One should consider the context. For structural matters, such as enforcement and procedure, treaties and Model Laws have proven particularly useful. For substantive law, the emphasis on party autonomy in international commercial law suggests that soft law, which parties can select instead of a particular national law, may be preferable. At the same time, one cannot underestimate the likely continuing popularity of influential national laws, particularly where they are commonly invoked in relation to standard form agreements or forms of transaction.

What is more likely to assist parties engaged in international commercial disputes, however, is greater convergence in the treatment of international commercial law principles and international standard forms by different adjudicative bodies: national commercial courts; international commercial courts; and arbitrators. This will also have the benefit of continuing to develop the *lex mercatoria* as a corpus of law, as a list of consistent and harmonised interpretations of different instruments develops. There is a model for how such a complex legal order can develop – it is called the common law. The goal for arbitrators and judges should be consistency in interpretation of the heterogeneous legal instruments that comprise the *lex mercatoria*, to the extent that is consistent with party autonomy and national law.

One way of achieving this is through greater collaboration. There is another possibility, however, which may also go some way to addressing a criticism of the international

[152] UNCITRAL Model Law on International Commercial Arbitration Art 28(3).
[153] See *Channel Tunnel Group Ltd v Balfour Beatty Constructions Ltd* [1993] AC 334.

commercial dispute resolution system made in recent years – the purported negative impact of arbitration on the development of commercial law. As has been noted earlier, Lord Thomas, in his 2016 BAILII lecture, expressed concern about the popularity of arbitration impairing the development of the common law, as decisions are made confidentially and often unpublished. For the purposes of this chapter, it is unnecessary to enter that debate. However, it is appropriate to make the point that, as so much of international commercial dispute resolution occurs through arbitration, there is a case to be made for the publication of redacted versions of arbitral awards on the basis that the decisions of skilled international arbitrators can contribute to the development of the modern *lex mercatoria*, understood in all of its heterogeneity and complexity.[154] This already occurs in certain settings, such as those of the ICC and LCIA, and in maritime arbitrations under the auspices of LMAA or the Society of Maritime Arbitrators of New York. Greater publication of the decisions of arbitrators on points of international commercial law would be a significant step toward convergence, as they would grow the available corpus analysing the instruments of the *lex mercatoria* that could then be examined and adopted by other arbitrators and judges alike. It may well do more for convergence than further legal instruments. It may also promote greater collaboration between arbitrators and judges, if judges have greater access to the decisions of the best international arbitrators.

B. International Commercial Courts[155]

An expansion in the number of international commercial courts in existence has been a significant feature of the development of the international commercial dispute resolution system in the past decade. Professor Walker has argued that 'The new specialised international commercial courts were created in their various contexts to fill a need in international commercial disputes for a respected independent judiciary to produce a sound result'.[156] She suggests that international commercial courts possess the following features that may make them more attractive in a particular dispute than international commercial arbitration:

- capacity for joinder of parties and consolidation of claims;
- power to grant interim measures;
- ability for appellate review;
- tribunal expertise and availability;
- greater transparency; and
- greater efficiency.[157]

[154] Professor Doug Jones AO has also argued in favour of the greater publication of redacted arbitral awards; see D Jones, 'Arbitrators as Law-Makers' (2018) 6 *Indian Journal of Arbitration Law* 19.
[155] See for further detail Pt 2 of this book.
[156] Walker (n 9) 21.
[157] ibid 10–21.

Professor Walker suggests that these do not represent matters where arbitration is failing to meet the needs of commercial parties per se, but areas where in certain disputes the importance of one of these features may favour litigation in an international commercial court rather than international arbitration. This recognises that 'one-size fits all' is not necessarily the best way to resolve international commercial disputes in all their diversity.[158] Thus:

> [A]s we become even more sophisticated in our appreciation of the differences between them and the implications for the special needs of particular business relationships, there may emerge some meaningful bases to choose [between international commercial courts and international commercial arbitration]. For example, the need for appellate review, where it arises, will be a narrow but important consideration in some business relationships that will likely continue to weigh in favour of specialised commercial courts. Further, it will be possible to weigh the benefit of access to decision-makers with well-established public track records in the adjudication of complex commercial disputes in specialised courts against the opportunity to select specific arbitrators with the right expertise for the particular case. And to the extent that the needs alternatively for transparency and confidentiality in the resolution of disputes can be anticipated at the outset of the business relationship it may affect the choice between litigation in a nominated specialised court or arbitrating the disputes that might arise.[159]

In addition, it is likely that the advantages of international commercial courts for certain disputes will drive innovation in international commercial arbitration. This is a welcome consequence of the interlocking nature of the international commercial dispute resolution system.[160]

There are three features of international commercial courts that may promote convergence: (a) ability for appellate review; (b) tribunal expertise and availability; and (c) greater transparency. These features enable international commercial courts to contribute to the corpus of international commercial law in a principled way. International commercial courts enable skilled, experienced commercial judges, drawn from the host state and abroad, to decide international commercial matters in a transparent way, publishing judgments that can contribute to the body of transnational commercial law. The facility for appellate review enables the further development of that law, and the correction of error where apparent.

The SICC's structure and work shows how this can occur. The jurisdictional framework of the SICC enables disputes that are truly international to be decided in Singapore. The SICC's judges are comprised of skilled Singaporean judges and distinguished international jurists from Australia, Canada, France, Hong Kong, India, Japan, the UK and the US. The Court sits in a coram of one or three judges.[161] The bench is truly international and embraces a range of different judicial and commercial experiences. An appeal is available to the Singapore Court of Appeal, which is already an appellate commercial court of international distinction.[162] Other international commercial courts, such as

[158] ibid 14.

[159] ibid 22.

[160] See M Hwang SC, 'Commercial Courts and international arbitration – competitors or partners?' (2015) 31 *Arbitration International* 193.

[161] Supreme Court of Judicature Act 1969 (Singapore) s 18H(2).

[162] Supreme Court of Judicature Act 1969 (Singapore) s 30.

those in the Gulf, have also adopted a system of appointing distinguished international judges. Since its inception, the SICC has published over 100 judgments.[163] Several matters have also proceeded on appeal to the Singapore Court of Appeal. Their international character, both in the law to be applied and in the judges hearing the case can be seen from several examples (which are by no means exhaustive):

- *BNP Paribas SA v Agam* – a dispute which involved issues of subrogation under French law, with parties based in France and Israel, which was heard by Steven Chong J, Roger Giles and Dominique Hacher IJJ.[164] An expedited appeal was heard by a combination of resident and international judges.[165] The remitted matter was then heard by the original panel.[166] A further interlocutory hearing was heard by Sir Vivian Ramsey IJ,[167] and an appeal against that decision was heard by a different panel of resident and international judges.[168]
- *Macquarie Bank Ltd v Graceland Industry Pte Ltd* – a contract and fiduciary obligation dispute involving English law that was heard by Sir Bernard Eder IJ.[169]
- *Sheila Kazzaz v Standard Chartered Bank* – a case alleging negligence, misrepresentation and breach of regulatory laws of the Dubai International Financial Centre brought by British nationals resident in Dubai against the Bank, which was decided by Anselmo Reyes IJ.[170]
- *Solomon Lew v Kaikhushru Shiavax Nargolwala* – a dispute about ownership of a luxury villa in Phuket, Thailand, which involved a dispute as to whether Thai or Singaporean law applied, and which was decided by Simon Thorley IJ.[171]

One can see the benefits, in the terms of the continued development of a system of international commercial dispute resolution of these transnational disputes, involving nationals of different states and different systems of law, being heard by an internationalised bench of skilled judges, with their reasons for decision published and able to inform the ever developing *lex mercatoria*. Of course, it could be argued that this is really what the English Commercial Court has done for over a century, albeit with a solely English bench. It might be thought, however, that there is a distinction to be drawn between it as the premier Commercial Court in the Anglo-American world and an internationalised bench that is able to draw on the expertise of commercial jurists from across the world. There is room for both courts to reflect the pluralism of and complementarity within the system, just as the system is strengthened by use of both international commercial arbitration and court litigation.

[163] As at 31 December 2021. The judgments are available at www.sicc.gov.sg/hearings-judgments/judgments.
[164] *BNP Paribas SA v Jacob Agam and another* [2016] SGHC (I) 5, [2017] SGHC (I) 2.
[165] *Jacob Agam and another v BNP Paribas SA* [2017] SGCA (I) 1.
[166] *BNP Paribas SA v Jacob Agam and another* [2017] SGHC (I) 10.
[167] ibid 3.
[168] ibid 7.
[169] *Macquarie Bank Ltd v Graceland Industry Pte Ltd* [2018] SGHC (I) 5.
[170] *Sheila Kazzaz v Standard Chartered Bank* [2019] SGHC (I) 15.
[171] *Solomon Lew v Kaikhushru Shiavax Nargolwala* [2020] SGHC (I) 2.

It is useful to discuss a further means of greater convergence in the adjudication (and so case management and resolution) of international commercial disputes that is somewhat less radical, but potentially more significant. This mechanism is the continued development and strengthening of frameworks for cooperation between institutions of the international commercial dispute resolution system. Lord Thomas, when he was the Lord Chief Justice of England and Wales, was a strong advocate for commercial courts of skill, excellence and efficiency. Under his leadership, the Standing International Forum of Commercial Courts (SiFoCC) was established in 2017.[172] Its members include commercial courts from across the globe. Its aim is to develop and enhance the skill of commercial courts around the world, and to harmonise and improve upon important features of their operation in practical working areas such as the enforcement of judgments, case management and cost reduction, technology in court, litigation funding and arbitration issues.

As part of these activities, in June 2019 SIFoCC published a Multilateral Memorandum on Enforcement of Commercial Judgments for Money, contributed to by 32 of SIFoCC's member jurisdictions.[173] The aim of the SIFoCC Enforcement Memorandum was to 'provide a useful tool in global enforcement' and 'demonstrate cooperation, provide a mutual understanding of laws and judicial processes in this area, and improve public perception and understanding'.[174] A second edition of the SIFoCC Enforcement Memorandum was published in December 2020.[175]

In addition, in May 2020, SIFoCC published its Presumptions of Best Practice in Case Management,[176] which is the product of its First International Working Group. It 'provides a succinct approach to what constitutes best practice in Case Management' and:

> [S]eeks to state, at an appropriate level of generality, the fundamental elements of, and approach to, case management. The purpose of the document is to provide a principled framework for individual courts to develop more particular approaches, rules or practice notes suitable for their individual requirements, situations, legislative contexts and circumstances.[177]

The Case Management Memorandum will provide useful guidance for national commercial courts seeking to promote the development of a problem-solving-focused litigation culture, through their approach to case management. The principles set out have been drafted with such a philosophy of dispute resolution in mind. They include the following:

> Case Management, largely judicially developed, exists (in this context) to assist in the resolution of commercial disputes. It is not process for its own sake. The mindset, culture or ethos

[172] See Standing International Forum of Commercial Courts, 'About us', available at www.sifocc.org.

[173] See Standing International Forum of Commercial Courts, 'Multilateral Memorandum on Enforcement', available at www.sifocc.org/2019/06/24/multilateral-memorandum-on-enforcement ('SIFoCC Enforcement Memorandum 1st edn').

[174] ibid.

[175] Standing International Forum of Commercial Courts, 'Multilateral Memorandum on Enforcement Second Edition', available at https://s3-eu-west-2.amazonaws.com/sifocc-prod-storage-7f6qtyoj7wir/uploads/2020/12/6.7053_JO_Memorandum_on_Enforcement_2nd_Edition_WEB.pdf ('SIFoCC Enforcement Memorandum 2nd edn').

[176] Standing International Forum of Commercial Courts, 'Presumptions of Best Practice in Case Management', available at sifocc.org/app/uploads/2020/05/SIFoCC-Presumptions-of-Best-Practice-in-Case-Management-May-2020.pdf ('SIFoCC Case Management Memorandum').

[177] ibid.

is central. It should be seen as a means to an end to resolve disputes, that is, to solve problems recognising that problems are mutual.

- Case management entails a judicial 'grip' on proceedings.
- Fundamental to Case Management is the early identification of what is common ground and what are the real issues.
- Save exceptionally, delay is the enemy of justice and Case Management requires that applications for adjournments should be subjected to rigorous scrutiny.
- Judicial leadership is necessary for successful Case Management.
- The cooperation of the legal profession/s is fundamental; judicial time spent achieving it is time well-spent.
- It is important that the Court retains overriding control over Case Management matters, including timelines, notwithstanding any agreement between representatives.
- Case Management must be seen as an integral part of the judicial role in commercial disputes.
- Technological developments should be harnessed to improve Case Management, as in all areas of commercial proceedings.[178]

In May 2020, SIFoCC also published a Memorandum on Delivering justice during the Covid-19 pandemic and the future use of technology.[179] These documents, and the work of SIFoCC generally, are examples of how convergence can be attained through more informal processes of cooperation and collaboration. They show how convergence does not need to be achieved solely through formal legal instruments or the setting up of formal institutions. Effective convergence can also be attained through collaboration between different institutions and actors of the international commercial dispute resolution system. SIFoCC has set up a framework for cooperation and collaboration between commercial courts, including international commercial courts. The next step may be the setting up of a collaborative organisation between commercial courts and arbitral institutions, as both come to appreciate their roles of competitive collaboration in the international commercial dispute resolution system.

C. A Facilitative Dispute Resolution Culture[180]

The most effective step that could be taken towards convergence is the development of a litigation culture (encompassing parties, lawyers, judges, arbitrators and scholars) that recognises the need to deal with international commercial disputes appropriately. The development of institutions such as the international commercial courts are steps in this direction, as are bodies such as SIFoCC. The facilitative instruments like the New York Convention and the Model Laws also play a role. However, culture is not only institutions, meetings or instruments. It is a state of mind and set of practices. How our legal cultures have changed in relation to the international commercial dispute resolution

[178] ibid [2]–[9], [14].

[179] Standing International Forum of Commercial Courts, 'Delivering justice during the Covid-19 pandemic and the future use of technology', available at sifocc.org/app/uploads/2020/05/SIFoCC-Covid-19-memorandum-29-May-2020.pdf ('SIFoCC COVID-19 Memorandum').

[180] See for further detail Pt 4 of this book.

system can be seen in how the common law of Australia's attitude to arbitration (one component of the system) has evolved.

Justice Keane, when Chief Justice of the Federal Court of Australia in 2010, suggested that a 'judicial shift' was underway in Australia 'in favour of the view that the UNCITRAL Model Law should be interpreted to confine intervention by the court as organs of the State to the minimum necessary to ensure the integrity of the arbitral process'.[181] More recent decisions have now definitively confirmed that the proper judicial approach is one that is supportive of international commercial arbitration. In *TCL Airconditioner (Zhongshan) Co Ltd v Judges of the Federal Court of Australia*,[182] the High Court of Australia held that section 16(1) of the International Arbitration Act 1974 (Cth), which gave the Model Law the force of law in Australia, did not provide for the exercise of judicial power in a manner contrary to the provisions of the Australian Constitution. It followed that the fact the Federal Court was not permitted by Articles 5 and 36 of the Model Law to refuse to enforce an arbitral award on the ground of error of law was not unconstitutional. The reasoning of the High Court paid particular regard to the nature of an arbitration as a contractual agreement between the parties, with the final and conclusive nature of the award being the result of that agreement.[183] The result is one that gives weight to the authority of the arbitrator to decide a dispute, with the arbitrator having authority even to err under the Model Law.

Subsequently, as discussed above, in *TCL Airconditioner (Zhongshan) Co Ltd v Castel Electronics Pty Ltd*,[184] the Full Court of the Federal Court of Australia held that an arbitral award was only to be set aside or denied recognition or enforcement under Articles 34 or 36 of the Model Law or Art V of the New York Convention if there was some 'real unfairness or real practical injustice in how the international litigation or dispute resolution was conducted or resolved'.[185] The result is one that limits the opportunity for a national court to deny recognition or enforcement of an arbitral award. Again, it is a decision that respects the parties' decision to refer their dispute to arbitration. Most recently, in *Hancock Prospecting Pty Ltd v Rinehart*,[186] the Full Federal Court of Australia confirmed that the principle of *kompetenz-kompetenz* that is incorporated into Article 16 of the Model Law extends to giving the arbitrator jurisdiction to hear an attack on the validity of the arbitration agreement itself under the proviso in Article 8 of the Model Law.

These decisions can all be viewed as a judicial recognition of the legitimacy of the international commercial dispute resolution system and of a developing culture that accords appropriate respect to other participants in that system, such as arbitrators, up until the point where it becomes appropriate for the court to intervene in the proper

[181] PA Keane, 'Judicial Support for Arbitration in Australia' (Financial Review International Dispute Resolution Conference, 2010).

[182] *TCL Airconditioner (Zhongshan) Co Ltd v Judges of the Federal Court of Australia* [2013] HCA 5, 251 CLR 533.

[183] ibid [108] (Hayne, Crennan, Kiefel and Bell JJ) and 555 [34] (French CJ and Gageler J).

[184] *TCL Airconditioner (Zhongshan) Co Ltd v Castel Electronics Pty Ltd* [2014] FCAFC 83, 232 FCR 361.

[185] ibid 377 [55].

[186] *Hancock Prospecting Pty Ltd v Rinehart* [2017] FCAFC 170, 257 FCR 442. Though a domestic arbitration, the governing statute (the Commercial Arbitration Act 2010 (NSW)), was one based on the Model Law.

exercise of its supervisory role. Commercial parties have already, to a large extent, embraced the culture of the international commercial dispute resolution system. They have embraced the opportunities afforded by the existence of a dedicated, heterogenous system for the resolution of international commercial disputes. This can be seen through the popularity of international commercial arbitration, through their use of non-national law in favour of international instruments, and through their use of standard form international agreements to govern their activities.

Lawyers, judges and arbitrators have also embraced the international commercial dispute resolution system, particularly in those renowned commercial courts and arbitral centres. What needs to continue to develop, however, is a culture that recognises that international arbitration, national courts and international commercial courts are all legitimate components of this system. One does not need to attain ascendancy over the other. As has been highlighted, arbitration depends on national commercial courts for supervision and enforcement. Similarly, courts need to continue to recognise the legitimacy of international commercial arbitration, recognise the authority given to the arbitrator under the arbitration agreement, and seek to fulfil their part of the bargain – the effective supervision of the arbitration. Although, as discussed earlier in this paper, appropriate supervision does not mean a laissez-faire approach to supervision. It means a willingness to intervene where it is appropriate to do so.

This does not mean that courts cannot legitimately compete to be the preferred dispute resolution institution for international commerce. The international commercial courts seek to do that, and their innovations will flow to international commercial arbitration. Above all, there needs to be a continued convergence in our litigation cultures in respect of international commercial disputes – a continued move towards collaboration, harmonisation, efficiency and fairness – in order to continue to strengthen the international commercial dispute resolution system as a whole as a mechanism for maintaining the international rule of law in international commerce. It is for these reasons that the human elements of the system are so important. The promulgation of soft law instruments like the SIFoCC Case Management Memorandum are important steps towards convergence in litigation cultures. However, the litigation culture that is required for the continued legitimacy of international commercial dispute resolution is not solely one that is sympathetic to international commercial dispute resolution. It must also be one that is focused on problem solving, rather than process. It must also be a culture that protects the legitimacy of the arbitral components of the system, through enabling the proper intervention of commercial courts in appropriate circumstances.

VI. COVID-19, the International Order and the System of International Commercial Dispute Resolution[187]

The first draft of this chapter was prepared prior to the outbreak of COVID-19. The pandemic has had, and continues to have, an unprecedented impact upon humanity.

[187] See for further detail Pt 6 of this book.

In December 2019, Professor Frankopan presciently described the risk of a pandemic posed by our increasingly interconnected world:

> We live in an interconnected world: more people live in cities than at any time in human history, and they live closer to each other than ever before. As this new decade starts, travel between cities is quicker and cheaper than ever: more than half the world's population live less than an hour from a major city; flight networks mean that almost every city in Africa, Asia and Europe is less than 18 hours apart – including with flight transfers.
>
> This produces all sorts of wonders – from fashions to food, from Instagram experiences to cheaper prices. But exchange is not just about commerce or even the spread of ideas. Contact brings unforeseen and unexpected consequences, too. Disease is perhaps the most important – and is potentially catastrophic.[188]

In addition to the impacts on human health, the pandemic's economic impact will be felt for years to come.

Like all sectors of society, the legal system has been significantly impacted by COVID-19. Across the world, judges and the profession have worked together to ensure that the administration of justice could continue as effectively as possible, primarily through remote video conferencing software such as Microsoft Teams and Cisco Webex. Many national courts have issued detailed practice notes to formalise procedures.[189] These mechanisms are not perfect, nor are they a total substitute for in-person proceedings. Conducting proceedings by web conference removes a significant amount of reality from the proceeding. It presents potential issues for the cross-examination of witnesses. Jury trials have had to be suspended in many jurisdictions. The technology has permitted the resolution of disputes in national courts to continue, albeit in a very different way. The cooperation and efforts of the legal profession to facilitate this in the aid of the administration of justice have been exemplary. Similar arrangements have been made around the globe.[190]

The changed conditions have required significant adjustment, and initially caused some uncertainty. In terms of commercial disputes, there have been requests for adjournment based on COVID-19 related reasons.[191] In *JKC Australia LNG Pty Ltd v CH2M Hill Companies Ltd*,[192] Buss P and Vaughan JA dismissed an application to adjourn an appeal hearing that, due to the pandemic, had to be heard by telephone or video link. Their Honours observed that:

> In the extraordinary circumstances presented by the COVID-19 pandemic the arrangements provided for in the public notice of 18 March 2020 are a necessary but proportionate

[188] P Frankopan, 'We live in the age of the pandemic. This is what we need to do about it' *Prospect* (8 December 2019), available at www.prospectmagazine.co.uk/magazine/pandemic-likelihood-preparedness-uk-who-global.

[189] See, eg, in the Federal Court of Australia: Special Measures in Response to COVID-19 Information Note (SMIN-1) (23 March 2020, revised 31 March 2020); Special Measures Information Note: Admiralty and Maritime (SMIN-2) (1 April 2020); Special Measures Information Note: Appeals and Full Court Hearings (SMIN-3) (7 April 2020); Special Measures Information Note: Court Attendance (SMIN-4) (19 June 2020).

[190] See, eg, for a useful summary of the arrangements made in England and Wales: DAC Beachcroft, 'COVID-19: Litigation in the Time of a Pandemic' (19 June 2020), available at www.dacbeachcroft.com/en/gb/articles/2020/march/covid-19-litigation-in-the-time-of-a-pandemic-latest-updates.

[191] The disruption was more significant in terms of criminal proceedings, with the suspension of jury trials in many parts of Australia. See, eg, *UD v The Queen* [2020] HCATrans 61; *R v Pentland* [2020] QSC 78.

[192] *JKC Australia LNG Pty Ltd v CH2M Hill Companies Ltd* [2020] WASCA 38.

> alteration to the normal practice and procedure of the court consistent with the due administration of justice. Were the submission of senior counsel for the respondents to be accepted this court would be unable to conduct any court hearings for an indeterminate time. That would be antithetical to the due administration of justice in the State of Western Australia and at odds with achievement of the goal and objects in O 1 r 4A and r 4B of the Rules of the Supreme Court 1971 (WA).[193]

In *Capic v Ford Motor Company (Adjournment)*,[194] Perram J dealt with an application for an adjournment of a six-week trial by reason of the COVID-19 related restrictions. The respondent argued that the limits of technology meant that the trial should not proceed, while the applicant contended that the technology was such that the trial could continue. His Honour noted the limitations of the technology, particularly in relation to the cross-examination of witnesses.[195] Ultimately, however, his Honour considered that it was appropriate to refuse the adjournment. Justice Perram explained that:

> [T]here is simply no guarantee that the situation will be any better in six months' time. It may be that this is a state of affairs which persist for a year or so. It is not feasible nor consistent with the overarching concerns of the administration of justice to stop the work of the courts for such a period. Nor is it healthy for the economy. A prolonged cessation of business will be very poor outcome. Those who can carry on should, in my view, do their best to carry on as inconvenient and tedious as this is going to be.[196]

In another case, Perram J ordered an adjournment.[197] This matter required cross-examination of seven witnesses located in China. Due to travel restrictions, they were unable to attend the hearing in Australia. Furthermore, Chinese law prevented cross-examination by video link from China and would have required permission to be obtained through the Hague Convention on the Taking of Evidence Abroad in Civil or Commercial Matters.[198] There was insufficient time to obtain such permission. The consequences of these matters meant, in all the circumstances, it was appropriate to grant an adjournment.

In order to assist Commercial Courts around the world in responding to the consequences of the pandemic, the SIFoCC COVID-19 Memorandum of May 2020 outlines 'the way courts from across the world are responding to the COVID 19 pandemic and is a collaborative effort of the SIFoCC membership.'[199] It addresses the: 'underlying principles for the fair and open delivery of justice'; 'use being made of technology' in commercial dispute resolution during the pandemic; 'sharing of experience' between jurisdictions; 'assistance on the use of platforms'; 'Options for holding jury trials'; 'detailed issues that need to be addressed'; and 'wider dimensions' of the pandemic's

[193] ibid [8].
[194] *Capic v Ford Motor Company (Adjournment)* [2020] FCA 486.
[195] ibid [19]. See also *Desira v Airservices Australia* [2020] FCA 818 [36].
[196] *Capic v Ford Motor Company (Adjournment)* [2020] FCA 486 [23].
[197] *Motorola Solutions Inc v Hytera Communications Corporation Ltd (Adjournment)* [2020] FCA 539.
[198] Opened for signature 18 March 1970. 847 UNTS 231 (entered into force 7 October 1972).
[199] Standing Forum of International Commercial Courts, 'Resources', available at sifocc.org/resources/resources-2.

impact on commercial dispute resolution.[200] Some of the 'detailed issues' that SIFoCC identified as necessitating resolution included issues relating to:

- '[d]elivery of online litigation';
- the conduct of online hearings;
- 'the judiciary and judicial administration' in a virtual environment; and
- the conduct of ADR and mediation online.[201]

The effects that the pandemic has had on international commercial dispute resolution are explored in part six of this book.

It is clear that the pandemic has also caused significant disruption to international arbitration around the world. The restrictions on international travel and on gatherings has led to the postponement or relocation of arbitration hearings to different jurisdictions.[202] There have also been changes to arbitral procedures, including the greater use of remote hearings as has occurred in national courts, together with greater use of electronic documents.[203] Although case management conferences in international arbitration have regularly been conducted remotely prior to the pandemic, hearings on the merits have traditionally remained as physical meetings.[204]

Despite all its negative consequences, there will be some benefits to dispute resolution arising from the experiences of the COVID-19 pandemic. For international dispute resolution, it has been argued that the myriad commercial issues that have arisen will, eventually, lead to an increased demand for dispute resolution by components of the international commercial dispute resolution system.[205] Some of the lessons learned will enable courts and other institutions to do their work more effectively. The experience of using remote hearing technology during the pandemic may well lead to a greater use of technology, where appropriate, in both international arbitration and in national courts. In the context of international arbitration, it has been argued that greater use of remote hearings may have potential to enhance the practice of international arbitration as a dispute resolution mechanism.[206] Chahat Chawla, of the Singapore International Arbitration Centre (SIAC), has described the SIAC's use of remote hearings during the pandemic, observing that if 'managed properly and applied in appropriate disputes, virtual hearings can save considerable time and costs'.[207] Three 'key considerations'

[200] SIFocc COVID-19 Memorandum (n 179).

[201] ibid.

[202] GL Benton, 'How Will the Coronavirus Impact International Arbitration?' Kluwer Arbitration Blog (13 March 2020), available at arbitrationblog.kluwerarbitration.com/2020/03/13/how-will-the-coronavirus-impact-international-arbitration/?doing_wp_cron=1592953502.0642220973968505859375.

[203] ibid.

[204] M Scherer, 'Remote Hearings in International Arbitration – and What Voltaire Has to Do with It?' Kluwer Arbitration Blog (26 May 2020), available at arbitrationblog.kluwerarbitration.com/2020/05/26/remote-hearings-in-international-arbitration-and-what-voltaire-has-to-do-with-it/?doing_wp_cron=1592963475.0728108882904052734375.

[205] Benton, 'Coronavirus' (2020).

[206] Scherer, 'Remote Hearings in International Arbitration' (2020).

[207] C Chawla, 'International Arbitration During COVID-19: A Case Counsel's Perspective' Kluwer Arbitration Blog (14 June 2020), available at arbitrationblog.kluwerarbitration.com/2020/06/04/international-arbitration-during-covid-19-a-case-counsels-perspective/?doing_wp_cron=1592963783.4222838878631591796875.

put forward by Chawla for effective use of remote hearings include: 'developing best practices for hearings'; conducting a 'practice run'; and, 'using reliable technology'.[208] Chawla concludes that:

> In the coming months and after the travel restrictions are eased, it is expected that users of arbitration will continue to refine and enhance the use of technology for virtual hearings. These hearings may become a 'new normal' for cross-border disputes, at least for less complex cases, which may be better suited for online platforms. The arbitration community will also need to consider the question of whether virtual hearings should directly replicate 'in-person' hearings or whether further efficiencies may be achieved to streamline the arbitral process.[209]

National courts, and international commercial courts, will also have to decide what use they make of remote hearings following the pandemic. There is potential for the continued use of remote hearings for case management hearings and other types of hearing, in order to make the court system more effective. Courts in the post-pandemic world will, however, have to resolve difficult practical, philosophical, and psychological questions about the importance of evidence being given, and argument being made, live and in a face-to-face environment. There is a real risk that use of remote hearing technology can remove the necessary reality from proceedings. Although this is a matter one may be willing to tolerate to keep the international commercial dispute resolution system functioning during a pandemic, there are questions about the future ideal and appropriate use of such a modality of proceedings once the spectre of the pandemic fades.

At the same time, as was recognised in the SIFoCC COVID-19 Memorandum published in May 2020:

> The consequences of the pandemic will likely place longer term demands on and challenges for courts, and perhaps Commercial Courts in particular. This is in light of:
>
> a. lasting damage to economies;
> b. both increased defaults and changes in strengths within the business sector;
> c. increased use of technology by business itself as a result of the pandemic;
> d. the build-up of dispute backlog;
> e. damage at least to some parts of the legal profession;
> f. increased calls for better arrangements for access to justice for those without means.[210]

It is important also to step back and note that the COVID-19 pandemic has taken place at a time where, although the world continues to become increasingly connected, there has been a fraying of the bonds making up the international order. Over the past few years, at a time of continued globalisation and shifting of global commerce to the Asia-Pacific, there has been a reaction in different countries and cultures, against the current international system. Long before COVID-19, that system was being disrupted, even as aspects of it have continued to grow and develop. We have seen a conscious pulling away by many liberal democratic states from aspects of the international order

[208] ibid.
[209] ibid.
[210] SIFoCC COVID-19 Memorandum (n 179) 2.

that for decades they had advocated. For example, the UK and Brexit; and the US and its attitude to the WTO under the previous administration. We have also seen nations assert greater strength and influence outside of the rules-based international order. Much of this has occurred in the context of the shifts in geopolitical and economic power that have occurred over the last few decades. Focusing on the international commercial dispute resolution system, there have been significant challenges as it has continued to develop. Criticisms have been made of international commercial arbitration. More fundamental criticisms have been made of the legitimacy of investment arbitration.[211]

The existing international order, and the international commercial dispute resolution system, is not perfect or free from flaws. Far from it. A system can never be perfect. However, it is in the nature of the system that the system can always develop and be improved. A number of the criticisms made in respect of international commercial arbitration and investment arbitration have some truth to them, and steps are being taken to address them by the international dispute resolution community. The concern that arises from present international events, even before the disruption wrought by COVID-19, is one that operates at a higher level of international affairs. It evinces a change in mindset, attitude and approach in many nations towards the international order. It has potential to cause damage to the international commercial dispute resolution system as part of the existing international order. The events of the past few years suggest an increasing scepticism towards, and reaction against, a rules-based international order in the form that has dominated international affairs in recent decades. We see it in increasingly illiberal trade policies, in a preference for unilateral action rather than action through institutions based upon principles. There appears to be less of an appetite for an international order founded on an international law which is accepted and contributed to by states and private parties. The international commercial dispute resolution system is part of that international order, and depends upon that order for its continued vitality.

The world that emerges from the COVID-19 pandemic will not be the same as that which existed before it. It remains to be seen whether that world will include a renewed commitment to a rules-based international order, or a continued trend towards closed borders, closed economies, and unilateral action. Returning to the matters considered earlier in this chapter, it remains to be seen whether the concept of an 'international commercial dispute' will narrow in the post-pandemic world. Such narrowing should be resisted. In any event, such narrowing is likely to arise due to the exacerbation of underlying tensions in the international order rather than the pandemic on its own. Ironically, despite the reaction against the international order that can be seen in some parts of the world, the COVID-19 pandemic has actually afforded an opportunity for greater global cooperation in some instances: for example, researchers and pharmaceutical companies around the world have collaborated on vaccine and treatment research, and special groupings of national governments have come together to discuss the best response to this virus. It may be that COVID-19 focuses the international mind on the

[211] For a discussion of some of these criticisms and some suggestions for reforms to address them, see Pt 3 of this book and Allsop (n 20).

need for greater collaboration and on the importance of the different systems that make up the international order.

Beyond that, we do not comment on these broader geopolitical matters. However, we would suggest that the international commercial dispute resolution system is a signal example of how a rules-based international order can be used to facilitate greater international cooperation, respect for other economic and legal cultures, economic development and, above all, the just resolution of disputes between commercial people from around the globe according to law. We should also consider the fact that, if we abandon a rules-based international order, we will inevitably also abandon our harmonised, cooperative international commercial dispute resolution system.

VII. Conclusion

The international community has recognised the importance of treating international commercial disputes in an appropriately unique manner for millennia. Over the course of the twentieth century and into this present century, an international system of commercial dispute resolution of unprecedented scope, sophistication and reach has developed. It is comprised of interlocking but competing institutions. It also involves competing interests – public and private, national and international – and requires a balancing of such interests through a process of accommodation. This chapter has sought to emphasise its character as a *system* and as a component of a rules-based international order. It has suggested that a system focus should influence what approach we take toward further strengthening this mechanism for applying the international rule of law to global commerce. In an increasingly uncertain period of history, whether due to COVID-19 or broader geopolitical challenges, the successful achievement of an international system of commercial dispute resolution should not be forgotten. The question should be how this system can be further strengthened and improved, as an aspect of an effective rules-based international order.

PART II

The Swinging Pendulum: International Commercial Arbitration and the Rise of Specialist Commercial Courts

3

The Landscape of International Commercial Courts

JIANPING SHI

I. Introduction

It is no exaggeration to say that new International Commercial Courts (ICCs) have spread like wildfire as more countries have established commercial courts to adjudicate multinational business disputes. By 2018, countries including the PRC, the UK, the US, France, Australia, Qatar, the UAE, Singapore, India, Kazakhstan and the Netherlands had set up their own ICCs.[1] With the establishment of new ICCs, there is inevitably considerable interest in exploring the reasons, particularly the advantages, behind this global phenomenon. At the same time, however, one cannot ignore the potential problems associated with this trend. This chapter will accordingly outline the characteristics of different ICCs, and the pros and cons underlying their establishment. The chapter consists of four sections. In section II, the development of ICCs in different countries will be outlined. In section III, the reasons for the establishment of ICCs will be explored. In section IV, the benefits of setting up ICCs will be discussed. Finally, in section V, the problems associated with ICCs will be addressed.

II. ICCs in Different Countries

A. The Commercial Court in London

Unlike the new breed of ICCs which have only emerged in the last two decades, the Commercial Court in London was set up in 1895. Strictly speaking, the Commercial Court is not an ICC in the sense that it is simply a specialised domestic court within the English High Court system. It is however undoubtedly one of the most popular

[1] Qisheng He Research Group, 'The Development of Contemporary International Commercial Courts – A Comparison with China International Commercial Court' (2019) *Business and Economic Law Review Volume 2* 60.

courts for the adjudication of commercial disputes arising among international business enterprises and entrepreneurs. It is regularly designated in international commercial contracts which have little or no connection with England for the resolution of disputes arising out of such contracts. As a result, its caseload, procedures, practices and judges have played a highly influential role in the development of ICCs around the world. Therefore, the dynamics of the London Commercial Court can serve as a benchmark against which to compare the ICCs covered here.

The new ICCs have been established to cater for the unprecedented growth of international trade witnessed in recent years. The ICCs, which are typically established as specialist courts within the existing court systems, are thus 'business-driven' in the sense that they are intended to service the increase in commercial disputes which is a corollary to the growth in international trade.[2] In essence, there is a perceived need among commercial enterprises and entrepreneurs for specialist courts that can resolve their disputes in a time-efficient, cost-effective and predictable manner. There are echoes of the same refrain in the history of the London Commercial Court.

In the City of London, there was, in medieval times, the Mayor's Court which became the most important court for personal actions, especially debt.[3] However, the history of the modern Commercial Court probably began with the establishment of a Commercial List by the Judges of the Queen's Bench Division by way of a Notice dated October 1895. It quickly became known as the 'Commercial Court' although it was, in truth, not a separate court at all but part of the existing Queen's Bench Division of the High Court. The reasons for the creation of this new 'Court' are vividly outlined in the Introduction to the first volume of an old set of law reports called *Commercial Cases*.[4] It was stated that the driving force behind this development was the 'businessmen' of London and the frequent 'complaints' by, in particular, 'commercial men' about the 'delay and expense' of the existing system under which actions were ordinarily tried in the High Court. It is plain from a reading of this short document that there was great dissatisfaction with the existing court procedures which had been introduced only 20 years previously with the enactment of the Judicature Acts 1875. *Commercial Cases* directed a tirade against the existing 'complicated procedures' and the fact that the heavy tome containing the Court's procedural rules (known as the *Annual Practice* and now commonly referred to as the *White Book*) had, in those 20 years, grown to

> two volumes of closely printed matter and contains references to over 7,000 decisions for the most part on points of practice, pronounced at the expense of litigants. They wished to recover property or debts due to them; They found themselves embarked in a long inquiry, with dubious results, into the meaning of rules more or less obscure. It is not to be wondered at that the cost of carrying a case through this maze of rules and judgments has often far exceeded the amount originally in dispute.

It was noted that the existing procedure was 'particularly objectionable to men of business'. It was also emphasised the need for disputes to have a 'prompt decision' and the fact that liabilities that are unsettled at the end of the year are 'intolerable to mercantile men'.

[2] ibid 61.

[3] A Thomas, 'Calendar of Early Mayor's Court Rolls Preserved among the Archives of the Corporation of the City of London at the Guildhall A.D. 1298-1307' (The University Press, 1924).

[4] (1895) Com Cas 1 i-viii.

A comparison is drawn with arbitration to secure a 'speedy result' although the author notes that 'if legal rights were not always understood and recognised by lay tribunals [ie in arbitration] their awards had the merit of finality'. It is against this background that the judges of the Queen's Bench Division decided to establish a separate Commercial List for the 'despatch of commercial business' in respect of 'commercial causes'.[5] The Notice issued by the judges declared that there would be a judge in charge of commercial business (who would generally have experience of commercial matters) and that such judge 'may at any time after appearance and without pleadings make such order as he thinks fit for the speedy determination, in accordance with existing rules, of the questions really in controversy between the parties'.

The reasons given for the establishment of the London Commercial Court are of particular interest as much today as they were some 125 years ago. In other words, it was the speed, finality and cost that the Court can offer to parties in commercial disputes. By all accounts, the London Commercial Court became a great success in the succeeding century and continues to be so. Although there are no hard statistics, a cursory review of *Lloyd's Law Reports* (which focuses on cases in the Commercial Court) would suggest that this was, at least in part, due to the fact that many commercial contracts (including charterparties and bills of lading) incorporated clauses providing for English jurisdiction. In 2015, the Lord Chief Justice of England and Wales announced the introduction of a specialist Financial List to deal with financial claims of £50 million or more or cases that raise issues concerning the domestic and international financial markets: the equity, derivatives, foreign exchange and commodities markets. Interestingly, it includes provision for an innovative test case procedure, the aim of which will be to facilitate the resolution of market issues on which there has been no previous authoritative English precedent.[6]

B. The International Chamber of the Paris Commercial Court

Before delving into the international commercial chambers (ICCs) in France, it is useful to look at the background of the establishment of the country's local commercial courts which, like their English counterpart, come with a colourful history. At present, there are 134 commercial courts in France, of which that in Paris is by far the largest with 180 judges. The development of the commercial courts in France originated in the Middle Ages. The Paris Commercial Court in its present form was established in 1792. It was the successor to the Paris Merchant Court which was created in the sixteenth century pursuant to a Royal Order issued in 1563. In that era, the initial way that parties dealt with commercial disputes was to select referees from respected merchants and accept

[5] 'Commercial causes include causes arising out of the ordinary transactions of merchants and traders; amongst others, those relating to the construction of mercantile documents, export or import merchandise, affreightment, insurance, banking, and mercantile agency and Mercantile usages.'

[6] The Civil Procedure (Amendment No 4) Rules 2015, available at www.judiciary.uk/you-and-the-judiciary/going-to-court/high-court/courts-of-the-chancery-division/financial-list/history; T Etherton and J Flaux, 'Guide to Financial List' (1 October 2015), available at assets.publishing.service.gov.uk/government/uploads/system/uploads/attachment_data/file/644030/financial-list-guide.pdf.

their judgment.[7] This method subsequently became popular throughout the country. Nowadays, most judges in the Paris Commercial Court (including its International Chamber) have been, and some continue to be, entrepreneurs, general counsel for major corporations, and senior managers engaged in the provision of engineering, trade, insurance, banking and financial services.

It is against this history of commercial courts in France that the International Chamber of the Paris Commercial Court (ICPCC) was established in 1995 as a division of the Paris Commercial Court.[8] In 2015, the international chamber was merged with the chamber for EU Law, which had been set up in 1997 to deal with international commercial cases within the EU.[9] The ICPCC now has jurisdiction over transnational disputes of an economic and commercial nature in which a respondent is a non-resident of France or in which a foreign governing law applies.[10] While the ICPCC Protocols do not give specific or express definition as to what amounts to an 'international' commercial dispute, one can ascertain the coverage of the phrase by reference to the examples of disputes heard by the ICPCC, which include disputes relating to commercial contracts and the termination of commercial relationships, transport, unfair competition, damage due to anti-competitive practices and disputes concerning financial instruments and products.[11] As part of the modernisation of the French justice system, in 2018 a new chamber was established under the Paris Court of Appeal, known as the International Chamber of the Paris Court of Appeal (ICPCA), to hear appeals and actions to set aside arbitration awards made in Paris, appeals against orders denying recognition or enforcement of an international arbitration award made in France, and appeals against orders granting or denying recognition or enforcement of an international arbitration award made abroad.[12] The ICPCA conducts rehearings by way of a full merits review on both the facts and the application of the law. The jurisdiction of the ICPCA is reflected in the chamber's model clause which states that it has jurisdiction over

> all disputes arising between the parties in connection with the validity, interpretation or performance or, more generally, with the present contract, shall be submitted, in first instance, to the jurisdiction of the International Commercial Chamber of the Paris Commercial Court and, on appeal, to the jurisdiction of the International Commercial Chamber of the Paris Court of Appeal.[13]

[7] J-B Blaise and R Desgorces, '*Droit des Affaires: Commerçants, concurrence, distribution*' (2013) Librairie générale de droit et de jurisprudence, 156.

[8] Rödl & Partner, 'The International Chamber of the Commercial Court and the International Chamber of the Paris Court of Appeal' (4 May 2021), available at www.roedl.com/insights/litigation-arbitration/france-paris-international-chamber-commercial-court-of-appeal#1.

[9] Qisheng He Research Group, 'The Development of Contemporary International Commercial Courts' (2019) 63.

[10] Protocole relatif à la procédure devant la chambre internationale du tribunal de commerce de Paris ('ICPCC Protocol') Art 1.1.

[11] A Reyes and K Tan, 'International Commercial Courts' (2020) *Dispute Resolution in China, Europe and World* (Springer, 2020), 32.

[12] *ICPCA Protocole relatif à la procédure devant la Chambre Internationale de la cour d'appel de Paris* (the ICPCA Protocol) Art 1.3; French Code of Civil Procedure Arts 1519, 1523 and 1525.

[13] C Vialard, 'The International Chambers of the Paris Courts and Their Innovative Rules of Procedure' (2018), available at www.shearman.com/perspectives/2018/04/paris-courts-and-their-innovative-rules-of-procedure; D Kühner and J Noy-Gsell 'The international chambers of the Paris Commercial Court and of the Paris Court of Appeal' (2019), available at bmhavocats.com/en/2019/07/30/the-international-chambers-of-the-paris-commercial-court-and-of-the-paris-court-of-appeal/#_ftnref11.

Language may be a distinctive feature of the Paris ICCs. Although the Paris ICCs are based on English-French bilingualism, the use of English remains limited. French is the main language of the proceedings including evidence and oral submissions, unless the judge and parties agree otherwise. While written submissions in English may be given without translation, pleadings must be in French.[14] In addition, simultaneous interpretation is available on the application of a party who undertakes to bear the costs. Parties, witnesses, experts and counsel are allowed to interact with the court in English. The judgments of the Paris ICCs are written in French, though an official English translation can be requested at the parties' own cost.[15] Judges sitting in the Paris ICCs are bilingual in French and English, and most have studied or worked in English-speaking countries. Further, the Paris ICCs have the power to appoint judges from the Paris Commercial Court who have specific expertise to hear cases.

C. The Singapore International Commercial Court

The Singapore International Commercial Court (SICC) was established on 5 January 2015 as a division of the High Court of Singapore. As with judgments handed down by the High Court, an appeal against a judgment of the SICC lies to the Court of Appeal of Singapore,[16] unless the parties agree to exclude such right of appeal.[17] In terms of jurisdiction, the SICC has jurisdiction only over the following three categories of cases.[18] The first category concerns cases which fulfil the following four criteria: (1) the action is one that the High Court may hear and try in its original civil jurisdiction; (2) the claim(s) concerned are of an international and commercial nature; (3) the parties have submitted to the SICC's jurisdiction under a written jurisdiction agreement made either before or after the dispute has arisen; and (4) the parties do not seek any relief in the form of or connected with a prerogative order (such as an order of *mandamus*, an order of *certiorari*, or an order of *habeas corpus*).[19] The second category concerns cases relating to international commercial arbitration under the International Arbitration Act 1994.[20] The third category concerns cases transferred to the SICC from the High Court, either on the basis that they are international and commercial in nature, or that they fall within the second category.[21] The SICC is prohibited from declining to assume jurisdiction 'solely on the ground that the dispute between the parties is connected to a

[14] ICPCC Protocol Art 2.3; ICPCA Protocol Art 2.2.

[15] ICPCC Protocol Art 7; Art 7, ICPCA Protocol Art 7.

[16] W Cai, 'International Commercial Court: Institutional Comparison, Conflict of Rules and Construction Path' (2018) 5 *Global Law Review* 177.

[17] Supreme Court of Judicature Act 1969 (Singapore) s 29(*b*) read with Fourth Schedule, para 3.

[18] In addition, the SICC has jurisdiction to hear proceedings for contempt of court in respect of any judgment or order that it has made: Rules of Court (2014 Rev Ed) (Singapore) ('ROC (Singapore)'), O 110 r 7(2)(*b*). From 1 April 2022, the rules of court governing the SICC will be contained in the SICC Rules 2021 (Singapore), but this will not substantively change the SICC's jurisdiction.

[19] Supreme Court of Judicature Act 1969 s 18D(1); ROC (Singapore) O 110 r 7(1); User Guides Note 1. For provisions relating to the High Court's original civil jurisdiction, see Supreme Court of Judicature Act 1969 (Singapore) ss 16–17.

[20] Supreme Court of Judicature Act 1969 s 18D(2); ROC (Singapore) O 110 r 57(1).

[21] ROC (Singapore) O 110 r 7(2)(*a*).

jurisdiction other than Singapore, if there is a written jurisdiction agreement between the parties'.[22]

As to the appointment of judges, in addition to the judges of the Supreme Court of Singapore, the SICC currently has 16 International Judges who come from civil and common law jurisdictions.[23] A person can be appointed as an International Judge if the Chief Justice of Singapore considers that the person has the 'necessary qualifications, experience and professional status'. As the International Judges have practised in different specialised areas of commercial law before their appointment to the SICC, they provide the SICC with expertise in different aspects of international commercial law (including shipping, construction, intellectual property, fintech, joint ventures and international trade). The International Judges are typically assigned to hear cases by matching their experience with the context of the cases. As to foreign lawyers' right of audience before the SICC, contrary to the rest of the Singapore High Court where only lawyers with the requisite Singapore qualification are allowed to practise, the SICC allows foreign lawyers to appear before it in 'offshore cases'.[24] Under Section 36P of the Legal Profession Act, foreign lawyers may be granted full or restricted rights of appearance before the SICC.[25] Foreign lawyers who wish to be registered must be sufficiently proficient in the English language and agree to abide by a Code of Ethics.[26] They must also have at least five years' experience in advocacy.[27]

In terms of applicable law, on the application of any party to proceedings, foreign law may be determined based on submissions (which can be oral or written, or both) instead of the usual common law method of proving foreign law as a matter of fact (which necessitates expert witness testimony).[28] As to the recognition and enforcement of judgments, since the SICC forms a part of the High Court of Singapore, the enforcement of SICC judgments is no different from the enforcement of regular judgments of the High Court. The SICC's judgments can be also enforced extraterritorially by virtue of international arrangements, such as those reflected in the Reciprocal Enforcement of Commonwealth Judgments Act 1921 (RECJA) and the Reciprocal Enforcement of Foreign Judgments Act 1959 (REFJA). Further, Singapore is a party to the 2005 HCCH Convention on Choice of Court Agreements.[29]

[22] ibid r 8(2).

[23] Reyes and Tan, 'International Commercial Courts' (2020) 47.

[24] See *Teras Offshore Pte Ltd v Teras Cargo Transport (America) LLC* [2016] SGHC(I) 02 per Eder IJ.

[25] Legal Profession (Foreign Representation in Singapore International Commercial Court) Rules 2014 (Cap 161) Part 2 sets out the requirements for registration under s 36P of the Legal Profession Act. This registration (and any renewal) is valid for one year: Legal Profession (Foreign Representation in Singapore International Commercial Court) Rules 2014 (Singapore) r 10.

[26] Legal Profession (Foreign Representation in Singapore International Commercial Court) Rules 2014 (Singapore, Cap 161,851/2014) rr 4–6. The Code of Ethics is set out in Sch 1.

[27] ibid r 4(1)(b).

[28] ROC (Singapore) O 110 r 25.

[29] RECJA facilitates the reciprocal enforcement of judgments and awards in the UK and other commonwealth countries such as New Zealand, Malaysia and Australia. REFJA presently only extends to the Hong Kong, not the rest of the PRC: Reciprocal Enforcement of Foreign Judgments Act (Section 3(1)); Reciprocal Enforcement of Foreign Judgments (Hong Kong Special Administrative Region of The People's Republic of China) Order, O 1 (GN No S 93/1999, Rev Ed 2001).

D. The Dubai International Financial Centre Courts

The Dubai International Financial Centre (DIFC) was established in Dubai, one of the seven emirates of the UAE, in 2002. It is the 'first special economic zone' in Dubai with its own independent and internationally regulated regulator and judicial system which is largely based on a common law framework. The Dubai International Financial Centre Courts (DIFCC) were established in 2006 to oversee all financial matters within the DIFC. Originally, the DIFCC's jurisdiction was limited to civil and commercial cases within the geographical areas of the DIFF. In 2011, after the enactment of the Dubai Law No 16,[30] that the DIFCC was empowered to hear any local or international commercial cases with the consent of all parties in dispute.

As to organisational structure, the DIFCC include the Court of First Instance and the Court of Appeal. The Court of First Instance is composed of a judge and has exclusive jurisdiction over: (1) civil or commercial cases and disputes involving the DIFC, any of the DIFC's bodies, or any of the DIFC's establishments; (2) civil or commercial cases and disputes arising from or related to a contract that has been fulfilled or a transaction that has been carried out, in whole or in part, in the DIFC or an incident that has occurred in the DIFC; (3) objections filed against a decision made by the DIFC's bodies, which are subject to objection in accordance with the DIFC's laws and regulations; and (4) any application over which the DIFCC have jurisdiction in accordance with the DIFC's laws and regulations.[31]

The Court of Appeal is composed of at least three judges, chaired by the Chief Justice or the most senior judge, and has exclusive jurisdiction over: (1) appeals filed against judgments and awards made by the Court of First Instance; and (2) the interpretation of any article of the DIFC's laws based upon the request of any of the DIFC's bodies or the request of any of the DIFC's establishments provided that the establishment first obtains leave from the Chief Justice.[32] Foreign judges can be appointed to the DIFCC. At present, the Chief Justice of the DIFCC is a Malaysian and there are three Emirati judges, two English judges, one Singaporean judge, and three Australian judges on the bench.[33] Foreign lawyers can appear before the DIFCC if they are registered with the Dubai Academy of Law and comply with relevant professional ethical practices.[34]

Unlike other UAE legal proceedings, which are conducted in the Arabic language, English is the official language of DIFCC.[35] Further, in the event of any inconsistency between the Arabic and English versions of any judgment, order or direction, the English version shall prevail.[36] In terms of the enforcement of DIFCC judgments, DIFCC judgments can be enforced by the Dubai Courts within the UAE in accordance with the requirements of Dubai Law. For instance, since DIFCC judgments are in English, they

[30] Dubai Law No 16, available at www.kbh.ae/media/law16.pdf.

[31] Court structure, the DIFC, available at www.difccourts.ae/court-structure.

[32] ibid.

[33] ibid.

[34] The Academy of Law's register is made up of two parts. Part I concerns law firms to conduct proceedings before the DIFCC. Part II concerns individual legal practitioners to obtain Rights of Audience before the DIFCC.

[35] DIFCC Rules Para 2.3.

[36] ibid Para 2.4.

must first be translated into Arabic before enforcement is sought.[37] For enforcement outside of the UAE, DIFCC judgments can be enforced by virtue of the international conventions and treaties entered into by the UAE with other countries.

E. The Netherlands Commercial Court

The idea of establishing a commercial court in the Netherlands arose as early as July 2017 when a motion was submitted to the Dutch Parliament. The motion was passed in December 2018. The Netherlands Commercial Court (NCC) consists of the District Court, the Court of Appeal and a Court for Summary Proceedings (principally for interim measures). The NCC opened its doors at the beginning of 2019.[38] In accordance with Article 1.3.1 of the Rules of Procedure of the Netherlands International Commercial Court 2018,[39] parties may bring an action before the NCC District Court if the following elements are present:

(1) The action is a civil or commercial matter in connection to a particular legal relationship within the autonomy of the parties and is not subject to the jurisdiction of the NCC Sub-District Court or the exclusive jurisdiction of any other chamber or court.
(2) The matter concerns an international dispute.
(3) The parties to the proceedings have designated the Amsterdam District Court as the forum to hear their case or the Amsterdam District Court has jurisdiction to hear the action on other grounds.
(4) The parties to the proceedings have expressly agreed in writing for proceedings to be before the NCC District Court in English.

In this respect, the scope of 'civil' and 'commercial' in the provisions is broad and includes contractual disputes, tort claims, property law disputes and some insolvency-related matters, such as directors' liability in insolvency. Similarly, 'international dispute' has a broad meaning. A dispute can be considered 'international' when: (1) there is at least one party to the proceedings living out of the jurisdiction; (2) there is a multinational treaty or foreign law applicable to the dispute; (3) the dispute arises from an agreement written in a language other than Dutch; or (4) where the dispute involves cross-border interests.[40] Article 1.3.3 of the Rules of Procedure[41] sets out the circumstances in which an appeal may be made to the NCC Court of Appeal. Both the NCC District Court and the NCC Court of Appeal have the power to decide whether a case complies with the abovementioned elements and thus whether the court has jurisdiction over the case.

The language used in the proceedings in the NCC is English unless the parties unanimously request the use of Dutch.[42] The NCC however retains the power to request

[37] Dubai Law No 12 of 2004 Art 7.
[38] Home, the NCC, available at www.rechtspraak.nl/English/NCC/Pages/default.aspx.
[39] Rules of Procedure of the Netherlands International Commercial Court 2018, available at www.rechtspraak.nl/SiteCollectionDocuments/draft-ncc-rules-june-2018.pdf.
[40] Reyes and Tan (n 11) 46.
[41] Rules of Procedure of the Netherlands International Commercial Court 2018, available at www.rechtspraak.nl/SiteCollectionDocuments/draft-ncc-rules-june-2018.pdf.
[42] NCC Rules Art 2.1.1.

the translation of the parties' submissions into other languages. In general, case law, analysis and documents in Dutch, English, German or French need not be translated unless the NCC so directs.[43] The judges of the NCC are all selected from judges on the Dutch bench. With the exception of summary proceedings, trials heard before the NCC are usually conducted by a three-judge panel.[44] Parties' pleadings, such as a statement of claim or a defence, must be submitted through a lawyer who is a member of the Dutch Bar.[45] Lawyers who are members of the EU Bar, the European Economic Area or Switzerland may act for a party together with members of the Dutch Bar. But they cannot represent a party alone.[46] The procedures for hearings before the NCC are relatively flexible, as the parties are free to make agreements on most procedural matters. For instance, the parties can agree to exclude the statutory evidentiary rule or to create extra rules on the confidentiality of documents presented in the proceedings. They can also agree on costs.[47] The NCC is equipped with an e-NCC system which facilities the exchange of information.[48] As with other judgments handed down by European courts, the NCC's judgments can be enforced pursuant to the agreements and conventions entered into between the Netherlands and other states.

F. The China International Commercial Court

On 29 June 2018, the China International Commercial Court (CICC) was established by the Supreme People's Court of China (SPC) and became part of the SPC. The CICC has two branches; the First International Commercial Court located in Shenzhen in Guangdong Province; and the Second International Commercial Court located in Xi'an in Shanxi Province. International commercial disputes before the CICC are heard by a panel of three or more judges. The CICC applies the law as agreed by the parties, which can sometimes be the common law. The judges can hear cases in English or Chinese. Distinctively, the CICC adopts a system of 'first instance is final'. In other words, the judgments handed down by the CICC are final and binding on the parties, without further avenue of appeal.

In terms of the CICC's jurisdiction, Article 2 of the Provisions of the SPC on Several Issues Concerning the Establishment of International Commercial Courts issued in September 2018 (the CICC Provisions) provides that the CICC shall have jurisdiction over: (1) international commercial cases within the jurisdiction of the SPC whose subject matter is worth more than RMB 300 million and which the parties have agreed to submit to the CICC; (2) subject to approval, international commercial cases that the Higher People's Courts deem should be tried by the SPC; (3) international commercial cases which are likely to have a major impact nationwide; (4) cases relating to international commercial arbitration, such as applications for setting aside an

[43] ibid Art 2.1.2.
[44] ibid Art 3.5.1.
[45] ibid Art 3.1.
[46] Reyes and Tan (n 11) 45–46.
[47] NCC Rules Art 8.3.
[48] M Requejo Isidro, 'International Commercial Courts in the Litigation Market' (2019) MPILux Research Paper Series.

award or for the recognition and enforcement of an award; and (5) other international commercial cases that need to be tried by international commercial courts as deemed by the SPC.[49] However, despite the CICC Provisions, the CICC's jurisdiction is as yet not entirely clear as its judicial ambit stems from the SPC's interpretations and is technically subject to the rules of the Chinese Civil Procedure Law, which are constantly undergoing revision.[50] It is the CICC's goal to provide a one-stop dispute resolution platform, rather than simply function as a specialised commercial court. As can be seen from the CICC Provisions:

> [T]he SPC will select competent international commercial mediation institutions, international commercial arbitration institutions and international commercial courts to build together a dispute resolution platform which integrates mediation, arbitration and litigation, and form a 'one-stop' international commercial dispute resolution mechanism.[51]

In the event the parties choose to mediate, the CICC can appoint a mediation institution. The CICC is even prepared to incorporate the terms of a mediated settlement agreement reached by the parties into a judgment.

Remarkably, the CICC has set up a subcommittee known as the International Commercial Expert Committee (ICEC) to which renowned experts, lawyers, judges and scholars in the field of international or Chinese commercial law are nominated. There were 31 experts on the CICC's first ever list of International Commercial Expert Committee. There are now over 50 ICEC members. The functions of these experts are wide and cover both judicial and administrative areas, ranging from providing mediation upon parties' request, advising on specific issues concerning mostly foreign law at the request of the CICC, and providing recommendations for the development of the CICC and the SPC. As a part of China's judicial modernisation, the CICC has launched online service platforms including an electronic litigation service platform and a trial process information disclosure platform.[52] These platforms aim to enable parties to file documents, make payments, exchange documents, or even attend hearings completely online.

At present, China has entered into approximately 40 bilateral judicial assistance treaties and conventions with other countries, pursuant to which the CICC's judgments can be recognised and enforced.

III. Reasons for the Establishment of ICCs

A. International Trade and Dispute

Different countries have their own considerations for the establishment of ICCs. In general, the establishment of ICCs and the models chosen by each country are rooted

[49] CICC Provisions Art 2, available at cgc.law.stanford.edu/wpcontent/uploads/sites/2/securepdfs/2018/10/BRText-20180701-provisions-re-intl-commercial-courts-english.pdf.

[50] L Ang, 'International Commercial Courts and the Interplay Between Realism and Institutionalism: A Look at China and Singapore' (2020), available at harvardilj.org/2020/03/international-commercial-courts-and-the-interplay-between-realism-and-institutionalism-a-look-at-china-and-singapore.

[51] CICC Provisions Art 11.

[52] ibid Art 18.

in their historical traditions, judicial level and the background of the times. Viewing the establishment of ICCs from a micro-perspective, the straightforward reason for the establishment of ICCs in many countries is to tackle the shortcomings of the existing international commercial dispute settlement mechanism. On the other hand, viewing from a macro-perspective, the reasons for the emergence of ICCs may perhaps be divided into two categories.

First, the establishment of some ICCs has been driven by the needs of the business community. In other words, it was driven by the rapid development of the economy as a result of which there is practically no geographical limit to doing business nowadays. As the number of commercial disputes increased and became more complex, they required a higher standard and degree of specialisation for their resolution. They needed judges with the professional ability and experience to handle commercial disputes in accordance with best international practice.[53] The London Commercial Court and the Paris ICCs are good examples of such courts.

Second, the other category is driven, at least in part, by the aim of becoming a regional centre for dispute resolution. Most of the new ICCs including the SICC, the DIFCC and the CICC are of such a category.[54] That aim may also have underlying geopolitical or economic purposes. These ICCs are mainly courts for the settlement of commercial disputes that have been specifically set up by a relevant state for political or economic purposes.[55] Such courts are usually established later in time and focus on the flexibility of institutional design to attract more parties to settle international commercial disputes before those courts. From a political or economic perspective, the establishment of ICCs and specialist courts has become an international trend in Asia and Europe. ICCs in Asia include the DIFCC established in 2006, the Qatar International Court and Dispute Resolution Centre established in 2009, and the SICC in 2015. Subsequently, Kazakhstan, India and Abu Dhabi respectively established the Astana International Financial Centre Court (AIFCC), the Commercial Court of India, and the Abu Dhabi Global Market Court (ADGMC). The CICC was established in 2018. In Europe, the UK established the Business and Property Courts of England and Wales in 2016 to challenge traditional commercial courts.[56] The Netherlands and France respectively established the NCC and the International Chambers of the ICPCC. International commercial courts have also been established in Stuttgart and Mannheim in Germany. Belgium has also considered the introduction of an ICC into its court system, although the proposal has not been carried forward.

The point is that, to enhance their competitiveness in the field of international commercial dispute resolution, an increasing number of countries have reformed their traditional litigation system and set up special international commercial dispute settlement bodies to meet international trends. The underlying rationale is (it is submitted) a strong belief that the rule of law and an efficient court system for the resolution of commercial disputes performs an important – perhaps crucial – part in the economic

[53] Qisheng He Research Group (n 1) 60.
[54] ibid 61.
[55] ibid 64.
[56] H Gu and Y Lin, 'A preliminary study on the construction of China's international commercial tribunals' (2018) 17 *Journal of Dalian Maritime University* 7, 8.

development of a country or region. It is fair to say that ICCs can be income-generating both for the courts and for the local legal community as well as service providers (lawyers, accountants, etc) closely linked to dispute settlement. Countries hope to develop their ICCs and attract dispute resolution work from other states. The establishment of an ICC might thus enhance a country's standing and yield economic benefits at the same time. For instance, the most successful of the new wave of ICCs would seem to be the SICC, the DIFCC and the CICC. The direct reason for establishing SICC was an urgent need for an effective forum in Asia to resolve the cross-border commercial disputes due to the rapid growth of commercial activity there. More importantly, Singapore hopes to broaden the scope of Singapore's own legal services and turn Singapore into the International Dispute Resolution Centre of Asia.[57] The DIFCC, on the other hand, provides judicial dispute resolution service to its particular area – the DIFC. 'Making Dubai a global financial centre' and 'building the world's leading international commercial court' are the main visions of the DIFC.

The CICC is an interesting variation on the foregoing theme. The establishment of the CICC is a typical national strategy-driven achievement. General Secretary Xi Jinping first proposed the Belt and Road Initiative in 2013, the core purpose of which is to build 'political self-confidence, economic integration, culturally inclusive community of shared interests' and a 'community of shared future'.[58] The Belt and Road Initiative has built a platform for the economic development of countries along the main maritime and land routes from China to Europe and Africa. It should be noted that the economic and trade exchanges under the Belt and Road Initiative are different from traditional business activities. The Belt and Road Initiative builds a long-term development platform and pays more attention to the maintenance of commercial trade between commercial parties. It is a great challenge to commercial dispute resolution bodies, because it not only requires that disputes be resolved fairly, but that the disputes are resolved in ways that maintain the relationships between the commercial subjects involved. Although there are many dispute resolution bodies in the countries along the relevant routes, considering the different subjects involved in the dispute, the wide variation in cultures, and the increasing number and complexity of international disputes, it has been difficult to meet the Belt and Road market participants' needs for cross-border dispute resolution by relying solely on the existing judicial systems of every country along the Belt and Road. To obtain a fair judgment of a dispute, it is necessary to have a unified and orderly dispute resolution model. In addition, the political turmoil, weak economic base, and relatively young legal systems in some countries along the Belt and Road will challenge the construction of a unified and complete commercial dispute settlement mechanism. With the further development of the Belt and Road Initiative, China, as the initiator, shoulders a responsibility and obligation to build a more professional and pluralistic mechanism for resolving disputes among the countries along the route. Obviously, China would like to develop the CICC as an attractive forum for the resolution of commercial disputes arising from the Belt and Road Initiative. The CICC is thus the product of the Belt and Road initiative and

[57] S Menon, 'Response by the Honourable Chief Justice Sundaresh Menon at the Opening of the Legal Year 2013 and Welcoming Reference for the Chief Justice' (4 January 2013), para 33.

[58] See, for example, 'Belt and Road helps build community with a shared future' *China Daily* (19 November 2021), available at www.chinadaily.com.cn/a/202111/19/WS6197a3a6a310cdd39bc76700.html.

directly serves the Belt and Road dispute settlement needs. It reflects China's aim to 'create a stable, fair, transparent and convenient international business environment and serve and safeguard the Belt and Road construction'.

B. Providing an Alternative to Arbitration

There has been a diversification of international commercial dispute resolution mechanisms. At present, the main mechanisms are conciliation, mediation, arbitration and litigation. Pending a wider adoption of the Singapore Convention, agreements reached by way of conciliation and mediation may not be readily enforceable across borders. This possibility gives rise to concerns that the parties might take a lot of time and effort at conciliation and mediation, but eventually fail in enforcing a resulting agreement. On the other hand, the high cost of arbitration, the length of time taken to arbitrate disputes, and the increasing technicality of arbitration may deter parties from opting for international commercial arbitration to resolve their disputes.[59] This is undoubtedly a key reason motivating countries such as Singapore and China to set up their own ICCs. In the past, international commercial disputes were almost always settled by way of arbitration or litigation before domestic courts. However, court procedures, which are based on non-dispositive and pre-established rules, were mostly designed for domestic settings (as opposed to cross-border ones).[60] Only in a few legal systems have the court procedures take into account the international dimension of commercial dispute resolution.[61] This situation has graphically been described as a 'market failure'.[62] As a result, legislators in different countries have tried to overcome this failure by establishing specialised courts or chambers tailored for international commercial proceedings. At the very least, the presence of ICCs offers international commercial parties a choice between arbitration and litigation for the resolution of their disputes.

IV. The Benefits of ICCs

A. Making Up for the Shortcomings of Arbitration

Traditional international arbitration attaches great importance to the protection of the privacy of the parties. Arbitral proceedings and the arbitration awards are usually not

[59] T Qi and X Rui, 'The Innovation of Civil and Commercial Dispute Settlement Mechanisms along the 'Belt and Road' (2017) 5 *Chinese Review of International Law* 41.

[60] M Isidro, 'International Commercial Courts in the Litigation Market' *Max Planck Institute Luxembourg for Procedural Law Research Paper Series No 2019(2)*, available at www.mpi.lu/fileadmin/mpi/medien/research/WPS/MPILux_Research_Paper_Series_2019_2_Requejo_ International_Commercial_Courts.pdf.

[61] F Gascón Inchausti and M Requejo Isidro, 'EU Procedural Law Study: Mutual Trust General Report' (2017) *EU Publications*, available at publications.europa.eu/en/publication-detail/-/publication/531ef49a-9768-11e7-b92d- 01aa75ed71a1/language-en.

[62] K Ramesh, 'International Commercial Courts: Unicorns on a Journey of a Thousand Miles' (13 May 2018), para 3, available at www.sicc.gov.sg/docs/default-source/modules-document/news-and-article/international-commercial- courtsunicorns_23108490-e290-422f-9da8-1e0d1e59ace5.pdf.

open to the public. Confidentiality measures are taken even for cases that do not involve trade secrets. While on the surface, this may seem to protect the privacy of the parties to the greatest extent, this has also bred problems – including reducing the predictability of arbitration outcomes. As such, fairness has become more difficult to guarantee. However, insofar as litigated cases are open to the public, the reasoning of courts is therefore for all to behold and assess. It allows commercial parties to have more realistic expectations of the likely outcome of their disputes before commencing the same. Judicial transparency reduces frivolous commercial disputes and leads to the more efficient use of public resources.

Further, the arbitral tribunal's jurisdiction derives from the parties' agreement to arbitrate. However, since the arbitration agreement binds only signatories, third parties are not bound by the arbitration agreement, and may not be joined to the arbitral proceedings at will without the consent of the signatories. In response to this limitation, one of the attractions of ICCs is that, whether the parties agree or not, the court generally has the right to join third parties or consolidate disputes, as long as the third parties or consolidated disputes are closely related. For instance, the SICC can merge two cases on the application of a party. This is particularly helpful for international construction disputes where multiple contractors and consultants are often involved.[63]

Litigation costs in ICCs are also different from international arbitration. In litigation, the parties generally do not have to bear the fees and other costs of the judge hearing their case. On the other hand, the parties to an arbitration are required to bear the tribunal's fees and provide financial support for trial facilities and logistics.[64] In addition, the cost of filing proceedings in ICCs may be lower than the cost of participating in international commercial arbitration. Thus, the emergence of ICCs can lead to competition between the two modes of dispute resolution and reduce the currently high costs of international commercial arbitration. Some countries or regions may have designed their ICCs to attract more commercial parties by subsidising the costs of litigation before such forums. That would mean that litigation before ICCs could be substantially less expensive than the cost of arbitration.[65]

ICCs are generally efficient. Efficiency is a comparative concept. Unlike arbitration, the structure and rules of the court proceedings are already in place and there is no need to draw up terms of appointment for the tribunal or Terms of Reference for the dispute. Accordingly, ICCs can process cases faster than arbitration. Many ICCs are not only speedier than arbitration, but also more efficient than courts in various countries. Domestic courts usually have one or more possible levels of appeal. However, commercial cases before ICCs may be confined to a decision at first instance, with no appeal available, as with the CICC. Long processes at first instance and appeal are not conducive to commercial predictability. ICCs have special provisions for the trial

[63] S Brekoulakis, 'Subcontracts and multiparty arbitrations in construction disputes' in *The Guide to Construction Arbitration* (Law Business Research Ltd, 2017).

[64] ibid 20.

[65] For a further discussion of the costs of appearing before an ICC, see A Reyes, 'Choice of Court: Considering an International Commercial Court for the Resolution of Contractual Disputes' in M Moser and C Bao (eds), *Managing 'Belt and Road' Business Disputes: A Case Study of Legal Problems and Solutions* (Wolters Klower, 2021) 118.

of commercial disputes, which will greatly save the time for dispute resolution and determine the rights and obligations between two or more parties early, thereby protecting their interests more effectively.

B. Greater Professionalism, Expertise, and Flexibility

In terms of jurisdiction, ICCs may not require the parties to submit a dispute that has a close connection with the country where the ICC is located. It will be enough to found jurisdiction if the parties have entered into a choice of court agreement designating an ICC as the forum to deal with disputes arising out of a commercial transaction. The jurisdictional requirements are lenient. An example is the SICC. As long as the parties have designated the SICC as the forum to deal with their disputes, the court may not refuse to accept the case on the ground that the parties or the case has no connection with Singapore. Compared with ordinary courts, ICCs are specialised in resolving international commercial disputes. This professionalism may be reflected (among others) in the appointment by ICCs of foreign judges with considerable expertise in the handling of transnational commercial disputes, by ICCs allowing foreign lawyers to represent parties, and by an ICC's adoption of bespoke rules of procedure catering especially for problems (such as the involvement of multiple parties) commonly associated with commercial disputes.

Nationality is often a problem with arbitrations. The rules of many arbitral institutions (such as those of the International Chamber of Commerce and the Hong Kong International Arbitration Centre) usually do not allow the president of a tribunal to have the same nationality as any party to an arbitration. In contrast, in addition to appointing national judges, emerging ICCs such as the SICC, the DIFCC, the ADGMC, Qatar International Court and Dispute Resolution Centre and the AIFCC in Kazakhstan have recruited judges all over the world. Their benches of judges are characterised by internationalisation. Their judges not only speak English but also have rich experience in dealing with international commercial disputes, and more importantly, they have different legal backgrounds and professional strengths. This breakthrough and innovation on the nationality of judges largely avoids a restriction encountered in arbitration.

Another feature in proceedings of ICCs is that foreign lawyers are often allowed a right of audience at least in certain circumstances (for example, in 'offshore cases'). There is no doubt that the choice of lawyer is important to parties. Therefore, ICCs which eliminate the normal prohibition against representation by foreign lawyers can be attractive to parties. For instance, the SICC adopts a registration system which allows foreign lawyers to represent their clients before the SICC as long as the lawyers have registered with the SICC. There are two types of registration: full and restricted. Foreign lawyers with full registration may participate in 'offshore cases'[66] as lawyers, while foreign lawyers with restricted registration may only appear in specific cases to

[66] ROC (Singapore), O 110 r 1(2)(f).

make submissions on specific questions of foreign law.[67] In contrast, foreign lawyers are more likely to be qualified to appear as advocates in the DIFCC because the jurisdictional system of the DIFCC does not have the concept of 'offshore cases'. Therefore, the registration of foreign lawyers does not distinguish between those with full registration and those with only restricted registration. This means that registered lawyers have the same authority as local lawyers to appear before the DIFCC once registered. Further, in the UAE, foreign lawyers can appear as representatives of UAE citizens, and lawyers from foreign law firms can advise on issues related to international and national law.[68] As there is no restriction on the scope of powers of the agent of foreign lawyers in Dubai, foreign lawyers can in theory represent their clients in any type of civil and commercial cases in the DIFCC.

The ICCs, even if part of a national court system, will often enjoy a degree of independence as a separate division. As just mentioned, the jurisdictional basis of ICCs will often be different from that of domestic courts. More particularly, ICCs will frequently have their own tailor-made rules for dealing specifically with transnational commercial disputes. An example is the SICC which, from April 2022, has had its own set of rules.[69] These have been designed to incorporate the best features of litigation in civil and common law jurisdictions as well as features from the world of arbitration. The rules should considerably enhance the SICC's ability to deal with cross-border commercial disputes in ways that may not be open to the normal Singapore courts.

C. Diversity

It has been noted (for instance, in connection with the SICC's new procedural rules) that ICCs can combine the advantages of arbitration and litigation. That is, they can give full play to party autonomy on the one hand and judicial authority and transparency on the other. This system which takes account of the advantages of litigation and arbitration is the core innovation of ICCs. Nonetheless, litigation before ICCs and international commercial arbitration should (it is submitted) best be regarded as complementary rather than competitive. The emergence of ICCs provides one more option for parties to resolve disputes and this is perhaps the major benefit of ICCs. As Justice Quentin Loh, now President of the SICC, stated:

> Arbitrators should not think of the SICC cannibalising their work. Instead they should look upon it as an integral part of a vibrant dispute resolution hub. … If Singapore succeeds in becoming the premier dispute resolution hub of Asia, the pie will grow, hopefully enormously,

[67] T Hwee Hwee, J Yeo and C Seow, 'The Singapore International Commercial Court in Action – Illustrations from the First Case' (2016) 28 *Singapore Academy of Law Journal* 692, 708–09. See also Singapore Legal Profession Act 1966, s 36P.

[68] J Kumar Krishnan and P Purohit, 'A Common Law Court in an Uncommon Environment: The DIFC Judiciary and Global Commercial Dispute Resolution' (2015) 32 *The American Review of International Arbitration*.

[69] The Singapore International Commercial Court Rules 2021.

> your [ie, the arbitration practitioner's] share will also grow, hopefully enormously too, even though it forms a smaller percentage of the whole.[70]

This is the reason why the SICC and SIAC can exist at the same time in Singapore and be equally successful. ICCs are about increasing the choices available to commercial parties for the determination of their disputes. Diversity in available options enables parties to go for the mode best suited to their circumstances.

D. Breaking through the Limits of National Boundaries

With the increase of international trade and commercial disputes, establishing a unified legal system and commercial dispute resolution mechanism has become one of the biggest aspirations of commercial parties. If the disputes between cross-border commercial parties are simply resolved by local courts, there would be a strong temptation for each country's courts only to apply their own domestic rules with rare, if any, reference to the laws of other countries. This would certainly not be the best way for developing a unified set of cross-border business law.[71] This means that every time a cross-border commercial transaction is agreed in some country, the parties must ensure that the activities which they carry out comply with all relevant local commercial laws. Where there are many different legal regimes involved, there is a risk of failing to consider one country's commercial laws with potentially disastrous consequences. That would deter cross-border trade which would then be regarded as only for the brave or possibly foolhardy.

Although, by itself, the emergence of ICCs will not bring about uniform commercial legal regimes, they are a positive step towards harmonisation. This is because most ICCs will not require the application of the law of the country in which they are located, and the specific applicable law (often as agreed by the parties in their contract) can be identified and the law's content determined by the ICC. The resulting judgment by the ICC would constitute a publicly available precedent which would at least have persuasive value when cited in similar cases in the courts of other countries, thereby gradually constructing a jurisprudence applicable to international commercial transactions. As the Chief Justice of Singapore has observed:

> [C]ourts can no longer operate in jurisdictional silos. It is desirable that the international commercial courts, together with courts in the major commercial centres, continue to establish links with their counterparts with a view to collectively developing international commercial law in a consistent manner that is supportive of transnational business.[72]

[70] Quentin Loh's opening address at the Regional Arbitral Institutes Forum Conference 2014 (see the Singapore Institute of Arbitrators September 2014 Newsletter (1 August 2014)), available at www.siarb.org.sg/images/Events/Newsletters/SIArb_Newsletter_Sep2014.pdf.

[71] See, eg, PwC, '21st CEO Survey: The Anxious Optimist in the Corner Office' (2018), observing that CEOs worldwide believe that the world has been moving towards multiple commercial law regimes as opposed to converging towards a single global system.

[72] S Menon, 'Transnational Commercial Law: Realities, Challenges and a Call for Meaningful Convergence' (2013) *Singapore Journal of Legal Studies* 231, 250–51.

E. Simplification of Proceedings

The convenience and flexibility of proceedings is one of the major advantages of ICCs. Take the SICC as an example. Parties are free to choose the evidentiary rules which will apply to their case and may opt to waive their right to appeal or to object to the recognition and enforcement of the SICC judgments. Such features have been described as 'completely alien' to the European landscape.[73] In addition, the SICC, the DIFCC and the AIFCC's disclosure systems are similar to discovery in arbitration under the International Bar Association (IBA) Rules on the Taking of Evidence in International Arbitration.[74] With regard to the rules of evidence, the DIFCC has the right to apply the rules it deems appropriate in the circumstances. It is not bound to treat foreign law as a fact to be proved and can instead apply such rules as it considers appropriate including determining issues of foreign law by direct legal submission.[75] While the AIFCC states that 'any procedural requirements may be waived if it is satisfied that it meets the overriding objective', the most important objective remains that of dealing with cases fairly.[76]

The simplification of proceedings and the associated reduction of paperwork is relevant to the use of advanced technological facilities, particularly in the ICCs in Asia. The SICC, the CICC, the DIFCC and the AIFCC are committed to integrate the use of technology into their procedures. Examples are the CICC electronic litigation service platform, the SICC electronic system for the filing of the court documents, and the AIFCC electronic archiving system. These electronic systems allow parties to file lawsuits and send electronic files almost anytime from anywhere. This is no doubt convenient for parties located in different countries and regions.

F. Unification of Litigation Language

In general, domestic courts require use of the official language of a country, even when hearing foreign-related cases. Parties who are unable to give evidence in such language usually have the right to apply for interpretation. Most ICCs are able to have litigation conducted in English, which is essentially the global language. The unification of the language used in ICCs makes it relatively fair to parties from different countries. The 'unification' referred to here does not mean that all ICCs are solely using English, but merely reflects that fact that ICCs on the whole use English as the dominant language of litigation. At the same time, in almost all ICCs, domestic and foreign judges are required to be proficient in English. The importance of language and communication skills should not be overlooked when it comes to the resolution of international commercial disputes.

[73] Isidro, 'International Commercial Courts in the Litigation Market' (2019), available at www.mpi.lu/fileadmin/mpi/medien/research/WPS/MPILux_Research_Paper_Series_2019_2_Requejo_International_Commercial_Courts.pdf.

[74] DIFCC Rules rr 28.15 and 28.16.

[75] DIFC Law, No 10 of 2004, Art 50(c). See also *Fidel v Felecia Faraz* [2015] DIFC CA 002 [47].

[76] AIFCC Regulations Reg 8.

V. The Problems of ICCs

ICCs have been created in response to the growth of cross-border trade and to overcome the shortcomings of international dispute resolution mechanisms including arbitration. ICCs have many attractive advantages. However, nothing is perfect. Problems exist. While some problems are common to all ICCs, others are unique problems to one or more specific ICCs. Some problems may be addressed by learning from experience, whereas some shortcomings need to be explored jointly by ICCs in various countries.

A. Recognition and Enforcement of Judgments

In general, judgments are recognised and enforced in other countries on the basis of bilateral treaties, multilateral conventions, Memorandums of Guidance (MOGs) between courts, or the domestic laws of a particular state. The difficulty of the bilateral treaty approach is that these may take a long time to negotiate, and treaties must then be signed and ratified by each state. Take China as an example. At present, China has entered into approximately 36 treaties for the recognition and enforcement of judgments. Under the Belt and Road Initiative, if China's goal is to establish a network of bilateral treaties to recognise and enforce judgments among countries along the Belt and Road, it means that more than 60 separate bilateral treaties will have to be negotiated and concluded in the future. This is clearly not an easy task and may not provide any short-term benefit to the Belt and Road Initiative.[77] Multilateral conventions may take an even longer time to negotiate and come into effect.

An MOG, on the other hand, can serve as a more convenient approach to the recognition and enforcement of judgments, based on the concept of reciprocity between the judicial organs of two or more states. An MOG is a non-legally binding document that sets out the criteria and procedures which will be applied when the courts which are parties to the MOG decide whether to recognise and enforce each other's judgments. It is generally signed by the judicial organs of the respective countries as opposed to a bilateral treaty or multilateral convention, which typically involve the executive or legislative branches of a state. Therefore, when compared with international treaties and conventions, the time needed for negotiation and conclusion of MOGs is usually shorter in practice. This, however, comes with an obvious disadvantage in that MOGs are non-binding in nature. A court is not obliged to comply with the relevant provisions of an MOG when it comes to the recognition and enforcement of a foreign judgment. In this regard, it is important to bear in mind that, where parties have agreed on the jurisdiction of a foreign court, the position is that the judgment of that foreign court will generally be enforceable subject to limited exceptions (such as fraud).[78] It is understood

[77] Reyes and Tan (n 11) 34.

[78] See, eg, in Hong Kong, P Harris SC, *The Conflict of Laws in Hong Kong*, 3rd edn (Sweet & Maxwell, 2017) at para 9.007.

that the position is similar in common law as well as civil law jurisdictions. The underlying rationale is that an agreement between the parties as to the jurisdiction of a foreign court constitutes a submission to the jurisdiction of that court. The ability for parties to agree that a particular ICC shall have jurisdiction and to be able to enforce a judgment of that court in a foreign country on the basis of such an agreement is an important advantage which is often forgotten.

The position with respect to the enforcement of arbitration awards is different. Originally, it was often difficult to enforce an arbitration award in a foreign country.[79] This gave rise to a problem of finality. This problem was solved to a large extent by the 1958 New York Convention. At the international level, the question of finality was further addressed in 1985 by the UNCITRAL Model Law which, in effect, prohibited any right of appeal. Thus, Article 5 of the Model Law provides that 'in matters governed by [the Model Law], no court shall intervene except where so provided in [the Model Law]'; and the grounds on which an award may be challenged are limited to those stipulated in Article 34(2).[80] Many countries around the world have adopted the Model Law in either its 1985 or 2006 version.[81] This has led to a boom in international commercial arbitration.

B. Imperfection and Ambiguity of Regulations

Each ICC operates in accordance with its own rules. But it is a challenge for foreign parties and lawyers to understand the laws and regulations of different countries. For example, in the Netherlands, the Rules of Procedure of the NCC do not specify what evidentiary rules the court may apply. Presumably, the rules of evidence which the court should apply are the rules of evidence provided for in the Dutch Code of Civil Procedure. Thus, parties and their lawyers will have to know what those evidentiary rules are. Vague and ambiguous features of the regulations governing litigation in ICCs are possibly more apparent in the CICC. While the CICC Provisions adopted in the 1743rd meeting of the Judicial Committee of the SPC in 2018 stipulated that the CICC's goal is to provide a 'one-stop' dispute resolution platform by integrating mediation, arbitration and litigation institutions, there has been no clear guidance on how these modes of dispute resolution are to be linked in a 'one-stop' platform. There is no specified criterion as to how mediation and arbitral institutions are to be selected. Nor is there any provision as to which judicial body has the power to select such institutions. In addition, on a plain reading, the CICC Provisions reflect the problem of 'forum-centricity' by effectively requiring cases to have a connection

[79] ibid at paras 10.002–10.003, Hong Kong's Arbitration Ordinance (Cap 609) passed in 1 June 2011, which is largely based on the UNCITRAL Rule, substantially increased the ease of recognition and enforcement of foreign awards.

[80] UNCITRAL Model Law on International Commercial Arbitration, available at www.uncitral.org/pdf/english/texts/arbitration/ml-arb/06-54671_Ebook.pdf.

[81] Legislation based on the Model Law has been adopted in 84 states in a total of 117 jurisdictions. See, eg, United Nations, 'Commission on International Trade Law', available at uncitral.un.org/en/texts/arbitration/modellaw/commercial_arbitration/status.

with China notwithstanding the broad definition of an 'international commercial case' under Article 3 of the CICC Provisions.[82] By virtue of Article 2(1) of the CICC Provisions,[83] despite a consensual agreement between the parties having been reached, the CICC will only have jurisdiction over a case if Article 34 of the Civil Procedure Law applies. That requires that the court chosen by the parties have a connection with the dispute depending on 'where the defendant is domiciled, where the contract is performed, where the contract is signed, where the plaintiff is domiciled or where the subject matter is located'.[84] Similarly, with respect to Article 3(3), there is ambiguity as to what amounts to 'a significant impact on the country'.[85] This term may also suggest an actual connection with the forum in light of the near identical words used in Article 20 of the Civil Procedure Law.[86] As a result, it appears that the CICC's jurisdiction is subject to the requirements of the Chinese Civil Procedure Law. These are likely to restrict the judicial ambit of the CICC significantly.

C. Disadvantages of Litigation in Some ICCs

Unlike arbitral awards, judgments are typically subject to appeal. Different ICCs may have different appeal mechanisms. This may contradict a core purpose behind the establishment of ICCs which is to resolve international commercial disputes quickly and efficiently. Appeal bodies have been set up for the NCC, the SICC and the DIFCC. For example, the judgments of the SICC may be appealed to the Court of Appeal of Singapore. Similarly, judgments of the DIFCC can be appealed to the Court of Appeal of the DIFCC. In France, cases first come to the International Chamber of the ICPCC, and appeals (if any) will be heard by the International Chamber of the ICPCA. Some cases may, with leave, even go to the *Cour de cassation*, where some highly significant judicial interpretation is involved.[87] In the Netherlands, cases decided by the District Court of the NCC are appealable to the Court of Appeal of the NCC. There is also a court of cassation. In England, court judgments can be appealed to the Court of Appeal and, in

[82] Art 3 of the CICC Provisions provides that 'A commercial case with one of the following circumstances may be determined to be an "international" commercial case as referred to in the [CICC Provisions]: (i) one or both party/-ies is/are (a) foreigner(s), stateless person(s), or foreign enterprise(s) or organization(s); (ii) the habitual residence(s) of one or both party/-ies is/are outside the territory of the People's Republic of China; (iii) the subject property is outside the territory of the People's Republic of China; (iv) the legal facts that generated, changed, or eliminated the commercial relationship occurred outside the territory of the People's Republic of China'.

[83] CICC Provisions Art 2(1) oprovides that 'the [CICC] shall accept … first-instance international commercial cases where the parties have, in accordance with Article 34 of the Civil Procedure Law, agreed to select the jurisdiction of the Supreme People's Court and where the subject amount is at least RMB 300 million'.

[84] Civil Procedure Law of the People's Republic of China Art 34 (revised in 2017), available at cicc.court.gov.cn/html/1/219/199/200/644.html.

[85] CICC Provisions Art 2(3) provides that 'the [CICC] shall accept … first-instance international commercial cases that have a significant impact on the country as a whole'.

[86] Civil Procedure Law Art 20 provides that 'the Supreme People's Court shall have jurisdiction as the court of first instance over the following types of civil cases (1) cases with significant impact on the whole country; and (2) cases that the Supreme People's Court deems it should try itself'.

[87] Attributions de la Chambre Commerciale, Financière et Économique, available at www.courdecassation.fr/jurisprudence_2/chambre_commerciale_574/commerciale_financiere_11638.html.

limited circumstances, to the Supreme Court and usually only with leave. The requirement of leave operates as an important filter and, in recent times, has restricted the number of appeals save in the most important and difficult cases. In contrast, the CICC features a one-level one-trial system. According to the CICC Provisions, the CICC is a permanent judicial body of the SPC, the judgments of which are final. Aggrieved parties therefore simply cannot appeal against the CICC's judgments. The CICC's one-trial system favours the quick and efficient resolution of international commercial disputes at the expense of parties' right to appeal.

D. Lack of Foreign Lawyers in Some ICCs

Foreign judges and foreign lawyers in ICCs are one of the main advantages of attracting commercial parties to bring their disputes there. However, not all ICCs allow for foreign judges to sit or foreign lawyers to appear. In this regard, the CICC is a remarkable example. The judges appointed to the bench of the CICC are restricted to current judges of the Chinese courts and Chinese nationals who must be experienced in international commerce with a strong ability to work in both English and Chinese. Further, the parties to a dispute before the CICC can only be represented by Chinese law-qualified lawyers, as foreign lawyers do not have a right of audience in Chinese courts. The prohibition on parties' ability to appoint foreign lawyers constitutes a hurdle which may deter parties from choosing the CICC as a forum for dispute resolution, since foreign lawyers are likely to be preferred by foreign nationals in cases where the applicable law is a foreign law agreed by the parties.[88] These constraints on the nationality of judges and lawyers constitute limitations to the internationalisation of the CICC and will likely constrain the popularity of the CICC. The CICC was established for the Belt and Road Initiative, so that most of the disputes before it will be between Chinese commercial parties on the one hand and parties from countries along the Belt and Road on the other. In the face of such disputes, if the CICC only has Chinese judges, foreign parties may question the neutrality of the court. The NCC has a similar problem as NCC judges are all from the Netherlands. It remains to be seen how the bench of these courts will be broadened in the future to maintain their competitiveness up with other ICCs.

VI. Conclusion

ICCs have emerged with the growth of international trade. ICCs are professional and independent in general. But they are not all the same. Each possesses different strengths and weaknesses in terms of jurisdiction, flexible procedures, experienced judges and foreign lawyers' right of audience. Nor are they a perfect solution in terms of overcoming

[88] J Chaisse and X Qian, 'Conservative Innovation: The Ambiguities of the China International Commercial Court' (2021) 115 *American Journal of International Law* 17.

the difficulties of international commercial dispute resolution. The new ICCs are clearly still a work in progress whose advantages and limitations will no doubt attract some and deter others. Those deterred will then likely stick to international commercial arbitration as their preferred mode of cross-border dispute resolution. But ICCs are constantly evolving and over time are poised to have a significant impact on the development of a transnational commercial law.

4

The Driving Forces behind the Swinging Pendulum

BERNARD EDER[1]

I. Introduction

The concept of international commercial courts (ICCs) may sound intriguing yet paradoxical. Strictly speaking, proceedings before ICCs are neither arbitration nor litigation in its conventional sense before a national court. Rather, in nature proceedings before ICCs are more akin to a combination of both. In recent years, the attention of the international arbitration community has been drawn to the establishment of ICCs in various jurisdictions in Europe, Asia and the Middle East. Some have claimed that ICCs are competitors of arbitration as they offer an alternative forum to the international business community.[2] Others, however, have remained sceptical about the practical values of these new worldwide dispute-resolving platforms. Some years and one pandemic later, arbitration continues to thrive. How have these ICCs been performing? Are they now in a better position to challenge arbitration? Summing up the questions raised, and opinions expressed, during the discussion session in the 3rd Judicial Roundtable on Commercial Law ('Judicial Roundtable') held virtually on 29 September 2021, the account here will build on the panorama provided by the previous chapter and further explore the changing trend of international businesses in choosing between arbitration and ICCs for dispute resolution.

In section II of this chapter, reasons for the changing relationship between court litigation and arbitration as a mode of dispute resolution will be outlined. In section III, the pros and cons of the pendulum's swing towards arbitration as international businesses' currently preferred mode of dispute resolution will be considered. Section IV centres on the rationale behind the rise of ICCs. Finally, section V considers various supposed shortcomings of ICCs as compared with arbitration.

[1] The author would like to acknowledge and thank Anselmo Reyes and Ho Ching Him for their input and assistance in preparing this chapter.

[2] See, for example, M Hwang, 'Commercial courts and international arbitration – competitors or partners?' (2015) 31 *Arbitration International* 193; X Kramer and J Sorabji, 'International Business Courts in Europe and Beyond: A Global Competition for Justice?' (2019) *Erasmus Law Review* 1, available at www.elevenjournals.com/tijdschrift/ELR/2019/1/ELR-D-19-00023.pdf.

II. Historical Perspective: What are the Reasons for the Swinging Pendulum?

As this title suggests, the relationship between arbitration and litigation is not a fixed one. It is not so much a tug-of-war, but rather a gradual ebb and flow or, even more figuratively speaking, a pendulum swinging from time to time in favour of arbitral tribunals or litigation before the courts. Embodied within the expression 'swinging pendulum', there is a presumption that it is possible to attract legal work from one platform (arbitration) to another (litigation) and vice versa. Of course, this presumption might be true in the modern world where the rapid advancement of technology and the globalisation of commerce have given business entities a much greater variety of choices for dispute resolution. However, it is not something unique to this century.

For example, in medieval times, an English Court might stay proceedings in favour of arbitration, that is, allowing the parties to have what was referred to in the court records as a *jour d'amour* or 'love day'. On a love day, the parties to a dispute were supposed to resolve their differences through arbitration rather than the courts.[3] This suggests that, even then, arbitration was looked upon favourably as a method of what we would now call 'alternative dispute resolution'. The swinging pendulum can also be seen in the approach taken by foreign merchants for dispute resolution in Europe during later stages of the medieval ages, when merchants doing business in foreign states preferred to avoid disputes, to the point of being prepared where necessary to write off their losses.[4] If, for whatever reason, the practice of writing off losses could not be adopted, they preferred to resort to mediation or arbitration to resolve their disputes. In particular, merchants would avoid a country's central courts, almost at all costs, because of the notorious consumption of time and money in legal proceedings. Eventually, this common approach taken by the merchants to have their disputes resolved out of court led to the creation of specialised courts dealing with commercial and maritime issues in various European countries. As a result, several European cities found themselves in a situation where local merchants were eager to conduct business elsewhere and the cities' relative judicial autonomy gave them the power for institutional arrangements to make courts more attractive platforms for cross-border commercial dispute resolution. The pendulum has thus been swinging to and fro between arbitration and litigation in Europe over a long period.

Another example of this swing comes from Asia. In China and Japan, there have been strong tendencies for judges to promote reconciliation between parties by non-adversarial means even after litigation has begun. In modern times, the Japanese family courts invariably require parties to mediate almost all disputes first before the courts proceed to hear substantial arguments. It is said that such high emphasis on the mediation system is built upon Asian values, which stress the maintenance of family and

[3] E Powell, 'Settlement of Disputes by Arbitration in Fifteenth-Century England' (1984) 2 *Law and History Review* 21.

[4] J Waters Bennett, 'The Mediaeval Loveday' (1958) 33 *Speculum* 351; O Gelderblom, *Cities of Commerce: The Institutional Foundations of International Trade in the Low Countries, 1250–1650* (Princeton University Press, 2013).

social harmony.[5] In eighteenth-century China, to remove the huge backlog of cases that had built up in the Chinese court system, the emperor's advisors suggested that parties should be actively dissuaded from going to court. The advice to the emperor was that anyone who went to court should face financial ruin. Apart from that, parties were encouraged to settle their disputes by some form of ad hoc mediation or arbitration before 'elders', that is, persons valued for their wisdom and who held a position of responsibility and authority in the parties' villages. Even in China during late imperial times, different clans (the predominant form of kinship organisations at that time)[6] maintained formal intra-clan mechanisms for dispute resolution with the objective of not enforcing a party's strict legal rights against another party but arbitrating a 'compromise' between them. The Chinese clan rules thus discouraged litigation and favoured arbitration.[7]

The pendulum has continued to swing in recent years. Many Chinese courts today are overwhelmed by the number of cases being brought, especially after the Supreme People's Court reformed and streamlined procedures for the commencement of litigation with the aim of providing citizens with easier access to justice.[8] As a result, it is estimated that the average Chinese judge may need to handle around 200 cases annually. On the other hand, the swinging pendulum in China has been influenced by the pro-arbitration attitude of the Chinese judiciary.[9] An example may be seen in the signing of the Supplemental Arrangement Concerning Mutual Enforcement of Arbitral Awards[10] between Hong Kong and Mainland China on 27 November 2020. The Supplemental Agreement clarifies the Arrangement Concerning Mutual Enforcement of Arbitral Awards between Mainland China and Hong Kong[11] in force since 1 February 2000. The Supplemental Agreement enables awards rendered under the arbitration law of Mainland China to be enforced in Hong Kong. The strong pro-arbitration attitude in China is also reflected in the number of cases handled by the courts. The number of cases before the Shanghai Financial Court in the past two to three years has been lower

[5] A Saito, 'International Commercial Arbitration and International Commercial Courts: Towards a Competitive and Cooperative Relationship' in *Harmonising Trade Law to Enable Private Sector Regional Development*, Faculty of Law, Victoria University of Wellington Hors Serie Volume XX (2016) 33, 51 available at www.victoria.ac.nz/__data/assets/pdf_file/0004/1186978/Saito.pdf.

[6] P Ebrey and J Watson, *Kinship Organization in Late Imperial China, 1000–1940* (University of California Press, 1986).

[7] A Greif and G Tabellini, 'Cultural and Institutional Bifurcation: China and Europe Compare' (January 2010) CEPR Discussion Paper No 7648, available at repec.cepr.org/repec/cpr/ceprdp/DP7648.pdf.

[8] The Supreme People's Court of China, 'Chinese Court Judicial Reform (2013–2018)' (1 March 2019) 105, available at english.court.gov.cn/specials/ChineseCourtJudicialReform2013-2018.pdf.

[9] See, eg, O Browne and I Devendra, 'Chinese Court Takes Pro-Arbitration Approach to Validity of International Arbitration Agreement' (26 February 2019), available at www.latham.london/2019/02/chinese-court-takes-pro-arbitration-approach-to-validity-of-international-arbitration-agreement/#_edn3.

[10] The Supreme People's Court of China and the Government of Hong Kong SAR, 'Supplemental Arrangement Concerning Mutual Enforcement of Arbitral Awards between the Mainland and the Hong Kong Special Administrative Region (Courtesy English translation)' (27 November 2020), available at www.doj.gov.hk/en/mainland_and_macao/pdf/supplemental_arrangementr_e.pdf.

[11] The Supreme People's Court of China and the Government of Hong Kong SAR, 'Arrangement Concerning Mutual Enforcement of Arbitral Awards between the Mainland and the Hong Kong Special Administrative Region' (21 June 1999) (Courtesy English translation), available at www.doj.gov.hk/en/legal_dispute/pdf/mainlandmutual2e.pdf.

than the number submitted to the Shanghai International Arbitration Center, especially cases related to private investment disputes.

Looking beyond Asia, in more recent times, the momentum of the swinging pendulum in England has been subject to radical changes owing to the Arbitration Act 1996.[12] The situation in England in the first half of the twentieth century was best described by Lord Scrutton's memorable phrase in *Czarnikow v Roth, Schmidt & Co*[13] that 'there must be no Alsatia in England in which the King's writ does not run'. Thus, the English courts had been exercising considerable interference in the arbitral process although that was eventually swept away in England by the enactment of the Arbitration Act 1979, culminating in the Arbitration Act 1996, in favour of party autonomy.[14]

By the old special case procedures which existed before the 1979 Act, the English courts placed increasing emphasis on the application of legal principles to arbitration.[15] The supervisory jurisdiction of the courts developed in a way that resembled more of an appellate process in arbitration. However, scholars at that time argued that this approach made London a much less attractive venue for dispute resolution in the eyes of commercial entities worldwide.[16] To alleviate this problem without completely abolishing the mechanism of allowing courts to intervene, it was suggested that the overall landscape between arbitration and subsequent appeals in courts would have to be modified to achieve greater finality and certainty in arbitral awards.[17] To achieve this, the Arbitration Act 1979 repealed the special case procedures, although the new legislation did not provide specific rules as to how the matter of leave to appeal from arbitrators to the courts should be handled, save and except for providing that leave could only be granted on a question of law which may 'substantially affect the rights of one of the parties'.[18]

However, the circumstances in which leave to appeal against an arbitration award might be granted were clarified by the important decision of the House of Lords in *Pioneer Shipping Ltd v BTP Tioxide Ltd (The Nema)* by way of an exposition of certain guidelines generally referred to as the 'Nema Guidelines', which were subsequently enshrined by statute in the Arbitration Act 1996, s 69. In summary, an applicant seeking leave to appeal against an arbitration award must show not only that the appeal involves a question of law which 'substantially affects the rights of the parties' but also that either: (i) the arbitral tribunal's decision on that issue was 'obviously wrong'; or (ii) if the issue is of 'general public importance', is, at the very least, open to 'serious doubt'. In practice,

[12] M Lewis, 'An Alsatia in England' (1984) 47 *MLR* 171.

[13] [1922] 2 KB 478.

[14] See, for example, s 1(b) which stipulates that parties 'should be free to agree how their disputes are resolved'; s 46(1)(a) which stipulates that the arbitral tribunal 'should decide the dispute in accordance with the law chosen by the parties as applicable'.

[15] B Conrick, 'Where the King's writ does not run: The Origins and Effect of the Arbitration Act 1979' (1985) 1 *Queensland Institute of Technology Law Journal*, available at www5.austlii.edu.au/au/journals/QITLawJl/1985/1.pdf.

[16] A Colman, 'Arbitrations and judges – how much interference should we tolerate?' (2006) 72 *Arbitration* 217–18.

[17] K Diplock, 'The Alexander Lecture' (1978) 44 *Arbitration* 107.

[18] Arbitration Act 1979, s 1(3)(b).

this has had the effect of severely restricting the number of appeals. As a result, arbitration has thrived in England as a demonstration of party autonomy and choice within a tolerant 'light touch' of statutory supervisory regime.[19] The relationship between arbitration and litigation in England was succinctly summarised by Lord Thomas as one of 'maximum support, minimum interference'.[20]

However, the balance between, on the one hand, the importance of maintaining finality in arbitral awards and, on the other, the effect on the development of the common law by allowing appeals on points of law is extremely difficult to strike. In this regard, Lord Diplock noted the importance of the court's role in the development of English commercial law as he put it in *The Nema*:[21]

> It is only if parties to commercial contracts can rely upon a uniform construction being given to standard terms that they can prudently incorporate them in their contracts without the need for detailed negotiation or discussion. Such uniform construction of standard terms had been progressively established up to 1979, largely through decisions of the courts upon special cases stated by arbitrators. In the result English commercial law has achieved a degree of comprehensiveness and certainty that has made it acceptable for adoption as the proper law to be applied to commercial contracts wherever made by parties of whatever nationality.

As at today, only a small portion of arbitration cases reaches the courts in England.[22] In the same vein as Lord Diplock when deciding *The Nema*, the former Lord Chief Justice of England and Wales, Lord Thomas, also expressed his concerns in the diminishing number of appeals in courts:[23]

> As I have explained reform was effected to promote the use of London as a centre for dispute resolution largely based on contracts based on the common law as developed in the Commercial Courts of London. However, the consequence has been the undermining of the means through which much of the common law's strength – its 'excellence' was developed – a danger not merely to those engaged in dispute resolution in London, but more importantly to the development of the common law as the framework to underpin the international markets, trade and commerce.
>
> …
>
> In my view, therefore, we must address what has happened and restore an essential part of the way in which courts are able to continue the development of the law that underpins our trade, financial system and our prosperity.

[19] Peter Gross's speech at Jonathan Hirst QC Commercial Law Lecture (1 May 2018, London) at [6], available at www.judiciary.uk/wp-content/uploads/2018/05/speech-by-lj-gross-hirst-lecture-distribution-may-2018.pdf.

[20] See Lord Thomas's speech at the National Judges College, 'Commercial Dispute Resolution: Courts and Arbitration' (6 April 2017, Beijing) at [25], available at www.judiciary.uk/wp-content/uploads/2017/04/lcj-speech-national-judges-college-beijing-april2017.pdf.

[21] [1982] AC 724, 737.

[22] See 'Arbitration in Court', a report by Osborne Clarke containing an analysis of some 538 arbitration cases which came before the English Courts over the period 2010–20.

[23] See Lord Thomas's speech at The Bailii Lecture 2016 'Developing commercial law through the courts: rebalancing the relationship between the courts and arbitration' (9 March 2016, London) at §§22, 24.

Lord Thomas considered various ways of achieving the objective of 'the development of the law' including the possibility of widening the limb of 'great public importance':[24]

> One answer might be to suggest that we go back to a more flexible test for permission to appeal before Lords Denning and Diplock restricted the ability to appeal by the interpretation he gave to the 1979 Act and before this was codified in the 1996 Act. That would enable the courts more readily to develop the law whilst leaving arbitration as an important means of dispute resolution.

He continued:[25]

> So far there has been no change, but I have no doubt that change to the section 69 test is one of the options that must be considered. The restriction in relation to appeals where the question is one of general public importance is, I have little doubt, a serious impediment to the growth of the common law. The benefits to the development of the common law is therefore obvious as it would increase the potential for greater numbers of appeals which would provide the means to maintain a healthy diet of appellate decisions, capable of developing the law particularly on issues of general public importance.

In this regard, it is worth noting that Lord Toulson even described the diminishing number of appeals as transferring the common law from a living instrument to an 'ossuary'.[26] However, by limiting the extent to which courts are allowed to intervene in arbitral awards, it would seem that arbitrations in England thrived at the expense of the diminished potential for the courts to develop and explain commercial law. It still remains for us to work out how the balance between the two should be struck.[27]

Apart from the drastic reforms brought about by the new legislations as discussed above, another obvious driving force of the pendulum towards arbitration is the very nature of arbitration. Arbitrations are generally perceived by many to be cheaper and quicker than conventional litigation in court which also come with the benefit of confidentiality. However, in the author's own experience, on the contrary, arbitration is hardly ever cheaper and is often much slower when one views this mode of dispute resolution as a whole. The service offered by certain ICCs is often faster and cheaper with a strong focus on robust case management.[28] As for confidentiality, some ICCs, such as the Singapore International Commercial Court (SICC), also allow for confidentiality in appropriate circumstances.

Another reason why it is often said that the pendulum has swung in favour of arbitration in the last 50 years is the perception that, because of the Convention on the Recognition and Enforcement of Foreign Arbitral Awards (New York Convention), arbitration awards are easier to enforce than a court judgment. This is not necessarily true: in summary, the position (at least as a matter of English law) is that if a contract provides that

[24] ibid §32. However, such a suggestion is highly controversial and has been subject to strong views to the contrary. See for example my own Keynote Address to the Chartered Institute of Arbitrators 'Does arbitration stifle development of the law? Should s.69 be revitalised ?' (28 April 2016), available at www.arias.org.uk.

[25] ibid §34.

[26] *Kennedy v The Charity Commission* [2014] 2 WLR 808 [133].

[27] For further discussion, see Pt IV of this book.

[28] See, for example, K Hart, 'Arbitration: The Good, the Bad and the Ugly' (May 2015) *Business Credit*, available at www.bellnunnally.com/27F299/assets/files/News/BC-May15_Hart.pdf.

all disputes between the parties shall be referred to the exclusive jurisdiction of a foreign court, that court is deemed to have jurisdiction over the parties[29] with the result that, in such circumstances, the enforceability of the judgment of that foreign court is no different in reality to the enforceability of an arbitration award. It was also suggested during the Judicial Roundtable that a reason why the pendulum swung towards arbitration is the parties' ability through that mode to the use of another country's law as governing law in an attempt to avoid domestic courts (which may, for example, be perceived as corrupt or too slow). The swing in this regard has arguably been accelerated by decolonisation in the late 1950s where businesses at that time had a general suspicion about the justice as administered by fledgling courts in newly established countries. Commercial parties, therefore, turned to new platforms in the form of arbitration of their own choice which appeared to be more independent than traditional institutions.

Of course, one cannot downplay the effects on arbitration brought by the rapid growth of international trade globalisation, which gave rise to the dramatic rise in high-value cross-border transactions. For instance, if party A in country X enters into a transaction with party B in country Y, the method and choice of venue for the resolution of any disputes that may arise will be important. Arbitration in a neutral venue had always been the obvious and perhaps the only answer, until ICCs provided the prospect of a neutral venue with highly experienced international judges to resolve cross-border commercial disputes.

III. Pros and Cons of the Swing

Having reviewed the changing dynamics between litigation and arbitration, it is equally important to consider the potential effects of the swing towards arbitration as a preferred means of international commercial dispute resolution. In broad terms, is such a swing a good thing?

It must always be remembered that arbitration is purely voluntary. Without a valid arbitration agreement, no one can force a party to go to arbitration. It follows that, logically, if commercial parties opt for arbitration, they should not be prevented from so doing. In that sense, the swing in favour of arbitration is of course a good thing as it reflects a higher degree of choice and freedom in the market of the platforms for dispute resolution. On the other hand, and as already mentioned above, there is a strong view that the growing popularity of arbitration as a means to resolve global business disputes hinders the development of the common law.[30] Against the trend towards judicial transparency, the popularity of international arbitration is often criticised for falling short of the paramount legal doctrine of open justice of public proceedings and of judgments. That doctrine would apply if the disputes are brought to litigation, rather

[29] Compare, for example, *Dicey, Morris & Collins on the Conflict of Laws*, 15th edn (Sweet & Maxwell, 2012), Rule 43 Fourth Case, at §14-076.

[30] See, eg, B Rix, 'Confidentiality in International Arbitration: Virtue or Vice?' Singapore Management University, Jones Day Professorship in Commercial Law Lecture, Singapore (12 March 2015) in which he said 'As more and more international commercial cases go to arbitration rather than the courts, we are more and more losing sight of the basic feedstock of our commercial law', available at law.smu.edu.sg/sites/default/files/

than arbitration. As pointed out by Lord Thomas, 'an effective justice system is no less than fundamental to the rule of law'.[31] Scholars have observed that the development of jurisprudence is highly dependent on the notion of open justice where court judgments are open for scrutiny by appeal judges, by practitioners, by academics and by the public at large. Novel ideas publicly discussed and explored can subsequently feed into counsel's future submissions. It is by such debate that the law develops.[32]

In contrast, arbitrations, in which hearings and awards almost invariably take place in private, are the complete antithesis of these processes. Since 'both the arbitration and the arbitral award are not generally a matter of public record',[33] there is at least some force in the argument that the growing popularity of international arbitration hinders the development of jurisprudence, at least to the extent which may not be easy to evaluate quantitatively. In this regard, Lord Briggs made some strong comments in a speech about the importance of case law delivered to a financial conference in the Netherlands in 2018. He said:[34]

> The just determination of disputes by independent judges in public courtrooms, and the publication of the reasons for their judgments, is a corner stone of the rule of law, as much in the commercial and financial spheres as it is in crime and public law. However complex the law has become, there can be no rule of law unless its development takes place in public, for all to be able to see and learn what the law is, and for academics to be able to apply and proclaim their invaluable criticism of judicial thought processes.

This was echoed by the Chief Justice of Singapore Sundaresh Menon:[35]

> Arbitration, by its very nature, cannot provide a complete solution to propel the vessel of global commerce forward. Arbitration was conceived as an ad hoc, consensual, convenient and confidential method of resolving disputes. It was not designed to provide an authoritative and legitimate superstructure to facilitate global commerce. It cannot, on its own, adequately address such things as the harmonisation of substantive commercial laws, practices and ethics.

Given the validity of the foregoing disadvantages of the swing of the pendulum, a second question naturally follows: does it matter? From a practical point of view, lawyers have suggested that the migration of cases from litigation to arbitration does matter in significant ways. For example, in the context of shipping law, it has been a matter of controversy whether the one-year time limit for bringing suit in cargo claims under Article III Rule 6[36]

law/CEBCLA/Notes_Confidentiality_in_International_Arbitration.pdf, and John Thomas's speech at The Bailii Lecture 2016 (n 23).

[31] John Thomas's speech at the DIFC Academy of Law Lecture, 'Commercial Justice in the Global Village: The Role of Commercial Court' (1 February 2016) at [7], available at www.judiciary.uk/wp-content/uploads/2016/02/LCJ-commerical-justice-in-the-global-village-DIFC-Academy-of-Law-Lecture-February-2016.pdf.

[32] S Malik, 'The Empire Strikes Back: Derivatives disputes, the financial list, test case scheme and arbitration' (2021) 16 *Capital Markets Law Journal* 251, 262.

[33] *Halliburton Company v Chubb* [2020] UKSC 48 [6].

[34] M Briggs, 'Dispute Resolution in Uncertain Times' at P.R.I.M.E. Finance conference, The Hague, The Netherlands (22 January 2018), available at www.supremecourt.uk/docs/speech-180122.pdf.

[35] S Menon, 'International Courts: Towards a Transnational System of Dispute Resolution' DIFC Courts Lecture Series 2015.

[36] Art III of Rule 6 of the Hague-Visby Rules provides that 'in any event the carrier and the ship shall be discharged from all liability in respect of loss or damage unless suit is brought within one year after delivery of the goods or the date when the goods should have been delivered'.

of the Hague-Visby Rules applies to cases of misdelivery after discharge of the cargo from the ship. Different textbooks offer different answers on this issue.[37] Unsurprisingly, different tribunals have given different reasons in support of their contrary conclusions. Such lack of consistency in the application of the law is unsatisfactory when predictability is a vital requirement of an effective dispute resolution mechanism.

It is submitted, however, that 'hindering the development of jurisprudence' may be too strong a way of characterising the swing of the pendulum in favour of arbitration. This is because there is a dearth of concrete empirical evidence establishing that the relationship between arbitration and litigation is ultimately a zero-sum game in which a prima facie 'win' for arbitration means a corresponding 'loss' for the courts and vice versa.[38] Analysing the trend in the number of cases in commercial courts, Cara North has remarked that:[39]

> It is impossible to conclude from these figures that the decline in the number of claims issued before English courts is a consequence of the popularity of arbitration. Such a conclusion would require the collection of data over a longer period of time, a better understanding of the court statistics and comparative analysis of arbitration and litigation trends. Absent such information, it is difficult to confidently assess the decline in the number of cases, the reasons for such a decline, and whether the success of arbitration is truly having the negative impact on commercial litigation that academics and judges fear. This is an area that warrants further research and consideration.[40]

It would also be unreasonable to put the blame of the so-called 'hindering' on the parties who prefer private dispute resolution mechanisms over public ones. For one reason, analytically, the ultimate and legitimate wish of these parties is simply to resolve their commercial disputes. It is therefore within their party autonomy to opt for arbitration if they consider it to be a better option over litigation. It is at heart a business decision. For another reason, these parties have no duty (business, legal, moral or otherwise) to take the route of litigation, which naturally comes with the risk of subsequent appeals against the award by an aggrieved party. Parties have no obligation to develop the case law on a particular subject. This point was emphasised by Lord Saville of Newdigate, a former Law Lord and Supreme Court Justice, when he said:[41]

> People use arbitration to resolve their disputes, not to add to the body of English commercial law. Why should international parties be put to the expense and delay occasioned by appeals to the court, often followed by further appeals to the Court of Appeal and the Supreme Court?

[37] See, eg, A Abid and Y Khalid. 'Rule of Prescription Under Article III, Rule 6 of Hague/Hague-Visby Rules: When Does the Clock of Limitation Start Ticking?' (2020) 14 *The Open Transportation Journal* 38; *cf*, A Kasi, 'Hague/Hague-Visby Rules: Carriers' Obligation and Defences' in A Kasi, *The Law of Carriage of Goods by Sea* (Springer, 2021) 271–322.

[38] M Saville, 'Reforms will threaten London's place as a world arbitration centre' *The Times* (28 April 2016), available at www.thetimes.co.uk/article/reforms-will-threaten-londons-place-as-a-world-arbitration-centre-02t50mgrd.

[39] C North, 'The Erosion of Commercial Common Law – the relative merits of litigation and arbitration' *JUSTICE* (8 January 2018).

[40] See also, B Rix, 'Judicial Review of the merits of arbitration awards under English Law' in JC Betancourt (ed), *Defining Issues in International Arbitration: Celebrating 100 Years of the Chartered Institute of Arbitrators* (OUP, 2016) 29.49.

[41] *The Times*, 28 April 2016.

> Why, in other words, should they be obliged to finance the development of English commercial law? The same point was made in 1979 by Lord Devlin, answering those who were against curtailing the then-existing right of appeal on the grounds that the development of English commercial law would suffer if decisions on debatable points were not published in the law reports. 'So there must be an annual tribute of disputants to feed the minotaur. The next step would, I suppose, be a prohibition placed on the settlement of cases concerning interesting points of law'.

In any event, commercial cases involving significantly important legal issues have found their way to courts via appeals from arbitral proceedings.[42] An example is *Globalia Business Travel SAU v Fulton Shipping Inc.*[43] In that case, the judge in the London Commercial Court disagreed with, and reversed, the arbitrator's decision. Subsequently, the English Court of Appeal reversed the judge's ruling. The UK Supreme Court finally allowed the appeal and restored the commercial judge's ruling. This is a classic case of how commercial law can be refined and developed even by way of a dispute originating in an arbitration. Some have expressed the view that the inherent confidentiality of arbitration proceedings exacerbates the problem of the erosion of the principle of open justice. That view, however, overlooks the fundamental distinction between respect for the 'transparency of process and procedure' and respect for the 'confidentiality of the substance of the dispute'.[44] The fact that the latter is preserved in arbitration does not of itself reduce the need for the former. In actuality, arbitrations have struggled to address the requirement of transparency when there is little or no assistance from a supportive court system. The well-known decision of the UK Supreme Court on the arbitrator's duties of disclosure in relation to the issue of apparent bias in *Halliburton v Chubb Bermuda Insurance Ltd*[45] is a telling example.

Thus, it would be wrong to label the swing of the pendulum in favour of arbitration in a binary way as either a good or a bad thing. The position is not one of 'either/or, but not both'. Arbitration should not be taken as the only beneficial way ahead for commercial dispute resolution. This would be particularly true for the disputes which are not subject to a valid arbitration agreement. Courts should instead take the occasion of the swing in favour of arbitration to build their strengths and reduce their weaknesses as commercial dispute resolution service providers. They need to raise their game insofar

[42] See, for example, *The Simona* [1989] AC 788; *The Golden Victory* [2007] UKHL 12; *The Achilleas* [2008] UKHL 48; *The New Flamenco* 7 [2017] UKSC 43.

[43] [2017] UKSC 43. In that case, charterers repudiated a time charterparty. Owners accepted the breach and sold the vessel for a larger sum than they would have if the vessel had been sold at the end of the charterparty. Charterers argued in arbitration that owners should give credit for their financial gain on the sale. The arbitrator held that credit should be given.

[44] C Galway, 'The tensions between confidentiality and transparency in international arbitration' (2003) 14 *American Review of International Arbitration* 121.

[45] [2020] UKSC 48. In that case, the parties could not agree on the identity of the third arbitrator. After a judge of the Commercial Court appointed M, it transpired that M had been nominated by Chubb as an arbitrator in two other arbitrations concerning overlapping subject matters. Halliburton applied for M's removal on the ground of apparent bias but failed. The Supreme Court upheld the judge's ruling and provided guidance on the application of the apparent bias test to arbitrators appointed to adjudicate overlapping issues by a common party as well as the nature of the disclosure that needs to be made and the consequence of non-compliance of disclosure requirements.

as international commercial dispute resolution is concerned. Courts could then offer a compelling alternative to arbitration which businesses can opt for because litigation and court judgments are able to address difficulties that arbitration and arbitral awards are unable to deal with effectively. Such considerations lead to the third question: To the extent that the swing towards arbitration does create problems, what steps (if any) can courts take to address them?

One obvious answer is the lack of an avenue of appeal from an arbitration award on a question of law. That form of recourse was rejected by the UNCITRAL Model Law.[46] Nevertheless, the possibility of an appeal on a question of law has been retained in England[47] although only in very limited circumstances, and then only with permission of the court.[48] It is also subject to an opt-out by agreement of the parties.[49] As already noted, the result is that the number of appeals in England has remained small. On the issue of possible appeals from arbitral awards, a consultation took place in 2019 in Singapore which considered whether to allow appeals to the courts on a question of law arising out of an international, as opposed to domestic, arbitral award.[50] It is understood that no final decision has yet been taken by the Singaporean authorities in this regard.[51] This prompts the question of whether it would be a good idea to allow an appeal on a question of law at least in limited circumstances and subject always to the permission of the court. Would it assist to swing the pendulum back in favour of courts? The position in Hong Kong is somewhat like that in England so that an appeal on a question of law arising out of an award can be brought before the court under the Arbitration Ordinance.[52] But there is a significant difference. This avenue of appeal is only available on an opt-in basis. Interestingly, this mode of recourse does not appear to have been widely adopted by commercial parties in their contracts. Prior to the present opt-in regime, there was a system in Hong Kong of applying for leave to appeal against arbitral awards on a point of law. But that mechanism resulted in cases where a question of fact was dressed up as a question of law to obtain leave for the purpose of reversing the factual findings of the arbitral tribunal.

It is submitted that, considered in the round, the possibility of an appeal to the courts on a question of law in limited circumstances with the permission of the court is beneficial. One can argue about the details, such as whether there should be an 'opt-out' or an 'opt-in' choice for the parties. While it is readily accepted that there are some disadvantages such as delay and increased cost, it is in the author's own experience of the English system that, overall, such means of recourse is hugely beneficial

[46] For example, Arts 35 and 36 of the Model Law provide that an arbitral award is to be recognised as binding and the enforcement of which may only be refused on specified grounds.

[47] Arbitration Act 1996,s 69(1), which provides that 'Unless otherwise agreed by the parties, a party to arbitral proceedings may (upon notice to the other parties and to the tribunal) appeal to the court on a question of law arising out of an award made in the proceedings'.

[48] Arbitration Act 1996, s 69(2)(b).

[49] Arbitration Act 1996, s 69(1).

[50] The Ministry of Law, 'Public Consultation on International Arbitration Act', available at www.mlaw.gov.sg/news/public-consultations/public-consultation-on-international-arbitration-act.

[51] L Ying Tan and C Sim 'Appeals on Questions of Law in International Arbitration – A Comprehensive Perspective from New York' [2020] SAL Prac 18, available at journalsonline.academypublishing.org.sg/Journals/SAL-Practitioner/Arbitration-and-Mediation/ctl/eFirstSALPDFJournalView/mid/590/ArticleId/1530/Citation/JournalsOnlinePDF.

[52] Arbitration Ordinance (Cap 609), Sch 2, S 5.

not only to the development of the law but also to the parties themselves by providing an inroad for some limited extent of court intervention on important issues of law. The effect of this suggestion remains unclear at this stage given that in England the number of appeals from awards has remained small. But the proposal echoes with Lord Thomas's remarks:[53]

> [I]t must always be remembered that:
>
> (a) It is the courts that develop the law. Arbitration does not.
>
> (b) Courts articulate and explain rights, including definitive rulings on the scope and interpretation of contractual clauses, financial instruments and so on. Arbitration does not.
>
> (c) As has been very rightly noted, 'open court proceedings enable people to watch, debate, develop, contest, and materialize the exercise of both public and private power'. Arbitration does not.

It may be true that 'the idea of courts being in competition with arbitration and with each other for international work would not be universally accepted, because courts are public goods, and their purpose is the administration of justice'.[54] But the existence of the swinging pendulum is a good thing by itself when one views it from a macroscopic perspective. The tension between what arbitration can offer and what the courts can offer is ultimately beneficial. Over the years, the 'competition' between arbitration and litigation has brought innovative changes in courtroom systems. These innovations are not limited to new technical advancements, but also include the courts' own initiative to renew their practice directions. France's Civil Code on contract law was substantially amended in order to render contract law in France more 'accessible, predictable, influential and commercially attractive'.[55] In 2009, Justice Barrett[56] of the New South Wales Supreme Court and Lord Neuberger[57] respectively suggested that video-conferencing was a feasible way for court proceedings to take place.

Such innovations have no doubt assisted the hearings in courts worldwide during the pandemic. In the UK, cases such as *Pyrrho Investments Limited v MWB Property Limited*[58] saw the English court ordering resort to artificial intelligence (AI) in the form of predictive coding to reduce time and costs for the review of over three million documents. The same justification was used subsequently in *Brown v BCA Trading Ltd*[59] when the English court ordered the use of predictive coding to replace traditional methods of reviewing trial documents. That resulted in estimated savings of costs of

[53] Lord Thomas's speech at The Bailii Lecture 2016 (n 23) §49.

[54] W Blair, 'The New Litigation Landscape: International Commercial Courts and Procedural Innovations' (2019) *International Journal of Procedural Law* 212, 219, available at sifocc.org/app/uploads/2020/04/The-New-Litigation-Landscape-International-Commercial-Courts-and-Procedural-Innovations.pdf.

[55] S Rowan, 'The New French Law of Contract' (2017) 66 *International & Comparative Law Quarterly* 805, available at eprints.lse.ac.uk/75815/1/Rowan_New%20French%20law_2017.pdf.

[56] Reginald Barrett's Closing address to the Current Issues in Insolvency Conference 'Thoughts on Court-to-Court Communications in Insolvency Cases' (31 July 2009) University of Sydney.

[57] David Neuberger's keynote address at Butterworths' Financial Institutions Litigation Conference, 'A Judicial Perspective on the Conduct of Claims in the Current Climate, (23 October 2009) [23], available at webarchive.nationalarchives.gov.uk/20131202164909/http://judiciary.gov.uk/Resources/JCO/Documents/Speeches/mor-financial-inst-conf-23102009.pdf.

[58] [2016] EWHC 256 (Ch).

[59] [2016] EWHC 1464.

over £100,000.[60] Other innovations in courtrooms include the use of speech-recognition systems which can provide simultaneous and quality transcription of in-court speeches. It is reported that in 2020 the Shanghai courts launched a pilot scheme for the use of a speech-recognition system.[61] Witnesses have been able to give evidence using virtual reality technology supported with speech-recognition systems in trials in Beijing courts.[62] These cost-saving systems contribute significantly to the efficiency and cost-effectiveness of litigation and arbitration regimes alike. The fact is that the two modes of dispute resolution can coexist in a quasi-competitive but also symbiotic environment. That is an important development which calls for support and recognition.[63] It is as Lord Parker once commented, 'the two systems (arbitration and litigation) ought indeed to be properly regarded as co-ordinate rather than rival'.[64]

IV. The Rise of ICCs

Since the turn of the century, the rise of ICCs has been observable around the world, notably in Singapore with the establishment of the SICC. In truth, the existence of such courts can be traced back to mediaeval times. What has driven this new trend? What has caused ICCs to be structured in the way they stand today? Unlike commercial arbitration, which operates as a private form of dispute resolution, ICCs have systematically been incorporated within their respective country's judicial system. Each such ICC is accordingly 'not a court newly and specially established to deal with international disputes'.[65] It does not come as a surprise to note that ICCs in general have relatively wide jurisdiction as their purpose is to attract as many international commercial disputes as possible. As such, what ICCs have in common is the aim to provide efficient and credible means of dispute resolution, especially to international commercial matters in support of a particular centre, with some of the characteristics of a free trade zone or in support of the court processes already provided by the country.

The mobility of disputes remains a crucial characteristic of specialist commercial courts today. It is a feature which distinguishes them from, for example, public law disputes. The parties have a choice. Within limits, they can choose to have their disputes decided by a court or in arbitration. If the dispute is brought before a court, they can choose which

[60] C Pache, L Medcraft and A Chan, 'Courtrooms of the Future – The Virtual Courtroom' *Epiq*, available at www.epiqglobal.com/en-hk/thinking/blog/courtrooms-of-the-future.

[61] S Dai, 'Shanghai judicial courts start to replace clerks with AI assistants' *South China Morning Post* (1 April 2020), available at www.scmp.com/tech/innovation/article/3077979/shanghai-judicial-courts-start-replace-clerks-ai-assistants.

[62] L Chenyu, 'VR Technology Called to the Stand in Beijing Court' *Sixth Tone* (2 March 2018), available at www.sixthtone.com/news/1001846/vr-technology-called-to-the-stand-in-beijing-court.

[63] See, for example, Peter Gross's speech at 35th Annual Donald O'May Maritime Law Lecture, 'A good forum to shop in: London and English Law post-Brexit' (1 November 2017, London) [20], available at www.judiciary.uk/wp-content/uploads/2017/11/gross-lj-omay-maritime-law-lecture-20171102.pdf.

[64] H Parker, 'London: still the cornerstone of international commercial arbitration and commercial law?' (2004) 70 *Arbitration Volume* 256, 269.

[65] M Warren and C Croft, 'An International Commercial Court for Australia – Looking beyond the New York Convention' (13 April 2016).

country the court is to be in. If, on the other hand, the dispute is brought for an arbitration, they can choose to arbitrate ad hoc, or under the rules of an organisation (such as the LCIA, the ICC or SIAC), and choose the seat. In England, the establishment of the Commercial Court in 1895 was driven by the merchants of London who were frustrated with the delays in the ordinary court system and the huge expense of litigation in terms of money and time. They wanted something better and quicker where disputes could be resolved more efficiently before judges with commercial expertise at reasonable cost.[66] These desires have no doubt helped to propel the modern rise of ICCs around the world. In addition, there are also broader considerations of both a political and economic nature.

What commercial parties want is honest, quick, skilled dispute resolution by competent judges.[67] New ICCs have introduced procedures which are designed to meet the expectations of the commercial community. In so doing, they have often adopted practices which originated in arbitration. Two examples are the use of witness statements or affidavits of evidence in chief (which were unheard of 40 years ago in England) and the use of what are now known as 'Redfern Schedules' in dealing with applications for discovery of documents. As such, ICCs are typically equipped with new procedural rules to overcome the shortcomings of arbitration, such as over-formalisation, delays, rising costs, concerns about legitimacy and ethical issues, lack of consistency and absence of appeals, as mentioned above.[68]

A recent webinar in Singapore carried the title 'SICC: Arbitration in Litigation'. While there is a large variety of specialist commercial courts nowadays, arguably the SICC is perhaps the best of all worlds for, among others, the following unique features that it can offer:

(1) the Court offers independent specialist judges from different jurisdictions;
(2) it allows foreign lawyers to appear as counsel in certain circumstances;
(3) instead of calling 'evidence' to prove foreign law, the latter is 'proved' by way of submissions, just as is often done in arbitration;
(4) it has a flexible but robust court system which encourages strong case management;
(5) in appropriate circumstances, the court has power to order that the proceedings be heard in private, that is, allowing the parties the confidentiality which is often trumpeted as one of the main advantages of arbitration; and
(6) unlike arbitration, there is an automatic right of appeal to the Court of Appeal.[69] The experience shows that these appeals are dealt with swiftly.

In addition, the SICC offers substantial advantages which are not available in arbitration including:

(1) The ability to join third parties. This can often be very important especially when (for instance) a claimant sues a shipbuilder, and the defendant shipbuilder wishes to make claims over for an indemnity against the designer or the engine supplier.

[66] See Introduction to *Commercial Cases* Vol 1 (1895).

[67] New York State Courts, 'A Forum for Business Disputes: The Commercial Division of the Supreme Court of the State of New York' (22 December 2016), available at www.nycourts.gov/courts/comdiv/PDFs/CommercialDivision2016Transcript.pdf.

[68] D Demeter and K Smith, 'The implications of international commercial courts on arbitration' (2016) 33 *Journal of International Arbitration* 441.

[69] Although it is possible for parties by agreement to opt out of an appeal stage.

(2) The power to order costs against a non-party. This can often be very important when the respondent is being financially supported by a third party.

An ideal solution might be to adopt a mechanism whereby certain cases (for example, those requiring simple immediate resolution) should be dealt with by way of arbitration whereas others (for example, those involving significant legal issues) should be dealt with by way of court litigation. However, this would be difficult, if not impossible, to achieve in practice. This is because parties would have to decide on the dispute resolution mechanism at the time when they sign a contract. It would be hard for them to foresee at that moment the types of dispute which they might ultimately have. If the parties have agreed to proceed to arbitration for resolving disputes arising from their contract, eventually all disputes will end up in arbitration regardless of a dispute's nature. Meanwhile, with the wide subscription to the Singapore Convention[70] on international mediation, it remains to be seen whether and, if so, to what extent the swinging pendulum might be distorted into another dimension as international commercial parties turn to mediation as a cheaper and more friendly mode of dispute resolution than either arbitration or litigation.

Looking ahead, with the rise of ICCs, is a swing in favour of specialist commercial courts likely to transpire? In which direction will the pendulum swing over the next 20 years? It is submitted that a swing in favour of commercial courts generally (and ICCs in particular) will occur provided such institutions can adapt their procedures to meet the expectations of the commercial community. Many jurisdictions have in fact taken, or are taking, the initiative to consider having a commercial court for the handling of international trade disputes.[71] But, at the same time, states can promote or upgrade their international commercial arbitration regimes. The options of litigation and arbitration are not mutually exclusive; they can be worked on concurrently.

Singapore is a good example, where the Singapore International Arbitration Centre (SIAC) and the SICC have both flourished side by side. Japan is also a good example. Since 2017, the Japanese Government has worked to promote Japan as an international arbitration and dispute resolution centre.[72] This has resulted in the opening of a new mediation centre in Kyoto in 2018 and new arbitration hearing facilities in Osaka and Tokyo in 2018 and 2020 respectively. In September 2020, the Japanese Minister of Justice commissioned the Legislative Council to consider possible amendments to the Arbitration Act and related statutes to make Japan more arbitration-friendly.[73] In 2021, the Japan Commercial Arbitration Association updated its commercial rules to

[70] United Nations: United Nations Commission on International Trade Law 'The United Nations Convention on International Settlement Agreements Resulting from Mediation' (2019), available at uncitral.un.org/sites/uncitral.un.org/files/singapore_convention_eng.pdf.

[71] A recent striking development is the passing of legislation by Kosovo in February 2022 for the establishment of a commercial court to deal with all business and administrative disputes initiated by business organisations in the country; see www.usaid.gov/kosovo/news-information/news/kosovos-assembly-passes-law-creating-commercial-court.

[72] 'An overview of the Proposed Amendments of Japan's Arbitration Act' Nishimura & Asahi (31 May 2021), available at www.lexology.com/library/detail.aspx?g=eeeea580-fac8-4887-9e80-dff2f5c0d2dc.

[73] See, for example, Y Furuta, 'Enforcement in Japan of Foreign Judicial and Extrajudicial Instruments' (2021) 2 *Japan Commercial Arbitration Journal* 88, available at www.jcaa.or.jp/common/pdf/publication/browsing-jcaj_02_2021.pdf?211004.

bring the latter in line with current international standards.[74] Amendments were also made to the Japanese Foreign Lawyers Act in 2021 to expand the scope of services that foreign lawyers can render in international arbitration proceedings.[75] At the same time, it is understood that Japan is exploring the possibility of having its own international commercial court.[76] Thus, it is conceivable that the future will see ICCs functioning in tandem with international commercial arbitration. The pendulum may not simply swing one way or the other. Arbitration and ICCs each have their own unique features and strengths. Forming a part of an international system of dispute resolution, they do not have to be 'islands unto themselves'.[77] The two modes can complement each other, offering commercial parties a choice on how all or some of their disputes can be resolved.

V. Supposed Shortcomings of ICCs

Litigation and arbitration are not identical as modes of dispute resolution. They have different strengths and weaknesses. Having accentuated the many positive aspects of the rise of ICCs, it is important to address some of the particular criticisms or suggested shortcomings which have been raised, although in truth the present author considers that these are often somewhat theoretical and of marginal practical significance.

First, while ICCs allow some scope for party autonomy in the way that proceedings are conducted, the parties do not enjoy the same extent of freedom as in international arbitration. As far as interlocutory proceedings and the merits hearing are concerned, parties before ICCs are usually constrained by the procedural laws of such forums.[78] For instance, when it comes to the service of documents, the procedures for the commencement of an arbitration are usually embodied in the rules stipulated in the parties' arbitration agreement. In general, no special procedure is necessary for overseas service of the notice of arbitration on a party. Therefore, it is usually sufficient to serve documents by fax or email unless the arbitration agreement provides (or the tribunal directs) otherwise. For proceedings before ICCs, parties must employ the designated mode of service specified in the court rules. For overseas service, the 1965 HCCH Convention on the Service Abroad of Judicial and Extrajudicial Documents

[74] Japan Commercial Arbitration Association, 'Amendment to Arbitration Rules and Enactment of Appointing Authority Rules' (10 July 2021), available at www.jcaa.or.jp/files/news_attach/detail_attach00000202-31.pdf.

[75] Ministry of Justice of Japan, 'Act on Special Measures concerning the Handling of Legal Services by Foreign Lawyers (Foreign Lawyers Act) has been amended', available at www.moj.go.jp/content/001331477.pdf.

[76] There are several hurdles that need to be overcome if Japan is to have an international commercial court. For instance, Art 74 of Japan's Court Act requires that court proceedings take place in Japanese. It will be difficult to attract businesses to designate a Japanese international commercial court as the forum for the resolution of their disputes, if everything will need to be translated into Japanese.

[77] Borrowing an expression from Lord Justice Peter Gross's speech at 35th Annual Donald O'May Maritime Law Lecture (n 63) [26]; Peter Gross's speech at Jonathan Hirst QC Commercial Law Lecture (n 19) [15].

[78] S Wilske, 'International Commercial Courts and Arbitration – Alternatives, Substitutes or Trojan Horse?' (2018) 11 *Contemporary Asia Arbitration Journal* 153.

in Civil or Commercial Matters[79] will often facilitate matters when the states involved are contracting parties to the instrument. However, even then, it can still be costly and time-consuming to effect services overseas. Thus, service on a respondent in connection with an action before an ICC may currently be more cumbersome than notifying a party of an arbitration.

Second, it is important to consider the steps sometimes necessary for the taking of evidence across borders for use in ICC proceedings. International arbitrations are a consensual form of proceeding. The tribunal is appointed pursuant to the parties' agreement and derives its authority from such agreement. Evidence from witnesses is usually taken with the consent of the witnesses giving the same. So long as a witness is willing to give evidence, there is usually no objection to the witness in country A giving evidence by remote technology to an arbitration tribunal sitting in country B. In contrast, ICCs are part of a nation's judicial establishment. The ICC's acts are accordingly a manifestation of a nation's sovereign activity. As a result, some countries (relevant countries) take the view that the taking of evidence from a witness in their territory for use in proceedings before an ICC seated elsewhere would constitute an affront to the relevant countries' national sovereignty. In such situations, it seems that the fact that the witness is giving evidence voluntarily or through a video link would usually be an irrelevant consideration and that any taking of evidence which a relevant country has not officially authorised would constitute an offence against the relevant country's laws.

The problem is that the procedure for obtaining official permission to take evidence from a witness situated in such countries is not always clear. Even when known, the procedure for obtaining permission may be time-consuming and costly. Although there is no easy solution to this potential problem, it should not be overstated for at least four reasons. First, the number of relevant countries which restrict the taking of evidence in this way is thought to be relatively small. Second, the problem can be eliminated or at least alleviated by obtaining the necessary official permission (where that is possible) or making arrangements for the particular witness(es) to give evidence in the traditional way at the seat of the ICC in question or perhaps at some other venue. Third, mechanisms can be developed for the taking of evidence by video link in a foreign country through the 1970 HCCH Convention on the Taking of Evidence Abroad in Civil or Commercial Matters, to which there are presently 64 contracting states. Fourth, courts in different jurisdictions can conclude memoranda of guidance setting out procedures for obtaining permission to take video link evidence in conjunction with an ICC case.

Third, there is the important question of enforcing an ICC judgment. The swing towards arbitration may largely be attributed to the 1958 New York Convention, which enables parties to enforce arbitral awards in commercial matters in nearly 170 jurisdictions. An international survey conducted by Queen Mary University of London and White & Case in 2015[80] found (65 per cent of interviewees agreeing) that the

[79] Hague Service Convention, available at assets.hcch.net/docs/f4520725-8cbd-4c71-b402-5aae1994d14c.pdf.

[80] '2015 International Arbitration Survey: Improvements and Innovations in International Arbitration' QMUL and White & Case, available at www.arbitration.qmul.ac.uk/docs/164761.pdf. The interview was conducted on 763 interviewees who are parties frequently involved in international commercial arbitrations

recognition and enforcement of awards under the New York Convention was the major draw of international arbitration. It was not until the HCCH Convention on Choice of Court Agreements[81] was adopted in 2005 that there was any near equivalent to the New York Convention as far as the recognition and enforcement of judgments is concerned. However, although the 2005 HCCH Convention has been adopted by only 32 state parties and does not therefore have the coverage of the New York Convention, they include notable major financial centres (including the UK, Germany, France and Singapore as well as the EU).

Moreover, as more fully discussed in part four of this book,[82] the fact is that many civil and common law jurisdictions today have updated their civil procedure codes and statutes so that commercial judgments (including those of ICCs) can in actuality readily be recognised and enforced. For instance, the position as a matter of English law is that, where parties have agreed in a commercial contract to submit their disputes to a specific court (for example, the SICC), such agreement operates as a voluntary submission to that court. This means that the judgment of that court in a dispute between the parties arising out of their commercial contract will generally be enforceable subject to limited exceptions, which are broadly similar to the exceptions in the New York Convention and the 2005 HCCH Convention. In truth, the regime established by the New York Convention imported into the world of arbitration the position that had long existed as a matter of English law in respect of court judgments where the court's jurisdiction derived from the agreement of the parties. Therefore, in the author's view, the suggestion that the New York Convention provides arbitration with a fundamental advantage over litigation is, at least as a matter of English law, largely illusory.[83]

Further, the notion that the international enforcement of arbitral awards is overwhelmingly easier than that of court judgments seems questionable in light of the steps taken by courts to foster the recognition and enforcement of their judgments worldwide. The SICC, for example, has concluded memoranda of guidance on the mutual recognition and enforcement of judgments with several courts, including courts in the UK, Australia, New Zealand, Malaysia, Brunei and India.[84] There have also been creative innovations. In 2015, the Dubai International Financial Centre (DIFC) Courts leveraged on the concept of recognition and enforcement of awards in the New York Convention. By amending Practice Direction No 2 of 2012 on the DIFC Courts' Jurisdiction, the DIFC Courts now allow parties to 'convert' a monetary judgment by the DIFC Courts into a DIFC-LCIA arbitration award to avoid any potential difficulties in enforcing a

from March to May 2015. The interviewees came from a wide spectrum of the legal profession, including researchers (4%), arbitration body staff (2%), arbitrators (11%), almost equally involved as lawyers and as arbitrators (12%), expert witnesses (2%), corporate in-house lawyers (8%), independent lawyers (49%), and others (judges, funding lenders, government related parties) (12%).

[81] The Hague Convention on Choice of Court Agreements came into force in October 2015; see www.hcch.net/en/instruments/conventions/specialised-sections/choice-of-court.

[82] See ch 7 section III and ch 8 sections IV and V.

[83] For the position with regard to the enforcement of SICC Judgments, reference should be made to the Guidance Notes on the Enforcements of Money Judgments, available at www.sicc.gov.sg/guide-to-the-sicc/enforcement-of-money-judgments, and Enforcement of SICC Judgments and Orders, available at www.sicc.gov.sg/guide-to-the-sicc/note-on-enforcement-of-sicc-judgments.

[84] By virtue of the Reciprocal Enforcement of Commonwealth Judgments Act (RECJA) and the Reciprocal Enforcement of Foreign Judgments Act (REFJA).

DIFC Judgment outside the UAE.[85] While 'conversion' may be an over-simplified word to describe this innovative mechanism, Chief Justice Michael Hwang noted that:[86]

> The targeted effect of this initiative was that, following a money judgment of the DIFC Courts, the judgment creditor would be able to demand payment of the judgment sum and, if payment were not made pursuant to that demand for any reason, the judgment creditor would be able to consider that an enforcement dispute (which we will now rename 'Judgment Payment Dispute' for greater accuracy) had arisen, and could refer the Judgment Payment Dispute to arbitration at our Arbitration Centre (or indeed any other arbitration centre). The latter might not be the wisest course to be taken by the parties, but they would be entitled to choose another centre if they wish, although this protocol might not work as well as it should if the arbitration were referred to our Arbitration Centre. The Arbitration Centre in turn would progress the arbitration, and the LCIA Court (which the parties would have chosen in their arbitration agreement) would appoint one arbitrator so as to ensure relative expedition, and the dispute would then be referred to the tribunal for its decision in the usual way in accordance with the Arbitration Rules of the Arbitration Centre.

He continued on what was really meant by the word 'conversion':[87]

> This process is what I meant to explain by the term 'conversion' of a judgment into an arbitration award. But it is not a 'conversion' in the strict sense of that word. The process enables a judgment creditor to have an additional option for securing payment of his judgment without losing its rights under the judgment in any way, so the judgment will remain intact and fully enforceable without regard to the progress of the arbitration. The term 'convert' is therefore simply a metaphor. Perhaps a more accurate (if less striking) characterization of the process is 'enhanced enforceability of DIFC Courts judgments'.

This mechanism of converting a judgment into an award allows parties to benefit from the worldwide enforcement afforded by the New York Convention and essentially 'enhance the enforceability of a DIFC Court judgment'.[88] Some, however, suggested that more time is likely to be taken in the 'conversion' process as parties would first have to go through the DIFC Courts, followed by an arbitration process and eventually by enforcement proceedings abroad.[89]

VI. Conclusion

The rise of ICCs has had a huge effect on the litigation landscape. The number of judgments handed down by ICCs is growing and it is something that can only improve over time as ICCs become more familiar to the business community. Arbitration as a means

[85] DIFC Courts Practice Direction No 2 of 2015 – Referral of Judgment Payment Disputes to Arbitration, available at difccourts.ae/amended-difccourts-practice-direction-no-2-of-2015-referral-of-judgment-payment-disputes-to-arbitration.

[86] M Hwang, Lecture Series No 5, Practice Direction providing for the wider enforcement of Court Judgments through DIFC-LCIA Arbitration Centre, 19 November 2014, at [9]–[10], available at www.difccourts.ae/wp-content/uploads/2018/01/DIFC-Courts-CJ-Lecture-Notes2.docx.

[87] ibid [10].

[88] ibid.

[89] C Lilley and C Johnson, '"Converting" DIFC Court judgments into arbitral awards.' (5 November 2014), available at constructionblog.practicallaw.com/converting-difc-court-judgments-into-arbitral-awards.

of resolving transnational commercial disputes was supposed to save parties money, time and the technicalities of litigation. But it has been shown to have its drawbacks. With the rise of the option of litigation before ICCs, another option becomes available for parties to consider for the resolution of their international commercial disputes. It is therefore incumbent upon commercial enterprises to review the options, advantages, and risks of both sides of the pendulum and to make an informed decision about which mode or what combination of the two modes to employ. Arbitration and litigation need not be perceived as being in conflict. A more constructive approach would be to work out how the two can coexist and complement each other.

PART III

David and Goliath: Investor–State Dispute Settlement

5

An Introduction to Investor–State Dispute Settlement

JIANJIAN YE

I. The System of Investor–State Dispute Settlement

A. Jurisdiction under the ICSID Convention and UNCITRAL Rules

The practice of hauling a sovereign state before an arbitration tribunal and requiring it to resolve its dispute with a private investor is a relatively recent development. Traditionally, an investor with a grievance relating to how its investment had been treated by a foreign state, was required to seek diplomatic protection from its home state and specifically to persuade it to pursue the investor's claims in the state's own name under the usages and practices of public international law, that body of law concerned with the law governing nations.[1] Such diplomatic protection was not readily available, because it depended entirely on the willingness of the investor's home state to act as enforcer when it might have other economic, diplomatic or security considerations to take into account. A private investor could alternatively seek a remedy in the courts of the host state. However, these domestic courts were not always satisfactory as a venue for seeking relief especially in situations where the investor harboured doubts over the independence or impartiality of the domestic court. Following the establishment of the International Centre for Settlement of Investment Disputes (ICSID) and the issuance of its model clauses in 1969, bilateral investment treaties (BITs) incorporating provisions on investor–state arbitration began to feature with growing regularity. By the end of the twentieth century, it had become common for a BIT to include a term enabling an investor from one state party to the BIT to invoke an international dispute settlement mechanism against the other state party to the BIT.[2]

[1] M Molinuevo, *Protecting Investment in Services: Investor-State Arbitration versus WTO Dispute Settlement* (Kluwer Law International BV, 2011) 13.

[2] ibid.

The principal instruments that make up the present investor–state dispute settlement (ISDS) system are: (1) the ICSID Convention; (2) bilateral or multilateral free-trade agreements (FTAs) or economic partnership agreements (EPAs), such as the North American Free Trade Agreement (NAFTA, now renegotiated and renamed the US–Mexico–Canada Agreement (USMCA)), the Comprehensive and Progressive Trans-Pacific Partnership (CPPTPP) and the Regional Comprehensive Economic Partnership (RCEP); (3) multilateral sectoral treaties such as the Energy Charter Treaty (ECT); and (4) BITs and multilateral investment treaties (MITs).[3] These instruments generally stipulate substantive legal standards and procedures for the resolution of investment disputes. In terms of dispute resolution procedures, some instruments opt for specialised dispute resolution regimes (such as under the ICSID Arbitration Rules), while others designate general institutional arbitration rules (such as the UNCITRAL Rules). Many provide a choice of different dispute resolution mechanisms. Because the ICSID and UNCITRAL rules are the most common choices, it is imperative to examine their respective jurisdictional scope.[4]

i. ICSID

ICSID is an inter-governmental body specifically designed to address international investment disputes. The Convention on the Settlement of Investment Disputes of 1965 ('the ICSID Convention') established ICSID as part of the World Bank Group with the aim of promoting economic development through the creation of a favourable investment climate.[5] ICSID administers arbitrations. ICSID has jurisdiction over any legal dispute arising directly out of an investment between a contracting state and a national of another contracting state.[6] But the ICSID Convention does not provide an independent basis for arbitrating particular disputes.[7] Instead, a foreign investor and a host state must have separately consented to ICSID arbitration for ICSID to have jurisdiction. Such consent usually takes the form of (1) an arbitration clause in an investment contract or (2) a consent in a foreign investment law, a BIT, or some other treaty.[8] Countries can limit ICSID's jurisdiction to certain matters by notifying ICSID. For example, China has accepted ICSID's jurisdiction only for disputes over compensation for expropriation or nationalisation.[9] Saudi Arabia excludes controversies relating to oil or acts of sovereignty.[10] Such reservations are only prospective in effect and cannot override any consent previously given to ICSID arbitration. ICSID awards are not enforced through the 1958 New York Convention. Instead, the ICSID Convention has its own mechanism for the recognition and enforcement of ICSID arbitration awards in Contracting States.

[3] G Born, *International Arbitration: Law and Practice*, 2nd edn (Kluwer Law International, 2012) 418.
[4] Molinuevo, *Protecting Investment in Services* (2011) 14–15.
[5] Convention on the Settlement of Investment Disputes between States and Nationals of Other States, which was adopted on 18 March 1965 and entered into force on 14 October 1966) 575 UNTS 159 Art 1.
[6] ibid Art 25.
[7] Born, *International Arbitration* (2012) 419.
[8] ibid.
[9] ICSID, Contracting States and Measures Taken by Them for the Purpose of the Convention (February 2019), ICSID/8-D at 1.
[10] ibid at 3.

ii. UNCITRAL Rules

Investment arbitrations under the UNCITRAL Rules differ from ICSID or other administered arbitrations. Arbitrations under the UNCITRAL Rules are ad hoc arbitrations. They do not rely on the support of a permanent organisation specialised in the management of arbitral proceedings. It is up to the parties to establish the administrative and logistical framework for their arbitration. However, nothing prevents the parties from agreeing to use UNCITRAL Rules for an arbitration administered by an institution such as ICSID or the International Chamber of Commerce (ICC). The UNCITRAL Rules address all matters that may arise in international arbitral proceedings, from the notice of arbitration, to the appointment of arbitrators, to interim measures, to procedural rules and the form and effect of an award, including awards of damages and costs. Awards rendered under the UNCITRAL Rules are, like all commercial arbitrations, recognised and enforced domestically through the 1958 New York Convention and lack the more simplified recognition and enforcement procedures of ICSID awards.

B. What is a Minimum International Standard?

Investor–state disputes typically involve allegations by investors that states have breached one or more of their obligations under a BIT, MIT, FTA or EPA. These are binding instruments under international law as between the state parties to the instrument. Within those instruments, the obligations owed by a state party to the investors of another state party are usually to be found in most favoured nation (MFN) clauses, fair and equitable treatment (FET) clauses, full protection and security (FPS) clauses, favourable treatment clauses, anti-expropriation clauses, and umbrella clauses. An arbitral tribunal constituted pursuant to the terms of such instruments will need to decide whether a state has breached one or more of such obligations by reference to an international minimum standard of state behaviour.

The international minimum standard is a principle of customary international law that requires states to afford a common standard of treatment to aliens in their territory. Historically, states did not have an international law obligation to offer rights or protection to aliens in their territory. But with the development of international trade and investment, states gradually recognised the importance of providing aliens with certain rights.

Two divergent standards of alien treatment developed during the nineteenth and early twentieth centuries. Developing countries advocated the Calvo doctrine, also known as the equality doctrine or national treatment standard. This posited that foreign investors should be treated in the same way as (and cannot expect to be treated more favourably than) the nationals of a host state. In contrast, the international minimum standard approach, as advocated by developed countries, provides that states must at least afford a common standard of treatment to aliens in their territory.

In the context of international investment, many BITs, MITs, FTAs and EPAs have expressly adopted an international minimum standard approach. For example, NAFTA chapter 11, Article 1105 (*cf* USMCA Article 14.6) requires treatment 'in accordance with international law, including fair and equitable treatment and full protection and security'. But different NAFTA tribunals have disagreed as to whether such standards as FET are included in or additive to the so-called international minimum standard. Subsequently, the NAFTA Free Trade Commission (FTC) issued Notes of Interpretation of Certain Chapter 11 Provisions[11] to clarify that FET and full protection and FPS clauses are comprised within the international minimum standard. More generally, arbitral tribunals have attempted to articulate what the international minimum standard entails. In the context of denial of justice, the *Mondev International Ltd v USA* tribunal held that the proper standard to decide whether an investor was unfairly and inequitably treated is to ask whether 'in the light of all the available facts … the impugned decision was clearly improper and discreditable'.[12] Tribunals in other cases, such as *Loewen Group Inc v USA*, have also adopted a similarly broad approach in defining the international minimum standard.[13] Although there has not been (and it may not be possible to have) a precise definition of the minimum standard, the general trend has been to afford more (rather than less) protection to investors.

C. Favourable Treatment and MFN Clauses

A favourable treatment clause obliges a state to treat an investor from a state party to a BIT, MIT or similar instrument no less favourably than it treats its own domestic investors in a like industry.

The MFN clause in an instrument casts a wider net. It generally means that an investor from country A investing in country B will not be treated less favourably by country B than an investor from any other nation investing in country B. An MFN clause accordingly reflects principles of equality and non-discrimination, and 'provide[s] a level playing field … between foreign investors from different countries'.[14] It also reduces the burden on the negotiating parties to review their treaty partner's prior treaties, because the MFN clause will automatically incorporate any better protection or concession afforded by the treaty partner to any other countries. If the treaty partner grants more favourable treatment in later negotiations with other countries, the MFN clause will likewise automatically ensure that countries bound by prior investment treaties are not disadvantaged, because the subsequent more favourable treatment will automatically apply to them via the operation of the MFN clause. In practice, investors often invoke MFN clauses for better protection substantively and procedurally.

In terms of substantive protection, it is generally accepted that MFN clauses will operate to incorporate stronger substantive protection standards from other similar treaties (comparator treaties) into the base treaty, although cases in which investors have successfully invoked the MFN clauses and obtained better protection have been rare.

[11] NAFTA Free Trade Commission, Notes of Interpretation of Certain Chapter 11 Provisions (31 July 2001).

[12] *Mondev International Ltd v USA*, ICSID Case No ARB(AF)/99/2, Award (11 October 2002) (Stephen, Crawford, Schwebel) 127.

[13] *Loewen Group Inc v USA*, ICSID Case No ARB(AF)/98/3, Award (26 June 2003) (Mason, Mikva, Mustill) 133.

[14] *Bayindir Insaat Turizm Ticaret Ve Sanayi AŞ v Islamic Republic of Pakistan*, ICSID Case No ARB/03/29, Award (27 August 2009) (Kaufmann-Kohler, Böckstiegel, Berman) 386.

There are generally four ways in which an MFN clause can operate as a substantive protection standard. First, investors invoke MFN provisions to expand or add content to substantive treatment provisions already included in a base treaty. For example, the claimant in *ATA Construction, Industrial and Trading Company v Hashemite Kingdom of Jordan* invoked the MFN clause to expand the types of treatment prohibited by the base treaty's FET clause.[15] Second, MFN provisions can incorporate standards of treatment additional to those already included in a base treaty. In *Gold Reserve Inc. v Bolivarian Republic of Venezuela*, for instance, the claimant sought to introduce entirely new substantive obligations from comparator treaties to the base treaty through the operation of an MFN provision.[16] Less commonly, investors have also invoked MFN clauses to eliminate unfavourable provisions in the base treaty[17] or prohibit host states from granting more favourable treatment to investors from another state.[18]

With respect to procedural protection, however, arbitral tribunals have split over the question of whether MFN clauses apply to forms of dispute settlement.[19] On the one hand, the *Maffezini v Spain* tribunal took a liberal approach and stated that

> if a third-party treaty contains provisions for the settlement of disputes that are more favorable to the protection of the investor's rights and interests than those in the basic treaty, such provisions may be extended to the beneficiary of the most-favored-nation clause as they are fully compatible with the *ejusdem generis* principle.[20]

On the other hand, the *Plama v Bulgaria* tribunal took a narrower approach and refused to import the dispute settlement framework in a comparator treaty to the base treaty.[21]

D. Expropriation, FET and FPS Clauses

Expropriation and FET clauses are distinct provisions, often seen in BITs, aiming at protecting the interest of foreign investors. Expropriation clauses prohibit host states from expropriating foreign investors' assets without compensation. FET clauses ensure

[15] *ATA Construction, Industrial and Trading Company v Hashemite Kingdom of Jordan*, ICSID Case No ARB/08/2, Award (18 May 2010) (Fortier, Sadek El-Kosheri, Reisman) ¶ 73.

[16] *Gold Reserve Inc v Bolivarian Republic of Venezuela*, ICSID Case No ARB(AF)/09/1, Award (22 September 2014) (Bernardini, Williams, Dupuy) 625–28.

[17] See eg *Talsud SA v United Mexican States*, ICSID Case No ARB(AF)/04/4, Award (16 June 2010) (Veeder, Fortier, Magallón Gomez).

[18] See eg *GEA Group Aktiengesellschaft v Ukraine*, ICSID Case No ARB/08/16, Award (31 March 2011) (van den Berg, Landau, Stern).

[19] Y Derains and J Sicard-Mirabal, *Introduction to Investor-State Arbitration* (Kluwer Law International, 2018) 150; A Newcombe and L Paradell, *Law and Practice of Investment Treaties: Standards of Treatment* (Kluwer Law International, 2009) 208–10; M Kinnear, G Fischer, J Minguez Almeida et al, *Building International Investment Law: The First 50 Years of ICSID* (Kluwer Law International 2015) 253–62.

[20] *Emilio Agustin Maffezini v Kingdom of Spain*, ICSID Case No ARB/97/7, Decision on Jurisdiction (25 January 2000) (Vicuna, Buergenthal, Wolf) 56; see also *Siemens AG v Argentine Republic*, ICSID Case No ARB/02/8, Decision on Jurisdiction (3 August 2004) (Sureda, Brower, Janeiro) 68.

[21] *Plama Consortium Limited v Republic of Bulgaria*, ICSID Case No ARB/03/24, Decision on Jurisdiction (8 February 2005) 240(c); see also *Salini Costruttori SpA and Italstrade SpA v Hashemite Kingdom of Jordan*, ICSID Case No ARB/02/13, Decision on Jurisdiction (9 November 2004).

that foreign investors are not unfairly treated by host states. A single action by a host state might constitute breaches of both clauses and foreign investors consequently often bring actions alleging the breach of these two provisions. It is therefore important to distinguish these two clauses. Expropriation are of two kinds: direct and indirect. Direct expropriation involves a host state directly confiscating a foreign investors' assets, such as President Hugo Chavez's nationalisation of foreign investors' property after his rise to power in Venezuela. Indirect expropriation, in contrast, takes place when a host state's measures have 'an effect equivalent to expropriation'.[22] It will typically be in indirect expropriation cases that FET and expropriation clauses overlap. More specifically, when tribunals refer to the 'expectations' of a claimant investor, they are usually concerned with allegations by the investor that a host state has acted contrary to the investor's legitimate expectations of FET and the payment of proper compensation for expropriation of an investment.

Some have referred to the investor's expectations as the core factor in deciding whether there has been indirect expropriation. Others have referred to an investor's expectations as an important indicator of whether there has been a failure to accord FET. A brief survey of tribunal decisions suggests that, in the absence of substantial interference with an investment, government assurances upon which an investor has relied when making an its investment weigh little in a tribunal's determination of indirect expropriation. But the contravention of an investor's legitimate expectations can amount to a breach of FET by a host state. For example, in *Saluka Investments BV v Czech Republic*, the claimant argued that the Czech authorities' refusal to secure a financial aid package for its bank and the subsequent suspension of trading in its bank's shares amounted to expropriation and a breach of FET. However, the tribunal concluded that there had been no expropriation because the various measures at issue could be 'justified as permissible regulatory actions'.[23] Despite this, the tribunal found that there had been a violation of FET under the relevant treaty because the Czech authorities had failed to treat the claimant fairly when negotiating and handing out state financial aid.[24]

An FPS clause is similar in effect to FET, but is usually treated as restricted to an undertaking by a state that it will take appropriate steps to protect the person and property of foreign investors within the state. Appropriate steps are evaluated by reference to the minimum international standard.

E. Dealing with Corruption

Corruption is a prevalent issue in international investment arbitration, especially in cases involving public procurement. When disputes emerge between an investor and a host state, the latter sometimes raises allegations of corruption in an attempt to avoid

[22] See, eg, Agreement Between Government of the Republic of Korea and Government of the Republic of Tajikistan on the Promotion and Protection of Investments (adopted on 14 July 1995, entered in force on 13 August 1995) Art 5(1).

[23] *Saluka Investments BV v Czech Republic*, Partial Award (17 March 2006) 265.

[24] ibid 446.

its contractual obligations. This is typically the situation where a new government has recently come to power and is critically reviewing the acts of its predecessor government. By way of a defence to a claim by an investor, the new government will contend that the investor only secured its investment by bribing its predecessor. In that case, it will be suggested that the investment (and therefore the investor's claim) is vitiated by illegality and consequently void.

There does not seem to be a clear-cut rule on deciding whether and how allegations of corruption taint an investment contract. Host states have argued that their national laws contain mandatory rules that nullify an investment contract that has been secured through bribery or some other form of corruption. Arbitral tribunals have adopted such views.[25] Host states might also argue that the investment contract is void or voidable because it violated international anti-corruption norms.[26] The difficulty, however, is that even though the international community has made progress in combating corruption, there is no transnational consensus on the legal consequences of corruption on the validity of an investment contract.[27]

Investors, on the other hand, have objected to host states' claims, relying on the principle of state responsibility. As a general rule, states must meet their contractual obligations, notwithstanding the corrupt activities of their officials. To hold otherwise would give the state an easy escape from its contractual obligations because the state can simply indict a relevant government official for corruption, whenever breaching a contract appears more advantageous. Therefore, investors argue, allegations of corruption should not nullify an underlying contract.

F. Umbrella Clauses

An umbrella clause in a BIT, MIT or similar instrument obliges a host state to observe past undertakings made to a foreign investor under an investment contract concluded before the BIT, MIT or similar instrument came into effect. An umbrella clause thus protects prior foreign investments by bringing the commitments that the host state undertook in connection with those investments, under the protection of the later BIT, MIT or similar instrument. Investors often rely on an umbrella clause as a catch-all provision to pursue claims against a host state where the latter's actions do not otherwise constitute a breach of the relevant treaty. Such action by an investor would allow it to elevate a contractual claim under its prior contract with the state to the level of a claim under the subsequent treaty. This would have the benefit, from the investor's viewpoint, of bypassing the dispute resolution clauses in its prior contract with the state. It would enable the investor to seek redress instead before an international arbitral body constituted pursuant to the BIT, MIT or similar instrument. An example of an umbrella clause

[25] *World Duty Free Co Ltd v Republic of Kenya*, ICSID Case No ARB/00/7, Award (4 October 2006) 49–62.

[26] *American Bell International Inc v Iran*, Award in Case No 48 (255-48-3) of 19 September 1986, 12 YB Comm Arb 292, 292 (1987).

[27] H Raeschke-Kessler and D Gottwald, 'Corruption' in P Muchlinski, F Ortino and C Schreuer (eds), *The Oxford Handbook of International Investment Law* (OUP, 2008) 595.

is Article 2 of the 1967 OECD Draft Convention on the Protection of Foreign Property: 'Each Party shall at all times ensure the observance of undertakings given by it in relation to property of nationals of any Party'.[28]

When called upon to rule on the effect of umbrella clauses, arbitral tribunals have diverged in their construction of such clauses. Some tribunals following the ruling in *SGS v Pakistan* have interpreted umbrella clauses narrowly, insisting that 'in the face of a valid forum selection clause' in a prior investment contract, there was no need to elevate claims grounded in that investment contract into claims under the later investment treaty.[29] Other tribunals have taken a wider reading of the scope of an umbrella clause. An example is the tribunal in *SGS v Philippines*. Faced with a near identical umbrella clause to that in *SGS v Pakistan*, the tribunal held that the host state's breach of contractual commitments could constitute a breach of the relevant BIT through the operation of the umbrella clause in the same.[30] So, in essence, whether an umbrella clause is of any use for investors depends not just on the specific text of the BIT, but also on the construction of that text adopted by arbitral tribunals. A recent trend in international investment law appears to be against the inclusion of an umbrella clause in a BIT. This may be inferred from the fact that the model BITs used by the US, France, and Canada, and a number of prominent multilateral investments agreements (including NAFTA and the ASEAN-Australia-New Zealand FTA) do not have umbrella clauses.

G. The Mauritius Convention

The UN Convention on Transparency in Treaty-based Investor–State Arbitration (the Mauritius Convention) is a multilateral treaty that was concluded in 2014. It entered into force in 2017. Its aim is to promote the wider application of the UNCITRAL Rules on Transparency in Treaty-based Investor–State Arbitration ('the Transparency Rules'). The Transparency Rules are a set of procedural rules dealing with, among others, the disclosure of case-related documents, public access to hearings, and submissions by *amici curiae* and non-disputing state parties.

The Mauritius Convention applies to Investor–State arbitrations conducted pursuant to investment treaties, whether or not under the UNCITRAL Arbitration Rules, in which the respondent state is a party to the Convention and the claimant is 'of a' state that is a party to the Mauritius Convention. When these conditions are satisfied, the Mauritius Convention provides for the mandatory application of the Transparency Rules, unless the respondent or the claimant's home state has made a 'relevant reservation'. By making a reservation, a party may exclude the application of the Mauritius Convention from arbitrations conducted under a specific treaty or using a specific set of arbitration rules. In addition, the Transparency Rules will also apply to investment-treaty arbitrations in which only the respondent is a party to the Mauritius Convention, but the state of the

[28] OECD Publication No 23081, November 1967.

[29] *SGS Société Générale de Surveillance SA v Pakistan*, ICSID Case No ARB/01/13, Decision on Jurisdiction (6 August 2003) 307.

[30] *SGS Société Générale de Surveillance, SA v Republic of the Philippines*, ICSID Case No ARB/02/6, Decision on Jurisdiction (29 January 2004) 128.

claimant's nationality is not, provided that the claimant agrees to the application of the Transparency Rules. If widely adopted, the Mauritius Convention could significantly change the way in which investment-treaty arbitrations are conducted. This is because it would greatly increase transparency in such arbitral proceedings.

Though widely applauded by practitioners and academics, the actual effect of the Mauritius Convention has been limited in the short-term and remains to be seen. Several reasons have contributed to its limited impact so far. Most importantly, only a few states have ratified the Mauritius Convention: among 23 signatories, only five have ratified it so far (Cameroon, Canada, Gambia, Mauritius and Switzerland). Consequently, the Mauritius Convention only applies to investment treaties among these states. There does not seem to be much interest from other signatories in ratifying the Mauritius Convention any time soon. In addition, the Convention does not apply to investor–state arbitrations initiated pursuant to contracts or domestic investment-protection laws. Such arbitrations constitute almost one-sixth of all cases initiated at ICSID to date.[31] Because of the limited scope of application of the Convention, many cases will fall outside its scope.

H. Set-Offs and Counterclaims

In investor–state arbitrations, a set-off is a defence that money owed by an investor to a host state should be counter-balanced against the investor's claim against the host state.[32] If the arbitral tribunal entertains the host state's set-off defence, it could reduce or extinguish the potential amount for which the host state is liable. In addition, the life of a set-off depends on the principal claim raised by the investor. Therefore, if a tribunal finds against the principal claim, the set-off defence will not be heard.[33] Different from (but related to) a set-off defence, a counterclaim is a new and independent cause of action, raised by the host state against the investor. However, the counterclaim must arise from the same legal and factual context as the principal claim. It was not common for states to bring counterclaims in the past. Both set-off defences and counterclaims centralise the hearing of related issues and avoid duplication, thereby promoting procedural economy. But unlike a set-off, which is dependent upon the principal claim, a counterclaim might raise a question of jurisdiction that the tribunal must resolve. Under ICSID Convention Article 46, tribunals can only exercise jurisdiction over counterclaims that 'are within the scope of the consent of the parties'.[34]

In recent cases, tribunals have diverged on whether there is sufficient consent for them to assert jurisdiction. The tribunal in *Roussalis v Romania* rejected jurisdiction on the grounds that the investor's mere filing of a claim with ICSID was insufficient of itself

[31] B Wasiak, 'The Mauritius Convention on Transparency Enters into Force' (Investment Claims, October 19, 2017), available at www.arnoldporter.com/en/perspectives/publications/2017/10/the-mauritius-convention-on-transparency.

[32] SR Derham, *The Law of Set Off*, 3rd edn (OUP, 2003) [1.01]; see also C Kee 'Set-off in International Arbitration – What Can the Asian Region Learn?' (2005) 1 *Asian International Arbitration Journal* 141, 146.

[33] Kee (ibid) 146.

[34] Convention on the Settlement of Investment Disputes between States and Nationals of Other States (adopted 18 March 1965, entered into force 14 October 1966) 575 UNTS 159, Art 46.

to constitute consent to the bringing of a counterclaim.[35] The tribunal reasoned that 'the scope of the consent' of the parties must be determined by reference to instruments external to the ICSID Convention, such as by the dispute resolution clause in a BIT. In the case, the relevant dispute resolution clause did not cover counterclaims against investors.[36] On the other hand, the tribunal in *Goetz v Burundi* found that the Belgium-Burundi BIT covered disputes concerning the interpretation or application of any investment authorisation granted by host state authorities.[37] Therefore, the tribunal held that Burundi's counterclaims for a bank's alleged non-compliance with its operating certificate fell within this definition, and the tribunal could hear Burundi's counterclaims.[38]

I. Multi-Party Arbitration and Consolidation

Consolidation is a procedural mechanism through which two or more claims are united into a single procedure concerning all parties and their disputes. The need for consolidation arises when there are multiple arbitration proceedings with common questions of law or fact, often stemming from the same governmental measures. The UNCITRAL Rules and the ICSID Conventions do not have any provision for the consolidation of claims, whereas NAFTA and many investment treaties provide for consolidation.[39] In cases where consolidation of claims is possible, tribunals have to balance the advantages and disadvantages of consolidation when deciding whether to consolidate at a party's request. Consolidation can increase the efficiency of arbitration and avoid conflicting awards. But consolidation may be unfair to an objecting party. The objecting party may not have a say in the appointment of the tribunal hearing the consolidated claims. It may also not have consented to its claims being adjudicated in a consolidated manner. Further, it might be prejudicial to the objecting party's substantive rights in that consolidation could affect confidentiality where additional parties are joined to arbitral proceedings, especially where the other parties are an objecting investor's competitors.

J. A Word on Awards

Depending on the governing rules of an investment arbitration, the review of an arbitral award may be left to international tribunals (for ICSID arbitrations) or national courts (under the ICSID Additional Facility[40] and UNCITRAL arbitrations). Because national laws adopt different approaches towards the review of investment arbitral awards, this section focuses on the review process of ICSID arbitration.

[35] *Roussalis v Romania*, ICSID Case No ARB/06/1, Decision Concerning the Respondent's Counter-Claim (31 March 2009).

[36] ibid.

[37] *Antoine Goetz and others v Republic of Burundi*, ICSID Case No ARB/95/3, Award (10 February 1999).

[38] ibid.

[39] NAFTA, Art 1126(2)(b), US Model BIT, Art 33(6)(b), and Canada Model Foreign Investment Protection Agreement (FIPA), Art 32(2)(b).

[40] Non-parties to the ICSID Convention may still be able to have an ICSID-style arbitration under the ICSID Additional Facility.

Under Article 52 of the ICSID Convention, parties may request the annulment of an ICSID award. Grounds for annulment include: (1) the tribunal was not properly constituted; (2) the tribunal has manifestly exceeded its power; (3) there was corruption on the part of a member of the tribunal; (4) there was a serious departure from a fundamental rule of procedure; and (5) the award failed to state the reasons on which it was based. The application must be submitted to the ICSID Secretary-General within 120 days from the date on which the award was rendered, except in cases of corruption. Having received the request, the Chairperson of the ICSID Board of Directors appoints a three-person committee from the ICSID Panel of Arbitrators to hear the annulment application. The ICSID annulment procedure functions under the principle of 'limited cassation'. The ad hoc committee may only confirm or annul the award. If the award is annulled, the dispute may be remitted for rehearing to a new tribunal constituted in accordance with the ICSID Convention.

Scholars have suggested that there have been at least three generations of annulment decisions. The first generation comprised the decisions of the ad hoc committees in *Klöckner v Cameroon* and *Amco v Indonesia*.[41] The ad hoc committees in these cases did not assess procedural defects, but reviewed the merits of the decisions of the original arbitration tribunals. The second generation comprised the decisions in *MINE v Guinea* and subsequent decisions in *Klöckner v Cameroon* and *Amco v Indonesia*. These reversed the trend of the first generation by affording greater deference to first instance arbitral decisions.[42] Scholars argue that the third generation of annulment decisions reached an equilibrium between the first two generations. An example of the third generation is the decision in *Wena v Egypt*.[43] At the end of the day, the key question for an ad hoc committee dealing with an annulment request is how much deference it should accord to the tribunal of first instance. One end of the spectrum would be only to assess procedural shortcomings as is done in international commercial arbitration. On the other end of the spectrum is a full appellate hearing, which would be similar to the appellate mechanism in WTO disputes.

II. Problems with ISDS

A. Transparency

Confidentiality is a major advantage of commercial arbitration. However, the involvement of a state as a party in international investment arbitrations has raised questions

[41] *Klöckner Industrie-Anlagen GmbH and others v United Republic of Cameroon and Société Camerounaise des Engrais*, ICSID Case No ARB/81/2, Ad Hoc Committee Decision on Annulment (3 May 1985); *Amco Asia Corporation and others v Republic of Indonesia*, ICSID Case No ARB/81/1, Ad hoc Committee Decision on the Application for Annulment (16 May 1986).

[42] *Klöckner*, Second Ad Hoc Committee Decision on Annulment (17 May 1990); *Amco*, Decision on the Applications for Annulment of the 1990 Award and the 1990 Supplemental Award (17 December 1992); *Maritime International Nominees Establishment v Republic of Guinea*, ICSID Case No ARB/84/4, Decision of Ad Hoc Annulment Committee (22 December 1989).

[43] *Wena Hotels Ltd v Arab Republic of Egypt*, ICSID Case No ARB/98/4, Decision (Annulment Proceeding) (5 February 2002).

about the appropriateness of principles of privacy and confidentiality. Stakeholders have called for more procedural transparency, because of the important public interest at stake. Indeed, more policymakers have recognised that investor–state disputes have unique features that require specifically tailored rules to strike a balance between protecting business and state secrets on the one hand and the need to inform the public on the other. But the arbitration rules for ISDS do not provide much guidance on the issue of confidentiality and leave it to the discretion of a tribunal. The absence of explicit standards has generated much legal and procedural uncertainty. For example, the ICSID Convention initially did not contain any explicit reference to the submission of amicus curiae briefs.[44] Similarly, prior to the Transparency Rules, the UNCITRAL Rules did not offer guidance on transparency. Given the regulatory void in terms of transparency, the authority to make relevant decisions shifts to the arbitral tribunals. A case in point was the ICSID case of *Suez-Vivendi*, in which there was a request for participation as an *amicus curiae*. The tribunal acknowledged that matters of public interest were at stake, because 'the investment dispute center[ed] around the water distribution and sewage systems of … Buenos Aires and surrounding municipalities' and '[a]ny decision rendered in this case … has the potential to affect the operation of those systems and thereby the public they serve'.[45] As a result, the tribunal held that it had the authority to accept *amicus curiae* briefs.

A recent development was the incorporation of the Transparency Rules into the UNCITRAL Rules in 2014. However, the scope of application of the Transparency Rules is generally limited to UNCITRAL arbitrations commenced under treaties concluded after 1 April 2014, unless the parties otherwise consent. Most present BITs remain outside the scope of the automatic application of the rules. This, in turn, limits the effect of the Transparency Rules. In addition, the ICSID Secretariat published proposals for amendments to its Rules. The proposed amendments include clarifications on the publication of ICSID Convention awards and amendments on participation of non-disputing parties. To sum up, although a lack of transparency has long been a source of criticism of ISDS, recent developments (such as more explicitly expressed rules regarding transparency and third-party participation in dispute-settlement proceedings) demonstrate positive changes in this regard.

B. Certainty

A legal system generates certainty when its decisions are coherent and consistent. Certainty engenders predictability, thereby increasing the credibility and legitimacy of this legal system. On the contrary, if a legal system produces inconsistent outcomes, it is unpredictable and uncertain. That would consequently increase the parties' associated

[44] E De Brabandère, 'NGOs and the "Public Interest": The Legality and Rationale of Amicus Curiae Interventions in International Economic and Investment Disputes' (2011) 12 *Chicago Journal of International Law* 85, 86.

[45] *Suez, Sociedad General de Aguas de Barcelona, SA and Vivendi Universal, SA v Argentine Republic*, ICSID Case No ARB/03/19, Order in Response to a Petition for Transparency and Participation as Amicus Curiae (19 May 2005) 19.

costs to settle disputes and drive parties away from the legal system. ISDS has been criticised for its lack of certainty.

The best example to illustrate the uncertainty inherent in ISDS are the contrasting outcomes in *Lauder v Czech Republic* and *CME v Czech Republic*.[46] The two cases concerned the same conduct by a single host state toward a single investment. In both, the tribunals were called upon to decide whether the Czech Republic had unlawfully expropriated foreign investors' property. But the tribunals came to different results. In addition, the tribunals differed on the issue of whether the Czech Republic's conducts caused the foreign investors any harm. Due to these differences in reasoning and findings, *CME* and *Lauder* has brought uncertainty as to what acts and measures host states can legitimately take without incurring liability under international investment law.

The causes of the uncertainty in the ISDS system are multifold. First, legal issues in investment arbitrations often concern legal concepts that are designed to be applied to a broad range of situations and therefore are generally open to different interpretations. As the example of *Lauder* and *CME* suggests, the concept of expropriation is itself subject to more than one interpretation. Second, investment arbitrations have the feature of decentralisation which amplifies the problem of uncertainty. Different treaties contain different wordings of the same concept; different arbitral institutions have different procedural rules. More importantly, there is no appellate body in investment arbitrations to correct inconsistent awards and generate certainty in outcomes. Although *stare decisis* has been a long-established principle in domestic courts, arbitral tribunals are not bound by *stare decisis* so that different tribunals may reach different outcomes based on similar facts. In addition, courts faced with similar parallel claims will often have recourse to well-established and robust case management measures, such as a stay of proceedings, to prevent the same dispute from being litigated in parallel in multiple fora.[47] Third, international investment law is a relatively new field of law. ICSID was not established until 1965, and significant case law did not start to take shape until the late twentieth century with the end of the Cold War. Therefore, the result that international investment law appears to offer less certainty than domestic law might be attributed to the fact that it is still in the process of being developed. However, one might question whether certainty is necessarily a desirable goal in international investment arbitration. Some commentators have suggested that inconsistency is an inherent feature of investment arbitration and the elimination of that characteristic could jeopardise the tribunal's duty and authority in deciding a dispute accurately.[48] But the majority view remains that certainty is desirable and more measures should be taken to improve certainty in investment arbitrations.[49]

[46] *Ronald S Lauder v Czech Republic*, Final Award (3 September 2001); *CME Czech Republic BV v Czech Republic*, Final Award (14 March 2003).

[47] See ch 8 section III.D.

[48] T Schultz, 'Against Consistency in Investment Arbitration' in Z Douglas, J Pauwelyn, and JE Vinuales (eds), *The Foundations of International Investment Law: Bringing Theory into Practice* (OUP, 2014).

[49] See eg G Kaufmann-Kohler, 'Is Consistency a Myth?' in E Gaillard and Y Banifatemi (eds), *International Arbitration Institute, Precedent in International Arbitration* (Juris Publishing, 2008) 137–48.

C. Accountability

Accountability of international investment arbitrations has often drawn criticism. In domestic court settings, various mechanisms have been designed to ensure the accountability of judges. For example, before appointment to the bench, a candidate normally has to go through a comprehensive vetting processes to establish one's qualifications and impartiality. Judicial appointment often comes with life tenure which reduces the likelihood of judges being beholden to other branches of government. In addition, judges receive fixed compensation from the state which helps combat corruption. Finally, there are usually disciplinary proceedings to remove misbehaving or incompetent judges. Matters are different when it comes to international investment arbitration. Arbitrators are appointed by the parties or the arbitration institution. Arbitrators do not have life tenure. They are appointed on an ad hoc basis. So their decision in a case may inevitably affect their position and reputation in the market and influence their chances of being reappointed. This feedback loop represents a different form of accountability.

It might be suggested that arbitrators have stronger incentive to be responsive and accountable because they do not have life tenure and their career largely depends on their reputation on the market. But it might equally be suggested that arbitrators are beholden to the party appointing them. Consciously or subconsciously, arbitrators may be influenced by the possibility that by deciding a case in a manner contrary to the interests of the party appointing them may lead to the latter not appointing them in the future. Second, arbitrators receive compensation from the parties. However, because the costs are normally apportioned equally between the parties, there is no obvious incentive for the arbitrators to play favourites between the parties. Third, arbitrators face much less disciplinary oversight in the international investment context. In some rare situations, an arbitrator might be disqualified. If an award is subject to procedural errors, it might be subject to annulment. But such supervision as there is appears to be weak when compared with what domestic judges face. In the absence of clear rules regulating the conduct of arbitrators, their accountability will inevitably come into question.

D. Expense

The high expense of international investment arbitration has long been an area of concern. The cost of arbitration includes fees for arbitrators, administration, legal representation and experts. Because few publicly available awards provide a detailed accounting of legal and arbitration costs, it is hard to gauge the exact expenses involved in many arbitrations. Nevertheless, a 2007 report of the ICC Commission on Arbitration found that legal expenses for counsel and experts on average accounted for about 82 per cent of the total costs of both parties, arbitrators' fees for 16 per cent, and institutional costs for two per cent.[50] A study also indicates that the share of legal costs

[50] ICC, Techniques for Controlling Time and Costs in Arbitration: Report from the ICC Commission on Arbitration (2007).

may even exceed 90 per cent of total costs, determining that disputing parties' costs for lawyers and experts average US$9 million.[51] The high legal cost has generated debate about the role of law firms in driving up the costs of investment treaty arbitration.[52] It is common for lawyers to charge several hundred dollars per hour; and even US$1,000 per hour at leading law firms.

Moreover, the parties also have to bear the costs associated with experts and witnesses, which can be prohibitively expensive. In terms of the allocation of costs, there are usually two approaches. The most prevalent approach is 'pay your own way' whereby parties share the costs of the proceedings and bear their own legal costs. The alternative is 'loser pays' in which the losing party bears all or part of the costs of the prevailing party. Tribunals usually have a discretion in deciding how to award costs and they frequently adopt the 'pay your own way' rule in investment treaty arbitration. Some arbitral rules (such as UNCITRAL Rules Article 42) stipulate that in principle the losing party has to pay for all legal and arbitration costs, but the tribunal has the discretion to decide a different cost allocation. In practice, the 'loser pays' principle is rarely adopted.[53] Daunting legal fees have become a major obstacle for developing countries to defend their cases meaningfully. Such states will not have the in-house capability to litigate an investment treaty case, because ISDS is a highly specialised area. Although outside counsel can help these governments better defend their cases by reason of counsel's knowledge and experience in representing claimants and respondents, developing countries might not be able to afford their legal fees. Therefore, the question of how developing countries can keep down legal costs without compromising their defence remains unanswered.

E. Enforcement

Enforcing a favourable arbitral award against a state can be difficult, especially when the state declines to pay. However, when a respondent state refuses to pay, an arbitral tribunal has little ability to enforce the award. Therefore, investors will have to enforce their awards through the national courts of jurisdictions in which respondent states have assets. Articles 53 and 54 of ICSID Convention make clear that domestic courts should accord a high degree of deference to final arbitral awards and treat them much as a 'final judgment of a court in that State'.[54] But Article 55 allows a respondent state to raise sovereign immunity as a defence to enforcement of an ICSID award.[55]

Sovereign immunity is a principle of public international law that protects states by conferring immunity on them from enforcement and execution against their assets. In many jurisdictions, there are exceptions to the sovereign immunity principle when a state's acts are commercial, rather than sovereign, in nature. ISDS case law

[51] M Hodgson, Costs in Investment Treaty Arbitration: The Case for Reform, TDM 1 (2014).

[52] Organization for Economic Co-operation and Development (OECD), 'Investor-State Dispute Settlement Public Consultation: 16 May–9 July 2012' (2012).

[53] B Sabahi, *Compensation and Restitution in Investor-state Arbitration: Principles and Practice* (OUP, 2011) 163.

[54] ICSID Convention, Art 54.

[55] ibid Art 55.

recognises this possible limitation to sovereign immunity. For example, in *LETCO v Liberia*, the claimant sought to enforce an award against Liberia's assets in the US.[56] The US court confirmed the award in accordance with ICSID Convention Article 54 and granted an ex parte order directing entry of the judgment for the amount specified in the award.[57] A writ of execution was issued by the US Marshal. In response, Liberia sought to vacate the ex parte judgment or (in the alternative) the execution order on the basis of sovereign immunity. The US court rejected Liberia's request to have the recognition of the award vacated, because Liberia had waived sovereign immunity in the US when signing the ICSID Convention.[58] But the US court granted Liberia's motion to vacate the executions because the assets at issue were not commercial in nature. The assets were tax revenues, and 'The levy and collection of taxes intended to serve as revenues for the support and maintenance of governmental functions are an exercise of powers particular to a sovereign'.[59]

Similarly, in *AIG Partners v Kazakhstan*, when the claimant sought to seize assets of the Central Bank of Kazakhstan in the UK, the English court considered the question whether the bank's assets were immune from execution.[60] The English court decided that the assets were not for commercial purposes and were thus shielded from execution on the basis of sovereign immunity. Most recently, Ukraine attempted to resist enforcement of an award in the UK by arguing that it had not waived sovereign immunity. It contended that it had not agreed to submit two of the claims to arbitration.[61] The English court held that because Ukraine had explicitly agreed in the relevant BIT to submit 'Any dispute' between a contracting party and an investor of the other contracting party 'in connection with investments' to a competent court or arbitration, Ukraine could no longer raise sovereign immunity.[62]

In conclusion, obtaining a favourable award is not the end of the story. There will still be significant hurdles to overcome in enforcing an award, especially when respondents aggressively resist execution in domestic courts. The case law suggests that domestic courts in general will comply with the ICSID Convention and recognise the validity of the awards. But claimants still have to prove that there has been a waiver of sovereign immunity or that the assets to be seized have been earmarked for commercial rather than sovereign purposes so as to repel a sovereign immunity defence.

F. Diversity of Arbitrators

The lack of diversity among arbitrators is notable in international investment law. Early studies have found that between three and seven per cent of arbitrators in ICSID cases were female.[63] A recent study covering arbitrators in ICSID and non-ICSID cases found

[56] *Liberian E Timber Corp v Government of Republic of Liberia*, 650 F Supp 73, 75 (SDNY 1986).
[57] ibid.
[58] ibid 76.
[59] ibid 77–78.
[60] *AIG Capital Partners Inc & another v Kazakhstan* [2006] EWHC 2239 (Comm).
[61] *PAO Tatneft v Ukraine* [2018] EWHC 1797 (Comm).
[62] ibid.
[63] SD Franck, 'Empirically Evaluating Claims about Investment Treaty Arbitration' (2007) 86 *North Carolina Law Review* 1, measured 3% in 2006; L Greenwood and CM Baker, 'Getting a Better Balance on International

that 11 per cent of arbitrators were female.[64] But among all female arbitrators, two women account for 57 per cent of all appointments given to female arbitrators.[65] Gender is not the only diversity criterion against which the international investment arbitration community fails. When it comes to nationality, investment arbitration is dominated by arbitrators from Western countries. A study has found that, as at 1 August 2019, only 35 per cent of 695 individual arbitrators who sat in at least one investment case were from non-Western countries.[66] Half of non-Western arbitrators were from Latin America and the Caribbean. Only two per cent were from Sub-Saharan Africa.[67] 90 per cent of the arbitrators received their higher education in OECD countries.[68]

The result is more troubling if one looks at the reappointment rates of arbitrators. More than 700 arbitrators have been appointed in investment arbitrations, but the same arbitrators tend to be reappointed multiple times. For example, a group of 50 arbitrators accounted for 1,710 appointments, almost half of all the appointments through to 1 January 2019.[69] Lack of diversity in the pool of arbitrators contributes to the concern that tribunals are biased against developing states, because representatives from developing states are excluded from decision-making bodies. The investment arbitration regime has been criticised for fostering neocolonialism and perpetuating the values of the global North. This criticism is exacerbated by the fact that the majority of arbitrators tasked with interpreting the rules and adjudicating disputes are from the same dominating culture and background.

III. Proposals for Reform and Possible Future Trajectories

As one can see from the problems listed above, ISDS continues to be controversial, spurring debate in the investment community and the public at large. In response, states have put forward various reform proposals to mitigate or eliminate these problems. Almost all recently concluded international investment agreements contain one or more of the proposed reforms. Some suggestions are more radical than others. For example, proposals have ranged from limiting the relief that tribunals can grant to investors, to

Arbitration Tribunals' (2012) 28 *Arbitration International* 653, found 5.63% in 2012; G Van Harten, 'The (Lack of) Women Arbitrators in Investment Treaty Arbitration' (2012) 59 *Columbia FDI Perspectives*, measured 4% in 2012; S Puig, 'Social Capital in the Arbitration Market' (2014) 25 *European Journal of International Law* 387, found nearly 7% in 2014; L Greenwood and CM Baker, 'Is the Balance Getting Better? An Update on the Issue of Gender Diversity' (2015) 31 *Arbitration International* 413, found 5.61% in 2014; and M Waibel and Y Wu, 'Are Arbitrators Political? Evidence from International Investment Arbitration' (2017) Working Paper, found less than 10% in 2017.

[64] TSt John, D Behn, M Langford and R Lie, 'Glass Ceilings and Arbitral Dealings: Gender and Investment Arbitration: (2018) PluriCourts Working Paper.

[65] M Langford, D Behn, and L Létourneau-Tremblay, 'Empirical Perspectives on Investment Arbitration: What do We Know? Does it Matter?' ISDS Academic Forum Working Group 7 Paper (15 March 2019).

[66] M Langford, D Behn, and M Usynin, 'Does Nationality Matter? Arbitral Background and the Universality of the International Investment Regime' (2018) PluriCourts Working Paper.

[67] W Kidane, The Culture of International Arbitration (OUP, 2017) 134–35.

[68] M Waibel and Y Wu, 'Are Arbitrators Political? Evidence from International Investment Arbitration' (2017) Working Paper 15.

[69] A Bjorklund, S Franck, C Giorgetti, W Kidane, A de Nanteuil and E Onyema, 'The Diversity Deficit' ISDS Academic Forum Working Group 5 Paper (30 March 2019) 5.

encouraging greater resort to mediation, and to enabling the participation of interested third parties in proceedings.[70] Among the proposals, a number which are of particular interest are discussed in more detail below.

A. Appeal Mechanism

A proposal that has attracted much attention is that of establishing an appeal mechanism. The current ISDS system has been criticised for a lack of consistency and certainty. Some also question the correctness of investment treaty arbitral awards. The creation of an appeal mechanism could ensure the procedural and substantive correctness of decisions, thereby promoting certainty. Under this proposal, the appellate body will be able to review and correct awards. In the long run, arbitrators should become more accountable as a result and a body of consistent legal authority will be developed so as to increase the coherence and predictability of ISDS. Questions remain as to how such an appeal system should be designed. It will be necessary to decide how broad the grounds of appeal should be. If appeal is restricted to issues of law, the appeal procedure could be relatively streamlined and faster. By contrast, some recently investment treaties include an appeal mechanism providing for appeal on factual and legal issues.[71] Another question is the standard of review. Should an appeal mechanism should provide for a review of issues *de novo* or should a degree of deference be accorded to the findings of the tribunal at first instance? If an appeal is successful, what remedies should the appellate body be able to provide? Will the body only be able to affirm, reverse or modify the initial award or should it remand a case to the original or another tribunal for further consideration? Remitting the case would cause further delay and increase the parties' costs.

Finally, stakeholders have suggested three different ways of establishing an appeal mechanism. First, the mechanism can be treaty-specific, so that states can tailor a system of appeal to the needs of particular BIT or FTA.[72] This approach might be easier to adopt because there would be a fewer number of states involved and the negotiation costs would be relatively lower. But it might still give rise to inconsistencies among different treaty-specific appeal bodies. Second, the mechanism can be set up on a purely ad hoc basis, just as what happens in the current ISDS framework. Third, institutions currently handling ISDS cases can develop their own appeal mechanisms. The 2004 ICSID Appeals Facility proposal has suggested possible features of an appeal mechanism.[73] This approach might be more desirable than the other two because it can help promote consistency and certainty in ISDS overall.

[70] UNCTAD, "Reforming Investment Dispute Settlement: A Stocktaking', available at investmentpolicy.unctad.org/publications/1194/reforming-investment-dispute-settlement-a-stocktaking.

[71] See eg EU-Singapore Investment Protection Agreement, Art 3.19 (signed on 19 October 2018).

[72] See eg Canada-EU Comprehensive Economic and Trade Agreement (provisionally in force since 21 September 2017).

[73] ICSID, 'Possible Improvements of the Framework for ICSID Arbitration' (22 October 2004) 14–16.

B. Appointment of Arbitrators

Under the current ISDS regime, members of ISDS tribunals are selected and appointed by a disputing party, by the parties jointly, or by an arbitral institution. This existing mechanism for constituting ISDS tribunals is based on party autonomy. However, arbitrators appointed through this mechanism have been criticised for lack of independence, expertise and diversity. Therefore, stakeholders have also advocated reforms of the process for selection and appointment of tribunal members. The goal of reform would be to guarantee that tribunal members are independent, impartial, and competent. Furthermore, methods of selecting and appointing arbitrators should also reflect standards of diversity and guarantee neutrality and accountability. A suggestion has been for membership of ISDS tribunals to be based on a pre-established roster. The roster would take into account gender balance, geographical distribution and balancing between arbitrators from developing and developed countries. Under the current regime, some arbitral institutions keep a roster of arbitrators but members are normally directly designated or appointed by states. So the reform of the roster should involve not only states, but also investors in deciding persons to be selected. Along the same lines, the procedures for inclusion of an arbitrator on the roster should be more transparent and open. This will in turn lead to greater accountability among arbitrators themselves. Moreover, this roster should be renewed regularly, so that new arbitrators can be introduced into already established circles of arbitrators.

There are also suggestions for a system of full-time adjudicators. This idea is part of the EU's broader proposal of establishing a standing mechanism for ISDS. With respect to selection and appointment of arbitrators, it is suggested that these adjudicators should be full-time ISDS arbitrators who would not have any outside professional engagements. They would be paid salaries comparable to those paid to judges in international courts and be subject to ethical requirements. To ensure independence from governments, they will serve non-renewable terms of office and be subject to a robust and transparent appointment process.

C. Reducing Costs and Duration

There are also proposals aimed at reducing the costs and duration of ISDS arbitrations. The current ISDS regime has been said to be time-consuming and expensive. First, it is suggested that states should devise creative ways to reduce the excessive burden of ISDS proceedings. For example, wider adoption of ADR mechanisms such as mediation should be encouraged. ISDS institutions should set up expedited and simplified procedures for relatively smaller claims. Because expense has become an obstacle for parties, it is also proposed that there should be formalised rules, addressing third-party funding not only for claimants but also for states. Similarly, some espouse the establishment of advisory centres similar to the Advisory Centre on WTO Law or the creation of funds to support parties in ISDS similar to the Trust Fund established for the purposes of the ICJ. Second, stakeholders seek to shorten the duration of an ISDS arbitration through the imposition of stricter timelines.

For instance, to contribute to a more efficient proceeding, the arbitral rules should introduce time limits for parties to nominate arbitrators, file disqualification applications, and raise preliminary or jurisdictional objections. Unreasonable delays should not be tolerated. Actions by a party after expiry of a time limit should be disregarded unless the party establishes special circumstances justifying the delay.

Tribunals, however, should in turn be under an obligation to use best efforts to meet time limits for issuing orders, decisions and awards. Third, there are also suggestions on better management of the overall costs of proceedings. For example, the tribunal and the parties might have an early consultation at the outset to work out a budget for the proceedings. When discussing the budget, a schedule of fees can be introduced as a benchmark. If possible, the parties can also set a ceiling for overall costs and conduct periodic assessments of the case and its expenses. If this initiative is to be successful, arbitrators would need to take a more pro-active role so as to avoid unnecessary expenses.

D. The Future

While it is too early to gauge the actual effect of the foregoing reform proposals, there are two important takeaways. First, the reform proposals should be not viewed in isolation. They interact with each other and are directly related to changes in substantive international investment law principles. Therefore, when considering which proposals to adopt and which to reject, one must be aware of the context of the relevant proposals and their consequences in that context. Second, reform proposals should be oriented toward today's sustainable development imperative. A fundamental goal should be effectively to direct and deploy investments towards sustainable and realistic goals.

IV. A Radical Proposal: Formation of an Investment Court and Use of International Commercial Courts

The EU has proposed a radical approach to reform the existing ISDS system: a multilateral investment court. The goal of the proposal was to address concerns about unpredictability, impartiality and costliness of ISDS in a more systematic manner. Its rationale was that these concerns are all intertwined and fixing them in a piecemeal fashion would inevitably leave unresolved questions. In July 2014 European Commission President Jean-Claude Juncker pledged to replace the 'outdated' ISDS system. Following a public consultation and impact assessment by the European Commission from 2016 to 2017, the European Council mandated the Commission to negotiate a convention establishing a multilateral investment court on behalf of the EU and its Member States. In the EU's recently negotiated international investment agreements with Canada, Mexico, Singapore and Vietnam, there are provisions replacing the ISDS system with a bilateral international court regime as well as provisions anticipating the transition from bilateral international courts to a permanent multilateral investment court. On 30 April 2019, following a request by Belgium in 2017 regarding the investment agreement between Canada and the EU, the Court of Justice of the EU confirmed the compatibility of an international court system with the Treaties of the EU. A number of features of the proposed system are examined below.

A. Two Levels of Adjudication

The most significant feature of the multilateral investment court is that it will have two levels of adjudication. A first instance tribunal will hear disputes, conduct fact-finding, and apply the law to the facts. It will also deal with cases remitted by the appeal tribunal. It will have its own rules of procedure. Grounds of appeal will include errors of law, manifest errors in the appreciation of facts, and serious procedural shortcomings. However, the appeal tribunal will not undertake a *de novo* review of facts. The appeal tribunal will have authority to affirm, reverse, or modify the lower tribunal's decision. It can also remit a case to the first instance tribunal if it cannot otherwise dispose of the case.

B. Adjudicators

The adjudicators in the multilateral investment court will be employed full-time. They will not have any outside activities. The number of adjudicators will be based on the workload of the multilateral investment court. They will be paid salaries comparable to those paid to adjudicators in international courts. They will be subject to stringent requirements regarding qualifications and impartiality. Under this proposal, parties to a dispute will not be able to choose who will hear their case. Tribunal members will be selected and appointed on a rotational basis from a group of adjudicators who will have limited tenure. It is also suggested that the pool of adjudicators should be carefully selected to ensure geographical and gender diversity.

C. Enforcement

The proposed multilateral investment court will have its own enforcement regime, which would not provide for review at the domestic level. In addition, the proposal is that awards under the future multilateral investment court be capable of enforcement under the New York Convention on the basis that enforcement is possible for awards made by 'permanent arbitral bodies'.[74]

[74] New York Convention, Art 1(2).

D. Financing

The financing of the multilateral investment court will come from contracting states. The amount payable by a state will be weighted according to its level of development, so that the less developed and developing countries will bear a lesser burden than developed countries. The weighting applied in other international organisations could serve as a benchmark in determining the appropriate contribution obligation of a contracting state.

E. Application to Existing Treaties

The future multilateral investment court regime will be available for the resolution of disputes under existing and future investment treaties following: (a) accession to the instrument establishing the multilateral investment court; and (b) specific notification that an existing or future treaty will be subject to the court's jurisdiction.

6

The Way Forward in Investor–State Dispute Settlement

How Do We Balance the Needs of States with the Demands of Investors?

ANSELMO REYES

I. Introduction

This chapter will advance four propositions. First, closely examined, current approaches to fair and equitable treatment (FET), anti-expropriation (AE), national treatment (NT) and most favoured nation (MFN) clauses by investor–state arbitration tribunals all essentially involve striking a balance between the legitimate purposes of a state and the legitimate expectations of an investor. Second, it follows from Proposition 1 that investment treaty arbitration at heart involves an evaluation by a tribunal of the 'proportionality' of the government measures being challenged by an investor. More specifically, to be 'proportionate', an impugned government measure must meet four conditions:

(1) It must be shown that as a matter of domestic or international law, the state had the power to impose the challenged measure.
(2) If the state had the requisite power, it must be shown that, in taking the measure, the state was exercising the power to achieve a legitimate (that is, bona fide) purpose.
(3) Where conditions (1) and (2) are met, it must further be shown that the measure taken by the state was no more than what was necessary to achieve the identified purpose.
(4) Where conditions (1), (2) and (3) are met, the tribunal must be satisfied that, taking account of all circumstances and balancing the investor's legitimate expectations against the state's legitimate objectives, the measure taken by the state was justified.[1]

[1] On proportionality generally, see AS Sweet and J Matthews, *Proportionality Balancing & Constitutional Governance: A Comparative & Global Approach* (OUP, 2019). There is an extensive literature on proportionality

Proposition 3 is that, if the first two propositions are accepted, it is difficult to see how a tribunal which has simply been constituted in the traditional manner (that is, with the state and the investor each designating their arbitrator of choice and the two arbitrators so designated nominating a presiding arbitrator) can have the capability or mandate to determine investor–state disputes. Proposition 4 is that, consequently, a more transparent and sustainable method of dealing with investor–state disputes would be the creation of special investment courts along the lines envisaged in the 2018 EU–Singapore Investment Protection Agreement[2] or the future EU Multilateral Investment Court (MIC).

By way of methodology, this chapter will proceed by examining current formulas for FET, AE, NT and MFN clauses used in investment treaties or free-trade agreements and then engaging in a close reading of how such clauses have been dealt with by the tribunals in two cases: *El Paso v Argentina* (ICSID, 2011)[3] and *UPS v Canada* (NAFTA, ICSID, 2007).[4] The close reading will suggest that, in reality, the clauses examined deal with one or more of the questions in the proportionality test just summarised. This chapter will conclude with observations on technical questions that are likely to arise in the future in connection with setting up the special investment courts called for in Proposition 4. The conclusion will also touch on the difficulties of using: (1) international commercial courts (ICCs)[5] to resolve investment treaty disputes; and (2) international commercial mediation[6] to settle investor–state disputes.

II. Four Propositions

A. Proposition 1

Current approaches to standard investment treaty provisions essentially involve a balancing exercise between the needs of states and expectations of investors.

The objective of this section is to show that, regardless of whether a tribunal is analysing a state's obligations under an FET, AE, NT or MFN clause, the exercise in each case is essentially the same.

in investment treaty law, see (for example) GV Harten, *Investment Treaty Arbitration and Public Law* (OUP, 2007); GV Harten, *Sovereign Choices and Sovereign Constraints: Judicial Restraint in Investment Treaty Arbitration* (OUP, 2013) 34–38; G Bücheler, *Proportionality in Investor-State Arbitration* (OUP, 2015); V Vadi, *Proportionality, Reasonableness and Standards of Review in International Investment Law and Arbitration* (Elgar, 2018).

[2] The text of the Agreement is available at trade.ec.europa.eu/doclib/press/index.cfm?id=961.

[3] ICSID Case No ARB/03/15, available at www.italaw.com/sites/default/files/case-documents/ita0270.pdf. The Tribunal consisted of Professor Lucius Caflisch (Swiss, president), Professor Piero Bernardini (Italian) and Professor Brigitte Stern (French).

[4] ICSID Case No UNCT/02/1, available at www.italaw.com/sites/default/files/case-documents/ita0885.pdf. The Tribunal consisted of Sir Kenneth James Keith (New Zealand, president), Dean Ronald A Cass (American), and L Yves Fortier QC (Canadian).

[5] ICCs are discussed in detail in Pt 2 of this book.

[6] International commercial mediation is discussed in Pt 1 of this book.

i. FET Clauses

A typical FET clause (often combined with a full protection and security (FPS) provision) would be as follows:[7]

> 1. Each Party shall accord to covered investments treatment in accordance with applicable customary international law principles, including fair and equitable treatment and full protection and security.
> 2. For greater certainty, paragraph 1 prescribes the customary international law minimum standard of treatment of aliens as the standard of treatment to be afforded to covered investments. The concepts of 'fair and equitable treatment' and 'full protection and security' do not require treatment in addition to or beyond that which is required by that standard, and do not create additional substantive rights. The obligations in paragraph 1 to provide:
>   (a) 'fair and equitable treatment' includes the obligation not to deny justice in criminal, civil or administrative adjudicatory proceedings in accordance with the principle of due process embodied in the principal legal systems of the world; and
>   (b) 'full protection and security' requires each Party to provide the level of police protection required under customary international law.

In connection with FET and FPS, it is now usual to add a clarification along the following lines somewhere in a bilateral or multilateral investment treaty (BIT or MIT) or free-trade or economic partnership agreement (FTA or EPA):

> The Parties confirm their shared understanding that 'customary international law' generally and as specifically referenced … results from a general and consistent practice of States that they follow from a sense of legal obligation. The customary international law minimum standard of treatment of aliens refers to all customary international law principles that protect the investments of aliens.[8]

The breach of an FET obligation is alleged in almost every investor–state dispute. It is probably the most common breach raised in an investment treaty arbitration. In theory, to determine whether there has been such a breach, a tribunal must ascertain the 'international minimum standard' of fair and equitable treatment that states are obliged to accord investors and covered investments under customary international law.[9] But that is a vague test to use for identifying the content of an FET obligation and therefore of limited or even no utility. It is difficult (if not impossible) to identify an international minimum standard, typically by reference to customary international law, with any degree of objectivity and precision, so that it can be directly applied to a dispute.

To a large extent, what constitutes fair treatment is fact-sensitive and will differ from case to case depending on the peculiar circumstances of each. It may be perfectly possible to identify a broad principle – for example, that investors should at a minimum be entitled to the speedy resolution by domestic courts of their complaints against a state

[7] CPTPP Agreement, Ch 9 (Investment), Art 9.6.

[8] CPTPP Agreement, Annex 9-A (Minimum Standard of Treatment).

[9] See M Paparinskis, *The International Minimum Standard and Fair and Equitable Treatment* (OUP, 2013). A norm of customary international law is usually established by evidence that the norm is adhered to by a substantial number of nations not as a matter of habit, but because of the belief (*opinio juris*) that the norm is legally binding.

in respect of an investment contract. The problem is that the mere statement of such a general principle will not get a tribunal very far. The tribunal will still have to assess what constitutes 'speedy resolution' where (say) a state has only limited resources to invest in a judicial system and even cases brought by the state's own nationals take a long time to be processed. If the 'international minimum standard' test is not of much assistance, how do tribunals go about determining in practical terms whether there has been a breach of FET in practice?

The award in *El Paso v Argentina* is illustrative. El Paso (a US company) alleged that Argentina had promulgated laws and regulations that effectively rendered its shareholdings in certain Argentinian electricity and oil companies worthless. El Paso accordingly contended that Argentina had breached the terms of a US-Argentina BIT. Argentina countered that the laws and regulations against which El Paso was complaining were imposed to deal with an unprecedented economic crisis that the country was facing at the time, and the BIT did not preclude Argentina from imposing such financial measures as it thought were called for to deal with the emergency and prevent its economy from total meltdown.

The tribunal in *El Paso* began its analysis of FET by identifying two approaches to FET:

> 332. Under the first approach, FET has to be equated with the minimum standard of treatment provided for by general international law …
>
> 333. The second approach deals with FET as an autonomous concept, considered in general as more demanding and more protective of investors' rights than the minimum standard of treatment provided for by general international law …
>
> 334. Between these two approaches, some tribunals chose not to decide …
>
> 335. The Tribunal considers this discussion to be somewhat futile, as the scope and content of the minimum standard of international law is as little defined as the BITs' FET standard, and as the true question is to decide what substantive protection is granted to foreign investors through the FET. The issue is not one of comparing two undefined or weakly defined standards; it is to ascertain the content and define the BIT standard of fair and equitable treatment.
>
> 336. This being said, it is the view of the Tribunal that the position according to which FET is equivalent to the international minimum standard is more in line with the evolution of investment law and international law and with the identical role assigned to FET and to the international minimum standard. The Tribunal wishes to emphasise what is, in its view, the specific role played by both the general international minimum standard and the FET standard as found in BITs. The role of these similar standards is to ensure that the treatment of foreign investments, which are protected by the national treatment and the most-favoured investors' clauses, do not fall below a certain minimum, in case the two mentioned standards do not live up to that minimum …
>
> 337. In conclusion, it is the Tribunal's view that the FET is not to be viewed with reference to national law – in which case it could be lower than required by international law – but has to be interpreted with reference to international law, the result being that it cannot go below what is required by international law, which is the standard to be applied. But if national law or the treatment accorded to some foreigners exceeds this minimum international standard, it is one of the former that has to be applied. In a sense, it could be said that the foreign investor is entitled to the most favourable treatment, be it national law, rules applied to some foreigners or the international minimum standard embodied in FET. The Tribunal thus considers that the FET of the BIT is the international minimum standard required by international law, regardless of the protection afforded by the national legal orders.

It is respectfully submitted that the foregoing discussion of FET is contradictory. It says everything and nothing. On the one hand, the tribunal seemingly (and, in the author's view, rightly) rejected the minimum international standard as too vague to be of help. What should instead be done (the tribunal suggested) is to deduce the requisite FET standard from the terms of a BIT. It is not spelled out just what such inferential exercise entails or whether it is even practically possible. On the other hand, the tribunal concluded that the international minimum standard nonetheless remains relevant after all as setting a bottom line for FET. Where national law is more favourable than the minimum standard, investors should be afforded such better standard of treatment. Thus, according to tribunal, the international minimum standard test for FET is at the same time too vague for determining whether there has been a breach of FET and sufficiently ascertainable to constitute a bottom line for the treatment that a state should accord to investors.

The tribunal went on to consider case law on FET. It identified 'different conceptions' of FET that have been used by arbitral tribunals in other cases. Examples of these conceptions are: (1) the view that 'the State has a duty to adopt a proactive behaviour in favour of the foreign investment';[10] (2) the view that 'the State is under an obligation to stabilise the legal and business framework in which the foreign investment was made';[11] and (3) the view that 'FET is only violated by *wilful bad faith behaviour* of the State'.[12] The tribunal found that these three conceptions were untenable for various reasons. The tribunal opted instead (again in the author's view rightly) for an approach premised on legitimate expectations:

> 355. The Tribunal, for its part, is inclined to accept the overwhelming jurisdictional trend … which considers that the concept of fair and equitable treatment must be analysed with due consideration of the legitimate expectations of the Parties … If legitimate expectations of the foreign investors are to be taken into account at all, it has to be stressed that of course all the elements that the investors would like to rely on in order to maximise their benefits, if they are indeed expectations, cannot be considered legitimate and reasonable. The Tribunal will thus endeavour to specify what it thinks can be viewed as legitimate and reasonable expectations.
>
> 356. On the one hand, if this Tribunal indeed agrees that FET can be linked to foreign investors' legitimate and reasonable expectations, it insists, on the other hand, that these expectations, as well as their violation, have to be examined objectively … The Tribunal considers that the notion of 'legitimate expectations' is an objective concept, that it is the result of a balancing of interests and rights, and that it varies according to the context.
>
> 357. This means, firstly, that the Tribunal considers that a violation can be found even if there is a mere objective disregard of the rights enjoyed by the investor under the FET standard, and that such a violation does not require subjective bad faith on the part of the State …
>
> 358. This means also, secondly, that legitimate expectations cannot be solely the subjective expectations of the investor, but have to correspond to the objective expectations than

[10] *El Paso v Argentina* [341].
[11] ibid [344].
[12] ibid [347].

> can be deduced from the circumstances and with due regard to the rights of the State. In other words, a balance should be established between the legitimate expectation of the foreign investor to make a fair return on its investment and the right of the host State to regulate its economy in the public interest …
>
> 359. Moreover, according to this Tribunal, legitimate expectations necessarily vary with the surrounding circumstances …

More specifically, the Tribunal identified two principles for assessing whether there has been a breach of FET in light of the parties' legitimate expectations. The first principle is that FET implies that a state has acted reasonably and justifiably in modifying its legal framework in the manner of which complaint is made. The second principle is that FET implies that a state has not modified its legal framework in a manner that is contrary to specific commitments made towards an investor. The tribunal's chosen methodology therefore boils down (it is submitted) to applying a proportionality test to the breaches of FET being alleged by an investor. If one unpacks the tribunal's analysis, the two principles highlighted in actuality require a tribunal to ask itself four questions:

(1) Did the state have to power to impose the impugned measures?
(2) If so, were the measures imposed for a legitimate (bona fide) purpose?
(3) If so, were the measures no more than what was necessary to achieve that purpose?
(4) if so, to what extent (if at all) should the state's legitimate purpose override an investor's legitimate expectations arising from any express or implied commitments made by the state to the investor at the time of investment?

The first two questions will in all likelihood usually be answered in the affirmative (that is, in the state's favour).[13] A state will usually have in place (or be able to pass on an emergency basis) legislation empowering itself to act in a manner adverse to an investor. Further, it will be difficult for an investor to muster compelling evidence that a state has acted in bad faith and deliberately set out directly or indirectly to harm the investor's investment. The real battleground in an investor–state arbitration will therefore be in relation to questions (3) and (4). Under those questions, a state may still breach be in breach of FET despite acting in good faith. The state may have conducted itself in a way which constitutes 'overkill', going beyond what is necessary to achieve its legitimate purpose. To establish such excess, the investor will typically put forward alternative, less disruptive means, by which a state could have attained its avowed objective. But, even if the state acted in a manner which was not excessive, it may still have acted in a way that was contrary to specific commitments or representations made to the investor at the time of investing. Such commitments or representations would have engendered legitimate expectations on the investor's part that the state would not act in the way that it has done in the circumstances that have occurred.

In *El Paso*, the tribunal considered the various economic measures imposed by the Argentine Government to protect its currency (the peso) and their effect on the investor's investment. The tribunal concluded that, although each of the measures considered

[13] I am indebted to Professor Alec Stone Sweet for this insight.

in isolation would not amount to a breach of the FET obligation, their combined effect amounted to such a breach:

> 515. Although they may be seen in isolation as reasonable measures to cope with a difficult economic situation, the measures examined can be viewed as cumulative steps which individually do not qualify as violations of FET, as pointed out earlier by the Tribunal, but which amount to a violation if their cumulative effect is considered. It is quite possible to hold that Argentina could pesify [that is, require that prices be quoted in Argentine pesos], put a cap on the Spot Price, etc., but that a combination of all these measures completely altered the overall framework.
>
> …
>
> 517. It cannot be denied that in the matter before this Tribunal the cumulative effect of the measures was a total alteration of the entire legal setup for foreign investments, and that all the different elements and guarantees just mentioned can be analysed as a special commitment of Argentina that such a total alteration would not take place …
>
> 518. The Tribunal considers that, in the same way as one can speak of creeping expropriation, there can also be creeping violations of the FET standard. According to the case-law, a creeping expropriation is a process extending over time and composed of a succession or accumulation of measures which, taken separately, would not have the effect of dispossessing the investor but, when viewed as a whole, do lead to that result. A creeping violation of the FET standard could thus be described as a process extending over time and comprising a succession or an accumulation of measures which, taken separately, would not breach that standard but, when taken together, do lead to such a result.
>
> 519. The Tribunal, taking an all-encompassing view of consequences of the measures complained of by El Paso, including the contribution of these measures to its decision to sell its investments in Argentina, concludes that, by their cumulative effect, they amount to a breach of the fair and equitable treatment standard.

It is respectfully submitted that the tribunal's analysis was insufficient. The tribunal's conclusion instead strikes one as highly subjective and inadequately motivated. The tribunal accepted (at [398]) that, to the extent that legitimate expectations were concerned, 'any investor entering the energy market had to include the real possibility of reasonable changes and amendments to the procedures governing the WEM [wholesale electricity market]'. In those premises, one asks rhetorically: Why was Argentina not entitled to promulgate the impugned package of measures in the face of an unprecedented economic crisis? The difficulty with the tribunal's conclusion stems from its failure to grapple with question (3) of the proportionality test. Precisely how was the package of measures applied by the Argentine Government more than should have been necessary to deal with the difficult economic situation that the country was undergoing? It is not enough for a tribunal to say, in an omnibus way, that the cumulative effect of the Government's measures fatally undermined the investor's legitimate expectations. The tribunal must condescend to particulars and specify the economic measure or measures which went beyond what was required to deal with the crisis. Where and what precisely was the tipping point?

This problem is compounded because, from the comfort of one's armchair, an arbitrator might be able to say with the benefit of hindsight that such and such regulations were (or ultimately proved to be) unwarranted or of little effect in stemming the rapid devaluation of the peso and the threat of hyperinflation. But this is unrealistic. There is no recipe for dealing with an economic meltdown. In real time, it is hard to see how the Argentine Government can be faulted for promulgating a battery of measures to forestall financial collapse. Conversely, how can it plausibly be said that the investor had a legitimate expectation that Argentina would forbear from taking all of the economic measures that it took to avert a financial catastrophe?[14]

Nonetheless, putting to one side whether the tribunal's decision was substantively right or wrong, it is submitted that *El Paso* correctly questioned the usefulness of the 'minimum international standard' test and correctly applied a proportionality test in evaluating whether the state had run contrary to the investor's legitimate expectations by enacting the challenged measures.[15]

ii. AE Clauses

A typical AE clause would be as follows:[16]

1. No Party shall expropriate or nationalise a covered investment either directly or indirectly through measures equivalent to expropriation or nationalisation (expropriation), except:
   (a) for a public purpose;[17]
   (b) in a non-discriminatory manner;
   (c) on payment of prompt, adequate and effective compensation in accordance with paragraphs 2, 3 and 4; and
   (d) in accordance with due process of law.
2. Compensation shall:
   (a) be paid without delay;
   (b) be equivalent to the fair market value of the expropriated investment immediately before the expropriation took place (the date of expropriation);

[14] This does not mean that the tribunal should accord a wide degree of deference to a state when assessing whether its acts have been excessive. It simply means that the tribunal must establish, by reference to a clear economic analysis, why one or other measure taken by the state was excessive considering what was known and unknown at the time when the measure was implemented.

[15] In his award in *Pantechniki SA Contractors & Engineers v Albania*, ICSID Case No ARB/07/21 at [76]. Professor Jan Paulsson has suggested that proportionality would not apply where it is alleged that there has been a breach of FET as a result of a denial of justice. In his view, there are two reasons for this: 'The first is that international responsibility does not relate to physical infrastructure; states are not liable for denial of justice because they cannot afford to put at the public's disposal spacious buildings or computerized information banks. What matters is rather the human factor or obedience to the rule of law. Foreigners who enter a poor country are not entitled to assume that they will be given things like verbatim transcripts of all juridicial proceedings – but they are entitled to decision-making which is neither xenophobic nor arbitrary. The second is that a relativistic standard would be none at all. International courts or tribunals would have to make ad hoc assessments based on their valuation of the capacity of each state at a given moment of its development. International law would thus provide no incentive for a state to improve. It would in fact operate to the opposite effect: a state which devoted more resources to its judiciary would run the risk of graduating into a more exacting category.' There is force in this view. It is submitted, however, that it does not negate the relevance of proportionality. An investor would have a legitimate expectation that the courts of a host state will hear its case in a non-arbitrary manner and in accordance with due process. It is hard to see what 'legitimate purposes' of a state could ever override such expectation. Consequently, where there has been a denial of justice, a proportionality analysis will inevitably favour the investor.

[16] CPTPP Agreement, Ch 9 (Investment), Art 9.8.

[17] Footnote to the AE clause: 'For greater certainty, for the purposes of this Article, the term "public purpose" refers to a concept in customary international law. Domestic law may express this or a similar concept by using different terms, such as "public necessity", "public interest" or "public use".'

(c) not reflect any change in value occurring because the intended expropriation had become known earlier; and
(d) be fully realisable and freely transferable.

3. If the fair market value is denominated in a freely usable currency, the compensation paid shall be no less than the fair market value on the date of expropriation, plus interest at a commercially reasonable rate for that currency, accrued from the date of expropriation until the date of payment.
4. If the fair market value is denominated in a currency that is not freely usable, the compensation paid, converted into the currency of payment at the market rate of exchange prevailing on the date of payment, shall be no less than:

(a) the fair market value on the date of expropriation, converted into a freely usable currency at the market rate of exchange prevailing on that date; plus
(b) interest, at a commercially reasonable rate for that freely usable currency, accrued from the date of expropriation until the date of payment.

5. This Article shall not apply to the issuance of compulsory licences granted in relation to intellectual property rights in accordance with the TRIPS Agreement, or to the revocation, limitation or creation of intellectual property rights, to the extent that the issuance, revocation, limitation or creation is consistent with Chapter 18 (Intellectual Property) and the TRIPS Agreement.
6. For greater certainty, a Party's decision not to issue, renew or maintain a subsidy or grant, or decision to modify or reduce a subsidy or grant,

(a) in the absence of any specific commitment under law or contract to issue, renew or maintain that subsidy or grant; or
(b) in accordance with any terms or conditions attached to the issuance, renewal, modification, reduction and maintenance of that subsidy or grant,

standing alone, does not constitute an expropriation.

A clarification along the following lines may be added:[18]

The Parties confirm their shared understanding that:

1. An action or a series of actions by a Party cannot constitute an expropriation unless it interferes with a tangible or intangible property right or property interest in an investment.
2. Article 9.8.1 (Expropriation and Compensation) addresses two situations. The first is direct expropriation, in which an investment is nationalised or otherwise directly expropriated through formal transfer of title or outright seizure.
3. The second situation addressed by Article 9.8.1 (Expropriation and Compensation) is indirect expropriation, in which an action or series of actions by a Party has an effect equivalent to direct expropriation without formal transfer of title or outright seizure.

(a) The determination of whether an action or series of actions by a Party, in a specific fact situation, constitutes an indirect expropriation, requires a case-by-case, fact-based inquiry that considers, among other factors: (i) the economic impact of the government action, although the fact that an action or series of actions by a Party has an adverse effect on the economic value of an investment, standing alone, does not establish that an indirect expropriation has occurred; (ii) the extent to which

[18] CPTPP Agreement, Ch 9 (Investment), Annex 9-B (Expropriation).

the government action interferes with distinct, reasonable investment-backed expectations;[19] and (iii) the character of the government action.

(b) Non-discriminatory regulatory actions by a Party that are designed and applied to protect legitimate public welfare objectives, such as public health, safety and the environment, do not constitute indirect expropriations, except in rare circumstances.

It will be seen from the sample AE clause that a state can directly or indirectly expropriate an investor's property for a legitimate public purpose. But in such cases the state must compensate the investor by paying the fair market value of the property expropriated. Thus, even when a state does not violate its FET obligation (because it has acted for a legitimate purpose and not conducted itself in a manner contrary to an investor's legitimate expectations), the state may still be liable to compensate the investor where the state's conduct amounts to the taking of the investor's tangible or intangible property. However, there is a qualification to what has just been stated. That is because, as in the sample clause above, BITs, MITs and FTAs typically go on to provide expressly that non-discriminatory acts carried out to protect 'legitimate public welfare objectives' (including measures to protect public health, safety, and the environment) will only constitute indirect expropriation 'in rare circumstances'.

Direct expropriation will involve the transfer of an investor's property to a state by an express act to that effect. Such conduct will usually amount to blatant confiscation. More often, the debate will be whether there has been indirect expropriation due to conduct by a state that has not been expressly or ostensibly targeted at an investor. In *El Paso*, the tribunal took the view that indirect expropriation must involve the 'neutralisation of the use of an investment' by the state's conduct. That means (quoting the headings to some of the sections of the *El Paso* tribunal's award): (1) 'As a Matter of Principle, General Regulations Do Not Amount to Indirect Expropriation.' (2) 'By Exception, Unreasonable General Regulations Can Amount to Indirect Expropriation.' (3) 'At Least One of the Essential Components of the Property Rights Must Have Disappeared.' (4) 'A Mere Loss in Value of the Investment, even though Important, Is Not an Indirect Expropriation.'

The net result of the foregoing guidelines is that, in practical terms, indirect expropriation will be difficult to establish. It must be shown that the impugned conduct led to one's property becoming valueless or nearly so, and it must additionally be shown that the relevant conduct was not undertaken by the state to protect 'legitimate public welfare objectives'. One might wonder, then, whether there is any benefit to claiming indirect expropriation. What does such a claim add, that cannot be obtained by simply complaining of a breach of FET? In contrast to AE claims, where there has been unfair treatment, there will be a breach of the FET obligation regardless of whether one's investment has been completely deprived of value. In FET cases, there will be an obligation to restore an investor (typically through the payment of damages) to the same position

[19] Footnote to the clarification: 'For greater certainty, whether an investor's investment-backed expectations are reasonable depends, to the extent relevant, on factors such as whether the government provided the investor with binding written assurances and the nature and extent of governmental regulation or the potential for government regulation in the relevant sector.'

that it would have been in but for the state's wrongful conduct.[20] There will be no need to establish a taking or near taking of one's property or investment to qualify for such remedy. Even then, supposing that an investor can show that there has been a taking and its property or investment has been neutralised by a state's expropriatory conduct, the measure of compensation (that is, the fair market value of the property) will not differ significantly (if at all) from that arising from the breach of FET. It is consequently submitted that it will only be in 'rare circumstances' that there would be a need to rely on an AE clause. That would be where, despite there being no breach of FET (that is, no unreasonable or disproportionate act by a state and no contravention of an investor's legitimate expectations), there has still been an unwarranted taking of the investor's property. It is hard to imagine what such a situation would be.

The reality is that claims for indirect expropriation and breaches of FET will effectively overlap, with the measure of damages being the same in the two situations. The test for determining whether there has been a breach of FET and the test for indirect expropriation are in practical terms the same as the first three questions of the proportionality test. The only difference is that, with indirect expropriation, there is an additional evidential hurdle for the investor. If indirect expropriation is to be established, the investor must show that it has been deprived (or almost wholly deprived) of the value of its investment. But it is unclear why an investor would wish to take on that additional burden and make life more difficult for itself.

iii. NT and MFN Clauses

A typical NT clause would be as follows:[21]

1. Each Party shall accord to investors of another Party treatment no less favourable than that it accords, in like circumstances, to its own investors with respect to the establishment, acquisition, expansion, management, conduct, operation, and sale or other disposition of investments in its territory.
2. Each Party shall accord to covered investments treatment no less favourable than that it accords, in like circumstances, to investments in its territory of its own investors with respect to the establishment, acquisition, expansion, management, conduct, operation, and sale or other disposition of investments.

A typical MFN clause would be as follows:[22]

1. Each Party shall accord to investors of another Party treatment no less favourable than that it accords, in like circumstances, to investors of any other Party or of any non-Party

[20] Chorzów Factory, Judgment No 13 (Claim for Indemnity – The Merits) of 13 September 1928, ICJ Reports 1928, PCIJ, Series A, No 17, at 47. Frequently, a discounted cashflow (DCF) analysis is used to assess the investor's loss due to a breach of FET. Similarly, to determine fair market value, resort is often made to DCF analysis.

[21] CPTPP Agreement, Ch 9 (Investment), Art 9.4.

[22] CPTPP Agreement, Ch 9 (Investment), Art 9.5. A provision such as that in Art 9.5(3) is now routinely added to BITs or FTAs to make it clear the relevant MFN clause only covers substantive matters and does not enable an investor to take advantage of more liberal dispute resolution procedures found in other treaties entered into by a contracting state. Compare the conflicting approaches to whether an MFN clause covers both substantive and procedural provisions or only the former, in *Maffezini v Spain (Jurisdiction)* (ICSID, 2004) and *Plama v Bulgaria (Jurisdiction)* (ICSID, 2005).

with respect to the establishment, acquisition, expansion, management, conduct, operation, and sale or other disposition of investments in its territory.

2. Each Party shall accord to covered investments treatment no less favourable than that it accords, in like circumstances, to investments in its territory of investors of any other Party or of any non-Party with respect to the establishment, acquisition, expansion, management, conduct, operation, and sale or other disposition of investments.
3. For greater certainty, the treatment referred to in this Article does not encompass international dispute resolution procedures or mechanisms, such as those included in Section B (Investor–State Dispute Settlement).

Taken at face value, NT and MFN clauses concern discriminatory treatment. Ostensibly, they do not pertain to a minimum standard of conduct that a state must accord to all investors as a matter of international law. They apparently do not involve an 'absolute' obligation. Instead, they are relative obligations in that they require an investor to identify some 'treatment' which, as between the investor and a comparator class of like investors, is demonstrated to be discriminatory. A claimant must show that the identified comparator (that is, an identified class of domestic or foreign investors 'in like circumstances' to the claimant investor) is being treated more favourably by the state.

The difficulty with such test for discriminatory treatment is that much depends on the identification of an appropriate comparator. The claimant will seek to define the comparator as broadly as possible to increase its prospects of establishing discriminatory treatment between itself and some member of a wide class. The state will define the comparator as narrowly as possible, even to the point of arguing that the investor should be regarded for some reason as belonging to a limited special class (*sui generis*). The state will then argue that the very few investors within the unique class have been subjected to the same treatment. In such circumstances, the objective criteria by which a tribunal is to choose between the two comparators proffered are not self-evident.

The tribunal's difficulty in identifying an appropriate comparator can be illustrated by reference to *UPS v Canada*. UPS, which provides courier and small package delivery services, complained that Canada was treating Canada Post (a government corporation) and Purolator (a courier service, 96 per cent was owned by Canada Post) more favourably than UPS and UPS Canada, especially in relation to the treatment of packages at Canadian customs. By a majority (Judge Kenneth Keith (President) and Yves Fortier QC (designated by Canada)), the tribunal held:

98. The evidence before us demonstrates that there are inherent distinctions between postal traffic and courier shipments that require the implementation of different programs for the processing of goods imported as mail and for goods imported by courier.
99. The Tribunal is convinced that the importation of goods as mail and the importation of goods by courier require different customs treatments because of their different characteristics.
100. The manner in which mailed goods arrive for importation into Canada is different from the manner in which courier shipments arrive. As a result of these differences, Customs designed separate processes for the clearance of mailed goods and courier shipments.
101. Customs accords treatment to inbound international mail under the Customs international processing system. Clearly, this treatment is not in like circumstances with treatment that Customs accords to couriers under the Courier/LVS program.

> 102. The principal factors which demonstrate to the satisfaction of the Tribunal that Customs treatment of international mail is not 'in like circumstances' with the treatment accorded to UPS Canada and other couriers including Purolator include:
>
> - couriers provide detailed advance information on shipments, thus permitting Customs to carry out risk assessments and other checks;
> - self-assessment in the Courier/LVS Program as contrasted to officer determinations in the postal process;
> - greater security of courier shipments through secure shipping routes and trade chain controls;
> - the need for expedited clearance by couriers to meet time-sensitive and time definite delivery standards;
> - the existence of contractual relationships between couriers and their clients;
> - the different roles performed by couriers such as brokerage and warehousing.
>
> 103. The distinctions between postal traffic and courier shipments are recognized not only in Canada but by Customs experts in the United States, the United Kingdom, the World Customs Organization and the UPU [Universal Postal Union].

However, it is respectfully submitted that the majority's analysis is unconvincing. A person wishing to send a small package to Canada from abroad or vice versa would in effect have a choice between using a courier service (such as UPS) or using the postal service. Different factors, including price and length of time required for delivery, will impact upon the person's decision to use one or other service. The two services are essentially in competition with and substitutes for each other. It would be artificial to distinguish between them by holding (as the majority did) that as a matter of generality postal and courier services are not comparable. The real question is why the differences between the two types of service identified by the majority mean that there is no unfairness in denying the competitive advantages that are available to Canada Post (including Purolator) to UPS.

A more persuasive analysis may be found in the dissent of Dean Ronald Cass (designated by UPS). He first set out the rival comparators put forward by the parties:

> 9. In connection with the determination of like circumstances, … Canada argues that any public policy rationale for distinguishing between two entities or investors makes them unlike. It is sufficient, in Canada's view, for differences in treatment to be based on 'legitimate policy considerations or public interest grounds' or to have any 'rational basis,' and suggests that dispute resolution tribunals should not 'second-guess the validity of public policy objectives' or whether 'there is a better way to meet these objectives.'…
>
> 10. UPS begins with a radically different notion of what like circumstances means. UPS suggests that being in the same economic sector or being in competition makes investors or investments in like circumstances. According to UPS, the essence of the 'like circumstances' determination is finding a competitive relationship in the market.

He found neither version compelling. He instead propounded a different view of how 'in like circumstances' should be assessed:

> 14. NAFTA does not require the sort of near identity of circumstances urged by Canada, a test that if adopted would substantially undermine the efficacy of Article 1102 [the NT clause in NAFTA]. Canada's approach would require an excessively close fit between the complaining investor or investment and the compared domestic investor or investment. National treatment protection would be dramatically reduced under that approach,

as it would eliminate any right to protection whenever there were differences between the complaining party and the compared investment or investor even if those differences were slight enough not to affect the competitive relationship that Article 1102 was designed to protect.

15. Further, Canada's proposed test would grant the government of any NAFTA Party extensive power to avoid national treatment obligations, giving conclusive weight to a Party's assertions that public policy supports divergent treatment of domestic and foreign investors or of particular investments. That position has not persuaded other tribunals and does not persuade me.
16. At the same time, UPS understates the similarity required for a complaining party to show like circumstances. It is not sufficient for a complaining investor to show that the investor or investment is in the same economic sector as, or competes with, an investor or investment of the NAFTA Party charged with violating its national treatment obligation. Sharing the same economic sector may be evidence that two businesses are in like circumstances. So, too, being in competition, even if businesses might be classified in different economic sectors, may be evidence of like circumstances. Yet, neither showing is conclusive of like circumstances. It is possible for two investors or enterprises to be in the same sector or to be in competition and nonetheless be quite unlike in respect of some characteristic critical to a particular treatment.
17. The most natural reading of NAFTA Article 1102, however, gives substantial weight to a showing of competition between a complaining investor and an investor of the respondent Party in respect of the matters at issue in a NAFTA dispute under Article 1102. Article 1102 focuses on protection of investors and investments against discriminatory treatment. A showing that there is a competitive relationship and that two investors or investments are similar in that respect establishes a prima facie case of like circumstances. Once the investor has established the competitive relationship between two investors or investments, the burden shifts to the respondent Party to explain why two competing enterprises are not in like circumstances.

Given evidence that Canada Post itself treated UPS as a competitor in relevant sectors, it followed that Canada's position that UPS and Canada Post (including Purolator) were not 'in like circumstances' was untenable. In Dean Cass's view, the mechanical approach taken by the majority of regarding UPS and Canada Post as being in unlike circumstances due only to abstract or formal differences between the general sectors in which they operated, would 'dramatically circumscribe'[23] the NT obligation. The services provided by UPS and Canada Post were in practical terms substitutable.

Taking one's cue from Dean Cass's analysis, the argument being made in this chapter is that NT and MFN clauses are really about determining whether an investor claimant is being discriminated against by a state's treatment of some comparator consisting of one or more domestic or foreign competitors. Where there is discriminatory treatment, the state will be in breach of an NT and MFN clause unless it can justify its conduct by showing that the claimant is not actually in competition with the domestic or foreign investors receiving preferential treatment. But, if this is correct, there would be little discernible difference between the breach of NT or MFN clauses on the one hand and FET and AE clauses on the other. That is because discriminatory treatment of a claimant will prima facie be unfair and inequitable. Discrimination

[23] *UPS v Canada* [49].

by the state having been established, the burden shifts. It would then be for the state to justify such treatment by reference to legitimate public policy objectives. Showing that a claimant is in different circumstances from a comparator class would be tantamount to establishing that there are legitimate public policy justifications for treating the investor differently and imposing the impugned measures on it despite the investor's legitimate expectation that it will not be discriminated against. That would be equivalent to answering questions (2), (3) and (4) of the proportionality test.

In summary, whether a tribunal is assessing the breach of an FET, AE, NT or MFN clause, it is effectively conducting the same exercise. It is carrying out a proportionality test and balancing the legitimate interests of the state against the legitimate expectations of an investor.

B. Proposition 2

Investment treaty arbitration requires a tribunal to assess the proportionality of government measures being challenged by an investor.

Proposition 2 follows from the discussion in the previous section. A tribunal assesses whether there has been a breach of NT, MFN, FET, or AE clauses, by balancing the legitimate expectations of an investor against the legitimate objectives of a state. In relation to a state's objectives, a tribunal must first evaluate whether some measure taken by the state: (1) was legally valid; (2) had a legitimate purpose; and (3) was no more than what was necessary to achieve such legitimate purpose. Where a measure meets those criteria, the tribunal then determines whether there is liability on the part of the state by balancing the investor's legitimate expectations (including that it will be treated fairly and equitably and will not be subject to unjustified discriminatory treatment) against the state's legitimate objectives.

C. Proposition 3

Given Propositions 1 and 2, a traditionally constituted arbitral tribunal will not have the mandate or legitimacy to determine investor–state disputes.

It is hard to see why a tribunal consisting of three arbitrators (a co-arbitrator selected by the state, a co-arbitrator selected by the investor, and a presiding arbitrator selected by the two co-arbitrators) should, merely by reason of their selection, have the authority, knowledge, or experience to decide how a proportionality or balancing exercise should be carried out in the relevant circumstances. This is especially the case where (as in *El Paso*) a tribunal's decision will inevitably touch on a state's economic development priorities and policies and inevitably affect the lives of the state's ordinary citizens.[24]

[24] See further S Menon, 'A Tale of Two Systems: The Public and Private Faces of Investor-State Dispute Settlement', Lalive Lecture 2021 (27 May 2021); F Xavier SC, 'A Multilateral Investment Court – A Mirage in the Horizon', Keynote Speech, IPBA Shanghai Conference 2021; K Kim, 'Current Developments and Challenges in Investor-State Dispute Resolution', Keynote Speech, IPBA Shanghai Conference 2021. The latter two keynote speeches may be found in the June 2021 issue of *IPBA Journal* (No 102) at 21 and 25 respectively.

D. Proposition 4

A more transparent method of dealing with ISDS would be the creation of special investment courts along the lines envisaged in the 2018 EU-Singapore Investment Protection Agreement or by the future EU Multilateral Investment Court (MIC).

Not surprisingly, given the disconnect between the composition of an ISDS tribunal and its task (that is, the assessment of some policy pursued by the respondent state), there has been dissatisfaction with the current state of ISDS. Why should arbitrators (typically, eminent law professors or international lawyers), merely because of their designation by a party, have the mandate to determine issues that could affect the economic, social and political well-being of a state? An obvious counter may be that the chosen arbitrators are acting with the authority and consent of the parties who have agreed to arbitration (including the procedure under the operative arbitration rules for the appointment of the arbitral tribunal). But it is submitted that such view is unpersuasive. That is because the decision of the arbitral tribunal in an investment-state dispute will affect the interests not just of the parties (the investor and the state government of the day) before it. The tribunal's decision will almost certainly have an impact on the lives and interests of the public, especially within the respondent state to the arbitration. Investment treaty arbitration differs from international commercial arbitration (ICA) in that the parties' private interests are not the only matters at issue in the former. In ICA, the tribunal's award only binds and concerns the parties to the arbitration agreement. The award can be kept confidential and not disclosed to the rest of the world for that reason. In contrast, the public interest is very much at stake in an investment treaty arbitration and the citizenry in the state parties to the treaty should therefore logically have some involvement in who may be appointed to an arbitral tribunal that will have an impact on their lives. By the same token, there should be greater transparency in the investor–state process (as opposed to the degree of confidentiality shrouding ICA). That greater openness should ideally include the possibility for affected non-parties to take part (for instances, as *amici curiae*) in investment treaty arbitrations.

The EU has sought to address the situation by setting up an MIC. The MIC is still at the discussion stage. It is proposed that the MIC be staffed by full-time adjudicators, presumably drawn from Member States and possibly other states, who will be paid a fixed salary and are not supposed to engage in other activities.

A possible way in which the MIC would operate may be seen from the 2018 EU-Singapore Investment Protection Agreement (yet to come into effect). As a means of resolving investor–state disputes, the latter provides for the establishment of a Tribunal of First Instance and an Appeal Tribunal. Singapore and the EU each nominate two members to the first instance and appellate tiers. The two state parties then jointly nominate two further members to each tier, neither of whom is to be a Singapore or EU national. Members of the first instance tribunal should 'possess the qualifications required in their respective countries for appointment to judicial office or be jurists of recognised competence'. Members of the appellate tribunal should 'possess the qualifications required in their respective countries for appointment to the highest judicial offices or be jurists of recognised competence'. Of the members for both tribunals, the Agreement requires that they:

> [S]hall have specialised knowledge of, or experience in, public international law. It is desirable that they have expertise, in particular, in international investment law, international trade law, or the resolution of disputes arising under international investment or international trade agreements.

The difference with the existing system of ISDS arbitration is that the state parties to an instrument would have a significant say on who will be resolving disputes relating to their economic, trade, investment, environmental, health, public welfare and other policies. If this model gains traction beyond the EU and Singapore to other countries, there would come into existence networks of MICs (including appellate courts), staffed by full-time international judges (some nationals of the countries party to the relevant agreements, others not) associated with specific BITs, MITs, and FTAs.

A spin-off from a network of MICs could be the creation of a stable jurisprudence on the proper construction and application of FET, AE, NT, and MFN clauses. At present, no particular tribunal's award is authoritative, or even persuasive. Awards are at best examples of how principles might be interpreted. Not surprisingly, then, it is possible to find an award saying one thing about a principle and another coming to an opposite conclusion. It is difficult to develop a settled jurisprudence in such circumstances as there is no authoritative pronouncement by a court of what a particular obligation entails. The same debates have the potential of continuing to perpetuity. Where the professional judges of an MIC pronounce on the law, their ruling will at least have persuasive value, especially when endorsed at the appellate level.

Judge Schwebel has been critical of the proposals for an EU MIC.[25] First, he suggests that to have judges appointed by states may lead to the MICs being biased in favour of states. Second, he contends that the proposed pool of candidates from which EU MIC judges are to be drawn is too narrow. Third, his 'fundamental objection' is that the EU MIC would be replacing the current system of ISDS with 'a system that would face substantial problems of negotiation, ratification, establishment, functioning, and financing'. The critique boils down to an assertion that *plus ça change, plus c'est la même chose.*

But it is respectfully submitted that the first criticism is speculative. Within the model of networks of MICs advocated here, the state parties to an investment treaty or agreement would be designating judges for the MICs to be established under those instruments. Those judges would be determining disputes between an investor of one state party and another state party. Everything else being equal, the state parties would not know in advance whether the claimant in a future dispute will be an investor from their state. Thus, it would be in the interest of a state party to designate judges: (1) who would be neutral or impartial as between state and investor interests; or

[25] SM Schwebel, 'The outlook for the continued vitality, or lack thereof, of investor-State arbitration' (2016) 32 *Arbitration International* 1.

(2) a representative body of judges, some of whom are reputed to favour state interests and others of whom are thought to favour investor interests. It may be that in some instances the likelihood will be that investors will predominantly be from one state party and that one or other state party to an instrument will likely be the respondents in any dispute. For example, consider a treaty between China and a country X along its Belt and Road Initiative. The probability is that, in relation to disputes brought to an MIC under the treaty, Chinese nationals will be the investor claimant and X will be the state respondent. In those circumstances, it would be in China's interest to designate at least a few judges who are thought to be sympathetic to investor interests as MIC judges.[26]

There may be some justification in the second criticism.[27] However, is the objection a showstopper? As argued here, a major objective of revamping the current system would be to instil greater transparency in ISDS, by appointing judges who can rule authoritatively on matters that touch upon the economic, social and political welfare of a state. If so, to restrict the judicial pool simply to persons with expertise in international investment law, international trade law, or the resolution of disputes arising under international investment or international trade agreements may be too restrictive. A state may wish to appoint economists, political scientists and other experts to sit as judges. The qualifications of MIC judges are something that state parties would be best qualified to negotiate over when drafting their instrument. It would be for the state parties to decide from the outset, rather than leaving matters (as now) to the caprices of the moment when a dispute arises and the parties (whether investor or state) manoeuvre to come up with a tribunal that favours their particular stance in the instant arbitration, rather than take a longer-term view.

The third observation simply states a reality. It will take time to set up an MIC between states. A network of MICs will not spring up overnight. But with the passage of time, given that more and more MICs are constituted, a standard pattern will develop which states can use as a template for their instruments. This would mean that, in due course, there will be a degree of harmonisation in the practices of MICs throughout the world. The fact that there will be difficulties is not a reason for casting the model aside. The question is instead the extent to which states feel that there is a serious disconnect in the present ISDS system between the arbitrators deciding questions that will inevitably affect the well-being of a state's citizens in the long term on the one hand and those very citizens on the other. If it is felt that there is indeed a disconnect, then something should be done to address it.

[26] In like vein to Judge Schwebel's first criticism, Professor Born argues that the EU MIC proposal is a blatant form of 'court-packing', analogous to proposals to make the US Supreme Court less political by enlarging the current bench of nine judges. In Professor Born's view, the EU MIC proposals 'have originated from the same extremes of the political spectrum as domestic American court-packing plans, and share many of the fundamental objectives of those plans'. Thus, for instance, according to Professor Born, by eschewing the current tried and tested system of investor–state dispute settlement, the upshot of the EU MIC proposal will be 'to reduce or eliminate international and independent adjudicative limits on the exercise of sovereign authority' by state parties to an investment treaty. See G Born, '"Court-Packing" and Proposals for an EU Multilateral Investment Court' Kluwer Arbitration Blog, 25 October 2021, available at arbitrationblog.kluwerarbitration.com/2021/10/25/court-packing-and-proposals-for-an-eu-multilateral-investment-court.

[27] The EU MIC has yet to be established. Judge Schwebel was criticising a draft term similar to that found in the EU–Singapore Agreement and quoted in the previous paragraph.

III. A Glimpse into a Possible Future

What might the future look like under a regime of such networks of MICs?

Hard or soft law instruments for the enforcement of the judgments of MICs will have to be worked out. But this should not be difficult, particularly if the judgments of the networks of MICs can be attributed to the states that are party to the relevant BITs, MITs or FTAs. The judgments would then be recognised and enforced in the same way that the regular judgments of courts are now recognised and enforced.[28] A universal civil procedure for MICs (it is submitted) can also be worked out. Here the Singapore International Commercial Court (SICC) Rules 2021, which came into effect in April 2022, might serve as a possible model.[29] This is because those rules: (1) are the product of discussions among civil and common law judges; (2) are couched in plain English (the *lingua franca* of transnational commercial law); and (3) allow for flexibility so that a case is progressed as appropriate through one of three tracks: (a) a pleadings track (similar to that used by many common law jurisdictions); (b) a statements track where facts are largely agreed and the court is only to determine questions of law; or (c) a memorials track (similar to that used in many civil law jurisdictions).

The COVID-19 pandemic has accelerated the use of remote technology in the hearing of transnational cases by courts and tribunals.[30] This technological development coupled with the existence of networks of MICs should open up possibilities for ISDS to be delocalised. Where MICs have judges from different countries in different times zones, the problems associated with a court's geographical location and time zone can be overcome. Assume a bench of three judges, each situated in a different time zone – perhaps a Singapore judge, an EU judge, and an American presiding judge. The judges in time zones A and B may hear evidence or submissions asynchronously from a party or witness in time zone A or B. The proceedings can be recorded and disclosed to the party in time zone C and that party can adduce rebuttal evidence and submissions to the judges in time zones B and C. Because everything is done remotely, the cost of travel and hotel accommodation (which can be substantial) will be minimised. The carbon footprint of stakeholders (judges, lawyers, witnesses, interpreters and hearing administrators) will likewise be minimised.

It has been argued in France that international commercial courts are only for those who can afford them.[31] But remote technology should bring the cost of ISDS down to an affordable level so that even MSMEs and smaller investors will benefit. Obviously,

[28] On the principles for the recognition and enforcement of judgments generally, see A Reyes (ed), 'Recognition and Enforcement of Judgments in Civil and Commercial Matters' in A Reyes (ed), *Recognition and Enforcement of Foreign Judgments in Civil and Commercial Matters (Studies in Private International Law: Asia, vol 1)* (Hart, 2019), especially chs 1 (Introduction) and 17 (Conclusion).

[29] The SICC Rules 2021 are available at www.sicc.gov.sg/docs/default-source/legislation-rules-pd/sicc-rules-2021.pdf.

[30] For further discussion, see Pt 6 of this book.

[31] See, for example, A Biard, 'International Commercial Courts in France: Innovation without Revolution?' (2019) 1 *Erasmus Law Review* 24, 30–31, available at www.erasmuslawreview.nl/tijdschrift/ELR/2019/1/ELRD-18-00023.pdf.

protocols to ensure due process will need to be worked out. Other technological developments can be brought into play (for instance, blockchain and artificial intelligence (AI)). We need to become accustomed to what is currently characterised as a 'new normal' following COVID-19. The dividend would be that future MIC benches of national and foreign judges, drawing on their experience and expertise and working together to resolve investment disputes, will lead to a body of authoritative case precedents and greater transparency and certainty in ISDS.

It might be asked whether existing international commercial courts (ICC) (such as the SICC) can play a role in ISDS. The difficulty is that at present no BIT, MIT or FTA identifies an ICC as a possible forum for the resolution of investor–state disputes. Parties may agree after a dispute has arisen to bring the same before an ICC. But this is improbable. It is hard to see a state agreeing, whether in an investment treaty or after a dispute has arisen, to have its disputes resolved by the ICC of another state. There would be issues of sovereignty that arise, making it difficult for the state to agree to ICCs as a dispute resolution option in an international treaty or free trade agreement.[32]

There is a related difficulty with the development of investor–state mediation to resolve disputes arising out of a BIT, MIT or FTA. In principle, much as with MICs, it ought to be possible in BITs, MITs or FTAs to set up special panels for the mediation of disputes arising out of the relevant instruments. But states may ultimately find it problematic to approve mediated settlements to a dispute with an investor, however advantageous the proposed settlement would be for the state. There will likely be political fall-out from a settlement with one or other rival government faction alleging that the ruling party has 'sold out' to an investor by agreeing to the same. A consensus among many departments within government may be needed before a settlement can be approved, and that would take time. A department may not wish to take on the responsibility of approving a settlement which may later be criticised when the political wind changes. An election or the assumption of executive power by a new faction can lead to a U-turn in ongoing negotiations with an investor, even when they have been progressing well. Frequently, governments would likely prefer to accept a resolution, even if far

[32] For instance, as a result of such agreement, the state may be perceived by its citizenry as having abdicated its autonomy to the ICC of another state. ICCs might still hear investment-treaty-related cases. Thus, where an investor–state dispute goes to ad hoc arbitration (frequently pursuant to the UNCITRAL Rules or the Arbitration Rules of the Permanent Court of Arbitration), the arbitration will likely be seated in a neutral venue which is not associated with either party. Applications may then be brought by a state before the court of the seat of arbitration to set aside an adverse award. Examples, in the case of Singapore seated arbitrations, are *Sanum Investments Ltd v Government of the Lao People's Democratic Republic* [2016] 5 SLR 536 (CA) and *Swissbourgh and others v Lesotho* [2019] 1 SLR 263 (CA). There is an additional difficulty where a treaty provides, as an option for resolving investor–state disputes, that a case be brought before the ICC of a state party to the treaty. In that situation, the decision of the ICC may itself be impugned by a disgruntled investor as further evidence of unfair and inequitable treatment by the state in which the ICC is located. On that basis, the investor may then bring the matter before an investment treaty arbitral tribunal. If the tribunal overrules the ICC, the courts of the losing state could then be in the invidious position of being asked by the investor to enforce an award that is contrary to the judgment of the state's own ICC. For a discussion of these and other problematic scenarios, see RS French, 'Investor-State Dispute Settlement – A Cut Above the Courts?' Keynote Speech, Australian Supreme and Federal Courts Judges' Conference, 9 July 2014, available at www.hcourt.gov.au/assets/publications/speeches/current-justices/frenchcj/frenchcj09jul14.pdf.

less favourable than a mediated settlement, to be handed down by a court or tribunal. In that way, it can be claimed that the resolution to a dispute was 'forced' upon the state as a matter of international law and the existing regime cannot be held responsible for the outcome. If this is correct, the sad reality may be that there will be few mediated settlements of investor–state disputes.[33]

[33] For a discussion of the dynamics of mediation in ISDS, see the Japan International Mediation Center (JIMC) webinar held on 25 June 2021, available at www.youtube.com/watch?v=a8e5TOJwEgQ.

PART IV

The Perfect as the Enemy of the Good – The Importance of Finality and Certainty

7

The Need for Finality and Certainty in International Commercial Dispute Resolution

WILSON LUI

I. Introduction

A. The Virtues of Finality and Certainty

Finality and certainty are concepts that are subject to various formulations in different contexts. Hart characterised 'finality' as follows:

> A supreme tribunal has the last word in saying what the law is, and when it has said it, the statement that the court was 'wrong' has no consequence within the system: no one's rights or duties are thereby altered.[1]

Finality ensures that any dispute will achieve, at some point of time, a complete and unchangeable resolution. It therefore has a 'fundamental public importance'.[2] 'Certainty', on the other hand, is defined as 'the clarity, unambiguity and stability in a system of law allowing those within the system to regulate their conduct according to the law's dictates'.[3] It provides predictability and transparency through ensuring the consistency and integrity of the system or mode of operation. At heart, both concepts serve fairness and justice.[4]

Finality and certainty have proved to be crucial aims in international commercial dispute resolution. To start with, certainty in outcomes and potential risks is afforded through the high degree of control over the methods and processes of the resolution of

[1] HLA Hart, *The Concept of Law*, 3rd edn (OUP, 1994) 141.

[2] *Lawal v Circle 33 Housing Trust* [2014] EWCA Civ 1514, [2015] HLR 9 [65] (Sir Terence Etherton C).

[3] BA Garner et al (eds), *Black's Law Dictionary*, 11th edn (Thomson Reuters, 2019) 279.

[4] See eg Lord Mance, 'Should the Law be Certain?' (UK Supreme Court, 11 October 2011), available at www.supremecourt.uk/docs/speech_111011.pdf; Lord Dyson, 'Time to Call it a Day: Some Reflections on Finality and the Law' (UK Supreme Court, 14 October 2011), available at www.supremecourt.uk/docs/speech_111014.pdf.

disputes. Moreover, in international commercial arbitration, finality and certainty are key attractive features as arbitral awards are conclusive and binding, with only a limited ability to appeal or challenge under most national legislations and a limited opportunity to defend against its recognition and enforcement, primarily under the framework of the 1958 United Nations Convention on the Recognition and Enforcement of Foreign Arbitral Awards (1958 New York Convention). The importance of finality and certainty has consistently been corroborated by the regular empirical surveys conducted by the School of International Arbitration at Queen Mary University of London, with a significant proportion of about 60 per cent of respondents considering the enforceability of awards and about 20 per cent of them considering finality as valuable characteristics of international arbitration.[5] International commercial mediation has also moved towards an efficient and harmonised framework that favours finality and certainty by the recent 2018 United Nations Convention on International Settlement Agreements Resulting from Mediation (2018 Singapore Convention on Mediation), which attracts at least 55 signatories and 10 contracting parties.[6]

The importance of finality and certainty also emerges from Professor Richard Fentiman's risk analysis. On his view, 'commercial activity depends on the assessment and management of risk. Risk determines transaction costs, and the willingness of the parties to contract'.[7] He identified two species of risk: (1) transaction risk and (2) litigation risk. Transaction risk is the risk that the parties' expectations will be defeated by the application of a law which does not give effect to the objective of their transaction. It is (for instance) the risk that any governing law clause in a contract will be ineffective or overridden. Where the parties to a contract do not have such a choice of law clause, it is the risk that their expectations as to governing law will be overridden by public policy concerns, or the mandatory rules of the place where their dispute is being argued or where their contract is to be performed.[8] Litigation risk is the risk to a claimant that it must sue to enforce its rights and the risk to a respondent that it must defend proceedings. In cross-border disputes, litigation risk pertains to the venue, that is, the risk that a dispute will not be resolved in a party's preferred forum, with the claimant prevented from suing in its preferred forum or the respondent compelled to defend proceedings in a non-preferred court. Litigation risk also arises in connection with enforcement, that is, the risk that a claimant's rights, even if validated by proceedings, cannot be enforced effectively. In international commercial litigation, there is a risk where a judgment is rendered ineffective, because the judgment-debtor has removed its assets from the jurisdiction of the judgment court, or because its assets are in a place where enforcement is difficult.[9] In essence, ensuring finality and certainty in international dispute resolution

[5] See eg the 2021 report, available at arbitration.qmul.ac.uk/media/arbitration/docs/LON0320037-QMUL-International-Arbitration-Survey-2021_19_WEB.pdf and the 2018 report, available at arbitration.qmul.ac.uk/media/arbitration/docs/2018-International-Arbitration-Survey---The-Evolution-of-International-Arbitration-(2).PDF.

[6] See also Y Zhao, 'The Singapore Mediation Convention: A Version of the New York Convention for Mediation?' (2021) 17 *Journal of Private International Law* 538.

[7] R Fentiman, *International Commercial Litigation*, 2nd edn (OUP, 2015) para 1.01.

[8] ibid, para 1.02.

[9] ibid.

processes will be able to reduce transaction costs, minimise unnecessary risks and promote efficient outcomes.[10]

B. The Limits of Finality and Certainty

But this does not mean that finality and certainty ought always to trump all other considerations. Concerns over fairness and justice also enter the picture. There may well be situations where states should be entitled to refuse to recognise or enforce a final judgment or award for some reason. There may well be also situations where a state should be entitled to ignore the fact of ongoing litigation or arbitration in another jurisdiction and allow concurrent proceedings to be initiated before its court. Conversely, there may well be situations where a court should be entitled to regard itself as the appropriate forum for the determination of a commercial dispute and to issue an injunction (commonly referred to as an 'anti-suit injunction') restraining a party from carrying on with litigation or arbitration elsewhere. The question is what those situations are. Clearly, concurrent proceedings in different states over the same subject matter, interference in ongoing proceedings by the issue of an anti-suit injunction, or the refusal to recognise a final judgment or award from some other jurisdiction should only be permitted in exceptional circumstances. Otherwise, there would be uncertainty at best and anarchy at worst. A claimant would be in danger of having its claim upheld in one jurisdiction but denied in another. Conversely, a respondent may be held not liable by the court of one state, only to be held liable by the court of another. Business enterprises would not know where they stand at any given moment and the transaction costs of managing the high degree of uncertainty and lack of finality would ultimately be prohibitive of trade. How do judges and arbitrators currently navigate between the demands of finality and certainty on the one hand and the interests of fairness and justice on the other? How should they carry out this balancing in the future? Those twin questions are ultimately what this chapter and chapter eight will be examining respectively.

Before launching into a detailed discussion, it is useful to highlight three constraining principles on how judges and arbitrators approach the two questions just identified. Those principles are party autonomy, comity and sovereignty.

Party autonomy is emphasised and respected in all commercial matters, including those of a cross-border nature.[11] When considering issues relating to commercial dispute resolution, party autonomy should normally prevail in the absence of compelling reasons to the contrary. Parties should be free to agree the forum for the resolution of their contractual dispute and the governing law to be applied. The parties should be allowed to allocate their risks and liabilities as between themselves through their agreement.

[10] See also JJ Spigelman, 'Transaction Costs and International Litigation' (2006) 80 *Australian Law Journal* 438; J Gleeson, 'An Australian Perspective on International Commercial Litigation: The Challenges and Opportunities' (Hauge Conference on Private International Law, 23 September 2013), available at assets.hcch.net/docs/8b6453af-0102-44ee-b8f3-9edd0404e5b7.pdf.

[11] On party autonomy generally, see ch 1 of this book.

Comity can mean many things. It can connote mutual courtesy (as in ordinary language)[12] or a need for reciprocity. In international law, the rules of comity are the 'accepted rules of mutual conduct … which each state adopts in relation to other states and expects other states to adopt in relation to itself'.[13] The High Court of Australia has defined 'comity' as[14]

> neither a matter of absolute obligation … nor of mere courtesy and goodwill. But it is the recognition which one nation allows within its territory to the legislative, executive or judicial act of another nation, having due regard both to international duty and convenience and to the rights of its own citizens or of other persons who are under the protection of its law.

Comity is consequently relevant as a matter of transnational case management. It operates as a restraint, discouraging interference with the decisions of the courts of other states in the absence of compelling reasons.[15] It is a set of international norms that must be weighed against a state's domestic values before a decision touching on extraterritorial matters is made. For example, when a judge exercises a power to grant an interim measure having extraterritorial effect (such as a freezing order), 'it is becoming widely accepted that comity between the courts of different countries requires mutual respect for the territorial integrity of each other's jurisdiction'[16] and a court should 'refrain from making orders which infringe the exclusive jurisdiction of the courts of other countries'.[17]

Notions of sovereignty likewise act as a restraint in the sense that a sovereign state should not exercise jurisdiction over the affairs of another sovereign state or apply measures of coercion over property situated in another sovereign state, except in limited circumstances in accordance with international law principles.[18] There is likely to be a tension between the principles of sovereignty and comity. It might be argued, for instance, that a liberal regime for the recognition and enforcement of commercial judgments, such as the 2005 HCCH Convention on Choice of Court Agreements (2005 Hague Convention) or the 2019 HCCH Convention on the Recognition and Enforcement of Foreign Judgments in Civil or Commercial Matters (2019 Hague Convention), constitute an encroachment on a country's sovereignty. But such a view would run contrary to the principle of comity whereby enforcing courts should respect the judgments of another state subject to overriding public policy concerns.[19]

[12] See eg *Aziz v Aziz* [2007] EWCA Civ 712, [2008] 2 All ER 501 [89]–[90] (Lawrence Collins LJ).

[13] *Buck v AG* [1965] Ch 745 (EWCA) 770 (Diplock LJ).

[14] *CSR Ltd v Cigna Insurance Australia Ltd* (1997) 189 CLR 345 (HCA) 395–96, citing *Hilton v Guyot* 159 US 113 (1895) 163–64.

[15] See eg *Société Nationale Industrielle Aérospatiale v Lee Kui Jak* [1987] AC 871 (PC); *Airbus Industrie GIE v Patel* [1999] 1 AC 119 (HL); *Stichting Shell Pensioenfonds v Krys* [2014] UKPC 41, [2015] AC 616.

[16] *Credit Suisse Fides Trust SA v Cuoghi* [1998] QB 818 (EWCA) 827 (Millett LJ).

[17] *Masri v Consolidated Contractors International Company SAL (No 2)* [2008] EWCA Civ 303, [2009] QB 450 [36]–[39] (Lord Donaldson MR).

[18] This also relates to the question of state immunity. See eg H Fox and P Webb, *The Law of State Immunity*, 3rd edn (OUP, 2015); J Crawford, *Brownlie's Principles of Public International Law*, 9th edn (OUP, 2019) chs 20–22.

[19] A Reyes, 'Introduction: Towards a System for the Recognition and Enforcement of Judgments' in A Reyes (ed), *Recognition and Enforcement of Foreign Judgments in Civil and Commercial Matters* (Hart Publishing, 2019) 28.

II. Concurrent Proceedings

There appears to be a divide between the views in civil and common law systems on the proper approach to managing concurrent proceedings.

A. *Forum Non Conveniens* and *Lis Alibi Pendens*

Disputes as to where litigation should occur are now common given the ever-increasing international trade and investment. The doctrine of *forum non conveniens* in common law systems attempts to ensure that a dispute is litigated in an appropriate forum having a 'real and substantial connection' with the circumstances underlying the dispute.[20] Even if a court has jurisdiction over a case, it may decline to exercise the same on the ground that it is not an appropriate or convenient forum to hear the dispute in the interests of cost-effectiveness, time-efficiency and fairness. The common law court typically engages in a two-stage inquiry when deciding whether to exercise or decline jurisdiction. That inquiry requires the court: (1) to determine whether there is another available forum which is clearly or distinctly more appropriate to try an action; and (2) to consider whether any factors militate against the grant of a stay.[21] Originally, it was envisaged that such factual enquiry would be fast, uncontroversial and completed within 'hours and not days'.[22] The determination of the appropriate forum would be 'pre-eminently a matter for the trial judge' so that 'an appeal should be rare and the appellate court should be slow to interfere'.[23] Later cases have sadly suggested that this was 'a rather optimistic aspiration'.[24]

The extent and scale of arguments over the appropriate forum and challenges based on *forum non conveniens* have become so substantial and prevalent that the phenomenon has been heavily criticised; the UK Supreme Court stressed that engaging in such ancillary litigation and skirmishing had become an expensive and time-consuming exercise.[25] By ensuring that a case is heard in an appropriate forum, the doctrine of *forum non conveniens* enables justice to be done in a particular case. However, this justice is often attained at great expense in terms of time and money. Certainty is also undermined since it has become commonplace to challenge jurisdiction in cross-border commercial cases where factors may point to a several possible forums for the hearing of dispute. There is a recent attempt by Professor Adrian Briggs and Professor Andrew Dickinson to tackle these challenges of certainty, predictability and cost-effectiveness through a proposed scheme for reform of English jurisdictional rules.[26]

[20] See eg *Spiliada Maritime Corp v Cansulex Ltd (The Spiliada)* [1987] AC 460 (HL); *The Adhiguna Meranti* [1987] HKLR 904 (HKCA); *Rappo v Accent Delight International Ltd* [2017] 2 SLR 265 (SGCA). *Forum non conveniens* is Latin for 'the forum not being convenient'.

[21] *The Spiliada* (ibid) 476–78 (Lord Goff).

[22] ibid 465 (Lord Templeman).

[23] ibid.

[24] See eg *VTB Capital plc v Nutritek International Corp* [2013] UKSC 5, [2013] 2 AC 337 [88] (Lord Neuberger PSC).

[25] ibid [81]–[82] (Lord Neuberger PSC).

[26] A Briggs and A Dickinson, 'Reframing Jurisdiction: A New Scheme?' (May 2022), available at www.blackstonechambers.com/documents/Reframing_Jurisdiction.pdf.

In contrast, *forum non conveniens* is generally inconsistent with civil law systems in which comprehensive codes of civil procedure dictate when a court has jurisdiction. Such a mode of proceeding allows for predictability and certainty, with minimal (if any) discretion being allowed to the judge. When jurisdiction exists, that jurisdiction must be exercised. Consider, for example, the application in some civil law jurisdictions[27] of the doctrine of *lis alibi pendens*,[28] which requires a court to defer to the jurisdiction of another court that is first seised of the same case. There is no discretionary authority to decide otherwise. This can lead to an unseemly race among litigants to commence proceedings in their preferred forum. This race, with the party first seising a court winning the jurisdictional competition, can lead to what have been disparagingly referred to as 'torpedo' actions. The latter are attempts by a party to forestall the adjudication of a claim against it by starting an action[29] in a jurisdiction known for having a dilatory court system. This race to found jurisdiction may be contrasted with the corresponding race to judgment in common law courts that tend to allow parallel litigation, only exercising the discretion to decline jurisdiction when it is deemed appropriate to do so.[30]

It is interesting to note how the EU deals with parallel proceedings under Articles 29 to 34 of the Brussels I Recast Regulation.[31] If the same cause of action between the same parties is brought in the courts of different Member States, the court first seised is to take jurisdiction and there will be a mandatory stay of proceedings in any other courts later seised. This may stall the proceedings for a significant period of time. As for 'related actions', that is, actions which can give rise to inconsistent (as opposed to contradictory) judgments, although there will be a presumption for a stay of proceedings in any court not first seised, a later seised court will have a discretion to hear an action, taking account of factors such as: (1) the extent of the relatedness and the risk of mutually irreconcilable decisions; (2) the stage reached in each set of proceedings; and (3) the proximity of the courts to the subject-matter of the case.[32]

B. Anti-Suit Injunctions[33]

Anti-suit injunctions are orders that typically require the party enjoined not to commence or proceed with specified court or arbitration proceedings in a foreign

[27] Japan is an example. See M Dogauchi, 'Japan' in JJ Fawcett (ed), *Declining Jurisdiction in Private International Law* (OUP, 1995) 303.

[28] Latin for 'litigation pending elsewhere'.

[29] In its action, the party will usually seek a negative declaration, that is, a declaration that the party is not liable to the other party.

[30] RA Brand and SR Jablosnki, *Forum Non Conveniens: History, Global Practice, and Future under the Hague Convention on Choice of Court Agreements* (OUP, 2007) 121.

[31] See eg P Torremans et al (eds), *Cheshire, North & Fawcett Private International Law*, 15th edn (OUP, 2017) 442–59.

[32] Case C–129/92 *Owens Bank Ltd v Fulvio Bracco*; *Starlight Shipping Co v Allianz Marine and Aviation Versicherungs AG (The Alexandros T)* [2013] UKSC 70, [2014] 1 All ER 590 [92] (Lord Clarke); *Euroeco Fuels (Poland) Ltd v Szczecin and Swinoujscie Seaports Authority SA* [2018] EWHC 1081 (QB), [2018] 4 WLR 133 [92]–[103] (Nicol J).

[33] See generally T Raphael, *The Anti-Suit Injunction*, 2nd edn (OUP, 2019); S Gee, *Commercial Injunctions*, 7th edn (Sweet and Maxwell, 2021) ch 14.

jurisdiction. The principles for the grant or refusal of an anti-suit injunction are determined by the law of the court in which the injunction was sought. It is a discretionary remedy and will only be granted if the court considers it appropriate to do so in all the circumstances and the interests of justice. The remedy is usually invoked to safeguard a right or expectation not to be sued abroad or to prevent vexatious, oppressive or unconscionable proceedings abroad. It may also protect the public policy of the forum. When considering whether to grant an injunction, a court must balance the injustice to the claimant if the injunction is refused against the potential injustice to the respondent if the injunction is granted.[34]

Anti-suit injunctions are granted under the *in personam* jurisdiction of a court of equity.[35] It is directed to a party to the court proceedings, not the foreign court. It does not question the jurisdiction of the foreign court. A breach of such injunction will lead to punishment for contempt of court, usually the payment of a fine, imprisonment, or both. Some argue that anti-suit injunctions are 'irreconcilable with international comity and public international law, and amount to an unjustifiable interference with the sovereignty of the foreign state and the jurisdiction of the foreign court'.[36] Comity may circumscribe the grant of anti-suit injunctions in a limited number of ways.[37]

For this reason, the courts in various jurisdictions have been increasingly sensitive to comity when granting an anti-suit injunction. Before intervening in respect of foreign proceedings, a court must be satisfied that it has a sufficient interest in, or connection with, the matter in question to justify granting an anti-suit injunction. The principle of comity requires the court to recognise that, in assessing the appropriate forum for where litigation should proceed, different judges operating under different legal systems with different legal policies may legitimately arrive at different answers.[38]

Anti-suit injunctions may be met or pre-empted by anti-anti-suit injunctions and anti-anti-anti-suit injunctions. Despite the high threshold required to justify any adverse effects on comity, these orders have been increasingly deployed by courts around the world, particularly in the intellectual property context.[39] Looking forward, it will be useful to have a soft law instrument, setting out guidelines for the grant or refusal of anti-suit injunctions.[40]

[34] Raphael, *Anti-Suit Injunction* (2019) para 4.05.
[35] Gee, *Commercial Injunctions* (2021) para 14–003.
[36] Raphael, *Anti-Suit Injunction* (2019) para 1.02.
[37] ibid para 1.28.
[38] ibid para 4.05.
[39] See eg JL Contreras, 'It's Anti-Suit Injunctions All The Way Down – The Strange New Realities of International Litigation over Standards-Essential Patents' (2020) 26 *IP Litigator* 1; G Colangelo and V Torti, 'Anti-suit Injunctions and Geopolitics in Transnational SEPs Litigation' (2022) 14(2) *European Journal of Legal Studies*, OnlineFirst.
[40] W Lui and A Reyes, 'Introduction' in A Reyes and W Lui (eds), *Direct Jurisdiction* (Hart Publishing, 2021) 8–9. A potentially similar 'soft law instrument' is the Institut de Droit International's resolution in 2003, albeit it will give the court first seised the carriage of a case: Institut de Droit International, 'The Principles for Determining When the Use of the Doctrine of Forum Non Conveniens and Anti-suit Injunctions is Appropriate' (2 September 2003), available at www.idi-iil.org/app/uploads/2017/06/2003_bru_01_en.pdf.

C. Applications for the Stay of Arbitral Proceedings

The general approach among common law courts is non-interventionist insofar as granting orders for the stay of arbitration proceedings are concerned. The courts have the discretion to stay arbitration proceedings, but such discretion must only be exercised in rare situations and with reference to all the circumstances of the case. On the other hand, where litigation before a court is commenced in apparent breach of an arbitration agreement, courts normally grant stays in favour of arbitration. Where arbitration has yet to be commenced or an arbitral tribunal has yet to decide on its jurisdiction, many common law jurisdictions, such as Hong Kong and Singapore, adopt the low threshold of a prima facie approach regarding the existence and scope of the arbitration clause.[41] A party applying for a stay of proceedings in favour of arbitration need only establish a prima facie case that the dispute is subject to a valid arbitration clause, and the arbitration agreement is not null and void, inoperative or incapable of being performed. This approach is consistent with a pro-arbitration attitude. In adopting the approach, a court should grant a stay to arbitration without excessive scrutiny, leaving the tribunal to decide on its jurisdiction and determine the existence and scope of the arbitration clause, while preserving the ability to review the tribunal's finding on jurisdiction at a later stage as provided by a relevant statute. This gives full effect to the well-established principle of competence-competence and is in alignment with the UNCITRAL Model Law.[42] In England, there is a presumptive approach where arbitration agreements are construed with the presumption that the parties as 'rational businessmen' were likely to have intended arbitration as a 'one-stop' forum for the resolution of disputes.[43] Yet some other jurisdictions undertake a full merits review when hearing applications to stay proceedings pending arbitration.

Where the arbitral tribunal has rendered its decision on jurisdiction, and a party subsequently challenges the decision in court and asks for a stay of the arbitration pending determination of the jurisdictional challenge, a stay will only be granted if there exist special circumstances. In Singapore, special circumstances can include sufficiently grave conduct of the other party in relation to the arbitral proceedings, or manifestly and egregiously improper conduct by the tribunal.[44] The wasted costs if it turns out that an arbitration was unwarranted, or the detriment stemming from an invalid award by a tribunal which lacks jurisdiction, do not constitute special circumstances. Such a practice ensures that parties diligently participate in arbitration despite a jurisdictional challenge before the court of the seat. Otherwise, parties risk substantial prejudice in the arbitration proceedings should their challenge fail.[45]

[41] See eg *PCCW Global Ltd v Interactive Communications Service Ltd* [2007] 1 HKLRD 309 (HKCA) [48]–[51] (Tang VP); *Tomolugen Holdings Ltd v Silica Investors Ltd* [2016] 1 SLR 373 (SGCA) [25]–[70] (Sundaresh Menon CJ).

[42] *Tomolugen Holdings Ltd* (ibid) [32]–[44].

[43] *Fiona Trust & Holdings Corp v Privalov* [2007] UKHL 40, [2007] 4 All ER 951. This presumption is widely applied but has its limitations in cases with inconsistent dispute resolution clauses: *H v G* [2022] HKCFI 1327.

[44] *BLY v BLZ* [2017] 4 SLR 410 (SGHC).

[45] See also D Chan and C Neoh, 'To boycott proceedings or not? Recourse against arbitral awards on jurisdictional grounds by different categories of respondents under the Model Law' (2020) 36 *Arbitration International* 529.

D. Applications for the Stay of Court Proceedings on Case Management Grounds

Stays of court proceedings on case management grounds are possible. One situation where a stay may be granted is where an action depends on the outcome of an arbitration between the same or different parties, as for example where a creditor initiates judicial proceedings against a guarantor while the primary debtor's liability has yet to be decided in ongoing arbitration proceedings. In such situations, which are common in complex international commercial disputes, courts may exercise their case management powers and take a pragmatic approach. The court should take the lead in ensuring the efficient and fair resolution of a commercial dispute as a whole. The precise measures which the court will deploy to achieve that end will turn on the facts of each case.[46]

The Singapore case of *Tomolugen* is an excellent example in this regard. In *Tomolugen*, Silica Investors brought several claims involving multiple defendants. The court found that one of the defendants was party to an arbitration clause with the plaintiff that covered some of the issues in dispute, and therefore a mandatory stay in favour of arbitration was granted.[47] This leads to a multiplicity of proceedings with overlapping parties, issues and remedies, some to be ventilated in arbitration and some others in court. The court had to consider the question of case management of whether to stay some or all of the court proceedings brought against the remaining defendants until after the conclusion of the arbitration proceedings. The Court of Appeal considered an array of competing factors including the potential duplication of parties' resources and efforts, the circumvention of a valid arbitration clause, and the potential challenge by the other defendants on findings in the arbitration (which they are not bound to as they were not party to the arbitration).[48] It concluded that the court has to take the lead in facilitating the fair and efficient resolution of the dispute as a whole. The balance should be struck as follows:

> This does not mean that if part of a dispute is sent for arbitration, the court proceedings relating to the rest of the dispute will be stayed as a matter of course. The court must in every case aim to strike a balance between three higher-order concerns that may pull in different considerations: first, a plaintiff's right to choose whom he wants to sue and where; second, the court's desire to prevent a plaintiff from circumventing the operation of an arbitration clause; and third, the court's inherent power to manage its processes to prevent an abuse of process and ensure the efficient and fair resolution of disputes. The balance that is struck must ultimately serve the ends of justice. In this regard, we consider that the court's discretion to stay court proceedings pending the resolution of a related arbitration, at the request of parties

[46] *Tomolugen Holdings Ltd* (n 41) [186] (Sundaresh Menon CJ).

[47] This power is based on Art 8 of the UNCITRAL Model Law on International Commercial Arbitration, which is adopted in International Arbitration Act (Cap 143A, 2002 rev ed) (Singapore), s 6. Similar provisions can be found in other Model Law jurisdictions such as Hong Kong: Arbitration Ordinance (Cap 609) (Hong Kong), s 20.

[48] *Tomolugen Holdings Ltd* (n 41) [142] (Sundaresh Menon CJ). For the well-accepted proposition that a finding in arbitration or court proceedings between A and B is not binding on A in arbitration or court proceedings between A and C, see eg *Lincoln National Life Insurance Co v Sun Life Assurance Co of Canada* [2004] EWCA Civ 1660, [2006] 1 All ER (Comm) 675.

> who are not subject to the arbitration agreement in question, can in turn be made subject to the agreement of those parties to be bound by any applicable findings that may be made by the arbitral tribunal.[49]

Accordingly, any attempt by the defendants to subsequently relitigate the issues raised in arbitration would be deemed an abuse of process. In the end, the court stayed all of the proceedings before it in the interest of efficient case management. Although this might seem to be a generous position, recent cases have shown that this is not an easy test to satisfy. The Singapore Court of Appeal commented that:[50]

> [I]n order for case management concerns to be relevant at all, there must first be the existence or at least the imminence of separate legal proceedings giving rise to a real risk of overlapping issues. Until such time, it would be premature to consider, let alone grant, a case management stay. We emphasise that when considering whether to grant a case management stay, it is critically important that the court apply its mind to appreciate the nature and extent of the overlaps between the putative arbitration and the court proceedings. Otherwise, the court may find itself, as it did here, ordering a case management stay for no good reason, because it has been distracted by some abstract notion of potential or theoretical overlapping of issues, parties or proceedings. … [The court] must go further and examine precisely which are: (a) the potential fora for the resolution of the dispute; (b) the different parties before each forum; and (c) the issues to be determined before each such forum. The sort of overlap that would attract a case management stay is one where the proper ventilation of the issues in the court proceedings depended on the resolution of the related putative arbitration. In such circumstances, a case management stay would be needed in order to achieve the efficient and fair resolution of the dispute as a whole: *Tomolugen* at [186].

Some jurisdictions, such as England and New Zealand, have held that the grant of a case management stay should only be exercisable under a higher threshold of 'rare and compelling' grounds.[51] A stay pending the conclusion of a related set of proceedings should only be granted 'if there were very strong reasons for doing so and the benefits which were likely to result from doing so clearly outweighed any disadvantage to the plaintiff'.[52]

E. *Res Judicata* and Issue Estoppel[53]

Where a final decision has been pronounced by a court or arbitral tribunal having competent jurisdiction over the parties and the subject of a dispute, then the parties to the proceedings are estopped from later re-arguing the dispute or issues which have

[49] ibid [188] (Sundaresh Menon CJ).

[50] *Rex International Holdings Ltd v Gulf Hibiscus Ltd* [2019] 2 SLR 682 (SGCA) [11] (Sundaresh Menon CJ).

[51] *Reichhold Norway ASA v Goldman Sachs International (a firm)* [2000] 1 WLR 173 (EWCA) 186 (Lord Bingham CJ); *Danone Asia Pacific Holdings Pte Ltd v Fonterra Co-operative Group Ltd* [2014] NZHC 1681; affirmed on appeal: [2014] NZCA 536. These cases were considered (but not followed) in *Tomolugen Holdings Ltd* (n 41). Hong Kong courts have yet to express a view on the issue: *Pag Holdings Ltd v Gorthy Anil Kumar* (unreported, HCMP 282/2017, 21 July 2017) (HKCFI) [52]–[55].

[52] *Reichhold Norway ASA* (ibid) 180 (Lord Bingham CJ).

[53] See generally PR Barnett, *Res Judicata, Estoppel and Foreign Judgments* (OUP, 2001).

been determined in the proceedings.[54] Estoppel by record (*per rem judicatam*) can be further divided into that of cause of action estoppel and issue estoppel. Cause of action estoppel 'prevents a party to an action from asserting or denying, as against the other party, the existence of a particular cause of action, the non-existence or existence of which has been determined by a court of competent jurisdiction in previous litigation between the same parties'.[55] Issue estoppel prevents the parties to an action from contesting a particular issue which has already been determined in previous proceedings to which they were parties.[56] Both cause of action estoppel and issue estoppel can apply to foreign judgments.[57] Thus, for instance, where the court of one state (the originating court) has decided a dispute, the losing party can be estopped from relitigating the same dispute before the court of another state. The rationale for *res judicata* as far as finality and certainty are concerned has been aptly summarised as follows:[58]

> The *res judicata* doctrine provides for the finality of decisions with the aim to avoid lengthy and wasteful repetitions of proceedings leading to legal uncertainty and, perhaps, irreconcilable decisions. … The doctrine of *res judicata* is generally considered to be based on a public and a private interest. The public interest requires that there be an end to litigation to ensure general security and public good. It is in the interest of society that the courts work in a way that is efficient and economic. … Furthermore, the public interest requires the avoidance of inconsistent judgments as inconsistencies may undermine the credibility of the court and diminish respect and obedience of court judgments. It does not generally matter whether the decision is correct in law or fact. A competent court has the jurisdiction to decide wrongly, as well as correctly, and its decisions are final and binding unless corrected on appeal. The private interest is to protect the individual. It ensures that no person shall be tried more than once on the same matter.

Three conditions need to be satisfied before an estoppel can be established:

(1) The decision of the originating court must be final and conclusive on the merits and the originating court must have been a court of competent jurisdiction.
(2) The parties to the action before the originating court must be the same as the parties to any contemplated later proceedings.
(3) The cause of action or issues to be argued in the contemplated later proceedings must be the same as those raised before the originating court.

When applying the doctrine of issue estoppel, the courts have repeatedly stressed the need for caution.[59] There are good reasons for this. Consider, for instance, the situation where it is alleged that a party is estopped from bringing proceedings before

[54] *Carl Zeiss Stiftung v Rayner and Keeler Ltd (No 2)* [1967] 1 AC 853 (HL) 933. See also *Virgin Atlantic Airways Limited v Zodiac Seats UK Limited* [2013] UKSC 46, [2014] AC 160.

[55] *Thoday v Thoday* [1964] P 181 (EWCA) 197.

[56] *Carl Zeiss Stiftung* (n 54) 913–17, 933–35, 964–65.

[57] *The Sennar (No 2)* [1985] 1 WLR 490 (HL); *Republic of India v India Steamship Co Ltd (The Indian Endurance and the Indian Grace)* [1993] AC 410 (HL).

[58] S Schaffstein, *The Doctrine of* Res Judicata *before International Commercial Arbitral Tribunals* (OUP, 2016) paras PI.04–PI.07.

[59] See eg *Carl Zeiss Stiftung* (n 54) 917–18 (Lord Reid), 925–26 (Lord Hodson), 947 (Lord Upjohn), 967 (Lord Wilberforce).

a court (Court A) because the same matter has already been determined in foreign proceedings. The judge of Court A will be unfamiliar with the law and procedures of the foreign court and is likely to have difficulty ascertaining the precise issues which have been decided abroad, and whether each of them has been determined 'finally and conclusively' beyond the possibility of further litigation. Issues may not have been fully ventilated previously because (say) in cases of a trivial nature it may have been regarded as impracticable to defend all matters fully in terms of the time and expense involved.[60] It may consequently be unjust to treat a party as estopped from raising certain issues in Court A in the interests of justice.[61]

III. Recognition and Enforcement of Judgments and Awards

Most civil law and common law jurisdictions have modernised their laws and codes of civil procedure so that foreign judgments and awards relating to cross-border commercial disputes can be recognised and enforced in a relatively straightforward manner. However, the process of recognition and enforcement is typically subject to at least the following conditions:

(1) Judgments must meet a requirement of indirect jurisdiction.
(2) Judgments may have to meet a condition of reciprocity.
(3) Judgments and awards must have been obtained through due process.
(4) Judgments and awards must not be contrary to the public policy of the enforcing state.

These are discussed in turn below.

A. Indirect Jurisdiction

If a party is to be held bound by a judgment rendered by a foreign originating court, the enforcing court must have some assurance that it was reasonable and fair to expect that party to appear and defend proceedings before the originating court. The requirement of indirect jurisdiction ensures that there is a link between the state where a judgment was obtained on the one hand and the party or the subject matter of a dispute on the other. Otherwise, the party cannot reasonably be expected to have incurred the time and expense of appearing before the originating court to defend oneself. Indirect jurisdiction is also referred to as 'international jurisdiction' because it involves the identification of internationally accepted grounds for a court to assume jurisdiction over a party or an action. The difficulty is identifying what those grounds are. It appears that,

[60] Torremans et al, *Cheshire, North & Fawcett* (2017) 560.

[61] *Good Challenger Navegante SA v Metalexportimport SA (The Good Challenger)* [2003] EWCA Civ 1668, [2004] 1 Lloyd's Rep 67 [54], [75]–[79].

at a minimum, an originating court is generally accepted as having indirect jurisdiction in the following situations:[62]

(1) The state in which the originating court is situated is the habitual residence of the judgment debtor.
(2) The judgment debtor has a principal place of business or an establishment, branch, or agency in the state of the originating court, provided that such place of business, establishment, branch or agency was closely connected to the claim.
(3) The judgment debtor submitted to the jurisdiction of the originating court: (a) by express agreement (such as a choice of court agreement in a commercial contract), (b) by defending the claim on the merits before the originating court without challenging jurisdiction, or (c) by invoking the originating court's jurisdiction by bringing a related counterclaim there.
(4) The claim against the judgment debtor relates to title in immovable property within the state of the originating court.
(5) The claim relates to a non-contractual obligation and the act that gave rise to the damage (death, personal injury, damage to property) occurred in the state of the originating court.

There are other grounds which may be accepted by individual jurisdictions as bases of indirect jurisdiction, but these have not received international acceptance.

In many common law jurisdictions, an originating court can claim exorbitant jurisdiction over a person who is not present or resident within the territory on the basis that the person is a 'necessary or proper party' to proceedings that have been commenced against a party who is subject to the originating court's jurisdiction.[63] This has not yet become a generally accepted ground of indirect jurisdiction. Nonetheless, such joinder can reduce the risk of contradictory findings by courts in different countries, with one set of defendants being sued in one country and another set of defendants being sued in another country in respect of the same matter. Professor Ronald Brand has further suggested that there should be a mirror principle where grounds for indirect jurisdiction should be the same as a country's grounds for exercising direct jurisdiction.[64] This would address what Professor Brand calls the 'jurisdiction gap problem' where countries in effect discriminate against foreign judgments by only allowing narrow grounds of indirect jurisdiction for the recognition and enforcement of foreign judgments, but applying extensive grounds of direct jurisdiction for claims initiated before their own courts.

[62] Reyes, 'Introduction' (2019) 29–30. It should be noted that these 'minimal' grounds of indirect jurisdiction are largely similar to those of direct jurisdiction: Lui and Reyes, 'Introduction' (2021) 9–12.

[63] See eg in Hong Kong, Rules of the High Court (Cap 4A), Ord 11, r 1(1)(d); in Singapore, Supreme Court Practice Directions 2021, para 63(3)(c); in the UK, CPR PD 6B para 3(b).

[64] RA Brand, 'The Circulation of Judgments under the Draft Hague Convention' University of Pittsburgh School of Law Legal Studies Research Paper Series Working Paper No 2019-02 (February 2019) 17, 22–23, available at papers.ssrn.com/sol3/papers.cfm?abstract_id=3334647. But whether ideally the grounds of direct and indirect jurisdiction should be the same is open to discussion: Lui and Reyes , 'Introduction' (2021) 3–4. See also R Michaels, 'Some Fundamental Jurisdictional Concepts as Applied in Judgment Conventions' in E Gottschalk et al (eds), *Conflict of Laws in a Globalized World* (CUP, 2007) 29–62; E Jueptner, 'The Hague Jurisdiction Project – What Options for the Hague Conference?' (2020) 16 *Journal of Private International Law* 247.

There is no requirement of indirect jurisdiction in relation to the enforcement of arbitral awards. The wide international adherence to the 1958 New York Convention has made the enforcement of foreign arbitral awards often easier than the enforcement of foreign judgments. It remains to be seen whether the 2019 Hague Convention will be able to redress the imbalance.

B. Reciprocity

Reciprocity and comity are interlinked. Reciprocity is the notion that a state will act towards a state in the same way that the latter acts towards the former. Applying the doctrine to judgments, countries will only recognise and enforce the (commercial) judgments of other states to the extent that the latter recognise and enforce their (commercial) judgments. Consequently, where an originating state does not recognise the judgments of an enforcing state, the court of the enforcing state will refuse to recognise the judgments of the originating state. But there are signs of a movement away from strict reciprocity, or *de facto* reciprocity, in many countries. There has instead been a trend towards 'presumed reciprocity', or *de jure* reciprocity, in several jurisdictions in recent years. That is, in the absence of evidence to the contrary, an enforcing state will assume that there is reciprocity between the originating and enforcing state. An illustration of the trend may be seen in the Nanning Statement, which was released in June 2017 by the Asia Pacific judges attending the 2nd China–ASEAN Forum.[65] Article VII of the Nanning Statement stipulates:

> Regional cross-border transactions and investments require a judicial safeguard based on appropriate mutual recognition and enforcement of judicial judgments among countries in the region. Subject to their domestic laws, Supreme Courts of participating countries will keep good faith in interpreting domestic laws, try to avoid unnecessary parallel proceedings, and consider facilitating the appropriate mutual recognition and enforcement of civil or commercial judgments among different jurisdictions. If two countries have not been bound by any international treaty on mutual recognition and enforcement of foreign civil or commercial judgments, both countries may, subject to their domestic laws, presume the existence of their reciprocal relationship, when it comes to the judicial procedure of recognising or enforcing such judgments made by courts of the other country, provided that the courts of the other country had not refused to recognise or enforce such judgments on the ground of lack of reciprocity.

This movement towards a more liberal and pragmatic regime of presumed reciprocity is to be welcomed.

Insofar as reciprocity remains a requirement for the recognition and enforcement of judgments in commercial matters, courts in different states have been entering into memoranda of guidance (MOGs) with each other for the purpose (among others) of evidencing reciprocity between their respective states. For instance, the Supreme Court of Singapore has entered into MOGs or their equivalent with various foreign courts (such as the Abu Dhabi Global Market Courts, the Bermuda courts, the Dubai International

[65] Available at www.chinajusticeobserver.com/nanning-statement-of-the-2nd-china-asean-justice-forum.

Financial Centre Courts, the Qatar courts, the Chinese courts and the Supreme Court of Victoria (Australia)). The MOGs set out the procedures whereby judgments issued in one jurisdiction may be enforced in the other. Despite being non-legally binding and not involving any change in existing legal regimes, the MOGs will reassure commercial parties that judgments in their favour will be enforceable elsewhere.[66] They will also foster a better understanding of each other's judicial processes among judges and lawyers. Recent initiatives have gone further to produce a multilateral memorandum on the enforcement of commercial judgments for money, which provides states with the confidence in reciprocity.[67]

Reciprocity is not normally a problem with arbitral awards, given the large number of countries that are party to the 1958 New York Convention. The latter in effect obliges state parties to recognise and enforce awards made under each other's laws.[68]

C. Due Process

In general terms, due process concerns whether a party had a fair or reasonable opportunity to present its case before the rendering court or before an arbitral tribunal. It involves, for instance, whether there has been proper notice of proceedings according to the relevant procedural rules and whether there has been fraud, actual bias or the appearance of bias in the way that a judgment or award was obtained.[69] It does not include a consideration of the substantive merits of a party's case, such as whether an applicable law was correctly applied to the facts. At the level of detail, there can be different views as to what does or does not constitute due process.

In common law jurisdictions, an arbitral award or judgment may be refused recognition and enforcement on the ground of a lack of due process in the way that it was obtained. But this will typically apply 'only to sufficiently serious or egregious cases where a party was effectively denied due process',[70] and does not extend to a situation in which there might be reasonable disagreements on whether the procedure followed by a tribunal was appropriate. The major concern in such an exercise will always be with 'the structural integrity of the arbitration proceedings', not 'the substantive merits of the dispute, or … the correctness or otherwise of the award, whether concerning errors of fact or law'.[71]

[66] K Chng, 'Singapore' in A Reyes (ed), *Recognition and Enforcement of Judgments in Civil and Commercial Matters* (Hart Publishing, 2019) 160–61.

[67] Standing International Forum of Commercial Courts, 'Multilateral Memorandum on Enforcement of Commercial Judgments for Money' (April 2021), available at sifocc.org/resources/resources-2.

[68] 1958 New York Convention, Arts I(3) and V(1)(e).

[69] Hong Kong has a multitude of recent cases on due process in arbitrations: see eg *Sun Tian Gang v Hong Kong & China Gas (Jilin) Ltd* [2016] 5 HKLRD 221 (HKCFI); *X v Y* [2021] 2 HKC 68, [2021] HKCFI 147; *AB v CD* [2021] HKCFI 327; *W v AW* [2021] 5 HKC 476, [2021] HKCFI 1707; *Guangdong Shunde Zhanwei Trading Co Ltd v Sun Fung Timber Company Limited* [2021] HKCFI 3823. On apparent bias of arbitrators, see eg *Halliburton Co v Chubb Bermuda Insurance Ltd* [2020] UKSC 48, [2021] AC 1083. On fraud in obtaining a judgment, see eg *Takhar v Gracefield Developments Ltd* [2019] UKSC 13, [2020] AC 450; *Dale v Banga* [2021] EWCA Civ 240.

[70] See eg *Grand Pacific Holdings Ltd v Pacific China Holdings Ltd (in liq) (No 1)* [2012] 4 HKLRD 1 (HKCA) [91]–[94] (Tang VP); *Pang Wai Hak v Hua Yunjian* [2012] 4 HKLRD 113 (HKCFI) [29] (Recorder Anderson Chow SC).

[71] *Grand Pacific Holdings Ltd* (ibid) [7] (Tang VP).

For instance, the court will not evaluate the correctness of the arbitral tribunal's findings, for example, on the compliance with the contractual pre-conditions and escalation mechanisms for arbitration.[72] The 'due process' ground is frequently raised by parties when resisting the enforcement of an arbitral award, so much so that some have warned about the ground being abused.[73] The legal position with the cross-border enforcement of commercial judgments is likely to be the same.

D. Public Policy

The public policy ground may be invoked when enforcement of a foreign judgment or award would be repugnant to the fundamental legal, social, cultural or religious norms of an enforcing state. There will undoubtedly be differences in how states define 'public policy' and in the types of cases which states view as giving rise to 'public policy' issues. In Singapore, the public policy ground can only be invoked in narrowly defined situations, where enforcement will 'shock the conscience' or be 'clearly injurious to the public good'. Examples are 'egregious circumstances such as corruption, bribery or fraud which would violate the most basic notions of morality and justice'.[74] In Hong Kong, to refuse enforcement on public policy grounds requires being 'fundamentally offensive to … notions of justice' and 'contrary to the fundamental conceptions of morality and justice'.[75] It is worth noting that there is common law precedent suggesting a judgment obtained in defiance of an anti-suit injunction is likely to be denied recognition on the public policy ground.[76]

By way of contrast, some states do not have a concept of 'public policy'. They may instead use expressions in their law such as a judgment or award being refused recognition or enforcement because they are 'contrary to the fundamental principles of the country's law'. For example, there is no concept of 'public policy' in Vietnamese law. Vietnam, however, is a party to the 1958 New York Convention and has an international obligation to recognise and enforce foreign arbitral awards of a commercial nature unless (among other grounds for refusal) they are contrary to 'public policy'. To deal with this, Article 68(2)(e) of Vietnam's 2010 Law on Commercial Arbitration provides that an award 'shall be set aside' if it is 'contrary to the fundamental principles of the law of Vietnam'. The difficulty is in identifying the 'fundamental' principles of Vietnamese law. On one reading all principles of Vietnamese law might be regarded as 'fundamental'. But this would not be consistent with international jurisprudence on the meaning of 'public policy' under Article V(2)(b) of the 1958 New York Convention. It should not just be any mistake of Vietnamese law by an arbitral tribunal that leads to an award being set aside by the Vietnamese court. Something more is required.

[72] See eg the recent significant Hong Kong decision of *C v D* [2022] HKCA 729.

[73] L Reed, 'Ab(use) of Due Process: Sword vs Shield' (2017) 33 *Arbitration International* 361.

[74] *Sui Southern Gas Co Ltd v Habibullah Coastal Power Co (Pte) Ltd* [2010] 3 SLR 1 (SGHC) [48] (Judith Prakash J); *BLB v BLC* [2013] 4 SLR 1169 (SGHC) [100] (Belinda Ang Saw Ean J).

[75] *Hebei Import & Export Corp v Polytek Engineering Co Ltd* (1999) 2 HKCFAR 111 [31] (Bokhary PJ), [99] (Sir Anthony Mason NPJ).

[76] *Philip Alexander Securities & Futures Ltd v Bamberger* [1997] ILPr 73 (EWHC (Comm)); affirmed on appeal: [1997] ILPr 104 (EWCA).

The Supreme People's Court of Vietnam attempted to provide guidance on that 'something more' through its Resolution No 01/2014/NQ-HDTP (Resolution 01) issued on 20 March 2014. Article 14 of Resolution 01 equated the 'fundamental principles of the law of Vietnam' with 'basic principles of conduct, the effects of which are most overriding in respect of the development and implementation of Vietnamese law'. Accordingly, a court 'must determine that the arbitral award violates one or more fundamental principles of the law, and such principle(s) are relevant to the dispute resolution by arbitration'. The court is to highlight the 'fundamental principles of Vietnamese law that were not respected by the Tribunal in making the award' and explain how, as a result, 'the award violates the interests of the government, or the legitimate rights and interests of third party or parties'.

A similar problem arises in India, which had previously considered 'contrary to public policy' to be equivalent as (among others) 'contrary to fundamental policy of Indian law'.[77] While this does not entail a review on the merits of the dispute,[78] the previous view was that a breach or violation of Indian law (in that case, regulatory laws on exchange control) would be contrary to public policy.[79] However, the current approach in Indian courts has moved towards viewing the mere contravention of a legal provision as insufficient to invoke public policy. It 'must amount to a breach of some legal principle or legislation which is so basic to Indian law that it is not susceptible of being compromised'.[80] The expression 'fundamental policy of Indian law' should only refer to 'all such fundamental principles as providing a basis for administration of justice and enforcement of law in this country'.[81] These are 'the core values of India's public policy as a nation, which may find expression not only in statutes but also time-honoured, hallowed principles which are followed by the Courts'.[82] It is submitted that this modern view conforms better with the spirit of public policy.

i. *Mistake of Law*

Not every mistake in the application by a foreign court or arbitral tribunal of the law of the enforcing state, or every failure of a foreign court or tribunal to apply such law, should qualify as a reason for invoking the public policy ground to refuse recognition and enforcement. Similarly, not every enforcement of the resulting decision would be repugnant to the fundamental norms of the relevant state. Provided that there has been due process and a court has acted in good faith (as opposed to fraudulently), the possibility of any court applying incorrect facts or law is simply part of the litigation risk

[77] *Renusagar Power Co Ltd v General Electric Co* (1994) Supp 1 SCC 644 [66]; *Shri Lal Mahal Ltd v Progretto Grano SpA* (2014) 2 SCC 433 [29].

[78] Explanation 2 to the Arbitration and Conciliation Act 1996 (India), s 48.

[79] *Renusagar Power* (n 77) [76].

[80] See eg *Cruz City 1 Mauritius Holdings v Unitech Ltd* (2017) 239 DLT 649 (Delhi High Court) [85]–[109]; *Vijay Karia v Prysmian Cavi E Sistemi Srl* (2020) 11 SCC 1.

[81] *Oil and Natural Gas Corp Ltd v Western Geco International Ltd* (2014) 9 SCC 263 [26]–[30]. The Supreme Court in that case suggested three fundamental principles that are 'part and parcel' of the concept: (1) requirement to act judiciously; (2) principles of natural justice; and (3) reasonableness based on the *Wednesbury* principle.

[82] *Vijay Karia* (n 80) [83].

implicit in any commercial dispute. Mere error in the law by an originating state should not operate as a pretext for an enforcing court to review the merits of a judgment or refuse recognition and enforcement.

The English Arbitration Act 1996, s 69 gives parties to an arbitration conducted in the England and Wales and Northern Ireland the opportunity (subject to the grant of leave) to appeal to the court against an award on a point of law. Similar avenues of appeal exist in other jurisdictions.[83] Such procedures, although arguably inimical to the finality and certainty of arbitral awards, are hedged in by various safeguards. First, appeals on points of non-English law are not allowed. Second, parties may contract out of the appeal mechanism. International arbitration rules, such as the LCIA Rules (Article 26.9) and the ICC Rules (Article 28.6), have been drafted to exclude the appeal mechanism by default. Such rules have been held to be effective, at least under English law.[84] Third, under s 69(3)(c)(i), leave to appeal will only be granted if the error of law made by the arbitrator is 'obviously wrong'. So far, successful appeals through this avenue have been very limited.[85] Fourth, in some jurisdictions such as Hong Kong, a party which has been unsuccessful in challenging an arbitral award will be ordered to pay costs on an indemnity basis.[86] This disincentives parties to launch unmeritorious and hopeless challenges.

ii. *Arbitrability*

Article V(2)(a) of the 1958 New York Convention allows an enforcing court to refuse to recognise or enforce an award which concerns a dispute which is not capable of settlement by arbitration under the law of the enforcing state. For instance, the domestic laws of some countries will regard matters pertaining to land, competition or antitrust law, intellectual property rights, consumer protection, family or personal status, succession or inheritance, labour or employment law, and criminal liability as not being susceptible to resolution by arbitration. Thus, it may not be possible to enforce awards relating to such matters in particular states and it may be necessary in those states to bring a separate action in accordance with their laws.

E. Enforcing Awards Set Aside by a Supervising Court

The 1958 New York Convention does not oblige contracting states to refuse enforcement of awards that have been set aside at the seat. Article V(1)(e) only provides that

[83] See eg Arbitration Ordinance (Cap 609) (Hong Kong), Sch 2, ss 5–6, which parties may expressly provide for them to apply.

[84] *Lesotho Highlands Development Authority v Impregilo SpA* [2005] UKHL 43, [2006] 1 AC 221 [5].

[85] See Courts and Tribunals Judiciary, 'The Commercial Court Users' Group Meeting Report – March 2018' (29 April 2018), available at www.judiciary.uk/wp-content/uploads/2018/04/commercial-court-users-group-report.pdf.

[86] *A v R (Arbitration: Enforcement)* [2009] 3 HKLRD 389 (HKCFI). The position is now different in Singapore: *BTN v BTP* [2021] 4 SLR 603 (SGHC); *CDM v CDP* [2021] 2 SLR 235 (SGCA). See also W Lui, 'Defending the Indemnity Costs Approach to Unsuccessful Arbitral Award Challenges' (2021) 23(3) *Asian Dispute Review* 129.

an award *may* be denied recognition and enforcement if it has been annulled by the courts of the arbitral seat. It does not prohibit enforcement. Additionally, Article VII provides that the Convention shall not deprive any party of any right to benefit from an arbitral award as permitted by the law of the enforcing state. These provisions therefore leave room for national courts to exercise a discretion to recognise and enforce annulled awards, or to honour the seat-court's nullification. In the absence of an international standard, courts in different jurisdictions have taken diverging approaches to the question whether an award that has been nullified in its seat can still be enforced elsewhere. This depends on how enforcement courts characterise the nature and role of the arbitral seat. On a broad spectrum, there are three theories that gives validity to an award:[87]

(1) An award's validity derives from the law of the arbitral seat. The implication of this is that, when an award has been set aside by the competent authority in its seat, the award ceases to exist and is an unenforceable nullity.
(2) The award's validity derives from the totality of the laws of enforcing states. Under this theory, setting aside is a factor to be considered, but is not conclusive, in deciding whether to enforce an award.
(3) An award's validity is a matter of transnational legal autonomy. Under this view, awards are delocalised and are not linked to a particular jurisdiction or seat. Thus, the annulment of an award can have no conclusive bearing on enforcement. The award can be enforced, unless transnational principles of law (for example, good faith in the conclusion of contracts) render the award invalid.

Common law courts, such as those in Singapore and Hong Kong, favour the first theory.[88] English courts will ordinarily respect the decision of the court of the arbitral seat annulling an award, unless that decision is found to be contrary to basic principles of honesty and natural justice. For example, enforcement of a Russian arbitral award annulled by the Russian supervising court was refused in England, despite the English High Court's heavy criticism of the annulment decision.[89] The High Court held that, to refuse recognition of an annulment decision, there must be 'cogent' evidence that 'the decision of the foreign court must be deliberately wrong, not simply wrong by incompetence'.[90] The fact that a foreign court is manifestly wrong or is perverse is not sufficient. The decision must be so wrong as to be evidence of bias or must be such that no court acting in good faith could have arrived at it.[91]

[87] E Gaillard, *Aspects philosophiques du droit l'arbitrage international* (Martinus Nijhoff, 2008). See also Crina Baltag, 'Article V(1)(e) of the New York Convention: To Enforce or Not to Enforce Set Aside Arbitral Awards?' (2022) 39(3) *Journal of International Arbitration* 397.

[88] See eg *PT First Media TBK v Astro Nusantara International BV* [2014] 1 SLR 372 (SGCA) [76]–[77]; *Astro Nusantara International BV v PT Ayunda Prima Mitra* (unreported, HCMP 835/2014, 25 June 2014) (HKCA) [13]. For the *Astro* litigation, see also the appeal to the Hong Kong Court of Final Appeal: *Astro Nusantara International BV v PT Ayunda Prima Mitra* (2018) 21 HKCFAR 118, [2018] HKCFA 12.

[89] *Nikolay Viktorovich Maximov v OJSC Novolipetsky Metallurgichesky Kombinat* [2017] EWHC 1911 (Comm), [2017] 2 CLC 121.

[90] ibid [15] (Burton J).

[91] For an exceptional case where the English court recognised and enforced awards set aside in Russia due to Russia's 'partial and dependent judicial process', see *Yukos Capital Sarl v OJSC Rosneft Oil Co* [2011] EWHC 1461 (Comm), [2012] 1 All ER (Comm) 479.

F. The 2005 and 2019 Hague Conventions

The 2005 and the 2019 Hague Conventions are developed by the Hague Conference of Private International Law (HCCH). Their aims are similar. For example, the 2019 Hague Convention[92]

> will be essential to reducing transactional and litigation costs in cross-border dealings and to promoting effective access to justice for all. It also facilitates rule-based multilateral trade and investment. The Convention will increase certainty and predictability, promote the better management of transaction and litigation risks, and shorten timeframes for the recognition and enforcement of a judgement in other jurisdictions, providing better, more effective, and cheaper justice for individuals and businesses alike. This includes the attempt on a global level to harmonise the very different approaches taken by common law and civil law jurisdictions to concurrent proceedings and recognition and enforcement.

Analogous to the 1958 New York Convention in the context of international commercial arbitration, the two Hague Conventions are intended to increase certainty for litigants in international commercial disputes.

The 2005 Hague Convention came into force in 2015. As of 1 April 2022, there were 32 parties (including the EU). Five other states signed the Convention, including the US (2009) and China (2017). They have yet to ratify, or accede to, the instrument. The Convention applies 'in international cases to exclusive choice of court agreements concluded in civil or commercial matters' (Article 1). An 'exclusive choice of court agreement' is an agreement whereby the court of a Contracting State is designated as the exclusive forum for deciding disputes which have arisen or may arise in connection with a particular legal relationship (Article 3). Article 2 sets out a long list of exceptions, including, for example, matters relating to family law, wills and succession, insolvency and most intellectual property rights. The 2005 Hague Convention has two key components. The first component (essentially Chapter II (Articles 5 to 7)) ensures that the court designated by the parties in an exclusive choice of court agreement (and no other court) will hear a dispute arising out of the particular legal relationship. The second component (essentially Chapter III (Articles 8 to 15)) ensures that the judgment of the designated court will be recognised and enforced in all other contracting states, save only in limited and narrowly defined circumstances set out in Article 9. Apart from those grounds, there is to be no review of the merits of a judgment. A judgment shall be recognised provided that it is effective and enforceable in the originating state (Article 8(3)).

The 2019 Hague Convention currently has six signatories: Israel, Costa Rica, Ukraine, Uruguay, the US and Russia. Following the EU's accession and Ukraine's ratification on 29 August 2022, the 2019 Hague Convention will come into force on 1 September 2023. It complements the 2005 Hague Convention and sets out rules for

[92] 'It's Done: The 2019 HCCH Judgments Convention has been Adopted!' (Hague Conference of Private International Law, 8 July 2019), available at www.hcch.net/en/news-archive/details/?varevent=687.

the recognition and enforcement of judgments in the absence of a choice of court agreement. Judgments of contracting states are to be mutually recognised and enforced (Article 4(1)), provided that the judgments are effective and enforceable in the originating state (Article 4(3)). There shall be no review of the merits (Article 4(2)). Article 5(1) sets out the grounds of indirect jurisdiction for recognition and enforcement. Article 7(1) sets out the narrow grounds on which recognition and enforcement may be refused. These are broadly similar to the grounds for refusal in the 2005 Hague Convention. The 2019 Hague Convention includes employer and consumer contracts, which are not included in the 2005 Hague Convention.

So far, relatively few states have joined or indicated willingness to join the two Hague Conventions. Such reluctance may be due to the fact that[93]

> the means by which litigious disputes are resolved, and indeed the substantive laws from which actionable rights spring, are deeply enmeshed with cultural traditions and understandings very often valued well above the demands of international commerce; thus it is only understandable that national courts and legislatures have shown a proclivity for retaining means to protect their citizens and residents from foreign judgments rendered contrary to such traditions … [I]t is the sheer diversity of procedural and substantive systems and the reluctance of states and regions to forfeit their specific legal heritages in favour of uniformity that presents the most fundamental obstacle to the creation of a wide-ranging convention on the enforcement of foreign judgments.

This is perhaps unfortunate as an enhanced membership in the Conventions will significantly promote finality and certainty in relation to the cross-border enforcement of commercial judgments.

To continue the exploratory normative work under the Jurisdiction Project,[94] the Council on General Affairs and Policy (CGAP) of the HCCH established a Working Group in March 2021 on matters related to jurisdiction in transnational civil or commercial litigation. In particular, the CGAP mandated the Working Group:

(1) To develop draft provisions on matters related to jurisdiction in civil or commercial matters, including rules for concurrent proceedings, to further inform policy considerations and decisions in relation to the scope and type of any new instrument.
(2) To proceed in an inclusive and holistic manner, with an initial focus on developing binding rules for concurrent proceedings (parallel proceedings and related actions or claims), and acknowledging the primary role of both jurisdictional rules and the doctrine of *forum non conveniens*, notwithstanding other possible factors, in developing such rules.

[93] CR Einstein and A Phipps, 'Trends in International Commercial Litigation Part II – The Future of Foreign Judgment Enforcement Law' (Supreme Court of the New South Wales, 2005), available at www.supremecourt.justice.nsw.gov.au/Documents/Publications/Speeches/Pre-2015%20Speeches/Assorted%20-%20A%20to%20K/einstein_index.pdf. A similar argument that the states have to balance between affording certainty and protecting their nationals is made in A Reyes and W Lui, 'Conclusion' in A Reyes and W Lui (eds), *Direct Jurisdiction* (Hart Publishing, 2021) 334.

[94] A comprehensive overview of the work of the HCCH Jurisdiction Project since 1992 is available at www.hcch.net/en/projects/legislative-projects/jurisdiction-project.

(3) To explore how flexible mechanisms for judicial coordination and cooperation can support the operation of any future instrument on concurrent proceedings and jurisdiction in transnational civil or commercial litigation.

After the meetings in October 2021 and February 2022, the Working Group has produced a preliminary draft of provisions on parallel proceedings.[95] The detailed structure, contents and operation of this possible future instrument remain to be further discussed. The word 'instrument' is used here as it is not mandatory for the discussion results to take the form of a Convention. It can also be a soft law instrument setting out principles or international best practices that can be adopted by individual states as they see fit. More generally, it is argued that the HCCH should embrace the potential of soft law instruments to achieve international consensus by pursuing a better balance between conventions and soft law instruments.[96]

The current draft has proposed a system based on 'connections' of the courts involved in parallel proceedings. A distinction has been made between 'exclusive' and 'priority' connections. If one of the courts has or meets an 'exclusive' connection (for example, in cases involving rights *in rem* in immovable property, being the place where the immovable property is located), then the court having this 'exclusive' connection shall proceed with the case, and other courts shall suspend or dismiss the case. In the absence of 'exclusive' connections, 'priority' connections (for example, connections based on party autonomy) will give priority to one of the courts over other courts.

There are divergent views as to whether proceedings in the court first seised that is commenced 'within a reasonable timeframe' should also be given priority over proceedings in other courts. Moreover, there is also discussion on the specific criteria to determine situations in which parallel proceedings might be allowed to proceed for the interest of justice and efficiency, and on a voluntary, non-binding cooperation or communication mechanism among states. These are all open questions for the future Working Group meetings. The draft provisions also featured issues of 'clearly more appropriate forum' (similar to the *forum conveniens* exercise), respecting access of justice (or avoiding denial of justice) and public policy.

IV. Post-Pandemic Considerations

The COVID-19 pandemic has had, and will continue to have, a profound impact on everyone's lives. The legal arena has not been left untouched. COVID-19 will affect the

[95] Hague Conference of Private International Law, 'Report of the Working Group on Jurisdiction' (Prel Doc No 7, February 2022), available at assets.hcch.net/docs/d05583b3-ec71-4a5b-829c-103a834173bf.pdf.

[96] See also T John et al, 'Editors' Introduction to the Elgar Companion to the HCCH' in T John et al (eds), *The Elgar Companion to the Hague Conference on Private International Law* (Edward Elgar, 2020) xxix. Currently, the HCCH only has one soft law instrument: the 2015 Principles on Choice of Law in International Commercial Contracts.

ability of an obligor to perform contractual obligations in scenarios such as the following paradigms:[97]

(1) Government restrictions: An obligor's business cannot operate due to government-imposed restrictions to contain the spread of COVID-19. As a result, the obligor cannot perform a specified contractual obligation.
(2) Supply chain shortages: An obligor cannot perform its contractual obligation because a supplier faces a COVID-19-related impediment and, as a result, the obligor cannot obtain from the goods needed to perform its contract with the obligee.
(3) The effects of 'long COVID': An obligor has fallen ill with long COVID. This has prevented the obligor from complying with its contractual obligation.
(4) Self-imposed business lockdown: An obligor decides to protect itself and its employees, as well as society at large, from the spread of COVID-19. The obligor therefore temporarily closes its business and does not perform its contractual obligation.
(5) Economic chaos: An obligor cannot perform its contractual obligations as a result of the economic havoc and uncertainty brought about by COVID-19.

In relation to these scenarios, two broad sets of questions arise in connection with finality and certainty:

(1) In the wake of the pandemic, to what extent should finality and certainty continue to be lodestars in the field of international commercial dispute resolution? Should dispute resolution institutions ascribe greater weight to other considerations, such as national sovereignty, in their processes and adjudicative functions?
(2) Will existing doctrines and approaches commonly used in the resolution of international commercial disputes, in particular: (a) jurisdiction; (b) public policy; and (c) enforcement, be affected?

The questions are intertwined and will be dealt with together.

Plainly, finality and certainty will continue to play a key role to play in international commercial dispute resolution. Businesses will want to know where they stand at any given time, in terms of their cross-border commercial rights and obligations. The focus has therefore been on how existing law and institutions can deal with the impact of COVID-19 in a practical and predictable manner. Commentaries have discussed the extent to which current concepts of *force majeure*, frustration, supervening illegality, change of circumstances, good faith, etc, can be applied.[98] They have dealt with issues of damages.[99] They have also considered procedural issues, such as how adjudicative

[97] FT Schwarz et al (eds), 'Contractual Performance and COVID-19: An In-Depth Comparative Law Analysis' (Wolters Kluwer, 2021) 9–10.

[98] See eg British Institute of International and Comparative Law, '"Breathing Space" – Concept Note 2 on the Effect of the 2020 Pandemic on Commercial Contracts: September 2020 Update' (September 2020), available at www.biicl.org/documents/10423_revised_concept_note_2_004wb_21.pdf; Schwarz et al (ibid).

[99] See eg M Hodgson and F Nowak, 'Valuation of Damages in Light of COVID-19' (International Bar Association, 13 October 2020), available at www.ibanet.org/MediaHandler?id=81A53DE9-E17D-49B5-84F5-05DB010C4F84.

processes can take place remotely, and how HCCH instruments can be applied and operated, etc.[100]

Such approaches attempt to find ways of dealing with the current unprecedented crisis within the framework of the law and practice that already existed. This is perfectly natural and not to be criticised. But it is submitted that the pandemic should also be an occasion for international commercial dispute stakeholders (states, courts, arbitral tribunals, parties, lawyers) to rethink previous approaches and make concerted efforts to come up with new initiatives. For example, the 'Concept Note 3' published by the British Institute of International and Comparative Law (BIICL)[101] has proposed (among others) that there be increased resort to ADR and greater emphasis on amicable contractual relationships. It is also high time to reassess the role of information technology, artificial intelligence, etc, in facilitating finality and certainty in resolving international commercial disputes.[102]

As for what the future might hold in terms of the development of concepts such as jurisdiction, public policy and enforcement, it is likely that states in the post-pandemic era will be more willing: (1) to expand grounds of direct jurisdiction; (2) to enable anti-suit injunctions to be used more aggressively; and (3) to re-evaluate the use of sovereign immunity.[103] Resort to public policy[104] will likely be more prevalent, as a reason for refusing to recognise foreign judgments and awards in whole or part and thereby protecting an enforcing state's commercial enterprises from foreign creditors. Some jurisdictions have already passed laws to provide temporary measures in connection with jurisdiction and enforcement issues in order to mitigate the consequences of the COVID-19 pandemic,[105] for example, by requiring parties not to commence or continue an action, or enforce a security where a counterparty's inability to perform

[100] See eg Hague Conference on Private International Law, 'COVID-19 Toolkit' (4 May 2020), available at assets.hcch.net/docs/538fa32a-3fc8-4aba-8871-7a1175c0868d.pdf; M Giddings, 'Remote Hearings, Access to Justice and the Efficient Resolution of Disputes' (Lipman Karas, 22 March 2021), available at www.lipmankaras.com/2021/03/remote-hearings-access-to-justice-and-the-efficient-resolution-of-disputes.

[101] British Institute of International and Comparative Law, '"Breathing Space" – Concept Note 3 on Guidelines for the Resolution of Disputes Following the 2020 Pandemic' (September 2020), available at www.biicl.org/documents/10471_biicl_breathing_space_concept_note_3_-_the_guidelines642428154_22_141020.pdf.

[102] For an attempt to 'look beyond' the pandemic and consider the future use of technology in dispute resolution, see Standing International Forum of Commercial Courts, 'Second SIFoCC COVID-19 Memorandum' (March 2021), available at sifocc.org/resources/resources-2. See also Pt 6 of this book for a more detailed discussion.

[103] Reyes and Lui, 'Conclusion' (2021). Concepts of immunities have indeed been creatively redefined in recent cases such as *Basfar v Wong* [2022] UKSC 20, [2022] 3 WLR 208, where a bare majority of the UK Supreme Court held that diplomatic immunity cannot defeat a claim by a victim of modern slavery as it falls within the 'commercial activity' exception.

[104] See section III.D above. See also eg A Mills, 'The Dimensions of Public Policy in Private International Law' (2008) 4 *Journal of Private International Law* 201; K Chng, 'A Theoretical Perspective of the Public Policy Doctrine in the Conflict of Laws' (2018) 14 *Journal of Private International Law* 130; S Menon, 'Taming the Unruly Horse: The Treatment of Public Policy Arguments in the Courts' (Federal Court of Malaysia, 19 February 2019), available at judiciary.kehakiman.gov.my/portals/media/others/(Public%20Policy%20Lecture)%20Lecture%20(FINAL%20FOR%20PUBLICATION)%20(1%20March%202019).pdf; Monique Sasson, 'Public Policy in International Commercial Arbitration' (2022) 39(3) *Journal of International Arbitration* 411.

[105] See eg the COVID-19 (Temporary Measures) Act 2020 (No 14 of 2020) (Singapore); Corporate Insolvency and Governance Act 2020 (UK) and the relevant Regulations; Commercial Rent (Coronavirus) Act 2022 (UK); Temporary Protection Measures for Business Tenants (COVID-19 Pandemic) Ordinance (Cap 644) (Hong Kong).

has been materially caused by a COVID-19 event. Where claims are commenced or sought to be enforced in contravention of such measures, the relevant proceedings will be dismissed.[106] Furthermore, issues of digital economy[107] and climate change[108] will certainly bring new developments to the landscape of international commercial dispute resolution.

[106] See eg COVID-19 (Temporary Measures) Act 2020 (No 14 of 2020) (Singapore), ss 5, 8.

[107] The Digital Assets and Private Law Working Group, established by UNIDROIT, has produced a list of draft principles on the legal nature, transfer and use of digital assets, available at www.unidroit.org/work-in-progress/digital-assets-and-private-law. The HCCH and the UNCITRAL Working Group II are both considering the scope and nature of future work in relation to private international law implications of and dispute resolution in the digital economy respectively. For an overview, see Hague Conference of Private International Law, 'Developments with respect to PIL Implications of the Digital Economy' (Prel Doc No 4 REV, January 2022), available at assets.hcch.net/docs/b06c28c5-d183-4d81-a663-f7bdb8f32dac.pdf. See also eg UK Jurisdictional Taskforce, 'Legal Statement on Cryptoassets and Smart Contracts' (November 2019), available at technation.io/lawtech-uk-resources; UK Jurisdictional Taskforce, 'Digital Dispute Resolution Rules' (April 2021), available at technation.io/lawtech-uk-resources.

[108] See eg International Chamber of Commerce, 'Resolving Climate Change Related Disputes through Arbitration and ADR' (November 2019), available at iccwbo.org/content/uploads/sites/3/2019/11/icc-arbitration-adr-commission-report-on-resolving-climate-change-related-disputes-english-version.pdf; L Greenwood, 'The Canary is Dead: Arbitration and Climate Change' (2021) 38 *Journal of International Arbitration* 309; L Bizikova, 'On Route to Climate Justice: The Greta Effect on International Commercial Arbitration' (2022) 39 *Journal of International Arbitration* 79.

8

Towards the Just Resolution of Disputes

How Do We Balance Commercial Certainty and Achieving the Right Result?

NALLINI PATHMANATHAN* AND JOANNE TAN XIN YING†

I. Introduction

It is a touchstone of most legal systems and legal argumentation that finality and certainty are of enormous importance, often outweighing the need to achieve a 'right' result. This is bolstered by the reference to these two fundamental qualities as features undergirding the Rule of Law. But this leads to the question: what is meant by these features of finality and certainty?[1]

A. Finality

The concept of finality merely means that an adjudication on a particular dispute, whether by the courts or by way of arbitration, becomes at some point permanent, binding and final. This in turn means that the party which has succeeded is entitled to enforce the decision or to preclude the opposing party from pursuing the original claim made in any other subsequent proceedings. The basis for courts and arbitrations to adhere to the principle of finality is that the dispute between the parties has been resolved by means of an accepted procedure in accordance with the Rule of Law and a substantive opinion brought to bear.[2] The fact that one or both parties are dissatisfied with the ultimate decision cannot result in a reventilation of the same matter in other fora. Finality ensures stability and order in the resolution of disputes,

* Judge of the Federal Court of Malaysia.
† Senior Assistant Registrar of the Federal Court of Malaysia.

[1] SJ Bayern, 'Against Certainty' (2012) 41 *Hofstra Law Review* 53.

[2] K Gusarov and V Terekhov, 'Finality of Judgments in Civil Cases and Related Considerations: The Experience of Ukraine and Lithuania' (2019) 4 *Access to Justice in Eastern Europe* 6.

as the primary aim of dispute resolution is to resolve disputes, not to perpetuate or maintain them indefinitely. Finality also lends itself to legal certainty, and this is put into practice through doctrines such as *res judicata*, which we shall explore later in this chapter.

In arbitrations, particularly commercial arbitrations, finality is greatly prized; this is reflected in the UNCITRAL Model Law, which is adopted in the legislation of many national jurisdictions. That is ensured by narrowing or confining the ability to review to a few specified exceptions. However, there are exceptions to this doctrine of finality which are rare and exceptional. Primarily these exceptions arise when there has been an encroachment into the fundamental elements comprising the Rule of Law, for example, equality before the law, access to justice, breach of the *audi alteram partem* rule, and other fundamental principles. In short, the doctrine of finality cannot be used as a cloak of complete immunity where such fundamental elements of justice have been breached. In such cases, the requirement to correct errors and achieve a just result override the doctrine of finality. Put another way, the doctrine of finality is premised on the basis that the essentials of procedural fairness and substantive justice subsist in a particular dispute.

While the foregoing is true of both public and private law, the recognition that finality is not absolute is entrenched in the mechanism of judicial review. Sometimes this is embedded in a written constitution or is otherwise available by convention and statute. In essence, in public law matters, the right of judicial review is an exception to finality in that it allows access to justice by aggrieved parties. In Malaysia, the doctrine of judicial review is expressly encapsulated in Article 4(1) of the Federal Constitution: 'This Constitution is the supreme law of the Federation and any law passed after Merdeka Day which is inconsistent with this Constitution shall, to the extent of the inconsistency, be void'.

This provision ensures that challenges to legislation, or legislative or executive action on the grounds of a failure to comply with the provisions of the Federal Constitution renders such legislation, statutory provision, act or omission null and void. The provision signifies that constitutional supremacy rather than parliamentary sovereignty is paramount. In relation to civil actions in the courts, there is a provision for review in the form of Rule 137 of the Rules of the Federal Court 1995 which speaks of the apex court having 'inherent powers' to make 'any such order as may be necessary to prevent injustice or to prevent an abuse of the process of the Court'. However, this power has been interpreted to be exercisable only within limited grounds and under exceptional circumstances.[3] It is not meant to operate as a back door for the losing party to have a second bite of the cherry.

Finality, like certainty, is very much to be balanced against achieving a correct and just outcome. Ultimately, as with certainty, a balance has to be found between finality and achieving a just and correct result. Jurisdictions may differ in the weight they accord to each of these elements within their national courts systems and that really is the subject matter of the discussion in this paper.

[3] *Yong Tshu Khin & Anor v Dahan Cipta Sdn Bhd & anor and other applications* [2021] 1 CLJ 631 [77]–[78].

B. Certainty

'Certainty' refers to the fact that a legal principle or rule promotes a consistent and specific – or 'certain' – conclusion in any given case. Such certainty promotes the Rule of Law in the sense that citizens can predict the outcome of their acts or omissions in various aspects of life, from behaviour to the conduct of transactions. There is an assurance of a predictable outcome that promotes the feature of certainty. Legal certainty, however, is not absolute in the sense that there can be no absolute or conclusive determination of a legal dispute based almost entirely on legal principles without reference to context and factual matrix. In every instance of its application, it is the context within which a particular principle is applied that determines, at least in part, and often to a considerable extent, the legal conclusion or result.[4] This can be explained by the fact that doctrines, rules or principles of law are always applied within the context of a fact situation. It is not possible, nor is it the case in actuality, that such rules are applied mechanistically or automatically. This renders legal certainty less definite and certain.

Further, the consistency or certainty of a legal conclusion will also be determined by the choice of rule adopted to be applied in any given fact situation. Where there is a choice of the rule or doctrine to be applied, given a particular set of facts, it is important that such choice remains available to the adjudicator, rather than truncating the choice by promoting certainty at all costs. Therefore, is legal 'certainty' an absolute feature in itself, which is to be promoted relentlessly? Is it not an equally accepted tenet of the law that different or unexpected facts require treatment that may differ from an accepted and certain application of a doctrine, thereby producing a different legal result? This may well encroach on the principle of certainty but produce a correct and just result.

Additionally, given that social norms change, and that the law is evolving to meet a globalising world which introduces new viewpoints and considerations, legal certainty is bound to evolve similarly, to enable and accommodate different interpretations and social judgements. This too encroaches on legal certainty, but ensures that the law evolves to meet the needs of a changing society. Legal certainty ought not be utilised to stultify the growth of the law. This is not to say that the current approach of incremental changes to the law to ensure its consistent and logical growth is incorrect. It means that legal certainty ought not to be utilised to impede the progression of the law to ensure a just result. Following on from this proposition, it is equally important to recognise that it may be necessary to depart from a particular doctrine or principle in order that the law evolves. Therefore, a departure from what was held to be a sacrosanct doctrine or rule may well be required in order to meet change, particularly today, in the face of a legal world that is on the cusp of an evolution, brought about in no small part by the COVID-19 pandemic. We are moving towards virtual courts and a digitalised world, and the law needs to evolve to meet those needs. The pace of the real world is relentless, and this needs to be recognised and matched in the law.

[4] Bayern, 'Against Certainty' (2012) 55.

Legal certainty is a feature to be applauded and promoted but it ought not to be employed with rigidity. In this context, the importance of ensuring a coherent and just result cannot be expended in the name of legal certainty.

II. Defining and Evaluating the Policies of Finality and Certainty in International Commercial Dispute Resolution

What do the policies of finality and certainty entail? Why are they important, and are there any limits on them?

A. Finality

Finality is regarded as one of the primary features and attractions of international commercial dispute resolution as compared to litigation before the domestic courts, which involve tiered levels of appeal.[5] The absence of an appeals process produces a regime that saves time and costs, but some argue that it sacrifices fairness since there is no method by which to correct an arbitral award given in error. Typically, the courts in pro-arbitration nations adopt a non-interventionist stance, which precludes review of awards on the merits except in very limited circumstances.[6] The tension between finality and fairness arises within this restricted sphere where an impugned arbitral decision may only be challenged under very narrow grounds. It has also been recognised that while arbitration has the potential of offering speedier resolution of disputes than litigation, this potential is not guaranteed as it remains subject to party autonomy, dilatory tactics, and issues in obtaining evidence.[7]

B. Certainty

Legal certainty prioritises clear, foreseeable and equal rules. It is often seen to be contrary to the idea of equity, which considers the circumstances underlying a matter. In an ideal world, predictability as to the result of a dispute is achievable if we have a system of exclusive jurisdiction rules. However, such a regime is not without its flaws as it ignores considerations of proximity and the interest of at least one party to the dispute.[8] A US survey has found that parties value a 'fair and just result' in arbitration

[5] C Larson, 'Substantive Fairness in International Commercial Arbitration: Achievable through an Arbitral Appeals Process?' (2018) 84 *The International Journal of Arbitration, Mediation and Dispute Management* 104, 104.

[6] See, for example, the Malaysian Arbitration Act 2005 (Act 646), ss 8 and 37 and the Singapore International Arbitration Act 1994, ss 47 to 49.

[7] N Japaridze, 'Fair Enough? Reconciling the Pursuit of Fairness and Justice with Preserving the Nature of International Commercial Arbitration' (2008) 36 *Hofstra Law Review* 1415, 1419.

[8] C Schmon, *The Interconnection of the EU Regulations Brussels I Recast and Rome I: Jurisdiction and the Law* (Asser Press, 2020) 6.

above factors like cost, arbitrator expertise, speed and privacy.[9] One view holds that fairness should be assessed in terms of both procedure and substance.[10] In other words, the 'right process' should have been adopted in coming to a 'right result'.[11] If emphasis is to be given to the correctness of awards, one notes that there has been growing support advocating for a form of substantive review in circumstances of mistake.[12] The main criticism against the introduction of such an appeals process is that it offends against the basic premise of arbitration and could potentially result in additional expense and delays, which have the effect of making arbitration less efficient as a mode of dispute resolution.[13] Apart from that, the concern that critics of the non-reviewable aspect of arbitration have may be allayed when one considers that most arbitral systems impose a variety of duties and limitations on arbitrators to safeguard the integrity of the arbitral process.[14] Parties may also impose duties on the arbitrator such as delivering an award within a stipulated timeframe, observation of institutional rules, and being held liable by parties in the event of failure of performance of his or her duty as spelt out in the arbitration agreement.[15]

C. Comity, Sovereignty and Party Autonomy

How do finality and certainty interact with other policies such as comity, sovereignty and party autonomy? 'Comity' is a doctrine which acknowledges that 'nothing could be more inconvenient to commerce and international usage than that transactions valid by the law of one place should be rendered of no effect elsewhere on the account of a difference in the law'.[16] It has been associated with courtesy, politeness, deference, respect, convenience, goodwill, expediency, reciprocity, conflict and necessity.[17] Sovereignty may be defined as an expression of self-determination by a state as to how it chooses

[9] RW Naimark and SE Keer, 'What Do Parties Really Want from International Commercial Arbitration?' (2003) 57 *Dispute Resolution Journal* 78.

[10] Larson, 'Substantive Fairness in International Commercial Arbitration' (2018) 106.

[11] ibid.

[12] WH Knull III and ND Rubins, 'Betting the Farm on International Arbitration: Is It Time to Offer an Appeal Option?' (2000) 11 *American Review of International Arbitration* 531; IM Ten-Cate, 'International Arbitration and the Ends of Appellate Review' (2011–12) 44 *New York University Journal of International Law and Politics* 1109, M Aimore Carreteiro, 'Appellate Arbitral Rules in International Commercial Arbitration' (2016) 33 *Journal of International Arbitration* 185.

[13] Larson (n 5) 110.

[14] Japaridze, 'Fair Enough?' (2008) 1426.

[15] ibid 1434.

[16] J Allsop, 'Comity and Commerce' [2015] *Federal Judicial Scholarship* 27 [6].

[17] LF Oppenheim, *International Law: A Treatise*, vol 1 (Longmans, 1912) 24–25; H Yntema 'The Comity Doctrine' (1966) 65 *Michigan Law Review* 9; GC Cheshire, *Private International Law* (Butterworths, 1965); JR Paul 'Comity in International Law' (1991) 32 *Harvard International Law Journal* 1; JR Paul 'The Transformation of International Comity' (2008) 71 *Law and Contemporary Problems* 19; H Barry 'Comity' (1926) 12 *Virginia Law Review* 353; DE Childress, 'Comity as Conflict: Re-situating International Comity as Conflict of Laws' (2010) 44 *University of California Davis Law Review* 11; *Dicey, Morris and Collins on The Conflict of Laws*, 14th edn (Sweet & Maxwell, 2006) 5–9; MW Lien 'The Cooperative and Integrative Models of International Judicial Comity: Two Illustrations Using Transnational Discovery and Breard Scenarios' (2001) 50 *Catholic University Law Review* 591.

to govern itself through rules and political institutions.[18] In practice, the application of the doctrine of comity by states is but another exercise of state sovereignty dependent largely on the goals and values of a particular nation. It is through the recognition and enforcement of foreign judgments inter alia that one may observe how comity is practiced by the states. Most countries require 'reciprocity' before foreign judgments are automatically enforced.[19] If reciprocity is absent, the party who wishes to enforce a judgment must resort to the ordinary law.[20]

Reliance on this system is not without uncertainty and risk. One of the approaches devised to overcome this is enshrined in Articles 8 and 9 of the 2005 Hague Convention on Choice of Court Agreements, which provide that any judgment rendered by the chosen court must be recognised and enforced by other contracting states, except where a ground for refusal applies.[21] Central to the concept of party autonomy is the idea that parties are free to determine how their disputes should be resolved, including the freedom to choose the law and forum under which their disagreements may be settled. This freedom presents difficulties when there is ambiguity in what the parties intended. In the context of arbitration, legal measures have been developed to prevent parties who have entered into an arbitration agreement from reneging on their agreement to arbitrate, in order to uphold the reliability of arbitration.

One of the key measures is Article II of the New York Convention. According to Article II, a court of a state party to the Convention that is seised of an action in a matter in respect of which parties have referred to arbitration is obliged at the request of one of the parties to refer the matter to arbitration (*exceptio compromissi*), unless the agreement is 'null and void, inoperative or incapable of being performed'.[22] Furthermore, it is only natural for parties to seek to minimise the risk inherent in a commercial bargain between themselves if there is uncertainty as to the law, for example by deciding for themselves the consequences governing a particular breach. It has been argued that party autonomy and finality are incompatible vis-à-vis appeal and review.[23] If an arbitral award is subject to further appeal, it becomes a mere precursor to court proceedings and such situation would render the arbitration agreement between the parties meaningless.[24] However, parties are free to exclude appeals on a point of law by express agreement.[25] In addition, certain conditions can be attached to the finality of an arbitral award which diminish the importance of the arbitral proceeding. This includes clauses which negative the finality of an arbitral award.[26] Thus, despite the enactment of restrictive legislative grounds for review of arbitral awards, parties may

[18] SL Snell, 'Controlling Restrictive Business Practices in Global Markets: Reflections on the Concepts of Sovereignty, Fairness, and Comity' (1997) 33 *Stanford Journal of International Law* 215, 218.

[19] Allsop, 'Comity and Commerce' [2015] [47].

[20] ibid.

[21] ibid.

[22] P Ortolani, 'Anti-Suit Injunctions in Support of Arbitration and EU Law' in L Chen and A Janssen (eds), *Dispute Resolution in China, Europe and World* (Springer, 2020) 172.

[23] S Talwar Mouland, 'Comparing the Role of the Courts in English and German Arbitration Law: Should Party Autonomy or Certainty Preferred?' [2015] *ALSA Academic Journal* 144, 157.

[24] ibid.

[25] ibid. An appeal on a question of law is possible under English arbitration law (see the English Arbitration Act 1996, s 69).

[26] ibid 156.

still circumvent the finality of a decision by choosing their own set of rules in creative arbitration agreements.[27]

III. Managing Concurrent Proceedings

As in domestic litigation, a multiplicity of proceedings in international dispute resolution is undesirable as it strains the resources of litigants, perpetuates injustice against an economically weaker party, and exacts a toll on national judicial systems at the expense of the taxpayer.[28] In addition, concurrent proceedings are a primary threat to the certainty and finality of international judgments and arbitral awards.[29] This is especially because they may give rise to potentially conflicting outcomes which undermine the credibility of the system of dispute resolution in the eyes of users.[30] There is consequently a need to ensure the cohesiveness of results when a matter is the subject of adjudication between different dispute resolution bodies. Consistency and uniformity in the interpretation and application of commercial law and commercial dispute resolution process promotes and inspires confidence in the Rule of Law. How, then, do and should the policies of finality and certainty feature in relation to the following types of applications and proceedings?

A. *Lis Alibi Pendens*

Civil law jurisdictions, which typically grant limited discretion to judges, manage parallel proceedings by utilising *lis alibi pendens*, an approach codified in the EU's Brussels I Regulation[31] and its successor the Brussels Recast Regulation (BRR).[32] The parties' chosen forum is given priority under the BRR.[33] Under the doctrine of *lis alibi pendens*, a stay of proceedings in a particular forum may be sought on the ground that litigation is pending in another jurisdiction.[34] This doctrine has been suggested as a potential panacea to the problem of the initiation of a multiplicity of proceedings in relation to

[27] ibid 156–57.

[28] S Menon, 'The Transnational Protection of Private Rights: Issues, Challenges, and Potential Solutions' in *The Effectiveness of International Law* (2014) 108 *Proceedings of the Annual Meeting of the American Society of International Law* 219, 223.

[29] G Kaufmann-Kohler, 'Multiple Proceedings in International Arbitration: Blessing or Plague?' Herbert Smith Freehills and Singapore Management University School of Law Asian Arbitration Lecture, 24 November 2015.

[30] ibid.

[31] Art 27(1) provides: 'Where proceedings involving the same cause of action and between the same parties are brought in the courts of different Member States, any court other than the court first seised shall of its own motion stay its proceedings until such time as the jurisdiction of the court first seised is established.'

[32] Art 29(1) provides: 'Without prejudice to Article 31(2), where proceedings involving the same cause of action and between the same parties are brought in the courts of different Member States, any court other than the court first seised shall of its own motion stay its proceedings until such time as the jurisdiction of the court first seised is established.' The reference to Article 31(2) is new and crucial as it deals with the parties' choice of jurisdiction.

[33] J Lewis, '*Lis Pendens*: The Parties' Choice of Jurisdiction Matters under the Recast Regulation' (2016) 7 *Butterworths Journal of International Banking and Financial Law* 419A, 1, 1.

[34] RH Hickling, 'Stay of Actions and *Forum Non Conveniens*' [1994] 3 *Malayan Law Journal* xcvii.

the same dispute, which is a tactic employed by some parties to increase their chances of success.[35] While there is no doubt that *lis pendens* fosters certainty among parties, it is open to being misused by litigants in the race of the 'first-to-file'.[36]

Extended legal uncertainty may ensue if proceedings are commenced in jurisdictions where there are backlogs in the judicial system. Such uncertainty has been weaponised by litigants into what is known as the 'Italian torpedo' with the aim of compelling settlement or to disturb the dispute resolution process by driving up its costs.[37] One difficulty in the application of this doctrine is that it assumes that each of the fora that have been seised possesses legitimate jurisdiction over the same dispute.[38] This at odds with the practice of international arbitration under which a valid arbitration agreement suffices to confer exclusive jurisdiction on the arbitral tribunal that has been appointed to determine the dispute between the parties.[39] In other words, when a party requests a court to stay proceedings on the ground that the same dispute is pending elsewhere, it necessarily means that there are two courts of competent jurisdiction.[40] In arbitration, there can be no scenario of two competent tribunals for it is the arbitration agreement which confers exclusive jurisdiction on the arbitral tribunal. The other obstacle to the application of *lis pendens* arises when a party seeks to secure its favoured venue by submitting part of its claims to one tribunal and the balance to another, which would result in each tribunal being seised of different disputes, rendering the doctrine inapplicable.[41]

B. *Forum Non Conveniens*

Under this doctrine, courts have a discretion to refuse to exercise their jurisdiction over a matter which they would otherwise have jurisdiction to entertain. This is crucial to address the possibility of inconsistent judgments in parallel proceedings. The essence of the rule lies in the consideration of the factor of the 'appropriateness' of the forum. In Malaysia, the 'appropriateness of the forum' rule has been endorsed and applied by the highest levels of the judiciary. It entails the assessment of many factors, including whether it would be unjust to confine a plaintiff to remedies elsewhere and whether a forum is one with which the action has the most real and substantial connection.[42] *Forum non conveniens* has been criticised by the European Court of Justice (ECJ) in *Owusu v Jackson*[43] as being anathema to legal certainty, and inapplicable even in matters involving a non-party to the Brussels Convention. Considering that and the coming into

[35] E Gaillard, 'Abuse of Process in International Arbitration' (2017) *ICSID Review* 1, 11.

[36] K Qureshi and C Nicol, 'The Demise of *Forum Non Conveniens*?' [2014] *Butterworths Journal of International Banking and Financial Law* 509, 510.

[37] Ortolani, 'Anti-Suit Injunctions' (2020) 173.

[38] Gaillard, 'Abuse of Process' (2017) 12.

[39] ibid.

[40] Kaufmann-Kohler, 'Multiple Proceedings in International Arbitration (2015).

[41] Gaillard (n 35) 12.

[42] *Petrodar Operating Co Ltd v Nam Fatt Corporation Bhd & anor* [2014] 1 CLJ 18 FC, *American Express Bank Ltd v Mohamad Toufic Al-Ozeir & anor* [1995] 1 CLJ 273 SC.

[43] Case C-281/02 [2005] ECR I-1383.

effect of Article 5(2) of the 2005 HCCH Convention on Choice of Court Agreements, which expressly prohibits a chosen jurisdiction from declining jurisdiction on the basis of *forum non conveniens*,[44] it has been suggested that the doctrine's popularity is on the wane.[45] Ultimately, the future of the *lis alibi pendens* and *forum non conveniens* doctrines rests on whether stakeholders see the tension as a healthy competition in the international regime or a zero-sum game between two very distinct doctrines.[46]

C. Anti-Suit Injunctions

An anti-suit injunction is an order to discontinue litigation previously commenced in a different forum, in violation of an arbitration agreement.[47] It is a common law entity with no exact equivalent in most civil law jurisdictions.[48] The power to issue anti-suit injunctions is regarded as part of the judiciary's arsenal to protect the integrity of its own processes.[49] In Malaysia, the issuance of an anti-suit injunction by use of the inherent powers of the court has only been exercised in favour of a third party who was not party or privy to the subject arbitration agreement.[50] It has been remarked that, because of their 'unilateral, confrontational nature', anti-suit injunctions or anti-arbitration injunctions are 'not helpful' tools to manage duplicity of proceedings.[51] It is also true that an anti-suit injunction, while directed at the party in breach of an arbitration agreement, is indirectly disruptive of the judicial process of a foreign court.[52]

One weakness of the anti-suit injunction is that foreign courts are entitled to ignore it, although they may choose to recognise anti-suit injunctions voluntarily out of respect for international comity.[53] The anti-suit injunction may also be countered by an anti-anti-suit injunction granted by a foreign court to prevent a litigant from obtaining an anti-suit injunction against the other party, or to prevent the enforcement of the original anti-suit injunction.[54] These tactics may eventuate in 'interjurisdiction judicial warfare' and leave litigants without a meaningful remedy.[55] Consequently, the value of

[44] Art 5(2) of the Convention states: 'A court that has jurisdiction under paragraph 1 shall not decline to exercise jurisdiction on the ground that the dispute should be decided in a court of another State.'

[45] Qureshi and Nicol, 'The Demise of *Forum Non Conveniens*?' [2014] 512–13; J Burke, 'Foreclosure of the Doctrine of *Forum Non Conveniens* under the Brussels I Regulation: Advantages and Disadvantages' (2008) 3 *The European Legal Forum* 121, 121.

[46] RA Brand, 'Challenges to *Forum Non Conveniens*' (2013) 45 *New York University Journal of International Law and Politics* 1003, 1004 (U of Pittsburgh Legal Studies Research Paper No 2013–21), available at ssrn.com/abstract=2288697.

[47] Ortolani (n 22) 173.

[48] ibid 174.

[49] See the decision of the Australian High Court in *CSR Ltd v Cigna Insurance Australia Ltd and others* (1997) 146 ALR 402, 433, cited with approval by the Malaysian Federal Court in *Jaya Sudhir a/l Jayaram v Nautical Supreme Sdn Bhd & ors* [2019] 5 MLJ 1.

[50] *Jaya Sudhir a/l Jayaram v Nautical Supreme Sdn Bhd & ors* [2019] 5 MLJ 1 FC.

[51] Kaufmann-Kohler (n 29).

[52] *British Airways Board v Laker Airways Ltd* [1985] AC 58 95 per Lord Scarman.

[53] JE Dowler, 'Forging Finality: Searching for a Solution to the International Double-Suit Dilemma' (1994) 4 *Duke Journal of Comparative and International Law* 363, 379.

[54] ibid.

[55] ibid 380.

an anti-suit injunction as an effective mechanism in dealing with multiple proceedings is doubtful.

The European position on anti-suit injunctions can be gleaned from a few examples. In *Turner v Grovit*,[56] Turner brought an action for unfair dismissal in London while Grovit commenced litigation for damages against Turner in Spain. Turner sought an anti-suit injunction from the English courts restraining the defendants from continuing with the Spanish proceedings on the ground that that the suit had been filed in 'bad faith' to frustrate or obstruct the English proceedings. The English Court of Appeal issued an anti-suit injunction, and the defendants appealed the decision to the House of Lords, which referred the matter to the CJEU. The CJEU held that the Brussels Convention precluded the issuance of an anti-suit injunction by the court of a Member State restraining a party from commencing or continuing legal proceedings before the courts of another Member State. Essentially, the CJEU prioritised legal certainty in the interpretation of the principle of mutual trust underpinning the Brussels regime.[57]

Subsequently, in *West Tankers*, an English court granted an anti-suit injunction restraining the parties from pursuing litigation in Italy in breach of an English arbitration agreement. The CJEU held that the English anti-suit injunction was inconsistent with the mutual trust underpinning the operation of the Brussels I Regulation, a decision that was greeted with consternation as it appeared to sanction the use of judicial proceedings at a rival forum to 'torpedo' arbitration proceedings.[58] It is worth noting that before the Italian court delivered judgment on the merits, the owners of the vessel in *West Tankers* applied to the English court to enter judgment on the English arbitral award with the intention of obtaining a judgment in England that would take precedence over any later Italian judgment.[59] *West Tankers* thus illustrates the structural shortcomings of the rules of international dispute resolution at the material time to manage the phenomenon of concurrent proceedings, where a tactical advantage may be obtained from a race to judgment.[60] Here the principle of effectiveness limited the English court's ability to safeguard the arbitral proceedings as it restricted the court from issuing an anti-suit injunction against the court of another Member State.[61]

The power of municipal courts to control multiple proceedings was clarified later in *Gazprom*.[62] Here, one of the questions confronting the CJEU was whether the courts of a Member State have the right to refuse to recognise an arbitral award restricting the court's right to determine itself whether it has jurisdiction to hear the case under the rules on jurisdiction in the Brussels I Regulation. *Gazprom* distinguished *West Tankers*. The CJEU agreed that the Regulation does not preclude a court of a Member State from recognising and enforcing, or from refusing to recognise and enforce, an arbitral award

[56] Case C-159/02, ECLI:EU:C:2004:228.

[57] ibid [28].

[58] C McLachlan, 'Are National Courts and International Arbitral Tribunals in Two Worlds or One?' (2016) 7 *Journal of International Dispute Settlement* 577, 584.

[59] ibid.

[60] ibid 585.

[61] Y Farah and S Hourani, 'Recasting *West Tankers* in the Deep Water: How *Gazprom* and Recast Brussels I Reconcile Brussels I with International Arbitration' (2018) 14 *Journal of Private International Law* 96, 108.

[62] Case C-536/13.

prohibiting a party from bringing certain claims before a court of that Member State, since that regulation does not govern the recognition and enforcement, in a Member State, of an arbitral award issued by an arbitral tribunal in another Member State. It therefore follows that giving effect to an anti-suit injunction issued by an arbitral tribunal would not contradict the principle of effectiveness of EU law and any other general principles of EU law.[63]

Gazprom has thus relaxed the application of the principle of mutual trust and effectiveness of EU law, and bolstered the national courts' ability to manage concurrent proceedings.[64] By confirming the arbitration exception, *Gazprom* clarifies that the Brussels Regulation governs conflicts of jurisdiction between the courts of the Member States, and not between the courts and arbitral tribunals.[65] Following *Gazprom*, it is clear that, in Europe, arbitrators enjoy greater anti-suit powers than judges.[66]

D. Applications for Stay of Proceedings

In Malaysia, the principles governing a grant of a stay of court proceedings to non-parties was considered in *Protasco Bhd v Tey Por Yee*.[67] The appeal was against the lower court's stay of court proceedings against the two respondents pending the arbitration of a dispute between the appellant and PT Anglo Slavic Utama ('the company'). It is of note that the suit dealt primarily with issues of fraud involving numerous parties. The appellant initiated a court action against the company and the respondents. Since the appellant and the company were parties to an arbitration agreement, the company applied for, and was granted, a stay of court proceedings pursuant to the Malaysia AA. Later, the two respondents filed an action for a stay of the court proceedings against them pending the disposal of the arbitration between the appellant and the company. This was allowed by the lower court.

On appeal, the Court of Appeal referred to the decision of the Singapore Court of Appeal in *Tomolugen*,[68] which held that the grant of a stay of court proceedings to non-parties to the arbitration under the inherent jurisdiction of the court ought not to be relegated to such a high threshold as the 'rare and compelling circumstances' test articulated in *Reichhold Norway*.[69] The Malaysian Court of Appeal noted that there was an overlap in (1) the parties to the proceedings and the arbitration, (2) the issues and the factual matrix, (3) the principal witnesses, and (4) some of the reliefs sought. It observed that, even if the arbitration were to proceed, the appellant would still have to continue with the court proceedings once arbitration was complete, in order to prosecute both respondents personally. There was also the issue of the respondents seeking to utilise the arbitral proceedings to defer or avoid the personal actions against them relating to fraud.

[63] Farah and Hourani, 'Recasting *West Tankers* in the Deep Water' (2018) 111–112.
[64] ibid 109.
[65] E Kajkowsa, 'Anti-Suit Injunctions in Arbitral Awards: Enforcement in Europe' (2015) 3 *Cambridge Law Journal* 412, 415.
[66] ibid.
[67] [2018] 5 CLJ 299.
[68] [2015] SGCA 57.
[69] [2000] 1 WLR 173.

Furthermore, the arbitrator's findings would not be binding on the non-parties to the arbitration in relation to the court proceedings against them. All these would require adjudication of the matter twice. On the other hand, the resolution of the court proceedings against the respondents would facilitate the arbitration.

For these reasons, the stay against court proceedings obtained by the respondents was set aside, and the arbitration proceedings between the appellant and the company temporarily stayed pending the disposal of the court proceedings. The decision in *Protasco* affirms that the existence of an arbitration clause does not translate to an automatic stay of court proceedings if non-parties are involved, and the avoidance of multiple proceedings is necessary to prevent an abuse of process and ensure the efficient and fair resolution of disputes.

E. *Res Judicata* and Issue Estoppel

All developed states accept that preclusion in some form is a general principle of law.[70] Accordingly, one way of remedying the problem of multiplicity of proceedings in international commercial dispute resolution is the imposition of a requirement that all arguments or claims concerning the same dispute should be raised before the same tribunal, something that has been done in common and civil law countries under different legal rules.[71]

At common law, *res judicata* applies where there is a final judgment rendered on the merits by a court or tribunal of competent jurisdiction in respect of the same parties.[72] In other words, matters which have been definitely decided by a tribunal cannot be reopened (preclusive effect) and must be enforced (conclusive effect).[73] Issue estoppel, on the other hand, prevents the re-litigation of an issue of fact or law that has been previously determined. At common law, it is not only claims, but also issues which were not but ought or should have been litigated in the first instance, which are precluded by *res judicata* in subsequent proceedings.[74]

In the UK three requirements must be satisfied before an issue estoppel may arise. First, the judgment of the foreign court must be (1) of a court of competent jurisdiction in relation to the party who is to be estopped, (2) final and conclusive, and (3) on the merits. Second, the parties to the English litigation must be the same parties as in the foreign litigation (or their privies). Third, the issues raised must be identical.[75] The problem with invoking issue estoppel is a local court's unfamiliarity with the procedural laws of another jurisdiction, besides the difficulty in determining if a particular

[70] P Barnett, *Res Judicata, Estoppel, and Foreign Judgments* (Oxford University Press, 2001) 8. G Born, *International Commercial Arbitration*, 2nd edn (Kluwer, 2014) 3733. In *Waste Management Inc v Mexico (Mexico's Preliminary Objection)* ICSID ARB (AF)/00/3, 26 June 2003, it was stated: 'There is no doubt that *res judicata* is a principal of international law, and even a general principle of law within the meaning of Article 38(1)(c) of the Statute of the International Court of Justice.'

[71] Gaillard (n 13).

[72] Born, *International Commercial Arbitration* (2014) 3735–36.

[73] N Yaffe, 'Transnational Arbitral *Res Judicata*' (2017) 5 *Journal of International Arbitration* 795, available at ssrn.com/abstract=2817537 or dx.doi.org/10.2139/ssrn.2817537.

[74] Born (n 70) 3735.

[75] *Carl Zeiss Siftung v Rayner & Keeler Ltd (No 2)* [1967] 1 AC 853.

issue has been decided or was a basis of a foreign judgment and not merely ancillary to it or obiter.[76] It is perhaps unsurprising therefore that issue estoppel is controversial and not accepted in international law.[77]

The English courts have developed the *Henderson v Henderson*[78] principle, a rule which prohibits parties from raising matters in a subsequent proceeding that they could and should have raised in earlier proceedings but did not. More recently, the rule in *Henderson* was discussed by the UK Supreme Court in *Virgin Atlantic Airways Limited v Zodiac Seats UK Limited*,[79] where it was highlighted that the concurrent jurisdiction enjoyed by the national courts and the European Patent Office in the determination of questions of validity of European and domestic patents had the potential of leading to the undesirable outcome of inconsistent decisions. In *Virgin Atlantic Airways* Lord Sumption acknowledged that there is a 'more general procedural rule against abusive proceedings' which may be regarded as the policy underlying all *res judicata* principles apart possibly from the doctrine of merger.[80]

An analogous doctrine can be seen in the French courts' recognition of the duty on litigants to concentrate grounds (*l'obligation de concentrer les moyens*), where the French Court of Cassation has held that the *res judicata* effect of a decision would extend not only to grounds that a party actually raised in a first set of proceedings, but also to grounds that it could have raised, but did not.[81] The French Court of Cassation has also held that a litigant should raise all of its claims against an opponent in a single proceeding.[82] Taking Spain as another example, Article 400(1) of the Code of Civil Procedure states that:

> Where the claims advanced in the application be based on different facts, different grounds or different legal arguments, they must be advanced in the application when they are known or can be advanced at the time at which the application is lodged. It is not permissible to defer claims to later proceedings.

One drawback of *res judicata* is that it is limited to successive and not simultaneous proceedings.[83] It is only invokable upon the completion of a previous proceeding. On this basis therefore, *res judicata* is of limited assistance in reducing inconsistent decisions. The other difficulty with the application of this doctrine lies in the unpredictability with which various jurisdictions grant *res judicata* effect to other nations' judicial judgments.[84]

[76] Briggs et al (eds), *Dicey, Morris and Collins on the Conflict of Laws*, 15th edn (Thomson Reuters, 2012) 680–81.

[77] P Jooste, 'The Preclusive Effect of National Court Decisions in International Investment Arbitration – *Res Judicata* or Issue Estoppel Applicable or Not?' Victoria University of Wellington Legal Research Papers 15/2017, 8.

[78] (1843) 3 Hare 100.

[79] [2013] UKSC 46.

[80] [2013] UKSC 46 [17]. In Malaysia, *res judicata* is inapplicable in respect of a judgment in default which does not deal with the merits of the case. The doctrine only extinguishes a cause of action once a matter has been adjudicated upon its merits. See the Federal Court decision in *Tindak Murni Sdn Bhd v Juang Setia Sdn Bhd & anor* [2020] 4 CLJ 301.

[81] Gaillard (n 13) 14.

[82] ibid.

[83] Kaufmann-Kohler (n 29).

[84] Dowler (n 53) 368.

i. Res Judicata *and Arbitral Awards*

If a prior arbitral award exists, there is no cause for the second arbitral tribunal to go behind the award in order to determine whether the previous award constitutes *res judicata*.[85] This is because the arbitration agreement concerning the dispute is exhausted and cannot be relied on a second time after one tribunal has been constituted.[86] However, if the impugned prior arbitral award is in the process of being set aside before the supervisory state court, the second tribunal might then be justified in staying proceedings, notwithstanding the absence of arbitration law or institutional rules supporting such an action. This is for the simple reason that if the challenge is unsuccessful, the first arbitral award would be *res judicata*, whereas if the setting aside proceedings are successful this might be indicative of the arbitrability of the dispute.[87]

ii. Res Judicata *and Court Decisions*

It has been opined that an arbitral tribunal is not bound by the decision that a foreign court may render in respect of its jurisdiction, as the arbitral tribunal is only subject to the supervision and control of the state court that has local jurisdiction at the place of arbitration.[88] The arbitrators' mandate is based on the agreement between the parties and the application of that agreement cannot be influenced by what any court, apart possibly from the supervisory court at the place of arbitration, considers to be the correct solution.[89] On this point, it is instructive to refer to Umpire Plumley's opinion in the *Selwyn* case:[90]

> International arbitration is not affected jurisdictionally by the fact that the same question is in the courts of one of the nations. Such international tribunal has power to act without reference thereto, and if judgment has been pronounced by such court, to disregard the same so far as it affects the indemnity to the individual, and has power to make an award in addition thereto or in aid thereof as in the given case justice may require. Within the limits prescribed by the convention constituting it the parties have created a tribunal superior to the local courts.

It therefore follows that conflicting decisions are bound to ensue as there is no ultimate body capable of adjudicating and reconciling two separate regimes.[91] The extension of the preclusive effect of the decisions of domestic courts into the international arbitration regime necessitates acceptance that municipal courts and international tribunals inhabit the same legal order. This requires harmonisation of two divergent propositions, viz: (1) the lawfulness of an act under local law has no bearing on its wrongfulness under international law; and (2) international disputes may be solved by domestic courts applying local laws.

[85] C Soderlund, '*Lis Pendens, Res Judicata* and the Issue of Parallel Judicial Proceedings' (2005) 22 *Journal of International Arbitration* 301, 310.

[86] P Mayer, 'Conflicting Decisions in International Commercial Arbitration' (2013) 4 *Journal of International Dispute Settlement* 407, 417.

[87] Soderlund, '*Lis Pendens*' (2005) 310–11.

[88] ibid 309.

[89] ibid 314.

[90] (1903) 9 RIAA 380, 381.

[91] Soderlund (n 85) 322, Mayer, 'Conflicting Decisions' (2013) 409.

For instance, one cannot deny the inconsistency in the assertion that the laws of the host state govern an investment treaty and the principle that a state cannot refuse to perform its international obligations by reliance on local laws.[92] While the conflict is impossible to resolve, there have been proposals to alleviate this phenomenon. One is the adoption of a broad definition of the same claims centred around the defendant's conduct.[93] Second, it is important to recognise that alternative schemes with different institutional aims are equally capable of delivering justice.[94] This means that, at the international level, private individuals and states should be treated equally, for it is through such equal treatment that unity in the legal order can be promoted.[95] Thirdly, the limitation found in many of the aforementioned approaches lies in their unilateral nature. In order to achieve true coordination, it has been suggested that one way forward would be the adoption of a multilateral remedy in the form of a treaty that would instil some semblance of order into the current legal framework for the resolution of international commercial disputes.[96] The lack of harmonisation is not just about law and economics, but it is also about politics as the development of a set of common standards boils down to the domestic policies and interests of a particular country.[97]

iii. Res Judicata *and International Commercial Courts*

It goes without saying that certainty and finality are of paramount importance to the international business community because they enable more efficient choices to be made. For business persons, recovery from a commercial deal gone wrong is essential in assessing the viability and choice of jurisdiction for an investment. The risk of multiple proceedings and the consequent uncertainty over the outcome of a dispute drives up the cost of doing business. There is thus a need for international commercial courts to adopt and apply best practices from civil and common law jurisdictions in a more simplified fashion when it comes to dealing with parallel proceedings. It is only by instilling confidence in their respective regimes and maintaining accessibility to their system of dispute resolution that international commercial courts can become (and continue to be) viable concerns.

IV. Recognising and Enforcing Judgments and Awards

A court must recognise every foreign judgment which it enforces (although it need not enforce every foreign judgment which it recognises).[98] For example, at the European level, the provisions of the Brussels I Regulation on recognition and enforcement are

[92] J Crawford, 'Treaty and Contract in Investment Arbitration' (2008) 24 *Arbitration International* 351.

[93] M Swarabowicz, 'Identity of Claims in Investment Arbitration: A Plea for Unity of the Legal System' (2017) 8 *Journal of International Dispute Settlement* 280, 302.

[94] ibid.

[95] ibid.

[96] Kaufmann-Kohler (n 29).

[97] Menon, 'The Transnational Protection of Private Rights' (2014) 222.

[98] D McClean and V Ruiz Abou-Nigm, *Morris on The Conflict of Laws*, 8th edn (Thomson Reuters, 2012) 159.

designed to enable the free flow of judgments between EU Member States. Generally, therefore, obstacles to the recognition and enforcement are to be minimised. The court of a Member State in which enforcement is sought may not examine the jurisdiction of the court of another Member State which issued the judgment.[99] In other words, it is the original court that decides whether it has jurisdiction, and that determination usually cannot be questioned in another member state during the recognition and enforcement stage.[100]

A. Jurisdictional Considerations

Indirect jurisdiction is often called 'international jurisdiction' or 'international competence'.[101] It has been defined as 'judicial authority as determined under the law of the state in which application is made for the enforcement of a judgment rather than for initial adjudication of a claim'.[102] According to Nussbaum, the jurisdiction of a foreign tribunal is derived from its local legislation. Thus, a requested court cannot confer, vary or whittle down the jurisdiction of a foreign court. What the enforcing or requested court actually does is to assess, on its own terms, the requirements for granting territorial expansion to the *res judicata* effect of the foreign judgment.[103] This distinction has been the subject of exposition by Bartin, who suggested that the judicial power which a state confers on its own courts be called *compétence générale directe*, while the requirement for the recognition of foreign judgments should be referred to as *compétence générale indirecte*.[104] Direct jurisdiction would thus describe the question for the rendering court, since only the originating or rendering court is directly engaged with the question whether it should exercise jurisdiction or not.[105] Indirect jurisdiction describes the question for the enforcing court, since that court can control only indirectly, through the recognition procedure, whether jurisdiction was properly exercised or not.[106]

However, this distinction does not address the following matters:[107]

(1) Is the question whether the rendering court had jurisdiction the same question when asked by the rendering and when asked by the requested court?
(2) Is the question the requested court asks for recognition purposes the same question it would ask if it were the adjudicating court?

[99] ibid 160.
[100] ibid.
[101] A Nussbaum, 'Jurisdiction and Foreign Judgments' (1941) 41 *Columbia Law Review* 221, 225.
[102] RB Ginsburg, 'The Competent Court in Private International Law: Some Observations on Current Views in the United States', (1965) 20 *Rutgers Law Review* 89, 93.
[103] Nussbaum, 'Jurisdiction and Foreign Judgments' (1941) 225.
[104] ibid.
[105] R Michaels, 'Some Fundamental Conceptions as Applied in Judgment Conventions' 8 in E Gottschalk et al (eds), *Conflict of Laws in a Globalized World: A Tribute to Arthur von Mehren* (CUP, 2007) 8, available at scholarship.law.duke.edu/faculty_scholarship/1574.
[106] ibid.
[107] ibid.

Many authors assume the standard for direct and indirect jurisdiction to be the same. So do many legal orders.[108] Lord Justice Hodson put the matter like this: 'It must surely be that what entitles an English court to assume jurisdiction must be equally effective in the case of a foreign court'.[109] In reality, the simplicity of Lord Justice Hodson's statement belies the difficulty in determining if ultimately a judgment rendered by Court A would be recognised and enforced by Court B. Consider, for instance, the *Yahoo!* litigation.[110] Here, a French court asserted jurisdiction over Yahoo! on the mere basis that its web site was accessible from French computers. Commentators have been divided over the question whether the French court rightfully asserted jurisdiction, and whether US courts would have to recognise and enforce the ensuing decision.[111]

The consequence of a finding that indirect jurisdiction is lacking is that a foreign judgment is not recognised and cannot be enforced in a requested state.[112] A corollary of indirect jurisdiction is that 'the findings of the foreign court in respect to jurisdiction are not binding upon the forum [that is, the enforcing court]'.[113] Thus, an enforcing court applying its own conceptions of the jurisdiction of the foreign court may lead to a denial of recognition even though in the same circumstances the foreign court would have had jurisdiction.[114]

When the bases of direct and indirect jurisdiction vary there is what is known as a jurisdiction gap. The US, Japan and Germany are examples of states which have no jurisdiction gap between their rules of direct and indirect jurisdiction.[115] In many other legal systems, the direct jurisdictional bases are wider than the indirect jurisdictional bases.[116] A direct/indirect jurisdiction gap which discriminates against judgments from foreign courts discriminates against foreign litigants seeking to enforce judgments against defendants with assets located in the requested state.[117] According to Ronald Brand, the discriminatory jurisdiction gap problem is 'not a minor problem' of the existing regime for recognition of judgments which can be tackled by a global convention.[118] However, a mirror approach where the bases of direct and indirect jurisdiction are identical may not be reflective of an ideal international standard either. Considering the different stakes involved, national jurisdictional rules may give rise to incongruity when applied to international disputes.[119] It is thus not surprising that in

[108] ibid 9.

[109] *Travers v. Holley* [1953] P 246, 256 (CA).

[110] *UEJF et Licra c. Yahoo! Inc. et Yahoo! France* 22 mai 2000 (*Tribunal de Grande Instance Paris*), 2000 Communication et Commerce Electronique (Comm Com Électr Comm n° 92, Note J-Chr Galloux).

[111] Michaels, 'Some Fundamental Conceptions' (2007) 10.

[112] Nussbaum (n 101) 226.

[113] B Kulzer, 'Some Aspects of Enforceability of Foreign Judgments: A Comparative Summary' (1966) 16 *Buffalo Law Review* 84, 94.

[114] ibid.

[115] RA Brand, *The Circulation of Judgments Under the Draft Hague Judgments Convention* (24 February 2019) University of Pittsburgh Legal Studies Research Paper No 2019-02, 23, available at ssrn.com/abstract=3334647 or dx.doi.org/10.2139/ssrn.3334647.

[116] RA Brand, 'Understanding Judgments Recognition' (2015) 40 *North Carolina Journal of International Law and Commercial Regulation* 877, 891.

[117] ibid 904.

[118] Brand, *Circulation of Judgments* (2019) 22.

[119] N Meier, 'Undue Due Process: Why the Application of Jurisdictional Due Process Requirements to the Recognition of Foreign-Country Judgments Is Inappropriate' (2016) 18 *Oregon Review of International Law* 51, 57.

World-Wide Volkswagen Corp v Woodson[120] Justice Brennan warned that the national US direct jurisdictional 'minimum contacts test' may not be appropriate for an international setting:[121]

> [T]hat principle, with its almost exclusive focus on the rights of the defendant, may be outdated … Given the tremendous mobility of goods and people … I do not think that the defendant should be in complete control of the geographical stretch of his amenability to suit … People should understand that they are held responsible for the consequences of their actions and that in our society most actions have consequences affecting many States.

Returning to the European position, in several EU national recognition systems, indirect jurisdiction is benchmarked against direct jurisdiction, so that different national jurisdictional rules may also result in broader or narrower recognition bases.[122] The dissimilarities also affect the rules on *lis pendens* and related actions of Articles 33 and 34 of the BRR, which depend on a 'recognition prognosis'.[123] For these reasons, it has been suggested that a movement towards full unification of jurisdictional rules between various states would be ideal as it would enable BRR Member States to assert jurisdiction according to common rules without being constrained by the requirements of municipal law.[124] Contrast the position outside of the EU, in which the lack of harmonised international rules means that it is likely that sovereign states will adopt or continue to retain a system with some form of control over foreign judgments given on unreasonable or exorbitant jurisdictional grounds.

Nevertheless, while it is certainly possible to use the same standard in respect of jurisdictional rules, it is by no means necessary to do so.[125] This is because direct and indirect jurisdiction must be seen as different and unconnected kinds of legal positions which can be regulated differently.[126] A state may find it important to secure access to its courts and therefore provide certain bases of direct jurisdiction, but accept that other states do not automatically recognise such decisions, and might even reject foreign judgments rendered on such bases.[127] Apart from that, a state may accept certain bases of indirect jurisdiction, even if it does not utilise the same bases of direct jurisdiction.[128]

B. Grounds for Refusing to Recognise or Enforce Judgments and Awards

i. Due Process

Throughout the world, states apply different processes and procedures in their respective justice systems and produce varying judgments. One commonality that is shared

[120] 444 US 286 (1980).
[121] ibid 308–11.
[122] A Bonomi, 'European Private International Law and Third States' (2017) 37 *Praxis des Internationalen Privat- und Verfahrensrechts* 184, 186.
[123] ibid.
[124] ibid 186, 191.
[125] Michaels (n 106) 10.
[126] ibid.
[127] ibid 10–11.
[128] ibid 11.

by these differing systems is the requirement by most enforcing states that a judgment must satisfy minimum standards of fairness or due process when its recognition and enforcement is sought.[129] At the international level, the idea of 'due process' can be equated with 'a concept of fair procedure simple and basic enough to describe the judicial processes of civilized nations'.[130] For example, while there is no separate head of 'due process' by which a foreign judgment is assessed, the Malaysian Reciprocal Enforcement of Judgments Act 1958 (Act 99)[131] makes it mandatory for a registered foreign judgment to be set aside inter alia where the issuing court lacked jurisdiction,[132] where the judgment debtor (defendant) did not receive notice of the proceedings in sufficient time to enable it to defend the proceedings and did not appear,[133] or if the judgment was obtained by fraud.[134]

In the US, 'It has long been the law … that a foreign judgment cannot be enforced if it was obtained in a manner that did not accord with the basics of due process'.[135] US case law has identified due process (non-exhaustively) as consisting of an 'opportunity for [a] full and fair trial abroad before a court of competent jurisdiction', 'regular proceedings' and not ad hoc procedures, 'due notice or voluntary appearance of the defendant', 'a system of … impartial administration of justice between the citizens of its own country and those of other countries', and assurances against 'fraud in procuring the judgment'.[136] The law in the EU in relation to recognition and enforcement of judgments is demonstrative of a deepening faith in multilateral private international law.[137] In contrast, it has been observed that in the US there is increasing scepticism and a tendency to subject foreign judgments to more probing review.[138] This is attributable to the increasing adoption by US states of legislation based on the 2005 Uniform Foreign Country Money Judgments Recognition Act (the 2005 Act), which contains two new grounds for refusing enforcement:[139]

(1) if 'the judgment was rendered in circumstances that raise substantial doubt about the integrity of the rendering court with respect to the judgment'; and
(2) if 'the specific proceeding in the foreign court leading to the judgment was not compatible with the requirements of due process of law'.

This is in addition to the mandatory ground of refusal under section 4(b)(1) of the 2005 Act which stipulates: 'A foreign judgment is not conclusive if (1) the judgment

[129] CT Kotuby Jr, 'General Principles of Law, International Due Process, and the Modern Role of Private International Law' (2013) 23 *Duke Journal of Comparative and International Law* 411, 424.
[130] *Society of Lloyd's v Ashenden* 233 F 3d 473, 477 (7th Cir 2000).
[131] Act 99 (REJA).
[132] REJA, s 5(1)(a)(ii).
[133] REJA, s 5(1)(a)(iii).
[134] REJA, s 5(1)(a)(iv).
[135] *Bank Melli Iran v. Pahlavi* 58 F 3d 1406, 1410, 1412 (9th Cir 1995).
[136] Kotuby, 'General Principles of Law' (2013) 426–27, citing *Hilton v Guyot* 159 US 113, 202 (1895).
[137] C Whytock, 'Faith and Scepticism in Private International Law: Trust, Governance, Politics, and Foreign Judgments' (2014) 3 *Erasmus Law Review* 113, 113, citing the elimination of the declaration of enforceability (*exequatur*) as a requirement for the enforcement of EU member state judgments in civil and commercial matters by the BRR.
[138] ibid 113.
[139] Section 4(c) of the 2005 Act. See also Whytock, 'Faith and Scepticism in Private International Law' (2014) 116.

was rendered under a system which does not provide impartial tribunals or procedures compatible with the requirements of due process of law'. Section 4(b)(1) of the 2005 Act thus requires the requested court to decline recognition of the foreign judgment if the requested court finds that the entire judicial system of the foreign state where judgment was issued does not provide procedures compatible with the requirements of fundamental fairness.[140] In short, it focuses on 'the foreign country's judicial system as a whole'.[141] Compared to the EU's BRR regime, the US system provides broader grounds for non-enforcement under due process.[142]

However, it has been pointed out that the due process ground may render other non-enforcement grounds superfluous.[143] For instance, issues of fraud or case-specific due process can be dealt with adequately through the rehearing or appellate procedures available in a legal system that provides impartial tribunals and procedures compatible with the requirement of due process.[144] Given the foregoing, one may question the need for a separate head of refusal based on due process when judgments failing to meet basic due process standards might arguably be impugned as being against the 'public policy' of a state.[145] As will be seen under the next subheading, a breach of natural justice – one of the components of due process – has been expressly identified in Malaysian legislation as a contravention of public policy.[146]

It must not be overlooked that the 2005 Act's due process exception – while aimed at protecting the rights of judgment debtors – may increase uncertainty about whether particular judgments will be enforced and can lead to costly litigation at the enforcement stage.[147] Predictability and efficiency is diminished if a surge in litigation at the enforcement stage ensues.[148] It must also be borne in mind that condemnation of a foreign jurisdiction's judicial process could be injurious to foreign relations with that country. This, however, does not mean that courts should unquestioningly accept foreign judgments from jurisdictions which fail to comport to minimum standards of due process when said foreign judgments do not adhere to a basic level of procedural propriety. Instead of condemning a judicial system wholesale, it is suggested that the better approach would be to evaluate due process challenges on a case-by-case basis by focusing on the individual proceedings in question.[149]

An emerging phenomenon in the arbitral landscape is the rise of 'due process paranoia', where arbitrators exercise an overabundance of caution in conforming with due process requirements to avoid having their awards set aside or refused recognition on

[140] Section 4(c) of the 2005 Act. See also Whytock (n 137) 116.
[141] Section 4, Comment 11 of the 2005 Act.
[142] Section 4(c) of the 2005 Act. See also Whytock (n 137) 118.
[143] Whytock (n 137) 118.
[144] ibid.
[145] J Linarelli, 'Toward a Political Theory for Private International Law' (2016) 26 *Duke Journal of Comparative and International Law* 299, 331.
[146] Section 37(2)(b) of the Malaysian Arbitration Act 2005.
[147] Section 4(c) of the 2005 Act. See also Whytock (n 137) 121.
[148] Section 4(c) of the 2005 Act. See also Whytock (n 137) 122.
[149] MD Carodine, 'Political Judging: When Due Process Goes International' (2007) 48 *William and Mary Law Review* 1159, 1223.

the ground of a lack of due process. This overly cautious stance results in delays to the arbitral proceedings and an increase in associated costs.[150] Ultimately, it is the integrity and legitimacy of the arbitral regime that suffers. 'Due process paranoia', first coined in 2015, embodies an issue which remains relevant today as reflected in Queen Mary University of London's 2021 International Arbitration Survey, which noted that 'several respondents felt that arbitrators are still overly cautious when it comes to "due process paranoia"'.[151] It therefore becomes pertinent to inquire whether the 'paranoia' diagnosis is justified. In this connection, the available research suggests that the setting aside of an award on due process grounds is the exception rather than the norm.[152] Indeed, studies have demonstrated that courts are supportive of the arbitral process and a challenge on purely procedural grounds seldom succeeds in court.

This is the approach in Malaysia as illustrated in *Allianz General Insurance Company Malaysia Berhad v Virginia Surety Company Labuan Branch*.[153] Here, the High Court rejected the notion that natural justice meant that a party was entitled to receive responses to all submissions and arguments presented and held that an arbitral tribunal is not obliged slavishly to adopt the entire position of a party, but is instead allowed to pick and choose the arguments that it deems necessary for its consideration. Regionally, Singapore[154] and Hong Kong[155] authorities have adopted a similar, arbitration-friendly stance.

ii. *Public Policy*

The courts of any system of private international law retain a discretion to refuse to recognise and enforce rights acquired under foreign law on public policy grounds.[156] The reservation of public policy in matters of conflict of laws is a necessary one, but its precise limits are elusive[157] and there is no fixed category to which the rule applies. In the UK, it is well settled that public policy only comes into play in clear cases where the injury to society is significant and does not depend upon the 'idiosyncratic inferences of

[150] K Takahashi, *Exclusion of Arbitral Procedure from the Scope of Public Policy Scrutiny as a Measure to Curb Due Process Paranoia: A Proposal under the UNCITRAL Model Law* (7 December 2020) 579, (2021) 29 *Michigan State International Law Review* (posted with permission), available at ssrn.com/abstract=3853449.

[151] Queen Mary University of London, '2021 International Arbitration Survey: Adapting Arbitration to a Changing World' 12, available at www.arbitration.qmul.ac.uk/media/arbitration/docs/LON0320037-QMUL-International-Arbitration-Survey-2021_19_WEB.pdf.

[152] V Herman, 'Challenges on Grounds of Due Process Pursuant to Article (V)(1)(B) of the New York Convention' in E Gaillard and D di Pietro (eds), *Enforcement of Arbitration Agreements and International Arbitral Awards: The New York Convention in Practice* (Cameron May, 2008) 679, 692. KP Berger and JO Jensen, 'Due Process Paranoia and the Procedural Judgment Rule: a Safe Harbour for Procedural Management Decisions by International Arbitrators', (2016) 32 *Arbitration International* 415, 423, citing *Brandeis (Brokers) Ltd v Black* [2001] 2 All ER (Comm) 980 [56]; International Bar Association, 'Annulment of Arbitral Awards by State Court: Review of National Case Law with Respect to The Conduct of the Arbitral Process', October 2018 2, available at www.ibanet.org/MediaHandler?id=b4b532bb-90e1-40ab-ab3d- f730c19984fb.

[153] [2020] 5 CLJ 345.

[154] *China Machine New Energy Corp v Jaguar Energy Guatemala LLC & anor* [2020] SGCA 12.

[155] *Pacific China Holdings Ltd (in liquidation) v Grand Pacific Holdings Ltd* [2012] 4 HKLRD 1.

[156] McClean and Ruiz Abou-Nigm, *Morris* (2012) 47.

[157] ibid 49.

a few judicial minds'.[158] Thus the English courts' residual power to disregard a provision in the foreign law is exercisable only in exceptional cases with the greatest circumspection where there is an affront to basic principles of justice and fairness.[159]

In Europe, under the BRR, recognition of a judgment or an award may be refused 'if such recognition is manifestly contrary to public policy (*ordre public*) in the Member State addressed'.[160] Case law has established that this ground may only be invoked in 'exceptional circumstances'.[161] It has been acknowledged that the BRR must be construed so as to limit the use of municipal conceptions of public policy. Article 45 of the BRR may only be used to refuse recognition where recognition or enforcement would differ to a degree unacceptable to the legal order of the state in which enforcement is sought.

A clear breach of a Rule of Law essential to the legal order of that state or of a right recognised as being fundamental within that legal order is essential.[162] The courts in Malaysia recognise too that the doctrine of public policy must be a 'narrow and restrictive' one. In *Mann Holdings v Pte Ltd v Ung Yoke Hong*[163] the Court of Appeal held that the non-recognition of a Singaporean judgment would be in violation of the principle of international comity and substantial reciprocity as statutorily provided under the Reciprocal Enforcement of Judgments Act 1958, making the refusal to recognise the foreign judgment an exercise contrary to public policy. In other words, when a judgment is plainly not contrary to the public policy of Malaysia, it is the non-recognition of the judgment that offends public policy. In the Malaysian arbitral context, certain (non-exhaustive) instances have been statutorily recognised as conflicting with public policy: (1) when the arbitral award has been tainted with fraud or corruption;[164] or (2) when there has been a breach of natural justice.[165]

Beyond these legislative examples, it is clear that public policy is a broad concept with a narrow sphere of application. There is high judicial authority affirming that, while the public policy rule extends to both procedural and substantive aspects and may be invoked if there 'a violation of the most basic notions of morality and justice', the courts are to bear in mind other policies like arbitral finality and minimal interference.[166]

iii. Res Judicata

In some jurisdictions, *res judicata* is a matter of public policy, which means that the court can annul or refuse to recognise an arbitral award because a tribunal misapplies preclusion law.[167] When *res judicata* is sought to be relied upon, it involves recognising that a previous judgment is finally and conclusively adjudicative of the issues

[158] *Fender v St John Mildmay* [1938] AC 1, 12 per Lord Atkin,
[159] *Kuwait Airways Corp v Iraqi Airways Co (Nos 4 and 5)* [2002] UKHL 19.
[160] BRR, Art 45(1)(a).
[161] Case C-78/95 *Hendrickman v Magenta Dock & Verlag GmbH* [1996] ECR I-4943.
[162] Case C-7/98 *Krombach v Bamberski* [2000] ECR I-1935.
[163] [2019] 6 CLJ 475 [74].
[164] Section 37(2)(a), Malaysian Arbitration Act 2005.
[165] ibid, Section 37(2)(b).
[166] *Jan De Nul (Malaysia) Sdn Bhd & anor v Vincent Tan Chee Yioun & anor* [2019] 1 CLJ 1 (FC) [55], [57] and [58].
[167] Yaffe, 'Transnational Arbitral *Res Judicata*' (2017).

which arose between the parties. At the EU level, Article 45(1)(a) of the BRR enables a Member State court to refuse recognition and enforcement on public policy grounds. While public policy is still an amorphous concept at the EU level, it has been observed that national provisions on *res judicata* may in some Member States be regarded as important enough to constitute public policy.[168] Hence, it is arguable that if there is an existing arbitral award that produces binding effects on the requested state, the court of the latter may refuse to recognise an incompatible court judgment on public policy grounds.[169] Similarly, if there is an earlier judgment delivered by another EU Member State or a third state court which involves the same cause of action and same parties, recognition of the later Member State court judgment may be denied provided that the earlier judgment fulfils the conditions necessary for recognition.[170]

In Malaysia, *res judicata* has been long been accepted as forming the public policy of our jurisdiction, for it is in the public interest that there should be finality in litigation – *interest rei publicae ut sit finis litium*.[171] Indeed, it is essential to public policy that there be finality in litigation, otherwise given a burgeoning population and an increasing sophistication in the tactical use law, the resources of the courts will be strained by the resulting increase in litigation.[172] Nevertheless, due to the infinite permutations of fact and law that may arise from a matter and the breadth and scope of the public policy doctrine, it would be prudent for the judicial organs of a state to maintain a flexible approach to *res judicata*, attuned always to the exigencies of a case and the need to do justice.

iv. Mistake of Law

In England, a foreign judgment cannot be impugned on the merits.[173] Thus, in *Godard v Gray*,[174] the foreign court's mistake while purporting to apply English law was held to be no defence against recognition and enforcement by the English court. In Malaysia, the defence of mistake is absent from the provisions of the Reciprocal Enforcement of Judgments Act 1958. In Singapore, the courts do not re-examine the merits of the foreign judgment.[175] It follows therefore that it is no defence to say that a foreign judgment is tainted by an error of law.[176] If part of a foreign judgment is objectionable, while the rest is unobjectionable, the part which is objectionable may be severed and the unobjectionable part enforced, provided the parts can be clearly identified and separated.[177]

[168] Ortolani (n 22) 185.

[169] ibid.

[170] ibid.

[171] *Asia Commercial Finance (M) Bhd v Kawal Teliti Sdn Bhd* [1995] 3 CLJ 783 (SC) 791.

[172] ibid 793.

[173] McClean and Ruiz Abou-Nigm (n 98) 182.

[174] (1870) LR 6 QB 139.

[175] A Chong, *Recognition and Enforcement of Foreign Judgments in Asia* (2017) 1-240, 174, Research Collection SMU School of Law, available at ink.library.smu.edu.sg/sol_research/2496.

[176] *Ralli v Anguilla* (1917) 15 SSLR 33.

[177] *Alberto Justo Rodriguez Licea v Curacao Drydock Inc* [2015] 4 SLR 172 [28]; *Yong Tet Miaw v MBF Finance Bhd* [1992] 2 SLR(R) 549 [29]; Reciprocal Enforcement of Foreign Judgments Act (Cap 265, 2001 Rev Ed) section 4(7).

The outlier on this front is the Philippines where the courts are empowered to review the merits of a foreign judgment when a defendant challenges the recognition of a foreign judgment on the ground of 'clear' mistake of law or fact.[178] The reasoning is that any review of the merits would be tantamount to determining whether a foreign judgment should be denied recognition for contravening public policy or public order.[179] However, it remains uncertain whether this line of argument is likely to find favour with the Philippine judiciary.[180]

C. Enforcing Awards Set Aside by a Supervising Court

i. Competing Theories

The unenforceability of an arbitral award diminishes the value of international commercial arbitration. Thus, countries have sought to regulate the recognition and enforcement of arbitral awards, primarily through the New York Convention. A tricky proposition arises vis-à-vis arbitral awards that have been annulled by the court of the seat. Should the requested court proceed with the enforcement of such awards?

Broadly speaking, there are three schools of thought.[181] The first argues that recognition or enforcement of the award should always be refused. This opinion is based on the argument that an award that has been set aside ceases to exist and therefore nothing is left to recognise or enforce (*ex nihilo nihil fit*). This is known as the seat or territorial theory. The second contends that the setting aside does not prevent its recognition or enforcement. This opinion is based on the view that international arbitration is not linked to any national legal order, including that of the seat, but forms part of a specific national or transnational legal order. This is known as the transnational legal autonomy or delocalisation theory. The third is an intermediate position. It distinguishes among the grounds of a setting aside. Thus, setting aside based on domestic as opposed to international standards should not lead to a refusal of recognition and enforcement elsewhere. This is known as the Westphalian or multi-local theory.

It is instructive at this juncture to refer to Article V(1)(e) of the NY Convention, which states:

> Recognition and enforcement of the award may be refused, at the request of the party against whom it is invoked, only if that party furnishes to the competent authority where the recognition and enforcement is sought, proof that:
>
> …
>
> (e) The award has not yet become binding on the parties, or has been set aside or suspended by a competent authority of the country in which, or under the law of which, that award was made.

[178] A Reyes (ed), *Recognition and Enforcement of Judgments in Civil and Commercial Matters* (Hart Publishing, 2019) 319.

[179] ibid.

[180] ibid.

[181] M Scherer, 'Effects of International Judgments Relating to Awards' (2016) 43 *Pepperdine Law Review* 637, 639 fn 11.

The lack of express guidance from Article V(1)(e) of the New York Convention has generated divergent views in respect of its application as to whether to enforce an annulled award. The use of the word 'may' has stirred up considerable debate as to the extent of the domestic court's discretionary power to enforce or refuse to enforce an annulled award. In France, there is authority enforcing annulled arbitral awards which indicate that the international arbitral award is not rooted to a particular legal system, including the seat of arbitration.[182] On the other hand, there is US precedent distinguishing between national and international annulment standards when enforcing foreign arbitral awards which have been annulled.[183] Both approaches reason that local norms are applicable utilising the discretion derived from the term 'may'.[184]

Although such a reading is supported by a literal reading of Article V(1)(e) to the effect that the court does indeed have residual discretion whether to enforce the annulled award, the difficulty is exacerbated when it leads to a different understanding of the international norms which regulate the recognition and enforcement of foreign arbitral awards.[185] Some commentators exhort a narrow reading of the New York Convention's Article V grounds for refusal of enforcement. They highlight the phrase 'only if', which appears in the introductory sentence of Article V.[186] This was the view espoused in *Diag Human SE v Czech Republic*,[187] where the court said: '[U]nder the Convention, the grounds for refusing enforcement are restricted and construed narrowly: enforcement may be refused only if one of the listed grounds, which are exclusive, is satisfied'.[188]

Any discussion regarding the application of Article V(1)(e) would not be complete without reference to Article VII(1) of the NY Convention, which states:

> The provisions of the present Convention shall not affect the validity of multilateral or bilateral agreements concerning the recognition and enforcement of arbitral awards entered into by the Contracting States nor deprive any interested party of any right he may have to avail himself of an arbitral award in the manner and to the extent allowed by the law or the treaties of the country where such award is sought to be relied upon.

Article VII(1) is sometimes referred to as the 'more favourable right provision'. Since some state parties to the New York Convention do not list some grounds for refusal that come under Article V in their national arbitration laws, the national courts of these states have interpreted Article VII(1) in a way that allows the courts to enforce an arbitral award notwithstanding the presence of one of the grounds

[182] R Seyadi, 'Enforcement of Arbitral Awards Annulled by the Court of the Seat' (2018) 84 *International Journal of Arbitration, Mediation and Dispute Management* 128, 131; *Hilmarton Ltd v Omnium de Valorisation* [1994] Case No 92-15.137 French Court of Cassation, published in (1995) XX *Yearbook Commercial Arbitration* 663; *Société Egyptian General Petroleum Corporation v Société National Gas Company* [2011] 10/16525 Paris Court of Appeal.

[183] Seyadi, 'Enforcement of Arbitral Awards' (2018) 132. *Corporación Mexicana de Mantenimiento Integral v PEMEX* [2013] 962 F Supp 2d 642 (Southern District, New York).

[184] Seyadi (n 182) 132.

[185] ibid.

[186] ibid. AJ van den Berg, 'New York Convention of 1958: Refusals of Enforcement' (2007) 18 *ICC International Court of Arbitration Bulletin* 2; AJ van den Berg, 'Enforcement of Arbitral Awards Annulled in Russia: Case Comment on Court of Appeal of Amsterdam' (2010) 27 *Journal of International Arbitration* 179.

[187] [2014] EWHC 1639 (Comm).

[188] ibid [12].

listed in Article V.[189] This is illustrated by *Chromalloy Aeroservices v Arab Republic of Egypt*,[190] where a foreign arbitral award that was previously annulled by the Egyptian Court of Appeal was enforced by the Paris Court of Appeal and the US courts in reliance on Article VII(1). It is clear from the foregoing that Article VII(1) allows for domestic law to take precedence over international law.

ii. *Which Theory is Preferable?*

There is support for the view that an annulled award should only be refused enforcement if it was annulled based on 'international standards'. Proponents of this approach assert that if the annulment was based on 'local standards', then the annulled award is still enforceable in other countries.[191] This approach is not entirely free from difficulty for several reasons. First, it still begs the question of what criteria should be used to identify 'international standards' as opposed to 'local standards'.[192] Second, it flies in the face of the wording of the New York Convention, which does not require enforcing courts to examine if awards were annulled under 'international' or 'national' standards.[193] Third, this approach does not guarantee any measure of certainty as the cases below will demonstrate.

In the US, an award that was set aside in Egypt after review was enforced by a US court on the basis that US public policy favoured the final and binding arbitration of commercial disputes.[194] In another decision, an arbitral award that was set aside in Mexico on the ground that an entity deemed part of the Mexican Government could not be forced to arbitrate was enforced by the US court as it felt that deference to the Mexican court's annulment would run against US public policy.[195] In *Yukos Capital SARL v OJSC Rosneft Oil Company*[196] awards that were set aside in Russia were given effect by the English High Court. On the other hand, the court in *Maximov v OJSC Novolipersky Metallurgicheksy Kombinat*[197] refused to give effect to an arbitral award set aside in Russia. The argument of bias on the part of the Russian court failed to find favour with the requested court and the award annulled by the Russian court was denied enforcement.

This can be contrasted with the situation in France, where arbitral awards are generally given deference so long as they do not contravene French law. The French system, which embodies the delocalisation theory,[198] holds that arbitral awards are not

[189] Seyadi (n 182) 134.
[190] *Chromalloy Aeroservices v Arab Republic of Egypt* [1997] 95/23025 Paris Court of Appeal; *Chromalloy Aeroservices v Arab Republic of Egypt* [1996] Case No 94-2339 US District Court, District of Columbia.
[191] J Paulsson, 'Enforcing Arbitral Awards Notwithstanding a Local Standard Annulment' (1998) 6 *Asia Pacific Law Review* 1, 25.
[192] Seyadi (n 182) 136.
[193] ibid 137.
[194] *Chromalloy Aeroservices v Arab Republic of Egypt* 939 F Supp 907, 912–13 (DDC 1996).
[195] Corporación Mexicana de Matenimiento Integral, *S De RL De CV v Pemex-Exploración y Producción* No 13-4022 (2d Cir August 2, 2016).
[196] [2014] EWHC 2188 (Comm).
[197] [2017] EWHC 1911 (Comm),
[198] Seyadi (n 182) 137.

integrated in a particular legal system, but are self-sufficient. There is also no equivalent of Article V(1)(e) in French law. Thus, in *Hilmarton Ltd v Omnium de Valorisation*,[199] the Cour de Cassation permitted enforcement of an arbitral award which had been set aside in Switzerland. The approach of the French courts was subject to a cursory appraisal by the Singapore Court of Appeal in *PT First Media TBK v Astro Nusantara International BV*.[200] Here, Menon CJ suggested by way of obiter that 'the contemplated *erga omnes* effect of a successful application to set aside an award would generally lead to the conclusion that there is simply no award to enforce'.[201]

The delocalisation theory does not offer a satisfying answer as to how justice may be upheld if the award is not tied to a particular legal system. If there is no link between the arbitration proceedings and the *lex arbitri*, the arbitration regime is unfettered by any legal system until the enforcement stage. In a nutshell, the current state of affairs in this area is far from settled. What is apparent is that municipal courts are at liberty to depart from the provisions of Article V and elect to follow national legislation in the process of enforcing arbitral awards that have been set aside by the supervising court.

D. Requirement of Reciprocity

In the context of the recognition and enforcement of foreign judgments, reciprocity has two distinct senses. The first is the by now largely discarded view by the US Supreme Court in *Hilton v Guyot*[202] that a judgment rendered by the court of a foreign country would not be enforced unless that country would enforce a comparable judgment of the requested court.[203] This is the view which forms part of the law of many civil law jurisdictions, but has never been the law of England.[204] The second sense in which reciprocity is used is to describe the view that a court should recognise the jurisdiction of a foreign court if the situation is such that, *mutatis mutandis*, the former court might have exercised jurisdiction. Proponents of a reciprocity requirement assert that it is necessary to create incentives for foreign states to enforce judgments.[205] It is also logical to assume that a reciprocity requirement prevents foreign country neglect of a country's judgments.[206] Conversely, opponents of reciprocity condemn the policy as being both costly to administer and highly unlikely to bring about any change in foreign state practice.[207] Some argue that the judicial costs of administering reciprocal legislation are simply too great.[208] Others contend that it is unfair to hold foreign litigants responsible for actions

[199] (1995) *XX Yearbook Comm Arb* 663–65.

[200] *PT First Media TBK (formerly known as PT Broadband Multimedia TBK) v Astro Nusantara International BV* [2013] SGCA 57, [2014] 1 SLR 372 [77].

[201] Seyadi (n 182) 138.

[202] 159 US 113 (1895).

[203] Briggs et al, *Dicey* (2012) 706.

[204] ibid.

[205] JF Coyle, 'Rethinking Judgements Reciprocity' (2014) 92 *North Carolina Law Review* 1109, 1112.

[206] SL Stevens, 'Commanding International Judicial Respect: Reciprocity and the Recognition and Enforcement of Foreign Judgments' (2002) 26 *Hastings International and Comparative Law Review* 115, 117.

[207] Coyle, 'Rethinking Judgements Reciprocity' (2014) 1112.

[208] ibid 1120.

taken by their governments.[209] Still others denounce reciprocity requirements on efficiency grounds.[210]

It is submitted that the burden of establishing binding rules among sovereign nations and the expectation of reciprocity from other foreign courts cannot lie on the shoulders of the judiciary alone.[211] The requirement of reciprocity has to be laid out in a formalised fashion in the form of a multilateral agreement between international judicial forums.[212] A formal instrument explicitly laying out the parameters of reciprocity as a doctrine helps dispel many difficulties foreign courts and tribunals encounter in applying this rule in practice. The lack of a clear uniform procedure is the reason why, although the US has been generous in its recognition and enforcement of foreign judgments, many foreign countries have been unwilling to honour US judgments.[213]

From the perspective of another country, the 'state-by-state' system practised in the US, where recognition and enforcement of foreign judgments is left to the states and their respective legislative regimes, is not a system at all because it provides no unified procedure indicating under what conditions foreign country judgments will be recognised and enforced.[214] There are case studies suggesting that foreign state response to reciprocal legislation affecting private rights will be driven largely by the reaction of interest groups within those states.[215] Any evaluation of the likely success of any policy of judgment reciprocity, therefore, is to determine what benefit foreign judgment creditors in the relevant states stand to gain if this policy is adopted.[216] The ability of reciprocal legislation to bring about reform to the laws of foreign states would depend mainly on the economic impact that such legislation is likely to have on potential foreign judgment creditors.[217] If foreign judgment creditors from a particular country are unwilling, unable, or uninterested in lobbying their legislature, then any reciprocity provision relating to the enforcement of judgments is unlikely to have its desired effect in that state.[218]

V. Impact of 2005 and 2019 HCCH Conventions on the Recognition and Enforcement of Foreign Judgments

A. 2005 HCCH Convention

The 2005 HCCH Convention is a multilateral treaty with the potential of expanding the effect and enforcement of judicial decisions among its contracting states and

209 ibid.
210 ibid.
211 Dowler (n 53) 366.
212 ibid.
213 Stevens, 'Commanding International Judicial Respect' (2002) 115.
214 ibid.
215 Coyle (n 205) 1115.
216 ibid.
217 ibid 1144.
218 ibid 1147.

further harmonising international commercial law.[219] It was drawn up to create a mandatory legal regime for the enforcement of exclusive jurisdiction agreements in commercial transactions and the recognition and enforcement of judgments resulting from proceedings based on such agreements.[220] The choice of court agreement provisions in the 2005 Convention have been aligned with those in the BRR to ensure better coordination and secure the consistent enforcement of jurisdiction agreements both within the EU and globally.[221] The 2005 Convention is both a jurisdiction and judgments convention. It is limited to exclusive choice of court agreements in international cases concerning civil or commercial matters.[222]

Generally, the chosen court in an exclusive choice of court agreement must exercise jurisdiction[223] and the non-chosen court must decline proceedings subject to the provisions of Article 6. On the other hand, Article 8 requires that the judgment of the chosen court be recognised and enforced, unless one of the grounds of refusal under Article 9 is made out. Although the effect of Article 5(2), which prohibits the chosen court from declining jurisdiction based on *forum non conveniens* or *lis alibi pendens*, may be cut down by a state declaration under Article 19, which empowers a state's courts to refuse to enforce an exclusive choice of court agreement in the absence of a 'connection between that state and the parties or the dispute', no state has made an Article 19 declaration yet.

The 2005 HCCH Convention applies only to agreements in favour of states that are party to it. It entered into force on 1 October 2015. As at January 2022, only Denmark, the EU, Mexico, Montenegro, Singapore and the UK have ratified or acceded to the 2005 Convention.[224] Thus, it would appear to have limited influence for the time being as the majority of non-party jurisdictions would not be able to have choice-of-court agreements favouring their courts respected by party jurisdictions. The 2005 HCCH Convention is also smaller in scope than the BRR regime, as it does not cover exclusive choice-of-court agreements where the claim involves personal injuries, infringement of IP rights, or certain tort and debt claims.[225] In short, the 2005 HCCH Convention has yet to enjoy the success of the New York Convention due to limited global ratification and a narrower scope of application.

The 2005 HCCH Convention has recently been condemned by Gary Born as being ignorant of 'endemic corruption among various judiciaries' and deficient in 'important protections' such as party autonomy and procedural fairness.[226] The criticism in

[219] Menon (n 28) 235.

[220] A Mukarrum and P Beaumont, 'Exclusive choice of court agreements: some issues on the Hague Convention on choice of court agreements and its relationship with the Brussels I recast especially anti-suit injunctions, concurrent proceedings and the implications of BREXIT' (2017) 13 *Journal of Private International Law* 386, 390.

[221] ibid.

[222] 2005 HCCH Convention, Art 1(1).

[223] ibid Art 5.

[224] Available at www.hcch.net/en/instruments/conventions/status-table/?cid=98.

[225] 2005 HCCH Convention, Art 2(2).

[226] G Born, 'Why States Should Not Ratify, and Should Instead Denounce, the Hague Choice-Of-Court Agreements Convention, Part I', 16 June 2021, *Kluwer Arbitration Blog*, available at arbitrationblog.kluwerarbitration.com/2021/06/16/why-states-should-not-ratify-and-should-instead-denounce-the-hague-choice-of-court-agreements-convention-part-i.

this regard stems from a belief that the regime for the enforcement and recognition of arbitral awards enshrined in the New York Convention – which in turn inspired the 2005 HCCH Convention – is unsuitable to be transposed onto court judgments. Born argues that allowing the chosen court to determine its jurisdiction in an unreviewable fashion and excluding the possibility of challenges to the independence or integrity of foreign legal systems create a 'mandatory recognition' system by enforcing courts that is problematic.[227] Born further characterises the public policy safeguard under the 2005 HCCH Convention as an inadequate exception to the mandatory recognition rule as it only allows states to invoke their own laws in 'rare and unusual' cases.[228] It is undeniable that incompetent, biased or corrupt judges do exist. However, it is pertinent to remember that the 2005 HCCH Convention enables parties to select the state in which their dispute is to be heard.[229] It even allows them to select a particular court from the chosen state.[230] If a choice is made to have the dispute heard in a country where the judicial system is corrupt, then the parties only have themselves to blame.[231]

In addition, the 2005 HCCH Convention offers parties another method of dispute resolution besides the arbitral system created by the New York Convention. This only serves to reinforce party autonomy. Born's assertion that the 2005 HCCH Convention fails adequately to safeguard procedural fairness may also be addressed with reference to the provisions of Articles 6(c) and 9(e). Article 6(c) provides that the court of a contracting state (other than the chosen court) is under no duty to suspend or dismiss proceedings covered by an exclusive choice-of-court agreement if 'giving effect to the agreement would lead to a manifest injustice or would be manifestly contrary to the public policy of the State of the court seised'. Article 9(e), on the other hand, stipulates that the recognition and enforcement of a judgment rendered by the court of a contracting state designated under an exclusive choice-of-court agreement may be refused if 'recognition or enforcement would be manifestly incompatible with the public policy of the requested State, including situations where the specific proceedings leading to the judgment were incompatible with fundamental principles of procedural fairness of that State'. Hence, any accusation that the 2005 HCCH Convention lacks proper procedural fairness protections is a misrepresentation of its salient features. In a brief rejoinder to Born, Trevor Hartley has also demonstrated that semantics aside, the substance and effect of the protections under the New York Convention and the 2005 HCCH Convention are similar.[232] Consequently, it is incorrect to assert that the former is superior to the latter.

[227] G Born, 'Why It Is Especially Important That States Not Ratify the Hague Choice of Court Agreements Convention, Part II', 23 July 2021, *Kluwer Arbitration Blog*, available at arbitrationblog.kluwerarbitration.com/2021/07/23/why-it-is-especially-important-that-states-not-ratify-the-hague-choice-of-court-agreements-convention-part-ii.

[228] ibid.

[229] 2005 HCCH Convention, Art 3(a).

[230] ibid Art 3(a).

[231] T Hartley, 'Is the 2005 Hague Choice-of-Court Convention Really a Threat to Justice and Fair Play? A Reply to Gary Born', 30 June 2021, *European Association of Private International Law Blog*, available at eapil.org/2021/06/30/is-the-2005-hague-choice-of-court-convention-really-a-threat-to-justice-and-fair-play-a-reply-to-gary-born.

[232] T Hartley, 'The 2005 Hague Convention on Choice-of-Court Agreements: A Further Reply to Gary Born', 3 August 2021, *European Association of Private International Law Blog*, available at eapil.org/2021/08/03/the-2005-hague-convention-on-choice-of-court- agreements-a-further-reply-to-gary-born.

B. 2019 HCCH Convention

It should be borne in mind that the only judgments covered by the 2019 HCCH Convention are those issued by a court which has jurisdiction according to an agreement 'other than an exclusive choice of court' agreement.[233] Therefore, the 2019 HCCH Convention cannot be used as a substitute for the 2005 HCCH Convention.[234] The 2019 HCCH Convention should not be considered a gap-filler until the 2005 HCCH Convention has become widely applicable.[235] Instead, the 2019 HCCH Convention should be treated as complementing the 2005 Convention by extending its benefits 'to a broader range of cases' as asymmetric and quasi-exclusive agreements are also granted protection.[236]

A foreign judgment is eligible to be recognised and enforced under the 2019 HCCH Convention if it fulfils any one of the 13 bases of jurisdiction enumerated in Article 5(1). While it is true that these 13 bases enable a litigant to gauge in advance if a particular foreign judgment is capable of obtaining recognition and enforcement in another state, that predictability exists only insofar there is uniform interpretation of Article 5(1) by the contracting states.[237] This arrangement is further compounded by the fact that unlike the BRR regime, there will be no single court to provide the final binding interpretation of the 2019 HCCH Convention text.[238] On the contrary, it is the courts of every contracting state that will interpret each provision separately, having regard to the 'uniform interpretation' rule enshrined in Article 20.[239] The lack of authoritative interpretation emanating from a supranational judicial body means that the courts of each contracting state may well construe Article 5(1) in a manner consistent with their own municipal laws instead of adopting a construction consistent with other contracting states.[240]

Under the 2019 HCCH Convention, inconsistent judgments are addressed under Article 7. Under Article 7(1)(e), recognition or enforcement of a foreign judgment may be refused if the judgment is inconsistent with a judgment given by a court of the requested state in a dispute between the same parties, while under Article 7(1)(f), recognition or enforcement of a foreign judgment may be refused if the judgment is inconsistent with an earlier judgment given by a court of another state between the same parties on the same subject matter, provided that the earlier judgment fulfils the conditions necessary for its recognition in the requested state. Article 7(2), on the

[233] 2019 HCCH Convention, Art 5(1)(m).

[234] C Kessedjian, 'Comment on the Hague Convention of 2 July 2019 on the Recognition and Enforcement of Foreign Judgments in Civil or Commercial Matters – Is the Hague Convention of 2 July 2019 a useful tool for companies who are conducting international activities?' (2020) *Nederlands Internationaal Privaatrecht* 19, 22.

[235] ibid.

[236] R Kasem, 'The Future of Choice of Court and Arbitration Agreements under the New York Convention, the Hague Choice of Court Convention, and the Draft Hague Judgments Convention' (2020) 10 *Aberdeen Student Law Review* 69, 76.

[237] RA Brand, 'New Challenges in the Recognition and Enforcement of Judgments' (7 September 2018) in F Ferrari and Fernandez-Arroyo eds, *The Continuing Relevance of Private International Law and Its Challenges* (Elgar, 2019) 360.

[238] ibid.

[239] 2019 HCCH Convention, Art 20 provides: 'In the interpretation of this Convention, regard shall be had to its international character and to the need to promote uniformity in its application'.

[240] Brand, 'New Challenges' (2018).

other hand, deals with situations when proceedings are pending in the requested state and the recognition and enforcement of a judgment given in another state is sought. Here, the recognition and enforcement may be postponed or refused. It must be noted that refusal under Article 7(2) does not prevent a subsequent application for recognition or enforcement of the judgment. It has been observed that the *lis pendens* nature of Article 7(2) could be exploited by a party initiating court proceedings pre-emptively in breach of a choice of court agreement.[241]

A criticism that may be directed at the 2019 HCCH Convention is that parallel proceedings are still a likely consequence, since a court designated by an agreement between parties cannot be given priority owing to the absence of direct jurisdictional rules in the text of the Convention.[242] Perhaps the most striking feature of the 2019 HCCH Convention is Article 15, which enables foreign judgments to be recognised and enforced under national law, provided that they do not infringe Article 6. Article 15 of the 2019 HCCH Convention was inspired by and shares the philosophy underlying Article VII of the New York Convention.[243] The latitude given to states under this provision appears to be conducive to the creation of a 'minimum standard' for the mutual recognition and enforcement of judgments.[244] On this basis, the 2019 HCCH Convention may prove attractive to more states as the party requesting recognition has a choice of whether to utilise the procedure laid down in the Convention or the national legal rules of a particular jurisdiction for recognition and enforcement.[245] In the long run, this may have a significant impact on the development of the rules of private international law.

VI. Issues Arising from the COVID-19 Pandemic

The COVID-19 pandemic is surely the crisis of this lifetime because of its global impact. Its novelty means that the legal consequences arising out of the present crisis may not be immediately and easily transposed from previous case law and it will take some time before the attendant issues are authoritatively settled by the courts.[246] As always, the function of the law and dispute resolution mechanisms must be to uphold legal certainty in the application of legal principles and at the same time ensure that the interests of justice are not overlooked. In respect of the effect of the pandemic, it has been postulated that in countries with weak adherence to the Rule of Law, it may become more difficult to enforce foreign judgments or arbitral awards against local businesses if the public policy ground is invoked by the courts in those countries

[241] Kasem, 'The Future of Choice of Court and Arbitration Agreements' (2020) 109.
[242] ibid 108.
[243] Kessedjian, 'Comment on the Hague Convention of 2 July 2019 (2020) 25.
[244] I Rumenov, 'Implications of the New 2019 Hague Convention on Recognition and Enforcement of Foreign Judgments on the National Legal Systems of Countries in South Eastern Europe' (2019) 3 *EU and Comparative Law Issues and Challenges Series* 385, 390.
[245] ibid 402.
[246] W Blair et al, '"Breathing Space"' – Concept Note 2 on the Effect of the 2020 Pandemic on Commercial Contracts (British Institute of International and Comparative Law, May 2020) [69(4)].

as a reason for refusing recognition and enforcement.[247] A creditor might find itself without recourse in light of the ad hoc legislative measures put in place by the governments of countries where the adverse effects of the pandemic are sought to be alleviated.

Another effect of the pandemic has been to cause us to rethink what is meant by 'due process'. The pandemic has forced us all to embrace and adapt to technology at a rate which would previously have been unthinkable. Thanks to technology, the courts and other dispute resolution processes have not come to a complete halt. One of the measures adopted to ensure access to the judiciary and dispute resolution bodies is virtual or remote hearings. On the part of the courts, it has become imperative to establish the requisite procedural protocols governing online hearings,[248] which one predicts will become increasingly prevalent even after the pandemic. The arbitral regime, particularly cross-border arbitration, is no stranger to virtual hearings either. Under Article 24(4) of the ICC Rules of Arbitration, 'case management conferences may be conducted through a meeting in person, by video conference, telephone or similar means of communication', while under Article 26, the arbitral tribunal may after consulting the parties, decide that hearings be conducted 'remotely by video-conference, telephone, or other appropriate means of communication'. In Malaysia, the Asian International Arbitration Centre (AIAC) Rules 2018 similarly empower the arbitral tribunal to direct that witnesses, including expert witnesses, be examined through means of telecommunication that do not require their physical presence at the hearing (such as video conferencing).[249]

But how exactly does the general permission translate into actual procedures? We have seen that a significant factor in balancing between finality and certainty, on the one hand, and justice, on the other, is the notion of due process. If judgments or awards are to be treated as final and binding, the proceedings underlying them should have been conducted in accordance with natural justice. Parties should be treated with equality and afforded a full or reasonable opportunity to present their case. Where remote hearings are involved and there may be inequalities in the technical equipment available to the parties of a dispute, what does due process require?

Evidence-taking is another area that will have to be reviewed in the interests of ensuring due process when it comes to harnessing the remote technology that has become the new norm since the pandemic. The adoption of differing approaches by civil and common law jurisdictions in the taking of evidence and collection means that this is a ripe area for closer investigation, analysis and reconsideration. Traditionally, under the civil law system, 'proof' is mainly in written form. How it is gathered is the province of the judge in an inquisitorial system. Under the traditional common law system, 'evidence' is primarily oral, and what is to be submitted to court and how it is adduced

[247] N Teramura, SF Ali, and A Reyes, 'Expanding Asia-Pacific Frontiers for International Dispute Resolution: Conclusions and Recommendations' in L Nottage, S Ali, B Jetin and N Teramura (eds), *New Frontiers in Asia-Pacific International Arbitration and Dispute Resolution* (Wolters Kluwer, 2021) 364–68.

[248] See, for example, *Hong Kong SAR, China: Guidance Note for Remote Hearings for Civil Business in the High Court (Phase 1 – Video-Conferencing Facilities)* [2020] HKCFI 614.

[249] AIAC Rules 2018, Art 28(4).

and supplemented by documents is largely a matter for the litigants in an adversarial system.[250] Over the decades, the two systems have converged. However, a further refinement and synthesis of the two procedural styles is called for in the post-pandemic era. For one, the conventional concentrated oral hearings in international commercial cases requiring that everyone (judge or arbitrator, lawyers, factual and expert witnesses, interpreters, transcript writers and other support staff) must be in the same place at the same time are expensive. Such hearings leave a significant carbon footprint. If remote technology is to be increasingly used and hearings take place over several time zones, procedures will have to be worked out to ensure that the parties are treated equally. Greater emphasis may have to be placed on documentary evidence and, insofar as there is to be examination of the witnesses by video link, such examinations will need to be succinct, focused and to the point. It is doubtful that, post-pandemic, we can or even should simply go on in the same way as before.

[250] Permanent Bureau of the Hague Conference on Private International Law, *Practical Handbook on the Operation of the Evidence Convention*, 3rd edn (HCCH, 2016) [145].

PART V

The *Lex Mercatoria* and the Convergence of International Commercial Law

9

An Anatomy of the *Lex Mercatoria*

JASON LIN

I. The Concept of *Lex Mercatoria*

The concept of *lex mercatoria* or the 'law merchant' reflects the view that the relationship between international businesses and trading bodies is governed by a body of transnational law. In the words of Lawrence Friedman, a prominent proponent of a *lex mercatoria*:[1] 'The idea is that the transnational [commercial actors] today have their own customs, norms, and practices, and a sort of merchant law is emerging, without the benefit of legislation, from their patterns of behaviour.'[2]

Friedman's optimism for an international supranational legal order is by no means universally shared. Whilst the *lex mercatoria* has been hailed by some as a manifestation of the 'third wave of globalization',[3] the utility and existence of the *lex mercatoria* remain very much the subject of controversy. Before delving into why this is, care must be taken in defining the precise parameters of the debate.

Orsolya Toth has cautioned that discussions about the existence of a *lex mercatoria* can frequently be unhelpful:

> The fruitfulness of these debates [on whether a *lex mercatoria* exists] … remains doubtful. It has been acknowledged by commentators that the arguments do not always clarify matters and they are sometimes conducted beyond the desirable confines of a careful academic discourse.

[1] Modern scholars refer to the '*new*' *lex mercatoria*. to distinguish between the historic *lex mercatoria* and the rise of a new transnational body of commercial law (see C Windbichler, 'Lex Mercatoria' in *International Encyclopedia of the Social & Behavioral Sciences*, Vol 13, 2nd edn (Elsevier, 2015) 915). For the purposes of this book, it is unnecessary to draw a sharp distinction; the phrase *lex mercatoria* will be accordingly used to encompass the continuum of the law merchant as it has developed and evolved from historic times to the present day. Nonetheless, though rooted in the historical understanding of a body of law that had normative force, the contemporary idea of the *lex mercatoria* may differ in many respects from its previous incarnation and so is best viewed through a modern (as opposed to a purely historic) lens.

[2] LM Friedman, 'Erewhon: The Coming Global Legal Order' (2001) 37 *Stanford Journal of international Law* 347, 356, cited in C Brolmann, 'Deterritorialization in international Law: Moving Away from the Divide Between National and International Law' in A Nollkaemper and JE Nijman (eds), *New Perspectives on the Divide Between National and International Law* (OUP, 2007) 102.

[3] M Hertogh, 'What is non-state law? Mapping the other Hemisphere of the Legal World' in H van Schooten and JM Verschuuren (eds), *International Governance and Law: State Regulation and Non-State Law* (Edward Elgar 2008).

> It has been claimed that the existence of the *lex mercatoria*, 'like the existence of God' often depended on 'the will to believe' … For some, the *lex mercatoria* is an 'historical fact' which simply exists regardless of what opponents say. For others, it is a 'myth' or an 'enigma' adding that it is 'hardly necessary to emphasize that no such body of law exists'.[4]

Toth suggests that any debate on the *lex mercatoria* must distinguish between arguments as to its factual existence, on the one hand, and its source of legal recognition, on the other.[5] Supporters of a *lex mercatoria* often point to arbitral awards and court judgments that refer to general principles of international commercial law. They are therefore making a descriptive claim on the existence and recognition of *lex mercatoria*. The opponents argue in response that the *lex mercatoria* cannot possibly exist under any jurisprudential rule of recognition. The critics are thus making a normative argument on the recognition of *lex mercatoria*. As such, the two sides often talk past each other. It will consequently be necessary to keep Toth's distinction in mind for the purposes of the discussion in this chapter.

A. Is the Concept too Nebulous?

Several difficulties arise when asking whether it is realistic to speak of a *lex mercatoria*. These include ascertaining *lex mercatoria*'s normative source, contents and objects. This is important since the norms and contents of any international law of merchants must be capable of being ascertained to be of any practical utility to commercial parties. As Toth put it, the *lex mercatoria* must be a 'pragmatic concept'. For this reason:

> The study of the *lex mercatoria* cannot be pursued as a *l'art pour l'art* exercise. Rather, it must serve the interests of businessmen engaged in cross-border trade. The [*lex mercatoria*] must offer solutions which are accessible to parties, their legal advisors and to commercial arbitrators. Failing this, even the most appealing theoretical account will have served no useful purpose.[6]

i. A Historical View

One way of understanding the *lex mercatoria* is to view it through its historic roots in ancient merchant law. Legal historians generally recognise that there once existed a transnational legal space which was part of the *ius gentium*.[7] This body of customary law governed trade and was developed through agreements between traders and merchants. Over the centuries, this historical *lex mercatoria* was gradually absorbed into national laws. In common law jurisdictions. the norms which formed the *lex mercatoria* found their way into judge-made case law.[8] The blurring of any distinction between the historical body of supranational law and national law continued

[4] O Toth, *The Lex Mercatoria in Theory and Practice*, 1st edn (OUP, 2017) 6–7.
[5] ibid 5.
[6] ibid, 2.
[7] Windbichler, 'Lex Mercatoria' (2015) 915.
[8] See for instance *Lethulier's Case* (1692) 2 Salk 443, per Holt CJ, cited in Windbichler (n 1).

as legislatures in common and civil law jurisdictions incorporated principles of the historical *lex mercatoria* into codifying statutes (such as the English Sale of Goods Act 1893 and the American Uniform Commercial Code).[9] Therefore, while legal history does not directly explain the normative force of the *lex mercatoria*, it sheds light on the discussion in a number of ways. The fact that courts regarded transnational commercial principles as binding and adopted them as domestic law suggests that, over time, the principles must have been regarded as having normative force. The process whereby legislatures incorporated developments in transnational commercial practice into their domestic statutes further supports the view that the *lex mercatoria* was more than just a set of rules of convenience, but a coherent body of law. If this is correct, then can the *lex mercatoria*, as it has become today and as it continues to evolve, be characterised as a body of supranational law? More pertinently, in what sense (if any) can the *lex mercatoria* be considered as 'law' today?

ii. A Normative View

To a legal positivist, a supranational *lex mercatoria* cannot possibly exist, let alone acquire normative force of law. For the legal positivist, to be law, the *lex mercatoria* must satisfy a rule of recognition, which dictates that law must be made by a recognised law-making process. Accordingly, the fact that the *lex mercatoria* is a supranational body of norms not made by any state or by states acting in concerted fashion militates against it being considered 'law'.[10] In contrast, the proponents of a *lex mercatoria* often take a sociological or functional view of law. Their view is that a rule can rightly be described as 'law' if it serves the purpose of governing private commercial relationships, even if it has not been promulgated by an act of state sovereignty (for example, by legislation or ratification of a treaty).[11]

A third opinion, as advanced in particular by Christine Windbichler, holds that the normative debate is ultimately of no consequence for the *lex mercatoria*, since the reality is that the *lex mercatoria* is to be inferred from the terms in contracts drawn up by commercial parties. Thus, when one speaks of the *lex mercatoria* governing commercial relationships, what is really meant is that commercial parties interact based on transnational commercial usages and practices as reflected in the terms of their legally binding contracts. On Windbichler's view, the *lex mercatoria* should be treated as the consequence of contract, which is in turn governed by, interpreted, and enforced pursuant to national law. In addition, the usages and principles of the *lex mercatoria* can be and have been incorporated into international commercial conventions and model laws. Where these instruments are ratified or adopted by a national legal system, and that national law is chosen as the governing law of a contract, the principles and usages of the *lex mercatoria* are then applied to the parties' commercial relationship.[12]

[9] ibid.

[10] ibid 916.

[11] See U Stein, *Lex Mercatoria: Realitat und Theorie, Juristische Abhandlungen Vol 28* (Vittorio Klosterman, 1995), cited in Toth, *The Lex Mercatoria* (2017) 31. C Drahozal, 'Contracting out of National Law: An Empirical Look at the New Law Merchant' (2005) 80 *Notre Dame Law Review* 523.

[12] Windbichler (n 1) 916–17.

One might argue that Windbichler's view avoids, rather than answers, the question of whether the *lex mercatoria* has independent legal validity. For instance, the question remains: can contracting parties choose the 'law merchant' as the governing law, rather than simply incorporating it as terms of their contract? Nonetheless, Windbichler's insight is useful in that it brings us back to what should be the real focus of the normative debate: the question whether the *lex mercatoria* has any practical utility. This is important since empirical studies suggest that a common reason for not adopting the *lex mercatoria* is uncertainty over its content.[13] It is therefore critical that the content of the *lex mercatoria* be capable of ascertainment.

B. What Principles Make up the *Lex Mercatoria*?

Some commentators suggest that the core principles of the *lex mercatoria* are readily ascertainable. In Ross Cranston's view, 'The *lex mercatoria* is more difficult to identify … but it consists of principles like good faith, reasonableness, the duty to negotiate, set-off, and the obligation to compensate on expropriation'.[14] Several arguments have been advanced in support of the view that the *lex mercatoria* is a defined and discernible body of international commercial law.

First, there is the 'codification argument'. Supporters argue that the *lex mercatoria* is discernible from soft law instruments such as the UNIDROIT Principles of International Commercial Contracts ('UNIDROIT Principles') and the Vienna Convention on the International Sale of Goods (CISG).[15] Opponents argue that such instruments cannot, on their own, establish a *lex mercatoria*, because they are static and cannot be frequently updated. Consequently, they cannot constitute an accurate reflection of ever-developing international commercial practice. To rebut this criticism, supporters refer to the Trans-Lex Principles (TLP),[16] which is frequently updated online and accessible to all.

Second, there is the 'arbitral recognition argument'. For this, scholars rely on the citation of the *lex mercatoria* as the applicable law in arbitral awards. In Berthold Goldman's opinion, such awards are 'sufficiently numerous' to make an argument that the content of the *lex mercatoria* is capable of being ascertained and meaningfully applied as law.[17] Support for this can be drawn from Article 28(1) of the UNCITRAL Model Law on International Commercial Arbitration, which permits tribunals to give effect to 'rules of law' chosen by the parties. These 'rules of law' could potentially include supranational law, as is evident from the Model Law's *travaux preparatoires*.[18]

[13] Drahozal, 'Contracting out of National Law' (2005).

[14] R Cranston, 'Theorizing Transnational Commercial law' (2007) 42 *Texas International Law Journal* 597, 598.

[15] Toth (n 4) 13–16.

[16] See www.trans-lex.org/principles/of-transnational-law-(lex-mercatoria).

[17] B Goldman, *Lex Mercatoria* (3 Forum Internatiaonle on Commercial Law and Arbitration) (Kluwer 1983), cited in Toth (n 4) 7.

[18] See for instance [5] and [12] in the 326th Meeting on the UNCITRAL Model Law, 17 June 1985, available at uncitral.un.org/sites/uncitral.un.org/files/media-documents/uncitral/en/326meeting-e.pdf.

Third, there is the 'national court recognition argument'. Advocates have suggested that the *lex mercatoria* must have a reasonably clear content since it has been recognised by national courts. Three cases which are often cited in support all involve national courts upholding arbitral awards which applied the *lex mercatoria.*[19] In *Société Fougerolle v Banque de Proche Orient,*[20] the French Cour de Cassation upheld an award in which the tribunal applied 'general principles of obligation generally applicable in international trade'. The tribunal in *Pablk Ticaret v Norsolor*[21] was even more explicit in its support of a *lex mercatoria,* and applied the 'principle of good faith inspired by international *lex mercatoria*' instead of selecting a national law as the source of an obligation of good faith. In subsequent annulment proceedings in Austria and enforcement proceedings in France, Norsolor argued that the award should be set aside because, by applying a principle of good faith derived from the *lex mercatoria,* the tribunal had effectively acted as an *amiable compositeur* without the parties' authorisation.[22] The Paris *Cour d'Appel* upheld the award, as did the Austrian Supreme Court.[23] The third case of *Deutsche Schachtbau*[24] concerned an ICC award. The tribunal applied 'internationally accepted principles of law' as the governing law of the contract. The award was challenged at the place of enforcement (England) on the ground that it was against public policy to apply an ill-defined body of 'law'. The Court of Appeal rejected that submission and ruled that, since parties did not confine their choice of law to any state law, the arbitrators had acted within their jurisdiction under the ICC Rules when applying general principles of international commercial law. More generally, Article 3 of the Hague Principles on Choice of Law in International Commercial Contracts provides that 'The law chosen by the parties may be rules of law that are generally accepted on an international, supranational or regional level as a neutral and balanced set of rules, unless the law of the forum provides otherwise'. Article 3 thus evidences a meta-rule supporting the acceptability of the *lex mercatoria* as a body of law provided that it meets the criteria for acceptance identified by the Hague Principles.[25]

The three arguments are not without their critics. On the codification argument, it could be argued that the UNIDROIT Principles and CISG are the result of harmonisation efforts among participating states aimed at facilitating trade. This is claimed to be different from the codification of the *lex mercatoria* as a distinct body of supranational

[19] Considered in Lord Mustill, 'The New Lex Mercatoria: The First Twenty-five Years' (1988) 4 *Arbitration International* 86, 106–09, cited in Toth (n 4) 19.

[20] [1983] Rev Arb 183.

[21] [1983] Rev Arb 525.

[22] Article 28(3) of the Model Law provides: '(3) The arbitral tribunal shall decide *ex aequo et bono* or as *amiable compositeur* only if the parties have expressly authorized it to do so.' For further discussion on the possibility of arbitrators acting *ex aequo et bono* or as *amiables compositeurs,* see N Teramura, 'Ex Aequo et Bono' *as a Response to the 'Over-Judicialisation' of International Commercial Arbitration* (Wolters Kluwer, 2020).

[23] See decision of Cour D'Appel of Paris in P Sanders (ed), *YearBoook Commercial Arbitration,* Vol VIII (Kluwer Law International, 1983), 362; and Austrian Oberster Gerichtshof at ibid 159.

[24] *Deutsche Schachtbau-und Tiefbohrgesellschaft mbH v The Government of Ras al Khaimah and Rakoil* [1987] 3 WLR 1023. See original award: ICC Award No 3572/1982.

[25] Article 3, however, remains subject to the laws of the forum, such as the Rome I Regulation, which applies within the EU and prohibits the application of supranational laws. In practice, it may be the case that, while arbitral tribunals may apply the *lex mercatoria* as rules of law chosen by the parties pursuant to the Model Law,

law.[26] If a *lex mercatoria* existed, there would be no need for the UNIDROIT Principles and CISG. Neither those instruments nor the TLP can purport to represent the substance of the law merchant accurately or with any authority. Neither do the UNIDROIT Principles nor CISG comprehensively codify every aspect of international commercial law, let alone contract law or the law relating to the sale of goods. In fact, as the experience of drafting CISG has shown, obtaining international consensus on the governing principles, even for a single discrete area of commercial law – the sale of goods – has proved to be protracted and difficult.[27]

Further, formidable objections have been raised against the arbitral recognition argument. In reply to Goldman's claim that 'numerous' arbitral awards have referred to the *lex mercatoria*, Toth has suggested that the number of arbitral awards citing the *lex mercatoria* is comparatively small and that most of the cases cited by Goldman never actually referred to any specific norm within the *lex mercatoria*.[28] On Toth's view, the content of the *lex mercatoria* is simply not certain enough to be of practical utility in commercial transactions. As Windbichler puts it: 'the term lex mercatoria is not actually used in international trade but rather denotes an abstraction'.[29]

Finally, responding to the national court recognition argument, Toth argues that the three cases cited above neither evince a judicial acceptance of the *lex mercatoria* nor indicate that its contents are sufficiently certain. The cases (it is contended) do not directly confront the real issue, which is: if is there is a *lex mercatoria*, what are its contents? The cases instead focus on whether arbitral tribunals exceeded their jurisdiction and whether the awards were enforceable under national law.[30] Indeed, the national courts of some European jurisdictions applying the Rome I Convention 1980 have held that it is not possible to choose non-state law as the governing law of a contract.[31]

In short, one must conclude that there is no consensus on whether the *lex mercatoria* has discernible content that would be of practical utility to contracting parties. However, it is submitted that, much as the principles of the common law can only be ascertained on a case-by-case basis and can never be exhaustively enumerated, at any given moment in time we can at best only see the *lex mercatoria* in parts rather than as a whole. We can only infer the contents of the law merchant as applicable to a particular case from judgments, arbitral awards, multilateral conventions, bilateral treaties, domestic legislation, trade practices or usages, and soft law instruments. These features of the *lex mercatoria* described thus far are by and large shared in common with the common law. What sets the two apart, however, is that there is no system of courts or other authoritative body that claims responsibility for definitively ruling on

courts may be prevented from so doing by national law. See, for instance, Richards J's analysis in *Musawi v RE International (UK) Ltd* [2008] 1 ALL ER (Comm) 607 [19] and [22].

[26] Toth (n 4) 13–16.

[27] MJ Bonell, 'The CISG, European Contract Law and the Development of a World Contract Law' (2008) 56 *The American Journal of Comparative Law* 1, 3.

[28] Toth (n 4) 17.

[29] Windbichler (n 1) 916.

[30] Toth (n 4) 20–1.

[31] That said, parties can, by express terms, incorporate non-state law (provided that the contract specifically identifies the 'black letter' provisions of the relevant law to be incorporated) as terms of the contract, which the court may then have recourse to in the ascertainment of the parties' rights and obligations under the contract: see *Shamil Bank of Bahrain EC v Beximco Pharmaceuticals Ltd* [2004] 1 WLR 1784. The position would be the same under Rome I Regulation.

the content of the *lex mercatoria*. What we have, instead, is the multiplicity of legal and quasi-legal (soft) sources setting out similar principles, which is evidence (one puts it no higher) that the principles so discerned have normative force. Even then, the contents of the *lex mercatoria* as perceived by us should not be regarded as static or immutable for all time. They may instead evolve over time to deal with new cases and fresh insights into how cross-border commerce can more fairly, efficiently, and cost-effectively be conducted. At a given moment in time, it may be possible to discern a principle of the *lex mercatoria* applicable to a particular case. But that principle may have to be refined in light of a later case which although ostensibly similar, possesses material distinguishing features.

It will be apparent that the features of the *lex mercatoria* just described are shared with the common law, save for one unique feature of the *lex mercatoria*. That special feature is that there is no court or system of courts which claims responsibility for definitively ruling on the content of the *lex mercatoria*. The difficulty is therefore not that the *lex mercatoria* has to be pieced together from multiple sources or that it is constantly changing (which is also true of the common law), but is instead one of assessing whether certain rules or rulings are authoritative statements of the content of the *lex mercatoria* (as opposed to being authoritative by reason of some other body of law which happens to resemble the *lex mercatoria* on a particular matter).

C. Is it Fit for the Purpose of International Commercial Dispute Resolution?

We have seen that *lex mercatoria* must be sufficiently clear to be of use to business, or else the 'labyrinth of conflicting national laws would be replaced with a maze of conflicting *leges mercatoriae*'.[32] However, to be a body of law fit for our time, the *lex mercatoria* needs to be much more. It is submitted that the *lex mercatoria* must at least be capable of responding robustly to the pressing modern challenges identified by Sundaresh Menon in the Introduction to this book. Consider, for example, three areas identified in the Introduction. First, does the *lex mercatoria* incorporate norms that address the global demand for action by commercial enterprises on climate change? Second, does the *lex mercatoria* have the ability to safeguard the commercial interests of parties in weaker bargaining positions (typically, referred to as micro, small, and medium enterprises (MSMEs))? Third, can the *lex mercatoria* deal with disputes as to whether and when non-performance should be excused amidst the uncertainties induced by COVID-19? These are discussed in turn below.

i. *Fitness to Address Climate Change*

It is common today to hear of global businesses (especially those in the energy sector) coming under pressure from activist investors to take action on climate change. In the lead-up to the United Nation's COP 25 conference on climate change, investors

[32] Toth (n 4) 67.

with US$37 trillion in assets pressed for urgent action against global warming.[33] Does the *lex mercatoria* have anything to say about such concerns? Mathilde Hautereau-Boutonnet argues that there is an emerging *lex mercatoria climatique* that can prompt companies to take action on climate change by incorporating climate protection standards in contracts without the need for national or international legislative action or intervention. In this way, commercial parties can establish systems of climate protection obligations within the context of their private transnational contractual relationships. Over time, much like standard terms in widely used international commercial contracts,[34] this would allow for the gradual development of norms.[35]

ii. *Fitness for Protecting MSMEs*

Stefan Vogenauer contends that soft law instruments such as the UNIDROIT Principles

> display a certain openness towards protecting 'the economically weaker' or 'less experienced' party in a commercial context. Thus they go a long way towards meeting the concerns of those who believe that an optional instrument for B2B [Business to Business] contracts is particularly needed for small and medium-sized enterprises (SMEs) because these typically have less access to legal expertise and frequently find themselves in an inferior bargaining position vis-à-vis bigger businesses.[36]

In this regard, soft law instruments such as the UNIDROIT Principles serve as evidence of the content of the *lex mercatoria*. The more widely cited or accepted the instrument, the more compelling the case for characterising it as a statement of *lex mercatoria* principles. To the extent for instance that (as Ross Cranston persuasively argues) the *lex mercatoria* incorporates principles of good faith,[37] the *lex mercatoria* can be utilised to safeguard the interests of smaller or weaker parties. Application of the *lex mercatoria* would not simply lead to a laissez-faire free-for-all from which only the commercially strong emerge triumphant.

iii. *Fitness for Dealing with the Aftermath of a Pandemic*

If parties contracted for the application of the *lex mercatoria*, would it be capable of dealing effectively and appropriately with the challenges posed by COVID-19? For example, there will likely be a plenitude of cases in the future on whether a commercial party's pandemic-induced failure to perform should be excused. Johanna Hoekstra submits that the *lex mercatoria* can address such challenges.[38] She demonstrates this by

[33] See for example 'Global investor group urges action on climate change' *The Financial Times*, 9 December 2019, available at www.ft.com/content/c740ae38-192a-11ea-97df-cc63de1d73f4.

[34] See the discussion on the role of standard form contracts harmonising international commercial dispute resolution in Pt 1 of this book.

[35] M Hautereau-Boutonnet, 'Une illustration du droit global, la lex mercatoria climatique' (2017) 14 *Revista de Direito Internacional* 31 (*Brazil Journal of International Law*, Global Environmental Law supplement).

[36] S Vogenauer, 'Common Frame of Reference and UNIDROIT principles of International Commercial Contracts: Coexistence, Competition, or Overkill of Soft Law?' (2010) 6 *European Review of Contract Law* 143, 180.

[37] Cranston, 'Theorizing Transnational Commercial law' (2007) 598.

[38] J Hoekstra, 'Regulating International Contracts in a Pandemic: Application of the Lex Mercatoria and transnational Commercial Law' in C Ferstman and A Fagan (eds) *Covid-19, Law and Human Rights: Essex Dialogues* (University of Essex, 2020) 117, available at repository.essex.ac.uk/28030.

deriving relevant principles of *lex mercatoria* from transnational instruments such as the UNIDROIT Principles and CISG, and by working out which general principles of international commercial law and trade usage should be applied in the circumstances of a case. She highlights three key competing principles:

(1) *Favor contractus*. Under this principle, tribunals must 'interpret the legal provisions in a way that as far as possible upholds the contract. Termination is the last option'.[39] Given the value of certainty and predictability in commercial contracts, parties should generally be held to their bargain, and the threshold for relieving a defaulting party of its contractual obligations will be high.
(2) Good faith. In contrast, this principle requires that parties deal with each other transparently and honestly. It emphasises equity and fairness. On this footing, tribunals may take into account unexpected and significant hardship arising from (say) the COVID-19 pandemic that might be occasioned to a contracting party if it were held strictly to its contractual bargain.
(3) *Clausula rebus sic stantibus*.[40] This principle 'allows the parties to modify or terminate an agreement because of serious disruptions and is considered part of the *lex mercatoria*'. The reasoning underlying the principle is that, when a disrupting event which was not within the contemplation of the parties at the time of contracting occurs, they could not have intended for their contractual obligations to continue in the same way despite the radical changes that the disrupting event causes to the basis upon which those obligations were entered into in the first instance. Therefore, the parties may have a valid reason for seeking a renegotiation of their contractual obligations.

A decision-maker's task would be to balance among these three principles to arrive at a just outcome in the circumstances of a particular case. None of the foregoing is to say that courts, arbitrators, and other decision-makers should lose sight of a need for contractual certainty when applying the *lex mercatoria*. The only point being made is that the *lex mercatoria* is sufficiently diverse in its sources, as well as nuanced in what can or should be inferred from such sources, to meet modern challenges.

D. Do Parties Actually Choose the *Lex Mercatoria* as Governing Law?

i. *Empirical Evidence*

The discussion so far has assumed that parties actually contract for the *lex mercatoria*, in lieu of national laws, to govern their commercial transactions. However, an empirical study conducted by Christopher Drahozal suggests that in practice:

> Only a small percentage of parties provide for application of transnational commercial law in their arbitration clauses. Even when parties do rely on transnational law, they often do so to supplement rather than displace national law. Thus, as stated in one leading international

[39] ibid 123.

[40] That is, an implied term that performance of the parties' contractual obligations is premised on the matters remaining as they are at the time of contracting.

arbitration commentary: 'For all of its intellectual fascination, the debate over *lex mercatoria* to date does not appear to have had more than a marginal impact on the practice of international arbitration, and this is even more true of the attitudes and conduct of parties to international contracts.'[41]

Drahozal analysed data from ICC administered arbitrations in 2003 and found that non-national law was chosen as the governing law in just 1.2 per cent of cases.[42] The number of cases expressly designating the *lex mercatoria* was unclear, but was probably even lower than that. Drahozal hypothesised that parties might not choose the *lex mercatoria* unless the benefits of doing so (that is, contracting out of national law) outweigh the likely costs of uncertainty over the applicable legal rule:

> As applied to contractual choice of law, parties will choose the applicable law (including transnational law) that likewise maximizes the net difference between deterrence benefits and dispute resolution costs. Thus, parties will contract to have their disputes resolved under the new law merchant if the deterrence benefits from contracting out of national law (that is, the benefits of avoiding costly national law) exceed the likely costs of relying on transnational law (in the form of uncertainty over the governing legal rule).[43]

In Drahozal's view, the most plausible explanation why parties eschew the *lex mercatoria* is the vagueness and uncertainty of its content. In cost-benefit analysis terms, the cost of contracting for *lex mercatoria* is too high *ex ante* (uncertainty as to the rules governing a party's contractual relationship) and ex post (the higher costs of dispute resolution consequential upon uncertainty). More recently, the ICC Dispute Resolution Statistics 2019[44] indicates that 869 new arbitrations were registered with the ICC Secretariat in 2018, of which cases from Asia and the Pacific made up around 30 per cent of the case load. Of all arbitrations conducted under the ICC in 2018, 88 per cent of cases included a contractual choice of law provision. Of those, English law was the most popular (16 per cent) followed by Swiss law (12 per cent). Only one per cent of contracts provided for the application of non-national law. The latter choices included CISG, the UNIDROIT Principles, and 'international commercial law'.[45] Therefore, empirically few parties choose non-state law, let alone the *lex mercatoria* to govern their contracts and disputes.

ii. *Diversity and Legal Pluralism in the* Lex Mercatoria

a. *Societas Mercatorum*

The next logical question is, who may be those parties that choose *lex mercatoria* to govern their commercial relationships? If the *lex mercatoria* is supposed to encapsulate norms derived from established trade practices and usages within the international business community, it becomes important to define that community

[41] Drahozal (n 11) 526.
[42] ibid 539.
[43] ibid 531.
[44] ICC, 'ICC Dispute Resolution 2019 Statistics', available at iccwbo.org/publication/iccdispute-resolution-statistics.
[45] ibid 15.

or *societas mercatorum.*[46] Advocates of a *lex mercatoria* assume the existence of an identifiable *societas mercatorum*, while opponents say that there is no such international business community homogenous enough to be characterised as a unified body capable of creating international norms.[47] For instance, Sir Roy Goode posits that the *societas mercatorum* consists of individual businesses. Their collective behavioural norms are recorded by organisations such as the ICC or Trans-Lex, thereby producing a body of norms that are reflective of the practices of that community.[48] Klaus Peter Berger puts forward a broader definition which includes not only businesses, but also trade associations, individual traders and other constituencies (such as arbitral tribunals and publishing agencies (eg Trans-Lex).[49]

On the other hand, the French jurist Paul Lagarde argues that any *societas mercatorum* would at most comprise a 'plurality of merchant communities … [and] not a single unified organization'. Thus, there can be no single *societas mercatorum* generating a *lex mercatoria*. There can at most only be bodies of coexisting *leges mercatoriae* and the law merchant would not be a homogenous legal system as often claimed.[50] In a similar vein, Lord Mustill observes that the notion of a homogenous *societas mercatorum*:

> [W]ould have been sustainable two centuries ago. But the international business community is now immeasurably enlarged. What principles of trade law, apart from those which are so general as to be useless, are common to the legal systems of the members of such a community?[51]

Assessing these contrasting positions, Toth argued that reference to a *single* global merchant community is impossible if the *lex mercatoria* is to be representative of a diverse group of commercial parties. She contends that:

> [A] *societas mercatorum* … consist[s] of individual merchants who have the potential to create norms through their conduct and *opinio juris*, being various merchant subcommunities within the *societas mercatorum* which are organised on an industry specific, rather than a territorial basis …

What this all suggests is that the *lex mercatoria* is not monolithic, but instead constitutes a pluralistic or diverse body of international commercial trade practices and usages.

b. Trade Practices and Usages

If so, what counts as the common practices and usages of the *societas mercatorum*? The issue is whether it is enough that a practice has been commonly adopted or

[46] Toth (n 4) 62.
[47] ibid.
[48] ibid 63, citing R Goode, 'Usage and its Reception in Transnational Commercial Law' (1997) *International and Commercial Law Quarterly* 1, 12.
[49] ibid 64. KP Berger, *The Creeping Codification of the New Lex Mercatoria*, 2nd edn (Kluwer Law International, 2010) 137.
[50] ibid 67. See P Lagarde, 'Approche Critique de la Lex Mercatoria' in P Fouchard, P Kahn and A Lyon-Caen (eds), *Le Droit des Relations Economiques Internatioanles, Etudes offertes a B. Goldman* (Litec Droit, Librairies Techniques, 1982).
[51] Lord Mustill, 'The New Lex Mercatoria' (1988) 92, cited in Toth (n 4) 67.

observed, or whether it is necessary also to show that the practice was adopted because commercial parties regarded themselves as bound to follow the same. It is refreshing to note that, on this particular issue, unlike the one just discussed, there is less of a controversy. It is common ground, at least between Lord Mustill and Sir Roy Goode, that only the latter – established conduct of international business parties coupled with an *opinio juris* – has legal force. Commentators take the view that the normative force of trade usages and practices derives from contractual consent. Usages become binding because they are routinely incorporated into standard contracts which are widely used internationally or because they have been received into relevant national law.[52] As Lord Mustill explained:

> At its widest, usage is simply a practice which is generally followed. So understood it cannot be a source of law or of individual legal rights. It can be such only if the practice is generally followed because commercial men regard themselves as bound to follow it in the absence of express stipulation to the contrary. Nobody could deny that usage in this sense can be an important element in the assessment by a tribunal of the rights and duties created by the contract, either because in a codified or inexplicit form it is tacitly incorporated into the contract, or because it has been received into the relevant national law.[53]

c. Non-Western Norms

Any discussion on trade practices is a broad-brush exercise that encompasses activities conducted in, and across different countries. The pluralism inherent in the *lex mercatoria* allows for a degree of elasticity, enabling it to take account of different social, cultural, moral, religious and other norms, depending on the circumstances of the transaction. However, one might doubt this proposition. For example, to the extent that CISG is reflective of the *lex mercatoria* on certain aspects of the sale of goods, Gary Bell has observed that Islamic law and Hindu law appear to have been left out of the picture by the drafters of CISG.[54] Specifically, Article 78 of CISG provides for the payment of interest, whereas the concept of interest or *riba* is generally forbidden under Islamic law. It may be argued that this example demonstrates that the *lex mercatoria* does not sufficiently embody non-Western religious, cultural or social norms, or reflect the usages, customs and practices of the many trading communities around the world.

There is no simple answer to this critique. If (as advocated here) one accepts the view that the *lex mercatoria* must be representative of a diverse global trading community, then the diversity of social, cultural, religious and other norms around the world should somehow be mirrored in the global law merchant. Put simply, failure to accommodate non-Western norms will undermine its acceptability in much of the world and undermine its claim to be global in nature.

By the same token, there is a need for diverse cross-border dispute resolution mechanisms and forums. These play a crucial role in ensuring that the industry- or region-specific norms are reflected in the *lex mercatoria*. Regional arbitration, for

[52] cf Windbichler's view summarised in section I.A.ii of this chapter.

[53] Lord Mustill (n 19) 94.

[54] G Bell, 'Harmonisation of Contract law in Asia – Harmonising Regionally or Adopting Global Harmonization – the example of the CISG' [2005] *Singapore Journal of Legal Studies* 362.

example, can promote the development of international commercial laws by ensuring that they are inclusive of different cultural and legal orders. In the context of Asia-Africa trade, new and emerging arbitration centres have developed innovative solutions to cater to the needs of an increasingly diverse pool of commercial parties.[55] In 2013 the Kuala Lumpur Regional Centre for Arbitration (KLRCA)[56] introduced its i-Arbitration Rules which are *shari'a* compliant for international commercial dispute resolution. Under these rules, parties may refer questions of *shari'a* to a *Shari'a* Advisory Council whenever the tribunal is called upon to form an opinion on a point of Islamic law.[57] Thus, regional dispute resolution mechanisms arguably can make the *lex mercatoria* more inclusive.

II. Convergence of the *Lex Mercatoria*

A. Efforts at Identifying the Principles of the *Lex Mercatoria*

Convergence (that is, the harmonisation of commercial legal principles) is important because it reduces transactional costs for businesses as they move from one jurisdiction to another. It therefore encourages cross-border trade. Three categories of convergence may be identified in respect of the *lex mercatoria*: (1) harmonisation of the rules of enforcement; (2) harmonisation of commercial dispute resolution processes; and (3) harmonisation of substantive law. Is there a guarantee that efforts to harmonise the *lex mercatoria* in those three areas will succeed, in the sense of at least achieving a consensus of core norms, as opposed to ushering in a bewildering amalgam of contradictory principles? There can be no guarantee of complete agreement among commercial stakeholders, but absolute convergence is not necessary. Judges in common law jurisdictions have over the centuries developed a coherent and consistent body of core legal principles, even if there may be regional or national differences or disagreements in the way that non-core principles are applied. In much the same way, it is submitted that the pluralist initiatives catalogued in this section can lead to a broad agreement on the key principles of the *lex mercatoria*. That body of rules being part of a discursive dynamic, judges in different states may reasonably disagree on the formulation or application of an operative *lex mercatoria* principle in the context of a given case. Such differences are only to be expected and would not by themselves detract from the general coherence and workability of the *lex mercatoria* as a system of commercial norms.

Four institutions that have been, and continue to be, actively involved in identifying and harmonising commercial law principles on a global level are the United Nations Commission on International Trade Law (UNCITRAL), the International Chamber of Commerce (ICC), the International Institute for the Unification of Private Law (UNIDROIT) and the Hague Conference on Private International Law (HCCH).

[55] MA Raouf, 'Emergence of New Arbitral Centres in Asia and Africa: Competition, Cooperation and Contribution to the Rule of Law' in S Brekoulakis et al (eds), *The Evolution and Future of International Arbitration, International Arbitration Law Library Vol 37* (Kluwer Law International, 2016) 321, 330.

[56] In 2018, the KLRCA was rebranded as the Asia International Arbitration Centre (AIAC).

[57] Raouf, 'Emergence of New Arbitral Centres in Asia and Africa' (2016) 330.

UNCITRAL has made invaluable contributions to the crystallisation, promotion and harmonisation of a global commercial law. Formed in 1966, UNCITRAL aims (among other matters) to promote and harmonise the law of international trade and to produce negotiated legislative and non-legislative instruments through an international process involving Member States of UNCITRAL as well as non-Member States and other representative bodies.[58] Among UNCITRAL's notable achievements are the CISG (adopted in 1980), the New York Convention on the Recognition and Enforcement of Foreign Arbitral Awards (1958), the Model Law on International Commercial Arbitration (1985, amended 2006), the Model Law on Cross-Border Insolvency (2014) and the Singapore Convention on International Settlement Agreements resulting from Mediation (2019) (Singapore Convention). The ICC, which came into being in 1919, is now represented in over 130 countries. It established the ICC International Court of Arbitration in 1923 and published the first edition of the Uniform Customs and Practice for Documentary Credits (UCP) in 1933, with the latest edition (known as UCP 600) being issued in 2007. Its more recent contributions include INCOTERMS (International Commercial Terms), first published in 1936, defining trade terms for the purposes of a consistent and harmonised worldwide usage. INCOTERMS was most recently revised in 2019.

UNIDROIT was formed in 1926 as an auxiliary organ of the now defunct League of Nations. It is an independent inter-governmental organisation with 63 Member States.[59] One of its principal aims is to study 'needs and methods for modernising, harmonising and co-ordinating private and in particular commercial law as between States and Groups of States and to formulate uniform law instruments, principles and rules to achieve those objectives'.[60] UNIDROIT publications include the Convention on a Uniform Law on the Formation of Contracts for the International Sale of Goods adopted in the Hague in 1964. The UNIDROIT Principles might be considered as its flagship publication, first published in 1994 and now in its fourth edition. The UNIDROIT Principles is a form of soft law. Although lacking binding force, it contributes to convergence as it has persuasive value before courts and tribunals as a well-researched compilation of contract law as applied by many existing legal systems.

The HCCH has as its purpose 'the progressive unification of the rules of private international law'.[61] It has promulgated 39 international conventions and one soft law instrument (The Hague Principles on Choice of Law in International Commercial Contracts (2015)). Its conventions have served to harmonise key aspects of international civil procedure and legal cooperation between states, such as the use of the apostilles for the certification of public documents, the service of foreign process, the taking of evidence abroad, and the recognition and enforcement of foreign judgments.[62]

[58] UNCITRAL, 'A Guide to UNCITRAL: Basic Facts about the United Nations Commission on International Trade Law' (UN Vienna Office Publishing and Library Section, 2013) 1–2.

[59] UNDROIT, 'History and Overview' International Institute for the Unification of Private Law, available at www.unidroit.org/about-unidroit/overview.

[60] ibid.

[61] Statute of the Hague Conference on Private International Law 1955, Art 1. See also HCCH, 'Vision and Mission', available at www.hcch.net/en/about/vision-and-mission.

[62] HCCH, 'About HCCH', available at www.hcch.net/en/about.

A number of organisations are engaged in initiatives to map out differences between commercial legal principles prevalent regionally and elsewhere. Examples of such initiatives in Asia, for example, may be found in the work of the Asian Business Law Institute (ABLI), the Asian Principles of Private International Law (APPIL) project, and the Principles of Asian Contract Law (PACL) project. Founded in 2016, ABLI is based in Singapore. It 'initiates, conducts and facilitates research with a view to providing practical guidance in the field of Asian legal development and promoting the convergence of Asian business laws'.[63] As part of its Legal Convergence Series, ABLI has produced practical guides comprising concise summaries of the business laws in various Asian jurisdictions. Publications include 'Asian Principles for the Recognition and Enforcement of Foreign Judgments', which analyses legal processes for the recognition and enforcement of foreign money judgments in Association of Southeast Asian Nations (ASEAN) states as well as Australia, China, India, Japan, and South Korea.[64] ABLI has also produced guides on the 'Regulation of Cross-Border Transfers of Personal Data in Asia' (2018) and on 'Corporate Restructuring and Insolvency in Asia' (2020).

The APPIL project operates from Doshisha University in Kyoto. It is led by private international law academics from participating East and South-east Asian jurisdictions, including China, Hong Kong, Indonesia, Japan, Korea and Singapore. The APPIL project seeks to harmonise private international law rules and principles in Asia through the publication of model principles on various aspects of private international law.[65] The PACL project was started by a group of Asian scholars.[66] It focuses on the harmonisation of substantive contract law in Asia,[67] and is working towards publishing an Asian equivalent to the 'Principles of European Contract Law', which came out in 2009.[68] Those working on the project take the view that the PACL is a 'necessity'[69] for any convergence of private law in Asia.

B. Evaluating Efforts at Convergence

How successful are the soft law initiatives just described likely to be in shaping a *lex mercatoria*? It is helpful to consider how the success or failure of a soft law instrument in driving convergence can be measured. A practical way is to ask whether the relevant soft law instrument has made any meaningful, positive impact on the law. As Henry Gabriel put it:

> Regardless of how well drafted a soft law instrument is, if it does not ultimately have some positive effect on the law, it becomes no more than an interesting academic exercise. Soft law

[63] Asian Business Law Institute, 'About Us', available at abli.asia/Introduction.

[64] See A Chong (ed), *Recognition and Enforcement of Foreign Judgements in Asia* (Asian Business Law Institute, 2017).

[65] W Chen and G Goldstein, 'The Asian Principles of Private International Law: objectives, contents, structure and selected topics on choice of law' (2017) *Journal of Private International Law* 411, 434.

[66] Including the President of the Institute for Asia Private Law (South Korea) Young June Lee, Professor Shiyuan Han (Tsinghua University), Professor Naoki Kanayama (Keio University) and Professor Wan Zejiang.

[67] J Ka, 'Introduction to PACL', available at wgtn.ac.nz/_data/assets/pdf_file/0018/920106/Ka.pdf.

[68] See Chong, *Recognition and Enforcement* (2017).

[69] S Han, 'Principles of Asian Contract Law: An Endeavor of Regional Harmonization of Contract Law in East Asia' (2013) 58 *Villanova Law Review* 589, 591.

> instruments are not ends in themselves but are usually the basis for further developments in the law. As such, soft law instruments tend to be drafted with the express purpose of providing guidance for the best practices. They often are drafted as forward-looking by relying on current and potential industry usages and customs.[70]

Soft law initiatives have their advantages.[71] The first is speed. The cumbersome process of negotiating, drafting and ratifying a treaty makes it difficult for such instruments to keep pace with changes in commercial law. Once promulgated, a convention still needs to be ratified by a specified number of states before it takes effect. Thus, it would often be quicker to adopt and publish soft law guidelines with a view to allowing consensus to coalesce around them.[72] A second advantage is that 'soft law has the flexibility of selective harmonization'.[73] Hard law instruments have to be consistent with existing laws of Member States. It will take time to revise laws and remove contradictions before a country adapts a convention or hard law instrument. Third, soft law avoids some of the more political aspects of law-making. In Gabriel's words, 'The political interests that care about binding legal instruments show much less resistance to soft law'.[74] The promulgators of soft law enjoy the flexibility of crafting instruments that truly reflect desired best practice, as opposed to binding instruments which are subject to political compromises among drafting states. Such bargaining can render conventions shadows of formal, more ambitious drafts.

The fate of CISG is indicative of what can be achieved and what might remain elusive. Michael Bonell observes that the success of the CISG is reflected by a number of outcomes. First, CISG has helped to bring certainty to the contractual relationships to which it applies by eliminating uncertainty over the applicable law governing such contracts. Second, empirical evidence suggests that only a small segment of traders (typically, commodity traders) routinely exclude the application of CISG. That said, in common law jurisdictions (such as Australia[75] and Singapore), CISG is routinely excluded by contract drafters, raising questions as to whether there is general acceptance and utilisation of CISG in international commercial contracting at least in common law states. Third, the chaos that it was feared would ensue from CISG being construed differently by different courts has not materialised, largely due to the availability of increasingly accessible online databases of CISG opinions and decisions. Finally, CISG has been adopted as a model contract law and has influenced the reform of contract law in several jurisdictions.[76]

The success of the CISG as an agent of convergence has not been limited to domestic law reform. Some have gone as far as to suggest that CISG is responsible for driving international convergence on the concept of breach of contract and compensation for

[70] HD Gabriel, 'The Use of Soft Law in the Creation of Legal Norms in International Commercial Law: How Successful Has It Been?' (2019) 40 *Michigan Journal of International Law* 413, 420.

[71] ibid.

[72] ibid 416.

[73] ibid 419.

[74] ibid 419.

[75] See L Spagnolo, 'The Last Outpost: Automatic CISG Opt Outs, Misapplications and the Costs of Ignoring the Vienna Sales Convention for Australian Lawyers' (2009) 10 *Melbourne Journal of International Law* 141.

[76] Bonell, 'The CISG' (2008) 5.

delivery of non-confirming goods in Europe and Asia.[77] Nonetheless, the long and arduous process of drafting CISG raises the question of whether multilateral conventions are the best means of promoting convergence. CISG took a few decades to be negotiated and drafted, and even then there remains a sense that it has not bridged (and perhaps can never fully bridge) the many differences in the legal values, norms and principles of signatory states. Thus, for all its achievements, it is worth remembering that CISG does not deal with a substantial number of legal issues, such as the sale of shares and securities, negotiable instruments, and important sale of goods issues, such as liability for death or personal injury caused by goods.[78]

The UNIDROIT Principles are another example of mixed success. The instrument was meant to be a soft law method of promoting convergence in international commercial law. Although published under UNIDROIT's auspices, the principles were drawn up by an international group of scholars and lawyers acting in their personal capacities, not as representatives of their respective governments.[79] On one view, the UNIDROIT Principles demonstrates the ineffectiveness of soft law as an agent of convergence. Relatively few parties and courts and tribunals rely on the PICC (what might be termed the 'no practical impact argument'). One study found that, as of 2016, only 259 reported judgments and 193 arbitral awards expressly cited the UNIDROIT Principles.[80] Given the small number of decisions, it would appear that the instrument has had little impact on the development of international commercial law. In response to the no practical impact argument, Gabriel argues that the impact and influence that soft law instruments like the UNIDROIT Principles have might not manifest themselves in the form of judicial recognition. Their benefits might not be 'visible'. On statistics of court and tribunal decisions, Gabriel points out that the same exclude unreported decisions. Judicial and arbitral decisions cannot be the only indicator of an instrument's success or influence. There have in contrast been numerous law review articles and books on the instrument. Moreover, the statistics cannot account for contracts which designate the UNIDROIT Principles but over which no dispute requiring litigation or arbitration has arisen. In short, looking exclusively at reported cases can result in a misleading view of the true extent of the UNIDROIT Principles' influence.[81]

Bonell further argues that the instrument's impact may be multifaceted and take the following forms: (1) reception in academic and professional circles; (2) service as a model for national and international legislation; (3) guidance to commercial parties in contractual negotiations; and (4) rules of law referred to in judicial proceedings.[82] This more holistic assessment has been borne out by a subsequent study, conducted by Bonell, which surveyed some 150 decisions citing the UNIDROIT Principles. In nearly half of those cases, the UNIDROIT Principles were mentioned in connection with the application of provisions of domestic law. This suggests that the instrument influences

[77] J Basedow, 'Towards a Universal Doctrine of Breach of Contract: The Impact of the CISG' (2005) 25 *International Review of Law and Economics* 487, 498.

[78] Bonell (n 27) 3.

[79] Vogenauer (n 36) 154.

[80] Gabriel, 'The Use of Soft Law in the Creation of Legal Norms' (2019) 422.

[81] ibid.

[82] MJ Bonell, 'The UNIDROIT Principles in Practice – The Experience of the First Two Years' [1997] *Uniform Law Review* 34.

the interpretation and application of domestic law. In several decisions, the instrument was used to interpret or supplement international uniform law instruments (mostly in relation to Article 7 of CISG, which provides that the CISG must be interpreted by taking its international character and the need to promote uniformity into account). Even where parties did not expressly apply the instrument as governing law, some courts and tribunals applied the principles there as 'general principles of international commercial law.'[83]

Besides the no practical impact argument, there is the view that soft law, by its non-binding nature, is unsuitable for achieving convergence. This is because parties are free to exclude or include any combination of the principles set out in an instrument. Thus, soft law instruments (it is said) may lead to greater divergence in the legal principles used to govern transnational commercial relationships. In response, others have suggested that realistically speaking it is unlikely that commercial parties would exclude cardinal provisions (such as the principle of good faith) of the UNIDROIT Principles or similar instruments. As Vogenauer forcefully puts it:

> Derogating from these rules would effectively amount to one of the parties suggesting to the other during the negotiations: 'Let our transaction be governed by the UNIDROIT Principles, but, hey, even if I act fraudulently you shall not be able to avoid the contract.'[84]

Finally, while empirically few commercial parties may specify soft law instruments such as the UNIDROIT Principles as the governing law of their contract, the instrument can still serve the important function of bridging cultural differences between trading parties. Vogenauer states:

> At present, the relatively rare instances in which the parties choose the [UNIDROIT Principles] or arbitral tribunals apply them in the absence of a choice of state law seem to be triggered by the parties' inability to reach agreement on any state law at all. This is particularly the case where both parties find it difficult to accept the overall cultural and ideological background of the other's legal tradition. Thus, an optional instrument is perhaps particularly useful for transactions between parties from Western and non-Western, e.g. Arab, countries.[85]

Generalising from the foregoing, it will be apparent that there are limitations on resorting to soft law alone to bring about convergence. First, soft law instruments are often not well known. A lack of familiarity means that there will be little incentive for commercial parties and their lawyers to adopt soft law instruments as the applicable law of a contract. Commercial parties would understandably be reluctant to be the first or 'test' case. As Gabriel comments: 'Unfortunately, the aspect of uncertainty in soft law instruments … becomes a self-fulfilling circular argument: they are not understood because they are not understood.'[86] Second, soft law may prompt over-legislation. For instance, in the context of international commercial arbitration, Michael Schneider has cautioned that the standardising effect of soft law (in the form of procedural guidelines) can dull

[83] Bonell (n 27) 25.
[84] Vogenauer (n 36) 155–56.
[85] ibid 181.
[86] Gabriel (n 70) 422.

one of arbitration's best features – its ability to offer bespoke procedures catering to the particular needs of a dispute.[87]

Whether and when the bounds of appropriate legislation are exceeded is a subjective assessment and individuals may reasonably disagree on how much standardisation is too much. Paul Friedland suggests to the contrary that the ability of soft law to 'universalise' arbitral procedure is precisely what brings benefits. Soft law procedural guidelines can foster common expectations among parties as to the proper conduct of arbitral proceedings. Since parties will likely regard a process as fair if it conforms to their expectations, soft law can enhance perceptions of arbitral proceedings as impartial. In addition, soft law advances what Friedland refers to as the 'familiarity factor'. He argues that the reason why international commercial parties choose arbitration over litigation in established legal jurisdictions (such as England) is frequently unrelated to questions of neutrality or the integrity of judges, but is instead the perception that litigation before a court is too 'foreign' and so unfamiliar. The universalising effect of soft law helps to make international arbitration less foreign for commercial parties in comparison to the national court system of a country other than their own.[88]

Can there be too much convergence? There are two opposing views. One is that the promulgation of a unified private law code (even if only regionally) would be an achievement. This is because 'common rules and principles of private law will provide a superior basis for constructing a transnational civil society' and 'Development of a civil code, perhaps commencing with contract law, would serve as the next institutional step in creating a system of governance that reinforces the aims … of ever-closer unity whilst respecting the sovereignty of nation States'.[89] Others warn that an unbridled pursuit of convergence can be unwise as:

> International commerce is best served not by imposing deficient legal schemes upon it but by encouraging the development of the best schemes in a climate of free competition and choice … What should no longer be tolerated is the unthinking acceptance of a goal of uniformity and its doctrinaire imposition on the commercial community.[90]

Diversity will offer parties the benefits of flexibility and choice, especially when it comes to available dispute resolution procedures.[91] Therefore, while harmonisation can be helpful, complete convergence – pervasive identity – should not be the desired goal.

[87] M Schneider, 'The Essential Guidelines for the Preparation of Guidelines, Directives, Notes, Protocols and other Methods Intended to Help International Arbitration Practitioners to Avoid the Need for Independent Thinking and to Promote the Transformation of Errors into 'Best Practices' in L Levy and Y Derains (eds), *Liber Amicorum en L'Honneur de Serge Lazareff* (Pedone, 2011) 567, cited in PD Friedland, 'Soft Law and Power' in S Brekoulakis et al (eds), *The Evolution and Future of international Arbitration, International Arbitration Law Library Vol 37* (Kluwer Law International, 2016) 341, 342.

[88] PD Friedland, 'Soft Law and Power' in S Brekoulakis et al (eds) *The Evolution and Future of international Arbitration, International Arbitration Law Library Vol 37* (Kluwer Law International, 2016) 341, 343–44.

[89] H Collins, 'Why Europe Needs a Civil Code: Europe Identity and the Social Model' in M Andenas et al (eds), *Liber Amicorum Guido Alpa: Private Law Beyond the National Systems* (British Institute of International and Comparative Law 2007) 259, 268.

[90] (1990) 106 LQR 530.

[91] FJM De Ly, 'Paradigmatic Changes – Uniformity, Diversity, Due Process and Good Administration of Justice: The Next Thirty Years' in S Brekoulakis et al (eds) *The Evolution and Future of international Arbitration, International Arbitration Law Library Vol 37* (Kluwer Law International, 2016) 21, 27.

C. Will International Commercial Mediation Detract from the *Lex Mercatoria*?

If international commercial mediation takes off, disputes will increasingly be settled by the parties' agreement. There will then be fewer pronouncements by courts or arbitral tribunals on the substantive principles of the *lex mercatoria*. Would this outcome hinder the development of the *lex mercatoria*?

Owen Fiss argues that out of court settlement comes at the expense of justice. On this view, adjudication serves not just a private function (dispute resolution), but also a public interest by ensuring long-term development of legal principles through judgments.[92] Some have suggested, to the contrary, that encouraging mediation would not impact the development of the common law in English courts.[93] But it should be noted that not every case litigated in the courts will serve the public interest to the same extent. Even if mediation gains pre-eminence, it is unlikely completely to replace litigation in every type of case. Instead, more contentious cases involving novel issues are inherently more likely to proceed to litigation, regardless of the relative popularity of mediation. It is these latter types of cases, rather than the less legally complex cases that are well suited for mediation, that will make the biggest contribution to the development of the law.

Further, the possibility of mediation taking over from litigation and mediation as a preferred form of dispute resolution should not be taken as for granted. From a socio-legal perspective, mediation and ADR scholar Carrie Menkel-Meadow believes that it is unlikely that mediation will become the global norm in dispute resolution in the near future.[94] She divides socio-legal cultures into 'argumentative, adversarial, conversational or dialogic, face saving, and hybrid cosmopolitan' cultures (albeit acknowledging that this division of a vastly diverse global legal culture has an element of arbitrariness and simplification):

> Ordinarily I quite deplore the systematic and stereotypic descriptions of 'civilizations' or cultures … but in viewing the variations of mediation usage around the world, I have come to believe that something like these cultural formations deeply influence both legislation-rule-making and the actual practice of mediation as a form of dispute resolution.[95]

Due to these different cultures, it cannot be assumed that 'the uptake of mediation will … be a unitary development or following a clear trajectory throughout the world'.[96] In more adversarial cultures, adjudicatory form of dispute resolution (litigation or arbitration) may be preferred, whereas in face-saving cultures, mediation may be the more favoured option in comparison to adjudication, which is viewed as an undesirable

[92] See O Fiss, 'Against settlement' (1984) 93 *Yale Law Journal* 1073.

[93] See H Genn, 'ADR and Civil Justice' in *Judging Civil Justice: The Hamlyn Lectures 2009* (CUP, 2009) 78.

[94] C Menkel-Meadow, 'The Future of Mediation Worldwide: Legal and Cultural Variations in the Uptake of or Resistance to Mediation' in I Macduff (ed) *Essays on Mediation: Dealing with Disputes in the 21st Century, Global Trends in Dispute Resolution Vol 6* (Kluwer Law International, 2016) 29.

[95] ibid 39–40.

[96] ibid 41.

zero-sum game.[97] Thus, globally there is likely to be resistance to mediation, with a stronger preference for international commercial arbitration.[98]

Where an international commercial dispute is settled through mediation, the Singapore Convention enables the mediated settlement agreement to be enforced in contracting states. The aspiration is that, as a result of the Singapore Convention, mediation will in due course become as popular as arbitration. There is a concern that this might negatively impact on the development of the *lex mercatoria* or the convergence of international commercial law generally.[99] But, for the reasons just mentioned, it is too early to say whether the Singapore Convection will at some point lead to international commercial mediation becoming more popular than international commercial arbitration and reverse the current preference for the latter.

D. Will International Commercial Arbitration Detract from the *Lex Mercatoria*?

It is submitted that international commercial arbitration will be vital to the development of a body of global commercial law. This is because, as Harold Koh has noted, international arbitration is 'a process whereby public and private actors, including nation-states, corporations, international organizations, non-governmental organizations, and individuals, interact in a variety of fora to interpret, enforce, and ultimately internalize, rules of international law'.[100] The question then is: how dependent is the substantive development of transnational commercial law on international commercial arbitration? It might be suggested, for instance, that the difficulty with international commercial mediation as an engine for the development of the *lex mercatoria* identified in the foregoing section equally applies in the case of international commercial arbitration. The argument would be that, because arbitrations are confidential and private, even if arbitral tribunals make numerous pronouncements on the substantive content of the *lex mercatoria*, the public will never know. In assessing the validity of this argument, it is useful to start by considering what it is that confers validity on an arbitral award in the first place.

According to Emmanuel Gaillard, there are three competing views explaining the legitimacy of international arbitration and the award that results from such process.[101] The first is the mono-local vision. On this view, the legitimacy of international arbitration derives solely from the law of the state in which an arbitration is seated. The view asserts that an arbitration can only validly take place in a given jurisdiction (the seat)

[97] ibid 42.

[98] ibid 44.

[99] See Fiss, 'Against settlement' (1984).

[100] H Koh, 'Jefferson Memorial Lecture – Transnational Legal Process after September 11th' (2004) 22 *Berkeley Journal of International Law* 337, 339, cited in M Mitsi, 'Decision Making and Legal Argumentation' in *The Decision-Making Process of Investor-State Arbitration Tribunals (International Arbitration Law Library) Vol 46* (Kluwer Law International, 2018) 22, 29.

[101] See E Gaillard, 'The Present – Commercial Arbitration as a Transnational System of Justice: International Arbitration as a Transnational System of Justice' in AJ Van den Berg (ed), *Arbitration: The Next Fifty Years, ICCA Congress Series Vol 16* (Kluwer Law International; ICCA, 2012) 66–73.

by grace of that seat's legislation. The seat, far from being little more than a forum of convenience or neutrality for the parties, serves as the legitimating bedrock of their arbitration.[102] The second view is the Westphalian vision.[103] On this view, the legitimacy of international arbitration stems from the transnational legal order and derives from the willingness of states to recognise the legitimacy of an arbitral award and enforce the same within their jurisdiction. In contrast to the mono-local theory, the legitimacy of an arbitral award does not depend upon the legitimacy of a single state (the seat). Instead, an award is legitimised *a posteriori* insofar as it meets an enforcing state's criteria for recognition. Each state has the right to determine the conditions under which an award will be judicially recognised and enforced within the state's territory.[104]

The third vision is the transnational vision. On this view, the legitimacy of international arbitration stems from collective state practice and agreements, such as the 1958 New York Convention, the UNCITRAL Model Law, and other internationally agreed guidelines and best practices. Arbitral tribunals and their awards therefore derive their legitimacy from the plurality of state actions affirming the validity of international arbitration.[105] The transnational view is not the same as the Westphalian vision, since the transnational vision stresses global trends and developments in arbitration. According to Gaillard, the transnational view does not go so far as to suggest that international arbitration derives its legitimacy from a supranational law of merchants or *lex mercatoria*. For Gaillard, the transnational view does not envisage an arbitral 'anarchy' politically and conceptually detached from the sovereignty of a state. He posits to the contrary that 'the transnational vision considers that international arbitration is anchored in the collectivity of legal systems. As such, this vision of judicial collectivism embraces rather than rejects the laws derived from national legal systems.'[106]

Taking all three views together, none suggests that international arbitration is detached from national law or judicial systems. The differences between them concern the state or states whose laws serve as the source of legitimacy. This is not a wholly theoretical debate, however, because the differences carry practical significance, depending on which view is espoused. Suppose, for example, that an arbitral tribunal is tasked with ascertaining the applicable law on a particular issue that it has to determine. Should the tribunal apply the choice of law rules of the seat, of an enforcing state or states, or of

[102] ibid 67–68.

[103] The Peace of Westphalia, which resulted from the signing of treaties in Osnabrück and Münster, brought about an end to the Thirty Years' War (1618–1648) and Fifty Years' War (1598–1648) in Europe respectively. The Peace was essentially based on an understanding that it would be for the ruler of each state to regulate the affairs of the same. cf, for instance, in matters of religion, the maxim *cuius regio, eius religio* ('the religion of a region is for the region to determine') encapsulating the outcome of the Thirty Years' War. The Westphalian order ushered in by the Peace was thus premised on a territorial view of law with each state having the right as sovereign to determine the law applicable within its territory. In many ways, the Westphalian order and territorial principle established by the Peace continues to influence the development of law generally today, many centuries later.

[104] Gaillard, 'The Present' (2012) 68.

[105] The transnational vision is often characterised as a 'delocalised theory' because it does not attribute the validity of arbitration to the law of any given state (neither the law of the seat or of any particular enforcing state or states). In contrast, a cardinal tenet of the mono-local theory view is that every international commercial arbitration must have a seat. For the mono-localist, there can be no such thing as a delocalised international commercial arbitration.

[106] Gaillard (n 101) 68–69.

some other source? A tribunal adhering to the mono-local view may, in the absence of any express designation by the parties, consider itself bound to apply the seat's choice of law rules. A tribunal holding the Westphalian vision may, on the other hand, not feel itself bound by the choice of law rules of the seat. Rather, the tribunal might consider the rules of the multiple jurisdictions where its award can be enforced and select the conflict of law rules best suited to the parties' needs (usually, for want of any express designation by the parties, the choice of law rules of the place of closest connection to the matter in dispute). Finally, a tribunal preferring the transnational vision would also not view itself bound by the conflicts rules of the seat. But what distinguishes the transnational and Westphalian visions is that the former goes a step further by considering global trends in the development: what is the most accepted practice insofar as choice of law is concerned?[107]

Now suppose a national court is called upon to enforce a foreign arbitral award. A mono-local court will ask whether the court of the seat has set aside the award. If the court at the seat has done so, there is no award to be enforced. For a Westphalian court, the mere fact that an award has been annulled by the court of the seat is an important factor to take into account, but not a bar to recognition and enforcement of the award. The transnational court, on the other hand, will not view annulment by the court of the seat as fatal to a claim for enforcement and will instead assess the validity of the award by reference to internationally accepted standards. Gaillard argues that the New York Convention marks a shift from the mono-local to the Westphalian vision. He suggests that current global arbitration development is now in transition from the Westphalian to the transnational vision:

> Widespread acceptance of the New York Convention by States thus evidences a shift away from the traditional paradigm that grants unwarranted discretion to the seat of arbitration. By giving some discretion to the national legal systems at the place (or places) of enforcement to review arbitral awards, the Convention appears at the very least to accommodate the Westphalian representation of international arbitration/ But the convention is primarily a declaration of the overarching international standards to which contracting states agree to adhere, the boundaries within which they will exercise their discretion. In this way, the Convention exemplifies the normative, collective activity of the states in which the legitimacy and validity of the transnational arbitral legal order is anchored.[108]

What emerges from this discussion is that, because of confidentiality, international commercial arbitration is probably not well suited to any systematic development of substantive commercial law over time. International commercial courts which adhere to the principle of open justice may consequently be in a better position to contribute to the substantive development of the *lex mercatoria*. That being said, the *lex mercatoria* is not merely a set of substantive legal principles. It is also about what constitutes due process in cross-border commercial dispute resolution. In corresponding fashion, the New York Convention and the Model Law allow for awards to be struck down or refused recognition and enforcement if they were obtained without observance of due process,

[107] ibid.
[108] ibid 73.

if they cover a matter which is not susceptible to resolution by arbitration, or if they are contrary to the public policy (including adherence to rules of fairness and impartiality) of a given jurisdiction. This means that the public pronouncements of courts (including international commercial courts) in their judgments and of arbitration-related bodies in their rules, guidelines and other soft law instruments on what constitutes due process in international commercial proceedings, arbitrability, fairness or impartiality can significantly contribute to the articulation of transnational norms of fairness, impartiality and good faith insofar as the determination of commercial disputes is concerned. This would especially be the case to the extent that Gaillard's transnational vision gains prevalence.

10

Developing the *Lex Mercatoria*

TIONG MIN YEO

I. Focusing the Inquiry

The historical *lex mercatoria*, or law merchant, is said to have emerged from the customary practices of ancient and medieval seamen and traders who found themselves in need of a common set of rules to govern mercantile trade; rules which would be broadly applicable (and acceptable) to trading parties regardless of their places of origin.[1] To the extent that such a body of legal rules did in fact exist,[2] its significance derived from two main features: (1) its independence (since it was not promulgated by any one decision-maker or legislator, but was drawn from the established practice of the merchant community); and (2) relatedly, its practical utility and credibility (as a set of rules which were created in the marketplace and therefore reflected the actual practices and needs of those subject to it).[3]

Over the centuries, as looser feudal forms of governance gave way to a new, Westphalian order which emphasised the sovereignty of states and their monopoly on legal norm-setting and rule-making, this set of rules – the putative medieval *lex mercatoria* – was gradually incorporated into national municipal laws by various European codifications of commercial law and in England by judicial recognition of those principles and rules as forming part of the common law.[4] By the nineteenth century, the medieval *lex mercatoria* had been absorbed into and replaced by a patchwork of municipal commercial laws promulgated by states and developed henceforth in jurisdictional silos.

[1] KP Berger, 'The *Lex Mercatoria* (Old and New) and the Trans Lex-Principles', available at translex.uni-koeln.de/the-lex-mercatoria-and-the-translex-principles_ID8.

[2] See O Volckart and A Mangels, 'Are the Roots of the Modern Lex Mercatoria Really Medieval?' (1999) 65 *Southern Economic Journal* 427; see also N Hatzimihail, 'The Many Lives-and Faces-of Lex Mercatoria: History as Genealogy in International Business Law' (2008) 71 *Law and Contemporary Problems* 169.

[3] Berger, 'The *Lex Mercatoria* (n 1) at para 40, noting that it has been argued that 'the dimension and commendable significance of the medieval mercantile community lies in the creation of its own law out of its own needs and its own views'.

[4] C Cutler, 'Medieval *lex mercatoria*' in *Private Power and Global Authority* (CUP, 2003); see also Berger (n 1) at para 38.

Some have observed that that state-centric patchwork of laws is now beginning to look increasingly dated.[5] The ability of state-endorsed top-down law-making processes to keep pace with the rapidly increasing needs and sophistication of the international business community has increasingly been called into question. For evidence of this, one need look no further than the proliferation of industry-developed standard form contracts and other forms of bottom-up self-regulation developed by private or non-governmental entities to fill the gaps.[6] As commercial activity extends beyond borders and thereby implicates the jurisdiction of multiple states, the traditional rules for the resolution of conflicts of laws have come under ever-greater strain. The exercise of disaggregating what is in fact a global commercial transaction with multiple nodes of commercial activity in an attempt to identify a single jurisdiction most closely connected with the transaction is becoming more and more difficult and artificial. In this context, the notion of having a single set of rules that governs all commercial transactions irrespective of where the parties are from and regardless of the connections of the transaction with a specific country, is clearly attractive. It will significantly reduce the transaction costs of international commerce, and greatly simplify the dispute resolution process. So why is the *lex mercatoria* so controversial today?

In the academic discourse on the *lex mercatoria*, there is precious little common ground.[7] There is debate over its historical origins and whether the historical *lex mercatoria* ever existed. There is debate as to whether the *lex mercatoria* can justifiably be referred to as law, or whether the putative *lex* is in fact no more than a collection of best practices or convention. Even amongst those who agree that it is law, its juridical basis remains mired in controversy; is the *lex mercatoria* an independent, freestanding and supranational body of rules, or does it exist only as a creature of national laws to the extent permitted by the principle of party autonomy?[8] The way forward from these seemingly intractable theoretical difficulties and differences of views should be to move *past* them. Rather than attempting to resolve irreconcilable doctrinal differences of view, it would be more practical to focus on ascertaining the content of the *lex mercatoria*, for two reasons.

First, the main obstacle to a wider adoption of the *lex mercatoria* as a governing law arises not from difficulties as to its juridical basis, but from the vagueness of its content and the resultant uncertainty as to the effect of its application. Over the ages, there have been numerous attempts to codify commercial law principles which are applicable across borders. The ancient *lex maritima* was variously referred to in the Code

[5] Berger (n 1) at para 55. The role and influence of the state has diminished in significance following the globalisation of the economy. We now live in a world which is more interconnected and interdependent than ever before; and importantly, these global connections are formed not just on the inter-*national* plane but *directly* between all manner of actors – including corporations, non-governmental organisations and individuals – without the intervention of the state: see the Introduction to this book.

[6] Berger (n 1) at para 55.

[7] See ch 9.

[8] Berger (n 1) at paras 50–53: On one view, the *lex mercatoria* is a mass of rules and principles which derive their validity and enforceability from the principle of party autonomy in contract law, to the extent that doctrine is accepted and applied in domestic national laws. Another more radical view regards the *lex mercatoria* as an independent, supranational legal system which exists and derives validity autonomously. See also KP Berger, 'Berthold Goldman and the Dijon School', available at translex.uni-koeln.de/1/_/the-rebirth-of-the-lex-mercatoria-by-the-dijon-school.

of Hammurabi, the Rhodian Sea Law (*Lex Rhodia*) and later in the influential Rôles d'Olerón of England and France and the Sea Law of the Hanseatic League.[9] Likewise, the historical *lex mercatoria*, can trace its roots to the thirteenth-century Little Red Book of Bristol and later to a sixteenth-century Venetian treatise, the *Tractatus de Mercatura*.[10] As mentioned, the *lex mercatoria* later disappeared as it was absorbed into various European codifications of commercial law, like the English Sale of Goods Act 1893 and the French *Code de Commerce* 1807.[11] There have been major modern efforts at describing and even codifying (albeit typically in soft law form) aspects of the rules of transnational commercial law, such as in the United Nations Convention on Contracts for the International Sale of Goods (CISG), the various model laws promulgated by the UNCITRAL and the UNIDROIT Principles of International Commercial Contracts (UNIDROIT Principles).

But these past and modern instruments have usually been projects of limited and modest scope, covering specific areas of commercial law (for instance, the law of the sea, the law relating to the international sales of goods, or the law governing aspects of international commercial contracts), as opposed to comprehensive legislation capable of general application. None of these can, on their own, claim to be a *lex mercatoria* of universal applicability. Commercial parties will only designate the *lex mercatoria* as the governing law of their international commercial contracts if the benefits of doing so outweigh the costs. The main benefit of a *lex mercatoria* to commercial parties is the reduction of the transaction costs needed to investigate the similarities and dissimilarities of national laws and the sometimes intractable problems of conflict of laws. The main disadvantage of the *lex mercatoria* emerges from an important empirical study of cases in international arbitration, which found few parties choose the *lex mercatoria* to govern their contracts because of uncertainty resulting from the vagueness of its contents and (as a corollary) unfamiliarity with and lack of information about the *lex mercatoria*.[12] This means that on average respondents reckoned that the risks of relying on transnational law exceeded the benefits.[13]

This should not be surprising. Uncertainty as to the *content* of a legal rule is costly because parties have no clear idea what their obligations are and such ignorance makes it more likely that there will be disputes between the parties.[14] For the *lex mercatoria* to be a viable replacement for national laws to govern commercial transactions, there must be sufficient certainty as to its substantive contents. Unless the contents of the *lex mercatoria* are ascertained and developed, and restated or described in a manner

[9] Berger (n 1) at paras 4–23. See also 'Rhodian Sea Law' in *Encyclopaedia Britannica*, available at www.britannica.com/event/Rhodian-Sea-Law. For the principles of the Rôles d'Olerón, see translex.uni-koeln.de/116770/_/a-lex-mercatoria-of-the-sea-in-piergiovanni-vito-from-lex-mercatoria-to-commercial-laws-207-et-seq-.

[10] Berger (n 1) at paras 24–37.

[11] ibid at para 38.

[12] C Drahozal, 'Contracting out of National Law: An Empirical Look at the New Law Merchant' (2005) 80 *Notre Dame Law Review* 523, 546. Drahozal also notes that besides the vagueness of the rules of the *lex mercatoria*, another factor for its lack of popularity might be unfamiliarity with it; ie a 'lack of practical experience and the fact that no information has been available on the subject of transnational commercial law'. See also ch 9.

[13] ibid 547.

[14] ibid 546.

acceptable to the international business community, it will neither be helpful nor viable as a body of rules for the governance of global commerce.

Second, the ascertainment and development of the body of legal rules which comprise the *lex mercatoria* remains viable irrespective of its theoretical basis. Thus, in the context of *public international law*, nations adopt one of two diametrically opposed positions.[15] For states which hold a monist perspective, public international law rules (whether arising from a treaty, custom or other source) are immediately applicable as part of domestic law. For states which take the dualist view, public international law is not automatically applicable within the domestic legal system until integrated by a domestic juristic act (for example, domestic legislation or incorporation into the common law). But this difference has not been an impediment to the development of public international law.

A similar debate has crystallised around the nature of the *lex mercatoria* – whether it is a source of supranational law which is binding without more or whether it is merely abstract content with no independent legal force unless incorporated into domestic law. The point is that the development of the *lex mercatoria* remains viable regardless of one's view as to its juridical basis. Take, for instance, the development of the *lex mercatoria* in international commercial arbitration.[16] An arbitral tribunal that subscribes to a delocalised theory of arbitration would not be opposed to the development of the *lex mercatoria* as an independent, freestanding source of law. Arbitral tribunals which do not work within the delocalised theory may develop the same legal content, albeit within the framework of a national law.

The same holds true for the development of the *lex mercatoria* in courts of law.[17] Whether the historical practices of medieval courts in applying a *lex maritima* or *lex mercatoria* is evidence of a universal source of law or merely incorporation of best practices from abroad into domestic law has generated much academic controversy.[18] If that debate is to be any guide, there will be different views on how international commercial norms will be applied by municipal courts (including international commercial courts) today. Will it be because the courts recognise an international source of law or because they treat these norms as having been incorporated into their domestic rules? In either scenario, the point remains that it is possible to work towards the convergence

[15] See generally C Dubay, 'General Principles of International Law: Monism and Dualism', available at www.judicialmonitor.org/archive_winter2014/generalprinciples.html.

[16] Today, there is broad global acceptance of that arbitrators may apply the *lex mercatoria* to settle disputes within their jurisdiction, and such awards will enforced under national laws: see for example G Born, *International Commercial Arbitration*, 3rd edn (Kluwer Arbitration, 2021) 2871, noting that Art 28(1) of the UNCITRAL Model Law (as well as some other national arbitration statutes) provides for the arbitral tribunal to apply 'rules of law' selected by the parties, and that the reference to 'rules of law', rather than merely 'law' has been interpreted as permitting parties validly to select non-national legal systems in their choice-of-law agreements. While 'the textual basis for this distinction is not obvious … it has a degree of support in the Model Law's negotiating history and in commentary'.

[17] Note, however, that whether this means that the *lex mercatoria* is recognised as an independent source of law in courts of law is more controversial, because the recognition of the *lex mercatoria* within the context of international arbitration can be rationalised as being mandated by national law.

[18] See M. Petsche, 'The Application of Transnational Law (Lex Mercatoria) by Domestic Courts' (2015) *Journal of Private International Law* 489, noting that 'it is almost universally accepted that, contrary to arbitral tribunals, domestic courts cannot and do not apply transnational law'.

of the content of the rules comprising the *lex mercatoria* regardless of the theoretical standpoint one adopts as to the rules' juridical nature. Therefore, the debate as to the legitimacy of the rules should not be allowed to derail work on *ascertaining* the content of the *lex mercatoria*.

In short, the theoretical debate as to the normative basis of the *lex mercatoria* should be secondary to the question of what its contents are. Before we can get to the question of whether commercial parties *can* apply the *lex mercatoria* to their contracts as a freestanding body of law, the anterior question is whether commercial parties *would wish to* apply the *lex mercatoria* in the first place given the uncertainty as to its contents. We must therefore focus on ascertaining what the principles of the *lex mercatoria* are.

The conventional wisdom that the *lex mercatoria* is a freestanding body of delocalised international common law rules does not represent the way forward for two main reasons. First, it is impractical for commercial parties who place a premium on predictability. Second, there are no available institutions to undertake to develop and articulate these norms. Practically, there are at least two ways to move forward. First, the development of discrete pieces of international instruments through multilateral treaties or widely adopted model laws through existing international institutions like the UNCITRAL and the Hague Conference on Private International Law. Second, the recognition of a core set of widely accepted concepts. One example of this is the published result of the study by the Asian Business Law Institute (ABLI) on the recognition and enforcement of foreign judgments in Asia that shows a high degree of convergence on the principles found within the national laws of the surveyed countries.[19] This methodology may have application in other areas of private international law. Work to map these and other areas either in a descriptive way or through soft law instruments that promote the emergence of common core concepts offer the best promise of something approximating a workable *lex mercatoria*.

II. Finding Common Ground

How might we begin to ascertain the content of the *lex mercatoria*? The task of identifying the principles and rules comprising the new *lex mercatoria* will be the work of years, if not decades, and lies far beyond the scope of this chapter. A more modest goal is to offer suggestions on how we might approach the task of distilling the content of the *lex mercatoria*. The first point is that harmonisation does not necessarily entail the pursuit of perfect uniformity in the laws of all jurisdictions. The second point is that harmonisation does not rule out a diversity of approaches in particular areas of commercial law. The *lex mercatoria* is often conceived of – at least in its ideal form – as aspiring to a convergence of commercial laws resulting in a single universally applicable law to govern transnational trade and commerce. There are a number of examples of the convergence of commercial laws; the most ambitious projects – like the UNIDROIT

[19] See A Cheong (ed), *Recognition and Enforcement of Foreign Judgments in Asia* (Asian Business Law Institute, 2017) and A Cheong (ed), *Asian Principles for the Recognition and Enforcement of Foreign Judgments* (Asian Business Law Institute, 2019).

Principles[20] and CISG[21] – involve the development of substantive rules of law which are to have global applicability. Other projects have a more regional focus – the Principles of European Contract Law (PECL, sometimes referred to as 'the Lando Principles')[22] and the Principles of Asian Contract Law (PACL)[23] are aspiring model uniform laws drawn up by leading academics in Europe and Asia respectively. There are sectoral instruments designed for specific industries. An example is the International Swaps and Derivatives Association's (ISDA) Master Agreement,[24] the most commonly used form of agreement for over-the-counter derivatives transactions. Globally, the Uniform Customs and Practice for Documentary Credits (UCP 600)[25] can claim universal application in relation to the issuance and use of letters of credit, while the INCOTERMS of the International Chamber of Commerce (ICC)[26] are widely used in international commercial transactions, especially procurement transactions. But complete uniformity is not always attainable and may not be desirable in all cases. Some degree of divergence is inevitable and even necessary to account for national or municipal interests or because of reasonable differences among stakeholders.

A. National and Municipal Interests

An advantage of the *lex mercatoria* to contracting parties is the avoidance of national laws where they do not favour the interests of the contracting parties. The obverse perspective is that the *lex mercatoria* poses a potential threat to national interests, insofar as application of the *lex mercatoria* on a matter may cause states to forsake a national interest in order to achieve transnational convergence and uniformity. Thus, a major obstacle to the development of a *lex mercatoria* lies in the tension between the need for consistency in the way in which norms are applied internationally and the need to preserve policy space for the pursuit of municipal interests.

These municipal interests can manifest themselves in a variety of ways, including in the preservation of religious or cultural values. An oft-cited example is the compatibility of Article 78 of CISG, which provides that interest must be paid to an aggrieved party, with the prohibition in Islamic law of interest as impermissible usury.[27] This has raised questions as to the applicability of the CISG to contracts which expressly provide that they are to be interpreted in accordance with Islamic law principles.[28]

[20] Available at www.unidroit.org/wp-content/uploads/2021/06/Unidroit-Principles-2016-English-bl.pdf.

[21] Available at uncitral.un.org/sites/uncitral.un.org/files/media-documents/uncitral/en/19-09951_e_ebook.pdf.

[22] Available at www.jus.uio.no/lm/eu/contract.principles/parts.1.to.3.2002.

[23] For an outline, see J Ka, 'Introduction to PACL', available at www.wgtn.ac.nz/_data/assets/pdf_file/0018/920106/Ka.pdf.

[24] For a sample agreement based on the ISDA Master Agreement, see www.sec.gov/Archives/edgar/data/1065696/000119312511118050/dex101.htm.

[25] For further information, see iccwbo.org/global-issues-trends/banking-finance/global-rules.

[26] For further information, see iccwbo.org/resources-for-business/incoterms-rules/incoterms-2020.

[27] FA kaddaf, 'Application of the United Nations Convention on Contracts for the International Sale of Goods (CISG) to Arab Islamic Countries: Is the CISG Compatible with Islamic Law Principles?' (2001) 13 *Pace International Law Review* 1, 46.

[28] ibid 56. Akaddaf notes, however, that there remains some flexibility insofar as the CISG is silent on the determination of the rate of interest, which allows judges and arbitrators to fill the gap, and potentially to characterise interest as 'compensatory indemnity instead of interest', as some arbitral tribunals have done.

Accordingly, although many issues that arise in commercial transactions will be agnostic in nature, there may be cases which involve aspects of Islamic financing (even if only peripherally) that will require special consideration. Cultural differences may also arise. For example, cash payments for high-value items may trigger a duty of inquiry in certain cultures,[29] but may be perfectly routine in other cultures,[30] with consequences for the development of international norms aimed at combatting money laundering.

There are also differences arising from history or tradition, such as the well-known differences between the common law and civilian approaches to procedural and substantive issues. One should therefore expect that there will be considerable difficulties in pursuing a monolithic uniformity on a *global* scale. The legitimacy crisis facing the Investor–State Dispute Settlement (ISDS) system discussed in chapters one and two illustrates the pitfalls of a monolithic system of norms in the approach to the governance of claims by investors against host states, when developed at an international level without adequate regard for national interests. A single uniform *lex mercatoria* across the board presumes a single homogenous *societas mercatorum* or business community. But reality is not that of a single, unified business community but of a plurality of communities. In such case, any articulation of the substantive principles of the *lex mercatoria* must incorporate a capacity for pluralism[31] and will only receive widespread acceptance if convergence is subject to overriding interests which may differ from state to state.

B. Diversity and Competition

The previous section queried whether absolute uniformity was practicable or desirable. Convergence does not proceed in a straight line. It is instead best regarded as a dialogue or a dialectical process. Diversity within a system, such as in the form of competing versions of a particular rule, can be beneficial if it leads, through a process of argument and counterargument, to a better and more appropriate synthesis of the relevant rule. This can be illustrated by reference to the common law process, which embodies an evolutionary approach to the development of legal rules. Principles can converge and diverge over and over many times before they become fully settled and accepted.

Consider the question whether a proprietary claim is available against a bribed agent (the bribee) in respect of bribe monies. The issue arose before the Singapore court in 1992.[32] At the time, the prevailing position under English law (as stated in

[29] K Busse et al, 'Cash, Cards or Cryptocurrencies? A Study of Payment Culture in Four Countries', available at eusec20.cs.uchicago.edu/eusec20-Busse.pdf at fn 19, noting that 'cash usage is mostly adopted when people make low-valued transactions'.

[30] G Millar, 'Why the Swiss still love cash' BBC (17 April 2019), available at www.bbc.com/worklife/article/20190416-why-the-swiss-still-love-cash.

[31] The alternative, if one insists on abstracting only those principles common to a *global* business community, would be as Lord Mustill argues, futile. Lord Mustill's point was that since the business community has now been immeasurably enlarged, the principles of trade law truly common to the legal systems of members of such a community would be 'so general as to be useless': see Lord Mustill, 'The New Lex Mercatoria: The First Twenty-five Years' (1988) 4 *Arbitration International* 86, 92.

[32] *Sumitomo Bank Ltd v Thahir Kartika Ratna and others and another matter* [1992] 3 SLR(R) 638.

Lister & Co v Stubbs[33]), and indeed under the laws of many other common law jurisdictions, was that a proprietary claim was not possible. Despite this, the Singapore court ultimately declined to follow *Lister*, holding that the case was 'wrong and its undesirable and unjust consequences should not be imported and perpetuated as part of our law'.[34] The Singapore court instead decided that the bribee held the bribe monies on constructive trust for the principal, thus charting a course divergent from *Lister*. That was not the end of the matter. Subsequently, the Judicial Committee of the Privy Council,[35] hearing an appeal from the New Zealand Supreme Court, also declined to follow *Lister*, holding that bribes are held on constructive trust, thereby heralding reconvergence. Two decades later, the UK Supreme Court overruled *Lister*.[36]

In this way, divergence and diversity can be a catalyst for change. They contribute towards keeping the law in a dynamic state and act as a bulwark against ossification of the law. The same is true of the development of law in civil law jurisdictions. Most European civil codes trace their roots to Roman law, an initial source of legal convergence. Subsequent centuries saw divergence as each of these strands developed independently to form hybrid systems: for example, Roman-Dutch law fusing concepts drawn from traditional Dutch feudal customary laws with Roman law. That divergence has since been followed by the re-convergence of laws with even wider geographical reach. Today, Roman-Dutch law is the foundation of the legal systems in jurisdictions such as South Africa, Indonesia and even Scotland.[37]

C. Scope and Modality of Convergence

Given that harmonisation of transnational commercial law does not entail the pursuit of perfect uniformity of commercial laws, it is submitted that it would be more appropriate to regard the *lex mercatoria* as a network of interlocking principles, rules and guidelines which deal with different aspects of transnational commerce. Diversity and divergence within that network is to be expected, and can even be advantageous where rules diverge not out of ignorance, but due to a genuine need to accommodate special interests or cater for unique situations. On this view, harmonisation does not call for a homogenisation of different parts, but the development of mechanisms that ensure that different parts cohere as a system. If we accept that some measure of diversity and divergence can be beneficial, the question is: in which areas should convergence be pursued, and in which areas should we be content to live with divergence? Where convergence is preferred, when would it be appropriate to pursue convergence through the promulgation of hard law instruments (such as treaties), and when would it be more appropriate to do so through soft law (such as model laws or guidelines)?

[33] *Lister & Co v Stubbs* (1890) 45 Ch D 1.

[34] *Sumitomo Bank Ltd v Thahir Kartika Ratna and others and another matter* [1992] 3 SLR(R) 638 [241].

[35] *Attorney General for Hong Kong v Reid (New Zealand)* [1993] UKPC 2.

[36] *FHR European Ventures LLP v Cedar Capital Partners LLC* [2014] UKSC 45.

[37] DV Cowen, 'Roman-Dutch law' in *Encyclopaedia Britannica*, available at www.britannica.com/topic/Roman-Dutch-law. For the relationship between Roman-Dutch law and Scots law; see TB Smith, 'Scots Law and Roman-Dutch Law' (1959) *Acta Juridica* 36.

i. Harmonisation as Interoperability

It is generally more difficult to achieve convergence on matters of substantive law than it is for matters of procedure. Certain areas of law are more likely than others to engage or affect strongly held local or municipal interests. Family law, for instance, is often influenced by a society's views and attitudes towards potentially controversial issues (eg, same-sex marital unions, grounds of divorce, rights of custody). The same tends to be true for insolvency and restructuring, since insolvency regimes do not operate in a vacuum and are often interlinked with local law (such as corporate and financing structures). The challenge that legal fragmentation of this sort poses is, in the main, an issue of efficiency and increased transaction costs – having different versions of a legal rule creates inefficiency, since it gives rise to uncertainty as to which version of the rule applies, and obliges commercial parties to investigate the contents of each version. The pursuit of legal convergence tackles the problem at its root by seeking to eliminate differences among competing rules. But where pursuing the convergence of applicable substantive law proves difficult or undesirable, an alternative might be to establish protocols to facilitate communication and cooperation between the courts of various interested jurisdictions.

The Judicial Insolvency Network (JIN), for instance, is a platform for facilitating judicial communication in the context of cross-border insolvencies with a view to improving efficiency and reducing the costs of insolvency proceedings in all jurisdictions concerned. In 2016, the JIN issued a set of Guidelines that establish key areas where courts presiding over parallel proceedings can cooperate – for example, sharing orders, judgments and other documents relating to the proceedings; empowering courts to direct that a notice of proceedings in its jurisdiction be given to parties in proceedings in other jurisdictions; facilitating the recognition of orders, laws or regulations of the courts of other jurisdictions without further proof; and holding joint hearings.[38] In a similar vein, HCCH's International Network of Judges (INJ) facilitates judicial communications in proceedings for the return of children abducted by a parent from one country to another.[39] The INJ facilitates general judicial communication in the form of judicial capacity-building sessions conducted by judges for judges and the development of 'guides to good practice', as well as direct, case-specific judicial communication to assist judges who must decide a case and avert the possibility of conflicting decisions (for instance, on how quickly a hearing can be scheduled in the jurisdiction of habitual residence if the abducted child is to be returned to that jurisdiction and whether the left-behind parent has rights of custody under the law of the jurisdiction of habitual residence).[40]

[38] See Judicial Insolvency Network, 'JIN Guidelines', available at jin-global.org/jin-guidelines.html.

[39] The Hague Conventions on the Civil Aspects of International Child Abduction were developed in response to the rising number of international parental child abductions in the 1970s. This created a forum-shopping problem as such abductions effectively allowed the abducting parent to seek a judicial determination of custody in the forum of his or her choice. The Conventions put a stop to this by creating a mechanism under which abducted children would first be returned to their habitual residences so as to restore the status quo. This required close cooperation between the potentially interested jurisdictions and judiciaries, and the International Hague Judicial Network was established to facilitate judicial communications concerning issues arising from the operation of the Hague Conventions: see J Kreeger, 'The International Hague Judicial Network – A Progressing Work' (2014) 48 *Family Law Quarterly* 221.

[40] ibid 224–25.

A similar effort at facilitating communication between governments and regulators is in progress, under the auspices of the Asian Business Law Institute (ABLI), in relation to cross-border transfers of data in Asia. Recognising that countries have different standards of data privacy and protection, the project covers not just the convergence of differences in national laws, but also the development of protocols to ensure interoperability between different national legal systems. It is hoped that this will facilitate cross-border business operations.[41] Another of ABLI's projects is to develop a set of Asian Principles of Business Restructuring in collaboration with the International Insolvency Institute. This project concerns the interface aspect of cross-border restructuring – how courts of different countries may effectively communicate and collaborate with one another to resolve cross-border matters.[42]

Yet another means of addressing the uncertainty that may arise from there being more than one version of a legal rule is the establishment of a robust framework for determining which version of a legal rule applies when. That is, there should be rules on choice of law, on choice of forum, and on the recognition and enforcement of judgments. These rules can go a long way to creating an environment possessing a sufficient level of certainty, without affecting the content of substantive national laws. In the context of commercial contracts, certainty can be achieved by giving effect to the parties' choices – in other words, by relying on party autonomy as an organising principle for resolving commercial conflict of law issues.

Party autonomy is an important principle from a philosophical point of view – respecting the will of the parties – but there are also important practical dividends because it: (1) supports the free market and the competition of ideas (here, in the form of legal rules); and (2) provides opportunities for the parties to allocate risk as between themselves from the outset. This philosophy also accords with prevailing notions of the free market as applied in the legal sphere. Such an approach preserves diversity where it is beneficial to the parties (because diversity offers a range of choices that cater to different situations and preferences) and yet ensures commercial certainty (parties know in advance which rule applies). The corollary to this is that the pursuit of convergence will generally be appropriate in situations where the scope for the exercise of party autonomy is limited (that is, parties have little choice as to which rule applies).

The rules on the enforcement of foreign judgments and arbitral awards are a good example. Pursuing the convergence of the rules relating to the enforcement of judgments and awards is a move in the right direction because enforcement is an area where uniformity of rules is of utmost importance. This is so because unlike in the case of substantive rules or even some procedural rules, there is little scope for the exercise of party autonomy in relation to the place of enforcement. When deciding where to enforce a judgment, a judgment creditor simply has to follow the judgment debtor's assets.

[41] ABLI, 'Transferring Personal Data in Asia', available at www.abli.asia/NEWS-EVENTS/Whats-New/ID/134.

[42] ABLI, 'Asian Principles of Business Restructuring', available at www.abli.asia/Projects/Asian-Principles-of-Business-Restructuring.

There have been a number of successful and promising international efforts at pursuing convergence on this front. Today, there are three important international instruments governing enforcement: (1) the 1958 New York Convention for arbitral awards; (2) the 2005 HCCH Convention on Choice of Court Agreements for judgments by courts which the parties have designated in their international commercial contracts; and (3) the 2018 Singapore Convention on Mediation for international mediated settlement agreements. The first has been a runaway success.[43] It is early days yet for the other two, which will take time to gain traction. Thus far there have been encouraging signs. Another potentially important international instrument is the 2019 HCCH Convention on the Recognition and Enforcement of Foreign Judgments in Civil and Commercial Matters, which is expected to enter into force on 1 September 2023 with the EU and Ukraine as initial Contracting States.

ii. Fostering Convergence through Soft Law

Pursuing the convergence of substantive laws through hard law instruments like international conventions has its limitations. The direct involvement of governments in the negotiating process engenders the risk that political considerations may end up displacing legal ones. For instance, the legal and economic soundness of the proposed rules and principles may have to be compromised in the face of political constraints and the need to forge consensus. As one commentator observed, irreconcilable differences may result in unacceptable compromises.[44]

The negotiating history of the CISG is a case in point. Because consensus could not be reached, huge gaps were left where uniformity and convergence would have been important. Crucial issues like contract validity had to be omitted from the CISG's scope because no agreement could be reached on how to proceed.[45] Even where the competing interests of negotiating parties were ostensibly reconcilable, the task of bringing them together could end up emasculating the treaty of all utility. Common ground would only be attained at a level of abstraction so high as to render the treaty toothless.

For these reasons, decentralised methods of achieving convergence, such as the promulgation of soft law, can in many cases be preferable to hard law, particularly where substantive laws are concerned. While hard law instruments will usually have escape valves for the protection of national interests, there may be concerns whether these interests have been adequately addressed and protected. From this perspective, countries may be more receptive to soft law instruments as there will be much less concern about compromising national interests. In other words, because soft laws are

[43] New York Arbitration Convention, 'In Brief', available at www.newyorkconvention.org/in+brief, noting that the New York Convention is adhered to by more than 160 nations, and has been described as the most successful treaty in private international law.

[44] M Dennis, 'Modernizing and harmonizing international contract law: the CISG and the UNIDROIT Principles continue to provide the best way forward' (2014) 19 *Uniform Law Review* 114, 139.

[45] ibid 140–41, noting that 'Topics such as validity, mistake, and agency were left out of the CISG because they were not considered suitable for harmonization', and specifically in relation to Art 4, that 'questions of validity were expressly carved out in Article 4 of the CISG because there was no consensus on how to proceed'.

not mandatory, there is considerably less pressure on negotiators to strike bad compromises in the name of consensus. Further, negotiators in their personal or professional capacities (as opposed to sitting as representatives of their governments and therefore of various political interests) have greater freedom to develop and endorse solutions and approaches which, though perhaps different from the legal positions in their home jurisdictions, may be better suited for the regulation of transnational trade and commerce.

In the international context, convergence through soft law may be criticised as ineffectual and dilatory. But it is the inherent nature of soft law to influence the formulation and modification of national laws. Although hard law has the advantage of immediate application, it also risks of becoming outdated. Soft laws, equally, may become out of date too, but at least they are not binding and they are easier to modify as a general rule. More recently, there have been complaints about a proliferation of soft law as more institutions produce such work, which can cause uncertainty and confusion. As mentioned, contract law principles may be found in the UNIDROIT Principles, Principles of European Contract Law (PECL), as well as the forthcoming Principles of Asian Contract Law (PACL). Many provisions will be repetitive. But this is in fact a boon because duplication signals convergence of thinking from different institutions, and divergences signal differences of values or preferences which may ultimately have to be resolved by a court or lawmaker seeking guidance from such instruments. One might even say that there cannot be too much soft law.

Projects promoting convergence are ongoing in many areas and at different levels, from the HCCH Principles on Choice of Law in International Commercial Contracts (the HCCH Principles),[46] to public institutional projects like ABLI's Asian Principles for the Recognition and Enforcement of Foreign Judgments, and academic projects like the Asian Principles of Private International Law (APPIL). These are resources for lawmakers and policy-makers. One good example of highly influential soft law, though not in the context of international law, is the series of Restatements from the American Law Institute (ALI) that has had profound effect on the confluence of the laws of the 50 states of the US.[47] Harmonisation can also occur organically when national laws are made with reference to international standards or practices, or in accordance with what a nation deems to be best practice as followed in other countries. For instance, the much-anticipated Civil Code of the People's Republic of China, which was promulgated in May 2020, draws on norms and rules from the UNIDROIT Principles, among other sources.[48]

iii. Role of Dispute Resolution Mechanisms

Dispute resolution mechanisms are important avenues for the convergence of procedural and substantive aspects of commercial law, for if the *lex mercatoria* is to *function*

[46] See HCCH, '40: Principles on Choice of Law in International Commercial Contracts', available at www.hcch.net/en/instruments/conventions/full-text/?cid=135.

[47] See R Revesz, 'The American Law Institute and the US Supreme Court', available at www.law.nyu.edu/sites/default/files/2016--ALI-Winter_Quarterly_Letter_0.pdf, noting that the ALI Restatements are regularly cited by the US Supreme Court.

[48] M Zou, 'A Milestone in China's Civil Law System: the Passage of its First Civil Code', available at www.qmul.ac.uk/euplant/blog/items/a-milestone-in-chinas-civil-law-system-the-passage-of-its-first-civil-code.html.

as a coherent body of law it must be consistently and predictably interpreted and applied (at least to a reasonable extent). While international commercial arbitration remains a popular means of cross-border commercial disputes adjudication, the fact that arbitral awards tend to be confidential and the lack of a widely recognised system of precedent means that international commercial arbitration's ability to foster meaningful convergence is constrained.

A network of international commercial courts could prove a more effective agent for the convergence of commercial laws relating to transnational commercial disputes. This can work at both a formal and an informal level. At the formal level, citations or cross-references to the judgments of other courts can serve as a basis for the harmonisation of rules or principles on points of law. Where foreign authorities are followed by a court, convergence is fostered. Where foreign authorities are considered but distinguished or not followed, the relationship between the divergent rules or approaches as well as the reasons for the divergence is at least explained and in this way the basis for their coexistence within the same transnational legal system (albeit in tension with each other) is properly articulated. The tension may be resolved on a future occasion.

On an informal level, conferences and seminars can provide a forum for the exchanges of ideas, knowledge and experience. The Standing International Forum of Commercial Courts (SIFoCC),[49] a global network of commercial courts, provides a platform through which likeminded commercial courts can share their experience of best practices and work together to keep abreast of the rapid pace of commercial change. An interesting question is whether international commercial courts (as opposed to international commercial arbitration tribunals) may apply supranational laws like the UNIDROIT Principles as the governing law of a dispute.

Whatever the juridical basis may be for the legitimacy of international arbitral rulings, it is clear that there is greater scope for the immediate application of soft law in the international arbitration context than in courts of law. The power of arbitral tribunals to apply supranational rules is generally acknowledged, whereas courts have generally been reluctant to accept the possibility of applying non-national rules as the governing law of a contract. The HCCH Principles give a nudge towards a more widespread acceptance of non-national rules as the governing law of an international commercial contract, suggesting that contracting parties should be allowed to do so, unless expressly provided otherwise by the law of the forum.[50] The HCCH Principles do contain a qualification, however, to the effect that any chosen system of non-state rules should be 'generally accepted on an international, supranational or regional level as a neutral and balanced set of rules', thus addressing concerns of legitimacy, certainty and fairness. Subject to whether the supranational body of rules chosen by the parties is sufficiently ascertainable and certain, there seems no reason why the parties to what is an entirely private commercial arrangement should be prohibited from choosing any given body of rules as the applicable law of their contract. If international commercial

[49] Seesifocc.org.

[50] Y Tiong Min, 'Choice of Law for Contracts: the Hague Principles from a Singaporean and Asian Perspective', 10th Yong Pung How Professorship of Law Lecture, available at ccla.smu.edu.sg/sites/cebcla.smu.edu.sg/files/Paper2017.pdf at para 37, noting that 'Article 3 will probably allow contracting parties to choose the PICC, or the Principles of European Law of Contract'.

courts and national courts more generally are limited to the application of national laws, their potential to contribute to the development of the *lex mercatoria* will be needlessly constricted.

III. Towards a System of Transnational Civil Justice

Moving forward, echoing part one of this book, the *lex mercatoria* should not be viewed as a monolithic structure cut from a single stone, but rather as a system composed of a number of different parts. A harmonised system does not require perfect uniformity; different situations call for different rules. Harmonisation should instead be viewed in terms of enhancing interoperability – a system of different parts which work seamlessly together. On this view, the *lex mercatoria* must be developed with pluralism at its core. The law merchant is not so much a solitary set of uniform rules as it is a network of rules and principles – distinct but coherent and coordinated by a body of private international law animated by the guiding principle of party autonomy. Such a *lex mercatoria* would: (1) accommodate national and other local interests wherever appropriate; (2) allow commercial parties the freedom to choose the laws that should apply to govern their private commercial arrangements; (3) minimise the uncertainty that arises from having a multiplicity of rules; and (4) provide clear direction as to which substantive principle should apply to a given situation.

PART VI

The Impact of COVID-19

11

How the Pandemic has Changed the Landscape of International Dispute Resolution

CEDRIC YEUNG

I. Introduction

As this chapter is being written, the omicron variant of COVID-19 is outcompeting the delta variant. The delta variant was highly transmissible with potentially severe effects on individuals' health, especially for unvaccinated persons. Although the omicron variant has proved to be even more highly transmissible, it is comparatively more benign in its effects. So, despite having witnessed steep spikes in their daily numbers of omicron cases, many countries are now seeing declines in COVID-19 infections as herd immunity develops in their populations. It seems that the world is at last glimpsing the daylight at the end of a very sinuous tunnel. The prognosis, however, is that COVID-19 will continue to be with us for a long time, albeit endemic rather than pandemic in character. We will have to learn to live with it, much as we have coped with other coronaviruses, such as the common cold.[1]

For the international dispute resolution community, this is an opportune time to reflect on the progress made and to shape the future by using the strategies and tools that have been fashioned to overcome the travel, quarantine and other restrictions imposed all over the world as a result of COVID-19. In this spirit, this chapter is divided into three sections. Section II describes the past, focusing on the impacts of the COVID-19 pandemic on cross-border dispute resolution. Section III considers the present, summarising the innovations that the dispute resolution community has come up with to mitigate those impacts. Section IV looks to the future, exploring possible ways in which technology can transform, not simply facilitate, dispute resolution as we know it.

[1] On COVID-19 generally, see the World Health Organization (WHO) Dashboard, at www.covid19.who.int.

II. The Past

On 11 March 2020, the World Health Organization (WHO) declared COVID-19 a pandemic. At the time, there were around 118,000 diagnosed cases on the public record, across 110 countries and territories. In response, politicians of many countries introduced policies, laws and guidance meant to enforce physical separation amongst individuals. Stay-at-home orders, travel restrictions, shutting of borders, quarantines, and social distancing measures were implemented with the hope of stopping the pandemic in its fatal path. The restriction or prohibition of physical proximity struck at the core of dispute resolution processes as then understood, whether domestic, regional or international. That is because, before the pandemic, in-person or physical hearings were the main mode of hearings (particularly, evidentiary hearings). However, the various public health measures imposed, and the raging spread of COVID-19 itself, meant that these hearings became ill-advised or impossible, without violating official guidelines.

The consequence was that, at the beginning of the pandemic, dispute resolution processes all over the world over came to a screeching halt. Courts were closed, hearings were suspended and postponed, and filing deadlines were extended.[2] Jurisdictions and institutions which had long integrated remote hearing technology had a head start in adapting to the constraints necessitated by COVID-19, but, given the scale at which remote hearings had to be conducted, many operational, technical, practical and legal issues required an urgent answer.

III. The Present

With the benefit of hindsight, there is no doubt that the international dispute resolution community has risen to this challenge spectacularly. Almost immediately after the COVID-19 pandemic was declared, procedural innovations at various levels (from filing to service to the many aspects of a hearing) were quickly designed and introduced to keep the momentum of cases going and to clear the growing backlog. The majority of these innovations came from the conduct of remote hearings. Although the foundational technology required for a satisfactory remote hearing (such as basic teleconferencing software and cybersecurity capabilities) predates the pandemic, it was used only sparingly due to the strong predilection for physical hearings. It was (and probably still is) common to treat remote hearings as a lesser option to physical hearings owing to the engaging atmosphere, collaborative setting and superior situational experience of a physical hearing overall.

A case in point is the examination of witnesses, which was often thought to be more manageable, more revealing, and more effective in a physical setting. The relative unpopularity of remote hearings explains why, prior to the COVID-19 outbreak,

[2] See Reanimation Package of Reforms, 'How COVID-19 Forces Courts to Operate Creatively Under New Circumstances' (31 March 2020), available at www.rpr.org.ua/en/news/how-covid-19-forces-courts-to-operate-creatively-under-new-circumstances.

discourses and practical guidance on when and how one should be conducted were few and far between.[3] Nevertheless, when by the merciless force of necessity, remote hearings became the only viable option for moving a case forward, participants had to abandon their reservations about the feasibility of a satisfactory remote hearing, and to focus on ensuring that it took place in an optimum way. Thanks to their efforts, a full range of innovative techniques was developed during the pandemic to meet the challenges arising from a remote hearing: from the presentation of documents via a screen-share mechanism and the creation of confidential communication channels, to the remote supervision of witnesses and pre-recording of videos on technical topics so as to combat the diminished attention span and energy experienced by participants of video conferences (so-called 'Zoom fatigue').[4]

More radical is the idea of an asynchronous hearing, where parts are conducted without the real-time participation of all stakeholders. It was first conceived so as to overcome the time zone differences amongst international participants, and has since gained considerable traction. Here is an illustration by Professor Scherer (given in the context of international arbitration):[5]

> An asynchronous participation in an oral hearing could take the form of a video recording of the counsels' opening statements, for instance. They could be made available to the arbitral tribunal some time in advance of the evidentiary hearing (which could still take place in a synchronous fashion). The arbitrators could watch the opening statements at different times, at their leisure. They could also watch them as often as they wish, going back to specific points they are particularly interested in. The tribunal members could prepare the evidentiary hearing, check the oral submissions against the written submissions and evidence already on file, and possibly even pre-deliberate some questions in advance of the evidentiary hearing.

All these techniques and procedural innovations have greatly improved the remote hearing experience. This raises a question: from a user's perspective, are remote hearings now just as good as physical hearings? A survey of mostly international arbitration practitioners, completed in the summer of 2020, shows that a majority of respondents now considered fully remote hearings and in-person hearings to be the same in many crucial aspects, including the assessment of the evidence of witnesses and experts, the effectiveness of advocacy and tribunals' understanding of the case.[6]

To the extent that this is representative of the views of the general dispute resolution community, it forces us to challenge the ingrained assumption that an evidentiary hearing must, by default, take place in a physical setting where every participant is present

[3] Ahead of its time, the Seoul Protocol on Video Conferencing in International Arbitration, helpfully setting out the best practice for planning, testing and performing video conferencing in an arbitration, was published in November 2018.

[4] For our purposes, it is not necessary to go into the nitty-gritty, for which readers may turn to an excellent article by J Walker, 'Courts in Lockdown: Lessons from International Arbitration' (2020) 10 *International Journal of Private Law* 216.

[5] M Scherer, 'Asynchronous Hearings: The Next New Normal?' (Kluwer Arbitration Blog, 9 September 2020), available at www.arbitrationblog.kluwerarbitration.com/2020/09/09/asynchronous-hearings-the-next-new-normal.

[6] G Born, A Day and H Virjee, 'Empirical Study of Experiences with Remote Hearings: A Survey of Users' Views' in M Scherer, N Bassiri, MSA Wahab (eds), *International Arbitration and the COVID-19 Revolution* (Kluwer Law International, 2020) 146.

at the same time. This is an important point for policy-makers and tribunals, as they would have to decide whether physical hearings should be reinstated as the norm when the dust of COVID-19 settles. The benefits of a remote hearing, relative to a physical one, are easy to rehearse. A remote hearing lowers the carbon footprint of cross-border dispute resolution, by obviating the need for participants to travel from one country to another. This dovetails with recent initiatives aiming to make dispute resolution green.[7] Remote hearings also bring down the costs of the process by eliminating travel and accommodation expenses. Reduced costs have the further consequence of promoting access to justice, which should of course be the basic desiderata of any legal process.

On the other hand, there remains considerable resistance to the idea of making in-person hearings an exception rather than the norm. The summer 2020 survey shows that, although the majority of the respondents put remote evidentiary hearings on the same footing as physical ones across many important metrics, there remains a preference for the latter.[8] Moreover, so far as international commercial litigation is concerned, it is conceivable that lay witnesses may be struck by the majesty and solemnity of the physical setting of a courtroom, and thus more inclined to speak the truth than if the hearing is virtual.

There is a further problem facing international commercial litigation practitioners if remote hearings become the default position. It concerns a rule relating to the taking of evidence before foreign courts which exists in most civil law jurisdictions. By virtue of this rule, a court in country A cannot take evidence from a witness in country B without permission from country B. It is a rule based on the notion of sovereignty, but the specifics are often lacking. For instance, it is often unclear to which institution one should turn in order to obtain the necessary permission. The requirements are often opaque as well. To avoid treading such murky waters, witnesses generally prefer to travel to the foreign court for evidence to be taken. This would be out of the question if a remote hearing is arranged for, and problems would arise where a witness residing in a civil law jurisdiction (where the aforesaid rule applies) is to give evidence before a foreign international commercial court. By contrast, international arbitration would seem to be immune to the prohibition, because arbitration is essentially a matter of private arrangement, as opposed to an exercise of sovereign authority by a foreign body.[9] Unless something changes, this could mean that international commercial litigation would fall out of favour as international arbitration (or other transnational dispute resolution mechanisms) rises in popularity.

IV. The Future

By making physical separation a persistent social norm, the COVID-19 pandemic has led to a thorough and rapid adaptation of remote technology into the conventional

[7] eg Greenwood Arbitration, 'The Campaign for Greener Arbitrations – Guiding Principles', available at www.greenerarbitrations.com/greenpledge.

[8] Born, Day and Virjee, 'Empirical Study of Experiences (2020) 145 (Fig 7.6).

[9] See AT Reyes, 'The Delocalisation of International Dispute Resolution' (speech at the PRIME Finance Asia Conference on 10 December 2020).

process of dispute resolution. Nevertheless, the digital revolution is only just beginning. If its benefits are taken seriously, there is every possibility that remote technology would go beyond being an auxiliary part of the dispute resolution process – it holds the promise of transforming the process itself for the public good.

To illustrate the transformative potential of remote technology, we may consider an immutable procedural feature in most common law jurisdictions: a single continuous evidentiary hearing where all the evidence for every single issue of a dispute – central or peripheral – would be given and taken. This kind of 'concentrated trial' is to be the culmination of the entire dispute resolution process at first instance. Common lawyers (or at least those who have inherited the English common law system) have taken this feature as a given. As will be submitted below, remote technology offers the opportunity for the common law process to reform, and shift to a civil law model of episodic hearings. One may wonder why the common law adopts a concentrated trial model. One plausible theory is historical. In earlier times, a jury was involved for both civil and criminal trials in England. It would have been a logistical challenge for the court to convene the same panel of jurors together for a number of short, discrete hearings.[10] More attractive was a concentrated trial where the jury had to gather and participate in one continuous sitting, involving less trouble for both the court (in terms of appointment and ensuring attendance) and the jurors (in terms of travel time and expenses).

By contrast, most civil law jurisdictions have never introduced jurors to civil disputes. The latter could therefore be resolved with less concern about administrative or logistical inconvenience. This may explain why, instead of a concentrated trial, many civil law jurisdictions receive evidence in stages, the pace and content of which is dictated by the judge. Germany and France offer a helpful example. A civil jury has never been an element of the German civil justice system. It is the court rather than the parties which takes the main responsibility for collecting and filtering evidence. Crucially, the court gathers and evaluates evidence over as many discrete 'episodic' hearings as the circumstances require.[11] It is permissible, and indeed a common practice, for German judges to review the preliminary case materials, identify the 'jugular' issue of law or fact that may dispose of the entire case, and call an evidentiary hearing dedicated to that issue.[12] Similarly, under the French system, the judge may, of their own motion, issue a binding 'instruction' and order a fact-finding procedure for specific issues.[13] Like Germany, France has never adopted the idea of a civil jury.

Today the civil jury is generally a thing of the past for most common law jurisdictions. Why, then, do concentrated trials remain a stubborn feature? The probable, if banal, explanation is human inertia, or the difficulty of agreeing a date when all participants can attend a single hearing. This may be a sufficiently potent disincentive for one to keep the idea of episodic hearings at bay.

[10] The same point was made by JA Jolowicz, 'Adversarial and Inquisitorial Models of Civil Procedure' (2003) 52 *International & Comparative Law Quarterly* 281, 282 (albeit in relation to the origin of the broader adversarial model, involving, apart from a single evidentiary hearing, the oral presentation of submissions at trial).

[11] JH Langbein, 'The German Advantage in Civil Procedure' (1985) 52 *The University of Chicago Law Review* 823, 826.

[12] ibid 830.

[13] Reyes (n 9) 290–91.

Here is where remote technology enters the picture. By eliminating the need for stakeholders (for example, parties, lawyers, interpreters, transcribers, witnesses, arbitrators, judges) to travel and make incidental arrangements (and making participation a mere few clicks away), it greatly reduces the level of planning and commitment required to attend a hearing. This in turn increases the flexibility of scheduling. In this way, remote technology removes an enormous disincentive for common lawyers to switch to a German or French model of episodic evidentiary hearings. The benefits are obvious. If judges or arbitrators detect issues of fact on which the entirety of a party's case hangs (such as the existence of an oral contract in a breach of contract dispute), they could schedule a first evidentiary hearing for that issue and, depending on its resolution, either schedule further hearings in an episodic fashion, or dispose of the entire action then and there. This carries the potential of massively reducing the time and costs of the dispute resolution process. Lawyers may despair for the cutdown in billable hours, but the conscientious ones would rejoice for greater access to justice.

Another context in which remote technology may cause a paradigm shift is in effective case management of international commercial and investor–state arbitration. Before the use of remote technology became mainstream and sufficiently familiar to dispute resolution service providers, it was often impractical to schedule physical meetings to case manage arbitrations. That is because even a brief physical appearance requires participants to travel from one place to another, and also to block off days or weeks in their schedules. The cost and inconvenience involved are self-evident. Further, telephone conference calls were very limited in their effectiveness. Amongst issues usefully the subject of proactive case management are disclosure, experts, preliminary questions and limitation of evidence to the key issues in dispute. Many matters may be disposed of satisfactorily in writing, but there are also complex, open-ended issues that are more effectively addressed by a real-time meeting between the tribunal, counsel and the parties.

The logistical challenges implicit in organising a physical hearing have meant that tribunals have been reluctant to be proactive. These days, with remote hearings being a popular and necessary means of dispute resolution, a court or tribunal may exercise its case management power more proactively, as judges or arbitrators need not worry as much about the burden of case management hearings on the parties. A cost-effective video conference can be conveniently convened to deal with interlocutory matters, big or small on an ad hoc basis. In this way, remote technology has the opportunity to bring about a far more effective style of case management. This may in turn streamline the dispute resolution process and bring along attendant benefits in terms of costs, expediency and access.

These are but two examples of how remote technology may disrupt traditional patterns of international dispute resolution and inspire new ideas that would bring significant social benefits in terms of costs saving, time-efficiency, lower carbon footprints and greater access to justice. In addition, there is no obvious reason why asynchronous hearings of the kind described above should be discarded when there is no longer a strict necessity for participants to avoid physical participation. Prerecording the opening or closing submissions of a case would shorten proceedings, and consequently save costs, free up judicial resources and promote access to justice. Valuable procedural innovations have already been made, and others will be in the making. The silver lining of COVID-19 is that it has forced people to scrutinise assumptions, test novel ideas vigorously, and adapt to the 'new' normal. The next chapter will discuss how the international commercial arbitration community could channel the creative spirit of the COVID era to pave the way for future reforms in promising areas such as asynchronous dispute resolution.

12

Shaping the Future of International Dispute Resolution

DOUGLAS JONES AO AND JONATHAN MANCE

I. The Lessons of the Pandemic

History has taught us that crises, such as pandemics, are often catalysts of innovation. Researchers at the International Monetary Fund (IMF) found that 'pandemic events accelerate robot adoption, especially when the health impact is severe and is associated with a significant economic downturn'.[1] Gutenberg's labour-saving printing press (*c* 1440), for instance, has been linked to the decimation caused by the Black Death.[2] In our own time, the COVID-19 pandemic has forced us to find new ways to complete old tasks, so as to cope with, and limit, the spread of the virus. International dispute resolution has not been immune from this impetus for adaptation and change. In particular, the suspension of international travel and ordinary social interaction meant that the conventional way of resolving international disputes, in which everyone physically converges on one physical venue at one time, had to change. And change it did. Amongst other developments, the wide adoption of remote technology to conduct hearings is testament to that. As light emerges at the end of the COVID-19 tunnel, it is timely to ask ourselves whether we should go back to old practices – such as in-person hearings – when the pandemic blows over and (if so) to what extent. Since the pandemic has shown us that traditional dispute resolution processes are mutable, even within a very short span of time, it is worth reflecting upon whether they should be reinvented altogether.

This chapter is accordingly divided into two parts. Both were written with international commercial dispute resolution firmly in mind, especially the procedures of international commercial courts and international commercial arbitration. The first part (section II below) argues that the benefits of using technology to improve current arbitral procedures outweigh its costs. The second part (section III below) argues that

[1] TS Sedik and J Yoo, 'Pandemics and Automation: Will the Lost Jobs Come Back?' (2021) International Monetary Fund Working Paper No 2021/011.

[2] 'What history tells you about post-pandemic booms' *The Economist* (25 April 2021). The Black Death (1347–51) is estimated to have killed at least 40% of the population in Europe.

remote technology has greater potential to transform the process of arbitration and litigation. More particularly, section III will explore the idea of fully asynchronous hearings and commend it as a viable and important direction for future changes to international commercial dispute resolution.

II. COVID-19, Technology and Cross-Border Dispute Resolution Procedure

There can be little doubt that the COVID-19 pandemic has normalised the incorporation of technology into international dispute resolution. Notably, the pandemic has enlivened the debate about the effect of technology on civil procedure, and it has become apparent that technology can supplement and even enhance existing procedural innovations in many respects. We first examine procedural innovations which can be implemented to maximise efficiency irrespective of the use of technology. We will then consider the impact of technology on these procedural innovations, both positive and negative. We conclude that overall the adoption of technology adds value and reduces inefficiencies in cross-border dispute procedure and the benefits significantly outweigh the costs.

A. Innovations in Dispute Resolution Procedure

We first explore three procedural innovations which serve to optimise arbitration and litigation before international commercial (or similar) courts even without the use of technology. These are case management conferences (CMCs), the streamlining of document production, and the close management of expert evidence by the tribunal or court.

i. Case Management Conferences

CMCs are an important tool for a tribunal or court (the adjudicator) to proactively manage a case as it progresses. When used effectively, CMCs can significantly reduce inefficiencies in the procedure and substance of dispute resolution. Specifically, CMCs allow an adjudicator to have active oversight of the progression of the dispute resolution process. This is critical to conducting proceedings in the most efficient way possible, because rather than addressing problems with the parties' cases or evidence only at a substantive evidentiary or merits hearing (that is, a hearing where evidence is taken), the adjudicator can deal with such problems as soon as they are spotted.

Various types of CMC may be held at different stages of the life cycle of a dispute resolution process.

The first CMC. A first CMC is held immediately after the tribunal or court is constituted. It is a fundamental step for putting in place a broad procedural framework between the parties at the very beginning. The first CMC invariably culminates in a document known as Procedural Order No 1 (PO1), which sets out the foundational procedural features of a case. It is customary, and advisable, for a first CMC to begin the coordination of the following procedural steps:

(1) the scheduling of the main evidentiary hearing;
(2) the scheduling of any interlocutory hearings;
(3) the identification of the parties' representatives;
(4) the identification of communication channels between the parties and the adjudicator; and
(5) formalising the process whereby the parties identify the differences between them and communicate their respective positions in respect of those differences to each other.

At the same time, it is obvious that not all procedural matters can, or should, be settled at a first CMC. For one thing, the course of a dispute may change. It is important to be flexible and to permit procedures to evolve as the case itself does. For another, milestone dates aside (see below), there are procedural issues that are best left until later, including document disclosure, expert evidence and matters related to the evidentiary hearing (such as the calling of live witnesses). These procedures need only be briefly outlined at the first CMC, for they can only be properly tailored to the circumstances of a dispute once a better understanding of the issues dividing the parties (and their respective positions on those issues) emerges.

Subject to this caveat, the efficiency benefits of a first CMC are obvious. By setting various 'milestone dates' for various stages in the dispute resolution process at the outset, the first CMC imposes discipline in the proceedings. The parties know where they stand at any given moment, insofar as having to complete specified steps by, in the absence of compelling reasons, immutable dates. This puts pressure on the parties to comply within the stipulated timelines such that the dispute resolution process can progress smoothly. Moreover, by settling the basic features of the process, the first CMC prevents disputes on these basic matters from arising later down the road. Given these benefits, it is unsurprising that arbitral institutions, tribunals, and courts have embraced the idea of first CMCs and PO1s in their rules.[3]

A CMC on issues. A CMC on issues allows a tribunal or court to discuss with the parties its understanding of the parties' cases. Accordingly, it is best convened after the first exchange of cases. A CMC on issues plays a critical role in streamlining the dispute resolution process. It assists the parties and the adjudicator in mutually understanding the key issues in the parties' cases and, when the parties are preparing subsequent submissions, focuses their time and energy on those issues that are most relevant and necessary for resolving the dispute. A CMC on issues may increase the efficiency of the dispute resolution process when coupled with 'episodic hearings'. Once a dispositive issue[4] is identified, the tribunal can hold an evidentiary hearing for that issue only. Depending on how the dispositive issue is resolved, it is possible for the rest of the

[3] See, eg, The London Court of International Arbitration (LCIA) Arbitration Rules (1 October 2020), Art 14.1, read with the LCIA Notes for Arbitrators, para 23; 2021 Arbitration Rules of the International Chambers of Commerce, art 24, supplemented by its ICC Arbitration Commission Report on Techniques for Controlling Time and Costs in Arbitration (2018), para 29.

[4] That is, an issue which if decided in one party's favour may be dispositive of the entire or nearly the entire dispute.

issues to fall away completely. The potential savings in costs and time can be enormous. A CMC on issues facilitates the organisation of episodic hearings by shedding light on what these dispositive issues may be.

An experts CMC. The process of adducing expert evidence, if uncontrolled by the adjudicator, can significantly drive up the costs and length of an arbitration. Without the tribunal's directions, irrelevant, duplicative or otherwise unhelpful expert reports may be prepared, at the expense of the economy of the process. An experts CMC allows the tribunal to maintain active oversight and management by directing the parties and the experts properly. The subject matter of these directions is elaborated upon in section II.A.iii below.

A pre-hearing CMC. It is common practice for the parties to attend a pre-hearing CMC before the main evidentiary hearing. The purpose is to settle the details of the hearing procedures to be adopted. A pre-hearing CMC should take place sufficiently in advance of the evidentiary hearing to allow for the adequate management of these procedural issues. As alluded to above, many of these issues cannot be dealt with at the first CMC, as the shape of the arbitration may still be obscure at that time, and there are variables which can only be fixed when the hearing date draws closer.

Common issues addressed in the pre-hearing CMC include:

(1) identification of the live issues that fall to be determined;
(2) venue and hearing facilities or virtual hearing platform and technological logistics;
(3) transcription;
(4) hearing timetable (including the time allocation between parties);
(5) witnesses to be called for cross-examination;
(6) interpretation;
(7) the appropriate electronic or hard copy format for hearing bundles; and
(8) the necessity of written closing submissions.

ii. Document Production

In complex commercial arbitrations and litigation, document production will often be extensive. It is therefore essential that the tribunal or court remains actively involved in the document production and disclosure process, so as to control the procedure and ensure that documents requested by a party are relevant, and that relevant documents are produced efficiently.

To organise information relating to document production, it is customary for arbitral tribunals and courts to direct the parties to prepare 'Redfern schedules' to record document requests, party submissions, objections and responses, and the decisions of the tribunal or court on each document or class of documents requested. In a Redfern schedule, each of these items is set out in successive columns, with the document requests separated into rows, allowing the tribunal to see at a glance all the parties' submissions on each set of document requests.

In the absence of sufficient prior communications among the parties and an adjudicator, the use of Redfern schedules can be challenging. That is because, when faced with a contested document request in a Redfern schedule, the adjudicator may find it difficult to resolve the contest without the parties' assistance on their understandings of the dispute. For example, where a document request is opposed on the ground of irrelevance, it is often difficult for an adjudicator to decide if a document or class of documents is relevant without a detailed understanding of the issues in a dispute. To address this difficulty, a procedural innovation is to settle document production and disclosure issues by way of a short oral procedural hearing or video conference, called in a timely fashion ahead of the document production stage. By this process, the tribunal and the parties can work out, by reference to the nature of the dispute, what evidence is truly needed on which issues and why. Thereafter, when presented with a contested document request in a Redfern schedule, the adjudicator should be better placed to resolve the dispute on paper, without further need to convene a hearing with the parties. The whole document production procedure is thereby streamlined.

iii. Expert Evidence

The efficient management of expert evidence likewise requires proactive attention by an adjudicator at every stage of the dispute resolution process. Critically, the procedure should as much as possible limit the extent of extraneous variables left unsettled between the experts, particularly: (1) the issues on which to opine; (2) the materials to be relied upon; and (3) the methodology to be used. The best practice would be to start by identifying the disciplines in the dispute that need expert evidence, and to have the parties identify the types of experts that they wish to call for each discipline. This would be followed by the establishment within each discipline of a common list of questions, closely supervised by the adjudicator. The parties must then refrain from rushing to produce their expert reports. The latter should instead be deferred until all the factual evidence (documentary and witness) is available, so that as much as possible the experts can formulate their opinions on the basis of a common set of facts.

When it comes to the production of the expert reports, all of the experts within each discipline should be required to produce a joint expert report identifying areas of agreement and disagreement between them, before they produce individual expert reports focussing solely on their areas of disagreement. The experts might, where appropriate, be asked to produce reply expert reports based on the methodology or factual assumptions adopted by the experts of the opposing party. This would reveal what the differences in the experts' opinions can be attributed to, whether it be the use of a different method, factual assumption, or interpretation of the evidence. It would also allow the adjudicator to link the differences in opinion between the experts to the use of a particular method or fact, facilitating an understanding of what the expert opinion would be if the adjudicator ultimately accepts one method or set of facts. To adopt this procedure, the adjudicator would require active communication with the parties, whether by way of experts CMCs or other teleconferences. The rewards in terms of efficiency gained, however, are significant.

B. Positive Impact of Technology

As tribunals and litigants alike have adapted to the increasing presence of technology in dispute resolution proceedings and in everyday life, the use of technology has become prevalent. This naturalisation of technology in the dispute resolution process has resulted in a new approach to case management. Because tribunal engagement before the evidentiary hearing becomes far easier with the aid of remote technology, the innovations in procedure outlined in the previous section require less effort to implement and are therefore more accessible to adjudicators. As a result, an adjudicator is able actively to engage with a case with relative ease, far in advance of the evidentiary hearing, even if the case involves international parties scattered across various time zones. For example, instead of leaving procedural issues for the main evidentiary hearing, parties and tribunals are more likely to resolve these preliminary issues in a timely manner due to the convenience of remote CMCs. As a consequence, preliminary issues can be resolved much more efficiently.

The ease of addressing issues as and when they arise means that the merits hearing of a proceeding is reserved for the key substantive issues in dispute between the parties. Consequently, the hearings in the later stages of a dispute resolution process are free from distractions arising from interlocutory procedural issues. This is possible only because of the increasing sophistication of remote technology. In the past, video streams were often choppy, the interface unsuitable for a legal hearing (let alone one with a sizeable group of attendees), and the overall experience was not user-friendly. Today's video-conferencing technologies have largely surpassed these difficulties, and thanks in no small part to COVID-19, are now ubiquitous. There is no doubt that the digital environment created by modern video-conferencing solutions is sufficiently stable and serviceable for a virtual hearing to be conducted in most locations set up for business use around the world.

Once the virtual format is adopted, the logistics of hearings and CMCs may be easily organised. For a start, there is no longer a need to travel to meet in one destination for a CMC or a hearing. Scheduling is also much easier when travel time is not a consideration. Participants can thus fit remote CMCs and procedural hearings into their schedules much more easily than if they are to take place physically. Moreover, for these reasons, CMCs and procedural hearings can be called with much shorter notice, enabling urgent issues to be dealt with more swiftly. Quite simply put, issues which were dealt with unsatisfactorily previously can now be ventilated and readily resolved with the aid of remote hearings.

A virtual hearing may be facilitated and supported by other technologies. For instance, electronic document management affords easy access to hundreds of thousands of documents in a remote setting. The use of shared databases or cloud-based repositories for the purpose of electronic file-sharing enables digital searches and categorisation and thus makes locating and transferring documents easy. This can be combined with the screen-sharing function of video-conferencing platforms, which allows participants of a remote CMC or hearing to view the documents under scrutiny conveniently and simultaneously. Another branch of facilitative technology concerns document production. Recent years have seen the development of predictive coding technology to assist in filtering and sorting documents in extensive document production exercises. In some jurisdictions, such technology has been judicially approved for use in discovery.[5]

[5] See, eg, *Da Silva Moore v Publicis Groupe & MLS Group* 287 FRD 182 (affirmed in *Moore v Publicis Groupe SA*, 2012 US Dist LEXIS 58742) in the US; *Pyrrho Investments Ltd v MWB Property Ltd* [2016] EWHC 256 (Ch), and *Brown v BCA Trading Ltd* [2016] EWHC 1464 (Ch) in England and Wales; *Irish Bank Resolution Corporation Ltd v Quinn* [2015] IEHC 175 in Ireland.

It is anticipated that a wider adoption of technology assisted document reviews will reduce time and costs (while also enhancing the accuracy)[6] of such exercises.

C. Limitations of Technology

At this juncture, it must be acknowledged that when technology is used to facilitate the handling of procedural matters, such as the ones just reviewed, this may give rise to challenges as well as benefits. Particularly acute amongst these potential challenges are cybersecurity and confidentiality breaches. Specifically, because the digital environment is more porous than a brick-and-mortar repository, files that are shared online may be accessible to hackers, as may private remote meetings. Organisers of such online endeavours must therefore pay attention to cybersecurity and confidentiality risks and mitigate them in a reasonable and proportionate manner.

A helpful reference is the detailed protocol issued by the International Council for Commercial Arbitration and the New York City Bar Association,[7] which contains high-level principles and concrete guidelines. The protocol is intended to be applied by an arbitral tribunal, in consultation with the parties, in light of the particular circumstances and risk profile of each individual arbitration.[8] It might be hoped that, with the assistance of frameworks of this kind (and ever-improving technology), the risks of cybersecurity and confidentiality breaches can be kept at a manageable and tolerable level.

Apart from the cybersecurity and confidentiality concerns associated with remote technology, one should also recognise that the remaining risks of using such technologies are considerably lower in the context of procedural matters as compared to evidentiary hearings. The most common objections to the use of remote technology revolve around the perceived difficulties with witness examination in a remote setting. These objections carry no force when remote technology is used simply to settle procedures rather than to take evidence. Nevertheless, even in an evidentiary hearing, the proposition that remote hearings are inferior to in-person hearings must be tested, rather than taken for granted. The oft-repeated maxim that 'justice must not only be done, but also be seen to be done' could be said to capture two notions of justice: substantive and procedural justice. Substantive justice is achieved when an adjudicator correctly applies the relevant law to the facts of a given case. Procedural justice, meanwhile, has many dimensions. As a rule, a procedurally just process should ensure that the parties are given an opportunity to state and defend their case (including an opportunity to test their opponent's case), and also that the tribunal is independent and impartial.

Against the touchstones of substantive and procedural justice, do remote evidentiary hearings fare worse than in-person hearings? In this regard, it may be helpful to

[6] HL Roitblatt, A Kershaw and P Oot, 'Document Categorization in Legal Electronic Discovery: Computer Classification vs. Manual Review' (2010) 61 *American Society for Information Science and Technology* 70, 79.

[7] 'ICCA–NYC Bar–CPR Protocol on Cybersecurity in International Arbitration (2020 Edition)' (The ICCA Reports No 6, 2019), available at www.cdn.arbitration-icca.org/s3fs-public/document/media_document/icca-nyc_bar-cpr_cybersecurity_protocol_for_international_arbitration_-_electronic_version.pdf.

[8] See Principles 6–12 of the protocol.

distinguish between evidentiary hearings featuring factual witnesses, and those featuring only expert witnesses. Ultimately, in the context of international arbitration or litigation, for both types of evidentiary hearing, there is little basis to suppose that remote technology would be any less effective in achieving substantive and procedural justice.

Turning first to hearings featuring factual witnesses, remote hearings are often criticised for undermining substantive justice, in that an untruthful account by a factual witness is more likely to be accepted than if evidence is taken in person. The argument can be broken down into several strands, none of which are convincing. First, it may be thought that a factual witness is more likely to lie in a remote setting. In the context of litigation in court, this may be because the 'majesty' or 'solemnity' of a courtroom setting has a psychological impact on witnesses,[9] making them more truthful than they would otherwise be. This plainly has no relevance in relation to arbitration, which, if conducted physically, takes place in a conference room. More fundamentally, the assumptions underlying this argument may be questioned. First, the solemnity of the proceedings do not derive solely from the trappings of the physical location in which they are held, but also from the participants' consciousness of the seriousness and importance of particular proceedings, and this can be brought home to the participants even in a virtual setting.[10] Secondly, it seems doubtful that a truly determined liar would change his or her mind due to the room they are in or the mode of communications. Thirdly, it may be thought that a factual witness who does lie is less likely to be caught in a remote hearing. The argument is that the demeanour of a liar is more conspicuous when observed in a physical setting. But experience has shown that demeanour is a treacherous guide to determining the truth: the honest witness may be nervous and incoherent, whereas the practised liar may look the tribunal in the eye and lie with confidence. As Sir Brian McKenna has aptly observed, in a passage subsequently endorsed by Lord Devlin:[11]

> I question whether the respect given to our findings of fact based on the demeanour of the witnesses is always deserved. I doubt my own ability, and sometimes that of other judges, to discern from a witness's demeanour, or the tone of his voice, whether he is telling the truth. He speaks hesitantly. Is that the mark of a cautious man, whose statements are for that reason to be respected, or is he taking time to fabricate? Is the emphatic witness putting on an act to deceive me, or is he speaking from the fullness of his heart, knowing that he is right? Is he likely to be more truthful if he looks me straight in the face than if he casts his eyes on the ground perhaps from shyness or a natural timidity? For my part I rely on these considerations as little as I can help.

[9] See *Re Chow Kam Fai ex parte Rambas Marketing Co LLC* [2004] 1 HKLRD 161 [28]; A Langdon QC, 'Inaugural Address by Andrew Langdon QC Chairman of the Bar 2017' (14 December 2016), available at www.barristermagazine.com/inaugural-address-by-andrew-langdon-qc-chairman-of-the-bar-2017-delivered-in-middle-temple-hall-london-on-14-december-2016.

[10] See, for example, E Rowden and A Wallace, 'Remote judging: the impact of video links on the image and the role of the judge' (2018) 14 *International Journal of Law in Context* 504, 516–18, discussing whether various participants exhibited less inhibited behaviour when appearing in court proceedings remotely; see also R Susskind, *Online Courts and the Future of Justice* (OUP, 2019) 208–10, questioning whether physical courtrooms are indeed more 'majestic' than online courts, and arguing that online courts can be designed to capture and convey the authority of conventional courts.

[11] B MacKenna, 'Discretion' (1974) 9 *Irish Jurist* 1, 10, words which Lord Devlin said he would 'adopt in their entirety' in P Devlin, *The Judge* (OUP, 1979) 63.

As a result, the primary basis of an evidentiary finding should surely rest upon contemporaneous documentation and inherent probabilities, rather than witnesses' recollections, at least in the context of commercial disputes. As Lord Leggatt cautioned:[12]

> [T]he best approach for a judge to adopt in the trial of a commercial case is, in my view, to place little if any reliance at all on witnesses' recollections of what was said in meetings and conversations, and to base factual findings on inferences drawn from the documentary evidence and known or probable facts … Above all, it is important to avoid the fallacy of supposing that, because a witness has confidence in his or her recollection and is honest, evidence based on that recollection provides any reliable guide to the truth.

The materiality of the nuances supposedly lost in testimony received through video-link should therefore not be overstated. Fourthly, it is often said that cross-examination is less effective in a remote setting. Yet, experience – including that of the authors – suggests that this has more to do with a lack of familiarity than any immanent feature of the remote environment. With time, practice and adaptations, cross-examination in a virtual hearing should be as effective as its physical counterpart.[13] For those reasons, the supposition that a remote evidentiary hearing would be less effective in doing substantive justice than an in-person hearing does not seem, to us, to withstand scrutiny.

What about procedural justice? Switching the hearing format from physical to remote certainly does not affect the independence and impartiality of the tribunal, but does it curtail the parties' right to be heard? Provided that basic technical capabilities (such as access to an adequate bandwidth and a functioning video-link) are not an issue, it is hard to imagine how that could be the case. The authors' experience during the pandemic has shown that, with some adaptations, virtual advocacy can be just as effective as in-person advocacy. As to the giving of evidence, witnesses can present their narrative, and be cross-examined, remotely, just as effectively as they could in a physical setting. The well-worn concerns of abusive practices undermining the integrity of the process, such as witness coaching, can also be easily prevented in a remote environment with the adoption of relatively simple measures. For instance, the tribunal may require, in addition to a video feed of the witness, a video feed showing a 360-degree view of the witness's surroundings, or allow the opposing party to have a representative present at the witness's location. As for hearings featuring only expert witnesses, the superiority of an in-person hearing is even less obvious. It is not obvious that a physical hearing is more conducive to the correct resolution of expert issues. Even more so than in the case of factual witnesses, the adjudicator would be interested in what an expert has to say, not how they say it.

D. Conclusion

In a nutshell, it is suggested that the increasingly widespread adoption of technology in international commercial dispute resolution is a positive development which greatly

[12] *Gestmin SGPS SA v Credit Suisse (UK) Limited* [2013] EWHC 3560 (Comm) [22].

[13] See W Miles, 'Remote Advocacy, Witness Preparation & Cross-Examination: Practical Tips & Challenges' in M Scherer, N Bassiri and MSA Wahab (eds), *International Arbitration and the COVID-19 Revolution* (Kluwer Law International, 2020).

enhances the efficiency of the proceedings, without compromising the quality of justice that it delivers. It would be to the benefit of all stakeholders in international dispute resolution for these technologies to remain in use post-pandemic.

III. Fully Asynchronous Dispute Resolution Proceedings

Professor Richard Susskind, a leading legal futurist and technologist, has drawn a distinction between 'automation' and 'transformation'. According to him, automation 'involves grafting new technology onto old working practices' by way of 'process improvement', whereas transformation takes place when technology 'displace[s] and revolutionize[s] conventional working habits' and 'blast[s] old approaches out of the water'.[14] Thus far, we have considered how technology has 'automated' international dispute resolution in the sense described by Professor Susskind, but we have yet to consider how international dispute resolution may be 'transformed' by technological innovations.

The rest of this chapter concerns transformation. Building on recent proposals for 'partially asynchronous' arbitration, we consider whether it is possible (and desirable) to introduce 'fully asynchronous' processes for international disputes. In what follows, the concept of 'asynchronicity' will first be unpacked. We will then describe the 'generic' and 'specialist' fully asynchronous litigation models which are either already in use or have been proposed for future development. The potential of fully asynchronous arbitration will then be examined. We conclude that the benefits of introducing a fully asynchronous process (in terms of both efficiency and access) outweigh its potential disadvantages, making it a viable and commendable direction for future reform.

A. The Concept of Asynchronicity

A process is 'asynchronous' if its progression does not require the simultaneous participation of its participants. There is no need for everyone to be available in the same place at the same time. In other words, sequential participation is at the conceptual core of an asynchronous process. A classic example is an email exchange: the sender and the recipient do not have to be simultaneously online for the exchange to take place. It is 'fully asynchronous', because at no point are the sender and the recipient required to be available at the same time. In contrast, traditional evidentiary hearings are 'fully synchronous', in that all the parties (or their representatives) and the adjudicator(s) are expected to be present at the same time, from the beginning (marked by some form of oral opening submissions), through the middle (the taking of evidence), and right up to the end (concluding with some form of oral closing submissions).

Between these two extremes are 'partially asynchronous' processes. As the name suggests, these are processes where one part is asynchronous and one part is synchronous. Strictly speaking, an asynchronous process does not necessarily require the support

[14] Susskind, *Online Courts* (2019) 34.

of modern technology. An exchange of letters is fully asynchronous. However, asynchronicity without the aid of technology would typically be too time-consuming and impractical to meet the needs of modern dispute resolution. As such, the discussion that follows is devoted to asynchronous dispute resolution assisted by remote technology.

B. Asynchronous Dispute Resolution

The idea that at least some parts of an arbitration may be held asynchronously has generated considerable interest during the COVID-19 pandemic. Professor Maxi Scherer has drawn attention to this possibility.[15] She has proposed that asynchronous participation could take the form of a video recording of counsel's opening submissions, which would be made available to the tribunal in advance of an evidentiary hearing, with the rest of the hearing taking place in a synchronous fashion. In Professor Scherer's view, a partially asynchronous model can mitigate the logistical and administrative problems arising from participants being in different time zones and having conflicting schedules. On the other hand, Professor Scherer does not consider the asynchronous format to be well suited to the taking of evidence, considering that present practice requires real-time interaction amongst witnesses, counsel, and the tribunal and most stakeholders in international arbitration consider this to be essential.

What, then, are the prospects of fully asynchronous arbitration? There has so far been little (if any) discussion on its potential. This shall be our focus in the remainder of this chapter. To set the scene, we first look at some of the models already in use or under scrutiny, in the context of domestic litigation.

i. Existing Models – Generic and Specialist

Broadly speaking, there are two types of fully asynchronous litigation which are either in use or being examined for their potential.

The first involves the use of generic technology not specifically designed for asynchronous dispute resolution, whereas the second involves the use of specialist online platforms. Examples of the first model include dispute resolution by email. In Singapore, in response to the disruptions caused by COVID-19, 'asynchronous court dispute resolution hearings by email' were introduced in March 2020 for smaller value claims relating to motor accidents, personal injury, and negligence.[16] Under this system, parties and the court would communicate by email on such matters as case management directions, the appointment of a single joint expert, the court's 'early neutral evaluation' of liability, and the quantum of the claim. The process resembles the paper disposal mechanism that is familiar to many jurisdictions. Importantly, this system contemplates that most

[15] See M Scherer, 'Asynchronous Hearings: The Next New Normal?' (*Kluwer Arbitration Blog*, 9 September 2020), available at www.arbitrationblog.kluwerarbitration.com/2020/09/09/asynchronous-hearings-the-next-new-normal.

[16] 'Asynchronous Court Dispute Resolution Hearings by Email (aCDR) for Case Management Lists at the State Courts Centre for Dispute Resolution (SCCDR)' (Singapore State Courts, Registrar's Circular No 2 of 2020, 5 March 2020).

or even all of the pre-trial process can take place asynchronously, with all case management directions being sought from and issued by the court through email, unless there is a special need for an in-person hearing.[17] This is a fully asynchronous process, since none of the parties have to be online at the same time for it to move forward. Moreover, it does not involve the use of any specialist platform. Rather, it exemplifies an application of generic technology (namely, email) in the context of online dispute resolution.

Contrast that with the second model of fully asynchronous litigation, which employs specialist online platforms for court users. An example is the 'asynchronous trial' system in use at the Hangzhou Internet Court of the People's Republic of China. To participate in such a trial, litigants must log on to an online platform designed and developed specifically for that purpose.[18] The trial proper comprises three stages: (1) questioning and answering; (2) debating; and (3) closing statements.[19] Submissions may be in written or audio form. Stage (1) is divided into two sessions. In the first, questioning session, participants (including the judge) may ask questions as they wish, and parties can choose whether to answer immediately. In the answering session, the parties can only give answers to the questions raised. In stage (2), parties are expected to express their opinions on the answers given. Lastly, in stage (3), the parties are to close their case. This is a fully asynchronous process, since the parties do not have to be simultaneously online to participate: Party A may leave a question on the platform for Party B to answer without Party B's virtual presence at the same time. Likewise, the court can read or replay the parties' submissions at its leisure. It was designed to be an asynchronous process from start to finish, with no feature catering for a real-time exchange of arguments or evidence at any stage.

A similar 'online court' process has attracted interest in England and Wales. In 2016, Sir Ernest Ryder, then Senior President of Tribunals, described a process known as 'online continuous hearings' which was being trialled by the Social Entitlement Chamber of the First-Tier Tribunal, in which 'all participants are able to iterate and comment upon the basic case papers online, over a reasonable window of time, so that the issues in dispute can be clarified and explored'.[20] Meanwhile, 'the judge will take an inquisitorial and problem-solving approach, guiding the parties to explain and understand their respective positions'.[21] A similar idea was picked up later on by Sir Geoffrey Vos, then Chancellor of the High Court, who described its potential application to a much broader range of commercial cases before the English courts. As he imagined the proceedings, participants can log on to an online platform when they have the time to do so within a time window and make their submissions online. Questions can then be asked by the judge online and responded to by the parties online. Such an 'iterative

[17] ibid, paras 18, 21.

[18] See A Mingay, 'Size matters: Alibaba shapes China's first 'Court of the Internet' (Mercator Institute for China Studies, 17 October 2019), available at www.merics.org/en/analysis/size-matters-alibaba-shapes-chinas-first-court-internet.

[19] 《涉网案件异步审理规程（试行）》(PRC), aArts 6–8; see also G Du and M Yu, 'A Close Look at Hangzhou Internet Court: Inside China's Internet Courts Series -06' *China Justice Observer* (3 November 2019), available at www.chinajusticeobserver.com/a/a-close-look-at-hangzhou-internet-court.

[20] E Ryder, 'The Modernisation of Access to Justice in Times of Austerity' (5th Annual Ryder Lecture, 3 March 2016), paras 28–29.

[21] ibid para 30.

online process' could be as convenient as texting on a phone.[22] Importantly, judges would and should have a much greater role to play in controlling the conduct of the case than in a traditional trial, 'asking questions, directing evidence and resolving cases stage by stage'.[23] Sir Geoffrey expressed the hope that 'oral evidence at a synchronous hearing could become the exception rather than the rule'.[24]

ii. Fully Asynchronous International Dispute Resolution – Potential and Challenges

To what extent can, and should, fully asynchronous processes (whether generic or specialist) be adopted in international commercial dispute resolution (whether litigation or arbitration)? It is suggested that such reforms are possible, and that, in the light of its benefits and potential, asynchronous proceedings should be seriously considered as the next transformative step in cross-border dispute resolution.

The 'can' question divides into two issues. First, can the parties to a dispute agree to have their differences resolved by a fully asynchronous process? This is relatively straightforward. The arbitral process is determined by the parties. If parties agree that their dispute is to be determined entirely on the basis of exchanges of emails, that would be decisive. Secondly, do we have the technology for a fully asynchronous arbitration to take place? The answer is obvious for the generic model, since, *ex hypothesi*, such a model uses technology already in widespread use for other purposes. As for the specialist model, although there is yet to be an online platform dedicated to fully asynchronous arbitration, it seems that the foundational technology is already available. This may be evidenced by the platform currently deployed by the Hangzhou Internet Court,[25] and also by other existing platforms for domestic litigation, such as Matterhorn – an American online dispute resolution platform allowing litigants to communicate asynchronously with the judge and other participants in the case[26] – and the 'eCourtroom' used in the Federal Court of Australia for handling simple applications and the giving of directions asynchronously.[27] The technologies used to develop these litigation platforms would be capable of being used in arbitration and litigation, since the core functional requirement (namely, sequential participation among the parties and the adjudicator) is the same in both contexts.

The 'should' question is more difficult. To properly answer it, it is necessary to weigh the pros and cons of fully asynchronous arbitration for international disputes. The benefits of fully asynchronous arbitration are obvious.

[22] G Vos, 'Debate on how the adoption of new technology can be accelerated to improve the efficiency of the justice system' (20 June 2018), paras 16, 22.

[23] ibid para 22.

[24] ibid.

[25] See n 18 above.

[26] See Matterhorn's official website at www.getmatterhorn.com. According to the website, Matterhorn is currently in use in over 150 courts and 20 states in the United States.

[27] See Federal Court of Australia, 'eCourtroom – Online Courtroom for Registered Users', available at www.fedcourt.gov.au/online-services/ecourtroom.

First, by allowing participants to engage the arbitral process sequentially and at their leisure, it saves time, reduces costs and eliminates the inconvenience arising from time zone differences. Synchronous arbitration requires all participants to be present at the same time. Effectively, it locks up a fixed period of all the participants' time, even though the information that is exchanged during the hearing can for the most part just as easily be picked up without simultaneous participation. This generates wasted costs, both in terms of time and money. By contrast, fully asynchronous arbitration allows everybody to access the arbitral process as and when they see fit. The potential savings on the time and costs of the arbitral process may be huge. In Sir Geoffrey Vos' words, 'many cases and some aspects of the more complex cases' can be resolved asynchronously 'without paying for partners in law firms, assistant solicitors and barristers all to sit, sometimes for hours or days on end, listening to material they can pick up online in far less time'.[28] Moreover, as with remote hearings, fully asynchronous hearings conducted through remote technology obviate the need for international travel, saving time and costs. In addition, because fully asynchronous arbitration does away with the need for everyone to be available at the same time for any part of the proceedings, time zone differences would no longer pose a problem.

Second, and more importantly, because of these efficiency gains, fully asynchronous arbitration may significantly promote access to adjudication by less economically resourceful entities, such as low-income individuals and small and medium-sized enterprises (SMEs). The extent to which a fully asynchronous process may facilitate their access to arbitration may be analysed from a temporal and a material dimension. Temporally, because parties are relieved of the need to pre-schedule blocks of time to attend hearings, they are more able, and likely, to engage in the dispute resolution process. The investment of time is a significant consideration for individuals whose commitments (such as work and caregiving) would be disrupted by the current 'lock-up' period of legal proceedings.

For instance, in a survey conducted in Nigeria in 2018, a lack of time was cited as the fourth most common reason for not commencing proceedings in the face of a legal dispute.[29] This factor disproportionately affects individuals and smaller enterprises, since, compared to large entities, they have a much smaller margin in which to rearrange their commitments to meet the demands of traditional dispute resolution. Fully asynchronous arbitration can therefore prove attractive to individuals and SMEs, for the time investment required is much lower. Materially, the reduction in costs resulting from fully asynchronous arbitration would lower the financial barrier to cross-border dispute resolution.

Rightly or wrongly, international arbitration or litigation has a reputation of being serviceable only for the rich. For instance, in a recent English family law decision, it was observed that 'There is a common misconception that the use of arbitration, as an alternative to the court process in financial remedy cases, is the purview only of the rich who seek privacy away from the courts and the eyes of the media'.[30] According to the CIArb

[28] Vos, 'Debate' (2018) para 16.

[29] The Hague Institute for Innovation of Law, 'Justice Needs and Satisfaction in Nigeria 2018' (2018) 98, available at www.hiil.org/wp-content/uploads/2018/07/HiiL-Nigeria-JNS-report-web.pdf.

[30] *Haley v Haley* [2020] EWCA Civ 1369, [2021] 2 WLR 357 [5] (King LJ).

Costs of International Arbitration Survey 2011, the average costs incurred by each party in international arbitration was around £1.5 million, most of which was lawyers' fees.[31] By reducing lawyers' hours on a case, a fully asynchronous process has the potential of dramatically lowering such costs, making international arbitration more accessible.

Promotion of access to international dispute resolution is a facet of the promotion of access to justice, and, as such, is a deserving and valuable goal. This is all the more so in the wake of COVID-19, which has generated a large volume of disputes in need of a cost-effective and speedy forum for their determination.[32] Setting aside the question of whether organisations (such as arbitral institutions or international commercial courts) have a duty to contribute to the achievement of such goals, there are self-serving reasons for such institutions to make themselves accessible to the less economically well resourced. For one thing, this demographic represents an enormous 'latent legal market'.[33] For another, providing a cost-effective process would allow a dispute resolution system of choice. As Sir Rupert Jackson observed, 'Every dispute resolution system needs to adapt to the changing needs of society and the rapid advances of technology. That means an almost constant process of procedural reform.'[34] In this regard, 'Competition between dispute resolution systems or institutions is a driver of improvement'.[35] If the arbitral process can harness the efficiency benefits of asynchronicity while other dispute resolution processes lag behind, it would win that 'competition' and vice versa. Accordingly, for self-interested reasons, dispute resolution service providers should look into the potential of fully asynchronous proceedings.

So much for the benefits of fully asynchronous hearings. What are the disadvantages?

Ethically, it may be said that a fully asynchronous process would on the contrary widen the gap in access to justice between the haves and have-nots, on the basis that fully asynchronous hearings would essentially be 'economy class justice'[36] for the economically disadvantaged, as Professor Susskind has dubbed this argument, while the wealthy alone would be able to afford and choose the traditional synchronous process. Underlying this claim is the assumption that a synchronous process is superior to its asynchronous counterpart, and it is therefore this underlying argument that needs to be unpacked.

Is it fair to assume that, substantively, fully asynchronous arbitration would undermine the rectitude of decisions? So far as submissions are concerned, it is hard to imagine why they would be more helpful when delivered in real time than when made asynchronously. The greatest value of a synchronous hearing is that the tribunal can raise questions on the arguments being put before it. This allows the tribunal's specific queries to be clarified there and then. In an asynchronous process, the tribunal can still seek clarifications and assistance from legal representatives, just as it could in a synchronous hearing, albeit with some degree of delay. Indeed, submissions given

[31] Chartered Institute of Arbitrators, CIArb Costs of International Arbitration Survey 2011 (2011) 13.

[32] See *Haley v Haley* [2020] EWCA Civ 1369, [2021] 2 WLR 357 [5] (King LJ).

[33] R Susskind, *The Future of Law: Facing the Challenges of Information Technology* (Clarendon Press, 1996) 27.

[34] R Jackson, 'Arbitration: Is it still fit for purpose?' (Keynote Speech at the 11th International Conference on Construction Law and Alternative Dispute Resolution, 23 May 2018) para 4.1.

[35] ibid para 4.7.

[36] Susskind, *The Future of Law* (1996) 187.

asynchronously may even be more helpful because legal representatives would not be pressed to give an immediate response. They would have the time to produce a thoughtful, organised and coherent answer. For that reason, while synchronous remote hearings have been criticised by some for providing tribunals with a less thorough understanding of the case than in-person hearings,[37] the opposite might be true of asynchronous hearings. They may in fact improve the tribunal's understanding of the case.

As for matters of factual evidence, it may be thought that by ridding dispute resolution of an exchange of *viva voce* evidence, it becomes much harder to assess the credibility of witnesses in a fully asynchronous process. In such a process, it would be impossible to gauge witnesses' real-time demeanour, such as their immediate reaction to a question. However, as already explained, the demeanour of witnesses is an unreliable guide of their honesty and, at least in the context of commercial disputes, rarely would the resolution of factual issues turn on the witnesses' recollection of what happened. A more powerful concern is that, because a fully asynchronous process affords witnesses a time gap before answering questions, there is a greater risk of witness coaching and outright fabrication. That said, the value of a cross-examination technique that relies mainly on the element of surprise or the gradual wearing down of a witness over the course of a continuous session is questionable. As Toby Landau QC has put it: 'Cross-examination subjects witnesses to a process that can be highly artificial, high pressure, divorced from real life, and – on occasion – culturally inappropriate. It may reward resilience, but as a process may not be optim[al] for adducing genuine evidence'.[38] To this it may be added that much of the effort expended on this style of cross-examination yields little practical benefits, as Wendy Miles QC has observed:[39]

> Often all successful cross-examination achieves is a confirmation that actual recollection is patchier that what lawyers compose in witness statements. But if tribunals were to accept that as their starting premise, perhaps we could spend a whole lot less time and energy trying to prove it to them in every single instance.

When focused on more productive practices, cross-examination in an asynchronous setting is not necessarily lacking in efficacy. In these premises, a general statement that fully asynchronous arbitration provides 'second rate' justice does not seem to rest on solid grounds.

A different critique may be that fully asynchronous hearings have limited utility, in that they would be suitable only for small-value claims of the simplest kind. There appears to be a notion among even the most fervent of legal technologists that asynchronous dispute resolution of the kind described above should be confined to simpler claims of a relatively modest value. Professor Susskind, for instance, has suggested that the value of a case, the complexity of its legal and fact patterns, and the types of legal problem at issue, are relevant factors for assessing whether asynchronous adjudication

[37] G Born, A Day and H Virjee, 'Empirical Study of Experiences with Remote Hearings: A Survey of Users' Views' in M Scherer, N Bassiri, MSA Wahab (eds), *International Arbitration and the COVID-19 Revolution* (Kluwer Law International, 2020) 149.

[38] T Landau, 'Tainted Memories: Exposing the Fallacy of Witness Evidence in International Arbitration' (The Kaplan Lecture, 17 November 2010) 12–13, available at www.neil-kaplan.com/s/2010-Toby-Landau-QC-Tainted-MemoriesExposing-the-Fallacy-of-Witness-Evidence-in-International-Arbitr.pdf.

[39] Miles, 'Remote Advocacy' (2020) 128.

is or is not suitable for the disposal of the case.[40] However, it may be questioned whether such constraints are justified. The claim value is important because it would determine what would be a proportionate amount of resources to be invested in resolving the claim, and because it is a fairly useful proxy for the claim's factual and legal complexity.

This does not, however, preclude the use of an asynchronous process for high-value claims. Instead, as Professor Susskind has also observed, a threshold for claim value is often set for asynchronous dispute resolution, simply because such methods are commonly explored as solutions to the problem of disproportionate expenses being incurred in resolving smaller claims.[41] It is not the case that higher-value claims are unsuitable for asynchronous judging. Surely, the more cost-effective resolution of higher-value claims is also a salutary aim. The second reason is tied to the complexity of the underlying claim. Is a legally complicated dispute unsuitable for wholly asynchronous arbitration? For the reasons explored above, it is difficult to see why. As explained, the quality of legal submissions may well be enhanced in an asynchronous process. What about a factually complicated dispute? A dispute may be factually complicated because, quantitatively, a great number of factual issues are involved, or because, qualitatively, the factual issue is finely balanced. Concerns over quantitative factual complexity may be placed in perspective by the following remarks by Sir Geoffrey Vos:[42]

> [T]here are many cases where parts of the trial process are costly and unnecessary … Why do we need days of evidence, when in reality there are very rarely more than a handful of substantive factual disputes, and even those are often borne of misunderstanding or mistrust rather than substantive disagreement as to what has actually occurred? In many cases, a good proportion of the factual disputes are irrelevant to the outcome, and could be avoided altogether if the matter had been considered in sufficient detail at an earlier stage.

Thus, experience suggests that it is rare for a case to involve so many factual issues that asynchronous determination is unsuitable. For the rare case, a synchronous hearing may possibly well be more cost-effective and practical. But that would be the exception, rather than the rule. As for concerns over qualitative issues, it does not seem that having a real-time hearing would make a difference. Although it is impossible to gauge a witness's real-time demeanour in an asynchronous process, it is an unhelpful indicator of veracity, as we have explained. If the tribunal has to split hairs in order to rule on a factual issue, it is much more likely that it would do so on the basis of inherent probabilities, rather than the eye contact or verbal delivery of a witness. Inherent probabilities are the same whether or not a hearing is synchronous. It follows that, when it comes to finely balanced factual issues, an asynchronous hearing is probably just as good as its synchronous counterpart. For these reasons, it seems that, save possibly in exceptional circumstances, fully asynchronous arbitration can resolve claims both large and small, and both simple and complex.

Lastly, it may be asserted that technology-assisted processes of the kind we have been considering are unhelpful for promoting access to justice. That is because the intended beneficiaries, who are relatively economically disadvantaged, are less likely

[40] Susskind (n 10) 149–50.
[41] ibid.
[42] Vos (n 22) para 21.

to have access to the Internet, or have the requisite computer literacy, for engaging in the new processes. In other words, a new barrier (technology) would replace the old ones (time and financial costs), taking us back to square one. Although this is a valid concern, it does not appear to be a cogent one when one considers that those unable to access online dispute resolution for the foregoing reasons are unlikely to have been able to access traditional forms of international dispute resolution either. Statistics suggest that the potential reach of online dispute resolution is already massive. In 2021, 60 per cent of the world population are Internet users, and 54 per cent are active social media users.[43] Provided that there is sufficient education (and that the design is user-friendly), these persons should have no problem using either the generic or specialist model of fully asynchronous arbitration. Thus, technology-driven access reforms in international arbitration would be both progressive and effective.

There nevertheless remains a separate question as to whether *parties* would see fully asynchronous arbitration as inferior to a synchronous process. It is plausible that parties may prefer a traditional hearing, whether physical or remote, because of its deeper interpersonal elements. Research suggests that parties place higher value on procedural justice as informed by interpersonal connections than the quality of decision-making.[44] A traditional hearing offers real-time face-to-face interactions, whereas a fully asynchronous process does not. On this basis, the former may be considered a superior interpersonal experience. However, this preference may change over time. As pointed out by Professor Susskind, recent anecdotal accounts in the field of psychotherapy have indicated that the younger generation prefers texting to voice or video-based communications.[45] It is entirely possible that the 'selfie generation' will prefer fully asynchronous hearings, which can be conducted entirely by text, in contrast to traditional hearings.

A fully asynchronous process, whether of the generic or specialist kind, is quicker, cheaper and more convenient, without compromising the quality of decisions (at least for commercial disputes). It gives the parties the full opportunity to comment on the case materials as the case progresses. The process, as conceived by some, would be more intelligible and streamlined, for the adjudicator is expected to 'take an inquisitorial and problem-solving approach, guiding the parties to explain and understand their respective positions',[46] and to be 'totally *au fait* with the issues and the stage that her online "trial" had reached and what she truly needed to know to resolve the issues that really divided the parties in the case'.[47] Recent research shows that, by removing the need for face-to-face interactions, fully asynchronous dispute resolution may make adjudication fairer, because 'judges need not be exposed to parties' group-based identity traits' which may become a source of bias.[48]

[43] S Kemp, "Digital 2021: Global Overview Report" (*DataReportal*, 27 January 2021), available at www.datareportal.com/reports/digital-2021-global-overview-report.

[44] See generally TR Tyler and SL Blader, 'The Group Engagement Model: Procedural Justice, Social Identity, and Cooperative Behavior' (2003) 7 *Personality and Social Psychology Review* 349, 357.

[45] Susskind (n 10) 213.

[46] Ryder, 'Modernisation' (2016) para 30.

[47] Vos (n 22) para 22.

[48] A Mentowvich, JJ Prescott, and O Rabinovich-Einy, 'Are Litigation Outcome Disparities Inevitable? Courts, Technology, and the Future of Impartiality' (2020) 71 *Alabama Law Rev* 893, 975.

With these considerations in mind, it is difficult to see why informed parties would see fully asynchronous arbitration as an inferior offering. The 'economy class justice' argument is unconvincing. This would, of course, be a radical and inconvenient change for lawyers who are trained under, and invested in, the traditional model. But it must be the interests of the users, rather than lawyers and adjudicators, which are paramount. All in all, it is suggested that fully asynchronous proceedings are a promising innovation which could improve the efficiency of, and access to, justice in commercial cases. This proposal is not without its downsides, but they do not appear to outweigh its benefits. It is hoped that, in the future, work would be done on designing specialist platforms for fully asynchronous proceedings.

IV. Overall Conclusion

Drawing all the threads together, technology has been, and will continue to be, beneficial to the reform of international arbitral processes. Not only does it greatly enhance the efficiency and cost-effectiveness of international arbitration, but it also has the potential of facilitating access thereto. In *The Plague*, Albert Camus wrote, 'All that a man could win in the game of plague and life was knowledge and memory'.[49] COVID-19 has endowed us with knowledge and experience as respects the use of technology to resolve legal disputes. Our next task is to avail of what we have learned to improve the system of international dispute resolution further.

[49] A Camus, *The Plague* (Penguin, 2015) 224.

Conclusion: Transnational Dispute Resolution, International Commercial Courts, and the Future of International Commercial Law

PAMELA BOOKMAN AND ALYSSA KING

This book contains many thoughtful discussions about how to build a system of international commercial dispute resolution in a way that responds to current discontent over dispute resolution processes, the legitimacy of global institutions, and the system's ability to address global problems. From the beginning, Chief Justice Sundaresh Menon framed the project as cognisant both of globalisation's role in increasing economic growth, cultural exchange, and overall prosperity and of criticisms that globalisation has also contributed to global problems, from income inequality to climate change. One question presented was how the international commercial dispute resolution system, and the actors within it, can respond to these problems.

To address this question, this volume's authors have often raised old themes from arbitration in the new context of international commercial courts. Section I of this final chapter summarises the chapters that have preceded it, highlighting these common threads. Section II considers how the questions and answers that are familiar from debates about international commercial arbitration differ in the context of international commercial courts. To chart a path forward, section III traces how international commercial courts might contribute to a system of international commercial dispute resolution with greater potential to address global problems, as well was obstacles to their ability to do so. Section IV concludes.

I. New and Old Challenges in International Dispute Resolution

This section summarises the previous chapters to set the stage for considering the future of international commercial courts and their potential to address the global problems Chief Justice Menon raises in his Introduction.

A. Chief Justice Menon's Introduction

Chief Justice Menon began by building the argument that law has helped to sustain globalisation, and globalisation has shaped the law. The Chief Justice highlighted three ways that law has contributed to these developments. First, over the past several decades, legal rights matured as a 'currency of trust' – with legal frameworks and institutions that safeguard and realise those rights.[1] Foremost among these frameworks were methods for transnational dispute resolution, which strive to ensure international enforceability, neutrality and flexibility of law. It is perhaps no coincidence that international commercial arbitration rose to prominence in this era, with the 1958 New York Convention widely cited as the most successful international treaty. Second, global commercial laws have converged on certain shared principles, trending towards convergence and standardisation of commercial practices, building a common, recognisable framework across most jurisdictions. Third, these methods and principles together have 'encourage[d] commercial entrepreneurship and innovation while limiting the potentially ruinous consequences of business failure', serving, as Lord Bingham said, as 'the handmaid of commerce'.[2]

Globalisation also brought global threats. The 1997 Asian financial crisis sparked a worldwide downturn, and the 2008 New York financial crisis likewise created global chaos. One might add global terrorism, climate change, and COVID-19 to the list. The Chief Justice urges us to consider that globalisation can help solve these problems, which ultimately 'require global solutions'.[3] Law, he urges, can help resuscitate globalisation by placing globalisation 'on a more sustainable footing', building a more constructive space for globalisation discourse, and grounding globalisation in legitimacy.[4] Building a sustainable foundation includes global responses to climate change, for example, through the UN Sustainable Development Goals and including sustainability clauses in free-trade agreements. It also requires global responses to rising income inequality, cooperation on which can be particularly difficult because states may have differing interests. But the law, the Chief Justice urges, can both *facilitate promise-keeping* and *coordinate* the nature of the promises kept, for example, by calling for universal adherence to certain standards.[5] This is the role for transnational commercial law.

In addition, the law can help globalisation and its institutions regain legitimacy. The Chief Justice provided three areas in which law can guide the way. First, procedural design should include making sure justice is accessible and fit for purpose. Criticisms of investor–state dispute settlement (ISDS), for example, reflect a belief that this justice system is not fit for purpose, because ISDS – unlike *private* commercial dispute resolution – is concerned with issues of significant public interest, not limited to the vindication of the private rights of private parties. Thus, ISDS calls out for public values

[1] See Introduction section II.A of this book.

[2] See Introduction section II.A of this book (citing Lord Bingham of Cornhill, 'The Law as the Handmaid of Commerce' (5 September 2001), speech at the Sixteenth Sultan Azlan Shah Law Lecture 2001).

[3] See Introduction section III.B of this book.

[4] See Introduction section IV.A of this book.

[5] See Introduction section IV.A of this book.

like 'transparency, accountability, and consistency of outcomes'.[6] Second, he urged thinking about procedural reform in which each type of dispute resolution – whether commercial arbitration, ISDS, or international commercial courts – are complementary parts of a *system* of international commercial dispute resolution.[7] As such, the focus should not be on uniformity among these component parts, but on interoperability. Finally, individuals working in all these areas can contribute to norm-building and the institutionalisation of the Rule of Law.

At a time when globalisation's negative effects are all too apparent, these remarks remind us of its possibilities. They are a call to action to address some of globalisation's most pressing challenges, not by retreating within our respective borders, but by renewing and deepening our work across them. As the Chief Justice has said, doing so requires 'a concerted effort to develop a more *sustainable* vision of [globalisation]'.[8]

B. International Commercial Law in an Age of Uncertainty

This volume has explored six themes across 12 chapters: the nature of commercial disputes; the relationship between international commercial arbitration and the rise of specialist commercial courts; investor–state dispute resolution; the importance of finality; *lex mercatoria* and the convergence of commercial laws; and the impact of COVID-19 on international dispute resolution. Here, we briefly summarise each section, highlighting, as appropriate, the ways in which the chapters address familiar debates from arbitration, or consider the potential for a modern system of international commercial dispute resolution – with new specialised commercial courts – to address the global problems the Chief Justice identified in his Introduction.

i. Part I: What is an International Commercial Dispute?

The chapters in part one argue that international commercial disputes should be treated as a unique category, to which specific, and transnational, substantive and procedural rules apply. They consider different forms of dispute resolution in this arena to be complementary, but highlight the potential of courts to contribute to convergence and law development. In chapter one, Pak Hei Li suggests that there is a place for a freestanding international commercial law, including for a shared definition of what is 'international' and 'commercial'. Although model legal instruments like the UNCITRAL Model Law may be drafted at the international level, they must be adopted as domestic law if they are to have force. Thus, any international commercial law will emerge from a process of 'convergence' or 'harmonisation', which Li argues should take place not only with respect to substantive law, but also with respect to the way disputes are resolved.[9] Li argues that courts have a unique role to play in this process as, unlike mediation and arbitration, they operate in public and publish their decisions. Publication gives courts a unique opportunity to shape a *lex mercatoria*.

[6] See Introduction section IV.C of this book.
[7] See Introduction section IV.C of this book.
[8] See Introduction section I of this book.
[9] See ch 1 section IV of this book.

Chief Justice Allsop and Samuel Walpole continue these themes in chapter two, considering what it means to develop and maintain a 'decentralised – but globalised – system' of international commercial law.[10] Chief Justice Allsop and Walpole situate the discussion in the long history of international trade. They then consider the ways in which commercial disputes, often thought of as concerning only the parties, also bring in a host of 'public' rules of law with implications beyond the individual case. These authors, too, discuss *lex mercatoria*, arguing for an expansive definition that would encompass not only transnational legal rules but also convergence in practices. They see a greater role for arbitral institutions to develop *lex mercatoria* through published awards and also for courts, highlighting the work of the SICC and the Standing International Forum of Commercial Courts.

ii. Part II: The Swinging Pendulum: International Commercial Arbitration and the Rise of Specialist Commercial Courts

Over the past decade, international commercial courts (ICCs) have emerged as an alternative to international commercial arbitration, which remains popular but is sometimes criticised as being too expensive, technical, or time-consuming. Part two surveys the rise of these courts. Chapter three first discusses international commercial courts in Paris, Singapore, Dubai, Amsterdam and China (Shenzhen and Xian), noting their similarities – for example, all make proceeding in English more accessible than in national courts, have expert judges, and limit jurisdiction in some way to international commercial disputes – and some of their differences. For example, the Paris, Amsterdam and Chinese international courts all use domestic judges, while the courts in Singapore and Dubai use a mixed bench of local and international judges. Additional courts similar to the Dubai model have been established in recent years in Qatar, Kazakhstan and Abu Dhabi.

Professor Shi Jianping explains ICCs as intended to address the shortcomings of the existing international commercial dispute resolution system. Some ICCs, like the London and Paris courts, respond to the needs of the business community, while others strive at least in part to become a regional centre for dispute resolution. These include the Singapore International Commercial Court (SICC), the Dubai International Financial Centre (DIFC) courts, and the Chinese International Commercial Courts. The Chinese International Commercial Courts also aim to provide a forum for disputes arising out of the Belt and Road Initiative. These courts, Shi argues, are all established to enhance the country's competitiveness in international commercial dispute resolution and are based on a belief that strong courts and the Rule of Law promote economic development.

International commercial courts 'mak[e] up for the shortcomings of arbitration'. The confidentiality of arbitral awards, Shi argues, reduces predictability and fairness; judicial transparency in ICCs, on the other hand, could create more realistic chances of consistent outcomes. Unlike arbitral tribunals, ICCs can join third parties or consolidate disputes, offer lower costs because parties do not have to pay the judge or the tribunal's fees, and provide pre-established procedural rules, appellate bodies and efficiency measures. Like arbitration, moreover, ICCs often offer a neutral forum that need

[10] See ch 2 section I.A.

not have any relationship to the dispute; specialised, expert, sometimes foreign judges; the availability of bespoke procedural rules; the option of evidentiary rules similar to those available in arbitration; state-of-the-art technology; English language; and access for foreign lawyers. They 'break through the limits of national boundaries' by creating national courts that routinely consider other nations' laws, thus furthering the development of international commercial law.

In chapter four, Justice Bernard Eder continues these themes. After exploring parties' shifting preferences for litigation or arbitration for resolving their disputes in Europe and Asia over the centuries, he acknowledges the preference for arbitration in the last few decades, which has handicapped courts' ability to develop the common law. Justice Eder contends that the swinging pendulum of preferences for litigation or arbitration is overall beneficial both because the 'competition' between arbitration and litigation drives courtroom innovation and because the two modes complement each other, for example as the courts promote transparency and ethical regulation over arbitration (as in the *Halliburton v Chubb* case).

Like Shi, Justice Eder characterises ICCs' hybridisation as 'the best of all worlds', catering to commercial parties' desire for 'honest, quick, skilled dispute resolution by competent [decisionmakers]' from arbitration and litigation, and their procedures and practices respond to this desire. If ICCs adapt their procedures to the commercial communities' needs and expectations, Justice Eder predicts that preferences will favour ICCs, in tandem with other kinds of dispute resolution – not only arbitration but also mediation, for example – thus complementing and expanding the international system of commercial dispute resolution.

Nonetheless, ICCs also pose some problems, which they should focus on mitigating. For example, many countries do not allow foreign courts to take evidence by remote technology in their territory. Service of notice of a suit may be more cumbersome for litigation than simply notifying a party of an arbitration. Judgments enforcement is also less assured than enforcement of arbitral awards under the New York Convention. Some of these problems are more easily addressed than others. Justice Eder expresses confidence that the differences in enforcement, at least under English law, are not so dissimilar as between the enforcement of an arbitral award and the enforcement of a judgment coming out of a court where the parties have agreed to jurisdiction. The conclusion remains that arbitration and litigation can and likely will continue to enhance and complement each other.

iii. Part III: David and Goliath: Investor–State Dispute Resolution

The public/private tension discussed in part two is at the centre of current debates about ISDS and the future of investor–state dispute resolution.[11] Justice Anselmo Reyes argues

[11] See, eg A Roberts, 'Clash of Paradigms: Actors and Analogies Shaping the Investment Treaty System' (2013) 107 *American Journal of International Law* 45; J Alvarez, 'ISDS Reform: The Long View' (2021) 36 *ICSID Review – Foreign Investment Law Journal* 253, available at papers.ssrn.com/sol3/papers.cfm?abstract_id=3957514; J Alvarez, 'Is Investor-State Arbitration 'Public'?' (2016) *Institute for International Law and Justice Working Papers* Working Paper 2016/6, available at www.iilj.org/working-papers/is-investor-state-arbitration-public; J Allsop, 'Commercial and Investor-State Arbitration: The Importance of Recognising Their Differences' (ICCA Congress 2018, Sydney, 16 April 2018).

that the use of private institutional design norms has undermined the legitimacy of ISDS decisions with broad public implications. Investment cases often come down to judgements of proportionality, 'a balance between the legitimate purposes of a state and the legitimate expectations of an investor',[12] which the current system is ill-equipped to handle. As a result, investment arbitration has lost legitimacy with the public and reform is necessary. In chapters five and six, Jianjian Ye and Justice Reyes consider an investment court or set of investment courts as a possible solution.

Chapter five describes how ISDS's initial institutional design borrowed heavily from international commercial arbitration, with elements like party selection of arbitrators, lack of transparency, no appeals and high costs. These design choices have different consequences when applied to disputes with more public elements and where the legal issues have more naturally aligned 'sides'. The enforcement context is also different – states may rely on sovereign immunity to prevent enforcement. Party selection of arbitrators is particularly contentious in disputes that involve state resources and if arbitrators are seen as divided into 'investor'- and 'state'-friendly camps. ISDS proceedings are typically more transparent than commercial arbitration – with more published opinions and a documented trend of cross-citation in a manner that resembles precedent.[13] Investors and states routinely pick specific arbitrators. Arbitrators' perceived bias towards one side or another, or at least, towards the institution of ISDS, corrupts the institution's image.[14] This problem is exacerbated when there are splits between the investor- and state-side arbitrators, with no possibility of appeal. As a result, the authors note, investment tribunals have sometimes struggled with legitimacy. When tribunals decide for investors, states may attack the decision as the product of out-of-touch foreigners who do not take the public interest seriously.

In chapter six, Justice Reyes argues that several of the treaty elements often at issue in ISDS, including fair and equitable treatment, anti-expropriation, national treatment, and most-favoured-nation clauses, all ask the tribunal to engage in a proportionality balancing test similar to that used in administrative and constitutional law in many jurisdictions. Reyes argues that tribunals in the current system lack the legitimacy to make these decisions. As with commercial dispute resolution, current proposals to reform ISDS involve diversifying the modes by which it can take place, seeking both less and greater formality. ISDS treaty provisions now commonly call for mediation, using an interest-based mode of dispute resolution rather than going directly to law. The authors in this part of the book disagree over whether mediation will work, with Ye arguing that it can save time and costs, and Justice Reyes arguing that it is typically more politically expedient for governments to fight rather than settle their cases. If one must go to law, the EU has proposed a return to court – not to the national court systems that investors have found inadequate, but to a multilateral investment court. Unlike arbitrators, the courts' members would be appointed by states for a fixed term, reducing a

[12] See ch 6 section I of this book.

[13] See WMC Weidemaier, 'Toward a Theory of Precedent in Arbitration' (2010) 51 *William & Mary Law Review* 1895, 1915.

[14] See J Arato, 'The Elastic Corporate Form in International Law' (2022) 62 *Virginia Journal of International Law* 383, 422–23 (arguing that ISDS favours claimants, a narrow sub-group of investors, not investors as a whole).

source of perceived bias and bringing in actors more familiar with proportionality tests. Justice Reyes also argues that courts will be more transparent and will be able to develop and enforce rules that save time and costs, such as those allowing for remote hearings. The perceived benefits of a standing, multinational, public court to handle ISDS thus resemble the benefits perceived to be offered by international commercial courts: the option of a neutral forum less associated with one state, adjudicators with judicial experience and transparency of process and outcomes.

iv. Part IV: The Perfect as the Enemy of the Good: The Importance of Finality and Certainty

This part explored the importance of certainty and finality in the determination of commercial disputes. The debates about the particulars of these rules can be many and contentious. These may be areas in which international commercial courts are well suited to develop best practices and to move the law towards convergence and harmonisation of those best practices. In international commercial dispute resolution, party autonomy and principles of comity and sovereignty can sometimes come into conflict with the values of certainty and finality in the form of concurrent proceedings. In this context, common law systems tend to regulate this balance through *forum non conveniens*, while civil law systems reject that approach and instead apply the doctrine of *lis pendens*. Sometimes, courts are called upon to enjoin parallel proceedings in other courts (via anti-suit injunctions) or to stay arbitral proceedings. Parties may also seek to prevent relitigation of a dispute by invoking *res judicata*. Related issues arise when a court is called upon to recognise and enforce foreign judgments. To do so, the enforcing court must have jurisdiction to recognise and enforce the foreign judgment; it also must determine that the judgment rendered was reasonable and fair by some standard. The question is: what are the international standards for that kind of indirect jurisdiction and for the recognition of the judgment? Common law and civil law jurisdictions take different approaches.

In chapter seven, Wilson Lui submits that the pandemic presents an opportunity for stakeholders in the international commercial dispute resolution system to rethink approaches to finality and certainty (among other issues). Regulations and invocation of public policies relating to COVID-19 – for example, provisions requiring parties not to initiate proceedings to enforce a security if the counterparty's inability to perform is materially caused by a COVID-19 event and dismissing such actions if brought[15] – could provide a template for further expansion of other kinds of public-policy-based regulations of international commercial dispute resolution.

Justice Nallini Pathmanathan reflects on the same tension in chapter eight. In either arbitration or litigation, multiplicity of proceedings can be a major threat to finality. Justice Pathmanathan therefore calls for the international commercial dispute resolution system to be consistent across different adjudicatory bodies to inspire confidence in

[15] See ch 7 section IV of this book (citing COVID-19 (Temporary Measures] Act 2020 (No 14 of 2020) (Singapore), Arts 5, 8).

the Rule of Law.[16] As national courts play increasingly important roles in international commercial dispute resolution, they continue to develop doctrines and mechanisms like *lis pendens*, *forum non conveniens*, and anti-suit injunctions, many of which incorporate public policies closely tied to the forum state's priorities. Justice Pathmanathan argues that the international commercial dispute resolution system requires a broad commitment to finality to function cohesively. This commitment to finality must include a commitment to enforce foreign awards and judgments. Such a commitment raises difficult legal questions that may be mitigated somewhat by the 2005 and 2019 Hague Conventions on the Recognition and Enforcement of Foreign Judgments. On the other hand, the COVID-19 pandemic has raised other challenges, including questions about the meaning of due process in an age of virtual proceedings. These are challenges that international commercial courts should take on.

v. Part V: The Lex Mercatoria *and the Convergence of Commercial Laws*

The question of whether the needs of international commerce have created or should create a *lex mercatoria* is perennial. Its permutations in the discussion of international commercial arbitration are well known,[17] but reference to courts brings a different perspective. Jason Lin begins chapter nine by considering the history of *lex mercatoria* and the debate over its existence. He makes the intriguing observation that common law judges have developed a sort of *lex mercatoria* between them: a commercial law discussed and applied across jurisdictions.[18] He then discusses the well-trodden territory of soft law instruments like the CISG. Lin closes by considering the role of international arbitration in developing a *lex mercatoria*.

Professor Yeo Tiong Min argues in chapter ten that *lex mercatoria* is meaningful only if it has sufficiently certain substantive content with practical significance for current transnational business. Thus, Yeo sets aside the theoretical debate and issues of historical genealogy in favour of a more pragmatic analysis. Instead of seeing *lex mercatoria* as set of rules, à la Lord Mustill,[19] Yeo argues that we should see '*lex mercatoria* as a network of interlocking principles, rules, and guidelines' that does not require strict uniformity.[20] The job of *lex mercatoria* is not to resolve differences between systems, but to provide 'interoperability', enabling choice and creating clear rules of priority between legal systems.[21] Instead of ignoring national and local interests that diverge from international norms (which may reflect the interests of a few historical trading powers and ignore normative systems relevant in other parts of the world) *lex mercatoria* would structure how and when they are considered. Like Lin, Yeo sees

[16] See ch 8 section III of this book.

[17] See, eg M Pryles, 'Application of the *Lex Mercatoria* in International Commercial Arbitration' (2008) 31 *UNSW Law Journal* 319 (summarising debates); L Yves Fortier, 'The New New *Lex Mercatoria* or Back to the Future' (2014) 17 *Arbitration International* 121; P Kahn, 'La *lex mercatoria*: point de vue français après quarante ans de controverses' (1992) 37 *McGill Law Journal* 413.

[18] See ch 9 section II.A of this book.

[19] See Mustill, 'The New *Lex Mercatoria*: The First Twenty-Five Years' (1988) 4 *Arbitration International* 86, 88.

[20] See ch 10 section II.C of this book.

[21] See ch 10 section III of this book.

multiple elements as contributing to a common corpus of commercial law, including treaties, soft law instruments and domestic laws explicitly designed to promote convergence.

Yeo also raises the role of courts in maintaining this system by providing public discussion that is often missing with commercial arbitration. Both chapters eschew clean theoretical definitions of *lex mercatoria* and describe instead a dialogue with multiple players representing both private and state interests. Using this more pragmatic definition of *lex mercatoria*, it may be less important to identify a set of principles and more important to identify sources of law and authoritative voices in the dialogue. As discussed below, courts emerge as important interlocutors because of their ability to mediate between participants and the public nature of their work.

vi. Part VI: The Impact of COVID-19

This final part considers the evolution of the international commercial dispute resolution system during and after the COVID-19 pandemic, considering the past, present and future of the pandemic's impacts on innovation and technology.

With the onset of the COVID-19 pandemic in March 2020, in-person hearings ceased and created an urgent need for virtual, remote hearings at a vast scale. As Cedric Yeung recounts in chapter eleven, remote hearings quickly became the norm, and the entire international commercial dispute resolution system innovated to accommodate these needs – both in the form of synchronous hearings, often over Zoom, and sometimes through asynchronous hearings, for example via prerecorded opening statements in arbitration. Remote hearings offer several advantages, including convenience, lower environmental impact and reduced costs.[22] Nevertheless, some still greatly prefer in-person hearings. In addition, certain rules necessitate in-person hearings, including civil law rules requiring courts (but not arbitral tribunals) to have permission from foreign countries if they wish to take evidence from witnesses there. Yeung argues that remote proceedings could transform the international commercial dispute resolution system for the better, for example, by pushing common law jurisdictions away from the 'concentrated trial' and towards the civil law tradition's episodic hearings, which can increase flexibility of scheduling, reduce time and costs and increase accuracy and fairness.[23]

In chapter twelve, Lord Jonathan Mance and Professor Douglas Jones continue these themes. The authors first highlight three beneficial procedural innovations in international commercial arbitration and litigation – case management conferences (CMCs), streamlining document production and close management of expert evidence – and how technology has improved each.[24] The convenience of remote CMCs, for example, permits them to occur earlier and more often, as needs arise, which greatly enhance their effectiveness. The authors recognise that technology also creates challenges. The more that proceedings and documents are digital, the greater the cybersecurity risks

[22] See ch 11 section III of this book.
[23] See ch 11 section IV of this book.
[24] See ch 12 section II.A of this book.

and the concern for confidentiality breaches. There may also be concerns that remote hearings are inferior to in-person hearings in terms of accuracy and fairness.

On both accounts, the authors defend remote hearings. They rebut arguments that factual witnesses are more likely to lie, or to have their lies believed, in remote hearings, in part because adjudicators should not rely heavily on demeanour or other nuances supposedly lost in remote hearings in the first place.[25] As to fairness and the opportunity to be heard, they argue that remote hearings *increase* access to judges and that 'virtual advocacy [can] be just as effective as in-person advocacy'.[26] The authors predict that fully asynchronous processes for international disputes could provide an even more transformative innovation in international commercial dispute resolution. The benefits, the authors say, are obvious: 'it saves time, reduces costs, and eliminates the inconvenience arising from time zone differences'.[27] These efficiency gains may also increase access to justice, especially for small and medium-sized enterprises that face resource barriers. The authors rebut arguments that fully asynchronous processes are better suited to low-value or less complex disputes. Complex and high-value disputes, they argue, likewise have much to gain from innovations that promise increased efficiency without compromising quality.[28]

II. Commercial Courts: Old Private Wine, New Public Bottles

The preceding chapters have raised questions about the boundaries of international and commercial law, the relationship between public and private law, the aims of dispute resolution, forms of legal harmonisation, and the institutional arrangements needed to manage these debates. Their authors generally take a pragmatic approach – seeing international dispute resolution as part of a system with multiple institutions. Some of the challenges facing this system are longstanding questions of private international law while others involve new incarnations of older problems, exacerbated in some ways by globalisation and the very 'success' it has brought. The authors have offered suggestions for the role that international courts can play in resolving these questions.

Many of the themes discussed in this volume should be familiar to scholars and practitioners of international commercial arbitration. These issues come with different implications when they involve international commercial courts and are understood in the context of the broader international commercial dispute resolution system. This section first reviews the themes that have traditionally pervaded scholarly and practical understanding of international arbitration's global role and then explores the extent to which these themes have parallels in the context of international commercial courts. This discussion sets the stage for the next section, which considers the extent to which the international commercial dispute resolution system is better equipped to address global problems with the addition of international commercial courts.

[25] See ch 12 section II.C of this book.
[26] See ch 12 section II.C of this book.
[27] See ch 12 section III.B.ii of this book.
[28] See ch 12 section III.B.ii

A. Familiar Themes from Arbitration

In the latter decades of the twentieth century, arbitration became the forum of choice for international commercial dispute resolution (as well as for investor–state disputes).[29] Arbitration's rise has been founded on the several advantages it offers when compared to domestic courts, including private proceedings, the application of private law, expert decision-makers, rulings that apply (at least in theory) only to the parties, easily enforceable awards by virtue of the widely accepted New York Convention, and the ability to cater to parties' preferences for choosing their own arbitrators and their own procedures. Parties that choose arbitration also often cite an additional motivation: the desire to avoid domestic courts.

Today, arbitration remains a robust part of the international commercial dispute resolution system. Around the world, arbitral institutions report rising caseloads.[30] With this increased influence, the arbitration community has made various efforts to embrace a heightened sense of responsibility, with initiatives for increasing transparency in awards and diversity among arbitrators, greening the practice of arbitration and spreading the gospel of the benefits of ADR.[31] Moreover, many international commercial courts and commercial divisions work to support arbitration and develop expertise in arbitration law.[32] These courts tout their arbitration expertise – their ability to ensure that agreements to arbitrate are enforced, to issue orders in aid of an arbitral tribunal, and to confirm or enforce awards in a manner consistent with the expectations of the international business community.

International commercial courts also respond in part to complaints about existing options in arbitration. International arbitration can be costly and there are limits to the authority that party-appointed arbitrators can claim beyond the specific contract or treaty dispute. Although some have pushed for greater publication of awards, many commercial awards are confidential, as are the proceedings themselves. Scholars and practitioners have also expressed broader concerns about arbitration's ability to confront

[29] See ch 4 (discussing the swinging pendulum of parties' preferences that have recently favoured arbitration); but cf J Nyarko, 'We'll See You in … Court! The Lack of Arbitration Clauses in International Commercial Contracts: (2018) 58 *International Review of Law and Economics* 6 (finding that commercial contracts between US parties and foreign parties more often choose litigation over arbitration in their forum selection clauses).

[30] See eg S Chapman et al, 'Rise in Arbitration Cases in 2020 Despite Reduced Volume of In Person Hearings Due to Coronavirus Pandemic' (Arbitration Notes, 3 March 2021), available at hsfnotes.com/arbitration/2021/03/03/rise-in-arbitration-cases-in-2020-despite-reduced-volume-of-in-person-hearings-due-to-coronavirus-pandemic. Most arbitration institutions that released statistics for 2020 reported increased caseloads, with the Hong Kong, Singapore, International Chamber of Commerce and London Centres all reporting record-breaking years. In 2021, those numbers receded somewhat. R Campbell et al, 'Assessing the LCIA's 2021 Annual Casework Report' (JD Supra, 20 May 2022), available at www.jdsupra.com/legalnews/assessing-the-lcia-s-2021-annual-1612293.

[31] See, eg American Arbitration Association-International Centre for Dispute Resolution Foundation, 'About Us: The Foundation', available at\www.aaaicdrfoundation.org; J Karton, 'Diversity in Four Dimensions: Conceptualizing Diversity in International Arbitration' in G Colombo, J Karton, F Balcerzak and S Ali (eds), *Sustainable Diversity in International Arbitration* (Edward Elgar, 2022).

[32] See eg PK Bookman, 'The Adjudication Business' (2020) 45 *Yale Journal of International Law* 227, 229, 253.

the global problems Chief Justice Menon discussed in his Introduction.[33] Some of the more theoretical controversies over the source of arbitration's authority and the scope of its jurisdiction also provide real-world limitations on arbitration's ability to carry these heavy loads. We discuss each set of challenges – those presented by arbitration's practical advantages and by its theoretical controversies – in turn below.

i. *Practical Advantages as Challenges*

Arbitration alone is inadequate – and was never intended – to address many of the issues that this volume suggests the international commercial dispute resolution system should aim to address.[34] Arbitration's traditionally attractive factors also hinder its ability to perform more public functions, address globalised problems, and develop law. First, it is private – it relies on parties' consent for its authority, proceedings are private, and its awards are often confidential. These features make it difficult for international commercial arbitration to build up a body of decisions and establish a stable dialogue with an international commercial audience.[35] Even if arbitration could build up a body of publicly available decisions, arbitration's private nature hinders its ability to develop law and address problems beyond the parties' dispute. Parties find arbitration attractive in part because it can offer dedication to their preferences, bespoke procedure, and approaches to law that may differ from the courts of a specific jurisdiction. For example, arbitral tribunals may apply *lex mercatoria* or serve as *amiable compositeur* – although they rarely do so in practice.[36]

But these very attributes that enable arbitration to cater to parties' needs can also detract from arbitration's ability to attend to more public and non-party interests, including global problems like climate change. Perspectives from the ISDS debates are helpful to understanding the point.[37] As the chapters in part three describe, ISDS faces doubts about its ability to address global problems because it is not structured to achieve public purposes.[38] The public ramifications of these disputes have led to calls for more transparency, accountability and consistency of outcomes.[39] International commercial

[33] DR Hensler and D Khatam, 'Re-Inventing Arbitration: How Expanding the Scope of Arbitration is Re-Shaping Its Form and Blurring the Line between Private and Public Adjudication' (2018) 18 *Nevada Law Journal* 381, 386; CA Rogers, 'The Arrival of the 'Have Nots' in International Arbitration' (2007) 8 *Nevada Law Journal* 341, 343; M Grando, 'Challenges to the Legitimacy of International Arbitration: A Report from the 29th Annual IRA Workshop' (Kluwer Arbitration Blog, 19 September 2017), available at arbitrationblog.kluwerarbitration.com/2017/09/19/challenges-legitimacy-international-arbitration-report-29th-annual-ita-workshop.

[34] See S Menon, 'International Courts: Towards a Transnational System of Dispute Resolution' DIFC Courts Lecture Series 2015; see also ch 4 section III of this book.

[35] The ICC and Jus Mundi recently entered a partnership to provide public access to 'all publishable ICC International Court of Arbitration awards and related documents made as of 1 January 2019'. 'Publication of ICC Arbitral Awards with Jus Mundi' (International Chamber of Commerce, 4 January 2021), available at iccwbo.org/dispute-resolution-services/arbitration/publication-of-icc-arbitral-awards-with-jus-mundi (describing how the awards are anonymised). The stated purpose of this initiative was to provide information and support the legitimacy of arbitration, not (of course) to build a body of law; ibid.

[36] The degree to which arbitrators are bound to apply mandatory law is a matter of debate. See LA Mistelis, 'Mandatory Rules in International Arbitration: Too Much Too Early or Too Little Too Late?' in GA Bermann and LA Mistelis (eds), *Mandatory Rules in International Arbitration* (Juris Publishing, 2011) 291–309.

[37] See Pt III.

[38] See ch 6 section II.D of this book.

[39] See ch 6 section II.D of this book.

arbitration is not immune to similar requests, but its private nature makes such concerns more muted. With some exceptions, the ramifications of particular awards in commercial arbitration are limited to the parties. The same elements, however, limit arbitration's ability to develop international commercial law that either considers or directly impacts the interests of parties outside the arbitration.

ii. Obstacles from Theory

Debates about arbitration theory also have practical implications for arbitration's ability to address global problems effectively. Arbitration can be difficult to conceptualise in part because it grew organically, largely propelled by private actors and their vision of necessity, unconcerned with academic theory.[40] Yet it is also an area in which theory has practical ramifications. Two theoretical difficulties have particular relevance here: (1) the source of the arbitral tribunal's authority; and (2) the scope of its jurisdiction. In the next section, we will discuss how international commercial courts seek to provide an attractive forum that overcomes these difficulties.

(1) Source of authority. While arbitration thrives in practice and clearly has authority, the source of this authority is a font of theoretical debate. This issue may affect what arguments and what laws the tribunal can consider, and it limits the extent to which the tribunal can develop law with lasting effects beyond the parties' dispute. For example, the tribunal may perceive tighter restrictions on what arbitrators may consider when adjudicating as compared to judges, focusing on the contract to sidestep nuances of domestic laws. A tribunal that views its authority as localised may apply mandatory laws of the seat, regardless of the law the parties choose in their contract.[41] On the other hand, a tribunal whose members believe that its authority is delocalised may refer to *lex mercatoria* or to general principles of transnational law in the absence of an operable choice-of-law clause, or if the parties so choose.[42] In practice, arbitrators can often avoid such questions, but the theoretical debate highlights the real dilemma about the source of and limitations on an arbitral tribunal's authority to develop law – transnational or otherwise.[43]

In theory, every arbitral award could contribute to an abstract international commercial law as much as it contributes to the development of English law, Swiss law, or whatever state law the parties have chosen. At the same time, to the extent that the parties' consent to arbitration is a necessary condition of the tribunal's authority, the award legally binds only the parties that have consented to arbitration. Future tribunals have no responsibility to follow the award's reasoning, if they are even aware the award exists. The debates about the very existence of *lex mercatoria*[44] and arbitrators' authority

[40] See eg S Brekoulakis, 'International Arbitration Scholarship and the Concept of Arbitration Law' (2013) 36 *Fordham International Law Journal* 745, 746.

[41] Mistelis, 'Mandatory Rules' (2011) 36.

[42] E Gaillard, *Legal Theory of International Arbitration* (Martinus Nijhoff Publishers, 2010) 103.

[43] In addition, the theoretical debate also has consequences for courts reviewing awards. If awards are localised, then a decision to confirm or to refuse to enforce an award has special weight. If awards represent international commercial law, then they might be properly set aside for reasons of international, but not national, public policy. ibid 60–63.

[44] See chs 9 and 10.

to develop general principles of law highlight the limitations of arbitration in developing international commercial law in ways that might address global problems – which, by definition, affect parties beyond those party to the arbitration.

(2) Scope of jurisdiction. The scope of a tribunal's jurisdiction, founded in the parties' arbitration agreement, creates similar obstacles. Just as an arbitration agreement limits arbitrators' ability to take other parties' interests into consideration when making decisions, it also limits arbitral tribunals' ability to join and bind third parties, enforce interim and final decisions, or protect the assets involved in the dispute. These are reasons why the complementarity between courts and arbitration is so important – for courts to enforce arbitral awards, for example, and to issue interim measures when necessary. Arbitration's limits are not inappropriate – to the contrary, they are vital – but the limits that appropriately constrain arbitration also constrain its ability to address problems beyond the specific case.

These debates matter for arbitration's ability to address global problems and develop law. The practical reality of arbitration means that it develops rules – even while questions may remain about the proper legal characterisation of those rules, the source of arbitration's authority to make those rules, and the legitimacy of those rules. One question that emerges from this reality is whether there is a need for another institution, or other institutions, that might make rules in a different manner, and with a different effect.

B. The Role of International Commercial Courts

International commercial courts offer some of the same tantalising jurisgenerative possibilities as arbitration without some of the obstacles. Like arbitration, these courts offer a hopeful, if not utopian, vision of how the rule of commercial law might contribute to shared international rule of law norms.[45] Like arbitration, international commercial courts offer a dispute resolution system designed to be attractive to parties, offering features such as decision-makers with subject matter expertise, some choice of language, including English, and some ability to avoid 'regular' local courts. Some, like the SICC, also offer decision-makers with considerable international arbitration experience and who are foreign nationals. Courts can also avoid some of the institutional barriers to developing international commercial law responsive to global problems that arbitration faces. Courts are public, both in terms of proceedings and decisions. It may therefore be easier to build up a publicly accessible body of decisions and a more stable dialogue with its international commercial audience.[46] One might worry about the ease of enforcement of an international commercial court's judgments abroad, but there has been headway on greater international judgment enforcement and these courts are nonetheless less dependent on the authority of another institution.[47] Within their own

[45] See generally R Michaels, 'Dreaming Law Without a State: Scholarship On Autonomous International Arbitration As Utopian Literature' (2013) 1 *London Review of International Law* 35 (describing the utopian character of much of the literature on international commercial arbitration).

[46] See WMC Weidemaier, 'Toward a Theory of Precedent in Arbitration,' (2010) 51 *William and Mary Law Review* 1895; CR Drahozal, 'Is Arbitration Lawless?' (2006) 40 *Loyola of Los Angeles Law Review* 187, 190–91.

[47] See ch 4 section V (discussing why concerns about enforcement are overstated).

territorial jurisdiction, courts have state authority. Outside, thus far, the judgments of international commercial courts have been enforced.[48]

Some of the longstanding theoretical debates about arbitration can be avoided in the context of international commercial courts. International commercial courts might offer answers to the legitimacy questions raised by international arbitration. As domestic courts, created by domestic legal systems, they have the authority and legitimacy of the host state. Thus, the Paris International Commercial Chamber has the same authority as other French courts; the Singapore International Commercial Court, likewise, is a division of the Singapore High Court; the DIFC, Dubai's special economic zone, has established courts local to that jurisdiction. To the extent these courts have procedures or other features that mimic arbitration – like party autonomy to opt out of rules of evidence or the right to appeal, foreign judges or proceedings in English – those do not seem to detract from the court's authority as a state actor. Just as arbitration's authority is grounded in parties' consent to arbitration, many international commercial courts also exercise consent-based jurisdiction. Additionally, international commercial courts often have well-respected, expert judges, sometimes from foreign jurisdictions, in some ways resembling the expert and international bench of adjudicators available for international arbitration. International commercial courts thus both draw on similar sources of authority to arbitration, and address some of its perceived shortcomings by rooting courts' legitimacy in a state's sovereignty.

A court's authority to interpret law or public policy when making decisions, and to render judgments that bind third parties, is on far sturdier ground than that of arbitral tribunals. Courts assign judges rather than letting the parties choose and courts offer public hearings and decisions.[49] The authority comes from the parties' consent (where relevant[50]), from the host state's sovereignty, and from the support of the international community. This international support itself comes from multiple sources, including initiatives like the 2019 HCCH Judgments Convention, trans-judicial organisations like the Standing International Forum of Commercial Courts (SIFoCC), and cross-jurisdictional judicial networks and respect for the domestic and foreign judges who sit on these courts.[51]

[48] See, eg *Barclays Bank Plc v Shetty* [2022] EWHC 19 (Comm) (London court enforcing DIFC judgment); T Fox and J Paterson, 'English Commercial Court Enforces DIFC Court Judgment Under Common Law Rules' (National Law Review, 21 January 2022), available at www.natlawreview.com/article/english-commercial-court-enforces-difc-court-judgment-under-common-law-rules (discussing the case).

[49] One of us has argued that the international commercial courts that most resemble court-arbitration hybrids should be careful with expanding their jurisdiction, for example, joining foreign third parties who were not party to the forum-selection agreement when that agreement provides the sole basis for the court's jurisdiction. See P Bookman, 'Arbitral Courts' (2021) 61 *Virginia Journal of International Law* 161, 208. This hybridisation creates theoretical problems. But in practice, thus far, these institutions have been treated internationally as courts.

[50] For many cases in many international commercial courts, but not all, jurisdiction is established by virtue of the parties' consent, for example, through a forum selection clause or post-dispute consent agreement. See W Theus, 'International Commercial Courts: A New Frontier in International Commercial Dispute Resolution? Lessons from the Mixed Courts of the Colonial Era' in *European Yearbook of International Economic Law* (Springer, 2022).

[51] See AS King and PK Bookman, 'Traveling Judges', (2022) 116 *American Journal of International Law* 477, 489–490.

Thus, international commercial courts appear to offer answers to the legitimacy questions raised by international arbitration – but they may also raise their own questions. Some states establish international commercial courts so that the courts can buttress the states' legitimacy. As such, the legitimacy of international commercial courts can be complicated by their ties to their host states, even if they avoid the legitimacy complications that arbitration faces because of its separation from host states.[52] Public criticism of judges who travel to Hong Kong, Kazakhstan, or the UAE, whether founded or not, reflects a popular understanding of these dynamics.[53]

In addition, there are drawbacks to arbitration that international commercial courts share. The sort of denationalised posture that gives the courts credibility with an international audience may also leave them without domestic support. As Justice Reyes discusses in chapter six, investment tribunals have been accused of not properly balancing public policy concerns with rights under international investment law. There can be parallel concerns about international commercial courts. For example, efforts to establish a Brussels International Commercial Court faltered in Parliament following critiques that it was a 'caviar court' and would take resources away from other more deserving parts of the judiciary. Different complications have arisen in Dubai, where the onshore courts and the offshore DIFC courts have sparred with each other over the scope of their jurisdictions.

In other words, the emphasis on party choice and control that is shared between international commercial courts and arbitration sits uneasily with courts' broader mandate, which may include developing widely applicable law and addressing global problems. International commercial arbitration can maintain its focus on a party-oriented, commercial perspective precisely because it does not create a set of public decisions that can be referred to, or bind future parties, over time. As a dispute resolution system of and by the parties, it may be appropriate for it to cater primarily to parties. If international commercial courts are 'competing' with arbitration for parties' adjudication business,[54] they may be under similar pressures to cater to the parties. But the criticisms of globalisation can be linked to the development of a commercial law focused primarily on maximising short-term profit.[55]

Indeed, the interconnectedness of globalised threats – from financial crises to environmental crises to public health crises – reveal an interconnectedness between commercial law and non-commercial public law. Global terror is financed through

[52] Bookman, 'Arbitral Courts' (2021) 203.

[53] M Townsend, 'Head of Press Regulator Advised Kazakh Regime that Suppresses Free Speech' *The Guardian* (25 January 2020), available at www.theguardian.com/law/2020/jan/25/lord-faulks-ipso-head-kazakhstan-under-fire; A Harwood, 'Why is No One Talking About How 9 British Judges – including a Lord – Work for the UAE' *The Independent* (22 November 2018); 'Judgment Call' *The Times* (2 February 2022) (calling on British judges on the Hong Kong CFA to resign); 'Role of UK Supreme Court judges on the Hong Kong Court of Final Appeal – update', A statement from Lord Reed, President of the UK Supreme Court, 30 March 2022, available at www.supremecourt.uk/news/role-of-uk-judges-on-the-hong-kong-court-of-final-appeal-update-march-2022.html (announcing resignations of Lord Reed and Lord Hodge from the Hong Kong Court of Final Appeal).

[54] See, eg J Walker, 'Specialized International Courts: Keeping Arbitration on Top of Its Game' (2019) 85 *Arbitration* 2 (describing international commercial courts as competing with arbitration); but *cf* Bookman, 'Adjudication Business' (2020) (acknowledging the competition but also pointing out other dynamics at play).

[55] Cf *Peevyhouse v Garland Coal & Mining Co* 382 P 2d 109 (Okla 1962).

global, not localised, financial networks; climate change reflects a global exploitation of our planet and its resources for financial gain;[56] and COVID-19 highlights the interconnectedness of our lives and our economies, revealing fault lines in everything from global supply chains to intellectual property regimes. International commercial courts thus should be wary of identifying too strongly with the perspective of large commercial parties (the likely repeat players).

At least in theory, courts serve a greater community beyond just the parties. International commercial courts face the challenging task of defining that community. Is it a local community, a national community, or an international one? Is the community limited to commercial actors, or does it include others? If international commercial courts are to participate in an international commercial dispute resolution system that aspires to address global problems, created in part by international commerce's failure to internalise externalities like climate change impacts, it must define and uphold its responsibilities to a broader community.

Investment arbitration provides a warning. If the purpose of the investor–state regime is to protect covered investors generally and promote efficient investment, these are purposes that (in theory) should have positive ramifications for investors, states and the world. Still, Julian Arato argues, at least in relation to certain areas of the law, investment tribunals 'almost invariably prioritize the particular claimant in the particular case. Putting aside questions of the adjudicators' intentions, ISDS always seems to expand the availability of claims and to reduce the risk of making claims'.[57] In other words, both international commercial arbitration and investor–state arbitration have been criticised (or praised) for catering to the parties before them rather than considering broader interests. To avoid the fate of investment tribunals, international commercial courts should tie themselves to a mast of public service – by committing, for example, to transparency and to declining party requests for confidentiality – to avoid similar incentives drawing them into a posture that disproportionately favours parties and potential parties to the detriment of a community more broadly defined.[58] As such, they should resist the pressures of 'forum selling,' whereby courts develop procedures and even substantive law in ways that make the forum more attractive to some potential users.[59]

III. Charting a Course for the Future of International Commercial Courts

As international commercial courts are still relative newcomers to the international commercial dispute resolution system, one might wonder how they can affect the future of international commercial law. In this section, we consider the practicalities of how

[56] The Chief Justice in his Introduction noted the continuation from the age of colonialism to today of 'humanity's seemingly single-minded desire to maximally exploit global resources without restraint – relying on the trade and legal infrastructure provided by globalisation – in a bid to sustain what are, in truth, unsustainable levels of consumption and affluence, even though those levels will only be attained by very few and at inordinate cost'. See Introduction section III.A

[57] Arato, 'Elastic Corporate Form' (2022) 423.

[58] Bookman, 'Arbitral Courts' (n 49) 212.

[59] See D Klerman and G Reilly, 'Forum Selling' (2016) 89 *Southern California Law Review* 241.

these courts might have such influence, using the SICC as a case study; and then offer some warning notes, urging these courts to maintain transparency and to work towards defining the kind of jurisprudence that will balance their competing roles as dispute-resolvers and law-makers.

A. Why International Commercial Courts? A Bridge from the Past to the Future

International commercial courts draw on a long history and tradition of tribunals with judges from foreign jurisdictions[60] and cross-citation in the common law world. Their very personnel connect them to multiple domestic courts as well as to the international arbitration community, heightening their potential influence.[61] Nevertheless, one might think international commercial courts are unlikely to have much impact on legal development because they are relatively new institutions, and some do not yet have many cases. To some extent, we must wait and see.

Adding to this book's arguments that international commercial courts will shape the future of the international commercial dispute resolution system, we submit they are well positioned to contribute to such a system and to the development of an international commercial law in part because they bridge the past and the future. They do so in at least four ways. First, a subset of common law international commercial courts are, in some sense, modern transplantations of the London Commercial Court or cousins of the colonial and consular courts of the British imperial past.[62] These institutions all advanced a globalised common law. With many parties today still choosing English law for their contracts,[63] common law international commercial courts may build on and modernise this tradition, perhaps by centring their own national or regional interests rather than London's interests, by including civil law, and by providing a site for convergence. International commercial courts are also poised to develop interpretations of civil law – either in jurisdictions like France, Germany and the Netherlands, or in the SICC, hearing cases in which the parties have selected a civil law through a choice of law clause and been assigned civil law judges. The courts in Singapore, Dubai and Qatar, which have mixed benches of local and foreign judges from common law and non-common law traditions, can also be a site of convergence between legal traditions, affording opportunities for courts to develop new hybrid approaches to legal issues.

Second, international commercial courts also benefit from the legacy that international commercial arbitration has built over the past several decades, developing a kind of private transnational commercial law and international community. International commercial arbitration has provided a proof of concept of a dispute resolution system

[60] See King and Bookman (n 51) 482; Theus, 'ICCs: a New Frontier' (2022).

[61] King and Bookman (n 51).

[62] See King and Bookman (n 51). See also Theus (n 50) (explaining the earlier history of mixed courts, which also foreshadow the rise of international commercial courts).

[63] See, eg G Cuniberti, 'The International Market for Contracts: The Most Attractive Contract Laws' (2014) 34 *Northwestern Journal of International Law and Business* 455, 459; S Vogenauer, 'Regulatory Competition Through Choice of Contract Law and Choice of Forum in Europe: Theory and Evidence' (2013) 21 *European Review of Private Law* 13.

that builds its legitimacy based on consent of the parties; expert (sometimes foreign or multinational) decisionmakers; and the global support of the international community. The system of international commercial courts builds on this tradition.

Third, international commercial courts, whether in common law or civil law jurisdictions, often apply foreign or transnational law to international commercial disputes, and frequently engage in comparative exercises in their decisions. They may do so as they develop the local law of their own jurisdiction, which governs transnational actors and interactions, or as they consider applications of relevant foreign law. Comparative law inquiries can develop law in a manner that can cross borders regardless of how the source or authority of the law is theorised.[64] As their local law develops, international commercial courts may gain more global influence through cross-citation, including by other international commercial courts.[65] These courts may have a first-mover advantage in terms of shaping the law if they are among the first courts to address cutting-edge issues, especially if the opinion is well reasoned and written by judges with international reputations.

Fourth, international commercial courts have the freedom to experiment with procedure and with mixes of local and international judicial personnel that would be harder to replicate in a domestic court with wider focus.[66] Especially with their innovative and hybrid structures, international commercial courts offer the possibility of pushing the convergence of both substantive transnational commercial law and procedure across multiple legal traditions and states.[67]

B. How Convergence Might Happen

To illustrate how international commercial courts might contribute to the development of international commercial law, this section focuses on the Singapore International Commercial Court (SICC) as an example, though in some ways a unique one, of an international commercial court poised to influence transnational commercial law. The section then profiles the recent cryptocurrency decision, *Quoine v B2C2*, as a case study in the kind of influence SICC opinions can have.

i. The Rise of the Singapore International Commercial Court

The SICC is arguably the most innovative and boundary-pushing of the international commercial courts, and is poised to develop international commercial law.[68] The Court

[64] See Michaels, 'Dreaming Law' (2013); Bookman, 'Adjudication Business' (n 32) 274; *cf* F Marotta-Wurgler and S Issacharoff, 'The Hollowed Out Common Law' (2020) 67 *UCLA Law Review* 600.

[65] See eg M Shadmehr, CM Cameron and S Shashahani, 'Coordination and Innovation in Judiciaries: Correct Law vs. Consistent Law' (2022) 17 *Quarterly Journal of Political Science* 61.

[66] See PK Bookman and MS Erie, 'Experimenting with International Commercial Dispute Resolution' (2021) 115 *American Journal of International Law Unbound* 5.

[67] See AS King, 'Global Civil Procedure' (2021) 62 *Harvard Journal of International Law* 223; Bookman, 'Arbitral Courts' (n 49).

[68] The SICC furthers Singapore's efforts to become a financial, legal and entrepreneurial tech hub in the region. See M Erie, 'The New Legal Hubs: The Emergent Landscape of International Commercial Dispute Resolution' (2020) 60 *Virginia Journal of International Law* 225, 263.

as yet does not see an overwhelming number of cases, but if the rise of the SICC comes to parallel the rise of the Singapore International Arbitration Centre (SIAC), it has a busy future ahead. The SICC is a well-financed, internally supported institution run by a visionary Chief Justice in a state that seems to be working to solidify its position as the 'Switzerland' of Asia.[69] The court has also attracted a roster of prominent and well-respected judges from around the (mostly common law) world, including former Supreme Court justices from the UK, Australia and Canada; subject matter experts in areas like shipping and international insolvency; and respected judges from the civil law jurisdictions of France and Japan. Some of the growth of the SICC's docket may in part rely on the commercial world's disenchantment with private arbitration, but Singapore's approach – to grow its share of the international commercial dispute resolution pie, not just the litigation (or arbitration or mediation) slice – is a wise one.[70]

ii. Are Cryptoassets Property?: A Case Study of the SICC's Influence Over Transnational Commercial Law

A recent SICC case, *Quoine v B2C2*, illustrates the SICC's potential to influence law beyond Singapore's borders.[71] The case presented the question of whether a crypto asset is property. The subject is still contested and differs in nuance across jurisdictions and situations.[72] *Quoine* was an early case to tackle the issue. The court determined that 'Cryptocurrencies are not legal tender in the sense of being a regulated currency issued by a government but do have the fundamental characteristic of intangible property as being an identifiable thing of value'.[73] The case has been widely cited for this proposition – by English, New Zealand and Australian courts; British committees tasked with making proposals for how English law should govern cryptocurrencies; and academics.[74]

[69] See eg M Yip, 'The Singapore International Commercial Court: The Future of Litigation?' (2019) 12 *Erasmus Law Review* 82 (noting that the SICC 'helps to establish the norm that litigation can be neutral, effective and user focused').

[70] The vision of courts as complementary to, not just competitive with, arbitration, is widely shared among international commercial courts. See Bookman, 'Adjudication Business' (n 32); but *cf* PK Bookman 'The Arbitration-Litigation Paradox' (2019) 72 *Vanderbilt Law Review* 1119, 1192 (noting that the US Supreme Court often focuses on the competitive relationship between litigation and arbitration more than their complementarity).

[71] *Quoine Pte Ltd v B2C2 Ltd* [2020] SGCA(I) 02.

[72] TH Wu, 'Trustees' Investment Duties and Cryptoassets' (2020) 26 *Trusts & Trustees* 183, 186 (noting the issue is contested); ibid 188 (discussing Japanese case finding that bitcoins are not property under the Japanese Civil Code); RM Garcia-Teruel and H Simon-Moreno, 'The Digital Tokenization of Property Rights: A Comparative Perspective' (2021) 41 *Computer Law & Security Review* 1, 4. The following sources provide (mostly pre-*Quoine*) scholarship discussing whether crypto assets are property: KFK Low and EGS Teo, 'Bitcoins and Other Cryptocurrencies as Property' (2017) 9 *Law, Innovation and Technology* 235; D Fox, 'Cryptocurrencies in the Common Law of Property' in D Fox and S Green (eds), *Cryptocurrencies in Public and Private Law* (OUP, 2019) ch 6; M Solinas, 'Bitcoiners in Wonderland: Lessons from the Cheshire Cat' (2019) *Lloyd's Maritime and Commercial Law Quarterly* 434, 439; J Sarra and L Gullifer, 'Crypto-claimants and Bitcoin Bankruptcy: Challenges for Recognition and Realization' (2019) 28 *International Insolvency Review* 233.

[73] *Quoine* [38] (relying on 'the classic definition' of a property right in the House of Lords decision of *National Provincial Bank v Ainsworth* [1965] 1 AC 1175,1248).

[74] I Childs, et al, 'Cryptocurrency fraud Remedies Cryptocurrency as property' Lexology, 29 November 2021, available at www.lexology.com/library/detail.aspx?g=3a47f4cf-e5d7-47a2-b548-e4fe3fb8443c (noting London Commercial Court, New Zealand High Court and BVI High Court cases); S Cohney and DA Hoffman, 'Transactional Scripts in Contract Stacks' (2020) 105 *Minnesota Law Review* 319, 358 (discussing *Quoine*).

It appears in at least one US contracts casebook.[75] In part, the decision's influence may be due to a first-mover advantage or dearth of cases in the subject area – but it nevertheless contributes to shaping transnational law.[76] The decision's impact is facilitated by networks that help spread the decision to multiple courts. For example, several of the courts that have decided and cited the case – the SICC, the English High Court and the BVI commercial court – all include English judges who have overlapping professional circles. Additionally, some SICC international judges also work as arbitrators, potentially further facilitating the diffusion of Singaporean law into international commercial law. The common 'language' – based in both English language and the English common law – also creates a *lingua franca* that facilitates legal concepts migrating quickly.

Quoine further demonstrates that innovations such as blockchain, contrary to some accounts, neither render law obsolete nor demand legal revolutions to address modern problems.[77] The complicated world of cryptocurrency can come down to age-old questions of property, contract and trust, applied to new circumstances. This suggests a continued role for traditional courts, or perhaps, modern courts building off a traditional model. Moreover, this adaptability demonstrates the value of the common law, according to its fans.[78]

The SICC – both in its innovative international structure and perhaps in its proclivity for attracting transnational disputes raising cutting-edge legal issues – thus stands poised to influence the development of common law in new directions.[79] The *Quoine* judgment speaks only to Singapore law, but it builds on English law precedents and contributes to a common law tradition that has involved comparative law, cross-citation and, historically, unity under the Privy Council. Although Singapore (and other former colonies) have developed their common law in a way that diverges from English precedents in some areas,[80] there may be more incentives towards convergence and

[75] RS Summers, RA Hillman and DA Hoffman, *Contract and Related Obligation*, American Casebook Series, 8th edn (West Academic Publishing, 2021).

[76] A further question is whether rights in cryptocurrency are protected by a property rule or a liability rule. Early Canadian cases, for example, have protected it with a property rule – that is, when cryptocurrency was misappropriated, the court ordered the cryptocurrency returned. The Singapore precedent, by contrast, protected the crypto currency with a liability rule, awarding damages (instead of specific performance) to B2C2 for the improper cancellation of the trades. See R Sarel, 'Property Rights in Cryptocurrencies: A Law and Economics Perspective' (2021) 22 *North Carolina Journal of Law and Technology* 389, 418 (distinguishing between the treatment of property rights in cryptocurrencies in Canadian cases and in *Quoine*). Sarel explains that there is little information about how civil law countries will treat crypto. But *cf* Wu, 'Trustees' Investment' (2020) 189 (discussing a Japanese case rejecting a creditor's claim that Bitcoin held by a bankrupt exchange was the creditor's property); RM Garcia-Teruel and H Simon-Moreno, 'The Digital Tokenization of Property Rights: A Comparative Perspective' (2021) 41 *Computer Law & Security Review* 1.

[77] Cohney and Hoffman, 'Transactional Scripts' (2020) 361 (emphasising the continued importance of 'old-fashioned contract law').

[78] See, eg RJ Daniels et al, *The Legacy of Empire: The Common Law Inheritance and Commitments to Legality in Former British Colonies* (2011) 59 *The American Journal of Comparative Law* 111, 117.

[79] Professor Shi notes earlier in this volume: 'Although, by itself, the emergence of ICCs will not bring about uniform commercial legal regimes, they are a positive step towards harmonisation. This is because most ICCs will not require the application of the law of the country in which they are located, the specific applicable law (often as agreed by the parties in their contract) can be identified and the law's content determined by the ICC. The resulting judgment by the ICC would constitute a publicly available precedent which would at least have persuasive value when cited in similar cases in the courts of other countries, thereby gradually constructing a jurisprudence applicable to international commercial transactions.' See ch 3 section IV.D of this book.

[80] S Menon, 'The Somewhat Uncommon Law of Commerce' (2014) 26 *Singapore Academy of Law Journal* 23 (discussing three ways that Singapore contract law strayed from English).

harmonisation now, especially through international commercial courts, which could become institutional agents of harmonisation.

C. International Commercial Law and Global Problems: Cause and Solution?

Quoine is an example of an SICC case having an outsized global influence. In theory, international commercial courts, especially the SICC, may follow this model and develop globally influential legal principles to address some of the global problems that Chief Justice Menon has raised. ICCs, however, face obstacles created by courts' simultaneous role as dispute resolution provider to a certain cadre of international commercial business parties and developer of law aimed at serving an unspecified community – perhaps national, regional, or international; a business community or a broader one.

Chief Justice Menon began this volume by discussing the collective action problems facing the world, from climate change to global income inequality. The Chief Justice urged international commercial courts and the system of international commercial dispute resolution to consider their position vis-à-vis these problems and how to address them. To do so, judges may need to understand their roles not just as dispute resolvers, but also as law developers and global citizens. If one goal is to address these global problems through the development of international commercial law, international commercial courts face several obstacles. Most fundamentally, international commercial law and international commercial parties contribute to the problems the Chief Justice identified.

The climate change crisis is so intractable in part because current legal and economic systems allow companies to externalise environmental costs while internalising profit from environmentally harmful practices.[81] Many multinationals that may be involved in cross-border disputes are from heavily polluting industries, from cryptocurrency to mining.[82] The oil industry, for example, has significantly shaped modern international dispute resolution, from the Iran-US claims tribunal to contemporary Energy Charter Treaty disputes.[83] International commercial courts also cater to the international

[81] M Condon, 'Market Myopia's Climate Bubble' (2022) 1 *Utah Law Review* 63, 104–09.

[82] The servers needed to create and maintain stores of cryptocurrency are extremely energy intensive. See eg E Kim, 'Bitcoin mining consumes 0.5% of all electricity used globally and 7 times Google's total usage, new report says' *Business Insider* (6 September 2021).

[83] *Credit Agricole Corporate & Investment Bank, Singapore Branch v PPT Energy Trading Co Ltd* [2022] SGHC(I) 1 (dispute over letter of credit for the purchase of crude oil); *Zaur Leshkasheli & Rosserlane Consultants Ltd v Rep of Azerbaijan* (ICSIC Case No ARB/20/20) (dispute related to oil exploration under the Energy Charter Treaty); *Philips Petroleum Co Iran v Islamic Rep of Iran* IUSCT Case No. 39 (case brought by US oil company for expropriation and breach of contract before the Iran-US Claims Tribunal). According to the UNCTAD database, as of 7 July 2022, there were at least 10 pending investment disputes against Russia, six of which involved Ukrainian investors. UNCTAD Investment Policy Hub, Investment Dispute Settlement Navigator, 'Russian Federation', available at investmentpolicy.unctad.org/investment-dispute-settlement/country/175/russian-federation/respondent There were at least 10 such disputes pending against Ukraine, three of which involved Russian investors. UNCTAD Investment Policy Hub, Investment Dispute Settlement Navigator, 'Ukraine', available at investmentpolicy.unctad.org/investment-dispute-settlement/country/219/ukraine/respondent.

business community's preferences for dispute resolution.[84] Because they are focused on this audience and on attracting cases, international commercial courts are vulnerable to capture by repeat player parties or by the international commercial business community – to the detriment of affected third parties who might not be represented in proceedings. As the users of international commercial courts and international commercial arbitration are likely to be similar, it is possible that court users would be comfortable with an arbitration-inspired approach that sets issues of pressing public concern to one side to focus narrowly on the specific contract and the parties' more immediate interests.

International commercial courts also facilitate a system by which parties choose their law and forum, typically avoiding onerous regulations. The risk is that international commercial courts will develop a party-focused commercial law that perpetuates rather than ameliorates global problems, offering seemingly neutral and internationally accepted rationales for a specific point of view.[85] Other concerns stem from the fact that international commercial courts are hosted by states, which have their own interests both in terms of policy and in terms of their designs for the courts. Unlike arbitral tribunals, courts also depend on the state for their authority. Thus, there may also be concerns that international commercial courts may become beholden to or instruments of their host states and their interests in more or less obvious ways. National interests, however, can potentially conflict with each other and with the interests of the overall international community.

If international commercial law is to do an about-face and strive to ameliorate global problems, it may need to reorient its approach and internalise principles of global welfare. This is of course easier said than done. For example, where might these principles come from? International commercial courts raise questions about which social and political community these courts belong to, should cater to, and seek to be legitimate before.[86] In another sense, however, these courts seem focused on serving an international commercial community – aiming to provide more efficient procedures and expert decision-makers who satisfy multinational corporations' desires for a public arbitration-like dispute resolution system.[87] But will the substantive law they develop also serve this community – to the possible exclusion of other communities? Contract law, for example, often prioritises the legitimate interests of the contracting parties.[88] When and how might international commercial law overcome that default in the face of advancing non-party interests, such as sustaining the environment?[89]

One possible entry point for these interests could be through the application of mandatory rules of law. While international commercial courts, like arbitration, stand poised to enforce parties' contracts according to the law designated by the parties, there

[84] See ch 4 section IV of this book.

[85] K Pistor, *The Code of Capital* (Princeton University Press, 2020) 208.

[86] On these difficulties in the arbitration context see A King, 'General Principles and the Search for Legitimacy in International Arbitration: A Comparative Perspective' (2020) 1 *Ius Comparatum* 288.

[87] See ch 4 section IV of this book.

[88] See O Ben-Shahar, D Hoffman and C Hwang, 'Nonparty Interests in Contract Law' (forthcoming 2022) *University of Pennsylvania Law Review*, available at papers.ssrn.com/sol3/papers.cfm?abstract_id=4038584.

[89] See ibid. 'Courts may try to resolve contractual disputes in a manner that appears social, for example when they justify a decision to avoid 'social waste.' But what they view as 'social waste' could well reflect controversial values, selective norms, and empirical guesswork' (discussing *Peevyhouse* (n 5555)).

are some laws that parties cannot contract around.[90] In arbitration, there is a perennial debate about which mandatory laws apply – the mandatory rules of law of the seat and/or the law of the contract? In courts, even 'international commercial courts', the forum law's mandatory rules apply. For example, in the first year of the pandemic, Singapore passed legislation prohibiting parties from initiating proceedings to enforce a security if the counterparty's inability to perform was materially caused by a COVID-19 event.[91] When applicable, that law would apply whenever Singapore law governs a dispute. In theory, the legislature could have specified instead that the rule would apply in Singapore courts even if the parties had chosen a foreign law through a choice-of-law clause.

International commercial courts may also be called upon to apply domestic or international public policy when adjudicating disputes. Recent US scholarship on contract law considering non-party interests also provides a potential template for considering these interests when courts interpret or enforce contracts.[92] In determining the content of such public policy, however, international commercial courts must decide whether it is national or international public policy – and in either case, how such public policy is defined. A problem could arise, however, if an international commercial court gets too innovative. The assets concerned may be scattered around the globe, necessitating enforcement in other jurisdictions. In such a context, innovation has risks: outlier approaches to the law may not be recognised by other courts. Many international commercial courts are relatively new, and they need to build reputations for the quality of their work and the enforceability of their judgments if they are to attract more legal business and gain recognition abroad.

This chapter seeks only to point out the potential conflict between the desire for international commercial courts to address global problems and the obstacles to their ability to do so – not to determine which will prevail. Market-based legal development tends to cater to the parties before the court and to the international commercial community. But if the courts are to be attentive to global concerns like climate change and income inequality, as the Chief Justice rightly urges, that focus may be too narrow.

D. What Can a Court Do?

To address international commercial law's old and new problems, international commercial courts must cater to parties (to attract cases and adjudicate them well) but also resist the temptation to defer to parties' interests so much that they propagate rather than ameliorate global problems. Likewise, these courts should build on their sovereign authority but also exercise independence from the host state – both to maintain

[90] JB Martin, 'Contractualists Versus Jurisdictionalists: Who is Winning the Mandatory Law Debate in International Commercial Arbitration?' (2016) 27 *American Review of International Arbitration* 475, 480.

[91] See n 15 (describing ch 7)) (citing COVID-19 (Temporary Measures) Act 2020 (No 14 of 2020) (Singapore)).

[92] See DA Hoffman and C Hwang, 'The Social Cost of Contract' (2021) 121 *Columbia Law Review* 979; Ben-Shahar, Hoffman and Hwang, 'Nonparty Interests' (2022); A Bagchi, 'Other People's Contracts' (2015) 32 *Yale Journal on Regulation* 211, 243 (arguing that diffuse social interests should be considered when construing ambiguous contract terms).

their international legitimacy and to shape international commercial law in a globally beneficial way. To both of these ends, international commercial courts will have to avoid pushing the arbitration analogy too far and focus on being transparent and independent. International commercial courts should establish and preserve strong norms around transparency of hearings and publishing decisions and widen the scope of issues a judge considers when deciding the dispute.

i. Transparency

A fundamental distinction between arbitration and litigation is the extent of transparency and the public nature of litigation in courts. Some international commercial courts may offer parties the option of confidential proceedings, in part as a means to 'compete' with arbitration, but doing so should be the exception, not the rule. Instead, international commercial courts commit themselves to transparency. Transparency in the form of published opinions allows these courts to develop law. The public's ability to evaluate the work of international commercial courts – and the courts' ultimate influence – will depend in no small part on how much of the courts' operations and decisions the public can see and trust.[93] And it will help them contribute to a more open and interactive system of international dispute resolution. International commercial courts are public institutions.

Several common law international commercial courts have articulated their commitment to the principle of open justice.[94] The purpose of open justice, the UK Supreme Court recently stated, 'is not simply to deter impropriety or sloppiness by the judge hearing the case. It is wider. It is to enable the public to understand and scrutinise the justice system of which the courts are the administrators'.[95] Open justice is necessary 'to enable the public to understand how the justice system works and why decisions are taken'.[96] Open justice is an important part of protecting courts against baked-in incentives to cater to private parties, starting with their confidentiality requests, but also in terms of developing law. But what does open justice mean to a global audience for a delocalised court, with proceedings occurring virtually for the past two years? Because of their privileged position, international commercial courts can be standard-setters in this regard. Transparency is thus a crucial building block of international commercial courts' legitimacy, influence and independence.

[93] The short-lived experiment in Delaware of creating a confidential tribunal staffed by Delaware Chancery Court judges who operated much as arbitrators would, revealed the delegitimising force of courts operating in private. Bookman, 'Arbitral Courts' (n 49) 209.

[94] From early on, the SICC has urged careful balancing of 'both the public interest of open justice and the countervailing private interest of safeguarding confidential information' in order to 'mak[e] the SICC a pragmatic, flexible and attractive forum for dispute resolution'. HH Teh and J Yeo, 'Commentary: The Singapore International Commercial Court in Action: Illustrations from the First Case' Singapore International Commercial Court 47 (21 July 2016), available at tinyurl.com/yy9lxn2s (discussing *BCBC Sing Pte Ltd v PT Bayan Resources* [2016] SGHC(I) (Sing), available at tinyurl.com/y3r7pdst).

[95] *Cape Intermediate Holdings Ltd v Dring* [2019] UKSC 38 [37] (appeal taken from EWCA Civ) (allowing a non-party access to discovery produced in an asbestos litigation that settled).

[96] ibid [42]–[43].

ii. Substantive Law

It matters not only that the public can see international commercial courts operating, but what it sees when it looks. A jurisprudence that does not acknowledge global realities is unlikely to have as much positive impact. One might argue that commercial courts should narrowly focus their work on commercial issues, refusing to get in the middle of policy decisions that could have wider implications.[97] These issues, however, can be inextricably intertwined. Whereas most international commercial courts have limited jurisdiction, and may even stay within that jurisdiction, limiting jurisdiction to commercial cases does not always have the neutral impact that is often assumed.

Chapter one began with an effort to define what is 'commercial' and 'international' so that such cases can be properly distinguished from cases that are not. But as Chief Justice Menon stated at the beginning of the Judicial Roundtable, international commercial law is bound up with the most important issues and global issues of our day – from climate change to income inequality – and disputes before international commercial courts may likewise have lasting impact that reaches far beyond the particular parties before the court. Many prominent commercial and international commercial courts are in jurisdictions that will be heavily impacted by climate change and that are deeply implicated in flows of global wealth.[98]

We accordingly urge international commercial courts not to hide behind their limited commercial jurisdiction and the conceit that private disputes have only limited private consequences. To address global problems, international commercial courts may also need to adopt an internationalised outlook, not just one that prioritises national public policy or private interests. It may be easier to enforce mandatory rules in court than in arbitration. Moreover, judges, unlike arbitrators, have greater freedom to consider arguments and laws not raised by the parties and that have effects beyond the parties. An internationalised outlook may further suggest there should be an international perspective on the kinds of mandatory rules or international public policy enforced.

As a template for such considerations, one might look to courts' development of the meaning of Article V(2)(b) of the New York Convention, which allows courts to decline to recognise and enforce an arbitral award if recognition or enforcement 'would be contrary to the public policy of that country'. While that phrase can refer to the enforcing court's national public policy, many courts have interpreted the phrase to give it international scope, using international or transnational interpretations of public policy. For example, looking to international standards about arbitrators' conflict of interests,[99] fraud or bribery. Transnational public policy is defined as 'norms agreed

[97] On this view, the problem with current investor-state dispute resolution was that it strayed too far into policy-making territory. Yet the solution discussed in Pt III, an investment court, seems a step in the other direction, towards recognising that such questions might be unavoidable, and building institutions that might have greater sociological legitimacy than the current ones.

[98] All states are affected by these global forces, but island or oil-producing jurisdictions are particularly vulnerable to certain kinds of climate change impacts; likewise, tax havens and global financial centres are particularly sensitive to changes in global wealth migration.

[99] See M Moses, 'Public Policy: National, International and Transnational' (*Kluwer Arbitration Blog*, 12 November 2018), available at www.arbitrationblog.kluwerarbitration.com/2018/11/12/public-policy-national-international-and-transnational. See also, eg H Bilgen Özeke, 'International vs Domestic Public Policy in International Arbitration: Where Does It Begin, Where Does It End?' (*Lexology*, 5 September, 2019), available at www.lexology.com/library/detail.aspx?g=8edc0dee-29e9-45e9-9879-e0b4deb80105.

upon by all civilized nations'.[100] These norms are very narrowly defined. But might norms develop that protect climate change that fit this standard? International commercial courts in theory may be in the position to recognise these norms as such.

The challenge is translating this theory into practice. We would encourage courts to develop any such norms slowly and incrementally. They may not come up in every case. In certain cases, however, climate change is undeniably a commercial issue (as well as one implicating a host of human rights). As Justice Antonio Herman Benjamin, National High Court of Brazil and founding member of the Global Judicial Institute on the Environment, puts it: 'We should include courts in the climate change picture because we have no other option'.[101] Courts are well suited to these challenges in some respects because of their relative insulation from politics. It is argued that a well-functioning judiciary is not beholden to special interests in the way politicians may be. A specialist court may also find it easier to understand issues from the point of view of corporate repeat-players, not because it is biased, but because it hears certain kinds of disputes framed in a certain way.

Courts, however, also have limitations. The courts' vision is necessarily limited to the specific dispute as framed by the parties.[102] And a specialised dispute resolution system with many venue options can lay the groundwork for court capture.[103] These challenges give international commercial courts even more reason to look for opportunities to promote global welfare to address problems like climate change. Courts should define the international community they serve broadly and think creatively about the ways they can serve it – whether through the enforcement of mandatory rules, applications of public policy arguments, methods of contract interpretation, or otherwise.

Once again, investment arbitration provides a cautionary tale – tribunals have been accused of ignoring wider context when it comes to environmental concerns.[104] At the same time, arbitrators have a limited mandate under the applicable treaties. Commercial courts have the same delicate balancing act – their jurisdiction is often based in contract or territorial connection. Their decisions tangle them up in policy issues and those decisions will be public. To the extent that they develop global commercial law, or general principles thereof, they should not detach these principles from their wider implications.

IV. Conclusion

This conclusion has surveyed this volume's contributions and has compared narratives about international commercial courts and other forms of international commercial dispute resolution to reveal more clearly how these courts may contribute to the broader international commercial dispute resolution system. It has raised some familiar themes

[100] See Moses (ibid).

[101] Asian Development Bank, 'Climate Change, Coming Soon To A Court Near You National Climate Change Legal Frameworks In Asia And The Pacific' (December 2020).

[102] LL Fuller and KI Winston, 'The Forms and Limits of Adjudication' (1978) 92 *Harvard Law Review* 353; F Schauer, 'Do Cases Make Bad Law?' (2006) 73 *The University of Chicago Law Review* 883.

[103] JJ Anderson, 'Court Capture' (2018) 59 *Boston College Law Review* 1543.

[104] See V Vadi, 'Beyond Known Worlds: Climate Change Governance by Arbitral Tribunals?' (2015) 48 *Vanderbilt Journal of Transnational Law* 1285, 1349.

in relation to legitimacy and law development. Courts are positioned to develop commercial law in ways other types of institutions cannot. If judges are to handle the biggest disputes in transnational commerce, they will inevitably handle cases that touch upon issues of global importance that go beyond the direct interests of the contracting parties – like working conditions, security concerns, taxation and inequality and climate change – issues Chief Justice Menon highlighted in his Introduction. To do so successfully, they need to view themselves as more than dispute resolution providers – developing procedure with public access in mind and developing substantive law that addresses global concerns. To win public support and develop justice 'without fear or favour' is only a start.

POSTSCRIPT

When we started developing the themes for the 3rd Judicial Roundtable on Commercial Law in 2019, we began with the relatively modest aim of furthering discussion on the linkages between globalisation and the law. The two are, after all, inextricably linked. Just as the law and its institutions had served as the handmaid of commerce over the centuries past by creating the conditions necessary for merchants from different places to trade with each other with confidence and at arm's length, it has, today, developed and transformed and now serves as the handmaid of *transnational commerce*, by facilitating cross-border commerce and activity through the development of transnational *rules and rights* to govern cross-border transactions, as well as a transnational system of *dispute resolution* to enforce and vindicate them. In other words, just as the law has shaped and influenced globalisation, so too will it be shaped *by* globalisation. The themes for the Judicial Roundtable were conceived with these relationships in mind, and with a view to imagining how they might lay the groundwork for the development of a transnational system of justice that would better serve a globalised and interconnected world which has seen explosive growth in transnational trade and commerce.

However, by the time the Roundtable was convened in September 2021, just two years later, the global milieu had drastically changed, and several cataclysmic events prompted serious questions as to whether globalisation and the pursuit of greater interconnectedness remained our best path to the future. First, as we welcomed the new decade, the celebrations were quickly overshadowed by crisis as a global pandemic of a scale unprecedented in our lifetimes struck with frightening and devastating speed, destroying lives, livelihoods and completely changing our way of life. Borders were shuttered as it became clear that connectedness had become a conduit for contagion, and the consequent disruptions to global supply chains placed renewed focus on resilience and self-sufficiency. Second, in April 2021, the Intergovernmental Panel on Climate Change (IPCC) warned that the climate crisis has continued to worsen, and that many of its most worrying consequences – such as the rise in sea levels – are already irreversible over hundreds to thousands of years.[1] In March 2022, the IPCC delivered what some have called its 'final warning', because at present rates the world will likely have burned through its carbon budget by the time the panel releases its next climate mitigation report in five or six years.[2] Third, in August 2021, the chaotic US withdrawal from

[1] IPCC, 'Climate change widespread, rapid, and intensifying – IPCC' (9 August 2021), available at www.ipcc.ch/2021/08/09/ar6-wg1-20210809-pr: 'Many of the changes observed in the climate are unprecedented in thousands, if not hundreds of thousands of years, and some of the changes already set in motion – such as continued sea level rise – are irreversible over hundreds to thousands of years'.

[2] B Berwyn, Inside Climate News, 'One Last Climate Warning in New IPPC Report: "Now or Never"' (5 April 2022), available at insideclimatenews.org/news/05042022/ipcc-report-climate-change.

Kabul marked the end of its decades-long war in Afghanistan, but not of the scourge of transnational terrorism.[3]

These crises evidenced a shift in global sentiment away from globalisation for two reasons. First, these crises and their aftershocks have laid bare the fact that interconnectedness necessarily entails inter*dependence* and, therefore, *vulnerability*. Second, globalisation and the pursuit of greater global integration – particularly economic integration – was premised on the idea that the benefits that accrue to a global community of nations, as a whole, would be greater than the sum of its individual parts. Accordingly, the thinking was that globalisation would, like a rising tide, eventually lift *all* boats. But these and other crises have raised serious doubts as to the validity of that premise. While it may be that the world as a whole remains greater than the sum of its parts on certain metrics, if that benefit accrues only or very disproportionately to the advantage of a tiny minority, then the majority, who find themselves worse off, both in actual and perhaps more dramatically in relative terms, will take a different perspective, one based on what is best for them *individually* rather than collectively.

The Judicial Roundtable took place against this backdrop. Its discussions brought judges, arbitrators, academics and lawyers together to consider the impact that these tectonic shifts and the fault lines they have exposed might have on the law, legal practice and our justice systems. In many ways, those discussions raised more questions than conclusions. That was only to be expected, when dealing with issues which are complex, interconnected and not static, but dynamic. As the Roundtable discussions drew to a close, it became clear to us that the event could not be left as a one-off, standalone conversation. It could and should be developed into an ongoing dialogue.

Today, the situation is even more in flux. As the manuscript of this book was being finalised, Russian forces invaded Ukraine, sparking what has been described as the largest armed interstate conflict in Europe since the Second World War.[4] It is too early to predict how the conflict will influence the law and legal practice. But what is clear is that it will have a significant and far-reaching impact on the law and its institutions:

(1) *Private law.* In the sphere of private commercial law, contracts disrupted by the war and the sanctions imposed on Russia and Russian entities have placed renewed focus on familiar doctrines such as *force majeure* and frustration.[5] As the economic noose around the Russian economy tightens, there have been signs that domestic law may be used as an instrument of retaliation. For example, in March 2022, a Russian government decree essentially granted a no-cost licence to the use of patents held by owners located in 'unfriendly' countries. Although the decree only explicitly mentioned patents, a Russian court has already relied on it to authorise

[3] Atlantic Council, 'Experts reach: The US withdrawal from Afghanistan is complete. What's next?' (30 August 2021), available at www.atlanticcouncil.org/blogs/new-atlanticist/experts-react-the-us-withdrawal-from-afghanistan-is-complete-whats-next, arguing that the war has not ended but has merely entered its next phase – one which will likely involve the construction of an over-the-horizon counterterrorism programme to deny would-be terrorists the use of Afghanistan as a safe haven.

[4] 'Russia-Ukraine crisis: What we know so far' *The Straits Times* (10 March 2022), available at www.straitstimes.com/multimedia/graphics/2022/02/russia-ukraine-crisis/index.html?shell.

[5] DLA Piper, 'Ukraine conflict: Force majeure and frustration in commercial contracts' Lexology (29 March 2022), available at www.lexology.com/library/detail.aspx?g=bc37242d-fcff-46ec-b21e-c8f45aebe393.

the free use of certain foreign-owned trademarks, such as Britain's Peppa Pig.[6] Further, as the mass exodus of well-known global corporations and brands from Russia gathers pace, there are reportedly plans afoot to pass legislation that would allow the Russian Government to seize control of any foreign-owned company that is closed 'unreasonably', including powers to confiscate any assets left behind.[7] In a similar vein, a Russian law allows planes leased from foreign companies to be seized by Russian operators so that they can continue to be flown in Russia.[8]

(2) *Public law*. The Ukraine-Russia war represents yet another blow to the credibility of the multilateral rules-based system and another reminder of just how vulnerable the rule of international law is to power. In particular, the paralysis of the UN Security Council (which was itself chaired by Russia at the time of the invasion)[9] and its inability to enforce the rule of law has raised questions as to the relevance of international law. This is particularly the case where the means for enforcing it are limited and still depend to a large extent on the willingness of those in the global community to comply.[10] The optimist might point to the fact that states now frequently invoke international law in respect of their claims (for example, the US-led invasion of Iraq in 2003,[11] the US boycott of the Appellate Body of the WTO,[12] and the Russian invasion of Ukraine and the sanctions which have been imposed on Russia in response[13]) as evidence of the law's influence as a source of legitimation. But that itself could present difficulties if the law comes to be seen as being so malleable that it is at risk of serving as a conduit for power rather than as a check on it.

(3) *Geopolitics and the global order*. The war and the fault lines it has exposed have cast a pall over prospects for global cooperation and collective action. The sanctions imposed against Russia have been unprecedented in their scale and potency, and the widespread support they have garnered. The very fact that the economic and cultural *isolation* of the Russian economy has been used to such great effect

[6] D Davis and JD Supra, 'Putin v. Peppa Pig: How Russia's War in Ukraine Threatens Intellectual Property Rights' (21 March 2022), available at www.jdsupra.com/legalnews/putin-v-peppa-pig-how-russia-s-war-in-2435822.

[7] M Thompson, 'Russia says it could seize assets Western companies leave behind' CNN (10 March 2022), available at edition.cnn.com/2022/03/10/business/russia-nationalization-western-companies/index.html.

[8] T Leggett, 'Putin changes law on leased jets to keep them flying' BBC News (14 March 2022), available at www.bbc.com/news/business-60741161.

[9] H Akita and N Asia,: 'Russian invasion exposes UN Security Council's utter impotence' (17 March 2022), available at asia.nikkei.com/Spotlight/Comment/Russian-invasion-exposes-U.N.-Security-Council-s-utter-impotence.

[10] H Hannum, 'International law says Putin's war against Ukraine is illegal. Does that matter?' The Conversation (25 February 2022), available at theconversation.com/international-law-says-putins-war-against-ukraine-is-illegal-does-that-matter-177438; see also J Neal, 'The war in Ukraine and international law' *Harvard Law Today* (2 March 2022), available at today.law.harvard.edu/the-ukraine-conflict-and-international-law.

[11] AJ Bellamy, 'International Law and the War with Iraq' (2003) 4 *Melbourne Journal of International Law*, available at law.unimelb.edu.au/__data/assets/pdf_file/0008/1680362/Bellamy.pdf.

[12] CP Bown, 'Why did Trump end the WTO's Appellate Body? Tariffs.' Peterson Institute for International Economics (4 March 2020), available at www.piie.com/blogs/trade-and-investment-policy-watch/why-did-trump-end-wtos-appellate-body-tariffs; referring to the United States Trade Representative's Report on the Appellate Body of the World Trade Organisation, available at ustr.gov/sites/default/files/Report_on_the_Appellate_Body_of_the_World_Trade_Organization.pdf.

[13] M Milanovic, 'What is Russia's Legal Justification for Using Force against Ukraine?' EJIL:Talk! (24 February 2022), available at www.ejiltalk.org/what-is-russias-legal-justification-for-using-force-against-ukraine.

as a *punitive* measure[14] speaks volumes of the value of global *interconnectedness*. Unfortunately, despite the flushes of unity that the war has inspired *within* existing political and economic blocs, the war has also heralded an era of greater tensions *between* blocs.

The war has exposed and exacerbated geopolitical fault lines, and the worry is, as Edward Alden, a senior fellow at the Council on Foreign Relations put it, that we are now 'headed toward … a more divided world economically that will mirror what is clearly a more divided world politically'.[15] Some suggest that the war and the sanctions which have followed it presage a fracturing of the world into separate economic blocs. The potency of sanctions could present risks to the prospects of global cooperation – particularly in financial spheres – if the current situation incentivises states to disengage gradually from the global (Western-led) financial system, so as to reduce their dependence on it and thereby hedge against future threats of sanctions.[16] We could see, in time, alternative technological ecosystems,[17] alternative trade networks[18] and alternative payment and financial systems.[19]

While the US dollar remains the world's currency of choice for cross-border transactions, there are signs that its dominance as a global reserve currency is eroding; the proportion of global foreign exchange reserves denominated in US dollars has declined from 71 per cent in 1999 to 59 per cent in 2021.[20] Beyond

[14] Sanctions and other restrictive measures have tightened the stranglehold on the flow of goods, the flow of money and the flow of people in and out of Russia: sanctions on key Russian exports have wreaked havoc on its sources of foreign currency, financial sanctions have denied the government access to much of the country's foreign reserves, and embargoes on exports to Russia – particularly Western technological goods from semiconductors to aircraft parts – could cripple industries and activities dependent on those technologies: see J Frankel, 'These Russia Sanctions Are Different' Project Syndicate (18 March 2022), available at www.project-syndicate.org/commentary/russia-sanctions-severe-economic-geopolitical-impact-by-jeffrey-frankel-2022-03.

[15] E Wong and A Swanson, 'Ukraine War and Pandemic Force Nations to Retreat from Globalization' *New York Times* (22 March 2022), available at www.nytimes.com/2022/03/22/us/politics/russia-china-global-economy.html.

[16] ZZ Liu, Council on Foreign Relations, 'Besides China, Putin Has Another Potential De-dollarization Partner in Asia' (11 March 2022), available at www.cfr.org/blog/besides/china-putin-has-another-potential-de-dollarization-partner-asia.

[17] Ede la Bruyere and N Picarsic, 'Game of Phones' Octavian Report (Summer 2019), available at octavian-report.com/article/5g-us-china-standards-fight.

[18] See for instance the alternatives which have arisen in response to China's Belt and Road Initiative, such as the EU's Global Gateway and the US-supported Build Back Better World initiative: K Wong, 'China's belt and road plans face new EU, US competition, but 'space for cooperation' remains' SCMP (4 February 2022), available at www.scmp.com/economy/china-economy/article/3165794/chinas-belt-and-road-plans-face-new-eu-us-competition-space. See also the Regional Comprehensive Economic Partnership, which includes China and India, whereas the proposed Trans-Pacific Partnership (and the present Comprehensive and Progressive Agreement for Trans-Pacific Partnership) does not: see U Pullela, 'Regional Comprehensive Economic Partnership (RCEP) – Will it counter TPP?' (25 January 2021), available at www.clearias.com/rcep.

[19] Russia presently has the SPFS (System for Transfer of Financial Messages), its equivalent of SWIFT, and China has the CIPS (Cross-Border Interbank Payment System). India reportedly plans to link a service currently under development with Russia's SPFS which would connect with China's CIPS, and if this materialises the linked systems would cover most parts of the world: see Liu, 'Besides China' (2022).

[20] See 'Will dollar dominance give way to a multipolar system of currencies' *The Economist* (2 April 2022), available at www.economist.com/finance-and-economics/2022/04/02/will-dollar-dominance-give-way-to-a-multipolar-system-of-currencies. *The Economist* argues that the US dollar remains the dominant currency of transnational trade. According to the IMF, in 2020, over half of non-US and non-EU exports were denominated in US dollars, and in Asian emerging markets, the US dollar's share was 75%. In February 2022, only one in every five transactions registered under the SWIFT messaging system did not have a dollar leg,

these worries of an economic decoupling, there are also concerns that the world is growing further apart politically and diplomatically. Russia's refusal to rule out the use of nuclear weapons[21] has eroded the fragile trust built over decades of joint advocacy for nuclear non-proliferation and reductions in global stockpiles of nuclear weapons.[22] The international outcry against the Russian invasion has led to popular, but probably unproductive calls to expel Russia from various international organisations.[23]

These are but a few of the ramifications of the war that we could see playing out over the coming years. However, this geopolitical crisis is merely the latest in a succession of other major global crises. Tharman Shanmugaratnam, Senior Minister and Chairman of Singapore's Monetary Authority, warns that the world now faces a 'perfect long storm' caused by various interlocking 'sources of fragility'.[24] He identifies four other elements (to which we have added a fifth) that have contributed (and are continuing to contribute) to this 'perfect storm'. They are:

(1) *Macroeconomic risk.* We are likely to see the return of 'stagflation' as the world economy contends with both pandemic-induced economic stagnation and rising prices driven both by pandemic-related supply chain disruptions and the Ukraine-Russia war and sanctions.[25]
(2) *Climate crisis and sustainability.* A World Wildlife Fund (WWF) report estimates that we are now consuming 1.5 'Earths' of renewable resources annually (meaning that it will take 1.5 years to regenerate the renewable resources we consume in a single year). We are on track to exceed annual consumption at the rate of three 'Earths' by 2050.[26] A climate crisis looms[27] and those who will be hardest

a proportion which has remained largely unchanged over the past five years. See also E Prasad, 'Has the dollar lost ground as the dominant international currency?' The Brookings Institution (20 September 2019), available at www.brookings.edu/research/has-the-dollar-lost-ground-as-the dominant-international-currency, arguing that 'dollar supremacy remains unchallenged'.

[21] O Oshin, 'Kremlin won't rule out use of nukes in case of "existential threat"' The Hill (23 March 2022), available at thehill.com/policy/international/europe/599340-russia-would-only-use-nuclear-weapons-in-case-of-existential.

[22] A Umland and H von Essen, 'Putin's War Is a Death Blow to Nuclear Non-Proliferation: Russia has shown that an attacker with nuclear arms is fundamentally safe' Foreign Policy (21 March 2022), available at foreignpolicy.com/2022/03/21/nuclear-weapons-war-russia-ukraine-putin-nonproliferation-treaty-npt.

[23] There have, for instance, been calls for Russia's right to vote in the UN Security Council to be discounted, and for Russia to be expelled from international organisations, not just from the UN Security Council, but also the UN Human Rights Council and the World Trade Organisation, amongst others: F Ni Aolain, 'Why Pushing Russia Out of Multilateral Institutions is Not a Solution to the War' Just Security (22 March 2022), available at www.justsecurity.org/80787/why-pushing-russia-out-of-multilateral-institutions-is-not-a-solution-to-the-war, arguing that 'It is in times such as these that we truly discover the unsettling necessity of continued dialogue. Accountability does not require total ostracization. Moreover, the intent and purpose of the United Nations Charter might in fact compel the international community to consider resisting such impulses.'

[24] Monetary Authority of Singapore, 'Responding to a Perfect Long Storm', speech by Mr Tharman Shanmugaratnam, Senior Minister and Chairman, Monetary Authority of Singapore, at the IMAS-Bloomberg Investment Conference (9 March 2022), available at www.mas.gov.sg/news/speeches/2022/responding-to-a-perfect-long-storm.

[25] ibid.

[26] 'The Challenges of Resource Price Volatility, Investment and Disruptive Change', available at www.chathamhouse.org/sites/default/files/London Conference 2015 – Background Papers.pdf.

[27] A March 2022 report of the IPCC notes that 'the effects of melting glaciers and thawing permafrost are now approaching irreversibility; half the world now lives with annual periods of severe water scarcity; and global

hit also tend to be the ones least prepared for it. The most developed countries emit carbon dioxide and other greenhouse gases disproportionately, but it is the least developed who will have the most difficulty coping and will therefore bear the brunt of adverse climate change effects. For instance, it is estimated that low-lying Bangladesh could lose 10 per cent of its territory to the ocean within a few decades, displacing 18m people.[28]

(3) *Pandemic insecurity*. As the Senior Minister put it, Omicron will not be the last COVID-19 variant and COVID-19 will not be the last pandemic we see.[29] It is not a matter of 'if' but 'when'. One study estimates the annual probability of a pandemic on the scale of COVID-19 in any given year to be between 2.5 to 3.3 per cent, which translates to a 47–57 per cent chance of another global pandemic as deadly as COVID in the next 25 years.[30]

(4) *Rising inequality*. Ensuring that growth is inclusive, in that its benefits are shared fairly by all, remains a major challenge. The latest World Inequality Report estimates that the richest 10 per cent of the global population enjoy 52 per cent of the world's income, whereas the poorest half earn just eight per cent. The wealth gap is even wider: the poorest half of the world shares just two per cent of total global wealth, whereas the richest 10 per cent own over three-quarters of it.[31]

(5) *Truth decay*. To the foregoing four factors, we add the spectre of 'truth decay', a term coined by American researchers to describe the blurring of the line between fact and fiction in modern political discourse, which can be seen in increasing disagreement as to objective facts and data and declining trust in formerly respected sources of factual information. This can have serious consequences. That is because, without a common bedrock of facts, it is nearly impossible to engage in proper discourse on any of the major issues facing the world today. In the case of COVID-19, despite the fact that we now have more evidence than ever before about the effectiveness and safety of vaccines, vaccine scepticism remains rife and in the US is on the rise.[32]

Two points might be emphasised. First, as the Senior Minister pointed out, these are not one-off factors, but are products of structural shifts. The tensions and problems they create are here to stay, and we must learn to deal with them.[33] Second, we must

increases in heat-related deaths can be expected without more efforts toward adaptation': F O'Sullivan, 'The World's Fastest-Growing Cities Are Facing the Most Climate Risk' Bloomberg CityLab (1 March 2022), available at www.bloomberg.com/news/articles/2022-02-28/global-south-cities-face-dire-climate-impacts-un-report.

[28] 'Editorial: Wealthy countries are responsible for climate change, but it's the poor who will suffer most' *Los Angeles Times* (15 September 2019), available at www.latimes.com/opinion/editorials/la-ed-climate-change-global-warming-part-2-story.html.

[29] Monetary Authority of Singapore, 'Responding to a Perfect Long Storm' (2022).

[30] E Smitham and A Glassman, 'The Next Pandemic Could Come Soon and Be Deadlier' Center for Global Development (25 August 2021), available at www.cgdev.org/blog/the-next-pandemic-could-come-soon-and-be-deadlier.

[31] J Myers, 'These charts show the growing income inequality between the world's richest and poorest' World Economic Forum (10 December 2021), available at www.weforum.org/agenda/2021/12/global-income-inequality-gap-report-rich-poor.

[32] RAND, 'About Truth Decay', available at www.rand.org/research/projects/truth-decay/about-truth-decay.html.

[33] n 24.

recognise that none of these problems stand alone. They overlap and interlock, and that makes them all the more difficult to address. For example, economic stagnation and stagflation could complicate efforts at combating climate change by eating into the political capital available to governments to push through with unpopular and economically painful measures to address global warming, such as raising carbon taxes.[34] Climate crises, pandemics and economic stagnation are all likely to hit the poor hardest and thus exacerbate existing distributional injustices. Truth decay and the rise of fake news will make it more difficult to rally the public and build support for collective action – the example of vaccine scepticism is a case in point.[35]

What then might we do to address these global challenges? For a start, we might begin by recognising that these are *global* problems which require *global* solutions – nobody can or will solve these problems alone. Our best hope for doing so is not to abandon the system of globalism and global collective action, but to *reinvent* it.[36] The law and its institutions can play a crucial role in this endeavour in the *public* sphere, by governing interactions between states and providing a framework for collective action, and also in the *private* sphere, by serving as the handmaid of transnational commerce and thereby creating conditions conducive to cross-border exchange and integration at all levels.

More specifically, how should the perfect storm affect legal practice and our systems of commercial justice? What can we as judges, arbitrators and lawyers do to effect meaningful change for the better in the way our transnational dispute resolution system operates?

We have sought in this book to offer initial perspectives on how at least some of the challenges might be addressed. The Introduction highlighted four discontents with the way that transnational commercial disputes are resolved today. Those discontents corresponded to four constituents of the 'perfect storm'. The present system of transnational commercial dispute resolution stands accused of ignoring the problems of (1) sustainable growth, (2) climate change, (3) global health security, and (4) access to justice for those marginalised by globalisation. The individual parts of this book attempted to identify the ways in which these challenges might impact our legal and judicial systems, and how these can be approached going forward. Part I argued that international commercial dispute resolution should be viewed as a complex system of many different interlocking components. The discontents with transnational dispute resolution will require a multifaceted effort to address, and their solutions call for collaboration at multiple levels – not just across borders, but also across disciplines. Parts II and III focused on ongoing reforms in the institutional structures of international commercial dispute resolution (courts and arbitral tribunals) and the roles that these play in the transnational system of justice and in facilitating transnational and global access to justice. Parts IV and V examined how the procedural rules and substantive law (*lex mercatoria*) of international commercial dispute resolution offer ways (for example, through the principles of due process, equality of treatment, mandatory law, and public policy) of ventilating concerns over (among others) environmental effects, community health and well-being,

[34] n 24.
[35] RAND (n 32).
[36] See CJ Menon's Introduction to this book.

inequality, and access to justice in the course of court and arbitral proceedings. Part VI discussed how the technological innovations which the pandemic has accelerated can be harnessed to make transnational dispute resolution more accessible to all, while at the same time reducing the cost and the carbon footprint of the system as a whole. Finally, the Conclusion stressed the limits of international commercial arbitration in dealing with the concerns raised and suggested that international commercial courts play a special role in filling the gap.

To be sure, many of the potential solutions to the global challenges mentioned above lie outside the realm of the law, or will at least require the involvement of other diplomatic, political and socio-economic levers. In this regard, it is important that we focus not on any ideological differences that may exist as to how we understand and approach these issues, but on the undeniable and substantial *interests* that we share in addressing them. These common interests might then serve as a rallying point around which the law might facilitate the coalescence of a coalition and agreed plan of action.[37] Seen in this light, the law and its institutions have a crucial role to play in the global effort to address these issues, whether *directly*, by bringing stakeholders together and providing a framework for direct collective action on these issues (for example, through treaties or other more informal agreements), or *indirectly*, through the development of a fair, efficient and effective transnational system of justice with rules and processes which encourage and facilitate the pursuit of a more sustainable vision of global economic development. This could become manifest, for instance, in developments in the law on directors' duties to permit directors to consider environmental factors in determining what is in the company's 'best interests', whether through legislation or the development of judicial precedent,[38] or more informally through opinions issued by legal professionals and industry thought leaders.[39] These are just but a few of the ways in which the law

[37] For example, framing the Russian invasion of Ukraine as a clash of ideologies between democracies and autocracies might serve to alienate stakeholders and thus undermine efforts to build a coalition based on the real and substantial common interests at stake, such as upholding the rule of international law and preserving international respect of the sovereignty, independence and territorial integrity of states: see PM Lee Hsien Loong's remarks at the Dialogue with the Wall Street Journal Editorial Board (1 April 2022), available at www.pmo.gov.sg/Newsroom/PM-Lee-Hsien-Loong-at-the-Dialogue-with-Wall-Street-Journal-Editorial-Board-Apr-2022.

[38] See, for example, the Supreme Court of Canada's decision in *People's Department Stores Inc (Trustee of) v Wise* [2004] 3 SCR 461 [42], holding that 'in determining whether [the directors of a company] are acting with a view to the best interests of the corporation it may be legitimate, given all the circumstances of a given case, for the board of directors to consider, inter alia, the interests of the shareholders, employees, suppliers, creditors, consumers, governments and the environment'. Section 122(1.1)(b) of the Canada Business Corporations Act (RSC, 1985, c C-44) legislatively codifies that principle, stating that the directors and officers of a corporation may, when acting with a view to the best interests of the corporation, consider the environment as a factor in their decision-making.

[39] See, for example, the legal opinions issued by Noel Hutley SC and Sebastian Hartford Davis on climate change and directors' duties in 2016, 2019 and 2021: Centre for Policy Development, 'CPD releases new materials on directors' duties, climate risk and net zero' (25 April 2021), available at cpd.org.au/2021/04/directors-duties-2021. In Singapore, a team of independent legal counsel have, on the Commonwealth Climate and Law Initiative's request, issued a legal opinion on the obligations of directors to consider climate change and environmental issues in discharging their duties under Singapore law, arguing that directors are obliged to take into account, amongst other things, climate change risks insofar as these risks have a material and adverse impact on the financial performance of the company: see J Chan SC, J Chun, E Lim, P Doraisamy and G Quek, 'Legal Opinion on Directors' Responsibilities and Climate Change Under Singapore Law' (14 April 2021), available at www.tcfdhub.org/wp-content/uploads/2021/04/Legal-Opinion-on-Directors-Responsibilities-and-Climate-Change-under-Singapore-Law-2021.04.pdf.

and those who practise it can make a difference. Moving forward, it is imperative that we consider how else we, as stakeholders of our justice system, may contribute, and beyond that, how we may work with other stakeholders in the political and economic spheres to tackle these challenges.

As such, this book's chapters do not – nor do they purport to – provide complete answers to the questions raised by the Introduction and this Postscript. Their modest aim is to *start* a much-needed dialogue as to how the law shapes and is shaped by these wider, global trends, and what that means for the design and development of justice systems in an age of rising anti-globalism, pandemic and now – war.

List of Participants in the 3rd Judicial Roundtable

29 September to 1 October 2021

Judges

(1) Chief Justice James Allsop, Chief Justice, Federal Court, Australia
(2) Justice Madiyar Balken, Supreme Court, Kazakhstan
(3) Sir William Blair, Justice of the Qatar International Court, formerly Judge in Charge of the Commercial Court of England and Wales; currently Professor of Financial Law & Ethics, Centre for Commercial Law Studies, Queen Mary University of London, UK
(4) Sir Bernard Eder, formerly Justice of the High Court of England and Wales; currently International Judge, Singapore International Commercial Court (SICC)
(5) Justice Jiyong Jang, High Court, Republic of Korea
(6) Justice Douglas Jones AO, International Judge, SICC
(7) Justice Godfrey Lam, Court of Appeal, Hong Kong SAR
(8) Lord Jonathan Mance PC, formerly Deputy President, UK Supreme Court; currently International Judge, SICC
(9) Chief Justice Sundaresh Menon, Supreme Court, Singapore
(10) YA Datuk Justice Nallini Pathmanathan, Federal Court, Malaysia
(11) Justice Kannan Ramesh, Supreme Court, Singapore
(12) Justice Anselmo Reyes, International Judge, SICC
(13) Justice Ryutaro Seki, Tokyo District Court, Japan
(14) Justice Arjan Kumar Sikri, formerly Justice of the Supreme Court, India; currently International Judge, SICC
(15) Senior Assistant Registrar Joanne Tan Xin Ying, Federal Court, Malaysia
(16) Justice Susan Thomas, Chief Judge, High Court, New Zealand
(17) Justice Geoffrey Venning, High Court, New Zealand
(18) Justice Kai Xiao, Vice-President, Shanghai Finance Court, China
(19) Justice Shuijuan Yu, Chief Judge, Suzhou International Commercial Court Division, China

Academics

(1) Professor Pamela Bookman, Fordham University School of Law, New York, USA
(2) Professor Alyssa King, Queen's University Law School, Ontario, Canada

(3) Professor Xiaohong Liu, President, Shanghai University of Political Science & Law (SHUPL)
(4) Professor Jianping Shi, Deputy Dean, School of International Law, SHUPL
(5) Professor Lihua Wang, School of International Law, SHUPL
(6) Professor Guojian Xu, Dean, School of International Law, SHUPL
(7) Professor Tiong Min Yeo SC (Hon), formerly Dean, School of Law, Singapore Management University (SMU); currently Yong Pung How Chair Professor of Law
(8) Professor Zhengyi Zhang, Deputy Director, International Affairs Office, SHUPL

Practitioners and Legal Assistants

(1) Dr Vladimir Egiyan, lawyer (Russia and New York)
(2) Ching Him Ho, barrister, Hong Kong SAR
(3) Jiahui Huang, Supreme Court of Singapore, Assistant Registrar and Special Assistant to the Chief Justice
(4) Jason Karas, Managing Partner, Karas LLP, Hong Kong SAR
(5) Arvin Lee, Partner, Wee Swee Teow LLP, Singapore
(6) Pak Hei Li, barrister, Hong Kong SAR
(7) Jason Lin, trainee solicitor, UK
(8) Wilson Lui, Pre-Doctoral Fellow and Lecturer, Faculty of Law, The University of Hong Kong
(9) Reuben Ong, Supreme Court of Singapore, Assistant Registrar and Special Assistant to the Chief Justice
(10) Lysetta Teo, Associate, Wee Swee Teow LLP, Singapore
(11) Kenneth Wang, Supreme Court of Singapore, Assistant Registrar and Special Assistant to the Chief Justice
(12) Jianjian Ye, Associate, Quinn Emanuel Urquhart & Sullivan LLP, New York
(13) Cedric Yeung, barrister, Hong Kong SAR

INDEX

A

Accountability
  arbitrators 154–5
  legitimacy of globalisation and its institutions 314, 324
  problem with ISDS 19, 150
  sovereign immunity 17

Anti-expropriation (AE)
  current approaches 139, 159
  general principles 140–1
  propositions for balancing needs of states with demands of investors
    creation of special investment courts 174–6
    current approaches 166–9
    future practicalities 177–9
    traditional tribunal not to determine investor–state disputes 173
    tribunal to assess the proportionality of government measures being challenged 173

Anti-suit injunctions
  concurrent proceedings 188–9, 217–19
  importance of finality and certainty 319–20

Appeals
  Dubai International Financial Centre 97–8
  effect of swing towards arbitration 125–6
  key mechanism for future convergence 75–6
  reform of ISDS 154
  Singapore International Commercial Court 95–6

Applicable law
  choice of law
    emphasis on party choice 328
    facilitation by ICCs 335
    importance of national law 61–2
    lex mercatoria 253–7
    obstacles to wider adoption of *lex mercatoria* 270–3
    party autonomy 33–5
    subject to supranational body of rules 281–2
  CICC 112
  CISG 260
  decision-maker's task 33
  determination 96
  due process 197
  ICCs 107
  lex mercatoria 248, 254, 273
  Singapore International Commercial Court 95–6
  soft law instruments 262

Arbitrability 64–6, 200, 222, 268

Arbitration
  see also **International commercial dispute resolution; Litigation**
  complementary mechanism 24
  English Commercial Court compared 93
  ICCs as alternative 103
  ICC's as better alternative 103–5
  impact on development of *lex mercatoria* 265–8
  impact on *lex mercatoria* 265–8
  importance of finality 210
  key components of system 59
  origins 51
  overview of central themes
    obstacles from theory 325–6
    practical advantages as challenges 324–5
    robust part of system 323–4
  pros and cons of swing towards arbitration
    appeals 125–6
    good thing by itself 126
    higher degree of choice and freedom 121–2
    hinder to development of jurisprudence 122–4
    non-binary situation 124–5
    remote hearings 126–7
  purported negative impact 75
  res judicata 222
  swing away from litigation
    Asia 117–18
    effect of globalisation 121
    English courts 118–20
    gradual ebb and flow 116–17
    nature of arbitration as a driver of change 118–20
    overview of central themes 317
    recognition and enforcement of awards 120–1

Asynchronous dispute resolution proceedings
  'automation' and 'transformation' distinguished 287
  future potential and its challenges 305–11
  how ICDR rose to the challenge 287
  illustration 287
  impact of COVID-19 177
  two types of fully asynchronous litigation in use 303–5
  underlying concept of asynchronicity 302–3
Autonomy *see* **Party autonomy**
Awards *see* **recognition and enforcement of awards**

B
Bribery and corruption
  arbitrability 65–6
  investor-state dispute settlement (ISDS) 142–3
  mandatory rules 68

C
Certainty
  see also **Finality**
  balance with achieving just and correct result 210–11
  choice of law 211
  concerns over fairness and justice 185
  concurrent proceedings
    anti-suit injunctions 188–9, 217–19
    forum non conveniens 187–8, 216–17
    issue estoppel 192–4, 220–1
    lis alibi pendens 187–8, 215–16
    res judicata 192–4, 220–3
    stay of proceedings 190–2
  crucial aims in ICDR 183–4
  driver of greater convergence 72
  evolution to meet global considerations 211
  impact of COVID-19 204–7, 240–2
  importance 184–5
  obstacles to wider adoption of *lex mercatoria* 271–2
  overview of central themes 319–20
  policy considerations 212–13
  problem with ISDS 148–9
  recognition and enforcement of awards
    awards set-aside by a supervising court 198–200, 232–5
    due process 197–8, 226–9
    Hague Conventions 2005 and 2019 202–4, 236–40
    indirect jurisdiction 194–6, 224–6
    overview 222–3
    overview of conditions 194
    public policy 198–200, 229–30
    reciprocity 196–7, 235–6
    res judicata 230–1
  three constraining principles 213–15
    comity 186
    party autonomy 185
    sovereignty 186
  underlying concept 183, 211
China International Commercial Court (CICC)
  disadvantages of litigation 111–12
  establishment 99
  imperfection and ambiguity of regulations 110–11
  International Commercial Expert Committee 100
  jurisdiction 99–100
  mediation 100
  rationale for establishment 102–3
Choice of forum
  certainty 211
  facilitation by ICCs 335
  party autonomy
    forum non conveniens 35
    general rule 33–4
    limitations 35
  recognition and enforcement of awards
    HCCH 2005 237
    HCCH 2019 239
Choice of law
  emphasis on party choice 328
  facilitation by ICCs 335
  importance of national law 61–2
  lex mercatoria
    diversity and legal pluralism 254–7
    empirical evidence 253–4
  obstacles to wider adoption of *lex mercatoria*
    development and nature of *lex mercatoria* 272–3
    risks of relying on transnational law 271
    uncertainty as to content 271–2
    vagueness of content 270–1
  party autonomy
    forum non conveniens 33–4
    general rule 33–4
    limitations 35
  subject to supranational body of rules 281–2
Climate change
  fitness for purpose of *lex mercatoria* 251–2
  impact of Russian invasion of Ukraine 345–6
  shaping of modern international dispute resolution 334–5
  strengths and hopes for future of globalisation 11
  threat to globalisation 6–7

Comity
anti-suit injunctions 189, 217
constraining principle on certainty and finality 185, 186, 213–15, 319
defined 40
general rule 33
international commercial dispute resolution as a system 65
link with reciprocity 196
Commercial courts *see* **international commercial courts (ICCs); National courts**
Commercial dispute resolution *see* **International commercial dispute resolution**
Commercial disputes *see* **International commercial disputes**
Concurrent proceedings
anti-suit injunctions 188–9, 217–19
forum non conveniens 187–8, 216–17
issue estoppel 192–4, 220–1
lis alibi pendens 187–8, 215–16
stay of proceedings
arbitral proceedings 190
case management grounds 191–2
Consolidation of claims 75, 146
Convergence
achievement of continued convergence
drivers of greater convergence 71–2
facilitative culture 79–81
international commercial courts 75–9
lex mercatoria 72–5
no single means of achieving convergence 72
three key mechanisms for the future 72
history of gobalisation 4–5
lex mercatoria
benefits of diversity 275–6
effectiveness 259–63
efforts at identifying core principles 257–9
impact of international commercial arbitration 265–8
impact of international commercial mediation 264–5
scope and modality of convergence 276–82
meaning and scope 35–6
practical means to attain convergence
institutions 37–41
instruments 36–7
rationale for special treatment of ICDR 32–3
SICC as an example
potential to influence international law 332–4
prominent and well-respected judges 331–2
Corruption *see* **Bribery and corruption**
Costs
average costs 306–7
benefits of technology 22
driver of greater convergence 72
ICC's and arbitration compared 103–5
problem with ISDS 150–1
rationale for special treatment of ICDR 31–3
reform of ISDS 155–6
UNCITRAL Rules 151
Counterclaims
investor-state dispute settlement (ISDS) 145–6
need for finality and certainty 195
Courts *see* **international commercial courts (ICCs); National courts**
COVID-19
beginning of the pandemic 286
benefits of swing towards arbitration 126–7
changes to administration of justice 82–4
daylight at end of tunnel 285
effect on rules-based international order 86–7
evolution of certainty as concept 211
fitness for purpose of *lex mercatoria* to deal with aftermath 252–3
future uncertainty 45
how ICDR rose to the challenge
asynchronous hearings 287
continuing problems 288
examination of witnesses 286–7
overcoming ingrained assumptions 287–8
successful approach 286
impact of Russian invasion of Ukraine 346
impact on certainty and finality 204–7, 240–2
lessons of the pandemic
incorporation of technology 294–7
limitations on technology 299–301
overview 293–4
positive impact of technology 297–9
overview of central themes 321–2
strengths and hopes for future of globalisation 11–13
threat to globalisation 7
transformative potential of remote technology
overall conclusions 311
overview 289–91
unexpected benefits 84–6
unprecedented impact
economic impact 82
health risks 81–2
Cross-border insolvency
approach to convergence 5
crystallisation, promotion and harmonisation of a global commercial law 258
effect of non-binding legal instruments 16

international commercial disputes defined 48
UNCITRAL Model Law 57–8, 73
Cultures *see* **Legal cultures**

D
Dispute resolution *see* **International commercial dispute resolution**
Disputes *see* **International commercial disputes**
Dubai International Financial Centre (DIFC)
disadvantages of litigation 111
establishment 97
jurisdiction 97
language 97–8
organisational structure 97–8
recognition and enforcement of awards 132–3
Due process
AE clauses 166
application of mandatory rules 67
dark side to arbitration 38
FET clauses 161
need for convergence 35
recognition and enforcement of awards 197–8, 226–9
Due process paranoia
build up of costs 38
contested legitimacy 39
overabundance of caution 228–9

E
Efficiency
benefits of technology 22
ICC's
arbitration compared 104
comparative concept 104
key feature 75
ICDR as a system 81
part of justice 21
Enforcement of judgments *see* **recognition and enforcement of awards**
English Civil Procedure Rules
international commercial disputes defined 47–8
overriding objective 21
English Commercial Court
arbitration compared 93
disadvantages of litigation 111–12
establishment 91
key mechanisms for future convergence 77–9
original specialised court 46
popularity 91–2
reasons for establishment 93
recognition and enforcement of awards 327
reputation for interpretation 74
unprecedented growth of international trade 92

Estoppel *see* **Issue estoppel**
Expenses *see* **Costs and expenses**
Expertise *see* **Professionalism and expertise**

F
Fair and equitable treatment (FET) clauses 159
general principles 141–3
propositions for balancing needs of states with demands of investors
creation of special investment courts 174–6
current approaches 160–6
future practicalities 177–9
traditional tribunal not to determine investor–state disputes 173
tribunal to assess the proportionality of government measures being challenged 173
Finality
see also **Certainty**
balance with achieving just and correct result 210–11
concerns over fairness and justice 185
concurrent proceedings
anti-suit injunctions 188–9, 217–19
forum non conveniens 187–8, 216–17
issue estoppel 192–4, 220–1
lis alibi pendens 187–8, 215–16
res judicata 192–4, 220–3
stay of proceedings 190–2
crucial aims in ICDR 183–4
impact of COVID-19 204–7, 240–2
importance 184–5
importance for arbitration 210
may be subject to judicial review 210
overview of central themes 319–20
policy considerations 212
problems with ICCs 110
recognition and enforcement of awards
awards set-aside by a supervising court 200–1, 232–5
due process 197–8, 226–9
Hague Conventions 2005 and 2019 202–4, 236–40
indirect jurisdiction 194–6, 224–6
overview 222–3
overview of conditions 194
public policy 198–200, 229–30
reciprocity 196–7, 235–6
res judicata 230–1
three constraining principles 213–15
comity 186
party autonomy 185
sovereignty 186
underlying concept 183, 209–10

Forum *see* **Choice of forum**
Forum non conveniens
concurrent proceedings 187–8, 216–17
effect on party autonomy 34–5
Hague Convention 2005 237
importance of certainty and finality 319–20
inconsistent judgments in parallel proceedings 216–17
Jurisdiction Project 203

G

Globalisation
advantages and disadvantages outlined by Chief Justice Menon 314–15
collective action problems 334
defined 1–2
focus of this book 2
history
convergence towards set of shared principles 4–5
encouragement of commercial entrepreneurship and innovation 5
law as globalised currency of trust 3–4
legal frameworks as notional 'bank' of rights 4
role in advancing global economic prosperity, 3
Second World War 3
triumphs of the Rule of Law 5
Judicial Roundtable postscript 342
mutually transformative effect on law 25
need to consider the future of globalisation 2
need to reorient law's approach 335
reasons for fall of ideology
false sense of security by pas successes 9–10
fundamental failure to achieve consensus on objectives 9
role of the law 10
recent threats
climate change 6–7
COVID-19 7
demonstration of interlocking fragility 7–8
global terrorism 6
regional and global events 6
recognition of global problems 347–9
strengths and hopes for future
COVID-19 11–13
fight against climate change 11
irreversibility of globalisation 13–14
need for multilateral solutions 11
swing away from litigation towards arbitration 121
underlying concept of certainty 211
ways to confront the failings of globalisation
building legitimacy 18–25
more robust global discourse 17–18
place it on a more sustainable footing 15–16
two key propositions 14

H

Hague Conventions 2005 and 2019
foundational legal instruments 38–9
international commercial disputes defined 30–1
major draw of international arbitration 132
objectives 258
practical means to attain convergence 36
recognition and enforcement of awards 202–4
HCCH 2005 236–8
HCCH 2019 239–40
rules of law 249

I

Injunctions *see* **Anti-suit injunctions**
Interim measures
CICC jurisdiction 60
comity 186
key mechanism for future convergence 75–6
Netherlands Commercial Court 98
scope of jurisdiction 326
UNCITRAL Rules 139
International Arbitration Survey 2018
average costs 306–7
due process paranoia 229
rationale for special treatment of ICDR 32–3
use of sanctioning powers 63
International Centre for Settlement of Investment Disputes (ICSID)
administration of UNCTRAL Rules 139
amicus curiae briefs 148
consolidation of claims 146
diversity of arbitrators 152–3
enforcement 151
filing of claims 145
inter-governmental body 138
jurisdiction 138
principal instruments 138
review of awards 146–7
sovereign immunity 151–2
Transparency Rules 148
International Chamber of the Paris Commercial Court
background 93–4
establishment 94
language 95
International commercial courts (ICCs) *see also* **Litigation**
addressing commercial law's old and new problems
maintenance of legitimacy 336–7
substantive law 338–9
transparency 337

answers to the legitimacy questions 328
application of public policy 336
avoidance of longstanding theoretical debates 327
benefits
  alternative to arbitration 103–5
  diversity 106–7
  establishment of a unified system 107
  overview of central themes 328–9
  professionalism and expertise 105–6
  simplification of proceedings 108
  unification of litigation language 108
China International Commercial Court
  establishment 99
  imperfection and ambiguity of regulations 110–11
  International Commercial Expert Committee 100
  jurisdiction 99–100
  mediation 100
  rationale for establishment 102–3
China International Commercial Court (CICC)
  disadvantages of litigation 111–12
choice of law and forum 335
distinctiveness of system 50–1
Dubai International Financial Centre
  disadvantages of litigation 111
  establishment 97
  jurisdiction 97
  language 97–8
  organisational structure 97–8
  recognition and enforcement of awards 132–3
effect on the future of international commercial law
  a bridge from the past to the future 330–1
  SICC as an example 331–4
effect on the litigation landscape 133–4
English Commercial Court
  arbitration compared 93
  disadvantages of litigation 111–12
  establishment 91
  key mechanisms for future convergence 77–9
  original specialised court 46
  popularity 91–2
  reasons for establishment 93
  recognition and enforcement of awards 327
  reputation for interpretation 74
  unprecedented growth of international trade 92
future prospects 129–30
International Chamber of the Paris Commercial Court
  background 93–4
  establishment 94
  language 95
interpretative role 327
jurisgenerative possibilities 326–7
key components of system 60
key mechanisms for future convergence
  necessary features 75–6
  SICC 76–7
Netherlands Commercial Court
  disadvantages of litigation 111
  establishment 98
  jurisdiction 98
  language 98–9
problems
  disadvantages of litigation 111–12
  imperfection and ambiguity of regulations 110–11
  lack of foreign lawyers 112
  recognition and enforcement of awards 109–10
rapid spread 91
rationale for establishment
  aims of becoming regional centre for dispute resolution 101
  alternative to arbitration 103
  CICC 102–3
  existing shortcomings of dispute settlement 100–1
  needs of business community 101
  reform of traditional legal system 101–2
reasons for world-wide rise of ICCs
  importance of mobility of disputes 127–8
  procedures to meet commercial expectations 128
  unique features of SICC 128–9
res judicata 223
shortcomings of system 316
Singapore International Commercial Court
  applicable law 95–6
  appointment of judges 96
  establishment 95
  future prospects 129–30
  international commercial disputes defined 31, 47
  jurisdiction 95–6
  key mechanisms for future convergence 76–7
  Memorandums of Guidance (MOGs) 132
  part of world-wide rise of ICCs 127
  rationale for special treatment of ICDR 32
  unique features 128

still a work in progress 112–13
supposed shortcomings
party autonomy 130–1
recognition and enforcement of awards 131–3
taking of evidence 131
unprecedented impact of COVID-19
changes to administration of justice 82–4
unexpected benefits 84–6
world-wide rise of ICCs
SICC 127

International commercial dispute resolution
see also **Arbitration**; **Litigation**
achievements in recent decades 43
aims for continuation of system 43–4
broader function 44–5
complex and multifaceted issues 43
components of system
complexity, reach and dynamism 55
foundational legal instruments 56–8
institutions 58–61
persons involved 62
rules and principles 61–2
shared norms 55–6
how system can be further strengthened and improved 87

International commercial disputes
achievement of continued convergence
drivers of greater convergence 71–2
facilitative culture 79–81
international commercial courts 75–9
lex mercatoria 72–5
no single means of achieving convergence 72
three key mechanisms for the future 72
balancing competing interests
arbitrability 64–6
centrality of party autonomy 62–3
key concepts 63–4
mandatory rules 66–8
procedural rules 62–3
public interests 63
public policy 68–71
defined
Hague Principles 30–1
SICC 31
UNCITRAL Model Law 29–30
distinctiveness of
interconnected nature of global trade 49
maritime law 51–3
need for specialised body of law 49–50
overview 315
rationale for continuing special treatment 54–5
role of commercial parties 51
unique system of courts 50–1
identification and description of
cross-border insolvency 48
English Civil Procedure Rules 47–8
investor-state dispute settlements distinguished 48–9
key feature 45
limits on defining 'commercial' 47–8
overview 316
SICC 47
UNCITRAL Model Law 45–7
rationale for special treatment 31–3
unprecedented impact of COVID-19
changes to administration of justice 82–4
economic impact 82
effect on rules-based international order 86–7
health risks 81–2
unexpected benefits 84–6

Investor-state dispute settlement (ISDS)
consolidation of claims 146
dealing with corruption 142–3
FET clauses 141–3
impact of design choices 318
international commercial disputes distinguished 48–9
jurisdiction
ICSID 138
overview 137–8
UNCITRAL Rules 139
Mauritius Convention 144–5
MFN clauses 140–1
minimum international standard 139–40
overview of central themes 318–19
proposals for reform and possible future trajectories
appeals 154
appointment of arbitrators 155
overview 153–4
reduction of cost and time 155–6
two important takeaways 156
propositions for balancing needs of states with demands of investors
creation of special investment courts 174–6
current approaches – AE 166–9
current approaches – FET 160–6
current approaches – MFN 169–73
current approaches – NT 169
future practicalities 177–9
traditional tribunal not to determine investor–state disputes 173
tribunal to assess the proportionality of government measures being challenged 173

radical approach to reform
financing from contracting states 158
full-time adjudicators 157
jurisdiction under existing and future investment treaties 157
overview 156–7
own enforcement regime 157
two levels of adjudication 157
review of awards 146–7
set-offs and counterclaims 145–6
umbrella clauses 143–4
underlying problems
accountability 150
certainty 148–9
costs 150–1
enforcement of awards 151–2
lack of diversity among arbitrators 152–3
transparency 147–8
use of private institutional design norms 317–18
ways to confront the failings of globalisation 19
Issue estoppel
concurrent proceedings 192–4, 220–1
controversial issue 221

J
Judgments *see* **recognition and enforcement of awards**
Judicial Roundtable
broader function of international commercial dispute resolution system 44–5
how ICCs are performing 115
postscript
changes to global milieu 341–2
Russian invasion of Ukraine 342–5
shift away from globalisation 342
transnational system of justice 341
Jurisdiction
China International Commercial Court 99–100
Dubai International Financial Centre 97
investor-state dispute settlement (ISDS)
overview 137–8
UNCITRAL Rules 139
Netherlands Commercial Court 98
possibilities of ICCs 326–7
proposed multilateral investment court 157
recognition and enforcement of awards 194–6, 224–6
scope of jurisdiction 326
Singapore International Commercial Court 95–6

L
Language
benefits of ICCs 108
Dubai International Financial Centre 97–8
International Chamber of the Paris Commercial Court 95
Netherlands Commercial Court 98–9
Law
see also **Applicable law**; **Rule of Law**
addressing commercial law's old and new problems
maintenance of legitimacy 336–7
substantive law 338–9
transparency 337
choice of law *see* **Choice of law**
convergence towards set of shared principles 4–5
example of how convergence might happen 332–4
focus of this book 2
as globalised currency of trust 3–4
importance of national law 61–2
infrastructure to encourage of commercial entrepreneurship and innovation 5
legal frameworks as notional 'bank' of rights 4
mutually transformative effect on globalisation 25
need to reorient its approach 335
role in decline of globalisation 10
triumphs of the Rule of Law 5
Lawyers
development of facilitative culture 81
embracing of system 81
lack of foreign lawyers in some ICCs 112
ways to confront the failings of globalisation 24
Legal cultures
achievement of continued convergence 79–81
majority of arbitrators 153
possibility of mediation taking over from litigation 264
variation among dispute resolution bodies 102
Legitimacy
addressing commercial law's old and new problems 336–7
authority given to the arbitrator under the arbitration agreement 81
benefits of certainty 148
Chief Justice Menon 314
criticisms of investment arbitration 86, 128
due process paranoia 39
enduring success of international commercial dispute resolution 55
global institutions 313

greater scope for the immediate application of soft law 281
investor-state dispute settlement 48, 173, 275
judicial recognition 80
lex mercatoria 266, 273
rationale for the separate treatment of international commercial disputes 32
system of international commercial courts 326–8, 336–40
use of private institutional design norms 318
ways to confront the failings of globalisation 18–25

Lex mercatoria
absence of common academic analysis 270
ascertaining the content of *lex mercatoria*
avoidance of national laws and municipal interests 274–5
benefits of diversity 275–6
no need for perfect uniformity 273–4
scope and modality of convergence 276–82
choice of law by parties
diversity and legal pluralism 254–7
empirical evidence 253–4
conceptual issues
its factual existence and source of legal recognition distinguished 245–6
ways of understanding the lex mercatoria 246–8
convergence
benefits of diversity 275–6
effectiveness 259–63
efforts at identifying core principles 257–9
impact of international commercial arbitration 265–8
impact of international commercial mediation 264–5
scope and modality of convergence 276–82
core principles
'arbitral recognition argument' 248
'codification argument' 248
'national court recognition argument' 249
objections to the three arguments 249–51
diversity and legal pluralism of parties who chose it
non-Western norms 256–7
societas mercatorum 254–5
trade practices and usages 255–6
fitness for purpose
aftermath of pandemic 252–3
climate change 251–2
failure to keep pace with modern needs 270
minimum requirements 251
protection of MSMEs 252
historical development 269
key mechanism for future convergence 72–
obstacles to wider adoption
development and nature of *lex mercatoria* 272–3
risks of relying on transnational law 271
uncertainty as to content 271–2
vagueness of content 270–1
overview of central themes 320–1
as a system of different parts 282
ways of understanding the lex mercatoria
historical view 246–7
normative view 247–8

Lis alibi pendens
concurrent proceedings 187–8, 215–16
Hague Convention 2005 237

Litigation
see also **International commercial courts (ICCs); International commercial dispute resolution**
asynchronous dispute resolution proceedings
future potential and its challenges 305–11
two types of fully asynchronous litigation in use 303–5
complementary mechanism 24
pros and cons of swing towards arbitration
appeals 125–6
good thing by itself 126
higher degree of choice and freedom 121–2
hinder to development of jurisprudence 122–4
non-binary situation 124–5
remote hearings 126–7
res judicata
court decisions 222–3
international commercial courts (ICCs) 223
simplified processes for uncontested divorces 20
swing towards arbitration
Asia 117–18
effect of globalisation 121
English courts 118–20
gradual ebb and flow 116–17
nature of arbitration as a d
change 118–20
overview of central
recognition and
awards on language 108
underlying
h Commercial Court
unificati

Londor

datory rules
balancing competing interests 66–8
entry point for legitimate interests 335–6

Maritime law
distinctiveness 54
example of a system of international commercial law 51–3
respect for English commercial judges 74
Mediation
benefits 40–1
China International Commercial Court 100
CICC's goal 100
finality 184
impact on development of *lex mercatoria* 264–5
impact on *lex mercatoria* 264–5
Memorandums of Guidance (MOGs)
convenient approach to the recognition and enforcement of awards 109–10
reciprocity 196–7
Singapore International Commercial Court 132
Minimum international standard 139–40
Mistake of law 199–200, 231–2
Most-favoured nation (MFN) clauses
current approaches 159
general principles 140–1
propositions for balancing needs of states with demands of investors
creation of special investment courts 174–6
current approaches 169–73
future practicalities 177–9
traditional tribunal not to determine investor–state disputes 173
tribunal to assess the proportionality of government measures being challenged 173

…al commercial courts
[illegible] International commercial courts
key role of national law 61
recogn[illegible] of arbitration awards 59, 81
National trea[illegible] [illegible]-19 85–6
[illegible] system 59–60
minimum inter[illegible]ment of awards 70
propositions for ba[illegible]
demands of inv[illegible]ard 139–40
creation of special invest[illegible] of states with
current approaches 169
future practicalities 178 174–6
traditional tribunal not to determine investor–state disputes 173
tribunal to assess the proportionality of government measures being challenged 173

Netherlands Commercial Court (NCC)
disadvantages of litigation 111
establishment 98
jurisdiction 98
language 98–9
New York Convention 1958
arbitrability 64–6
awards set-aside by a supervising court 198–200
foundational legal instrument 56–7
preference for international commercial arbitration 37–8
public policy 68–70
recognition and enforcement of awards 38–9
swing towards arbitration 131–2

P
Paris *see* **International Chamber of the Paris Commercial Court**
Party autonomy
balancing competing interests 62–3
benefits of ICCs 106–7
benefits of swing towards arbitration 121–2
choices of law or forum
forum non conveniens 34–5
general rule 33–4
limitations 35
constraining principle on certainty and finality 185, 213–15, 319
paradigm issues 33
supposed shortcoming of ICCs 130–1
Professionalism and expertise
benefits of ICCs 105–6
China International Commercial Court 100
key mechanism for future convergence 75–6
Public policy
application by ICCs 336
balancing competing interests 68–71
recognition and enforcement of awards
arbitrability 200
general principles 198–9
mistake of law 199–200, 231–2
scope of application 229–30

R
Reciprocity
breaches of Rule of Law 230
comity 186
defined 39
interaction with finality and certainty 213–14
MOGs 109
promise-keeping 16
recognition and enforcement of awards 196–7, 235–6

Recognition and enforcement of awards
awards set-aside by a supervising court
certainty and finality 198–200
competing theories 232–4
preferred approach 234–5
certainty and finality
awards set-aside by a supervising court 198–200, 232–5
due process 197–8, 226–9
Hague Conventions 2005 and 2019 202–4, 236–40
impact of COVID-19 240–2
indirect jurisdiction 194–6, 224–6
overview 222–3
overview of conditions 194
public policy 198–200, 229–30
reciprocity 196–7, 235–6
res judicata 230–1
Hague Conventions 2005 and 2019
HCCH 2005 236–8
HCCH 2019 239–40
Netherlands Commercial Court 99
New York Convention 1958 38–9
problem with ISDS 151–2
problems with ICCs 109–10
proposed multilateral investment court 157
public policy 68–71
supposed shortcoming of ICCs 131–3
swing away from litigation towards arbitration 120–1
Res judicata
certainty and finality 192–4
concurrent proceedings
arbitral awards 222
court decisions 222–3
general principles 220–1
international commercial courts (ICCs) 223
general principle of law 220–1
recognition and enforcement of awards 230–1
Rule of Law
achievements in recent decades 43
adaptation of commercial courts 55
benefits of unification and convergence 72
certainty *see* **Certainty**
connection to international commercial arbitration 59
finality *see* **Finality**
impact of Ukraine-Russia war 343
importance 101
importance of human elements of the system 81
institutionalisation of Rule of Law values 24
international support for the system 63
need for system focus 87
New York Convention as key pillar 57
prioritisation of values 20
promotion of economic development 316
provision of accessible and proportionate justice 23
role of effective justice system 122
role of international commercial courts 326
role of international dispute resolution system 48
triumphs of globalisation 5
UN Sustainable Development Goals 10
Rules
effect of COVID-19 on rules-based international order 86–7
mandatory rules
balancing competing interests 66–8
entry point for legitimate interests 335–6
UNCITRAL Rules
ad hoc arbitrations 139
aims of Mauritius Convention 144
consolidation of claims 146
costs 151
guidance on transparency 148
Russian invasion of Ukraine
climate change 345–6
geopolitics and the global order 343–5
macroeconomic risk 345
pandemic insecurity 346
rising inequality 346
significant and far-reaching impact on the law 342–3
truth decay 346

S

Set-offs
investor-state dispute settlement (ISDS) 145–6
lex mercatoria 248
Singapore International Commercial Court (SICC)
applicable law 95–6
appointment of judges 96
establishment 95
example of how convergence might happen
potential to influence international law 332–4
prominent and well-respected judges f 331–2
future prospects 129–30
international commercial disputes defined 31, 47
jurisdiction 95–6
key mechanisms for future convergence 76–7
Memorandums of Guidance (MOGs) 132
part of world-wide rise of ICCs 127
rationale for special treatment of ICDR 32
unique features 128

Sovereignty
basis for courts' legitimacy 327
constraining principle on certainty and finality 186, 213–15, 319
constraint on policy choices 18
ICSID jurisdiction 138
impact of COVID-19 12
nature of international commercial disputes 43, 48
propositions for balancing needs of states with demands of investors 178
Russian invasion of Ukraine 348
taking of evidence 131, 288
Westphalian order 269
Standard form contracts 37
Stay of proceedings
arbitral proceedings 190
case management grounds 191–2

T
Technology
arbitrability of disputes 66
asynchronous dispute resolution proceedings
'automation' and 'transformation' distinguished 302
future potential and its challenges 305–11
illustration 287
impact of COVID-19 177
two types of fully asynchronous litigation in use 303–5
underlying concept of asynchronicity 302–3
lessons of the pandemic
limitations on technology 299–301
positive impact of technology 297–9
three procedural innovations resulting from pandemic
case management conferences 294–6
document production 296–7
expert evidence 297
transformative potential of remote technology
overall conclusions 311
overview 289–91
ways to confront the failings of globalisation 22–3
Terrorism 6, 11, 314, 328, 342
Transnational system of justice
courts and arbitral tribunals 347
need for 1
potential solutions to the global challenges 348
role of Judicial Roundtable 341
Transparency
addressing commercial law's old and new problems 337
benefits of ICCs 106–7
key mechanism for future convergence 75–6
legitimacy of globalisation and its institutions 314, 324
problem with ISDS 147–8
UNCITRAL Rules 148

U
Ukraine *see* **Russian invasion of Ukraine**
Umbrella clauses 143–4
UNCITRAL Model Law
arbitrability 64–6
balancing competing interests 62–3
convergence with *lex mercatoria* 257–8
cross-border insolvency 57–8, 73
development of facilitative culture 80
foundational legal instrument 57
impact on convergence 36
international commercial disputes defined 29–30, 45–7
as notional 'bank' of rights 4
public policy 68–70
stay of proceedings 190
ways to confront the failings of globalisation 16
UNCITRAL Rules
ad hoc arbitrations 139
aims of Mauritius Convention 144
consolidation of claims 146
costs 151
guidance on transparency 148
UNIDROIT Principles
convergence with *lex mercatoria* 257–8
key mechanisms for future convergence 74
practical means to attain convergence 36
protection of MSMEs 252

W
World Bank
broader function of international commercial dispute resolution system 44
establishment of ICSID 138
impact of globalisation 15
World Trade Organisation (WTO)
broader function of international commercial dispute resolution system 44
ways to confront the failings of globalisation 18

Ingram Content Group UK Ltd.
Milton Keynes UK
UKHW020353210623
423772UK00005B/110

9 781509 954971